SELECTED WORKS OF
JOSEPH CARDINAL BERNARDIN

Selected Works of
Joseph Cardinal Bernardin

VOLUME 2

Church and Society

Alphonse P. Spilly, C.PP.S.
Editor

A Liturgical Press Book

 THE LITURGICAL PRESS
Collegeville, Minnesota

Volume 2: ISBN 0-8146-2584-3

1	2	3	4	5	6	7	8

Library of Congress Cataloging-in-Publication Data

Bernardin, Joseph Louis, 1928–
    [Selections. 2000]
    Selected works of Joseph Cardinal Bernardin / Alphonse P. Spilly, editor ; foreword by Roger Cardinal Mahony.
        p.   cm.
    Includes bibliographical references and index.
    Contents: v. 1. Homilies and teaching documents.
    ISBN 0-8146-2583-5 (alk. paper)
    1. Catholic Church—Doctrines.   I. Spilly, Alphonse P., 1939– .
II. Title.

BX4705.B38125 A25   2000
282'.77311—dc21   99-039499
                                                                    CIP

Contents

Health Care

Evangelization

Pastoral Ministry

Pastoral Outreach

Appendix

Part One

THE LIFE OF SOCIETY

Introduction to Part One:
The Life of Society

It is rare for a U.S. Catholic bishop to be featured on the cover of a national secular magazine, but Cardinal Bernardin was so honored twice. In November 1982, when the bishops were considering a third draft of a pastoral letter on war and peace, a text prepared by a committee of bishops chaired by Bernardin, his portrait appeared on the cover of *Time*. In November 1996, his picture appeared on the cover of *Newsweek* a few days after his death. The cover story spoke about the way he had taught us how to die. Both instances reflect the extraordinary status of Cardinal Bernardin within the Church and in society.

As archbishop of Chicago, Cardinal Bernardin made major contributions in several areas of the Church's teaching, but he is especially widely known for his contributions to peacemaking, the consistent ethic of life, religion and society, health care, Catholic-Jewish dialogue, and the Catholic Common Ground Initiative.

Cardinal Bernardin drew on many sources. Many of his talks in Part One of this volume were particularly influenced by two documents of the Second Vatican Council, the Pastoral Constitution on the Church in the Modern World and the Declaration on the Relation of the Church to Non-Christian Religions as well as by papal teaching of Popes Paul VI and John Paul II.

How he made his contributions in these six areas was also important to Cardinal Bernardin, for each topic was controversial and marked by differences of opinion and approach. He had learned from two important mentors, Archbishop Paul Hallinan of Atlanta and John Cardinal Dearden of Detroit, that differences can be resolved through open and honest dialogue, and that conviction made Cardinal Bernardin an expert reconciler, a person who could lead others to consensus. For him dialogue did not mean compromise of the truth of Catholic doctrine. Rather he diligently searched for the truth that can bind people together.

Peacemaking

Cardinal Bernardin served as chairman of the National Conference of Catholic Bishops' (NCCB) ad hoc Committee on War and Peace that drafted the pastoral letter, "The Challenge of Peace: God's Promise and Our Response." The committee used extensive consultation in its work, presenting three successive drafts for consideration by the NCCB. The collaborative process of its development marks a kind of watershed in the history of the Catholic Church in the United States. Many bishops were initially rather hawkish, but attitudes were changed by the time of the final vote on the pastoral letter. On May 3, 1983, it was adopted by the bishops at a special meeting in Chicago by a vote of 238–9.

In recognition of his leadership on the ad hoc committee, Cardinal Bernardin received the 1983 Albert Einstein Peace Award. He was often asked to speak about the pastoral letter. In January 1984, at a memorial service in honor of Dr. Martin Luther King, Jr., the cardinal linked civic harmony and social justice with peacemaking. Two days later, he spoke at the University of Chicago about the pastoral letter in the context of the Church's role in the public policy debate. A week later, he examined the letter's ecumenical foundations and implications at the University of San Francisco. And eight days later at the Catholic University of Louvain he compared "The Challenge of Peace" with the pastoral letters on war and peace adopted by the French and German episcopal conferences. He continued to highlight the importance of dialogue in peacemaking (Rome, 1986) and to assess the value of the pastoral letter in the light of new global developments (University of South Carolina 1990 and Washington, D.C., 1991).

Consistent Ethic of Life

The pastoral letter on war and peace specifically linked the nuclear arms question with abortion and other life issues (no. 285). However, it did not provide a fully articulated theological framework for this linkage. Cardinal Bernardin began to develop the theme of the consistent ethic precisely to provide a more comprehensive theological and ethical basis for the linkage of war and abortion and for the bishops' Respect Life Program. Moreover, in October 1983 he was asked to chair the NCCB Pro-Life Activities Committee, and he knew that both abortion and defense-related issues would play an important role in the upcoming U.S. presidential campaign.

In the 1983 Gannon Lecture, Cardinal Bernardin first articulated the need for a consistent ethic of life, linking the full range of life issues from conception to natural death while acknowledging each as a distinct issue that required its own specific moral analysis. The public response greatly exceeded his hopes and expectations. In the ensuing years there has been a lively exchange by both those who agree and disagree with the theme and its implications. By far, the majority of the reactions have been supportive. But it has also been used and misused by those who tried to push their own, more narrow agendas. Some opponents even accused the cardinal of heresy. While he was confident that the consistent ethic of life was fully consonant with Catholic teaching, he sent copies of his addresses on the topic to the Holy See for an unofficial review. The answer came back that his views on the consistent ethic were, indeed, in accord with Catholic teaching.

In subsequent addresses he applied the consistent ethic of life to such issues as capital punishment (Amnesty International, 1984) and poverty (The Catholic University of America, 1985). In November 1985 the NCCB officially adopted the consistent ethic of life as the theological basis for its Plan for Pro-Life Activities. He further developed the underpinning of the consistent ethic (Seattle, 1986). In 1987, a symposium on the consistent ethic was held at Loyola University in Chicago. Ten of the cardinal's talks on the topic from 1983–86 and the papers given at the symposium were published as *Consistent Ethic of Life* (Sheed & Ward, 1988).

RELIGION AND SOCIETY

Initially, Cardinal Bernardin's contributions to this topic flowed from his involvement with the pastoral letter on peace and his articulation of the need for a consistent ethic of life. Cardinal Bernardin often pointed out that all life issues have a serious moral dimension that needs to be taken into consideration in the formulation of public policy. He also insisted that the Church has a right to participate in public policy debates, but it must earn its right to be heard by the quality of its arguments.

His insights about religion and society went well beyond defending the Church's participation in the public policy debate and, as noted above, were especially influenced by the Pastoral Constitution on the Church in the Modern World (e.g., Notre Dame University, 1985, and Catholic Theological Union, 1990). He was also interested in the interaction between religion and society, between Catholic institutions and the secular world (Fordham University, 1991), and the Church and U.S. culture (Columbia University, 1993).

On September 9, 1996, two months before his death, Cardinal Bernardin received the Presidential Medal of Freedom, the highest civilian honor bestowed on individuals who have made important contributions to their communities and the nation. In presenting the medal, President Clinton cited Cardinal Bernardin's work on behalf of racial equality and arms control and noted that he "has been a persistent voice for moderation."

HEALTH CARE

One of his first major addresses on Catholic health care as archbishop of Chicago was at Loyola University in Chicago in May 1985, where he examined traditional medical ethical issues and social justice issues in the light of the consistent ethic of life. He articulated a concern that there was no clear evidence that Catholic hospitals in general donated more health care to the poor than other hospitals, although many particular ones had outstanding records in this regard. The Catholic Health Association had already begun to address this issue by appointing a Task Force on Health Care of the Poor in late 1984. Its final report was issued in a prepublication version in April 1986, and Cardinal Bernardin was invited to respond to it in the Flanagan Memorial Lecture during the annual CHA meeting in San Diego in June.

By 1994 health care reform had become a national obsession. In May, Cardinal Bernardin addressed the topic at the National Press Club, examining reform in the light of the consistent ethic of life. In early 1995 he argued the case for not-for-profit health care before the Harvard Business School Club of Chicago, noting that health care is not simply a commodity.

In June 1995 his keen interest in health care issues took on a more personal dimension when he discovered that he had pancreatic cancer and, later, when he began to suffer considerable pain from spinal stenosis and the eventual collapse of four vertebrae. He issued a pastoral letter on health care, "A Sign of Hope," in October 1995. (It is included in the first volume of this collection of his selected works.) In December 1995, he addressed the House of Delegates of the American Medical Association on "Renewing the Covenant with Patients and Society," arguing passionately for recovering the moral center of medicine lest its moral authority be lost, perhaps irrevocably. It was a powerful challenge to physicians by a cancer patient who was also a widely respected moral leader.

In recognition of Cardinal Bernardin's many outstanding contributions to the health care debate, the American Hospital Association presented its Award of Honor posthumously to Cardinal Bernardin in 1999 "for teaching others how to die with grace and live with compassion."

CATHOLIC-JEWISH DIALOGUE

Cardinal Bernardin's relationship with the Jewish community in metropolitan Chicago developed early in his ministry in Chicago. The ground had already been well prepared. The first Catholic-Jewish dialogue began in metropolitan Chicago shortly after the end of the Second Vatican Council. There were several groups and multiple levels of dialogue and cooperation when Archbishop Bernardin arrived on the scene. Moreover, he brought with him well-established relations with national Jewish leaders.

When invited by diverse Jewish religious and social organizations to speak about various aspects of Catholic-Jewish relations, Cardinal Bernardin relied greatly on the developing thought of Pope John Paul II whose contributions to Catholic-Jewish relations have been extraordinary. In part, Cardinal Bernardin's addresses on the topic made available to a wider audience this papal teaching as well as ongoing efforts of the U.S. episcopal conference.

Cardinal Bernardin's relationship with the Jewish community was greatly deepened during an interfaith trip to the Holy Land in March 1995. Jewish and Catholic representatives from metropolitan Chicago spent twelve days with him visiting the holy sites and indigenous religious communities in Israel, the West Bank, and Gaza. The highlight of the visit was Cardinal Bernardin's address on anti-Semitism at the Hebrew University in Jerusalem on March 23. It was well received and widely disseminated. Again, a small but vocal minority charged the cardinal with heresy, an accusation entirely without merit. Indeed, Cardinal Bernardin later showed me a letter from Cardinal Cassidy, the Holy See's head of the office for relations with the Jewish people, who commended Bernardin for his well-founded and clear presentation of authentic Church teaching in his Jerusalem address.

In an unprecedented tribute, Jewish representatives from metropolitan Chicago conducted a testimonial wake service in Holy Name Cathedral on the day before Cardinal Bernardin's funeral. The eloquence of their tributes and grief gave great affirmation to his contribution towards improving the relations between Catholics and Jews.

CATHOLIC COMMON GROUND INITIATIVE

Although this final major contribution of Cardinal Bernardin occurred during the last three months of his life, it was vintage Bernardin. He was always a firm believer that what unites us is more important than what divides us. So, it is no surprise that his name remains widely associated with the Catholic Common Ground Initiative.

Cardinal Bernardin announced the inauguration of the Catholic Common Ground Project, as it was first called, at a press conference in Chicago on August 12, 1996. The announcement caught the imagination of and received immediate approval from many within and outside the Church as well as the immediate public opposition of Cardinals Bernard Law of Boston, James Hickey of Washington, D.C., and Anthony Bevilacqua of Philadelphia. Cardinal Bernardin replied that their criticisms indicated the very need for a common ground of dialogue. He was well aware that there was a tension in the postconciliar Church about dialogue. While some, like Bernardin himself, saw dialogue as essential for building up the unity of the Church, others saw in it a danger of compromising the truth. All of the cardinal's statements about the Catholic Common Ground Project clearly state that the dialogue he envisioned would take place within the bounds of authentic Church teaching.

Over the next two weeks, in order to build on the momentum of the August 12 announcement and to respond to its critics, the cardinal worked with staff on a statement in question-and-answer form. It was released to the media on August 29, 1996, the same day that he announced publicly that an MRI two days earlier had revealed that his cancer had returned and spread to his liver. His condition was now considered terminal, and his doctor had told him that he had six to twelve months left to live.

On October 24, 1996, as the cardinal's health was deteriorating at an alarming pace, the first meeting of the Catholic Common Ground Project committee met in Chicago, and that evening he delivered his first and last major address on the topic, "Faithful and Hopeful: The Catholic Common Ground Project." In a sense, he left us a very precious gift in that address, "a vision of the Church that trusts in the power of the Spirit so much that it can risk authentic dialogue." Three weeks later, on November 14, 1996, Cardinal Bernardin died.

*   *   *

In a sense Cardinal Bernardin's efforts in these six areas have continued beyond his death. The Joseph Cardinal Bernardin Center for Theology and Ministry at the Catholic Theological Union in Chicago fosters research and discussion in these six areas, building upon Cardinal Bernardin's vision and insights. The Catholic Common Ground Initiative is carrying out its mandate throughout the nation. The Archdiocese of Chicago sponsors an annual Bernardin Lecture to honor his contributions to the Catholic-Jewish dialogue and to further that work. And the Joseph Cardinal Bernardin Center at the Spertus College of Judaica, established in 1987, continues to promote interfaith understanding between Jews and Catholics.

Moreover, his own voice continues to be heard. In addition to the four volumes in this collection of selected works, *Consistent Ethic of Life* (Sheed & Ward, 1988) is still in print. Nearly all of Cardinal Bernardin's talks and writings about Catholic-Jewish relations are available in *A Blessing to Each Other* (Liturgy Training Publications, 1996). Several of his important public policy addresses are included in *A Moral Vision for America* (Georgetown University Press, 1998), and all of his addresses on health care are contained in *Celebrating the Ministry of Healing: Joseph Cardinal Bernardin's Reflections on Healthcare* (Catholic Health Association, 1999).

Reverend Alphonse P. Spilly, C.PP.S., PH.D.

Peacemaking

1983 Albert Einstein Peace Laureate

Chicago, Illinois

— November 9, 1983 ────────────────────────────

It is a high honor and a distinct privilege to receive the Albert Einstein award. The honor is to be measured by the genius and humanity of the man in whose name the award is given and by the goal of peace to which the award is dedicated. The privilege is to be associated with the previous recipients of the Einstein award. For the honor and the privilege I express my deepest gratitude. I accept this award in the name of the National Conference of Catholic Bishops and particularly in the names of the other bishops who served on the drafting committee: Bishops George Fulcher, Thomas Gumbleton, John O'Connor and Daniel Reilly.

I am grateful, too, for the opportunity to give this address, even though preparing for it proved to be a rather difficult assignment. This was so for two reasons. First, I am acutely conscious of the contributions which previous Einstein award addresses have made to the public debate. Second, the audience which assembles annually for this ceremony represents a distinguished body of wisdom and experience on questions of war and peace in the nuclear age.

Nevertheless, I appreciate the opportunity to reflect upon the message of the pastoral letter, *The Challenge of Peace: God's Promise and Our Response*. It is meant to have long-term value, but this requires that its contents be reviewed and related to changing issues.

I shall address three themes: the pastoral letter after six months; arms control after twenty years; and the public, politics and morality—the next twenty years. Throughout, I shall examine the relationships of public opinion, policy, and morality.

13

THE PASTORAL AFTER SIX MONTHS

The pastoral letter was passed by the bishops by a vote of 238–9 last May 3. Its purpose was to make a moral/religious assessment of the challenge of the nuclear age. We wrote as bishops within the Catholic moral tradition and as citizens within the American political tradition. The political and strategic complexity of the nuclear age beggars our intellect and imagination. The effort to examine this complexity within the structure of moral reason, informed by the light of the Christian gospel, stretches the resources of faith and reason. Neither the peril of the nuclear age nor the paradoxes of nuclear strategy are lessened when the perspective is moral analysis rather than political or technical.

In many ways both the dangers and the dilemmas are magnified when the assessment is cast in terms of what we ought to do morally rather than in terms of what we can do technically. In essence, the question pervading the entire analysis of the pastoral letter is a product of the technological character of the age: When we *can* do almost anything, how do we decide what we *ought* to do?

The pastoral pursues this theme through the arcane logic of the nuclear argument. Its position can be sketched in a series of propositions. Strategically, it classifies nuclear weapons in a category qualitatively distinct from other weapons. One reason for this distinction is the radical skepticism expressed throughout the letter about the ability to control nuclear weapons within morally meaningful limits.

The pastoral proceeds to state a series of moral judgments about these unique instruments of destruction:

- On the basis of principle, it forbids directly intended attacks on civilian populations even in retaliation for attacks on our own civilian centers;

- On the basis of prudential judgment, it opposes any first use of nuclear weapons;

- While expressing the most extreme skepticism about morally acceptable uses of nuclear weapons, the letter provides a carefully defined justification for the strategy of deterrence. The terminology—"strictly conditioned moral acceptance" of deterrence—is meant to acknowledge the significance of deterrence in a world of nuclear superpowers and to specify the inadequacy of this strategy as a long-term basis for peace. The conditional acceptance of deterrence is designed to challenge the idea that it promises a secure future and yet to give space for that challenge to be worked out. A previous Einstein award recipient, McGeorge Bundy, caught the sense of our moral analysis when he commented: "In our current debate (the Bishops') strict conditions may be more significant than their approval."

Having sketched the strategic and moral character of the era of deterrence, the bishops propose a political response. They advocate a broad range of arms control measures designed to cap, contain, and reverse the quantitative and qualitative growth of nuclear arsenals. The objective is not simply standard pursuit of arms control, but a larger effort to displace the deterrence dilemma with a more secure basis, morally and politically, for national and international security.

The pastoral was written to address both the general public and the specific forum of the policy debate. At the level of the general public, it is now being communicated through the normal channels of the Catholic Church's diocesan, parish, and educational system. In the long run, such activity may be our most significant contribution, for the letter addresses Catholics as citizens, parents, and professionals in many walks of life. While the bishops expected a substantial response to the letter within the Church, a surprise awaited us in the widespread public interest shown by other Christian churches, sectors of the Jewish community, the scientific and university worlds, and the national media. Attention in these circles does not mean universal agreement, but, rather, serious consideration of the arguments made in the letter.

In the policy community, the letter's fundamental contribution has been to open space in the policy debate for explicit analysis of the moral dimension of policy. As many of you know, during the writing of this letter we had a series of public exchanges with the U.S. government. This kind of Church/state examination of the moral quality of public policy is crucial to test the moral status of prevailing policy. We profited from the exchange even though several substantial areas of difference emerged—from "no-first-use" through the comprehensive test ban treaty.

It does seem to me that in the last year the rhetoric surrounding nuclear policy has been significantly restrained and the emphasis placed on arms control has increased. While many factors, I am sure, contributed to both of these developments, it seems that public pressure—not least in its moral assessment of policy—has been a crucial catalyst.

The deeper dilemma of deterrence remains, however, and the pastoral urges that the very structure of the deterrence relationship be addressed. Hence, I wish to leave the assessment of the pastoral and concentrate on where the past twenty years have brought us and where the next twenty may take us.

Arms Control After Twenty Years

I use the period from 1963–1983 for two reasons. First, the twentieth anniversary of the Limited Test Ban Treaty is significant because the treaty is properly regarded as the fruit of serious arms control policy and it was seen as the first of several steps to reverse the nuclear arms race. Second, in 1963 Pope John XXIII wrote the encyclical Peace on Earth, a document which has had a profound effect within the Catholic community on issues of war and peace. The firm "no" to nuclear war found in the American bishops' pastoral is prefigured in the argument of that encyclical.

Twenty years of effort on arms control have not produced startling results. It would be all too easy to disparage both the process and its basic concepts. The pastoral letter itself is not expansive about arms control; it places primary emphasis on the need to go beyond anything yet accomplished. Nonetheless, our expectations of arms control are themselves a tribute to its success. We need periodically to think about the kind of competition we would have if arms control negotiations had not been pursued over the past twenty years.

Our problem, therefore, is not that nothing has been done. It is the gap between what has been done and what must still be done for the clear and present danger to be replaced by a more stable peace. The hope which accompanied the Limited Test Ban Treaty and the moral imperative stated by John XXIII—"that the arms race should cease" and "that nuclear weapons should be banned"—have not been realized. Why have the hopes not been fulfilled?

One factor, not sufficiently emphasized in my view, is the fact that the general public has given only sporadic attention to arms control and disarmament. In the pastoral letter the bishops described a "new moment" in the nuclear age, marked by the increased public awareness of these questions. They called attention to Pope John Paul II's statement that a vigorous public opinion is central to a morally enlightened public policy. We must, however, be especially conscious just now, when the public is acutely sensitive to the nuclear issue, that previous periods of public interest have been followed by long stretches of public apathy. When apathy prevails, policy lacks both the discipline and the support afforded by public opinion.

Unscrutinized policy decisions are among the costs of public apathy. In reviewing the last twenty years, few decisions appear more fateful for arms control than the deployment of MIRVed missiles by both superpowers. Questions remain even to this day about why the U.S. failed to seek a ban on MIRVing when we had the technology and the Soviets did not. Without trying to solve the historical question, I simply want to use the MIRVing decision to exemplify why arms control is not today at the point one might have hoped.

The decision was taken without widespread public interest. Indeed, by comparison with the intense debate of the last several years surrounding deployment of the MX, the relative silence about MIRVs in the 1970s is all the more striking. If an earlier Scowcroft Commission had aired the implications of MIRVed missiles, the 1983 Scowcroft Report might not have had to call for retreat from a ten-year buildup of MIRVed missiles.

Public apathy and policy mistakes are complemented by a third factor: the U.S.–Soviet relationship. There is a fundamental connection between the political level of superpower relations and their strategic content. It was a common experience during SALT II to find 75 percent of the American public in favor of arms control and an equally high number profoundly skeptical of our ability to deal with the Soviets. This pervasive mistrust—identified in 1963 by Pope John XXIII as a root cause of international tension—is fueled by objective events and subjective perceptions. Events like the destruction of the Korean airliner give anyone pause about the capacity for cooperation. But our own policy definitions—like a comprehensive doctrine of linkage as a test for any progress on arms control—can also set standards virtually impossible to meet. Such a doctrine ties the preeminent aspect of U.S.–Soviet relations—their need to curb their military competition in their own interests and the interests of the world at large—to issues which, though no doubt important in themselves, are nevertheless peripheral by comparison.

While these three factors do not constitute an exhaustive explanation of why the hopes of 1963 remain frustrated in 1983, they do provide some criteria for assessing where we have been.

This sketch brings us, of course, to the chapter of arms control entitled START (Strategic Arms Reduction Talks) and INF (Intermediate-range Nuclear Forces). One can readily sympathize with the great difficulty of carrying these talks forward in the present climate. At the same time, we need to evaluate INF and START in 1983 in terms of the overall priority accorded them in U.S.–Soviet relations. Although we are now deep in the negotiating process, precious time was lost in getting to this point. The larger issue is the priority given arms control on a sustained basis in U.S. policy. Obviously, our political differences with the Soviets fuel the strategic competition. But the complex task of moderating and reversing the dynamic of the strategic dimension must be pursued consistently as a priority across administrations. Arms control should be insulated from the multiple factors which make the superpower political relationship volatile and unpredictable.

PUBLIC, POLICY AND MORALITY— THE NEXT TWENTY YEARS

The last twenty years have been a mix of success and failure; nuclear weapons have not been used, but the nuclear relationship has grown more dangerous. Speculating on the next two decades from the perspective of

the pastoral letter, my concerns are: (1) nuclear politics and public understanding; (2) nuclear technology and policy choice; and (3) nuclear nations and the needs of others.

Nuclear Politics and Public Understanding

The bishops describe their perspective on the U.S.–Soviet relationship
as one of "cold realism." At first that may not sound appropriate for pastors of the Christian gospel. But one function of theology has been to
teach us how to read history soberly—not devoid of hope, but not de-
ceived by easy optimism. The cold realism of the letter has particular
relevance for the way policymakers and the public understand our political situation in a deeply divided world under the nuclear threat.

Cold realism recognizes the divided character of our international life
and the ever-present possibility of open conflict. Indeed it affirms, sadly
but surely, that some use of force in international relations can be justifiable. But then it makes some distinctions.

Cold realism rules out crusades and definitions of the world which lead
to a crusading mentality. It resists, therefore, simplistic definitions of the
world cast in terms of unqualified good or evil. From the perspective of
this kind of cold realism the pastoral acknowledges the depth of U.S.–
Soviet division, based on differences of history, philosophy, and ideology,
and then affirms the existence of a narrow band of common interests upon
which efforts to contain the nuclear arms race should be based.

This cold realism is very much in line with Pope John XXIII's encyclical which encouraged Catholics to work with others whose worldview is
not ours but who share our nuclear fate and future.

This reflection speaks directly to nuclear politics and public understanding. Realism today requires that we understand our divisions but not
be blind to our mutual interests. Realism requires the capacity to recognize hard facts and to make fine distinctions. It calls us to face the dual
truth that nuclear conflict would be irrational, but all conflict is not therefore impossible. We can cooperate with the Soviets where we share common ground and dispute with them on other grounds. Realism would be
served if these other grounds were precisely and wisely defined so that all
conflict in the world is not seen as superpower conflict. But that is a topic
for another time.

Realism in our public understanding of the nuclear age should not seek
to establish a detailed consensus in the United States on all aspects of the
U.S.–Soviet relationship. It should instead seek a narrow but firmly held
set of shared convictions which could undergird a coherent arms control
policy over the long term. Such a consensus might seek support for the
following propositions:

- The use of nuclear weapons is not a rational moral goal; deterrence is but as a transitional strategy.

- Arms control is not a function of trust nor a favor to others; it serves mutual interests in avoiding the use of nuclear weapons.

- Negotiation is hardly the only form of risk-taking in a nuclear age; we may risk much more by refusing to give arms control a consistent priority.

Nuclear Technology and Policy Choice

I began by suggesting that the relevant moral question concerns the tension between what we can do technologically and what we ought to do morally. The relationship of technology, politics, and moral choice is a central theme in the pastoral letter. It is also the way in which John Paul II defines the challenge of the nuclear age. How is political choice to direct technology—and moral choice to direct politics?

I have already noted the decision to proceed with MIRVing in the 1970s. The decisions of the 1980s involve similar questions of politics and technology. These decisions are undoubtedly shaped and driven by the wider political atmosphere of superpower relations.

We define MX as a response to Soviet 18s and 19s; we describe Pershing IIs as a response to SS-20s. The political logic of these decisions is clear; the strategic logic is widely debated. Some see in the MX a dangerous response to a bad decision by the Soviets to deploy weapons with first-strike characteristics. Others focus on the Pershing II deployment as more dangerous than MX in its impact on Soviet perceptions and plans.

In the pastoral letter we accorded a real but narrow justification to deterrence. That justification hangs almost totally on the role of the deterrent in preventing the use of nuclear weapons in a politically divided world. But marginal justification of deterrence is contingent upon containing the character of the deterrent to the specific function of preventing nuclear war. Every increment to the deterrence arsenal must be tested by this question. Additions which may have political utility or allow us to match the other side symmetrically, but which increase the danger of the deterrence relationship should not escape very careful public scrutiny. I shall not engage here in a detailed discussion of these proposed deployments, but I wish to set them in the context of what we have learned from the MIRVing decision of the 1970s. We should not have to recoup in the 1990s what might be salvaged for arms control by a decision in the 1980s.

Nuclear Nations and the Needs of Others

A final theme of the pastoral must be mentioned here in light of the next twenty years. The nuclear dilemma is so dangerous and so devilishly complex that it can mesmerize us. It is a central aspect—perhaps *the* central aspect—of superpower relations. But much of our increasingly interdependent world lives daily with other challenges, some no less stark.

Avoiding nuclear war is a central moral and political task of our time. It is not the only moral and political challenge. Part three of the pastoral letter addresses the question of building the peace under conditions of interdependence. The recently released estimates on global military and social expenditures described a world in which $660 billion is spent on armaments in a world marked by grinding poverty and injustice.

I do not wish to make this point as a footnote to an address on the nuclear question. I am simply saying that many in the world live close to death, but the potential destructiveness of nuclear arms is not the only reason. We cannot forsake the quest for nuclear peace, but neither can we confine our foreign policy to that alone. While the specifics of the non-nuclear challenge are a matter to be considered another time, they are too central simply to be ignored here.

I close, however, on a more personal note. I come to accept this award as a bishop—a person of faith entrusted with the teaching and preaching of Catholic faith. The experience of drafting the pastoral letter opened a whole vista of problems for me that tested my capacity for understanding, imagination, and insight. Many of you have spent your lives struggling with these questions, seeking to contain and control power through the resources of reason. I stand in admiration of your efforts; the entire Catholic tradition respects this use of the resources of reason.

But the experience of the last two years has constantly forced me to draw on the resources of faith as well—on trust in a God who so loved the world he sent his Son to save it, on the power of prayer which sustains us when the resources of reason are stretched to their limit. Perhaps the most significant aspect of faith in this process has been the need I have experienced to rekindle in myself and others the virtue of hope. The danger, size, and complexity of the nuclear question tend to paralyze us. Hope gives us the capacity to sustain courage, conviction, and constancy in the face of issues which transcend our individual capabilities. Several themes sustain my hope; my faith is the principal source, but the spirit of a man like Einstein is also a beacon of hope. May the universal day of prayer to which the Einstein Foundation has called all the religious communities of the world, and which I personally and wholeheartedly commend, be itself a source of the hope we all need in the pursuit of world peace.

Address

Memorial Service in Honor of the 55th Birthday of Dr. Martin Luther King, Jr.*

Washington, D.C.

——*January 14, 1984* ——————————————————

It is both an honor and a privilege to participate in this 55th birthday memorial for Dr. Martin Luther King, Jr. I come as a bishop and pastor of the Roman Catholic Church to pay tribute to one of the great pastors and prophets of the Christian Church in the United States. I rejoice that I am able to join Mrs. Coretta Scott King, members of the King family and all of you here today as we celebrate the fact that Dr. King has now been rightfully recognized as a national hero by the United States Congress.

Other individuals in American history have been honored for their political wisdom or military skill; Dr. King earned his place in the history of the nation through a role of moral leadership. Others spent their lives in the service of the security of the nation; Martin Luther King, Jr., spent his life caring for the soul of the nation.

It is fitting, therefore, that this memorial service is held in the church where Dr. King ministered to the people of God. He was first and foremost a man of the gospel and the Church. He fused the Old Testament cry for justice with the New Testament witness of nonviolence to create a social revolution which reshaped the substance of our public life in the United States.

*Also published in *Origins*, vol. 13, no. 33, January 26, 1984, pp. 545, 547–49.

Dr. King was not only an outstanding pastor and eloquent preacher, he was also a prophet. Today the term is used too often and we tend to debase its meaning by applying it so broadly. But Martin Luther King, Jr., earned the title. He sought to do in our day what the biblical prophets did in theirs. The Hebrew prophets were distinctly different people and they faced diverse problems but a single theme united them: The prophets always tested the quality of Israel's faith by the character of justice in its society.

A prophet's purpose is not primarily to describe the future, but to illuminate the moral issues of his own time. Prophets serve the word of God by their vision, not their power of prediction. Prophets remain with us through the power of their words; others in later generations receive the prophet's word and share his vision. To honor Martin Luther King, Jr., requires that we understand his vision and what it calls us to be today.

The prophetic message is preeminently focused on the issue of justice: the community's right relationship with God as that is measured by our relationships with one another. Dr. King took the measure of justice in American society in the 1960s and found it wanting. In the style of Isaiah and Amos, he concretized the meaning of justice in terms of the specific questions of the day: fair wages and social welfare; voting rights and political power; employment, equity and economics.

The prophets always called the people they served to the crucible of decision; the prophets defined problems in clear moral terms, challenged the people and forced a social decision. Two decades before Martin Luther King, Jr., became a national figure, Gunner Myrdal had defined the treatment of black Americans as "The American Dilemma"; Dr. King knew the dilemma would be resolved only by a series of political-moral decisions reaching from personal relationships to public institutions. The issue of race was so deeply embedded in American life that it required profound changes in the way we thought and the way we acted; in the way we voted and the way we allocated resources.

The decisions required were essentially moral; the drive toward these decisions needed to be a moral force. Using the constitutional principles of justice and the gospel's power of nonviolence, he called us to a national process of deciding anew to resolve the American dilemma; that process continues to this day.

We have seen some of its fruits. Yet we see perhaps even more clearly what has not been decided and remains to be done. But we will never again be the same as a nation because of the prophetic vision of Martin Luther King, Jr. It forced us to face squarely the moral, political and constitutional crisis caused for us, as individuals and as a nation, by basing our *political system* on the principles of human dignity and equality, while basing our *practice* on a systematic denial of those principles.

The remarkable feature of Dr. King's prophetic vision was its combination of specific roots and universal scope. His passion for justice and equality was rooted in his faith, grounded in the prophets and galvanized by the ministry and message of Jesus.

His immediate purpose was shaped by the black experience of the people he served in Atlanta and the black community he led across the nation. But his perspective grew to embrace an even larger constituency: By the time he was assassinated he spoke for the poor and dispossessed of the nation and he was a symbol of justice and peace in the world. His perspective and his personal witness transcended both race and nation.

He was prophetic in style and substance. He accepted the prophetic vocation and he paid the prophet's price—his life for the people. The substance of his vision is contained in Isaiah (32:17): Peace is the fruit of justice. He knew what we have yet to learn fully as a nation: that a stable peace within nations and among nations cannot exist apart from the claims of justice, claims which must be acknowledged by individuals and groups alike. An imposed peace is a transitory illusion. Those who said Dr. King disturbed the peace failed or refused to see what he knew from the Scriptures: An unjust peace is purchased for some at the price of the lives of others. There is a moral duty to disturb that peace.

Dr. King disturbed the domestic peace of the United States in a nonviolent way. He forced us to face the reason why the peace in the strongest nation on earth was precarious and unstable: One dimension of that peace was rooted in the denial of full human and civil rights to a whole sector of the nation. Dr. King created a constitutional crisis because only by exposing the constitutional question could the crisis of conscience in the nation be addressed. By making the crisis of conscience and the constitution visible, he made it possible to address it personally and publicly. He began the process and we must continue it; his death enhanced this work, it did not stop it. The prophet lives in the vision he leaves us; we are moved and measured by the prophetic vision.

It would be sufficient tribute to the memory of Martin Luther King, Jr., for us to concentrate on the contributions he made to the work of justice in the United States. But his vision was larger than that and so our objectives must be larger also.

A crucial step in Dr. King's life and ministry was the way he linked the pursuit of justice to the pursuit of peace. The truth that peace must be based on justice is beyond dispute; but in a complex, changing world both objectives must be pursued simultaneously. A lasting peace must be rooted in justice, but in the nuclear age keeping the peace provides the space in which we can work for greater justice. This is one of the decisive characteristics of our time: A failure to keep the nuclear peace will foreclose our quest for justice and all the other values which make life meaningful.

Dr. King did not live to see the frightening upward spiral of the nuclear arms race in recent years, but his vision and message are relevant to our efforts to address—and redress—the new realities.

In this spirit, the Catholic bishops of the United States decided to weigh the nuclear question, to place it before the Church and the nation. We did so in our pastoral letter, *The Challenge of Peace: God's Promise and Our Response*. In a way, we were seeking to learn from the lesson of Dr. King. As pastors in a nuclear nation, we wanted to make the political and moral challenge of nuclear weapons a visible question of conscience for the American public. We addressed a series of issues which I shall not try to summarize here.

Instead, I will focus on one topic which is a direct link between the preaching of Dr. King and the pastoral letter of the Catholic bishops. When Dr. King tied the pursuit of justice to the pursuit of peace in his opposition to the Vietnam War, one of his reasons was that he recognized that resources used for war are taken from resources needed for building a just peace.

At times one must make war to secure the peace; but these are rare occasions and the political-moral task of our time is to consign this dilemma to history. The more fruitful task is to build a peace which makes war unnecessary.

The need to build the peace is a favorite topic of Pope John Paul II. He returned to the theme in his Christmas Message last month; he prayed that God would:

> Look with eyes of the newborn child upon the men and women who are dying of hunger while enormous sums are being spent on weapons. Look upon the unspeakable sorrow of parents witnessing the agony of their children, imploring them for that bread which they have not got but which could be obtained with even a tiny part of the sums poured out on sophisticated means of destruction, which make ever more threatening the clouds gathering on the horizon of humanity (Christmas Message, "Urbi et Orbi," December 25, 1983).

This was not the first time the Pope had contrasted the disparity between the needs of the world and the way we use its resources. His statement focuses our attention on one of the great tragedies of the age: the glaring clash between what we spend to enhance our capacity to destroy life and what we are willing to spend to promote life.

The Pope's statement was aimed at the global level, but he made special reference during the Christmas season to the distorted priorities of the major nations. His statement, I am convinced, has direct meaning for our national decisions. It is very much in accord with the thinking of the American bishops who said in their pastoral letter: "When we consider how and what we pay for defense today we need a broader view than the equation of arms with security. The threats to the security and stability of an interdependent world are not all contained in missiles and bombers" (*The Challenge of Peace*, no. 270).

There are those who claim that the substantial and continually increasing amounts spent on the arms race are justified as contributions to security. The Pope's words of last month and Dr. King's vision of the relationship of peace and justice force us to examine what we mean by security. We cannot be secure in a world in which, according to reputable studies, 450 million people go hungry and 30 children die every minute for want of food and vaccines while global military expenditures are $1.3 million per minute (Ruth L. Sivard, *World Military and Social Expenditures*, 1983).

Yet in the face of this reality, the United States has just reduced for a second time its rate of contributions to the International Development Agency which provides subsistence aid to the poorest countries of the world. We must ask what view of stable peace and what conception of security support such a policy. We must not only ask, we must demand something different.

The disparity between what we should do for peace based on justice and what we are doing under a distorted conception of security extends into our domestic policy. The competition for scarce resources has been played out vividly for the last several years. The fact we must all face is that we are clearly in a situation where every dollar spent for military measures is in competition with increased resources needed for human and social needs.

Severe cuts in social programs which fed, housed and cured those for whom Dr. King spoke in the 1960s have been accompanied by an astoundingly consistent rise in military spending. Faced with stubborn deficits, there will be another pitched battle on the budget this year. Already the targets for cuts are medical and nutrition programs. What view of security moves us as a nation to believe that hungry and homeless people in the world's wealthiest democracy is a basis for a stable domestic peace?

What kind of political vision is at work when we have intricate national debates about whether hunger is a national crisis or only a human catastrophe? What are we to think about our future as a compassionate society when these detailed debates about people going hungry are not matched at all by a similar scrutiny on spending for our capacity to destroy others and possibly ourselves?

I am not arguing that there is no military component to a true definition of security. A nation has an obligation to defend itself against unjust aggressors and a certain military capability is needed for this in today's world. I am saying, however, that to be truly secure, peace must also be linked to a conception of justice nationally and internationally.

There are two reasons, both found in the Pope's message, which require a more stringent test for military spending and a more generous view of social spending. First, we are now building weapons which themselves endanger a stable peace in the nuclear age; this is sufficient reason to stop them. Second, we know that direct competition exists today for every dollar; to allocate it to an almost exclusively military view of security forecloses even the possibility that it will be used for human needs.

The national budget debate now before us stands under the shadow of Pope John Paul II's severe criticism of our present priorities and Martin Luther King's vision of how a compassionate nation should build the peace at home and abroad.

The Scriptures tell us that where there is no vision, the people perish. Dr. King had a vision, one that saw peace as the fruit of justice. It was this vision that shaped his dream for America and the world, but we have yet to measure up fully to it. His legacy calls us to bring this vision into clear focus so that it can shape our dreams and actions as we move toward the third millennium of the Christian era. May this memorial service in his honor, and the national holidays we will observe in the future, motivate us to complete the work he began.

Address

"The Church in the Public Life of the Nation: The American Bishops' Pastoral Letter"*

University of Chicago, Chicago, Illinois

—*January 16, 1984* —————————————————————

The last three days have been a very interesting and meaningful experience for me. On Saturday, I spoke on the American bishops' pastoral letter, *The Challenge of Peace: God's Promise and Our Response*, at Ebenezer Baptist Church in Atlanta, commemorating the 55th birthday of Dr. Martin Luther King, Jr. Yesterday, I gave the keynote address at a meeting sponsored by the Education Department of the U.S. Catholic Conference where Catholic school administrators and others involved in the Church's educational ministry had gathered to discuss the implementation of the pastoral presently underway across the country. This evening, in this academic setting, I have the privilege of participating in this symposium on some of the issues addressed in the pastoral letter. These diverse but uniquely significant forums, each with a distinct constituency—ecumenical, academic and ecclesial—fulfill my hopes, and those of all the Catholic bishops, for the way in which the pastoral letter should be communicated, critiqued and discussed.

Obviously each forum treats the letter differently, but this is necessary if its content is to permeate the public life of our nation. The setting here at the University of Chicago has specifically shaped my lecture. The experience of chairing the committee which drafted the pastoral had several

*Also published in *Origins*, vol. 13, no. 34, February 2, 1984, pp. 566–69.

dimensions. While reflecting upon them would indeed make an interesting presentation, I do not believe that this would be the best way to use
our time this evening. For I see this as a splendid opportunity to cross a
corridor separating bishops or church administrators from the theological
enterprise as it is cultivated in a university setting, a corridor which at
times assumes the proportions of a chasm.

Briefly, the experience of drafting not only surfaced a series of theological and moral questions which had to be addressed to complete the
letter, but it also highlighted more long-term pastoral and theological
questions which require continued assessment from this community and
other faculties like yours throughout the nation.

This faculty, through the work of a number of its scholars, has shown a
particular interest in the public ministry of the Church and the public
function of theology. Without addressing the specific dimensions of any
single author or argument, I have taken the public role of the Church as
my theme because it was so much a part of my experience during the last
three years, and because there remain many unanswered questions about
how we should fulfill our public role. Despite the complexities and ambiguities, however, I am certain of this: The Church's public ministry must
be cultivated.

In pursuit of this objective let me reflect briefly on three questions: (1)
The Church and public policy; (2) public opinion and public policy; and
(3) policy choices and "The Challenge of Peace."

THE CHURCH AND PUBLIC POLICY

Throughout the drafting process and in the months since the pastoral
was published, the Catholic bishops have been in the midst of a major
policy debate on war and peace. Participating in the debate has been a
two-dimensional experience: (1) deciding where to stand and what to say;
and (2) justifying our right to be this centrally involved in a public question affecting our society and the world as a whole. At first glance, the experience of the pastoral letter appears principally as an exercise of our
social ministry, a political and moral analysis of the nuclear age. But just
below the surface of the moral arguments lie the ecclesial questions; addressing them became an exercise in apologetics in the public forum.

Defining the Church's role in the public life of the nation fitted into
this ecclesial-apologetic category, requiring that three issues be examined:
the *place* of the Church; the *posture* we assumed; and the *perspective* we
used to guide our participation in the public debate.

Explaining the proper place of the Church in the public arena was a
continuous task. Most often it was done in response to charges that we

were violating the separation of Church and state. My experience of the last three years is that this precious tenet of our constitutional tradition holds a paradoxical place in the public mind. There seems to be an inverse relationship between the readiness of people to invoke the principle and their capacity to understand it clearly.

The phrase is used most often to tell religious bodies to be quiet. However, my reading of the constitutional principle—and the theology which affirms its truth—is that the separation of Church and state is designed to provide religious organizations space to speak. To put it succinctly, the separation of Church and state means that religious communities should expect neither favoritism nor discrimination in the exercise of their religious and civic functions. They are free to participate in any dimension of the public debate, but they must earn the right to be heard by the quality of their arguments. The place of the Church is separate from the state but, as John Courtney Murray continually reminded us, never separate from society. In society, churches are voluntary associations, free to address the public agenda of the nation. More specifically, they are voluntary associations with a disciplined capacity to analyze the moral-religious significance of public issues. That, at least, is how the Catholic bishops saw their place in the nuclear debate.

Accordingly, we assumed a posture which was designed to keep our role both ecclesial *and* public. The challenge was how to speak *as* a Church *to* a public issue; how to speak *from* a tradition of faith in a language which was *open* to public acceptance by citizens of several faiths and no faith. Early in the pastoral, the bishops defined their posture in this way: "As bishops we believe that the nature of Catholic moral teaching, the principles of Catholic ecclesiology and the demands of our pastoral ministry require that this letter speak both to Catholics in a specific way and to the wider political community regarding public policy. Neither audience and neither modes of address can be neglected when the issue has the cosmic dimensions of the nuclear arms race" (*The Challenge of Peace*, no. 19).

I need not stress the fact that, embedded in this description of our posture, are issues which go beyond a choice of language and a determination of relevant audiences for a pastoral message. The classical questions of faith and reason, nature and grace, church and world are cryptically contained in this paragraph. These perennial issues are honed to a specific sharpness by the nuclear question.

Historically, the moral issues of war and peace have spilled over into ecclesiology; today the cosmic dimensions of the nuclear question have moved many to say that the Christian posture can only be one of separation—personally, vocationally and ecclesially—from the societal enterprise of possessing nuclear weapons. Despite the radical moral skepticism of the pastoral letter about ever containing the use of nuclear weapons within justifiable limits, the bishops were not persuaded that this moral judgment should lead to an ecclesial posture of withdrawal from dialogue or participation in the public life of the nation. Rather, in accord with the traditional Catholic conception, they affirmed a posture of dialogue with the pluralistic secular world. I am the first to say—after the past three years—that it is a precarious posture, but one I find more adequate than either total silence within society or absolute separation from society.

Our understanding of our place and posture shaped our perspective in the letter. This perspective has classical roots but contemporary relevance. Since at least the time of Augustine, the moral teaching of the Church on warfare has had a pastoral and a policy function. In the words of the pastoral letter, "Catholic teaching on peace and war has had two purposes: to help Catholics form their consciences and to contribute to the public policy debate about the morality of war" (*The Challenge of Peace*, no. 16).

Both dimensions have public relevance. If the Church effectively carries out its teaching role, assisting in the formation of adult Christian conscience on matters of war and peace, this will inevitably have an impact on the public perception of these issues. Questions of the limits and obligations of citizenship, conscientious objection, selective conscientious objection and professional ethics in military service will all be sharpened. In a corresponding fashion, the engagement by the Church, as an institution in the public policy debate, opens space in the public argument for explicit consideration of the moral dimensions of policy. In the perspective of the bishops, the pastoral and policy purposes of the letter are complementary.

PUBLIC OPINION AND PUBLIC POLICY

Both the pastoral and policy dimensions of the teaching on war and peace are linked to the Church's role in the development of public opinion. In a democratic society, the Church's role in the public life of the nation is directly related to, though not exhausted by, the theme of public opinion. A major direction of the pastoral letter was set by a quotation from Pope John Paul II:

> Peace cannot be built by the power of rulers alone. Peace can be firmly constructed only if it corresponds to the resolute determination of all people of good will. Rulers must be supported and enlightened by a public opinion that encourages them or, where necessary, expresses disapproval (*World Day of Peace Message*, 1982).

In the perspective of this quotation, public opinion plays both a positive and a restraining role: At times it should provide support for necessary but perhaps unpopular initiatives; at other times public opinion should place limits on the direction of policy. The bishops tried in the pastoral letter to fulfill both functions.

If public opinion is a key vehicle for the Church in its public role, then we need some sense of both the possibilities and limitations of the function of public opinion in a complex democracy. My conception is that public opinion has a crucial but not guaranteed effect on major policy decisions. If we fail to cultivate an active, engaged public opinion on key questions, we lose an important moral as well as political resource. But even a carefully nurtured public opinion will not guarantee specific results.

To be more specific, public opinion does not usually translate immediately into concrete policy choices. Rather, on key major issues an atmosphere can be shaped in society which sets quite identifiable parameters within which detailed policy choices are then made. I believe it is possible to identify the role of such an atmosphere in recent U.S. history on issues as diverse as civil rights, tax and welfare policies and the use of U.S. troops in combat. This is not to say that public opinion is always wise and well formed politically or ethically. My point is simply to highlight that it does have an effect. If this is true, then the task of trying to shape a well-formed public opinion, which both provides positive direction and sets moral limits for power, is central to the public role of the Church.

Our experience at the Catholic Bishops' Conference provides the basis for distinguishing different kinds of influence through public opinion. On the war and peace question, there certainly has been a perceptible impact on the rhetoric of U.S. policy about nuclear war in the last few years; we no longer hear major officials talking about "winning" nuclear wars or even "prevailing" in them. The public opinion costs of such language are too high. When one moves from the level of rhetoric to concrete policy choices, however, the problem is more complex, as I will indicate briefly.

The bishops' experience in the Central America debate over the past four years highlights a different lesson: It is easier to prevent certain policy choices than it is to shape a redirection of policy. The Catholic bishops have opposed the basic direction of U.S. policy in Central America since 1980; in a series of policy statements reaching from 1980 through testimony by Archbishop James A. Hickey before the Kissinger Commission in October 1983, we have tried to contain the military option and emphasize the diplomatic element of U.S. policy. I think we have, along with others, been somewhat effective in preventing a larger U.S. military role; we have not been effective in substantially recasting the premises of U.S. policy.

My sense, in light of the recent Kissinger Commission Report, is that we are now about where we have been for the past four years. The commission reaffirms the basic direction of U.S. policy; we have never been convinced of the wisdom of that policy and I remain unconvinced of it today. New efforts will be needed to place limits on the military options, most especially placing firm public restraint on any idea of using U.S. troops in the region. The positive themes of using human rights criteria as a basis for U.S. aid and of providing humanitarian assistance should be supported. But the basic redirection which is so needed will be very difficult to accomplish. We should continue to press for it, but it will not be easily realized.

A third example offers other lessons. One finds a substantial body of common opinion relative to war and peace issues among those concerned with the ethics of policy. The translation of this moral consensus on nuclear issues, which is so real, to other related issues is extraordinarily complicated. If one takes the question of abortion, for example, the widely differing views within the community of articulate moral opinion make it very difficult to relate ethical discourse to policy discourse. In a sense the ecumenical debate must precede the policy debate.

I do not propose to enter either tonight, but it is precisely such further discussion that I commend to this academic community. I gave an address at Fordham University recently in which I emphasized the urgent need to look more carefully—within the ecclesial communities and our secular society—at the relationship among several issues which are analogously related. It is not a question of collapsing war and abortion or identifying either with capital punishment, but these three very visible public issues do require that those concerned with the ethics of policy examine our premises as well as the public conclusions we advocate. This broad topic is of profound interest to me, but I can only mention it here since I need to return to the more specific question of public opinion and policy choices on the war and peace agenda.

POLICY CHOICES AND "THE CHALLENGE OF PEACE"

In terms of my general topic—the Church's role in public life—the nuclear debate provides an interesting case study. It is clear that public opinion has played a significant role in the policy debate recently, and it is equally clear that the contribution of religious communities has been visible, vocal and effective.

Having said that, I think it is necessary to probe more deeply some specific questions about the future. We need to measure the effect of public opinion in the nuclear debate. In terms of setting an atmosphere it has been surprisingly successful: There is a perceptible public scrutiny of the direction of government policy on nuclear questions, and a demonstrable effect at the level of rhetoric. I suspect that the "peace movement," as it is sometimes called, has a greater consensus on what it opposes than on what it would support; it is probably more effective in pushing governments to negotiate than it would be if a specific treaty were in the Senate awaiting ratification. Since we do not now have the luxury of testing this last proposition, I believe we should push for effective negotiations and begin to think more concretely about how a positive consensus could be shaped about specific measures which might issue from such negotiations.

A more fundamental issue is that of paying attention to the need for *sustained* public scrutiny of policy. The danger of the moment is presuming we have a long-term effort in place. I agree, as I indicated, that there is more organized public attention to nuclear questions than ever before, but I think it is useful to recall a lesson from the 1960s. A similar, though less extensive, body of public opinion existed in the early 1960s. Shortly after the Limited Test Ban Treaty was ratified, however, the arms control constituency dissolved; there were several reasons for this, not least of which was the Vietnam War, but the effects of a sporadic interest by the public in the nuclear question are very costly. An apathetic public opinion sets the wrong atmosphere. In periods of apathy, like the 1970s, policy lacks both direction and discipline.

Unscrutinized policy decisions are one of the costs of public apathy. In reviewing the last 20 years of arms control, few decisions appear more consequential for efforts to restrain the arms race than the deployment of multiple independently targetable warheads (MIRVs). Questions remain to this day as to why the United States did not try in SALT I to ban MIRV-ing rather than take this fateful step in a qualitative escalation of the arms race. My purpose is not to settle the historical debate, but to highlight the policy consequences. The MIRVing decision has made every effort at arms control more difficult; we literally mortgaged the process of arms control through a policy choice which received very little public evaluation.

Decisions facing us in the 1980s have some of the characteristics of the MIRVing decision. One finds again policy choices with significant technological implications for the nuclear balance. The technological drive to proceed with new systems should be measured by broader criteria than are presently being used.

We define MX as a response to Soviet 18s and 19s; we describe Pershing IIs as a response to SS-20s. The political logic of these decisions is clear; the strategic logic, however, is widely debated. Many see in the MX a dangerous response to a bad decision by the Soviets to deploy weapons with first-strike characteristics. Others focus on the Pershing II deployment as more dangerous than MX in its impact on Soviet perceptions and plans, since it reduces the warning time for the Soviets and encourages "launch-on-warning" policies.

In the pastoral letter, we accorded a real but narrow justification to deterrence. That justification depends almost totally on the role of the deterrent in preventing the use of nuclear weapons in a politically divided world. But marginal justification of deterrence is contingent upon containing the character of the deterrent to the specific function of preventing nuclear war. Every increment to the deterrence arsenal must be tested by this criterion. Additions which may have political utility or allow us to match the other side symmetrically, but which increase the danger of the deterrence relationship should not, in my view, be supported. I shall not engage in a detailed discussion of these proposed deployments, but I wish to set them in the context of what we have learned from the MIRVing decision of the 1970s. We should not have to recoup in the 1990s what might be salvaged for arms control by a decision in the 1980s.

My purpose here is not to enter a casuistic process of assessing a range of weapons systems, but to say that an effective public opinion must have the capability to make such assessment. These decisions are, obviously, not purely moral questions, but they are not devoid of moral dimensions. The public role of the Church involves participation in a broad-based effort to set an atmosphere of moral scrutiny and to contribute to the public capability to move from general attitudes about war and peace to influencing specific directions in our policy.

The pastoral letter is one example of how the Church can function in the public life of the nation. It is hardly the answer to all of our questions—theological or moral, political or strategic—but it does provide an ongoing effort which needs not only to be cultivated but also to be critically examined. It is precisely such an effort of reflective examination which university faculties are uniquely suited to undertake. I invite and encourage a continuation of today's symposium in a sustained process of reflection on the public role of the Church in the life of the nation.

"The Challenge of Peace: Ecumenical Roots and Relationships"

Paul Wattson Ecumenical Seminar and Lecture Series

University of San Francisco, San Francisco, California

— January 23, 1984 ───────────────────────────────

I appreciate the opportunity to meet with you in an ecumenical setting to discuss the Catholic bishops' recent pastoral letter, *The Challenge of Peace: God's Promise and Our Response.* In the last six months I have been able to present this document to many groups of both a religious and secular nature. I feel a strong responsibility to do this as often as my pastoral duties allow.

Tonight's meeting, however, gives me a special opportunity to thank the Protestant community for the overwhelming support which it has given to the letter, and to illustrate the ecumenical roots and implications of this letter written by Roman Catholic bishops. Accordingly, I shall divide my presentation into three parts: the ecumenical foundations of the pastoral letter, a summary of its contents, and an examination of its ecumenical implications.

THE ECUMENICAL FOUNDATIONS OF THE PASTORAL

Many observers have noted the extraordinary response of the Protestant community to the pastoral letter. I shall return to that theme. But I wish to begin by focusing on an ecumenical dimension of the letter which is too little noticed: the contribution of Protestant theologians and ethicists to the content of the document.

The letter's use of the work of Protestant theologians, which is documented in the footnotes, is not an accidental development. While the decisive and primary intellectual framework for the bishops has recent papal teaching on war and peace, the theological argument in the letter has been enriched by work done by both Catholic and Protestant theologians in the past twenty years. Two major dimensions of the theology of the pastoral have been influenced by this recent work.

The first is the basic moral perspective—the moral theory—used to assess the question of warfare. The letter's dominant moral theory is the "just-war ethic" which has provided the principal perspective for addressing the use of force in the Catholic tradition since St. Augustine. Precisely because of the central position the just-war ethic has held and continues to hold in Catholic theology, it is significant that the pastoral letter also acknowledges that the other major perspective in the Christian tradition, the nonviolent or pacifist option, is a legitimate choice for an individual, even though it is clearly not the public policy position of our document. The relationship between the just-war ethic and the nonviolent perspective in the pastoral has received substantial attention from commentators. Both moral positions have benefited from the work of Protestant theologians in the last two decades. Historically, the nonviolent themes have been developed within the "peace churches" of Protestant tradition. Today one finds Christians across the spectrum of our churches, Catholic and Protestant, who draw inspiration and direction from this nonviolent perspective. The theological writing of Professors John Yoder and Stanley Hauerwas of Notre Dame (both Protestants) and the work of Jim Wallis and his associates at *Sojourners* magazine, as well as the cooperation among Catholics and Quakers in various aspects of the peace movement, are all ways in which the theology of nonviolence and peacemaking have influenced parts of the Catholic community.

From a historical perspective it may be more surprising that the just-war theology of the pastoral also is indebted to recent Protestant research. While it has been cultivated most extensively by Catholic authors the just-war ethic is not a doctrinal preserve of Catholics. Beginning in the 1960s and continuing to the present there has been a renewed interest in the just-war theory among Protestants who have produced some landmark studies cited in the pastoral letter. The analytical work of Professors Ralph E. Potter of Harvard, Paul Ramsey of Princeton, and James Childress of the University of Virginia as well as the superbly documented historical work of Professor LeRoy B. Walters of Georgetown and James Johnson of Rutgers has greatly contributed to our understanding of the content and capacity of just-war ethics to evaluate public policy.

Indeed, the second contribution of Protestant theology to just-war thought is precisely in the area of applying the principles to specific policy choices. Here the work of Professor Ramsey of Princeton in his two books *War and the Christian Conscience* (1961) and *The Just War* (1968) holds a unique place. Our letter does not follow Ramsey's conclusions but like many others we have immensely benefited from his research. The same debt can be acknowledged to the work of Dr. Alan Geyer of Washington, D.C., whose extensive writings on war and peace are used in the Catholic and Protestant communities and whose testimony to our drafting committee was particularly helpful.

It goes without saying that a list of contemporary Catholic authors could be developed to whom the bishops turned for guidance in writing the pastoral. I have specified these Protestant theologians in order to show that the ecumenical roots of the pastoral letter are very specific and very contemporary. Among other things, the pastoral demonstrates how the ecumenical dialogue has developed to the point where real theological exchange shapes our views on key issues across ecclesial lines.

Having discussed the foundations of the letter, let me now examine its content.

THE CHALLENGE OF PEACE: A SUMMARY

The pastoral letter devotes over thirty pages to the challenge of constructing peace in an increasingly interdependent world. The political and moral challenge it poses for world politics may be its most significant long-term teaching. This positive section on peace shows why the nuclear issue does not exhaust the challenges of the moment. Issues of human rights, economic justice and respect for rights of all nations, great and small, are unfinished tasks in the daily business of world affairs today.

The urgent need to build peace does not, however, dispense with the constant effort required to prevent any use of nuclear weapons and to limit other uses of force in international relations. It is this section of the letter which has attracted the most attention—the policy section containing an analysis of the moral problems related to the use of nuclear weapons and the strategy of nuclear deterrence.

The argument of the pastoral must be understood in the context of the just-war teaching which is clear about the duty of the state to defend society, the right of the state to use force as a last resort, and the need to assess state action by moral criteria whenever force is used. It is those moral criteria that the pastoral addresses. The argument moves in three steps: first a basic premise is established; then this promise is related to three cases of use; and, finally, to an assessment of deterrence.

The premise of the letter is that nuclear weapons and nuclear strategy constitute a qualitatively new moral problem. The nuclear age is not simply an extension of the moral questions on warfare addressed by our ancestors. Albert Einstein, one of the fathers of the nuclear age, said that everything is changed except the way we think. We have experienced the meaning of this statement as we have struggled with nuclear issues in the development of the pastoral.

From a moral tradition like ours, which judges *some* but not all uses of force to be morally legitimate, the nuclear era poses a profound—indeed a revolutionary—challenge. The extreme skepticism of the pastoral regarding our ability to control any use of nuclear weapons is a pervasive influence throughout the policy analysis of use and deterrence.

The first case is "counter-population" warfare. Directly intended attacks on civilian centers qualifies as murder in Catholic moral theology. It is not justified even in retaliation for an attack on our cities, and no exceptions of the principle are admitted.

The second case is the "initiation of nuclear war." This requires a different moral judgment. The pastoral opposes the first use of nuclear weapons and supports a "no first use" pledge in these words: "We do not perceive any situation in which the deliberate initiation of nuclear warfare, on however restricted a scale, can be morally justified. Non-nuclear attacks by another state must be resisted by other than nuclear means." The letter explicitly acknowledges that it will take time to implement such a policy. It also acknowledges certain objections to a "no first use" pledge. Hence this assessment does not have the same absolute character as the "counter-population" section; we have made prudential judgments, and we are aware that people can and will draw other conclusions based on a different reading of the factual data.

The third case, that of "limited nuclear war," involves an assessment of what the *real* as opposed to *theoretical* meaning of "limited" is. Taking into account the long debate—both strategic and moral—which surrounds this question, the pastoral argues that the entire burden of proof rests on those who would hold that limited nuclear exchange can indeed be contained within moral limits. The skepticism of the letter about the possibility of control shows through clearly in this section.

On the question of deterrence, the judgment of the pastoral is based on Pope John Paul's statement to the United Nations in June 1982. We have taken the Holy Father's judgment and applied it to the specific details of U.S. strategic policy. Such an application, of course, is done in our name. The judgment of the pastoral is "strictly conditioned moral acceptance" of deterrence. Devoid of all modifiers, the judgment is acceptance, not condemnation. But we have used the term "strictly conditioned" to stress that deterrence must be seen as a transitional strategy.

The pastoral highlights the meaning of transitional by attaching a series of conditions to the content of deterrence policy. The letter seeks to keep deterrence limited to a very specific function, it resists extending it to war-fighting strategies, and it calls for keeping a clear fire-break between conventional and nuclear weapons. Finally, we have called for an aggressive pursuit of arms control and disarmament objectives, including a halt to the testing, production and deployment of nuclear systems.

THE ECUMENICAL IMPLICATIONS OF THE PASTORAL

The reception accorded the pastoral letter in the Protestant community was truly a remarkable sign of ecumenical support. As you know, the National Council of Churches commended the pastoral to its membership; several national church bodies passed resolutions about the pastoral, and the religious press in the Protestant community gave us very generous support and coverage.

In light of this response, for which the Catholic bishops are extremely grateful, I wish in this final section of my remarks to reflect upon the future of the Church's witness to peace. Specifically, I wish to comment on the lessons of the pastoral concerning the role of the Church in public policy, and then the relationship between ecumenical dialogue and our public role.

Most of the public commentary about the pastoral letter focused on the specific moral conclusions we drew about deterrence and the use of nuclear weapons. My concern is to step back from the specific conclusions of the pastoral and assess how the Church has influenced the public debate.

There are lessons here, I believe, which go beyond the questions of war and peace. The premise of our analysis was that every major policy decision has a moral dimension. There is no such thing as a "nonmoral policy"; it may take a certain degree of analysis or probing to uncover the moral choices made in what is described as a "purely technical" decision, but the moral choices are always there, often embedded in the way political, strategic or technological choices are made. I should also add that our premise is based on the idea that there is no "purely moral analysis"; this means that moral conclusions on complex policy issues cannot be drawn in isolation from the technical data of the problem.

The style of analysis in the pastoral letter, therefore, was to construct a dialogue between the empirical dimensions of the nuclear question and the moral principles of the Christian tradition. The impact of the pastoral in the policy debate has been due, I believe, to this style of moral analysis. The major consequence has been to open space in the national debate on nuclear policy for the moral dimensions of the question. By opening space for the moral factor in the policy debate, we have helped set a framework for others to join the moral scrutiny. In the long run this may be the most significant contribution of the pastoral letter. We made very specific policy judgments and we want those to be considered, but we also are aware that no single document has the answer to the policy issues of the nuclear age.

By opening space for the moral dimension of the public debate we have tried to establish the principle that in every forum where the nuclear question is addressed, where decisions are made and policies shaped, there should be explicit public consideration of the moral issues. This means that several groups and individuals should participate in the analysis of the ethical and empirical issues. The explicit appeal to moral justification for policies which came from representatives of the U.S. government in their dialogues with the bishops, and the increased attention to moral factors which one finds in the secular journals are indications of either the pressure or the incentive participants in the debate feel to cast their policy conclusions in a moral framework. When this is done, either in government or outside, it is the beginning of moral analysis, for everyone's views (the bishops included) should be subjected to scrutiny.

The broader significance of our experience on the war and peace issue is the potential to which it points for the religious communities to open space for moral analysis of other public policy issues. Today we face a series of questions running from medical care to international relations, from equity and employment to budget priorities and national purpose, where the moral dimensions of issues are as important to our future as the technical calculations which absorb most of our public debates.

Religious groups should not expect or be given special treatment of any kind. We should earn a hearing in the public debate by the quality of our analysis. I am convinced that the moral factor of our public life is a topic which people inside and outside the churches are concerned about; if we can demonstrate how moral vision enriches the choices we face and the challenges which confront us as a nation, then space will be given to the moral factor in every public policy debate.

Such participation in the public arena will require a more extensive ecumenical exchange among the churches. On the war and peace question we share a common vision on a whole range of topics. This is not the case on every moral issue on the political and social spectrum. Nonetheless we are sufficiently well grounded in our ecumenical relationships that we can face our differences as well as our shared concerns.

I recently gave an address at Fordham University in which I set forth an argument linking the war and peace question with a series of other issues: capital punishment, abortion, and human rights in our domestic and foreign policy. It is not my intention to rehearse the main lines of that address here. I think it useful to say, however, that I realize it poses a delicate, indeed a difficult, set of questions for our ecumenical dialogue. I believe we agree on more issues than we differ about, but our differences on issues like abortion can be painful.

I purposely linked the issues for two reasons. First, I am convinced certain key moral principles in the pastoral letter, such as the prohibition of the direct killing of the innocent, relate to other issues as well. Second, I know that within the Catholic community these issues are treated selectively, with different groups appealing to the same principles, but not following the logic of the principles when it moves beyond one issue; I wanted to promote an explicit, conscious dialogue within the Catholic community about the question of consistency in our public policy positions.

I also believe the consistency question has relevance to the wider public debate. I am not saying the issues are either simple or identical. I do not believe consistency means that one has a single answer to several complex policy questions. I do believe, however, that consistency requires that within the churches and in our public debate, we should test our position and reasoning on similar issues. Precisely because we do not agree within the churches on some of these public questions, we could demonstrate in our own ecumenical debate how the wider public could work toward resolution of questions we cannot ignore but upon which we do not now agree. The quality of our ecumenical dialogue, in other words, can enhance the quality of our public debate.

In conclusion, let me express again to you, and through you to the wider Protestant community, my personal gratitude and that of my brother bishops for the support we have received. Let me pledge our continued involvement with you in the struggle to reverse the arms race and to move toward real peace and security in the world. And let me urge further consideration of how a disciplined moral debate in our ecumenical life might enhance the common good of our society.

Address

"The Challenge of Peace: Genesis, Principles and Perspectives of the American Bishops' Pastoral Letter"*

Catholic University of Louvain, Belgium

—February 1, 1984 ————————————————

I wish first to express my deep gratitude to the Catholic University of Louvain for the honor which will be bestowed upon me tomorrow. I will accept the doctorate *honoris causa* in the name of the other bishops of the United States in the collegial spirit which marked our many months of work on the pastoral letter *The Challenge of Peace: God's Promise and Our Response*. I will also accept this degree and I present this lecture today as a sign of the fruitful collaboration of the theological community and the episcopacy which has been a key element in the development and implementation of the pastoral letter in the United States. The complementary roles of the academy and the episcopacy in the pastoral life of the Church is a theme which I believe must be supported and cultivated in every way possible.

The purpose of my lecture today is to provide a framework for understanding the style and substance of the U.S. bishops' pastoral and for placing this American document in the life of the wider Church. I will address three themes: (1) the process of writing the pastoral; (2) the product of the process; and (3) the place of the letter in the Church.

————————————

*Also published in *Origins*, vol. 13, no. 36, February 16, 1984, pp. 605–08.

THE PROCESS OF WRITING THE PASTORAL: A DESCRIPTION

The decision to write a pastoral letter on the morality of war in the nuclear age was taken at the 1980 General Meeting of the National Conference of Catholic Bishops. The vote followed an extensive and wide-ranging discussion among the bishops in which a number of them, some young and newly appointed and others very senior members of the U.S. hierarchy, expressed a concern about the direction of the arms race and a conviction that the Church had something valuable to say about the fate and future of our nation and the world.

One question that commentators inside and outside the Church often raise is *why* the bishops came to the decision to move comprehensively into the public debate on war and peace in the 1980s. The question is put to us in two different ways: Some ask, why did you wait so long? Others ask, what made the events of the 1980s any more morally compelling or politically dangerous than the 1960s or the 1950s; why did you decide to speak now?

Behind these questions there is usually a lurking suspicion that the bishops' decision in 1980 was a narrowly political concern, directed against one party or specific individuals. Such suspicion is mistaken and misdirected. It ignores, for example, the fact that our Episcopal Conference has been addressing a wide range of foreign policy issues for a number of years. These include the role of human rights in U.S. foreign policy, the posture of the United States on issues of international economic justice, U.S. policy in Latin America and the Middle East, and, in a special way, the problem of the nuclear arms race. As many of you know, John Cardinal Krol's testimony on the SALT II agreements before the U.S. Senate Foreign Relations Committee in 1979 was a document of major interest in both theological and political circles.

But something even more important than our past record of addressing social issues must be clarified if there is to be a proper understanding of what propelled the U.S. bishops so visibly into the debate on war and peace in the 1980s. Our motivation was not narrowly political or partisan; it was rather due to a convergence of several forces of long-term significance which created basic consensus of opinion among the bishops.

In my view, three distinct forces were important in the 1980 decision to proceed with a pastoral letter. First, the U.S. bishops have been profoundly influenced by the teaching of the recent popes, particularly Pope John Paul II, on the issues of war and peace. This influence has been rooted in two characteristics: first, the intrinsic religious and moral power of the teaching itself; and second, the particular pastoral responsibility we feel in the United States to make the papal teaching applicable to the policies of one of the two nuclear superpowers.

A second motivating force for our episcopacy has been the experience we have had in opposing abortion in the United States; no institution in our country has been as vocal, as visible or as persistent in its opposition to abortion as the Catholic bishops. We have diligently and consistently worked for the maximum legal protection for the unborn. The experience of the abortion debate also had a double effect on us: On the one hand, we have experienced sustained involvement in a public policy debate at the center of American political life; on the other hand, we have always seen a direct parallel between the protection of human life in the womb and the preservation of human life in the face of the nuclear threat. In both cases we believe we have a pastoral responsibility to stand for the sanctity of life in the face of two menacing "signs of the times."

The third motivating force was a sense among many of the bishops that the nuclear arms race in particular was heading in an ever more dangerous direction, quantitatively and qualitatively, as we entered the 1980s. Faced on the one side by the urgent papal pleas for a redirection of global resources away from instruments of destruction and toward the satisfaction of the basic human needs of the poor and, on the other side, by proposals to expand the nuclear arsenals of both superpowers, the U.S. bishops were convinced by 1980 that a clear moral voice was needed in our country calling for a drastic change in our definition of security. Thus, we began the preparation of the pastoral letter.

The first step was the appointment of a special committee to draft the letter for consideration by the entire episcopate. Archbishop John Roach, then president of the NCCB, asked me to assume chairmanship and I accepted, knowing that the task was monumental, but convinced that the responsibility must be faced. The four other bishops who became indispensable collaborators on the committee were Bishop George Fulcher (who was killed in an automobile accident only last week), Bishop Thomas Gumbleton, Bishop John O'Connor and Bishop Daniel Reilly. We began our work in July 1981, and met at least monthly and often weekly for two years, completing our task at a specially convened meeting of the NCCB in Chicago on May 2–3, 1983.

Two aspects of the drafting of the pastoral are particularly interesting for the wider life of the Church: the hearings we held and the circulation of three drafts of the document to the general public.

The hearings were especially significant in the first nine months of the committee's work. During that time, we received testimony from thirty-five witnesses who represented a broad spectrum of views on the moral and strategic questions of the nuclear age and a great diversity of expertise. We listened to two former Secretaries of Defense (Mr. Harold Brown and Mr. Arthur Schlesinger), a number of arms control experts of very different convictions, many moral theologians who had addressed the issues of war and peace, retired military personnel, a physician, biblical scholars, and some Catholics who have been particularly active in the witness for peace over many years. We concluded our hearing process with a full day of meetings with senior officials of the U.S. government: Secretary of Defense Caspar Weinberger, the Under Secretary of State for Political Affairs, Mr. Lawrence Eagleberger, and the director of the Arms Control and Disarmament Agency, Mr. Eugene Rostow.

These hearings were very valuable to the committee for they immersed us in the political, strategic and moral debate. Along with the study that each of us was pursuing, these personal witnesses gave the bishops a very profound and wide-ranging sense of the complexity, the danger and the urgency of the present phase of the arms race.

Even while this extensive process of hearings was in progress, our committee was both shaping its views and beginning to write the first draft of the pastoral. We completed the initial draft in May 1982, and circulated it among the bishops the following month. We established at this time the procedure of sharing the drafts with other episcopal conferences and, of course, the Holy See, asking for comments and suggestions.

The first draft generated over 700 pages of written commentary and we found it necessary to revise our writing schedule, postponing a final vote on the document until the spring of 1983, so that we could give the responses adequate attention. Without going into detail, I wish simply to note that the public response to all three drafts of the pastoral was extraordinarily helpful to the committee. We took seriously the content of the commentary and shaped the writing of each successive draft in light of the reactions we had received.

The second draft was ready for circulation in October 1983; it was much longer than the first. Even while retaining many aspects of the first draft, it proceeded to expand the scriptural and theological sections of the document and it made a sharper criticism of the direction of the arms race and U.S. nuclear policy. The second draft was reviewed and discussed in detail at the General Meeting of the NCCB in November 1982. The debate among the bishops (which was open to the media) and their suggestions for revising the scriptural section, the treatment of the relationship between pacifism and the just-war teaching, the moral argumentation leading to our conclusion on deterrence, and the section on U.S.–Soviet relations had a decisive influence on our development of the third draft.

During the November 1982 meeting the Reagan Administration sent an extensive commentary on the second draft to every bishop. Many commentators attributed the changes from the second to the third draft to the very critical response made by the U.S. government. I believe a careful reading of the second and third drafts will show that the decisive influences on changes made were episcopal, not political. While we carefully considered the arguments raised by the government, we were neither surprised that it found the pastoral letter critical of U.S. policy nor were we convinced by the political commentary that we should change the basic direction of our moral analysis. We took particular note of the Reagan Administration's comments on targeting doctrine and we pursued this theme with officials of the administration in intensive discussions.

It was, however, the views of our own episcopacy, as I noted a moment ago, and the discussion which took place at the consultation convoked by the Holy See in January 1983, that had the really decisive impact on the third draft. The consultation in Rome gave Archbishop Roach and me the opportunity to hear the views of several European episcopal conferences. This consultation was, I believe, a valuable experience of collegiality; it was very helpful to the U.S. bishops involved and it established a framework within which we could proceed with our pastoral in the United States and other episcopal conferences, addressing issues proper to their countries, could proceed with their own statements.

The third draft was made public in April 1983, and sent to our bishops as the working document for the special General Meeting in May 1983. The public commentary emphasized the differences between the second and third drafts. There were differences, but the media commentary vastly overstated the degree of difference, often by concentrating on symbolic words rather than the main substantive arguments in the third draft. Prior to the Chicago meeting, the bishops submitted over 400 amendments which the committee had to review and take a position on when presenting the document at the Chicago meeting. During our two days in Chicago we considered, through a disciplined and complex parliamentary process, the 400 previously submitted amendments and some additional ones which were presented during the course of the meeting itself. Then, by a vote of 238 to 9, we approved a final text which reasserted a sharp, detailed critique of the nuclear arms race and the prevailing policies driving the race. It is that final text which I would like now to summarize for you.

THE PRODUCT: *THE CHALLENGE OF PEACE—* A SUMMARY

The pastoral letter devotes over thirty pages to the challenge of constructing peace in an increasingly interdependent world. The political and moral challenge it poses for world politics may be the most significant long-term teaching of the pastoral. This positive section on peace shows why the nuclear issue does not exhaust the challenges of the moment; issues of human rights, economic justice and respect for the rights of all nations, great and small, are unfinished tasks in the daily business of world affairs today.

The urgent need to build peace does not, however, dispense with the constant effort required to prevent any use of nuclear weapons and to limit other uses of force in international relations. It is this section of the letter which has attracted the most attention: the policy section containing an analysis of the moral problems related to the use of nuclear weapons and the strategy of nuclear deterrence.

The argument of the pastoral must be understood in a context of Catholic teaching which is clear about the duty of the state to defend society, the right of the state to use force as a last resort, and the need for state action to be assessed by moral criteria whenever force is used. It is those moral criteria that the pastoral addresses and the argument moves in three steps: first, a basic premise is established; then this premise is related to three cases of use and; finally, to an assessment of deterrence.

The premise of the letter is that nuclear weapons and nuclear strategy constitute a qualitatively new moral problem. The nuclear age is not simply an extension of the moral questions on warfare addressed by our ancestors. Albert Einstein, one of the fathers of the nuclear age, said that everything is changed except the way we think. We have experienced the meaning of this statement as we have struggled with nuclear issues in the development of the pastoral.

From a moral tradition like ours, which judges *some* but not all uses of force to be morally legitimate, the nuclear era poses a profound—indeed a revolutionary—challenge. The extreme skepticism of the pastoral regarding our ability to control any use of nuclear weapons is a pervasive influence throughout the policy analysis of use and deterrence.

The first case is "counter-population" warfare; directly intended attacks on civilian centers qualifies as murder in Catholic moral theology. It is not justified even in retaliation for an attack on our cities and no exceptions of the principle are admitted.

The second case is the "initiation of nuclear war." This case requires a different moral judgment. The pastoral opposes the first use of nuclear weapons and supports a "no first use" pledge in these words: "We do not perceive any situation in which the deliberate initiation of nuclear warfare, on however restricted a scale, can be morally justified. Non-nuclear attacks by another state must be resisted by other than nuclear means." The letter explicitly acknowledges that it will take time to implement such a policy. It also acknowledges certain objections to a "no first use" pledge. Hence this assessment does not have the same absolute character as the "counter-population" section; we have made prudential judgments, and we are aware that people can and will draw other conclusions based on a different reading of the factual data.

The third case, that of "limited nuclear war," involves an assessment of what the *real* meaning of "limited" is, as opposed to the *theoretical*. Taking into account the long debate—both strategic and moral—which surrounds this question, the pastoral argues that the entire burden of proof rests on those who would hold that limited nuclear exchange can indeed be contained within moral limits. The skepticism of the letter about the possibility of control shows through clearly in this section.

On the question of deterrence, the judgment of the pastoral is based on Pope John Paul II's statement to the United Nations in June 1982. We have taken the Holy Father's judgment and applied it to the specific details of U.S. strategic policy. Such an application, of course, is done in our name. The judgment of the pastoral is "strictly conditioned moral acceptance" of deterrence. Devoid of all modifiers, the judgment is acceptance not condemnation. But we have used the term "strictly conditioned" to stress that deterrence must be seen as a transitional strategy. The pastoral highlights the meaning of transitional by attaching a series of conditions to the content of deterrence policy. The letter seeks to keep deterrence limited to a very specific function; it resists extending it to war-fighting strategies, and it calls for keeping a clear fire-break between conventional and nuclear weapons. Finally, we have called for an aggressive pursuit of arms control and disarmament objectives, including a halt to the testing, production and deployment of nuclear systems.

THE PLACE OF THE PASTORAL IN THE CHURCH: A SURVEY

While I could continue my analysis of the pastoral letter in greater detail, I believe that it would be more useful now to step back from it and place it in the context of the concerns of the universal Church. I can do this only in the most general terms and I offer my remarks not as a definitive analysis but a preliminary comment on the complementarity and the contrasts which can be found in a series of statements made by several episcopal conferences in the last year.

The first observation is the widespread and profound degree of pastoral concern which has been expressed by the bishops of the Catholic Church about the arms race. At the center of this chorus of voices is, of course, the chief pastor, Pope John Paul II, but his example has been followed by individual bishops and by episcopal conferences as a body. I do not have an exhaustive list, but I am aware of statements from the episcopal conferences of Austria, Belgium, Brazil, Canada, England and Wales, the Federal Republic of Germany, France, the German Democratic Republic, Holland, Hungary, Japan and Scotland. This is an impressive manifestation of religious-moral involvement by the leadership of our Church. Indeed, before we proceed to a more detailed commentary, we should note the fact that two decades after *Gaudium et spes* called for a renewed commitment of the Church to contributing to the solution of the major problems of our time, we find the Catholic Church throughout the world identified with a vigorous effort to oppose one of the greatest dangers the human family faces.

A second observation which is crucial to understanding this worldwide opposition to the arms race is that each of the local episcopal statements fits into a well-defined framework. This framework is established by the teaching of the popes of the nuclear age from Pope Pius XII through Pope John Paul II, and by the conciliar teaching found in *Gaudium et spes*. The substantive details of the papal and conciliar framework are well known to this audience and they are far too extensive for me to summarize. In a recent major address in the United States at the University of San Francisco, Agostino Cardinal Casaroli, the Secretary of State of the Holy See, provided a detailed statement of these documents and of the work of the Holy See in the pursuit of peace. The cardinal noted that the Holy See's activity has three dimensions: (1) a doctrinal, teaching role, outlining moral principles concerning war and peace; (2) the influencing of public opinion, particularly among Catholics but also in the wider civil society; and (3) direct action addressed to governments and other centers of decision-making on questions affecting peace.

Speaking from the perspective of the U.S. bishops, I can say that it was precisely this threefold role which we sought to fulfill within our country. We saw our primary obligation in terms of an ecclesial tradition with the longest recorded history of assessing issues of war and peace in the Western world. We believed that the principal way our moral teaching would be effective was precisely in terms of its impact on public opinion, helping to form a constituency of conscience within the Church and in American society committed to reversing the arms race. As part of the process of shaping public opinion, the bishops addressed U.S. policy directly, always conscious that there are *two* nuclear superpowers responsible for the arms race, but especially aware of the pastoral responsibilities we hold for the direction of U.S. policy.

In light of these two observations, let me now move to a third consideration: a comparison of the American pastoral letter with the statements of the French and German hierarchies. I will do this only in the most general terms and as part of a larger dialogue among our local churches which must be pursued by theologians, social scientists and all members of the People of God. My comparison is meant to be a catalyst for further commentary, not a final word. I believe it is useful to make the explicit comparison, however, precisely because the complexity of the nuclear arms race requires diverse insights to reverse its dynamic and reorient our policies toward the shaping of a just and peaceful world order. The unity of the framework from which each of our episcopal statements proceeds is an established fact; the pluralism of the specific statements can be a step toward deeper analysis and a more effective witness for peace in each of our local churches. In this spirit, let me comment on the French, German and U.S. statements in terms of the tone of each, the themes addressed and the judgments made on specific issues.

The tone of all three episcopal statements reflects the urgency of the call of Pope John XXIII in *Pacem in terris* (1963), Pope Paul VI at the United Nations in 1965, and Pope John Paul II at Hiroshima in 1982. There is in all three episcopal documents an unmistakable determination to say to our governments and our people that the present direction of the arms race is unacceptable. It is unacceptable because of the danger it poses and because of the way it diverts resources from other tasks. A particularly vivid example of the distortion of our priorities is the way in which the industrialized nations have just reduced significantly their commitments to the funding of the International Development Agency of the World Bank, even as the spending for defense rises in our nations. The U.S. role in both failing to meet an adequate commitment to the poorest nations of the world and moving toward major expenditures for strategic weapons of doubtful value is something which is of great concern to me. The tone of all three episcopal statements appears, to me at least, to find our present direction in the industrialized nations a scandal to the poor of the world.

The *themes* of the documents can be analyzed in terms of two major questions. In a Catholic theology of peace, the two basic structural questions are: (1) how do we build the peace? and (2) how do we keep the peace? The concept of building the peace, of shaping the *shalom* of God in the midst of history, is the positive task to which Pope Paul VI called us in 1965 at the United Nations, which Pope John XXIII outlined in *Pacem in terris*, and which Pope John Paul II describes regularly in his addresses throughout the world. The idea of keeping the peace is the key to understanding Catholic teaching on the morality of war, for that teaching had always found it useful both to condemn the idea of war and to try to set limits to violence if no other way can be found to protect basic human values from unjust aggression.

The three episcopal statements we are considering all address these two questions but they do so with distinct orientations. The U.S. pastoral letter takes up the question of building the peace in chapter three and addresses the issue of keeping the peace in the nuclear age in chapter two. While we confronted both issues, our concern with nuclear weapons in chapter two was much more detailed than our proposals for building the peace in chapter three. The German letter by contrast, spends much more time and gives greatest emphasis to the concept of "peace-building" and is less detailed and less technically oriented in its assessment of nuclear weapons. The French statement is shorter than either the American or German, but proportionately it gives more attention to analyzing the dilemmas of nuclear strategy and less to the peace-building theme than the German document. In sum the U.S. and French bishops pay more detailed attention to the choices required to keep the peace in the nuclear age; the U.S. and German bishops both have more elaborate designs for peace-building than the French.

On specific *issues,* the three statements also show differences of style and substance. The principal specific issue which all three letters address is the "hard question" of the nuclear age: the morality of deterrence. None of the documents condemns the strategy of deterrence; all of them reflect the judgment of Pope John Paul II's message to the United Nations in 1982, a judgment of conditional acceptance of deterrence as a transitional strategy to be used while seeking to move the world to a more stable basis of security.

But there are differences in the three statements. The U.S. bishops' judgment of "strictly conditional acceptance" of deterrence in which the strict conditions are analyzed in a series of detailed judgments has generally been regarded as a more stringent criticism of the entire strategy of deterrence than the French bishops' analysis of the "logic of distress," with accompanying attention given to the distinction between threat and use in a policy of deterrence. The American letter has a strongly deontological or "absolute" tone to its ethical argument; the French letter is closer to a "consequentialist" and more contextual style of argument. The German letter is less detailed in its assessment of the inner dynamism of deterrence than the American pastoral, and its assessment of "moral toleration" of the deterrent probably stands between the U.S. and French judgments. All of this commentary would require a more extensive treatment; my purpose is simply to show both the solidarity of the concern in the three statements, without ignoring significant differences.

A second issue on which the three documents show some difference of orientation is the attention given to the political context of the arms race, more specifically the East-West confrontation which is the source of the strategic race. The French letter is very direct and forceful about the nature of the threat from the East; it is the theme which shapes the argument of the French statement. The German letter is less explicit about the threat, but quite sensitive to the political dimension of the balance of terror. The U.S. letter in its section entitled "The Superpowers in a Divided World," addresses the same political context of the U.S.–Soviet competition which the other episcopal letters confronts, but the U.S. letter does spend much more time on the *means* of the strategic competition than on the *nature* of the East-West divide.

To some degree, these differences between the French and German statements on the one hand, and the U.S. letter on the other, reflect differences of geography, but they also reflect the questions which each episcopate chose to emphasize. The perennial international problem of states and ideologies competing in a world devoid of an effective superior political authority is still with us; the new feature of this reality is that the competition is carried on with qualitatively new means of destructive power. The European letters are particularly sensitive to the perennial political dangers; the U.S. letter is equally sensitive to the awesome arsenals which today threaten all our political and human values.

This analysis of the three letters, and indeed of others—not least the Belgian statement—could and should go on, but I have exhausted my time in this address. My purpose has been not to give a definitive analysis, but to leave you with a sense of hope and a spirit of further inquiry. The sense of hope—even in the face of the terrible threats of the nuclear age—should come from an awareness that the immense resources of faith, reason and prayer in the Catholic tradition are being used today to help the world confront the nuclear "signs of the times." The spirit of inquiry should move this academic institution and others in the Church to continue the indispensable work of assisting the Church to fulfill its ministry of service: a ministry of faith, love, justice and peace in a world which needs all of these.

Conference Address
"Dialogue as Universal Foundation of Peace"
Rome, Italy
─*July 2, 1986* ─────────────────────────────────

This afternoon's panel is devoted to the general theme of "Dialogue and Peace." Since I am a bishop, a pastor and teacher, not a politician, strategist or economist, I find the broad scope of our topic appealing; it is open to philosophical and religious reflection as well as empirical analysis. The approach of my paper will be to draw upon Catholic teaching on international affairs, particularly as it has been developed by Pope John XXIII, Pope Paul VI and Pope John Paul II, to relate the ideas of dialogue and peace. I will address three points: (1) dialogue as the way to peace in papal teaching; (2) the elements of international dialogue; and (3) dialogue, public opinion and foreign policy.

DIALOGUE AND PEACE: PAPAL TEACHING

All three popes I have mentioned have strongly supported the method of dialogue as the way to peace, and they have contributed to the public dialogue of nations and peoples. Pope John XXIII's encyclical, *Pacem in terris* (1963), attracted attention and admiration in the East and West. Pope Paul VI's encyclical, *Ecclesiam suam* (1964), was a guide to the method of dialogue at every level of human life. His encyclical, *Populorum progressio* (1967), is regarded even today as a major contribution to the North-South dialogue.

Pope John Paul II, however, has most specifically and directly taken up the theme of dialogue itself, probing its potential, its elements, and its role in international relations today. I would particularly like to bring into focus two of his World Day of Peace Messages: (1) "Dialogue for Peace: A Challenge for Our Time" (1983) and (2) "Peace is a Value with No Frontiers" (1986). In the 1983 message the Holy Father examines dialogue as a method of addressing differences in the international system. In the 1986 message he examines the scope of the topics that dialogue must address today. Both messages point directly to the concerns of this conference.

In his 1983 message Pope John Paul II stated unequivocally his conviction about the absolute necessity of dialogue in world affairs:

> Peace will not be established, nor will it be maintained, unless one takes the means. And the means *par excellence* is adopting an attitude of dialogue, that is, of patiently introducing the mechanisms and phrases of dialogue wherever peace is threatened or already compromised, in families, in society, between countries or between blocs of countries (no. 2).

The Holy Father makes this strong statement with a clear understanding of the nature of international relations today and of the many obstacles to dialogue. He presumes the existence of an international system where sovereign states hold power and authority, even as he warns against an "exaggerated and out-of-date" concept of state sovereignty (no. 7). He recognizes that within the sovereign state system there are factual diversities of size, power and influence. He is acutely aware of the role of competing ideologies and how they can block the perception of nations to the common interest and the mutual responsibilities they share. In spite of all these factors, he affirms his conviction that dialogue is a human and political possibility as well as an ethical imperative for states in the world today.

The possibilities of dialogue being used effectively as a method of addressing international problems are rooted in the aspirations of people for peace, the lessons of history taught us in this century, and the nature of the problems confronting us as we move toward the next century.

The Pope is confident that the aspiration of people across national, racial and cultural lines is universally for peace; this provides a common foundation for dialogue.

Moreover, this century with its two "world" wars and over one hundred and fifty conflicts since the end of the Second World War has vividly impressed upon statesmen and citizens alike the truth that dialogue—however tedious and difficult—is infinitely superior to another resort to arms. There is a realism running through the papal message that recognizes that the lessons of history are learned slowly and implemented fitfully. But the lessons of failure to use dialogue are there to be learned, and the papal message is an appeal not to ignore them.

Finally, the lessons of the past are complemented by the challenges of the future: A growing interdependence of the world poses a range of political, economic and social problems that are transnational in their scope. No single nation—even the most powerful ones—can address its monetary, trade, security or ecological problems without cooperation. But cooperation requires dialogue. The dialogue that is required is not left in general terms by the Holy Father. In 1983 he specified the content of the international dialogue as concerned, "with the rights of man, with economics, with disarmament, and with the common international good" (no. 10).

In his 1986 World Day of Peace Message, Pope John Paul II returned to the content of the dialogue needed today. The focus of the 1986 message was a call to leaders, scholars and citizens to join the East-West dialogue and the North-South dialogue. Stated in very general terms, these two relationships encompass the major political, economic and moral questions of the day. Often the two sets of issues are discussed in such isolation that areas of common interest are not identified. The East-West questions focus on political-strategic concerns; the North-South questions relate to political-economic concerns.

Clearly, the substance of each agenda is sufficiently complex to require independent analysis. But failure to join consideration of the two areas of negotiation misses the interdependent character of international affairs today.

In a passage that illustrates the basic insight of the 1986 message, the Pope says:

> It is clear that "peace" built and maintained on social injustices and ideological conflict will never become a true peace for the world. Such a "peace" cannot deal with the substantial causes of the world's tensions or give to the world the kind of vision and values which can resolve the divisions represented by the poles of North-South and East-West.

I would now like to accept the Holy Father's invitation to think about the content of the international dialogue needed for a solid and lasting peace.

THE INTERNATIONAL DIALOGUE: ACTORS AND ISSUES

To examine the content of the dialogue, I believe it useful to state dominant characteristics of the contemporary international system, then to examine the key actors and, finally, to look at specific issues.

The international system today is both interdependent and nuclear in character. The interdependence of nations today—a theme stressed frequently in papal teaching—is a product of several forces. At one level, increased communication, facility of travel and increasing institutional linkages among nations create the foundation of material interdependence. At a second level, the nature of certain problems, like the management of the monetary and trading systems, requires a recognition of the welfare of other actors lest the system collapse for all.

At a third level, interdependence results from the erosion of the traditional distinction of domestic vs. foreign policy. Today many foreign policy issues—like trade policy—have direct and immediate consequences for domestic life in a nation. Similarly, some domestic issues—for example, interest rates in the United States—have major consequences for other nations. Interdependence has many implications for policy. One dominant effect is the recognition that we are all vulnerable to others in an interdependent world. Even the most powerful feel the effects of an oil shortage or a Chernobyl. Equally important, however, is the recognition that we are not all equally vulnerable. Within interdependence there exists both political and economic dependency.

The second characteristic of the system today is its nuclear potential. In one sense, all nations are part of the problem of interdependence. The nuclear fate of international affairs depends, for the present at least, on a very few states and uniquely on the Soviet Union and the United States. The studies on nuclear winter, while still being refined, illustrate the interdependent character of the nuclear danger. A major nuclear exchange would have fatal consequences in regions far beyond the targets of the attack.

Today, the interdependent world is split by enormous disparity of wealth and human welfare. A nuclear world lives daily with a danger that dwarfs previous conceptions of the damage war can cause. Who are the actors and what are the issues that influence the dialogue for peace?

There are three sets of actors in the contemporary system who should be part of the dialogue of peace. First, the traditional actors are states. In an interdependent world states do not have the same role they once played. Sovereignty today is contained by a series of forces. But states are still the unique actors in world affairs.

A second set of actors are transnational institutions. Generally speaking, transnational actors are based in one place, present in several places, possess a trained corps of personnel and a single guiding philosophy. Transnational actors have not replaced states, but they do pose a certain rivalry for states. There is a multiplicity of transnational actors ranging from international institutions, through privately owned corporations, to professional and scientific organizations, to religious bodies like the Catholic Church. A transnational capacity for action offers particular advantages in an interdependent setting. Dialogue between states and transnational entities is a necessary component of the dialogue for peace.

Third, organizations that represent the perspectives and positions of citizens, workers, and particularly of groups that often do not have access to centers of power and public attention are a necessary element in the dialogue for peace. This third set of actors in the dialogue are the least developed and have the most difficulty in finding access to represent its constituency. But from trade unions in Poland, to popular organizations in the Philippines, to peace movements in North America and Western Europe, the significance of such private organizations is today being demonstrated.

The mechanisms for dialogue among states are in place even if they are not always well utilized. The dialogue between states and transnational actors is still in a rudimentary stage of development. And the capacity to extend the global dialogue to local or citizen organizations is sporadic within countries and almost nonexistent in the international arena.

The issues of the dialogue for peace involve East-West and North-South questions. Three categories that illustrate the scope of the dialogue for peace are: (1) nuclear armaments, (2) economic justice, and (3) human rights.

The nuclear arms race poses uniquely dangerous issues. It illustrates how human technology might escape the control of its creators and return to destroy them. For much of the nuclear age, we have witnessed the race between technology and politics. Most of the time nations have shown themselves more capable of producing weapons than of controlling them.

The nuclear dialogue for peace is principally a task for states, although I will indicate later the crucial role for public opinion. The nuclear superpowers bear the primary responsibility for the arms race and share the primary burden for reversing its direction. The dialogue about nuclear questions had had a formal character for many years, since it has been conducted through an intermittent series of negotiations between the United States and the Soviet Union. The result of this institutionalized form of dialogue has been a series of agreements that should neither be underestimated nor oversold. The agreements include the Limited Test Ban Treaty (1963), the Nonproliferation Treaty (1968), and the SALT I Treaty (1972). In addition to these ratified treaties, there have been negotiations on a Comprehensive Test Ban Treaty that remain unfinished, and, of course, the negotiations that led to the SALT II Agreement which remains unratified but has been informally observed until this year.

Even taken together, these treaties are less than what is needed to protect the world from nuclear catastrophe. But the accomplishments of this arms control regime are too often understated today. I cite the limits of what has been done, not to denigrate the accomplishments of these various treaties, which I believe are significant, but to press the dialogue of peace forward by building on these agreements and completing the work begun through them.

The spirit of my commentary reflects a statement from Pope John Paul II's 1986 World Day of Peace Message:

> The only way to respond to this legitimate fear of the consequences of nuclear destruction is by progress in negotiations for the reduction of nuclear weapons and for mutually agreed upon measures that will lessen the likelihood of nuclear warfare (no. 2).

I believe the dialogue for peace on the nuclear issue is presently in a critical phase. Unless the superpowers can reverse their present direction of unilateral moves unconstrained by agreements, we will enter a new cycle of the arms race where technological developments will take us toward new instability and new dangers.

Precisely because the race between technology and politics is so central to the nuclear dialogue, I submit that the single most effective measure the two superpowers could take is to cease all testing of nuclear weapons immediately. I realize that voices and forces in both political systems regard such a move as a risk to national security. Nevertheless, continued testing—with all that lies beyond testing—is a disproportionate threat to global security. If testing were halted, the dialogue for peace could proceed to qualitative and quantitative restraints on the arms race that are needed for stability and safety.

The second issue, international economic justice, is the North-South issue *par excellence*. To cite again Pope John Paul II's 1986 message: "between the countries which form 'the North bloc' and those of 'the South bloc' there is a social and economic abyss that separates rich from poor." In one of his encyclicals the Holy Father referred to this abyss as a contemporary version, on a global scale, of the biblical story of Dives and Lazarus.

The dialogue for peace on this question must engage states, but it also must include transnational actors and institutions as well as groups that can authentically speak for various sectors of the population like unions and citizens' organizations.

Although the justice problem is primarily cast in economic terms, it has a significant political dimension. The poorer states have difficulty making their presence felt in major negotiating forums. The dynamic of North-South negotiations is quite different from the East-West dialogue. The disparity of political power reinforces disparities in economics. But, as with the arms question, there is no substitute for regular, serious negotiations aimed at fundamental reforms in the North-South relationship.

The most pressing issue for several nations today is their foreign debt. The factors that led to the situation are too complex to examine here. What is needed to meet the problem, however, is a more far-reaching and fundamental proposal than has thus far been offered, coordinating the efforts of debtor nations, major governments of the North, commercial banks and relevant international institutions. In designing such a plan, constant attention should be paid to a fundamental point: The poor in the debtor nations should not have to bear the burden of a debt that they had no part in assuming.

The third issue in the dialogue for peace, the protection and promotion of human rights, is the theme that Pope John Paul II chose for his address to the United Nations in 1979. In the dialogue for peace, both states and nongovernmental organizations have a particular role on the question of human rights. States are often the agencies that have violated human rights. But states, acting together, must be an essential part of any plan to protect human rights in a more secure fashion in the future.

Precisely because the action of states must be scrutinized when it threatens human rights and supported when it is designed to protect human rights, the role of nongovernmental agencies, within and among nations, is vitally important in international affairs today. These nongovernmental organizations include churches, legal associations, other professional groups and independent agencies like Amnesty International. They already have a proven record of identifying human rights abuses and arousing public opinion to address them.

The dialogue for peace faces a fundamental problem regarding the protection of human rights. Pope John XXIII identified the problem in his 1963 encyclical, *Pacem in terris*. He wrote that the world faced a number of transnational problems—issues that could not be contained within the scope of one nation—but we have no supranational authority capable of addressing these emerging transnational questions.

The protection of human rights involves precisely this kind of problem. Since no transnational legal authority exists, the protection and promotion of human rights today depends upon the moral vision of states and citizen organizations. This is not an adequate long-term solution, but it is what we have immediately available to us. It is precisely for this reason that the Church has taken such a direct role in the human rights question, seeking to act now on specific cases and to build toward the day when the international community will be organized in a fashion that can securely protect and promote the rights of each person.

THE DIALOGUE FOR PEACE AND PUBLIC OPINION

The dialogue for peace that is needed in the last part of the twentieth century involves many actors and a multiplicity of issues. Having sketched the key actors and some of the issues, I wish to focus in the final section of my remarks on a theme that is implicit in much that I have said, but one that requires explicit analysis: the role of public opinion in the dialogue for peace.

I again turn to Pope John Paul II who said in his 1982 World Day of Peace Message:

> Peace cannot be built by the power of rulers alone. Peace can be firmly constructed only if it corresponds to the resolute determination of all people of good will. Rulers must be supported and enlightened by a public opinion that encourages them or, where necessary, expresses disapproval.

The possibilities for public opinion to be expressed are not the same in every country, but the need to cultivate a role for public opinion is crucial for the future of an international dialogue for peace. Public opinion, when it is formed on the basis of sound information and can be expressed through channels which give it political significance, can act as a restraint and guide for the policy of states. It can also express the wider aspirations of citizens about key issues.

Several participants are needed to shape public opinion in contemporary society. The press is a crucial component, since access to information on a regular and reliable basis is the foundation of public opinion. Academic institutions are particularly important today since so many questions, from genetics to nuclear policy, involve information the general public does not command. Popular or community-based organizations are needed so that the shaping of public opinion will involve more than just the intellectuals of a society. Professional associations that possess a classical sense of the professions—that they exist for public purposes—can make a significant contribution to public opinion.

Along with these other actors, religious organizations have a definite role to play in the development of public opinion. Certainly in the Christian tradition, the Church is a place where the meaning of citizenship is shaped. Participation in a faith community should help a person prepare for contributing to the wider life of society.

In the United States the program of the Catholic Bishops' Conference in preparing the pastoral letters on peace and the economy has been designed, in part, to make a contribution to the public opinion of our society. Both the process we have used and the role we envisage for these pastoral letters relate to the formation of public opinion in the United States.

The process of drafting both letters has involved extensive consultation. The committees of bishops responsible for drafting the documents held a series of private consultations with representatives of various sectors of U.S. society. Then we circulated three drafts of each pastoral letter for public reaction. The debates among the bishops on the documents were held in open public meetings that were covered by the press. Through this process both pastoral letters have come to be seen as documents that have a role in the national policy debate in the United States. The letters were designed, in the first instance, for the community of the Church; but the audience for both of them has gone far beyond the Church.

Precisely because of the attention the letters have attracted, the bishops have taken great care to keep the role of these documents precisely defined. We wrote them as teachers of a religious-moral tradition, seeking to bring the resources of that tradition to bear upon the public questions of the day. The objective of the pastoral letters has been to open space in the public policy debate for explicit consideration of the moral dimensions of nuclear policy and U.S. economic policy. Since an effective public opinion must go beyond purely technical questions to evaluate the moral foundations of policy, the bishops believe they are making a significant contribution to the public dialogue by highlighting precisely the intersection of ethical and empirical considerations of public policy.

I began this address by focusing on papal teaching regarding dialogue and peace, and I conclude it by looking at the efforts of one part of the Church to contribute to that dialogue. But the Church's role must be seen as one piece of a larger societal process of dialogue—locally, nationally and internationally. It is that larger process that this conference is analyzing, and I offer my remarks as a contribution to our common reflection.

Address

"Ordering Our Destiny:
Politics, Strategy, and Ethics"*

University of South Carolina
Columbia, South Carolina

——— *February 8, 1990* ———————————————————————

I wish to begin by commending my *alma mater*, the University of South
Carolina, for undertaking this conference to examine the political, strategic, and ethical dimensions of nuclear deterrence. It is always a pleasure
to return to this university. But being invited to open this conference has
particular meaning for me because of my experience in chairing the U.S.
Catholic bishops' committee which drafted the pastoral letter *The Challenge of Peace* in 1983.

Most of you participating in this conference have spent your professional lives wrestling with the nuclear question. While I had always been
interested in the significance of the nuclear age as a citizen, the task of
writing the pastoral letter forced me to address the specific elements of
deterrence, strategic doctrine, and arms control in a new way. I drew from
this experience the conviction that the quality of the policy and academic
debate about nuclear strategy is one of the primary resources our society
possesses in exercising responsible control of nuclear weapons.

Official nuclear policy—the strategy which guides the actual development, deployment, and role of nuclear weapons—has a unique status. But

*Also published in *Origins*, vol. 19, no. 39, March 1, 1990, pp. 629, 631–34.

official policies are formed in light of our understanding of the meaning of the nuclear age, the relationship of strategic weapons and foreign policy, and the responsibilities of being one of the two nuclear superpowers. Although the world is clearly passing through political changes which will mark a new and hopefully safer chapter in the nuclear age, the need for continuing analysis will not decline. By this symposium the University of South Carolina demonstrates its willingness to exercise public responsibility for enhancing our national understanding of the nuclear age.

The intense involvement with the nuclear question which I had from 1980–1988, preparing both the pastoral letter and the 1988 review of the bishops' position, left a powerful impression on me. But it did not provide me with the detailed knowledge of the nuclear question which you take for granted. Hence, when I approached the challenge of opening this conference, I thought it best to shape my remarks as one interested in public policy but not a specialist in nuclear questions, and to offer a general framework of analysis rather than to focus on a particular aspect of the nuclear debate.

A general framework seems best suited to a conference on nuclear policy in the year 1990. Even among those who have studied this topic closely, I find a growing consensus that the next decade of analysis and action will clearly not be a continuation of the nuclear debate of the last four decades. What changes must be made, intellectually and politically, to adapt nuclear policy in the post-Cold War world is the question which today cuts across strategic doctrine, arms control, and budgetary policy.

Two books published at the end of the 1980s, McGeorge Bundy's *Danger and Survival* and Robert Jervis' *The Meaning of the Nuclear Revolution*, capture the historical drama of the nuclear age and the way nuclear weapons have reshaped standard expectations about international politics. Together they reflect much of the political wisdom which living with nuclear weapons has produced in the last half-century. But these books, published in 1988 and 1989 respectively, may come to be seen by historians as symbolizing the end of the first stage of the nuclear age. Clearly in 1990, one has the sense of living on the other side of a fault line from what has been the experience of nuclear politics in the first fifty years. Obviously, nuclear weapons are very much with us—over 50,000 jointly held by the superpowers. Negotiations which promise reductions proceed, but they remain to be completed. The physical means to threaten civilization as we know it stand ready to be used, either purposefully or accidentally.

But in spite of these signs of continuity with what has been, the historical fault line marked by 1989 is real. The rationale for superpower conflict has declined dramatically. The frailty of human nature and the folly often evident in political history keep us all vigilant and cautious, but even the most careful voices today say the superpower agenda for the 1990s will demonstrate change rather than continuity.

The nuclear question had been at the center of the superpower relationship. It will continue to be close to the center, but in a new context. I wish to highlight three themes from the 1980s which will be part of this new context, and then close my remarks by trying to locate where nuclear deterrence, strategy, and arms control will fit in the new context.

THE 1980S: POLICY, ETHICS, AND PUBLIC OPINION

One characteristic which set the 1980s apart from most of the nuclear age was the degree of public engagement in the policy debate. The nuclear debate had been an elite discussion, engaging a highly sophisticated but tightly knit corps of specialists drawn from the government, a few think tanks, and some major universities. Within this circle the nuclear discussion acquired the character which historically has been associated with the great doctrinal disputes within Christianity. There were canonical concepts, established patterns of reasoning, and views which were regarded as orthodox and heretical. A shift from massive retaliation to flexible response, or from superiority to sufficiency, was regarded as a doctrinal change—an event accorded the intellectual attention once reserved for the decisions of popes and their theologians. Books which trace these doctrinal shifts, like Fred Kaplan's *The Wizards of Armageddon* or Greg Herken's *The Counsels of War*, read like ecclesiastical history.

The general public seldom was aware of either the character of the debate or the specific conclusions which divided the experts. Even in the U.S. Congress, the intricacies of the argument were not the concern of all 535 members who voted on defense budgets annually, but only those who sat on specialized committees like the armed services, intelligence, or appropriations committees.

The 1980s saw the nuclear debate spill over the boundaries of elite discussion and engage the electorate. In the first six years of the decade, at least, the general lines of U.S. strategic policy, if not the intricate arguments, were debated in city councils in California and town meetings in New England. The merits and risks of deterrence were explored in parish halls and meetings of the local medical societies. The Nuclear Freeze movement was the most visible symbol of this broader public discussion. In retrospect, its significance lies less with its specific proposal than with its capacity to draw ordinary citizens into an argument which had always affected them but had hardly ever included them.

In his book *The Nuclear Debate*, Professor Robert Tucker contended that the upsurge in public engagement was sparked by a fear that the

U.S.–Soviet relationship in the early 1980s was slipping out of control. As an effort to reestablish confidence, the public wanted more attention paid to efforts for arms control. While it is always difficult to establish causality in large social movements, I believe this public pressure did influence the U.S. return to arms control negotiations, first through a series of proposals, then through the summits of 1985 to 1988.

By the end of the 1980s, however, with the INF Treaty signed and ratified, with START proposals for deep cuts on the negotiating table, and with the entire political order which generated the nuclear arms race in flux, the public in the United States was *not* focused on arms control. Primary concerns in 1989 ran to drugs and the environment, but this is not the product of a fickle public. To use Tucker's argument, the general public perceived the nuclear threat being addressed by responsible proposals and negotiations.

Some who are part of the elite debate would argue that the general public's reaction in the early 1980s was misplaced. The nuclear danger was not objectively greater than it had been in the immediate past, and the experts might contend that the present situation is more complex than the public believes. My own sense is that the public played a very useful role in pressing the policy process toward negotiations, and that the fact that attention has shifted to other issues like drugs does not mean that public engagement on the nuclear question is a thing of the past.

The interest generated in the last ten years has produced an increased understanding of the nuclear age, its dangers, challenges, and possibilities. In a sense, the U.S. public came out of the 1980s with a better grasp of their responsibility as citizens of a nuclear nation, a better understanding of how and when to engage their government, and a greater awareness that decisions taken in Moscow and Washington on the nuclear question are never purely national decisions, for they can threaten the international community. The elite debate about nuclear weapons is still the core of the policy argument, but in the 1990s it will be pursued in the context of an electorate more capable of entering the nuclear discussion when it believes the elite is either too complacent or too adventurous.

The second major theme of the 1980s nuclear debate was the attention paid to ethics and nuclear strategy. From the beginning of the Christian era, war has been regarded as not only a political but also a moral problem. The nuclear age transformed the moral problem. In the pre-nuclear period, the ethical question was the ethics of war—when force could be used, under what conditions, and by which means. In the nuclear age, these questions were joined with debates about the ethics of nuclear peace—whether deterrence, our way of keeping the peace, was morally acceptable. In the pre-nuclear age, right up through World War II, the moral arguments began with the war. Under conditions of nuclear deterrence, the key moral questions about targeting, declaratory doctrine, and the relationship of strategic policy and arms control were all discussed and decided under conditions of peace.

The new moral challenge posed by both the destructive capabilities of nuclear weapons and the dynamics of nuclear deterrence was grasped early by theologians like Reinhold Niebuhr and Paul Ramsey in the Protestant community, and by John Courtney Murray, S.J., in the Catholic community. But the arguments about the ethics of strategy and deterrence remained at the edge of the policy arguments until the 1980s.

In the last decade, the ethical issues moved into the center of the public discussion at both the elite and popular levels of the nuclear debate. The religious communities continued to address the moral questions, but with much greater systematic preparation. Moreover, the religious voices were now joined by many who were visible participants in the strategic literature. Robert Tucker, Stanley Hoffmann, Herman Kahn, Albert Wohlstetter, Joseph Nye, Bruce Russett, Lawrence Friedman, George Kennan, and George Quester were only some of the participants in the ethics and strategy arguments.

The range of participants and the centrality of the ethical concerns were new in the 1980s. The structure of the ethical argument, however, followed the categories sketched out in the 1960s and 1970s.

One pole of the deterrence debate held that moral limits of means and ends could be maintained with nuclear weapons; hence a credible and morally justifiable deterrent could be sustained. Ramsey and Murray had espoused this position in the 1960s; Albert Wohlstetter, James Johnson of Rutgers, and William O'Brien of Georgetown renewed the argument in the 1980s.

The other pole of the deterrence debate was given renewed emphasis and systematic statement in 1987 by John Finnis, Germain Grisez, and Joseph Boyle in their book, *Nuclear Deterrence, Morality and Realism*. This position held that an inevitable contradiction existed between the requirements of credible deterrence and the central moral tenet that one could never intend to kill the innocent; hence, one can never target civilians in any form of a deterrent threat.

Both of these polar positions offered internally coherent and very detailed policy judgments. Both positions conveyed a sense of confidence that the move from ethical assessment to policy conclusions was both possible and self-evidently imperative.

The third general position in the debate of the 1980s was the one found in the U.S. Catholic bishops' pastoral letter, *The Challenge of Peace*, and developed by other analysts. It was less confident than Wohlstetter and others that new technologies of accuracy and miniaturization could be used to reconcile moral and strategic objectives of deterrence. But even though it upheld strongly the principle of protecting civilians, it was reluctant to reduce the totality of the deterrence question to the role of moral intention, as Finnis and others seem to do in their analysis.

This third position sought to place restrictions on deterrence—restrictions governing targeting, deployment, and declaratory doctrines—and then to work for a transformation of the political and strategic relationship which surrounds the deterrence relationship. This position, described as a conditional acceptance of deterrence as an interim strategy for the nuclear age, sought to forestall use of nuclear weapons, reduce the risks of deterrence, and then relativize the role of deterrence over the long term. The third position was less clear and coherent than either of the poles of the ethical argument. It was a political ethic as much as a strategic one; it conditioned ethical acceptance of deterrence by seeking to reshape the political setting in which deterrence functioned.

As someone identified with this third position, I must admit that I conceived of the time frame needed to change the political setting as something to be measured in decades. Even while advocating political changes to reduce the central role of nuclear weapons, I never expected immediate steps in this direction in the 1980s.

But the final major theme of the last decade has been precisely the political changes we have experienced in the superpower relationship, in the Soviet Union, and in Eastern Europe. I have already noted the fragility of this process, but its significance for the nuclear question should be recognized. For the last forty years, both the strategic literature and the ethics of strategy were built on the premise that fundamental political change in the superpower relationship was nearly impossible. The presumption of the strategic debate was that, since political progress was not a realistic goal for U.S.–Soviet relations, the highest objective of policy should be to guarantee stability in the nuclear relationship. The threefold goal of crisis stability, arms race stability, and political stability was the centerpiece of the strategic and arms control literature. Ethical assessments often presumed this logic without spelling it out.

The possibilities opened by the political changes occurring in East-West relations—from U.S.–Soviet relations, through European politics, to the question of German reunification—make it necessary to review the political presumption which has been the foundation of strategic thinking. In the 1990s, fundamental political change is imperative, not optional. The strategic relationship, with its goal of stability, should take second place to the wider effort of shaping political relations which will reduce the danger, centrality, and saliency of the regime of nuclear deterrence.

If this assertion is correct, if the political dimension of superpower relationships should have primacy in the 1990s, then it is possible to locate the ethics of nuclear strategy in a new setting for the 1990s.

THE 1990S: ETHICS, ORDER, AND POLITICS

My purpose in these closing remarks is to sketch a framework, not to draw a blueprint, for the primacy of the political. The first imperative is to recognize that changing the content of political relationships will not do away with nuclear weapons, but could substantially relativize their role. For one hundred years France and Germany sustained a hostile military posture. In the post-1945 political setting, the evolution of their relationship has made war between them virtually unthinkable. This is the kind of political transformation which should be the long-term goal of the primacy of the political.

The second imperative is to address the strategic relationship, relying on the traditional objectives and methods of arms control. In the 1990s, three broad areas of arms control will need to be pursued simultaneously: the strategic relationship addressed in the START negotiations; the reduction of conventional forces in Europe targeted in the CFE negotiations; and the long-neglected topic of proliferation, now understood to mean preventing proliferation of nuclear weapons, chemical weapons, and ballistic missiles. The new possibilities of the political do not render these hard-core strategic objectives any less urgent.

Finally, allow me to return to a definition of the ethical issues we face in the 1990s. Here too, I believe, we need to recast the issues. Recasting does not mean moving away from the ethics of deterrence, but addressing it in a different context. The nuclear question retains its intrinsic importance and urgency. It must be addressed on its own terms, in continuity with the analysis of the 1980s which will have to be extended and deepened.

This analysis of nuclear deterrence, which we are examining in this meeting, has been an "ethic of control." Like its secular counterpart of arms control, nuclear ethics has tried to contain and control the nuclear threat. Since the threat still exists—embodied in 50,000 warheads—the work of control must continue.

But I would suggest for your consideration that the question for the 1990s is not the ethics of strategic control, but, rather, an ethic of political order. The shift in perspective from control to order arises from the need to address the political changes already occurring. They have in fact eroded the order of international relations which has sustained the nuclear relationship since 1945. Today, the task before the international community, as it was in 1815 and 1945, is to shape a viable order of political relations which can control, contain, and direct strategic relations.

The difference of the 1990s is that the call to order today is to the first international system which encompasses all the actors in the global community. In his 1987 encyclical *On the Social Concern of the Church*, Pope John Paul II argued that the East-West issues need to be related to

North-South issues. His appeal is for what he calls "a real international system."

The immediate task created by changes in the Soviet Union and Eastern Europe is to reshape the order of superpower and European relations. But the world is no longer either the superpowers or Europe. From proliferation to pollution, from deterrence to debt, the demands of world politics today, ethically and politically, require a new conception of order.

This broadly defined political challenge is both a moral and an empirical task. We need to construct an order which works, but one which works justly and can be maintained peacefully. At the heart of this order, the fact of nuclear weapons remains. The ethic of control, the ethic of reducing the nuclear danger must continue. But it is too narrow a conception of political responsibility to remain with this complex task.

Control in international relations—whether control of weapons, the environment, or our common economic future—requires cooperation. Cooperation, in turn, must be built on a common conception of a shared destiny. It is this common destiny of the international community which the moral argument about an ethic of order seeks to grasp. Two decades ago, the prophetic Jesuit Teilhard de Chardin said the task of this century was "to build the earth." The search for order is another way to say that we must build our common future in peace, in justice, and, ultimately, in love.

Address

"A Century of Social Teaching"*

Centennial of Rerum Novarum, *Washington, D.C.*
—— *February 25, 1991* ————————————————

As we mark the centenary of *Rerum novarum*, I appreciate this opportunity to reflect on the significance of "The Challenge of Peace." Very much has changed since we began our work on the pastoral letter ten years ago. The changes in Eastern Europe and the Soviet Union, for example, signal a significant shift in the geopolitical realities which helped shape the letter. That alone deserves careful analysis.

However, an even more critical issue demands our attention today: the war in the Persian Gulf which highlights both the failure and the success of the pastoral letter.

The very fact of the war sadly confirms that the challenge of peace still eludes us. While we were drafting the pastoral letter, we became convinced that the world cannot truly afford war today. The technology of modern weaponry, even so-called conventional weaponry, greatly multiplies death and destruction, as we have seen so vividly in news reports of the past five weeks. Moreover, the planet itself is wounded ecologically by modern warfare. Pope Paul VI's plea before the United Nations—"No more war! War never again!"—has more meaning today than in many a year; it resonates in all the victims of the current war.

Nonetheless, despite the disappointment of the war itself, there have been some positive signs in the debate about the conflict in the Middle

*Also published in *Origins*, vol. 20, no. 40, March 14, 1991, pp. 652–54.

East. Its moral dimensions have been widely recognized. The issue of a just war has rightly taken its place at the center of the debate. The coalition forces, for example, have underlined the importance of discriminating between civilian and military targets. The principles enunciated in the pastoral letter continue to influence such public policy issues as the proper motivations for going to war, ways to restrain its violence, and the path that will lead to a just and lasting peace in the region. President Bush, for example, without explicitly referring to the just-war theory, has justified the current war in the context of its criteria.

During the past six months, the U.S. bishops have commented extensively on the situation in the Persian Gulf. Before the war began, Archbishop Pilarczyk, on behalf of the bishops, wrote to President Bush that military action to drive Iraqi troops out of Kuwait "could well violate" the criteria for a just war. Because this teaching starts with a strong presumption against the use of force, meeting the criteria presents a formidable challenge. The purpose of the teaching is to limit sharply the justifiable recourse to war and, in the event war does occur, to confine its destructiveness to the minimum extent possible. Since the war began, however, most bishops have been reluctant to declare definitively that the war is either just or unjust. Why is this so?

First of all, some of the just-war criteria were clearly met. In many ways the invasion of Kuwait by Iraq presents a textbook case for *just cause*. In the final analysis, war can be justified only for the purposes of self-defense or the defense of others who have been attacked. Few suggest that Iraq's aggression should go unchallenged. In addition, the criterion that states that war may be initiated only by a *competent authority* was met by the resolutions of the U.N. Security Council and the U.S. Congress.

At the same time, many questioned whether two specific just-war criteria could be met. The first was *proportionality*, which requires that the harm caused—the destructiveness and cost of the war—be proportionate to the good that would be achieved. The costs to be measured, are, first, the human lives that would be lost, as well as the ecological, economic, strategic and even spiritual costs. The second problematic criterion was *last resort*, which means that all other means of resolving the conflict peacefully must have been exhausted. These two criteria, of course, demand that prudential judgments be made about the factual situation; people of good will may legitimately disagree when making such judgments.

The result of all this is that some people are convinced that the war is just; some are convinced that it is unjust; many feel that a moral ambiguity exists. Some too are pacifists, that is, they believe that no war is moral, regardless of circumstances.

No matter what judgment one makes about the start of this war, *moral discernment does not cease with the onset of hostilities. The moral analysis must continue now that the war, especially the ground war, is underway.*

This brings us to the third reason why many bishops are reluctant to pass a definitive judgment on the justice or injustice of the war. Just-war criteria for the actual conduct of war require that the military response be *proportionate* and *discriminate*. The criterion of proportionality requires that the military response not be more than is needed to accomplish the purpose of the war; that the resources expended—both human and material—and the resulting consequences not be excessive in relation to the justifiable goal. The criterion of discrimination requires that civilians not be directly targeted; the distinction between combatants and noncombatants must be adhered to scrupulously.

This means that, as the war continues, we must give careful attention to several issues.

(1) The first is the human and material cost of the war. The number of casualties to date, both combatants and noncombatants, remains unknown. But now, in the ground war, more than a million soldiers are at battle in the desert, and undoubtedly the number of casualties will escalate. Hundreds of thousands of people have already had to abandon their homes and/or jobs in Kuwait, Iraq, and Saudi Arabia. The financial cost of the conflict and its aftermath will involve many billions of dollars—money which is desperately needed to combat poverty at home and abroad.

(2) The second issue is the required discrimination between combatants and noncombatants. Iraq's shameful Scud missile attacks on Israel and Saudi Arabia merit unreserved condemnation. Despite repeated affirmations that the coalition's military strategy takes serious precautions to attack only military targets, there have also been many civilian casualties. Moreover, we know that the Iraqi infrastructure to deliver such essentials as electricity and water has been virtually destroyed, thus imperiling noncombatants as well as combatants.

(3) Third, the allied intentions in regard to the war must be known and evaluated. The liberation of Kuwait is surely a just cause. Other motivations, however, may not merit this judgment. If there are other goals, they must be clearly stated and judged on the basis of their own merits.

(4) Finally, what kind of peace do we seek? Is it a peace with justice that deals with the multiple issues facing the Middle East? Or is it one which sows the seeds for greater animosity in the future?

At this point, some may ask where I stand personally. I was opposed to initiating the war in mid-January because I was not convinced that all the other available means of resolving the conflict (economic sanctions, diplomacy) had been exhausted. I was saddened, therefore, when the war began and expressed the hope that it would end quickly. Only time would tell, I stated, whether the good accomplished would outweigh the evil— both in terms of the conflict's short- and long-range effects.

I still have grave reservations about the long-term implications of the war, especially now that the land war has begun. I am not prepared to state categorically, as some have, that it is unjust or immoral. For me there is considerable ambiguity in this regard. Nonetheless, even if it can be legitimately argued that the just-war criteria are substantially fulfilled, I continue to question the wisdom of going to war when we did. Surely the unjust and illegal seizure of Kuwait must be rectified. But, in addition to our own military forces, we must also be concerned about the havoc which the war is causing for the people of the region and the growing gap between the West and much of the Arab world which can give rise to even greater difficulties in the future.

Another unfortunate result of the war has been the sidetracking of international efforts to build peace elsewhere in the world. In this regard, the third and fourth chapters of the pastoral letter on war and peace (entitled the "Promotion of Peace" and the "Pastoral Challenge and Response"), perhaps the least well-known section of the document, deserve much more study and discussion. These sections, rooted in a century of papal social teaching, have a great deal to say about the values and shape of a new world order. They focus on the reality of the world's *interdependence*, a fact that continues to have enormous political, economic, social, and moral implications, even though the geopolitical realities extant when *The Challenge of Peace* was written have changed dramatically.

In the aftermath of the Persian Gulf war, an intriguing question will be what impact the Church's teaching on war and peace will have on the major issues that face what some have called a "unipolar" world. The pastoral letter dealt primarily with the nuclear arms race in a *bipolar* environment. We must now turn to the new reality and apply our tradition in ways that continue to seek to minimize the resort to armed force, and indicate the directions we might take to ensure greater justice in the world. The reduction of nuclear arms must continue to be a priority. Nuclear deterrence must give way to progressive disarmament. The growing sophistication and proliferation of conventional arms impels us to redouble our efforts to limit their production and distribution.

Greater attention and resources must also be focused on the growing gap between the North and the South. A just and lasting peace will never be achieved when so many people live in abject poverty.

In short, we must be committed to advancing the cause of peace which continues to challenge us as a Church. Returning to "business as usual" would be perilous, for other crises as serious as the one in the Persian Gulf loom on the horizon. As Pope John Paul said at Coventry Cathedral in England: "Peace is not just the absence of war. It involves mutual respect and confidence between peoples and nations. It involves collaboration and binding agreements. Like a cathedral, peace must be constructed patiently and with unshakable faith."

A Consistent Ethic of Life

Address

"A Consistent Ethic of Life: An American-Catholic Dialogue"*

Gannon Lecture

Fordham University, New York, New York

—December 6, 1983 ————————————————————————

It is a privilege to be invited to give the Gannon Lecture at Fordham University. Fr. Gannon's life as a priest, a Jesuit and a scholar offers a standard of excellence which any Gannon lecturer should seek to imitate.

I was invited to address some aspect of the U.S. Catholic bishops' pastoral letter, *The Challenge of Peace: God's Promise and Our Response.* I am happy to do so, but I want to address the topic in a very specific manner. The setting of today's lecture has shaped its substance. The setting is a university, a community and an institution committed to the examination and testing of ideas. A university setting calls for an approach to the pastoral which does more than summarize its content; six months after its publication, it is necessary to examine the document's impact and to reflect upon the possibilities for development which are latent in its various themes.

More specifically, Fordham is an American Catholic university, an institution which has consistently fostered the work of enriching American culture through Catholic wisdom and has simultaneously sought to

*Also published in *Origins*, vol. 13, no. 29, December 29, 1983, pp. 491–94; *Consistent Ethic of Life* (Sheed & Ward, 1988); and *A Moral Vision for America* (Georgetown University Press, 1998).

enhance our understanding of Catholic faith by drawing upon the American tradition.

Today I will discuss the pastoral letter in terms of the relationship of our Catholic moral vision and American culture. Specifically, I wish to use the letter as a starting point for shaping a consistent ethic of life in our culture. In keeping with the spirit of a university, I have cast the lecture in the style of an inquiry, an examination of the need for a consistent ethic of life and a probing of the problems and possibilities which exist within the Church and the wider society for developing such an ethic.

I do not underestimate the intrinsic intellectual difficulties of this exercise nor the delicacy of the question—ecclesially, ecumenically and politically. But I believe the Catholic moral tradition has something valuable to say in the face of the multiple threats to the sacredness of life today, and I am convinced that the Church is in a position to make a significant defense of life in a comprehensive and consistent manner.

Such a defense of life will draw upon the Catholic moral position and the public place the Church presently holds in the American civil debate. The pastoral letter links the questions of abortion and nuclear war. The letter does not argue the case for linkage; that is one of my purposes today. It is important to note that the way these two issues are joined in the pastoral, places the American bishops in a unique position in the public policy discourse of the nation. No other major institution presently holds these two positions in the way the Catholic bishops have joined them. This is both a responsibility and an opportunity.

I am convinced that the pro-life position of the Church must be developed in terms of a comprehensive and consistent ethic of life. I have just been named the chairman of the National Conference of Catholic Bishops' Pro-Life Committee; I am committed to shaping a position of linkage among the life issues. It is that topic I wish to develop today in three steps: (1) a reflection on the pastoral letter on war and peace; (2) an analysis of a consistent ethic of life; and (3) an examination of how such an ethic can be shaped in the American public debate.

THE CHURCH IN PUBLIC DEBATE: THE PASTORAL IN PERSPECTIVE

The pastoral letter on war and peace can be examined from several perspectives. I wish to look at it today in ecclesiological terms, specifically as an example of the Church's role in helping to shape a public policy debate. Early in the letter the bishops say that they are writing in order to share the moral wisdom of the Catholic tradition with society. In stating this objective the American bishops were following the model of the Second Vatican Council which called dialogue with the world a sign of love for the world.

I believe the long-term ecclesiological significance of the pastoral rests with the lessons it offers about the Church's capacity to dialogue with the world in a way which helps to shape the public policy debate on key issues. During the drafting of the pastoral letter one commentator wrote in the editorial section of the *Washington Post:*

> The Catholic bishops . . . are forcing a public debate on perhaps the most perplexing nuclear question of them all, the morality of nuclear deterrence. . . . Their logic and passion have taken them to the very foundation of American security policy.

This commentary accurately captures the purpose of the pastoral letter. The bishops intended to raise fundamental questions about the dynamic of the arms race and the direction of American nuclear strategy. We intended to criticize the rhetoric of the nuclear age and to expose the moral and political futility of a nuclear war. We wanted to provide a moral assessment of existing policy which would both set limits to political action and provide direction for a policy designed to lead us out of the dilemma of deterrence.

It is the lessons we can learn from the policy impact of the pastoral which are valuable today. The principal conclusion is that the Church's social policy role is at least as important in *defining* key questions in the public debate as in *deciding* such questions. The impact of the pastoral was due in part to its specific positions and conclusions, but it was also due to the way it brought the entire nuclear debate under scrutiny.

The letter was written at a time it called a "new moment" in the nuclear age. The "new moment" is a mix of public perceptions and policy proposals. The public sense of the fragility of our security system is today a palpable reality. The interest in the TV showing of *The Day After* is an example of how the public is taken by the danger of our present condition. But the "new moment" is also a product of new ideas, or at least the shaking of the foundation under old ideas.

Another commentary generated during the drafting of the pastoral letter, this one from *The New Republic,* identified the policy characteristics of the "new moment":

> The ground is not steady beneath the nuclear forces of the United States. The problem is not modes of basing but modes of thinking. The traditional strategy for our nuclear arsenal is shaken by a war of ideas about its purpose, perhaps the most decisive war of ideas in its history.

The significant fact to which this editorial points is that the "new moment" is an "open moment" in the strategic debate. Ideas are under scrutiny and established policies are open to criticism in a way we have not seen since the late 1950s. From the proposal of "no first use," through the debate about the MX, to the concept of a Nuclear Freeze, the nuclear policy question is open to reassessment and redirection. The potential contained in the "new moment" will not last forever; policies must be formulated, ideas will crystallize and some consensus will be shaped. As yet, the content of the consensus is not clear.

The fundamental contribution of *The Challenge of Peace*, I believe, is that we have been part of a few central forces which have created the "new moment." We have helped to shape the debate; now we face the question of whether we can help to frame a new consensus concerning nuclear policy.

The "new moment" is filled with potential; it is also filled with danger. The dynamic of the nuclear relationship between the superpowers is not a stable one. It is urgent that a consensus be shaped which will move us beyond our present posture. The pastoral letter has opened space in the public debate for a consideration of the moral factor. How we use the moral questions, that is, how we relate them to the strategic and political elements, is the key to our contribution to the "new moment." I could spend the entire lecture on the moral dimension of the nuclear debate, but my purpose is rather to relate the experience we have had in dealing with the nuclear question to other issues. Without leaving the topic of the war and peace discussion, I will try to show how our contribution to this issue is part of a larger potential which Catholic moral vision has in the public policy arena. This larger potential is to foster a consideration of a consistent ethic of life and its implications for us today.

A CONSISTENT ETHIC OF LIFE: A CATHOLIC PERSPECTIVE

The *Challenge of Peace* provides a starting point for developing a consistent ethic of life but it does not provide a fully articulated framework. The central idea in the letter is the sacredness of human life and the responsibility we have, personally and socially, to protect and preserve the sanctity of life.

Precisely because life is sacred, the taking of even one human life is a momentous event. Indeed, the sense that every human life has transcendent value has led a whole stream of the Christian tradition to argue that life may never be taken. That position is held by an increasing number of Catholics and is reflected in the pastoral letter, but it has not been the dominant view in Catholic teaching and it is not the principal moral position found in the pastoral letter. What is found in the letter is the traditional Catholic teaching that there should always be a *presumption* against taking human life, but in a limited world marked by the effects of sin there are some narrowly defined *exceptions* where life can be taken. This is the moral logic which produced the "just-war" ethic in Catholic theology.

While this style of moral reasoning retains its validity as a method of resolving extreme cases of conflict when fundamental rights are at stake, there has been a perceptible shift of emphasis in the teaching and pastoral practice of the Church in the last thirty years. To summarize the shift succinctly, the presumption against taking human life has been strengthened and the exceptions made ever more restrictive. Two examples, one at the level of principle, the other at the level of pastoral practice, illustrate the shift.

First, in a path-breaking article in 1959 in *Theological Studies*, John Courtney Murray, s.j., demonstrated that Pope Pius XII had reduced the traditional threefold justification for going to war (defense, recovery of property and punishment) to the single reason of defending the innocent and protecting those values required for decent human existence. Second, in the case of capital punishment, there has been a shift at the level of pastoral practice. While not denying the classical position, found in the writing of Thomas Aquinas and other authors, that the state has the *right* to employ capital punishment, the action of Catholic bishops and Popes Paul VI and John Paul II has been directed against the *exercise* of that right by the state. The argument has been that more humane methods of defending the society exist and should be used. Such humanitarian concern lies behind the policy position of the National Conference of Catholic Bishops against capital punishment, the opposition expressed by individual bishops in their home states against reinstating the death penalty, and the extraordinary interventions of Pope John Paul II and the Florida bishops seeking to prevent the execution in Florida last week.

Rather than extend the specific analysis of this shift of emphasis at the levels of both principle and practice in Catholic thought, I wish to probe the rationale behind the shift and indicate what it teaches us about the need for a consistent ethic of life. Fundamental to the shift is a more acute perception of the multiple ways in which life is threatened today. Obviously questions like war, aggression and capital punishment have been with us for centuries and are not new to us. What is new is the *context* in which these ancient questions arise and the way in which a new context shapes the *content* of our ethic of life. Let me comment on the relationship of the context of our culture and the content of our ethic in terms of: (1) the *need* for a consistent ethic of life; (2) the *attitude* necessary to sustain it; and (3) the *principles* needed to shape it.

The dominant cultural fact, present in both modern warfare and modern medicine, which induces a sharper awareness of the fragility of human life is our technology. To live as we do in an age of careening development of technology is to face a qualitatively new range of moral problems. War has been a perennial threat to human life, but today the threat is qualitatively different due to nuclear weapons. We now threaten life on a scale previously unimaginable. As the pastoral letter put it, the dangers of nuclear war teach us to read the book of Genesis with new eyes. From the inception of life to its decline, a rapidly expanding technology opens new opportunities for care but also poses new potential to threaten the sanctity of life.

The technological challenge is a pervasive concern of Pope John Paul II, expressed in his first encyclical, *Redemptor hominis,* and continuing through his address to the Pontifical Academy of Science last month when he called scientists to direct their work toward the promotion of life, not the creation of instruments of death. The essential question in the technological challenge is this: In an age when we *can* do almost anything, how do we decide what we *ought* to do? The even more demanding question is: In a time when we can do anything technologically, how do we decide morally what *we never should do?*

Asking these questions along the spectrum of life from womb to tomb creates the need for a consistent ethic of life. For the spectrum of life cuts across the issues of genetics, abortion, capital punishment, modern warfare and the care of the terminally ill. These are all distinct problems, enormously complicated, and deserving individual treatment. No single answer and no simple responses will solve them. My purpose, however, is to highlight the way in which we face new technological challenges in each one of these areas; this combination of challenges is what cries out for a consistent ethic of life.

Such an ethic will have to be finely honed and carefully structured on the basis of values, principles, rules and applications to specific cases. It is not my task today, nor within my competence as a bishop, to spell out all the details of such an ethic. It is to that task that philosophers and poets, theologians and technicians, scientists and strategists, political leaders and plain citizens are called. I would, however, highlight a basic issue: the need for an attitude or atmosphere in society which is the precondition for sustaining a consistent ethic of life. The development of such an atmosphere has been the primary concern of the "Respect Life" program of the American bishops. We intend our opposition to abortion and our opposition to nuclear war to be seen as specific applications of this broader attitude. We have also opposed the death penalty because we do not think its use cultivates an attitude of respect for life in society. The purpose of proposing a consistent ethic of life is to argue that success on any one of the issues threatening life requires a concern for the broader attitude in society about respect for human life.

Attitude is the place to root an ethic of life, but ultimately ethics is about principles to guide the actions of individuals and institutions. It is therefore necessary to illustrate, at least by way of example, my proposition that an inner relationship does exist among several issues not only at the level of general attitude but at the more specific level of moral principles. Two examples will serve to indicate the point.

The first is contained in *The Challenge of Peace* in the connection drawn between Catholic teaching on war and Catholic teaching on abortion. Both, of course, must be seen in light of an attitude of respect for life. The more explicit connection is based on the principle which prohibits the directly intended taking of innocent human life. The principle is at the heart of Catholic teaching on abortion; it is because the fetus is judged to be both human and not an aggressor that Catholic teaching concludes that direct attack on fetal life is always wrong. This is also why we insist that legal protection be given to the unborn.

The same principle yields the most stringent, binding and radical conclusion of the pastoral letter: that directly intended attacks on civilian centers are always wrong. The bishops seek to highlight the power of this conclusion by specifying its implications in two ways: first, such attacks would be wrong even if our cities had been hit first; second, anyone asked to execute such attacks should refuse orders. These two extensions of the principle cut directly into the policy debate on nuclear strategy and the personal decisions of citizens. James Reston referred to them as "an astonishing challenge to the power of the state."

The use of this principle exemplifies the meaning of a consistent ethic of life. The principle which structures both cases, war and abortion, needs to be upheld in both places. It cannot be successfully sustained on one count and simultaneously eroded in a similar situation. When one carries this principle into the public debate today, however, one meets significant opposition from very different places on the political and ideological spectrum. Some see clearly the application of the principle to abortion but contend the bishops overstepped their bounds when they applied it to choices about national security. Others understand the power of the principle in the strategic debate, but find its application on abortion a violation of the realm of private choice. I contend the viability of the principle depends upon the consistency of its application.

The issue of consistency is tested in a different way when we examine the relationship between the "right to life" and "quality of life" issues. I must confess that I think the relationship of these categories is inadequately understood in the Catholic community itself. My point is that the Catholic position on abortion demands of us and of society that we seek to influence an heroic social ethic.

If one contends, as we do, that the right of every fetus to be born should be protected by civil law and supported by civil consensus, then our moral, political and economic responsibilities do not stop at the moment of birth.

Those who defend the right to life of the weakest among us must be equally visible in support of the quality of life of the powerless among us: the old and the young, the hungry and the homeless, the undocumented immigrant and the unemployed worker. Such a quality of life posture translates into specific political and economic positions on tax policy, employment generation, welfare policy, nutrition and feeding programs, and health care. Consistency means we cannot have it both ways. We cannot urge a compassionate society and vigorous public policy to protect the rights of the unborn and then argue that compassion and significant public programs on behalf of the needy undermine the moral fiber of the society or are beyond the proper scope of governmental responsibility.

Right to life and quality of life complement each other in domestic social policy. They are also complementary in foreign policy. *The Challenge of Peace* joined the question of how we prevent nuclear war to the question of how we build peace in an interdependent world. Today those who are admirably concerned with reversing the nuclear arms race must also be those who stand for a positive U.S. policy of building the peace. It is this linkage which has led the U.S. bishops not only to oppose the drive of the nuclear arms race, but to stand against the dynamic of a Central American policy which relies predominantly on the threat and the use of force, which is increasingly distancing itself from a concern for human rights in El Salvador and which fails to grasp the opportunity of a diplomatic solution to the Central American conflict.

The relationship of the spectrum of life issues is far more intricate than I can even sketch here. I have made the case in the broad strokes of a lecturer; the detailed balancing, distinguishing and connecting of different aspects of a consistent ethic of life is precisely what this address calls the university community to investigate. Even as I leave this challenge before you, let me add to it some reflections on the task of communicating a consistent ethic of life in a pluralistic society.

CATHOLIC ETHICS AND THE AMERICAN ETHOS: THE CHALLENGE AND THE OPPORTUNITY

A consistent ethic of life must be held by a constituency to be effective. The building of such a constituency is precisely the task before the Church and the nation. There are two distinct challenges, but they are complementary.

We should begin with the honest recognition that the shaping of a consensus among Catholics on the spectrum of life issues is far from finished. We need the kind of dialogue on these issues which the pastoral letter generated on the nuclear question. We need the same searching intellectual exchange, the same degree of involvement of clergy, religious and laity, the same sustained attention in the Catholic press.

There is no better place to begin than by using the follow-through for the pastoral letter. Reversing the arms race, avoiding nuclear war and moving toward a world freed of the nuclear threat are profoundly "pro-life" issues. The Catholic Church is today seen as an institution and a community committed to these tasks. We should not lose this momentum; it provides a solid foundation to relate our concerns about war and peace to other "pro-life" questions. The agenda facing us involves our ideas and our institutions; it must be both educational and political; it requires attention to the way these several life issues are defined in the public debate and how they are decided in the policy process.

The shaping of a consensus in the Church must be joined to the larger task of sharing our vision with the wider society. Here two questions face us: the substance of our position and the style of our presence in the policy debate.

The substance of a Catholic position on a consistent ethic of life is rooted in a religious vision. But the citizenry of the United States is radically pluralistic in moral and religious conviction. So we face the challenge of stating our case, which is shaped in terms of our faith and our religious convictions, in nonreligious terms which others of different faith convictions might find morally persuasive. Here again the war and peace debate should be a useful model. We have found support from individuals and groups who do not share our Catholic faith but who have found our moral analysis compelling.

In the public policy exchange, substance and style are closely related. The issues of war, abortion, and capital punishment are emotional and often divisive questions. As we seek to shape and share the vision of a consistent ethic of life, I suggest a style governed by the following rule: We should maintain and clearly articulate our religious convictions but also maintain our civil courtesy. We should be vigorous in stating a case and attentive in hearing another's case; we should test everyone's logic but not question his or her motives.

The proposal I have outlined today is a multidimensional challenge. It grows out of the experience I have had in the war and peace debate and the task I see ahead as chairman of the Pro-Life Committee. But it also grows from a conviction that there is a new openness today in society to the role of moral argument and moral vision in our public affairs. I say this, even though I find major aspects of our domestic and foreign policy in need of drastic change. Bringing about these changes is the challenge of a consistent ethic of life. The challenge is worth our energy, resources and commitment as a Church.

Address

"The Death Penalty:
An International Human Rights Issue"

General Annual Meeting of Amnesty International

Loyola University, Chicago, Illinois

——*June 23, 1984* ———————————————————————

I first want to express my appreciation for the opportunity to address this annual meeting of Amnesty International. The objectives of Amnesty International and your work throughout the world are well known in the Catholic Church. Indeed, as you know, in the United States many members of Amnesty International are Catholics who find in your organization a particularly effective way to express their moral concern about leading questions in international relations, so many of which affect the welfare of the human person.

As a way of addressing the topic of this morning's session—the death penalty as an international human rights issue—I will offer my reflections on the larger context of the issue. That is, I plan to illustrate the common ground we share on a wide range of issues and to examine some common objectives which both the Church and Amnesty International should pursue in a world that is still too violent, still too unaware of the dignity of the human person. Accordingly, I will focus on three topics: (1) protecting the person in a world composed of independent states; (2) the issues shaping a shared agenda; and (3) capital punishment in the international arena.

First, protecting the person in a world of nation-states. The genius of Amnesty International has been that it has found a way to concretize a major concern of international relations, and to do so in a way that has caught the imagination of large numbers of people. International politics is a very complex subject. The foreign policy of our own nation, for example, is at times so complex that people cannot deal with it personally. They feel that it is so far removed from them that they cannot really influence it. Amnesty International's method, however, helps people to cut through the complexity of governments, institutions, laws, rules and conflicts. By adopting a prisoner of conscience, for example, you can become concerned about a specific individual in a specific country whose life and welfare are in danger. By identifying one human being for whom you feel a personal responsibility, a human being you know needs help, you concretize the meaning of international politics. The genius of this approach is demonstrated and proven in the way in which Amnesty International has become a major force in world politics.

I assure you that I do not make this assertion lightly. Amnesty International is known the world over. You are known both for the wide geographical scope of your concern—that is, the global range of your interest in protecting people from the reach of arbitrary power—and for your ability to form local, grassroots constituencies which can make and have made an impact on larger transnational problems. I hasten to add that the genius of your approach is not simply the result of an organizational technique. Rather, it is rooted in your ability to lift up the question of the protection of the individual person in the complex and often violent world of international affairs in a way that people can understand and act on.

I cite this accomplishment not only because you should be commended for the way in which you have protected and saved individuals whose lives and welfare were directly threatened, but also because you have engaged large numbers of people who otherwise might never have taken an interest in foreign policy, in the task of protecting human rights the world over. My other reason for highlighting the way in which you have focused on the protection of the person in international relations is that the person is the foundation of the Catholic Church's concern in its entire social ministry. The Catholic Church, as a worldwide institution, is involved in a broad range of social questions at the international, national and local levels. Indeed, if one were to list them all, it would be quite long because the concerns vary so much in the different countries and continents.

There is, however, a common element which links the many concerns of the Church's social ministry, namely, its conviction about the unique dignity of each human person. The person is the clearest reflection of the presence of God among us. To lay violent hands on the person—which is precisely the thing that Amnesty International seeks to prevent—is to come as close as we can to laying violent hands on God. Every social system—east or west, north or south, communist or capitalist—should be judged by the way in which it reverences, or fails to reverence, the unique and equal dignity of every person.

The person, then, is the key to the entire social presence and outreach of the Church. But the protection of the human person requires a broader view than simply the conviction that the person has a unique dignity. Protection of the person in a social setting requires that we have a clear conception of a doctrine of human rights. For rights are moral claims that persons make in light of their human dignity; they are moral claims that people can make against other persons and against the state. We protect the dignity of the human person in a social setting by surrounding each person with a spectrum of rights and responsibilities. These rights ensure that the individual's worth is rooted in his or her personhood, that the individual's worth is not swallowed up in a faceless collectivity. Those moral claims, in other words, provide a kind of space within which the fragile dignity of the human person is to be protected.

Catholic teaching argues that political relationships within and among states must be seen and developed within the context of human rights. This was the theme of Pope John Paul II when he visited the United Nations in 1979. He sought to examine problems as diverse as war and peace and economic justice from the perspective of the human rights of the person.

The affirmation that the person's human rights are to be respected both within and among states is fundamental and is critically important for our world today. It is a principle that Amnesty International puts into practice all the time. It affirms that in a world of states, the nation-state has real but only relative value; it is the dignity of the human person that has transcendent value and must be respected at all times. The nation-states do not have the right to so isolate themselves that they can ignore the moral concern of the rest of the world when, within their boundaries, there are serious allegations about human rights violations.

This relativization of the role of the state has implications for the way we view international relations. Indeed, one point of convergence between Amnesty International and the Catholic Church—even though our starting points may be different—is our affirmation of the primacy of the person in international affairs, the need to protect the person in a world of states, and the need to judge every state by the way it reverences and enhances, or fails to reverence and enhance, the dignity of each person.

A second point of convergence between Amnesty International and the Catholic Church is that we are both transnational actors in today's increasingly interdependent world. Interdependence, first of all, is simply a factual condition. It arises from the growing exchange of information, ideas, contacts, and political and economic ties among nations. All of these ties illustrate our mutual vulnerability; they show how we are influenced by each other; how we can touch each other, for good or for ill, across national boundaries by our policies, our practices, our concern for what happens within other states.

Now, of special importance in an increasingly interdependent world is the growing role of transnational actors. The world is still composed of states, and states are the unique organizing force in international politics. But they are no longer the only organizing force.

Transnational actors have the following characteristics: They are based in one place but are present in several places; they have a trained corps of personnel, a single guiding philosophy, and a sophisticated communication system. There are a handful of organizations that possess these characteristics. We readily identify corporate actors who have those characteristics and who exert enormous influence. But other organizations, perhaps to a less visible degree, also have the characteristics of transnational actors. The Catholic Church is clearly such an actor in the world today. In a less visible but real way, Amnesty International has become a recognized transnational actor which focuses on the protection of the person in a world of nation-states. Both in terms of the vision which motivates and guides our action in international politics and in terms of our organized presence in an increasingly interdependent world, the Church and Amnesty International have shared concerns and a capability to cooperate to the benefit of both.

Indeed, the second topic I would like to address is precisely our shared concerns, the issues shaping our shared agenda. Amnesty International is known today primarily for its protection and promotion of human rights. And here again, our shared vision of what we mean by human rights provides a common meeting ground. Both Amnesty International and the Catholic Church have a view of human rights which cuts across political and civil rights on the one hand and socioeconomic rights on the other. And this view shapes one's perspective relative to international affairs.

This seems self-evident, as it has been affirmed in United Nations' declarations and documents, as well as scholarly literature. But it is not universally accepted, even in our own country. The dominant view in the West, for example, is often to stress political and civil rights and to regard social, economic and cultural concerns as something less than rights. The dominant view in the East, on the other hand, is to stress socioeconomic and cultural rights and to pass off political and civil rights as peripheral or unnecessary, or even a hindrance in the organization of society. But if one adopts the view that the protection of the dignity of the person requires a spectrum of rights which extends from the right to life itself, to the right to basic nutrition, social welfare, housing, education, and a job, to the right of freedom of conscience and religion, freedom of association, and the right to know the truth—then one has a broader perspective of the relevant issues in a given country or in relationships among countries. My point is not to outline a whole doctrine of human rights but to emphasize the fact that when one sees the full spectrum of human rights, this influences the way one interprets issues in international relations. It should be evident to all of us how a shared vision of the full range of human rights provides the basis for a shared agenda of issues that are our concern.

Let me press this idea of a shared view of issues one step further, this time concentrating more on what goes on in my own faith community. However, it is a theme and a tendency that is relevant to the topic you have asked me to address.

Just as we see a linkage among human rights in the protection of the person, increasingly in the Catholic Church today we see a linkage among what I would call "life issues." Precisely because we reverence the dignity of the human person as a unique being, unlike any other creature in the world, the question of the protection of human life from attack becomes for us a central theme in our whole social ministry. I suspect we would not have difficulty sharing views on why human life is sacred and how important it is in the organization of a society, whether nationally or internationally, to give primacy to the sacredness of human life. But it is not enough simply to say *why* we believe life is sacred. It is also necessary to examine the challenges to the unique dignity and sacredness of human life today.

Human life has always been sacred and there have always been threats to it, but we live in a period of history when we have produced, sometimes with the best of intentions, a technology and a capacity to threaten human life which previous generations could not imagine.

The threat to life today can be illustrated by examining our technology. Technologically, we can do almost anything. In its effort to understand and shape our world, to push back the boundaries and barriers of our knowledge so that we can use the world well in all its dimensions, science has produced many marvelous and commendable inventions. It is simply a fact of life, however, that as we do one thing with science and technology, there are often side effects or unexpected effects, or even things we planned to do, that go far beyond what we expected would happen. The result is that life is often threatened. Today, for example, in areas as diverse as medical ethics and nuclear strategy, the challenge to human life is very great. When we cracked the atom and the genetic code—both tributes to human genius—we penetrated the recesses of the secrets of nature. In itself, this is good; we were created to do this. The consequences of these breakthroughs of knowledge present us with a complicated and sometimes problematic set of questions. For example, how do we control and direct the power we have created, whether it be in laboratories and hospitals or in arsenals? My point is that, if we begin by affirming the sacredness of all life, and then move to an examination of the threats to life, we soon realize that, if we want to protect the sacredness of life, we must do it in a number of places; there is no one place where the entire threat to life is lodged.

Certainly the nuclear question on which I have spent a substantial amount of time over the past four years represents in a unique way a threat to the sacredness of life which the Church and others in society must take with utmost seriousness. We must be convinced that only by concerted, sustained action can we move away from the perilous condition in which we find ourselves today because of the nuclear arms race. But as serious as it is, the arms race is not the only threat to life.

As you so well know, the Catholic bishops have been deeply involved in the effort to stem the increasing number of abortions in our society. I am fully aware that some who agree with us on the position we have taken on nuclear questions do not agree with us on abortion, and vice versa. But we are convinced that the same principle is at stake in both issues. That is not to say that the issues are identical. What we do say is that the protection of innocent human life from direct attack is a principle underlying both issues and it is this linkage, which goes far beyond nuclear warfare and abortion, that makes it necessary for us to examine a broad range of threats to life.

Indeed, our conviction that life is threatened at a number of points on the life spectrum prompts us to think more explicitly about how we relate one life issue to another. It has certainly influenced our view on capital punishment. The Catholic Church for many centuries has taught that in extreme circumstances the state has the right to take life, either to defend against external threats through what is called the "just war," or to defend society against threats from within through the use of capital punishment. That statement of Catholic moral teaching still prevails at the level of principle. Principles, however, must be applied. Each age must exercise its capacity for critical moral discernment in its particular circumstances. So, as the bishops became more involved in the questions of abortion and nuclear war, their convictions about the death penalty also came under review. Basically, we have taken the position that, while in principle, the state has the right to use capital punishment, that right should not be used in the United States. In other words, we have not reversed our traditional teaching on this point; what we have said is that there are other ways—more appropriate and effective than capital punishment—for the state to defend its people. For example, through a carefully considered process of moral discernment, the bishops of Kentucky in a recent pastoral letter concluded "that under the circumstances prevailing in society today, the death penalty as punishment for reasons of deterrence, retribution, or the protection of society cannot be justified." Their conclusion comes after an examination of the death penalty in itself and in relationship to American society today.

Another reason why the American bishops have concluded that the death penalty is inappropriate is their vision of the linkage among life issues, that is, the linkage among the life issues convinces us that one must foster a positive attitude toward life in society if life's sacredness is to be cherished and protected. While the state has the obligation to defend its people against attacks on their lives and to protect them against forces that threaten key societal values, we believe that the exercise of the right to capital punishment does not foster the kind of reverence for life that is needed to deal creatively and effectively with the whole range of life questions we face in our society today. In a complex, sophisticated democracy like ours, means other than the death penalty are available and can be used to protect society. Moreover, we recognize the need of society to move beyond mere justice in dealing with the victims of crime and their families. We must offer people afflicted by violence our deepest compassion, understanding, and support.

When we move to the question that you are particularly concerned about—the death penalty in the international arena—there are new problems: the diversity of legal systems in each country; the diversity of cultural traditions; the diversity of capabilities of states to maintain order and to protect their people. There is, in other words, a range of problems in the international sphere that does not confront us in precisely the same way in the United States. But I welcome this opportunity to come before you to affirm my support for your goal to eliminate the death penalty, especially as a means of dealing with political prisoners. I am convinced that this is a step which needs to be taken.

Pope John Paul II has addressed this very question. In his address to the diplomatic corps at the Vatican on January 15, 1983, he stated: "the Holy See, in its humanitarian concern, is prompted to recommend clemency and mercy for those condemned to death, especially those who have been condemned for political reasons, which can be changeable, linked as they are to the personalities of the authorities of the moment."

"The church likewise takes to heart the plight of all those who are subjected to torture, whatever the political regime may be, for in her eyes nothing can justify that debasement which unfortunately often accompanies barbaric, repugnant cruelties. Likewise she cannot remain silent about the criminal action which consists in causing a certain number of people to disappear without trial, leaving their families in a cruel state of uncertainty."

It should be noted that this statement from Pope John Paul II is in line with the thinking of his predecessor, Pope Paul VI. Pope Paul never made such a clear statement of principle or called for prohibiting capital punishment as a way of dealing with political prisoners although he intervened in a number of specific cases where political prisoners were sentenced to death.

Both the practice of Pope Paul VI and the teaching of Pope John Paul II, I believe, support and affirm Amnesty International's position and objective on this question.

I should like to add that the papal concern is humanitarian, as is yours. But the significance of what you are trying to do is in the fact that your efforts also seek to embody that human concern in political and legal measures which would restrain the power of a state in dealing with the question of political prisoners.

There are reasons to pursue this objective in spite of the difficulties which exist in the international system. Precisely because of the variety of governments and legal systems involved, there is a need for a common movement—one that cuts across states—seeking to ban capital punishment as a means of dealing with political prisoners.

It does seem to me that one way to pursue this objective is precisely to speak to states about their role in the world today. In a world marked by violence and often a disregard for the dignity of the person, the state must protect its people and the key values of its society, but it should do so in a way that promotes reverence for the life of each person. Forswearing the right to execute those it has declared to be political prisoners would be a remarkably useful public declaration by the state of its concern about the protection and enhancement of human life.

There is need for an organization not in the governmental sector to raise this question and to argue for its inclusion on the agenda of nation-states. You have proved your capability of doing just that. I wish to affirm the value of the task you have undertaken and to wish you godspeed in the work you have undertaken.

Thank you.

Address

"The Fact of Poverty Today: A Challenge for the Church"*

The Catholic University of America, Washington, D.C.

—*January 17, 1985* ————————————————————————

Let me begin by expressing my appreciation to Father Byron, President of Catholic University, for the invitation to deliver this address on the fact of poverty and the challenge it poses for the Church. Both the topic and the place of the lecture have special relevance.

The bishops of the United States are engaged in a major effort to help the U.S. Church in its analysis and response to the fact of poverty. The first draft of the pastoral letter, "Catholic Social Teaching and the U.S. Economy," is merely an initial step in an extended process. Its goal is to engage every level of the Church in study, discussion and decisions about how the Church can and must respond to the cry of the poor.

The opportunity for me to address an audience at Catholic University as part of this process has both symbolic and substantive significance. The Church always acts with a sense of its history and its tradition. The tradition of the U.S. Church's social teaching on poverty has been profoundly influenced by this university. To come to the intellectual home of Msgr. John A. Ryan and Bishop Haas, of Father Paul Hanley Furfey and Msgr. George Higgins is to acknowledge the U.S. Church's debt to this university. It also recognizes that the social tradition continues here, symbolized by Fr. Byron's own ministry and by the work of so many of your faculty.

*Also published in *Origins*, vol. 14, no. 33, January 31, 1985, pp. 543–48; *Consistent Ethic of Life* (Sheed & Ward, 1988).

My purpose this evening is to analyze the relationship of the Church to the fact of poverty in our time. I will examine where we stand as a Church, what we can bring to the struggle against poverty, and how we should proceed in this struggle precisely as the Church.

More specifically, I will address three questions: the nature of the problem we face, the role of the Church, and one aspect of the policy debate on poverty.

THE NATURE OF THE PROBLEM: THE FACT AND THE FACES OF POVERTY

Let me begin with two assertions: (1) much of the poverty in the world is hidden from us; (2) the poor usually live at the margin of society and too often at the margin of awareness of those who are not poor. Yet, in the world of the 1980s, although many of the poor are hidden, it is also impossible for the rest of us to hide from the poor.

The faces of poverty are all around us. Chicago and Washington are different cities, but I have lived in both of them long enough to know that the only way to hide from the poor is to stay in one's room or home. We cannot walk to work or to the bus stop, we cannot run a noontime errand without seeing the faces of poverty—on the heating grates, in the doorways, near the bus terminal and huddled in the winter around the places which serve the cheapest cup of coffee.

After walking through the poverty of the city during the day, we are confronted with the faces of poverty on a wider scale in the nightly news. Ethiopia is an extreme case, but not as extreme as we might first think. The fact of poverty is the dominant social reality for over a hundred countries of the world. Numbers can be numbing in their effect, but they can also crystallize a challenge.

The fact of global poverty means:

- *800 million people* live in conditions of "absolute poverty," that is, "a condition of life so limited by malnutrition, illiteracy, disease, high infant mortality, and low life expectancy as to be beneath any rational definition of human decency" (Robert McNamara, Speech to Board of Governors of the World Bank);

- *2.26 billion people*—half of the world's population live in countries with a per capita income of less than $400.00 per year;

- *450 million people* are malnourished.

Statistics illustrating the global reality of poverty could be given in much greater detail, of course. But statistics do not tell us all we need to know. The gospel points out that these poor people are our brothers and sisters. The first draft of the pastoral letter wisely devotes a substantial section to the U.S. relationship with the rest of the world because the resources of this nation and its role in the world constitute a serious responsibility in responding to the absolute poverty of our 800 million brothers and sisters.

My specific concern this evening, however, is not the faces and figures of *global* poverty, but poverty in the United States. The fact of world poverty is so massive that it can overwhelm us. The fact of poverty in the United States is a part of our national life, but it is not recognized as a dominant fact of our existence. It can easily blend into a larger picture which stresses—not poverty—but the power and productivity of the nation.

Poverty is surely present but, in the dominant national perspective—provided by magazines, media and movies—it is not a significant feature. Poverty is present but, when we plan for the future, the poor are not central to the planning. Poverty is present but, in the policy debates of the nation, the poor exercise little leverage.

The drafting of the pastoral letter on the economy is still in its early stages. However, it has already accomplished something which commentators have quickly noticed: The letter makes space in the policy debate for the fate of the poor in a way which has not been evident for some years now.

We need to make space for the faces of the poor in our personal consciences and in the public agenda because the facts tell us that poverty is not so marginal in this nation as we might think. At the end of 1983, by official government estimates, 35 million Americans were poor. That meant 15 percent of the nation was defined as poor. The hidden poor were another 20–30 million who lived just above the poverty line.

Who are the poor? They represent every race and religion in the nation. They are both men and women, and, so very often, they are children. The poor are a fluid population. People move in and out of poverty. With unemployment still affecting at least 7–8 million people, the condition of poverty touches millions for some part of their lives.

No group is immune from poverty, but not all share it equally. Some of the statistics in the pastoral letter are striking: blacks are 12 percent of the American population but 62 percent of those persistently poor; women who head households constitute 19 percent of the family population, but 61 percent of persistently poor families. The very old and the very young know the reality of poverty in disproportionate numbers.

The causes of poverty are a subject of honest disagreement, but the fact of poverty, even in a nation of our resources, cannot be disputed. It is the Church's response to this fact which is my major concern this evening.

THE ROLE OF THE CHURCH

The role of the Church in this question or any other must be shaped by the perspective of the Scriptures as these are read in the Catholic tradition. The draft of the pastoral letter develops the scriptural case in detail. Here I will simply indicate the lines of an argument which is self-evident to anyone who examines the biblical basis of our faith. The argument is quite simple: The poor have a special place in the care of God, and they place specific demands on the consciences of believers.

The biblical argument runs through both Testaments, as the draft of the pastoral letter has shown. The prophets, in particular, specify the theme. In spite of their different styles and personalities, the prophets converge on a single message: the quality of Israel's faith will be tested by the character of justice in Israel's life. For the prophets, the test cases for Israel are specific: The way widows, orphans and resident aliens are treated measures the link between faith and justice.

Jesus himself continues the prophetic tradition. He clearly identifies his ministry with the preaching of the prophets as, for example, in the fourth chapter of St. Luke's Gospel. He consciously finds those on the edge of society—the "widows, orphans and resident aliens" of his time—and lifts up their plight even as he responds to their needs. He identifies himself so concretely with the poor that the first letter of St. John can say that love of God is measured by love of neighbor.

The biblical mandate about the poor is richer and more powerful than I can convey in this address. I recommend further study of the pastoral letter because it concisely gathers these biblical themes in its first chapter. However, I can synthesize the lesson the Church is trying to learn from the biblical perspective. It is found in a phrase which runs throughout the letter: the Church must have a "preferential option for the poor." This concept, rooted in the Scriptures, developed with originality by the Church in Latin America and now becoming a guide for ministry in the universal Church under the leadership of Pope John Paul II, illustrates how the Church learns anew from the Scriptures in every age.

The power of the phrase, "preferential option for the poor," is that it summarizes several biblical themes. As the pastoral letter states, it calls the Church to speak for the poor, to see the world from their perspective, and to empty itself so it may experience the power of God in the midst of poverty and powerlessness.

This, in all honesty, is an extraordinarily demanding view of what we should be as a Church. It is clear we have a distance to go in implementing this view of the Church's mission and ministry. Nevertheless, we have begun by taking the imperative seriously.

The option for the poor, I would suggest, will be realized in different ways according to the situation of the Church in different societies and cultures. Now we need to ask what the phrase means for the ministry of the Church in the United States.

I do not have a blueprint for determining the specific meaning of the "option for the poor" or integrating the concept into our ministry in this country. However, one dimension of the task especially interests me—the role of the Church as a social institution in our society. The Church as a social institution has made two distinct responses to the fact of poverty. The first has been to organize itself to carry out works of mercy. The fulfillment of the command to feed the hungry, clothe the naked and care for the sick has found direct and immediate expression in the Church from the apostolic age until today. The methods of doing this work have varied, but all can be classified as direct, social service to the poor.

The manifestations of this dimension of ministry are well known in the United States. They include Catholic Charities and social services in every diocese, St. Vincent de Paul Societies in every parish, and institutions—such as orphanages, hospitals and shelters for the homeless—established by communities of men and women religious and others throughout the country.

This form of social ministry is well known, but it is not the only way the Church addresses the fact of poverty. The second and complementary witness to the option for the poor is the Church's role as advocate and actor in the public life of society. The roots of this dimension of social ministry are found in the prophets who teach us to ask questions about how we organize our life as a society. The prophets asked questions in Israel about patterns of land ownership and wages, about the rules and customs used to design the social life of the nation. The prophets did not stop at formulating the norm that the quality of faith is tested by the character of social justice. They pressed specific questions about the social patterns in the life of Israel.

The conditions of twentieth-century industrial society are radically different from eighth-century B.C. Israelite society. Nevertheless, the prophets' style of social questioning has been taken up in the Church's social teaching of this century. The purpose of this social teaching is to measure the social and economic life of society by the standards of social justice and social charity.

The leadership of the popes in this century has, in turn, produced a body of social teaching from the bishops. The best-known example was probably drafted in some faculty residence on this campus by John A. Ryan when he authored the 1919 pastoral letter of the U.S. bishops. The first draft of the 1984 pastoral letter on the economy stands in this tradition of social teaching.

These two dimensions of the Church's life—its ministry of direct social service and its role as an advocate for the poor in society—remain the principal channels for the Church's response to poverty. The challenge we face in making an effective option for the poor is how these two aspects of social ministry are integrated into the full life of the Church today.

In a large, complex, bureaucratic, secular society like the United States, the Church's social service role is more needed than ever. We should not try to duplicate what society does well in supplying social services, but, in particular, we should bring two dimensions to the system of social care. First, the delivery of some social services is best done in a decentralized local model. For many social services today, only the taxing power of the state can raise sufficient funds to meet human needs. But the state is often not the best agency to minister services to people in need. The Church and other voluntary agencies can often deliver, in a humane and compassionate way, services that only the state can fund.

Second, the Church's agencies of direct social service should be a source not only of compassion but also creativity. Public bureaucracy is not known for creative innovation. Its size and complexity often prevent it from acting in anything but routine patterns. In every field from housing to health care to hospices, there is room for new, creative methods of public-private cooperation to feed the hungry, shelter the homeless and heal the sick. We can do better what we are already doing. With 35 million poor in our midst, we can reach beyond what we are doing!

In saying this, I want to be correctly understood. I am aware that Catholic Charities, the Catholic health care system and other diocesan and national networks are already involved in significant efforts of creative and direct service. It is the very success of these efforts which will give us courage to extend our efforts.

There is another sense in which I want to be clearly understood. We cannot be consistent with Catholic tradition unless we accept the principle of subsidiarity. I fully support a pluralist social system in which the state is not the center of everything. Nevertheless, I do not want the principle of subsidiarity used in a way which subverts Catholic teaching on the collective responsibility of society for its poor. I am not endorsing a concept of decentralization or federalism which absolves the government from fulfilling its social responsibilities.

Both the Catholic and American traditions urge a pattern of public-private cooperation. This means the state has a positive social role, and we have social responsibilities as religious organizations. The churches alone cannot meet the social needs of this nation, and we should not try to do so. We should be prepared to play a major role, but part of our role is to enter the public debate and work for a compassionate, just, social policy.

This is the second challenge which confronts the Church today: how to fulfill the role of advocate in the public debate. This is the role which the Bishops' Conference is seeking to fulfill in its pastoral letters, first on peace and now on social justice. It is the role Bishop Malone stressed in his presidential address to the bishops last November. He argued that, on issues as diverse as abortion, Central America, nuclear war and poverty, failure of the bishops to speak would be a dereliction of civic responsibility and religious duty.

It is this role which puts the bishops in the midst of public controversy. Controversy is the companion of participation in public policy debate. That is why it should not be surprising that contributions of the scope and range of our two pastoral letters cause controversies.

At the same time, it is important to understand the purpose of the bishops' interventions. In the pastoral letters—and in many other documents, such as congressional testimonies, speeches and letters of individual bishops—we speak at the level of both moral principles and the application of these principles to particular policies. We regularly assert that we understand and want others to understand that the moral principles we present have a different authority than our particular conclusions. We invite debate and discussion of our policy conclusions. We know they must be tested in the public arena, in the academic community and in the professional community. We have been using the process of successive drafts to stimulate this discussion.

Since I was so directly involved in the pastoral letter on war and peace, I believe there is specific merit in joining principles and policy proposals in the same document. Its purpose is not to foreclose debate, but to foster it. The policy conclusions give a sense of how the moral principles take shape in the concrete situations our society faces. I think we would be mistaken as bishops if we did not distinguish principles from policy judgments. But I think we would fail to stimulate the public argument if we withdrew from the arena of policy choices.

Our role is not to design or legislate programs but to help shape the questions our society asks and to help set the right terms of debate on public policy.

We have an excellent example in the issue confronting the administration, the Congress, and the general public as we begin 1985—the deficit debate. It is the kind of highly technical and complex question which a modern state must face. The way the question is decided will shape the life of our society. The fact is that the deficit must be cut. The choices facing the Administration and the Congress are *how* to cut spending to reduce the deficit.

The technical details are admittedly immense, but the general policy question is not purely technical. At the core of the deficit debate is the trade-off between military spending and social spending. How that trade-off is adjudicated requires moral discernment as well as economic competence.

In the 1980s virtually every program for the poor has been cut:

• more than 2 million poor children lost health care benefits;

- half a million disabled adults lost cash and medical assistance; and

- one million poor families lost food stamp benefits.

In general, spending for the poor is less than 10 percent of the federal budget, but it has sustained 33 percent of all budget cuts.

These cuts in social spending have been accompanied by significant, steady increases in military spending. It is the responsibility of the federal government to provide for defense *and* to promote the general welfare. Military spending will justifiably be part of the budget. But the deficit forces us as a nation to ask who will bear the burden of the deficit. Military spending should not be insulated when plans for reducing the deficit are formulated.

I have no misconceptions about bishops being competent to write a national budget. But it is not beyond our competence or role to say that the burden of reducing the deficit should not be borne by the most vulnerable among us. Programs for the poor have been cut enough! The burden must be shared by *all* sectors of the economy. The specifics of how to do it fall beyond my responsibility, but shaping the question of how we face the deficit is clearly part of what the Church should do as advocate in the social system.

THE POOR AND THE POLICY DEBATE—ONE ISSUE

In the deficit debate, the fate of many of the poor is at stake. This evening I would like to focus attention on a particular group by addressing a specific dimension of poverty: the feminization of poverty. This phrase has been coined by Dr. Diana Pierce, a Catholic University faculty member who has made a significant contribution to the study of poverty. She has focused her research on the plight of women who are divorced, widowed or unmarried. She has surfaced data which have special relevance for the Church in the policy debate about poverty.

Dr. Pierce's pioneering work has helped many begin to understand the severe economic consequences of motherhood and sex discrimination in this country. Of course, men, especially minorities and youths, also suffer from unemployment and poverty, and millions of intact families have inadequate income. However, poverty is growing fastest among women and children.

As we look at this issue, it will be helpful to remember that nearly all (94 percent) women marry and nearly all of them (95 percent) have children. Reducing the economic price of motherhood should be a priority for our society. This disproportionate burden of poverty on women and children is appalling. Current statistics reflect some of this grim picture:

- two out of three poor adults are women;

- three out of four poor elderly are women;

- almost half of all poor families are headed by women, and half of the women raising children alone are poor;

- one in four children under six is poor;

- one in three black children under six is poor.

Even if poverty did not weigh so disproportionately on women, the growth of both the number and percentage of the poor would be cause for alarm and action. For those of us in the Church, this situation is profoundly disturbing. The fact that poverty is so concentrated among women and children should galvanize our energies and focus our attention on the conditions that create the situation.

A closer look at poverty among women reveals that it is strongly linked to two sets of factors: (1) job and wage discrimination and (2) responsibility for the support and care of children.

Job and wage discrimination leave women concentrated in the lowest paying jobs, with more problems finding full-time, year-round work. But even when women overcome these obstacles, they still earn substantially less than men. Dr. Pierce's data indicate that women college graduates working full-time and year-round still make less than male high school dropouts! Of course, most women workers are not college graduates, and so the disparity in incomes is even greater for those in the lowest paying jobs.

While this discrimination affects most women, those whose husbands are employed are partially insulated, at least temporarily, from its worst effects. For women raising children alone, of course, the situation is much worse because they are often financially responsible for most or all of their children's support. Despite some well-reported exceptions, child care and support fall mainly on women. The increased rates of divorce and out-of-wedlock births have left more women than ever solely responsible for the support of children.

Increasingly, it appears that it now takes the earnings of two adults to support a family in the United States. A single parent—widowed, divorced or unmarried—finds it difficult to stay above the poverty line. When that parent faces additional obstacles, such as the cost of day care (which can easily take more than a fourth of an average woman's salary) and sex discrimination in employment, the cards are overwhelmingly stacked against her.

The job market often offers little hope to a single mother trying to escape poverty. Unfortunately, other potential sources of supplemental income are also very limited. Child support is paid regularly to only a very small proportion of eligible mothers. Welfare benefits are so low that, in most states, the combined value of Aid to Families with Dependent Children (AFDC) and food stamps doesn't even approach the poverty line. For the fifty states and the District of Columbia, the median benefit is 74 percent of the poverty threshold.

I cite these statistics and the case of women in poverty not because it is the only issue we must face as a Church in the policy debate but because it is one we should face with special emphasis. I have argued the case for a consistent ethic of life as the specific contribution which the Church can and should make in this nation's public debate. Central to a consistent ethic is the imperative that the Church stand for the protection and promotion of life from conception to death—that it stand against the drift toward nuclear war which has been so evident in recent years—and that it stand against the trend to have the most vulnerable among us carry the costs of our national indebtedness.

To stand for life is to stand for the needs of women and children who epitomize the sacredness of life. Standing for their rights is not merely a rhetorical task! The Church has its own specifically designed social services to protect and promote life. Through them we must counsel, support and sustain women seeking to raise families alone and to provide their children with the basic necessities—necessities which the most well-endowed society in history surely should be able to muster.

But the Church cannot simply address the problem of the feminization of poverty through its own resources. It must also stand in the public debate for such programs as child care, food stamps, and aid to families with children. I do not contend that existing programs are without fault or should be immune from review. My point is that something like them is a fundamental requirement of a just society.

Whenever I speak about the consistent ethic, I am always forced by time limitations to omit or neglect crucial themes. In the past, I have stressed that our concern for life cannot stop at birth, that it cannot consist of a single issue—war or abortion or anything else. I have always considered that a substantial commitment to the poor is part of a consistent ethic and a concern for women in poverty a particularly pertinent aspect of this "seamless garment." This evening I am grateful for the opportunity to spell out why and how the Church should stand on these issues.

Ultimately, the pastoral letter on peace and the letter on the economy should help us as a Church develop the specific features of a consistent ethic. In the end, every social institution is known by what it stands for. I hope that the Catholic Church in this country will be known as a community which committed itself to the protection and promotion of life—that it helped this society fulfill these two tasks more adequately.

"The Consistent Ethic of Life: Its Theological Foundation, Its Ethical Logic, and Its Political Consequences"*

Seattle University, Seattle, Washington
—*March 2, 1986* ————————————————————

I wish to express my sincere appreciation to Seattle University, to its president, Fr. William Sullivan, S.J., and to the Board of Trustees for the honor bestowed on me today. The relationship between centers of scholarship and learning and the episcopacy is one of the preeminent issues in the Church in the United States today. I accept your honorary degree with the pledge that I will do all I can to strengthen that relationship—to keep it based on standards of intellectual honesty, professional respect, and a shared concern for the welfare of the Church and its witness in society.

It is the Church's witness to life that I wish to address this afternoon. It is now over two years since I first proposed consideration of a "consistent ethic of life" in the Gannon Lecture at Fordham University. Since that time there has been a sustained process of reflection and analysis in the Church about the multiple issues which come under the umbrella of the consistent ethic.

Last November, the National Conference of Catholic Bishops adopted the consistent ethic theme in its revised Plan for Pro-Life Activities. Obviously, I find that step particularly significant, for it gives the consistent ethic the status of policy within the Episcopal Conference. Nevertheless, I

*Also published in *Origins*, vol. 15, no. 30, March 20, 1986, pp. 655–58; *Consistent Ethic of Life* (Sheed & Ward, 1988).

believe the concept and consequences of the consistent ethic must be examined more deeply, its implications made clearer within the Church and in the wider civil society. So I am returning to the theme this afternoon at another Catholic university, seeking to press forward the dialogue of several disciplines in the quest for a comprehensive and consistent ethic of life.

During the past two years, as I have followed the commentary on the consistent ethic in journals and the media, and as I have carried on a wide-ranging personal correspondence with many bishops, theologians, philosophers, and social scientists, three topics emerged about the theme which I wish to address: its theological foundation, its ethical logic, and its political consequences.

THE THEOLOGICAL FOUNDATION: SYSTEMATIC DEFENSE OF THE PERSON

Some commentators, while very positive about the substance and structure of the call for a consistent ethic, have urged me to focus on its underlying theological foundations. I see the need for this and will comment here on two aspects of its theological substance, leaving for the next section some more detailed moral commentary.

The consistent ethic grows out of the very character of Catholic moral thought. By that I do not mean to imply that one has to be a Catholic to affirm the moral content of the consistent ethic. But I do think that this theme highlights both the systematic and analogical character of Catholic moral theology. The systematic nature of Catholic theology means it is grounded in a set of basic principles and then articulated in a fashion which draws out the meaning of each principle and the relationships among them. Precisely because of its systematic quality, Catholic theology refuses to treat moral issues in an *ad hoc* fashion. There is a continual process of testing the use of a principle in one case by its use in very different circumstances. The consistent ethic seeks only to illustrate how this testing goes on when dealing with issues involving the taking of life or the enhancement of life through social policy.

The analogical character of Catholic thought offers the potential to address a spectrum of issues which are not identical but have some common characteristics. Analogical reasoning identifies the unifying elements which link two or more issues, while at the same time it recognizes why similar issues cannot be reduced to a single problem.

The taking of life presents itself as a moral problem all along the spectrum of life, but there are distinguishing characteristics between abortion and war, as well as elements which radically differentiate war from decisions made about care of a terminally ill patient. The *differences* among these cases are universally acknowledged; a consistent ethic seeks to highlight the fact that differences do not destroy the elements of a *common moral challenge*.

A Catholic ethic which is both systematic in its argument and analogical in its perspective stands behind the proposal that, in the face of the multiple threats to life in our time, spanning every phase of existence, it is necessary to develop a moral vision which can address these several challenges in a coherent and comprehensive fashion.

If the theological style of the consistent ethic is captured by the two words, systematic and analogical, the theological rationale for the ethic is grounded in the respect we owe the human person. To defend human life is to protect the human person. The consistent ethic cuts across the diverse fields of social ethics, medical ethics, and sexual ethics. The unifying theme behind these three areas of moral analysis is the human person, the core reality in Catholic moral thought.

It is precisely the abiding conviction of Catholic ethics about the social nature of the person that ties together the emphasis—in the pastoral letter on the economy—on society's responsibility for the poor, the insistence of the bishops that abortion is a public not a purely private moral question, and the constant refrain of Catholic ethics that sexual issues are social in character.

The theological assertion that the person is the *imago dei*, the philosophical affirmation of the dignity of the person, and the political principle that society and state exist to serve the person—all these themes stand behind the consistent ethic. They also sustain the positions that the U.S. Catholic Bishops have taken on issues as diverse as nuclear policy, social policy, and abortion. These themes provide the basis for the moral perspective of the consistent ethic. It is the specifics of that moral perspective which now must be examined.

THE ETHICAL ARGUMENT: THE LOGIC OF LINKAGE

The central assertion of the consistent ethic is that we will enhance our moral understanding of a number of "life-issues" by carefully linking them in a framework which allows consideration of each issue on its own merits, but also highlights the connections among distinct issues. This is the moral logic of an analogical vision.

In essence the consistent ethic is a moral argument, and, therefore, its principles and perspective must be constantly measured and tested. The consistent ethic rejects collapsing all issues into one, and it rejects isolating our moral vision and insulating our social concern on one issue. What has been the response to the moral argument of the consistent ethic?

First, it has generated precisely the kind of substantive debate in the Catholic community and in the wider society which I believe is needed.

The response began immediately after the Gannon Lecture in the press and weekly journals; it has now moved also to scholarly journals. Second, the range of the commentary has run from the ethical theory of the consistent ethic, to debate about its specific conclusions, to assessment of its contribution to the public witness of the Church in U.S. society.

A particularly extensive analysis of the theme appeared in the "Notes on Moral Theology" in *Theological Studies* last March. This annual review of scholarly writing on moral theology has been highly respected for many years. Among the many commentaries on the consistent ethic, I cite this one because it engages bishops and theologians in the kind of disciplined debate which is needed if our theology is to be authentically Catholic, intellectually responsive to contemporary moral challenges, and pastorally useful to the Catholic community and civil society.

In a time when continuing respectful dialogue is urgently needed between bishops and theologians, I believe the kind of theological interest generated by the two pastoral letters of the U.S. bishops and the consistent ethic proposal is a healthy sign. The *Theological Studies* articles on the consistent ethic were a wide-ranging survey of several specific questions. On the whole, I found the commentary quite positive and very helpful. I lift it up for consideration by others even though I do not agree with every conclusion drawn by the authors.

One of the areas where I differ is the critique of the moral theory made by Fr. Richard McCormick, S.J. He supports the perspective of the consistent ethic, calling it "utterly essential," but he believes that I give the prohibition of direct killing of the innocent too high a status. Rather than calling it a basic principle of Catholic morality, Fr. McCormick would designate it a moral rule, "developed as a result of our wrestling with concrete cases of conflict." Furthermore, he argues that the rule has been formulated in teleological fashion, by a balancing of values which yield some exceptions to the presumption against killing.

While I do not consider it my role to engage in a full review of the moral theory of the consistent ethic, I think the reduction of the prohibition against the intentional killing of the innocent to a status less than an absolute rule is not correct. As I argued in the Gannon Lecture, the justification of the use of force and the taking of human life is based on a presumption against taking life which then allows for a series of exceptions where the presumption is overridden. But within this general structure of reasoning, for example in the just-war doctrine, the direct killing of the innocent has not been regarded as a legitimate exception.

This means, as Fr. John Connery, S.J., and others have observed, that Catholic teaching has not ruled out the taking of life in all circumstances. There is a *presumption* against taking life, not an *absolute prohibition*. But the cutting edge of the Just War argument has been its capacity to place a double restraint on the use of force. One limit is based on the calculation of consequences (the principle of proportionality) and the other based on an absolute prohibition of certain actions (the principle of noncombatant immunity).

As I read Fr. McCormick's proposal, both principles would become proportional judgments. My experience in addressing the nuclear question leads me to conclude that such an interpretation will weaken the moral strength of the ethic of war. In assessing the strategy of deterrence, having two distinct criteria of moral analysis provided the bishops with a perspective on the policy debate which was different from what a totally proportionalist view would have offered.

Because of my experience with this specific moral dilemma of deterrence and because I find the prohibition against the intentional killing of the innocent a crucial element across the spectrum of the consistent ethic, I find myself not persuaded by Fr. McCormick's recommendation, even though I appreciate the care with which he reviewed my lectures. I know adherence to the absolute prohibition creates very complex and difficult choices, not least in deterrence theory, but testing the absolute prohibition across the spectrum of life leads me to reaffirm it rather than reduce its status.

A very different objection to the consistent ethic arose—primarily from persons active in the right-to-life movement—immediately after the Gannon Lecture. The critique continues to this day. The objection is raised against the way I called for relating our defense of innocent life to support for social policies and programs designed to respond to the needs of the poor. The passage of the Gannon Lecture which attracted the most criticism read this way:

> If one contends, as we do, that the right of every fetus to be born should be protected by civil law and supported by civil consensus, then our moral, political and economic responsibilities do not stop at the moment of birth. Those who defend the right to life of the weakest among us must be equally visible in support of the quality of life of the powerless among us: the old and the young, the hungry and the homeless, the undocumented immigrant and the unemployed worker. Such a quality of life posture translates into specific political and economic positions on tax policy, employment generation, welfare policy, nutrition and feeding programs, and health care. Consistency means we cannot have it both ways: We cannot urge a compassionate society and vigorous public policy to protect the rights of the unborn and then argue that compassion and significant public programs on behalf of the needy undermine the moral fibre of the society or are beyond the proper scope of governmental responsibility.

Reviewing those words in light of the criticisms of the last two years, I still find what I said to be morally correct and, if anything, politically more necessary to say than it was two years ago. In the first half of the 1980s we have seen many of the programs designed to meet basic needs of poor people systematically cut. Perhaps the prototypical example is what is happening to children—precisely those who first evoke our right-to-life defense. In the second draft of the pastoral letter on the economy the bishops graphically describe the situation of children in our country:

> Today one in every four American children under the age of 6 and one in every two black children under 6 are poor. The number of children in poverty rose by 4 million over the decade between 1973–1983, with the result that there are now more poor children in the United States than at any time since 1965.

In a recent book of far-reaching significance, Senator Patrick Moynihan has made the point that children are the most vulnerable group in our society.

In the face of this evidence it is precisely the function of a consistent ethic to gather a constituency which stands against those social forces legitimating the taking of life before birth, *and* stands against other social forces legitimating policies which erode the dignity of life after birth by leaving children vulnerable to hunger, inadequate housing, and insufficient health care.

The criticism of my Gannon Lecture was twofold: that it confused two different moral issues and that it expected everyone to do everything. I have responded to this critique previously, but I wish to expand upon my response. Surely we can all agree that the taking of human life in abortion is not the same as failing to protect human dignity against hunger. But having made that distinction, let us not fail to make the point that both are moral issues requiring a response of the Catholic community and of our society as a whole.

The logic of a consistent ethic is to press the moral meaning of both issues. The consequence of a consistent ethic is to bring under review the position of every group in the Church which sees the moral meaning in one place but not the other. The ethic cuts *two* ways not one: It challenges pro-life groups, and it challenges justice and peace groups. The meaning of a consistent ethic is to say in the Catholic community that our moral tradition calls us beyond the split so evident in the wider society between moral witness to life before and after birth.

Does this mean that everyone must do everything? No! There are limits of time, energy and competency. There is a shape to every individual vocation. People must specialize, groups must focus their energies. The consistent ethic does not deny this.

But it does say something to the Church: It calls us to a wider witness to life than we sometimes manifest in our separate activities. The consistent ethic challenges bishops to shape a comprehensive social agenda. It challenges priests and religious to teach the Catholic tradition with the breadth it deserves. And it challenges Catholics as citizens to go beyond the divided witness to life which is too much the pattern of politics and culture in our society. Responding to this multiple challenge requires consideration of the public consequences of the consistent ethic.

THE POLITICAL CONSEQUENCES: SHAPING PUBLIC CHOICES

Some commentators on the consistent ethic saw it primarily as a political policy. They missed its primary meaning: It is a moral vision and an ethical argument sustaining the vision. But the moral vision does have political consequences. The consistent ethic is meant to shape the public witness of the Catholic Church in our society.

The first consequence is simply to highlight the unique place which Catholic teaching on a range of issues has given the Church in the public arena. As I have said before, no other major institution in the country brings together the positions the Catholic bishops presently hold on abortion, nuclear policy, and economic policy. Our positions cut across party lines, and they contradict conventional notions of liberal and conservative. I find that a healthy contribution to the public debate, and I believe we ought to stress the point.

The second public consequence of a consistent ethic is to establish a framework where we can test the moral vision of each part of the Church in a disciplined, systematic fashion. We will not shape an ecclesial consensus about the consistent ethic without the kind of vigorous public debate which has gone on in the Church in the last two years. But our debate will sharpen our ecclesial moral sense, and it can also be a public lesson to the wider society if it is marked by coherence, civility, and charity.

The third public consequence of a consistent ethic is that it provides a standard to test public policy, party platforms, and the posture of candidates for office. Here is where the challenge to moral reasoning, pastoral leadership, and political sensitivity reaches its most delicate level. But we should not shrink from the need to make specific the logic of the consistent ethic.

We are a multi-issue Church precisely because of the scope and structure of our moral teaching. But it is not enough to be interested in several issues. We need to point the way toward a public vision where issues can be understood as morally and politically interdependent. I propose the consistent ethic not as a finished product but a framework in need of development. I invite more debate about it, precisely at this concrete level where specific choices on issues are made, where candidates take positions, and where citizens must evaluate them.

I believe our moral vision is broader and richer than we have made it appear at this concrete, practical level of politics. Precisely because we are not yet in a national election year, we need to think about how a consistent ethic can be set forth in a convincing way. It will cut across conventional party lines, and it will not lead to crystal clear judgments on candidates, but it may give the Church, as an institution and a community, a better way to engage the attention of the nation regarding the intersection of moral vision, public policy, and political choices.

To think through the meaning of such a position, we need bishops who foster the debate, political leaders who enter the discussion, professors and policy analysts who can clarify categories, and members of the Church who exercise the supremely important role of citizens. It is my hope that we can have this kind of ecclesial and public debate in the months ahead.

Address

University of Illinois
Health Care Community

Chicago, Illinois

── *February 16, 1993* ─────────────────────

Thank you for inviting me to address you on an issue of great importance and enduring controversy in our nation today: abortion. During the
past ten years, as a pastor, I have given many presentations and written
many articles on the Catholic Church's stand on life issues, including
abortion. However, we are at a new moment in the public debate on abortion, and I am grateful for this opportunity to refine my own thinking on
the issue. I speak, of course, from my perspective as a Catholic bishop. I
realize that there are some who hold other views.

Three federal initiatives contribute to the newness of the moment.
They help shape the context of today's public policy debate on abortion
and call the Church and its pastors to reexamine their approach to the
discussion. The first is the U.S. Supreme Court decision last June on
Planned Parenthood of Southeastern Pennsylvania v. Casey. The second is
a series of executive orders on abortion policy issued by President Clinton
on January 22, reflecting the new administration's position on legalized
abortion which is quite different from that of the two previous administrations. The third is what is today called the Freedom of Choice Act currently before the U.S. Congress.

This afternoon, I will, first, briefly describe the broader contemporary
context of these issues and indicate the need for a consistent ethic of life
in the Church and society. Second, I will discuss the current status of the
abortion debate in the U.S. in the light of the three federal initiatives I

117

just mentioned. Third, I will explore how the Church might shape its pastoral response to the debate about, and the reality of, abortion in our society today.

RESPECTING LIFE TODAY

The Pastoral Constitution on the Church in the Modern World is the *magna carta* of the Catholic Church's social ministry since the Second Vatican Council. The document asserted that the social task of the Church in the modern world is to read the signs of the times and to interpret them in light of the gospel. In the contemporary signs of the times, three challenges pose different but interrelated questions for the Church's social ministry. There is a technological challenge, a peace challenge, and a justice challenge. The three must be interpreted in light of the biblical truth that human life, a gift from God, is sacred, and that everyone has an obligation to defend, protect, and nurture it.

The technological challenge arises from the unique capacities which contemporary science, especially its applications in the medical field, has produced in our generation. This challenge is most clearly visible at the beginning and the end of life.

At both ends of the spectrum of life—the mystery of conception and the mystery of death—our generation has developed capacities to intervene in the natural order in ways which earlier generations would have thought belonged solely to God. Today, from genetics to embryology, to the care of the aged and the terminally ill, we have the capacity to shape the beginning of life, make choices about its development, and sustain it by life-support systems.

At both ends of life's spectrum, the technological challenge has been both a blessing and a burden. Some discoveries help us to enhance life expectancy, to correct inherited genetic defects, and to relieve pain and suffering. But the new technologies have also placed in human hands decisions about life and death which were previously unknown to ethicists and for which there is little human experience to guide our choices.

The danger of our day is that we will use our technological genius to erode human dignity rather than enhance it. Technology has its own logic, but it does not have its own ethic. The danger is that our choices will be dominated by technology rather than directed by human wisdom and the light of religious faith.

These questions of technology, life, and death are not, of course, limited to the world of medicine. The unique moral character of our day is demonstrated by the linkage between the "micro-questions" of medical ethics and the "macro-questions" of war and peace in an age with the capacity of atomic, biological, and chemical warfare. The link between these two quite different areas of human existence is the technological revolution which has unlocked the genetic code and unleashed the power of the atom within the space of a lifetime. So, the technological challenge is also part of the peace challenge: How to keep the peace in an age when the instruments of war can threaten the very fabric of human existence as a whole. Now that the Cold War has ended, the new threats to life are posed predominantly by nuclear proliferation and the various forms of instability we find in such areas as the Middle East, the former Soviet Union, and especially the Balkans.

Technology provides the material link between the "micro" and the "macro" threats to life in our time. The moral link is the unique value of human life. In very different settings—in the laboratory and in the life of nations—our generation is called to protect the fragile fabric of human life against unprecedented dangers.

The justice challenge poses a different but related set of questions. It calls us to expand our moral concern beyond the question of protecting life from attack to promoting and enhancing the dignity of human life in society. Justice challenges us to build a society which provides the necessary material and moral support for every human being to realize his or her God-given dignity. We are aware of the limits of human nature and the impact of sin on human affairs. We know that this work of shaping a humane society is a never-ending task. But this must not prevent us from defending human life and dignity and protecting human rights. The justice challenge calls us to this effort.

Each of these challenges—technology, peace, and justice—has its own inner complexity. Each must be addressed on its own terms by slow, patient work. No one can do everything, and some may feel closer to some of the issues I have described; indeed, they may consider themselves better able to address them than others.

But acknowledging the relationship, the connection, among the three challenges—technology, peace, and justice—is very important. And it was that conviction that started my reflection several years ago on the need for a consistent ethic of life. A consistent ethic recognizes the need for specific approaches to concrete issues, but it also raises a broader question. Are the Church and society well served by addressing these questions in isolation from each other? Do we not learn more about the personal and social challenge of this moment in history by consciously connecting it with what has gone before and with its present implications which often are addressed separately?

The consistent ethic sees the convergence of these multiple and diverse challenges as a time of opportunity. It has seemed to me and others that the very nature of Catholic moral teaching offers us an opportunity to respond to multiple challenges under the guidance of an overall, coherent moral vision. The consistent ethic of life is a moral vision based on two principles regarding the sacredness of human life: the obligation to protect and nurture it, and not to bring direct harm to it. We hope the consistent ethic might provide, not only for us but also for others, a framework for moral analysis across the full spectrum of life-issues, from conception to natural death.

The concept of the consistent ethic is based upon two characteristics of Catholic teaching: its scope and its structure. Its scope is broad enough to encompass the three distinct challenges I have outlined. In terms of abortion, for example, the Catholic Church in the U.S. is committed to reversing a public policy of abortion on demand. But we are also convinced that we cannot have a just and compassionate society unless our care extends to both sides of the line of birth: We must protect the basic right of unborn children to live and, at the same time, promote the associated basic human rights of adequate nutrition, housing, and health care which enhance the lives which are saved.

The scope of a comprehensive ethic is matched by a systematic structure of moral argument. A broad moral concern must be based upon solid moral analysis. No two "life" issues are identical; they cannot be collapsed into one. At a given time, one may have to be given a higher priority than others. The solution to one may not be applicable to others. In short, each requires its own moral analysis. A systematic moral tradition is necessary for such analyses which enable the ecclesial community to take a position on a given issue and then project that position in the civil debate.

The consistent ethic draws upon the scope and structure of the Catholic moral vision to confront the full range of questions endangering human dignity today—from abortion to euthanasia. However, the idea must be linked to a community—a constituency—which holds and embodies the vision. Within our own Catholic tradition, we recognize that a vision without a community is not capable of influence. A vision tied to a committed community is the first prerequisite of serious social impact. This is why we try to build that community and invite others into this discussion.

Let us turn now to the status of the abortion debate in the United States today.

THE ABORTION DEBATE IN THE U.S. TODAY

I will briefly outline the legal dimensions of the issue after the U.S. Supreme Court decision on *Casey* and, then, explore its political dimensions, including the new administration's liberal approach to abortion and the Freedom of Choice Act.

Legal Dimensions

In effect, the U.S. Supreme Court's controversial 1973 decision, *Roe v. Wade*, and another one issued on the same day, prohibited states from completely protecting the unborn in our country. There is considerable confusion about these decisions in the minds of many Americans. Many people think that the Court said a woman has an *absolute* right, protected under the U.S. Constitution, to an abortion. Others presume that a woman has an unlimited right to do with her body whatever she pleases. Still others claim that a woman may terminate her pregnancy at whatever time, in whatever way, and for whatever reasons she herself chooses.

But that is not what the Court said in *Roe v. Wade*. Instead, the justices explicitly rejected these notions and said that the woman's right to an abortion is balanced by the state's "important and legitimate" interests in safeguarding the health of the mother, maintaining medical standards, and protecting "the potentiality of human life." Moreover, the justices said, these interests grow "in substantiality as the woman approaches term and, at a point during pregnancy, each becomes 'compelling.'"

Since 1973, many state legislatures and some municipalities have enacted new abortion laws in the light of the Court's rulings, especially its holding that the state has "important and legitimate" interests in the matter. Several of these statutes were subsequently challenged in the courts and eventually came up for review by the Supreme Court. While the Court upheld some provisions, it struck down many others.

Given the confusing history of the Court's decisions on this issue since 1973, it is not surprising that many people have assumed that abortion on demand is an absolute right, despite the Court's assertions to the contrary. Meanwhile, legal scholars and others—including four current members of the Court itself—continue to point out the inadequate reasoning on which *Roe v. Wade* was based.

Last June, the U.S. Supreme Court issued its decision on *Planned Parenthood of Southeastern Pennsylvania v. Casey*. By the narrow margin of 5–4, a majority of the justices decided to reaffirm the essential holding of *Roe v. Wade* which, as the justices pointed out, has three parts: (1) "the right of the woman to choose to have an abortion before viability and to obtain it without undue interference from the state . . ."; (2) "the state's power to restrict abortions after fetal viability, if the law contains exceptions for pregnancies which endanger a woman's life or health . . ."; and (3) "the principle that the state has legitimate interests from the outset of the pregnancy in protecting the health of the woman and the life of the fetus that may become a child."

The majority opinion in *Casey* rejected *Roe's* rigid trimester approach and substituted for it the concept of viability. While it also emphasized the state's "legitimate interests" in protecting both maternal health and protecting the life of the fetus, the majority opinion offered the new concept of "undue burden" as a guide for deciding which statutory provisions regarding the state's interests would be constitutional or not.

The four dissenting justices, including Chief Justice Rehnquist who wrote the minority opinion, argued, instead, "that *Roe* was wrongly decided, and that it can and should be overruled consistently with our traditional approach to *stare decisis* in constitutional cases." Chief Judge Rehnquist's dissenting opinion also points out that the "undue burden" standard "does not command the support of a majority of this court." (Only Justices O'Connor, Kennedy, and Souter supported the "undue burden" standard.) The sharp division within the Court reflects the divisiveness of the abortion debate in our society as a whole.

Pro-abortion forces rejoiced in the reaffirmation of the woman's constitutional right to an abortion but were much less happy with the Court's emphasis on the state's legitimate interests in the matter. They were most upset by the Court's declaration that several provisions of the Pennsylvania statute being challenged were, indeed, constitutional, and only one was deemed unconstitutional (and that by a single vote). The specific provisions of the Pennsylvania statute which were challenged are these:

> (1) The Pennsylvania statute required "that the woman be informed of the availability of information relating to fetal development and the assistance available should she decide to carry the pregnancy to full term." The Court upheld this informed-consent requirement by a vote of 7–2, judging that it is "a reasonable measure to ensure an informed choice."

> (2) A requirement that the woman's spouse be notified before an abortion was declared invalid by the simple majority of 5 of the 9 justices who argued that a spousal notification requirement is "likely to prevent a significant number of women from obtaining an abortion."

> (3) A requirement that a minor seeking an abortion obtain the consent of a parent or guardian, provided that there is an adequate judicial bypass procedure, was upheld by 7 of the 9 justices;

> (4) The record-keeping and reporting requirements of the Pennsylvania statute were also upheld by 7 of the 9 justices.

In short, while a narrow majority of the justices reaffirmed the woman's right to an abortion articulated in *Roe*, they, in effect, overruled many of the Court's decisions on abortion cases in the last twenty years.

While those of us who are pro-life were understandably disappointed by the Court's reaffirmation of abortion on demand, we also saw new possibilities for legislation at the state level which would finally reflect the state's "legitimate interests" in maternal health and protecting "potential" human life.

Despite the fact that the Court remains divided on the validity of *Roe*, it appears that we will have to live with its interpretation in *Casey* for the foreseeable future. Let us now turn to the political dimensions of the current status of the abortion debate.

Political Dimensions

As might be expected, public discourse on a politically divisive, moral issue like abortion has been lively and heated. While dedicated advocates of the pro-life and the so-called "pro-choice" positions are poles apart, the majority of our citizens seem to stand somewhere in the middle. There is great ambiguity and confusion among many about the various issues of the abortion controversy. And when public opinion is divided, it is difficult to make headway with thoughtful, effective legislation.

Let me explain the current dilemma. On the one hand, as has been true for many years, Americans remain overwhelmingly opposed to a permissive abortion policy on the model of *Roe v. Wade*. A recent issue of the Chicago *Sun–Times* carried a graph based on a Gallup poll which found strong majorities (about 70 percent) agreeing that abortion should be legally available either "never" (15 percent) or "only in some circumstances" (55 percent). Fewer than one out of three Americans think that it should "always" be available.

It has also become evident that many simply do not realize the scope and magnitude of legalized abortion in the U.S. According to a survey carried out by the Wirthlin Group in 1990, almost half of our citizens surmised that there are fewer than 500,000 abortions annually in the United States. The real total, as you know, is more than three times as many: 1.6 million—some 4,400 a day!

Again, Americans tend grossly to overestimate the extent to which so-called "hard cases" make up the abortions which are performed. According to the Wirthlin survey, people typically believe that over 20 percent of all abortions occur in cases of rape and incest, and over 15 percent in cases where the woman's life is endangered. Because of these beliefs, many are reluctant to support legislation which would ban all abortions. However, according to the research arm of Planned Parenthood, the actual percentages are quite different from popular belief. Fewer than 1 percent of abortions are performed in rape or incest cases, and only 7 percent of the women having abortions even cite "health" as a reason.

This means that the pro-life movement in this country—including the Catholic Church—faces a double challenge: (a) We need to educate people, who are opposed in principle to abortion on demand, to fundamental facts about the number of abortions, the reason for which they are performed, and the moral values which are often neglected or simply dismissed in the public debate. (b) We need to make some strategic choices which I will say more about later.

Often the public debate on abortion is intertwined with the concerns of many in the feminist movement, especially those who insist upon a woman's absolute right to choose an abortion. However, among others, Dr. Sidney Callahan, a lay theologian, has very persuasively argued the case for pro-life feminism. She argues that "women can never achieve the fulfillment of feminist goals in a society permissive toward abortion." She has also pointed out that

> permissive abortion laws do not bring women reproductive freedom, social equality, sexual fulfillment, or full personal development. Pitting women against their own offspring is not only morally offensive, it is psychologically and politically destructive. Women will never climb to equality over mounds of dead fetuses, now in the millions.

My point in raising this issue is simply this: being pro-life and being a woman are not inconsistent or contradictory; indeed, they are naturally compatible.

Let me turn now to two specific political initiatives which, in my opinion, ignore the disagreement of the vast majority of Americans with the current policy of abortion on demand and create a new moment in the abortion debate.

THE PRESIDENT'S EXECUTIVE ORDERS (JANUARY 22, 1993)

During the campaign President Clinton adopted a fairly aggressive platform embracing legalized abortion on demand, and, within 48 hours of his presidency, he reversed five executive orders of his predecessors in regard to abortion. Specifically, he lifted:

• a ban on privately funded abortions at military hospitals;

• a ban on abortion counseling in federally funded clinics;

• a moratorium on federal research using fetal tissue;

• a ban on the import of the French abortifacient pill RU 486 for personal use;

• the restriction of funds going to United Nation programs giving abortion advice.

President Clinton stated that he signed the executive orders as part of his efforts to keep abortion "safe, legal, and rare." As Cardinal Mahoney of

Los Angeles noted, how one keeps abortion rare by promoting and expanding its availability is difficult to comprehend.

It is unfortunate that the president chose a very symbolic day for the pro-life movement—the twentieth anniversary of *Roe v. Wade*—on which to issue these directives. However, his actions were in accord with his campaign promises and not unexpected. At the same time, he has said that he is personally opposed to abortion and wants to limit the number of abortions in this country.

The media has engaged in considerable speculation about the relationship between the Catholic Church and the new administration. We clearly disagree with the administration's pro-choice position and the executive orders which the president issued. But we agree with many of the administration's other positions; for example, putting children and families first, making health care more accessible to all our citizens, and lessening the gap between the wealthy and the poor of this nation. On February 5, President Clinton signed into law the Family and Medical Leave Act, long backed by the U.S. Catholic bishops. We hope that, through ongoing dialogue, the administration will come to see the necessary logic linking the various life-issues, including the right to life of the unborn. Our challenge is to keep making that case in a persuasive way in the public arena.

THE FREEDOM OF CHOICE ACT

A much more threatening initiative, which has very serious implications for the current debate on abortion, is the proposed legislation known as the Freedom of Choice Act (FOCA) which is before the U.S. Congress. As I have pointed out, in *Casey*, the U.S. Supreme Court, in effect, abandoned many of the Court's earlier decisions in abortion cases as ill considered. The legislation now before the Congress would impose a strict scrutiny standard and resurrect the kind of thinking which the Supreme Court has just abandoned.

I have been advised that, if FOCA is passed, it would likely prohibit the following kinds of statutes which *Casey* allows:

- laws designed merely to influence the woman's informed choice between abortion or childbirth;

- laws designed to inform pregnant women of the probable anatomical and physiological characteristics of the unborn child;

- laws designed to inform pregnant women of the existence of public and private agencies to help them if they decide to carry their child to term;

- laws designed to inform pregnant women of the availability of medical assistance benefits;

- laws designed to inform pregnant women that the father of their child is responsible for financial assistance should they carry the child to term;

- laws designed to inform pregnant women of the medical risks, including the physical and psychological effects of abortion;

- laws designed to ensure that for post-viability abortions, the physician choose an abortion procedure that will provide the best opportunity for the unborn child to be aborted alive unless use of that procedure would present a significantly greater medical risk to the life or health of the pregnant woman than some other procedure;

- laws designed to ensure that, during any abortion procedure that may result in the child's survival, a second physician is present to care for the child born alive and to take reasonable steps to preserve its life;

- laws promoting maternal health or unborn life, if the law results in *any* increased cost;

- laws requiring a physician (or someone other than the minor) to inform the minor's parents of her intent to obtain an abortion would be subject to challenge;

- laws requiring that physicians counsel their patients or provide them with relevant information before performing an abortion;

- laws requiring a 24-hour waiting period;

- laws protecting health care providers, like Catholic hospitals (as distinguished from unwilling individuals) from having to participate in abortion;

- laws designed to prevent public facilities from being used to perform abortions or to prevent public employees, in the course of their employment, from performing or assisting in abortions;

- laws requiring viability testing such as that upheld in *Webster*.

In effect, under the amended Senate bill, FOCA, with limited exceptions, would deny states their historic role in protecting unborn life and women's health—interests that the U.S. Supreme Court reaffirmed in *Casey!* In other words, FOCA is an attempt to overrule Supreme Court cases, like *Casey* and *Webster,* that permit state regulation of abortion. As the Justice Department pointed out in a letter to Representative Henry Hyde of Illinois, FOCA "represents an extraordinary and unprecedented act of constitutional revisionism that would raise grave questions concerning Congress' power under section 5 of the Fourteenth Amendment" (March 2, 1992).

The Freedom of Choice Act goes well beyond *Roe v. Wade* and all subsequent U.S. Supreme Court decisions on abortion since 1973 by absolutizing and isolating abortion. It is of doubtful constitutionality. It would make bad law and worse public policy.

THE CHURCH'S PASTORAL RESPONSE TODAY

How should the Church and its pastors respond to this new moment in the nation's debate on abortion? Our pastoral response is basically threefold: (a) working for legal protection for the unborn, (b) striving for economic justice for women and children, and (c) educating people about the reality of abortion and its moral dimension.

Because we are committed to establishing constitutional protection for the unborn child to the maximum degree possible, we will vigorously oppose the enactment of FOCA. Moreover, the House bill does not protect health care providers other than individuals, even if those providers have serious moral or religious objections to abortion. Can you imagine the dire consequences of such legislation on Catholic hospitals and other health care facilities which, as institutions, are opposed to abortion? As you may know, 25 percent of the hospitals in the United States are under Catholic sponsorship. How could these Catholic hospitals survive?

We will continue to urge federal and state legislators to work for laws and public policies which are both pro-life and pro-family and which address the legitimate concerns of women. Sadly, many women make a decision about an unwanted pregnancy in relative isolation from those who should help and support them—their family, their husband or boyfriend, close friends, their pastor or rabbi. Conception does not take place in isolation, and pregnancy should not be experienced in isolation. We must teach, insist on, and live out the reality that sexual activity carries with it significant and unavoidable social and moral responsibilities for men and women alike. Abortion harms both the mother and her unborn child. It also has tragically destructive effects on families and society as a whole. It erodes respect for human life. These are all reasons why the Church must address the issue and work for legislation which is both pro-life and pro-family.

At this moment, the most important response of the Catholic Church will be to continue to educate people—our own constituency and all who are willing to listen—about the reality and moral dimension of the abortion issue. In particular, I am concerned about reaching out in an effective way to the majority of Americans who do not accept the current permissive policy on abortion but do not want to see all abortions outlawed.

They have a right to know the number of abortions annually in this country, the reasons why women choose abortion over childbirth, and the moral dimension of the issue.

If the vast majority of Americans can agree that some restrictions are needed in regard to abortions, what are the limits which the majority of our citizens will support? Some refuse to accept the possibility of merely restricting abortions, because they are committed to eliminating all abortions. I understand their feelings and respect their conscience on this matter. I, too, am strongly opposed to all directly intended abortions, without exception. However, a public policy which would not allow abortions under any circumstances does not have the support of the majority of our citizens at this time. I, for one, cannot justify waiting until such a consensus is developed before I support measures that will save the lives of any unborn children.

In a religiously pluralistic society, achieving consensus on a public moral question is never easy. But we have been able to do it before—by a process of debate, decision-making, then review of our decisions. For example, civil rights, particularly in the areas of housing, education, employment, voting, and access to public facilities were determined—after momentous struggles of war, politics, and law—to be so central to public order that the state could not be neutral on the question. Today we have a public consensus in law and policy which clearly defines civil rights as an issue of public morality. But the decision was not reached without struggle; the consensus was not automatic. And the issue is not yet fully resolved. The fact, then, that a spontaneous public consensus is lacking at a given moment does not prohibit its being created. But, as I said earlier, even as we work toward such a consensus, we should do all we can to save the lives of as many unborn children as possible. This does not mean that I understand morality in incremental terms but that we must use available means to achieve the full realization of our moral vision.

When some accuse us of forcing a Catholic point of view in regard to abortion on others, I reply that the defense of innocent human life is, indeed, a cornerstone of Catholic social teaching. But it is not a specifically sectarian concern. Abortion is a human rights issue, not a narrowly Catholic one. While not all moral values and principles need be legislated, certain key values, principles, and practices must be protected and promoted by law and public policy. Protection for unborn children cannot rely only upon moral persuasion; their lives must be protected, as our lives are, by the civil law.

A consistent ethic of life demonstrates that it is not enough merely to protect and promote the rights of unborn children; we must also extend such protection and promotion of basic human rights to women and children. And this means working for economic justice. Besides advocacy and education, the Church offers many maternity-related services to women, such as free or low-cost prenatal and maternity care, adoption services, emotional and spiritual support, housing and continuing education. The Church also reaches out to console those women and men who have been victimized by abortion through our Project Rachel counseling network.

As I have intimated, the development of public policy requires a wider consensus than the personal conviction of any individual—including a public official. The beginning of the process is a series of conscious choices that something different must be done. Then the search for a deliberate, specific policy can begin, and the consistent ethic offers valuable guidance for reflection and discussion.

The value and appeal of the consistent ethic lies precisely in its ability to transcend considerations of mere political expediency and to ask where moral truth leads us. Thus, even if this message is inevitably misinterpreted, distorted, or abused in the political arena, in no way is the moral argument itself invalidated.

* * *

A consistent ethic of life seeks to defend and enhance human life across its full spectrum from conception to natural death, and in all its circumstances. As I stated earlier, the life-issues may not always be of equal importance, and they cannot be collapsed into one. But they are linked. One cannot, with consistency, claim to be pro-life if one applies the principle of the sanctity of life to one or more life-issues but rejects or ignores it in regard to others. It is essential that the Church—its pastors, its priests, and all its members—continue to address this moral dimension of the life issues in the public debate on abortion.

To prevent deeper divisions in our society, I call upon all who participate in the public debate about abortion to speak and act in an honest, mutually respectful manner that can seek the truth and find a common ground. In order to attain such a common ground for the common good of our society, we must take into consideration both the right of the unborn to life and the concerns of pregnant women. Ignoring either of these will not promote justice in our land.

"The Consistent Ethic of Life"
Archdiocese of Melbourne, Australia
—— *February 23, 1995* ————————————————————

I am deeply grateful to Archbishop Little and all of you for your warm welcome and kind hospitality. I am delighted to have this opportunity to address you on a topic to which I have devoted much thought during the past eleven years: the consistent ethic of life.

It was in December 1983, at Fordham University in New York City, that I first presented the idea and the rationale for it.

This evening, I will (1) give an overview of the concept, (2) point out the distinct levels of the problem, and (3) assess the contribution of the consistent ethic to the Church and society.

THE CONSISTENT ETHIC OF LIFE: AN OVERVIEW

The idea of the consistent ethic is both old and new. It is "old" in the sense that its substance has been around for years. For example, in a single sentence the Second Vatican Council condemned murder, abortion, euthanasia, suicide, mutilation, torture, subhuman living conditions, arbitrary imprisonment, deportation, slavery, prostitution, and disgraceful working conditions (*Gaudium et spes*, 27). Moreover, when the U.S. Catholic bishops inaugurated their Respect Life Program in 1972, they invited the Catholic community to focus on the "sanctity of human life and the many threats to human life in the modern world, including war, violence, hunger, and poverty."

The U.S. Catholic bishops' 1983 pastoral letter, *The Challenge of Peace: God's Promise and Our Response*, also emphasized the sacredness of human life and the responsibility we have, personally and as a society, to protect and preserve its sanctity. In paragraph 285, it specifically linked the nuclear question with abortion and other life issues:

> When we accept violence in any form as commonplace, our sensitivities become dulled. When we accept violence, war itself can be taken for granted. Violence has many faces: oppression of the poor, deprivation of basic human rights, economic exploitation, sexual exploitation and pornography, neglect or abuse of the aged and the helpless, and innumerable other acts of inhumanity. Abortion in particular blunts a sense of the sacredness of human life. In a society where the innocent unborn are killed wantonly, how can we expect people to feel righteous revulsion at the act or threat of killing non-combatants in war?

However, the pastoral letter—while giving us a starting point for developing a consistent ethic of life—did not provide a fully articulated framework.

It was precisely to provide a more comprehensive theological and ethical basis for the Respect Life Program and for the linkage of war and abortion, as noted by the pastoral letter, that I developed the theme of the consistent ethic. Another important circumstance that prompted me to move in this direction was that I had just been asked to serve as Chairman of the U.S. bishops' Pro-Life Committee. It was October of 1983, and I knew that both abortion and defense-related issues would undoubtedly play an important role in the upcoming U.S. presidential campaign.

It was urgent, I felt, that a well-developed theological and ethical framework be provided that would link the various life issues while, at the same time, pointing out that the issues are not all the same. It was my fear that, *without* such a framework or vision, the bishops would be severely pressured by those who wanted to push a particular issue with little or no concern for the rest. *With* such a theological basis, we would be able to argue convincingly on behalf of all the issues on which we had taken a position in recent years.

I first presented the theme, as I noted, in an address at Fordham University in New York City in December 1983. At that time, I called for a public discussion of the concept, both in Catholic circles and the broader community. In all candor I must admit that the public response greatly exceeded my hopes and expectations.

Since that time there has been a lively exchange by both those who agree and disagree with the theme and its implications.

By far, the majority of the reactions have been supportive. Nonetheless, it has been used and misused by those who have tried to push their own, more narrow agendas. I myself have made further contributions to the discussion through many subsequent addresses and writings.

The concept itself is a complex and *challenging* one. It requires us to broaden, substantively and creatively, our ways of thinking, our attitudes, our pastoral response. Many are not accustomed to thinking about all the life-threatening and life-diminishing issues with such consistency. The result is that they remain somewhat selective in their response. Although some of those who oppose the concept seem not to have understood it, I sometimes suspect that many who oppose it recognize its challenge. Quite frankly, I sometimes wonder whether those who embrace it quickly and wholeheartedly truly understand all its implications.

In November 1985, the U.S. bishops explicitly adopted the consistent ethic as the theological basis for their updated Pastoral Plan for Pro-Life Activities. In sum, to the delight of those who agree with its theological reasoning and to the dismay of the small minority who do not, the "consistent ethic" has entered into our theological vocabulary.

* * *

Let me now explain in greater depth the theological basis and strategic value of the "consistent ethic." Catholic teaching is based on two truths about the human person: human life is both *sacred* and *social*. Because we esteem human life as *sacred*, we have a duty to protect and foster it at all stages of development, from conception to natural death, and in all circumstances. Because we acknowledge that human life is also *social*, society must protect and foster it.

Precisely because life is sacred, the taking of even one life is a momentous event. Traditional Catholic teaching has allowed the taking of human life in particular situations by way of exception—for example, in self-defense and capital punishment. In recent decades, however, the presumptions against taking human life have been strengthened and the exceptions made ever more restrictive.

Fundamental to these shifts in emphasis is a more acute perception of the many ways in which life is threatened today. Obviously, such questions as war, aggression, and capital punishment are not new; they have been with us for centuries. Life has always been threatened, but today there is a new *context* that shapes the *content* of our ethic of life.

The principal factor responsible for this new context is modern *technology* which induces a sharper awareness of the frailty of human life. War, for example, has always been a threat to life, but today the threat is qualitatively different because of nuclear and other sophisticated kinds of weapons. The weapons produced by modern technology now threaten life on a scale previously unimaginable. Living, as we do, therefore, in an age of extraordinary technological development means we face a qualitatively new range of moral problems. The essential questions we face are these: In an age when we *can* do almost anything, how do we decide what we *should* do? In a time when we can do almost anything technologically, how do we decide morally or ethically what we should *not* do?

We face new technological challenges along the whole spectrum of life from conception to natural death. This creates the need for a consistent ethic, for the spectrum cuts across such issues as genetic engineering, abortion, capital punishment, modern warfare, and the care of the terminally ill. Admittedly, these are all *distinct* problems, enormously complex. Each deserves individual treatment. Each requires its own moral analysis. No single answer or solution applies to all. *But they are linked!* While each of these assaults on life has its own meaning and morality, they must be confronted as pieces of a larger pattern.

Given this broad range of challenging issues, we desperately need a societal *attitude* or climate that will sustain a consistent defense and promotion of life. When human life is considered "cheap" or easily expendable in one area, eventually nothing is held as sacred, and all lives are in jeopardy. Ultimately, it is society's attitude about life—whether of respect or nonrespect—that determines its policies and practices.

The theological foundation of the consistent ethic, then, is defense of the person. The ethic grows out of the very character of Catholic moral thought. I hasten to add that I do not mean to imply that one has to be a Catholic to affirm the moral content of the consistent ethic.

As I mentioned earlier, the concept of the consistent ethic is both complex and challenging. It joins the humanity of the unborn infant with the humanity of the hungry; it calls for positive legal action to prevent the killing of the unborn or the aged and positive societal action to provide shelter for the homeless and education for the illiterate. A consistent ethic identifies both the problem of taking life and the challenge of promoting human dignity as *moral* questions.

The theological assertion that the human person is made in the "image and likeness" of God, the philosophical affirmation of the dignity of the person, and the political principle that society and state exist to serve the person—all these themes stand behind the consistent ethic. They provide the basis for its moral perspective.

A consistent ethic does not say everyone in the Church must do all things, but it does say that, as individuals and groups pursue one issue, whether it is opposing abortion or capital punishment, the *way* we oppose one threat should be related to support for a systemic vision of life. It is not necessary or possible for every person to engage each issue, but it is both possible and necessary for the Church as a whole to cultivate a conscious explicit connection among the several issues. And it is very necessary for preserving a systemic vision that individuals and groups who seek to witness to life at one point of the spectrum of life not be seen as insensitive to or even opposed to other moral claims on the overall spectrum of life. Consistency does rule out contradictory moral positions about the unique value of human life. No one is called to do everything, but each of us can do something. And we can strive not to stand against each other when the protection *and* the promotion of life are at stake.

THE CONSISTENT ETHIC OF LIFE: THE LEVELS OF THE QUESTION

A consistent ethic of life should honor the complexity of the multiple issues it must address. It is necessary to distinguish several levels of the question. Without attempting to be comprehensive, allow me to explore *four* distinct dimensions of a consistent ethic.

First, at the level of general moral principles, it is possible to identify a single principle with diverse applications. In my Fordham address, for example, I used the prohibition against direct attacks on innocent life. This principle is both central to the Catholic moral vision and systemically related to a range of specific moral issues. It prohibits direct attacks on unborn life in the womb, direct attacks on civilians in warfare, and the direct killing of patients in nursing homes.

Each of these topics has a constituency in society concerned with the morality of abortion, war, and care of the aged and dying. A consistent ethic of life encourages the specific concerns of each constituency, but also calls them to see the interrelatedness of their efforts. The need to defend the *integrity of the moral principle in the full range of its application* is a responsibility of each distinct constituency. If the principle is eroded in the public mind, all lose.

A *second* level of a consistent ethic stresses the distinction among cases rather than their similarities. We need different moral principles to apply to diverse cases. The classical distinction between ordinary and extraordinary means has applicability in the care of the dying but no relevance in the case of warfare. Not all moral principles have relevance across the whole range of life issues. Moreover, sometimes a systemic vision of the life issues requires a combination of moral insights to provide direction on one issue.

In my Fordham address I cited the classical teaching on capital punishment which gives the state the right to take life in defense of key social values. But I also pointed out how a concern for promoting a *public attitude* of respect for life has led the Catholic bishops of the United States to oppose the *exercise* of that right.

Abortion is taking innocent human life in ever-growing numbers in our society. Those concerned about it, I believe, will find their case enhanced by taking note of the rapidly expanding use of public execution. In a similar way, those who are particularly concerned about these executions, even if the accused has taken another life, should recognize the elementary truth that a society, which can be indifferent to the innocent life of an unborn child, will not be easily stirred to concern for a convicted criminal. There is, I maintain, a political and psychological linkage among the life issues—from war to welfare concerns—which we ignore at our own peril. A systemic vision of life seeks to expand the moral imagination of a society, not partition it into airtight categories.

A *third* level of the question before us involves how we relate a commitment to principles to our public witness of life. As I have said, no one can do everything. There are limits to both competency and energy; both point to the wisdom of setting priorities and defining distinct functions. The Church, however, must be credible across a wide range of issues; the very scope of our moral vision requires a commitment to a multiplicity of questions. In this way the teaching of the Church will sustain a variety of individual commitments.

My addresses on the consistent ethic have not been intended to constrain wise and vigorous efforts to protect and promote life through specific, precise forms of action. They *do* seek to cultivate a dialogue within the Church and in the wider society among individuals and groups that draw on common principles (e.g., the prohibition against killing the innocent) but seem convinced that they do not share common ground. The appeal here is not for anyone to do everything, but to recognize points of *interdependence* which should be stressed, not denied.

A *fourth* level, one where dialogue is sorely needed, is the relationship between moral principles and concrete political choices. The moral questions of abortion, the arms race, the fate of social programs for the poor, and the role of human rights in foreign policy are *public* moral issues. The arena in which they are ultimately decided is *not* the academy or the Church but the political process. A consistent ethic of life seeks to present a coherent linkage among a diverse set of issues. It can and should be used to test party platforms, public policies, and political candidates. The Church legitimately fulfills a public role by articulating a framework for political choices by relating that framework to specific issues and by calling for systemic moral analysis of all areas of public policy.

This is the role our episcopal conference has sought to fulfill by publishing a "Statement on Political Responsibility" during each of the presidential and congressional election years in the past two decades. The purpose is surely not to tell citizens how to vote, but to help shape the public debate and form personal conscience so that every citizen will vote thoughtfully and responsibly. Our "Statement on Political Responsibility" has always been, like our "Respect Life Program," a multi-issue approach to public morality. The fact that this statement sets forth a spectrum of issues of current concern to the Church and society should not be understood, as I have already indicated, as implying that all issues are qualitatively equal from a moral perspective.

Both the statements and the Respect Life program have direct relevance to the political order, but they are applied concretely by the choice of citizens. This is as it should be. In the political order the Church is primarily a teacher; it possesses a carefully cultivated tradition of moral analysis of personal and public issues. It makes that tradition available in a special manner for the community of the Church, but it offers it also to all who find meaning and guidance in its moral teaching.

THE CONSISTENT ETHIC: ITS PASTORAL AND PUBLIC CONTRIBUTION

The Church's moral teaching has both pastoral and public significance. Pastorally, a consistent ethic of life is a contribution to the witness of the Church's defense of the human person. Publicly, a consistent ethic fills a void in our public policy debate today.

Pastorally, I submit that a Church standing forth on the entire range of issues, which the logic of our moral vision bids us to confront, will be a Church in the style both of Vatican II's *Gaudium et spes* and Pope John Paul II's consistent witness to life. The pastoral life of the Church should not be guided by a simplistic criterion of relevance. The capacity of faith to shed light on the concrete questions of personal and public life today is one way in which the value of the gospel is assessed.

Certainly the serious, sustained interest manifested throughout U.S. society in the bishops' letter on war and peace provided a unique *pastoral* opportunity for the Church. Demonstrating how the teaching on war and peace is supported by a wider concern for all of life led others to see for the first time what our tradition has affirmed for a very long time: the linkage among the life issues.

The *public* value of a consistent ethic of life is directly connected to its pastoral role. In the public arena we should always speak and act like a Church. But the unique public possibility for a consistent ethic is provided precisely by the unstructured character of the public debate on the life questions. Each of the issues I have referred to this evening—abortion, war, hunger and human rights, euthanasia and physician-assisted suicide, and capital punishment—is usually treated as a separate, self-contained topic in our public life. Each is indeed distinct, but an ad hoc approach to each one fails to illustrate how our choices in one area can affect our decisions in other areas. There must be a public attitude of respect for all of life, if public actions are to respect life in concrete cases.

Eleven years ago, the pastoral letter on war and peace spoke of a "new moment" in the nuclear age. The letter has been widely studied and applauded because it caught the spirit of the "new moment" and spoke with moral substance to the issues of the "new moment." I am convinced there is an "open moment" before us on the agenda of life issues. It is a significant opportunity for the Church to demonstrate the strength of a sustained moral vision. I submit that a clear witness to a consistent ethic of life will allow us to grasp the opportunity of this "open moment" and serve both the sacredness of every human life and the God of Life who is the origin and support of our common humanity.

But to take advantage of this new, "open moment," we must learn how to *work together* as a community of faith. Unfortunately, a great deal of polarization exists within the Church today. This has created at times a mood of suspicion, even acrimony. A candid discussion of important issues—and a common witness to them—is often inhibited, so that we are not always able to come to grips effectively with the problems that confront us. So what do we do?

As I conclude, I would like to suggest how we might *begin* to answer that question.

The reality is that those who take extreme positions are often the most noisy—they get most of the attention. Those in the middle—the majority—are often quiet. I submit that we must make a greater effort to engage those in the middle and, in the process, establish a common ground—a new space for dialogue—that will make it possible for us to reach those who are alienated or disillusioned or uninformed for whatever reason.

To establish this common ground—this space for authentic dialogue—a broad range of the Church's leadership, both clerical and lay, must recommit themselves to the basic truths of our Catholic faith. The chief of those truths is that we must be accountable to our Catholic tradition and to the Spirit-filled, living Church that brings to us the revelation of God in Christ Jesus. Jesus who is present in sacrament, word, and community is central to all we do. So our focus must constantly be on *him*, not ourselves.

This rules out petty criticisms and jealousy, cynicism, sound-bite theology, inaccurate, unhistorical assertions, flippant dismissals. It rules out a narrow, myopic appeal to our personal or contemporary experience as if no other were valid. It acknowledges that our discussions must take place within certain boundaries because the Church, for all its humanness, is not merely a human organization. It is rather a chosen people, a mysterious communion, a foreshadowing of the kingdom, a spiritual family, the body of Christ. When we understand the Church in this way, we will be able to see the full beauty and relevance of our heritage as it has developed under the influence of the Holy Spirit from the apostolic age to the present. It will also help us to become more tolerant of one another.

In sum, what we need in the Church today is a realization that there is room for considerable diversity among us. When there is a breakdown of civility, dialogue, trust, and tolerance, we must redouble our efforts to restore and build up the unity of the one body of Christ.

Dealing with each other in a *consistent, gospel-inspired* way will add greatly—I would say it is indispensable—to our public, collective witness to the consistent life ethic which is so desperately needed in today's world.

Religion and Society

Address

"The Pastoral Constitution on the Church in the Modern World: Its Impact on the Social Teaching of the U.S. Bishops"*

Notre Dame University, Notre Dame, Indiana

— October 1, 1985 ─────────────────────────

I appreciate this opportunity to return again to the campus of Notre Dame University. Besides being a pleasant experience, it gives me another occasion to acknowledge the contribution of this university, and in a particular way, its president, Father Hesburgh, to the life of the Church in the United States. In providing Cardinal O'Connor and me a common platform to examine the social ministry of the Church in the postconciliar era, Notre Dame continues its long history of service to the Church. This convocation is another in an already lengthy list of events in which the intellectual, spiritual and physical resources of this campus have been used to help the Church in the United States, at every level, reflect upon the meaning and the challenge of being Catholic in the twentieth century.

Cardinal O'Connor and I will give two presentations which are designed to address a single theme. The setting for my lecture is the particular moment of ecclesial history in which we find ourselves: It is twenty-five years since the convocation of the Second Vatican Council and twenty years since the promulgation of one of the council's major documents, The Pastoral Constitution on the Church in the Modern World. In this setting it is worthwhile to examine the role and impact of

*Also published in *Origins*, vol. 15, no. 18, October 17, 1985, pp. 306–08.

The Pastoral Constitution on the social ministry of the Church, and particularly on the bishops of the United States. My lecture will serve as a background for Cardinal O'Connor's examination of one example of the bishops' social teaching: the pastoral letter on Catholic social teaching and the U.S. economy.

In examining the content and consequences of The Pastoral Constitution, I will focus on three themes: first, Vatican II as the source of The Pastoral Constitution; second, the content and style of The Pastoral Constitution; and third, the postconciliar consequences of this document in the ministry and teaching of the U.S. bishops.

THE CONCILIAR EVENT: AN INTERPRETATION

By calling an Extraordinary Synod this November, Pope John Paul II has invited and urged the Church to reflect upon the meaning of Vatican II and its implications for the life of the Church and the world during the last fifteen years of this century. Ecumenical councils are powerful events in the life of the Church. In the two-thousand-year history of the Church only a few generations of Christians have experienced the event of a council, but every generation has been shaped by the work of the twenty ecumenical councils. There comes with the privilege of being a conciliar generation the responsibility to appropriate its meaning, interpret its content, and share its significance with future generations. The calling of the synod helps to focus attention on the last twenty-five years since Pope John XXIII called us to a profound renewal of Christian life and witness for the world.

In the postconciliar period there has appeared, of course, a voluminous corpus of commentary on Vatican II. Quite appropriately, most commentaries have focused upon one aspect or document of the council and sought to explain its meaning and press forward its implications. In the last five years there has appeared another kind of commentary which I think is particularly helpful in preparation for the synod and in evaluating any single aspect of Vatican II assessment which seeks to interpret the conciliar event in its *totality*, to evaluate its place in the historical and theological development of the Church.

Two examples of this kind of analysis are Karl Rahner's essay, "Toward a Fundamental Interpretation of Vatican II" (*Theological Studies*, 1979) and John W. O'Malley's essay, "Developments, Reforms and Two Great Reformations: Toward a Historical Assessment of Vatican II" (*Theological Studies*, 1983).

It is neither my purpose nor my role to provide a commentary on these extensive articles, much less to offer a systematic interpretation of my own. I cite them in an address on social ministry in the postconciliar era because they provide the kind of broad framework we need to connect the conciliar and postconciliar periods of Catholic life and ministry. Such a perspective helps us to dispel the popular notion that the council suddenly dropped from heaven (or emerged from Hades!) in finished form. Interpreting the conciliar event means identifying its historical roots, evaluating its theological content, and recognizing that the implementation of the council has been complex and even a bit untidy, but still a blessing. On several occasions recently the Holy Father has referred to the council as a positive event in the life of the Church.

By examining the event of the council we can show that it follows the law of development in Catholic thought—that is, the dynamic Father John Courtney Murray used to call "the growing edge of tradition." The Catholic style admits of change—indeed requires change, but it is change rooted in continuity. Anyone familiar with Catholic history knows that Vatican II was a surprise but not an aberration from the law of development.

In areas as diverse as liturgy, ecumenism and social thought a basic pattern is visible in the council. Everything said in the documents of the council had a history in nineteenth- and twentieth-century Catholic authors and movements, but both the authors and movements had been relegated to the edge of the Church's life. The movements (in the fields of liturgy, ecumenism, and social action) and the authors (Congar, de Lubac, Chenu, Murray and Rahner) had been in the Church but not at the center of attention. They had lived on the growing edge, saying and doing things which made some uncomfortable and others hostile. It was not a question of bad will, but the dynamic of a growing community and institution with its attendant tensions.

The significance of Vatican II, looked at through the history of these movements and authors, is not that it said brand new things, but that it took these ideas from the edge of the Church's life and located them in the center. In the process the council gave new legitimacy to the growing edge of the Catholic tradition and also added its own content to the ideas and movements. The council authenticated and also created. Precisely because it followed the law of continuity and change, Vatican II was an event which summarized a previous process of development, becoming at the same time the starting point for a new process of growth. Once the growing edge had been taken into the center of Catholic thought, it was time for new growth at the edge.

This dynamic of receiving from the past, adding to it in council, and opening the road for new growth is particularly clear in The Pastoral Constitution. By examining this document we will see the dynamic of the council at work.

THE PASTORAL CONSTITUTION OF VATICAN II: AN ANALYSIS

Many of the major themes of Vatican II had their roots in the previous one hundred years; one of them was the emphasis on social teaching and social ministry. Leo XIII had inaugurated the tradition of papal social encyclicals in 1891 and Pius XI had pressed the organizational dimension of social witness in his program of Catholic Social Action of the 1930s. The bishops of the U.S. had used this social teaching to address a broad range of issues from labor questions to race relations to war and peace. In both teaching and development, therefore, the social dimension of the Church's life had a history in the twentieth century. This is why it is surprising to find that, in preparing for the council, no provision was made for a document on the role of the Church in the world. When the first session of Vatican II opened in 1962, there was no thought of a document in the style of The Pastoral Constitution. There were social themes running through the draft documents on the liturgy and the Church, but no explicitly *theological* reflection on the Church's presence in the secular arena.

Assessing the council from the perspective of 1985, it is clear that The Pastoral Constitution, along with the dogmatic Constitutions on the Church and Divine Revelation, stands as one of the key texts of the council, yet no one thought so at the beginning. It is also significant that the call for a document on the Church in the world emerged directly from the experience of the council. When the bishops addressed the task of defining the nature and mission of the Church, it became evident that an explicit, extensive interpretation of the role of the Church in the political, economic, cultural and international arena was a theological fact which required expression. Few guessed, I think, how powerful a force such an expression would be in the postconciliar ministry of the Church. In recognizing the impact of The Pastoral Constitution, it is important at Notre Dame to remember the contribution of Monsignor Joseph Gremillion to the development of this document.

The contribution of The Pastoral Constitution to the Church's social ministry has been a threefold gift: in *theological style, ecclesiological substance* and *pastoral spirit*. I will comment briefly on each.

The theological style of The Pastoral Constitution is symbolized and represented by its use of the phrase "the signs of the times." Father Marie-Dominique Chenu, O.P., one of the great precursors of the council, has said of this phrase that "it might well be considered as one of the three or four most important formulas used by the Council, one which served as a source of its inspiration and guided its progress."

The phrase implied both a principle of theological method and a basic posture of the Church toward the world. The method is that theological assessment of secular history and reality should begin with an evaluation of empirical data. In carrying out the social ministry, the Church is not to impose *a priori* solutions. Rather, it is to join with others, of all faiths and no faith, in seeking to understand the scope and depth of the secular challenge the world faces. When the empirical challenge has been honestly evaluated, it should then be "interpreted in the light of the Gospel." This methodological position does not simply equate theology with a secular discipline, nor does it imply moral relativism, but it does determine a pastoral posture for the Church. This posture respects the contributions of the scientific, social and humanistic disciplines, and promises that the Church will have the humility and the seriousness to face the modern world in all its complexity and ambiguity.

The drafting of the pastoral "The Challenge of Peace" brought all the U.S. bishops face-to-face with this pastoral posture. The arcane complexity of deterrence had to be probed in all its dimensions before we could address its moral meaning. Now, after three years of work and the publication of the letter, we recognize that the danger of deterrence and the difficulty of containing the arms race mean that our moral surveillance is not finished. There has to be continual scrutiny of the technical "signs of the times" of the arms race and of the adequacy of the moral judgments we made in 1983.

The theological contribution of The Pastoral Constitution is not limited to methodology. The fundamental breakthrough of the conciliar text is that it provides an ecclesiological foundation for social ministry. Prior to the council, the papal encyclicals had provided a solid philosophical and moral doctrine centered on human dignity and human rights and applied to problems as diverse as war, labor-management relations, and agriculture and trade policy. But this extensive moral teaching was often regarded as a secondary concern of the Church. Those who took the social teaching seriously often had to defend their work and ministry against charges that it secularized the Church or was devoid of truly religious content.

The Pastoral Constitution addresses these claims forthrightly. The document ties the entire Catholic tradition's defense of the human person directly to the very center of the Church's life. The vision of the Church which emerges from the council is that of a community of faith committed to public defense of the person, to advocacy for the least and most vulnerable in society, and to the protection of human society in the face of the awesome technologies of war which this century has spawned. It is impossible to support the conciliar teaching and not support a socially engaged Church, for that is the theological mandate of The Pastoral Constitution.

The theological grounding of social ministry has produced a pastoral spirit of social leadership for the Church throughout the world. I hasten to add that my point here is hardly to be triumphal, for what remains undone is staggering. But a simple, descriptive account of the changes in the Church on social questions since Vatican II would force any observer to ask what is behind the change. From Soweto to Seoul, from San Salvador to Sao Paulo, from Warsaw to Washington—the Catholic Church is a major social force. The pressure of events in each place has called the Church into the public arena. However, we need to be honest enough to acknowledge that the Church has been challenged by injustice before and did not always respond. Today we still miss key moments, are timid about key choices, and do not see all the signs of the times acutely. But there has been a response which is worthy of note. I do not think it is because of random chance that the response has been made in all these places. It is the spirit of The Pastoral Constitution which has called forth the social resources of the Church. Today there is a consensus established by the council that there can be no retreat from an engaged public ministry. The specific choices and challenges remain to be faced, but the premise of our ministry is clear: A socially active Church is not a distraction from gospel ministry; it is an essential component of that ministry.

THE SOCIAL IMPLICATIONS OF THE COUNCIL: AN ASSESSMENT

This conviction that social ministry is a central element of the Church's pastoral ministry is reflected in the postconciliar record of the U.S. episcopal conference. In his presidential report to the Holy See in preparation for the Extraordinary Synod, Bishop Malone expressed the strong conviction of the U.S. bishops that Vatican II has been a gift and a blessing for the Church in this country. One of the gifts of the council is the consensus which has been created among our bishops about the significance of social ministry. We debate and disagree on specific choices, of course, but these debates about concrete issues never take the form of questioning *whether* we ought to be in social ministry. That point is now beyond dispute, and we have The Pastoral Constitution to thank for this consensus.

The same document has shaped the way in which the bishops have pursued social teaching and witness. A key passage in The Pastoral Constitution states: "And so the Council, as witness and guide to the faith of the whole people of God, gathered together by Christ, can find no more eloquent expression of its solidarity and respectful affection for the whole human family, to which it belongs, than to enter into dialogue with it about all these different problems" (3).

The U.S. bishops have adopted this theme of dialogue with the world and sought to adapt it to the style of the democratic, pluralistic culture in which we minister. The dialogue theme is at work at two levels.

First, as a general principle, the bishops take positions on a wide range of social issues, from abortion to nuclear war to Central America. Moreover, they do so in forums which guarantee they will have to defend, explain and argue their positions both inside and outside the Church. By taking concrete positions, rooted in religious and moral values, but applied to contingent realities, the bishops both state a position and stimulate the wider public dialogue.

The range of issues addressed is one of the distinguishing characteristics of the bishops' position. No other major institution in our society joins the defense of innocent human life in abortion with the defense of all life in the face of nuclear war in the way we have done. It is to highlight both the scope of our moral concern and the strength of Catholic social teaching that I have focused on the notion of a "consistent ethic of life" in a series of addresses I have given over the past two years.

Second, this method of dialogue has been at the core of both pastoral letters on peace and the economy. The subject matter of the letters demands that we be in dialogue with relevant disciplines. The process of publishing drafts requires that we listen and respond to a range of commentary on our work. Finally, the specificity of our conclusions requires that we make crucial distinctions in the pastorals between the moral authority of Catholic social and moral teaching and the less authoritative policy conclusions we draw, as bishops, from that teaching.

Committing the bishops to public dialogue in this way has been a demanding exercise in pastoral leadership. But I believe the vast majority of our bishops would agree with my view that it has been an effective method of presenting the social teaching, an important witness to the bishops' concerns about signs of our times, and a contribution to the wider civil dialogue in the United States.

I do not think we would have developed the method of the pastorals, nor do I believe we would have shaped the ecclesial consensus which is their foundation in the bishops' conference, if the council had not occurred and The Pastoral Constitution not been written. I am convinced that we express our gratitude for both by continuing the dialogue with the world, solidifying the social ministry in the Church, and standing publicly in our society on a range of social issues which bear upon the human dignity of the person.

Fourth of July Address

Chicago Historical Society

Chicago, Illinois

——July 4, 1987 ——————————————————————

Immediately after the Declaration of Independence was adopted, John Adams, filled with the enthusiasm of the moment, spoke these stirring words:

> The second of July 1776 will be the most memorable epoch in the history of America. I am apt to believe that it will be celebrated by succeeding generations as the great anniversary festival. It ought to be commemorated as the day of deliverance, by solemn acts of devotion to God Almighty. It ought to be solemnized with pomp and parade, with shows, games, sports, guns, bells, bonfires and illuminations, from one end of the continent to the other, from this time forward forevermore!

Thus it has been that for 211 years we have been celebrating Independence Day with the enthusiasm which John Adams predicted. However, if you listened carefully to that quotation, you may have noticed one significant error. John Adams thought that the day that would go down in history was the *second* of July, the day the resolution was adopted. However, it wasn't until two days later, on the *fourth* of July, that the Declaration of Independence was actually signed by John Hancock and the others.

There was a gap between what Adams thought would happen and what actually occurred. Isn't that the way reality is for all of us? There is a gap between the ideal and the real. There is a gap between what we hope to be as individuals and as a nation and what we actually are. There is a gap between our most cherished dreams and hopes and yearnings on the one hand, and the actual realization of those dreams on the other.

151

And yet, that gap does not vitiate or diminish our very real achievements. To celebrate the Fourth of July in an authentic manner, we need to consider three factors. First, we need to recognize and celebrate all the marvelous achievements of this great nation in the course of the past 211 years. Secondly, we must honestly acknowledge the gap between what we profess and what we actually do. Third, we need to set an agenda for the future so that we can close the gap, so that our deeds might more closely match our words.

So, then, what achievements do we celebrate today? We celebrate a people and we celebrate a way of forming a community, a true Union. We celebrate successive waves of people who journeyed to this rich and abundant land. We celebrate the Native Americans who crossed the Bering Strait in prehistoric times and taught us a profound respect for nature. We celebrate the initial European colonists who settled this land: Pilgrims and Puritans in New England; voyageurs, traders, and trappers in New France; explorers and missionaries in New Spain.

We celebrate the Africans who came here against their will in the cargo holds of slave ships and whose sweat, blood, and tears moistened the cotton fields of the South and the factories of the North. We celebrate the waves of early immigrants from Germany, Ireland, Italy, Poland, Eastern Europe, and China who fled from hunger, political oppression, and religious persecution to build our railroads, farm our fields, and populate our cities. We celebrate the Jewish people from many nations who brought an ancient tradition of faith and learning to this new nation.

The litany goes on and on. We celebrate the displaced persons and refugees who came here before, during, and after the Second World War—fleeing from Hitler and Nazism, from Stalin and Communism. We celebrate the people of the Philippines and Japan who brought many skills to enrich our society. We celebrate the diverse Spanish-speaking people who have come here from Mexico, the Caribbean, Central and South America to seek jobs, education, and a better life for their families. And we celebrate the most recent newcomers: the Vietnamese, Laotians, and Cambodians fleeing from war-ravaged lands; people from India, Pakistan, China, and the Middle East; the "boat people" from Haiti and Cuba; Poles bringing the hunger and thirst for freedom symbolized by the Solidarity movement.

The list paints a portrait of the American people. That is who we are. That is what we celebrate on this Independence Day. At the same time we also celebrate the system and the structures which enable us to live together in some degree of justice, peace, mutual respect, and harmony. We celebrate the great foundation principles and documents of our nation: The Declaration of Independence, the Constitution, which marks its 200th anniversary this year, the Bill of Rights and other amendments to the Constitution. We celebrate the system of three branches of government—executive, legislative and judicial—as well as the system of checks and balances which struggles to keep them functioning in some measure of harmony and effectiveness. We celebrate the pivotal values of our society: that a person is presumed innocent until proved guilty; that a person has a right to face his or her accusers and to be judged by a jury of peers. We celebrate the separation of Church and state; the principle of one person, one vote; and the sometimes controversial but always necessary freedom of the press.

These are some of our proudest achievements. These are our ideals, our vision, our values, our goals. Nevertheless, as I intimated earlier, there is, at times, a gap between what we profess as values and how we act as citizens and as a nation. What are some of the gaps between these magnificent ideals and the reality which we experience today in these United States? What is the unfinished business of our nation?

I would like to explore briefly six areas in which there are serious gaps between who and what we are and who and what we are called and challenged to become.

First, we are justly proud of the wonderful diversity of our population. Chicago reflects this reality very well: It is a truly cosmopolitan city, a kaleidoscope of the world's cultures. Yet, in this city and in our nation, there are continual signs of hostility, tension and suspicion among various racial and ethnic groups. Racism continues to raise its evil head among us. The defacing of the newly dedicated Holocaust memorial in suburban Skokie serves as an eloquent reminder that anti-Semitism still lives in our midst. Ethnic prejudice towards people whose accents, clothing, customs, or belief differ from ours is an ongoing challenge. We can do better. We must do better!

Second, we are dedicated to equal opportunity for all. Yet, we have a growing underclass in our society—people who face a future of mediocre education, dangerous living conditions, unemployment, and a demeaning existence on welfare assistance grudgingly granted. Often women are not paid equally for the same services provided by men. We can do better. We must do better!

Third, we believe in a system of freedom and justice for all. Yet, despite our best efforts, we must admit that there is one system of justice for the rich and powerful who can afford it, and a second system for the poor who cannot. The Operation Greylord investigations here in Chicago reveal how greed can corrupt our system of justice. And the system of influence-peddling and political contributions in Washington reveals how power can pervert the legislative and executive processes. We can do better. We must do better!

Fourth, as a people, we rightly and proudly pledge allegiance to the flag of the United States of America and to the Republic for which it stands. Yet, we encounter at times a false patriotism which seeks simplistic answers to complex questions, which sees the flaws and shortcomings in other nations but denies any flaws in our own. At times, some seem to believe that might makes right—that slogans and mere rhetoric can replace careful analysis, authentic compromise, and well-thought-out policies and strategies. We Americans are a vigorous, creative people. But we can become impatient, shortsighted, self-righteous, demanding of quick results. We can do better. We must do better!

Fifth, we are a deeply religious people who describe ourselves as "one nation under God." On our coins we print the motto "In God we trust." Yet, we are also subjected to the seduction and corruption of materialism and consumerism. We can become quite cynical, believing that everything and everyone has a price. We can believe that possessions in sufficient numbers can solve our problems and satisfy the deepest hungers of our hearts. We can do better than that. We must do better!

Finally, we are a people who value the dignity and uniqueness of every human person. We have taken great care that the will of the majority should never be able to coerce the free choice of an individual acting according to her or his conscience. And that is good. Yet, in that laudable goal we have become a nation where an exaggerated individualism has become an erosive, destructive force. Family life has begun to disintegrate. The sense of individual sacrifice in the name of the common good has diminished. Exploitation of resources for one's own personal gain is in the ascendancy. We can do better. We must do better!

I began by quoting John Adams, one of the signers of the Declaration of Independence. You recall that he mistakenly thought that July 2 would be celebrated as Independence Day. He forgot that unfinished business would take two additional days. I have tried to describe what I see as the achievements and glories of our nation as well as my analysis of the gaps between our admirable ideals and some of the less than beautiful realities of our nation.

Now I wish to address some of the unfinished business which lies ahead. When today's celebration is over, when the curtain rings down at midnight on another Fourth of July, what do we take with us in our hearts and minds and lives? What will be our personal agenda for the future? Let me suggest three things.

First, we need an attitude of deep gratitude. You and I are very fortunate to live in the United States of America! We need to resist the tendency to take things or one another for granted. We must resist the tendency to see only the problems and overlook the beauty, the achievements, the ideals already realized. Someone once observed that the two most "American" holidays are Independence Day and Thanksgiving Day. We need to hold fast to that sense of appreciation, that feeling of gratitude, that awareness of being a highly fortunate and richly blessed people.

Second, we need to hold fast to a passionate hunger and thirst for justice. That is one of the basic foundations of this great nation. Our traditions remind us that when one suffers, all suffer; when one is oppressed, all are oppressed; when one is victimized, all are victimized. We need to have a blessed rage for justice, equality, fairness, inclusiveness. That must be our standard and the criterion by which we measure our lives as individuals and as a nation.

Finally, we need to be hopeful people. We need to resist the tendency to be cynical about the possibilities of the future. The American Dream cannot be allowed to disintegrate into mere rhetoric. It cannot be allowed to be trivialized by pious platitudes. The American Dream cannot be allowed to become long-winded hot air from a Fourth of July orator, such as myself! Wealthy persons may say to themselves, "There are too many people who want everything for nothing. It won't work. Why bother?" The poor may say, "The cards are stacked against us. We don't have a chance. Why bother?" The middle class may say, "It's too complicated. What difference does one person make in the face of so many difficulties. So why bother?"

But I say, and I hope you will join me in saying, "It *does* make a difference! I *do* make a difference. Together, we *can* make a difference." Why bother? Because the Dream of America which has brought us this far is worth the best we can be, the best we can do, the best we can become.

"God bless America, the land that I love!"

"Vatican II's Pastoral Constitution on the Church in the Modern World Revisited— 25 Years Later"

Catholic Theological Union, Chicago, Illinois

—— December 7, 1990 ——————————————————————

The Second Vatican Council was an extraordinary event in the Church's history. This Twenty-First Ecumenical Council legislated and implemented more changes that directly affected the lives of Catholics throughout the world than any previous council. Moreover, no other council had ever called for such a radical change in viewpoint.

Vatican II was the first council in which the Church became universal in the fullest sense. In all, about 2,900 bishops participated in it, more than four times the number at Vatican I. Moreover, for the first time there was significant representation from the missionary churches of Asia and Africa. The council's dynamism was also fueled, in part, by experts drawn from among the Church's greatest scholars. Non-Catholic "observers" at the council had some indirect impact on the language of the conciliar documents. And the close attention of the media and global communications technology enabled virtually the entire human family to follow the course of the conciliar sessions and gave nearly everyone access to its teaching.

Perhaps the council's most significant feature was the fact that, unlike earlier councils, it did not condemn heresies or resolve crises. Rather, in attending to the "signs of the times," it reflected on, and responded to, some of the most important issues of our time. It set the course for the Catholic community as we approach the third millennium of Christianity.

The postconciliar period has been somewhat confusing, even chaotic at times. Some greeted the conciliar decrees with enthusiasm. The council's momentum swept through the Church, and some, in their eagerness to implement its teaching, unfortunately went well beyond what the council had taught. Others have resisted the conciliar teaching and opposed its more innovative dimensions. Many Catholics were simply confused at the dizzying pace of change in such vital areas of Church life as worship, the role of the laity, and ecumenism.

Cardinal Newman, an avid student of Church history, provides a helpful insight. A month after the closing of the First Vatican Council, he wrote that "it is uncommon that a council *not* be followed by great confusion." Having such an historical perspective helps us understand that, while much has changed in the past quarter century, it takes more than a single generation to assimilate fully the teaching of an ecumenical council, especially one whose purpose was primarily pastoral and whose scope embraced so many important topics and concerns.

The Catholic Theological Union is itself a result of conciliar teaching and innovation. This school emerged from the theological and pastoral ferment of the council and was deliberately located in the hustle and bustle of the Hyde Park intellectual community, not in the allegedly "safe" environment of a rural setting. Conciliar teaching has helped shape CTU's curriculum and formation programs. I am especially delighted to know that the council's documents have been the object of intensified research and discussion since my last visit here two years ago.

As you know, it is quite impossible to cover adequately the full scope of Vatican II's significance in a single presentation. But four of the council's documents are foundational: the Constitutions on the Liturgy, on the Church, on Divine Revelation, and on the Church in the Modern World. This evening I will focus on the last of these, *Gaudium et spes*. It was approved at the closing session of the council and, perhaps more than any other document, reflects the new thinking which began to take hold during the pontificate of Pope John XXIII and took deep root during that of Pope Paul VI. Moreover, it has had the greatest impact on the Church's relationship to the world.

First, I will explain the document's overall significance. Then, I will explore one of its major themes, dialogue between the Church and the world. Finally, I will briefly examine the subsequent response to the document and suggest some agenda for the future.

THE SIGNIFICANCE OF *GAUDIUM ET SPES*

Two key concepts were on Pope John XXIII's mind when he convoked the Second Vatican Council: *unity* and *world*. While he was deeply concerned about the long-standing disunity among Christians, his quest for unity embraced the entire human family. And while he wanted the council to reexamine and renew the Church's inner life, he also wanted the council fathers to take a close look at the Church's relationship to the world.

The text of what eventually became *Gaudium et spes* went through at least six major revisions over three years before its adoption. Its official description attests to its uniqueness and significance: Pastoral Constitution on the Church in the Modern World. It is called a *constitution* because the first part of the document, in particular, contains doctrinal statements which throw light on the Church's relationship with the world. The council fathers underlined its doctrinal authority by calling it a constitution. As I have intimated, it thus ranks as one of the four most important conciliar documents.

At the same time, *Gaudium et spes* threw light on the contemporary world itself and its problems. It was addressed to the entire human family, not only to Catholics and other Christians. So, the council called it a *pastoral* constitution, the first ever issued by an ecumenical council. Its very uniqueness has understandably caused some confusion.

Father Yves Congar, one of the most respected theologians at the council, has pointed out that a pastoral approach is also doctrinal. But it involves a more existential, synthetic way of understanding "doctrine" than the traditional, more analytical approach. The pastoral approach is more open to search, research, and new contributions. It is not satisfied with conceptualizations, definitions, deductions, and anathemas. As it explores contemporary issues and tries to answer current questions, its goal is to present the truth of salvation in a way that is understandable to people today. Because the entire scope of Vatican II was pastoral, the language of its documents differs considerably from the dogmatic style of the previous twenty ecumenical councils. This is especially true of *Gaudium et spes* which, perhaps more than any other conciliar text, was shaped by the conciliar experience itself.

The full title of *Gaudium et spes* also indicates that the Church is *in* the world. That may not come as a surprise to you or me, but it represents a radically new approach to understanding the relationship between the Church and the world. The traditional approach was either to set up a severe *dichotomy* between the Church and the world or to view the Church as being *dominant* over the world.

In the early centuries, Christian communities tended to isolate themselves from secular society. Since the Middle Ages, however, the Church has tended to exercise its influence over secular society. Both approaches still have adherents today. In his first encyclical, *Ecclesiam suam*, Pope Paul VI acknowledged both of these ways of relating to the world. He pointed out, however, that

> The fact that we are distinct from the world does not mean that we are entirely separated from it. Nor does it mean that we are indifferent to it, afraid of it, or contemptuous of it (63).

He concluded that the Church needs to "enter into dialogue with the world in which it lives" (65).

The encyclical had great impact on the council fathers and, especially, on the development of *Gaudium et spes*. The opening words of the pastoral constitution express this new understanding of the Church's relationship with the world in an eloquent way:

> The joy and hope, the grief and anguish of the men of our time, especially of those who are poor or afflicted in any way, are the joy and hope, the grief and anguish of the followers of Christ as well. Nothing that is genuinely human fails to find an echo in their hearts.

In other words, the Church does not go *to* the world; it is a community of Jesus' disciples *in the midst of* the human family. At the same time the council acknowledged that there is a legitimate secularity to the political, social, and economic orders. As Congar has pointed out, "the Church recognizes the positive values and autonomy of this world; it does not reduce the world to the role of a mere means of getting to heaven."

The full title of *Gaudium et spes* also underlines the fact that its contents deal with the Church in the *modern* world. Again, at first blush, that may seem quite insignificant. However, the Second Vatican Council took more explicit notice of history than any ecumenical council before it. Earlier, in the Dogmatic Constitution on the Church, the council had described the Church as the pilgrim people of God. As a result, we recovered a sense of ourselves as a dynamic community, not merely a fixed treasure or museum piece that is to be guarded until the end of time. We are a people on the move, and historical awareness is the consciousness of that movement.

The council fathers and their theologians were acutely aware of significant changes in the modern world—scientific discovery and technological application, mass communications, global interdependence, to name only a few. They knew that, because the conditions of modern life had changed, the Church had to find new, effective ways of addressing these existential concerns. Part two of the pastoral constitution singles out certain of these contemporary issues for in-depth treatment: the dignity of marriage and the family, the proper development of culture, economic and social life, the political community, and the fostering of peace and establishment of a community of nations.

In short, *Gaudium et spes* calls for a radical change of viewpoint. For many of us who grew up with a more traditional perspective, it is often difficult to understand fully and to embrace this new, challenging dimension of conciliar teaching.

DIALOGUE BETWEEN THE CHURCH AND THE WORLD

As I have intimated, the Second Vatican Council, following the lead of Pope Paul VI, pointed out that it is no longer sufficient to flee from the world or to work strenuously to reroute the world's direction. The Church does not see the world only as a danger from which to flee, or a flawed reality to be transformed, but also as a possible partner in dialogue. Ecclesial renewal now also means conversation with the world.

But how are we to understand such a dialogue? While the concept appears in several conciliar documents, it is never precisely defined. And that is understandable because there are different kinds of dialogue. A conversation between adults is different from one between an adult and a child. Dialogue among Catholics is different from a conversation between Christians and atheists. Ecumenical dialogue among Christians is different from interfaith dialogue between Christians and Muslims.

Nonetheless, we assume that certain common denominators underlie the various kinds of dialogue: a mutual respect among partners, a willingness to speak the truth in love, a capacity to listen, a common search for the truth. But is this how the Church understands authentic dialogue? The Church's primary mission is to proclaim Jesus Christ and his gospel. To what extent can the Church set that essential task aside to engage in open-ended dialogue? Or does it understand dialogue simply as a means to evangelize, as many potential dialogue partners fear?

Prior to the council, the Church was rather slow to engage in dialogue with others. In *Ecclesiam suam*, Pope Paul VI devoted nearly a third of the encyclical to the nature and function of dialogue. His approach was cautious and reflects the Church's earlier, more limited understanding of that process. He wrote that,

> although the truth we have to proclaim is certain and the salvation necessary, we dare not entertain any thoughts of external coercion. Instead we will use the legitimate means of human friendliness, interior persuasion, and ordinary conversation.

From the broader context of the encyclical, it is quite clear that the Holy Father understood that the basic objective of dialogue was conversion to the Catholic faith. Despite this more limited focus, however, he was the first to use the word "dialogue" in a papal document, and this had a great impact on the Second Vatican Council.

Something very significant happened to the council fathers during the course of Vatican II. A growing awareness developed that the Holy Spirit's influence extended well beyond the confines of the Christian flock to the entire world. This had great impact on the development of Catholic ecumenism and interfaith dialogue because it meant that the Church had something to learn from other communities of believers. This did not take away from the truth which the Church teaches, but it opened the Church to the possibility of discovering elements of the truth which others possessed.

This new awareness of the universal scope of the Spirit's activity also implied that dialogue between the Church and the world was a *mutual* exchange, not the conversation between a doctor and a patient. The world has something to contribute to the Church. In our relationship to the world, which has been touched by Jesus' saving acts and influenced by the Holy Spirit, we are an *ecclesia docens* but also an *ecclesia discens*—a teaching Church, but also a learning Church.

There are, of course, some dangers to be avoided in the dialogue with the world. To be faithful to the gospel, we cannot be satisfied with an uncritical acceptance of whatever the world offers. But neither should we be too quick to reject or distrust the world. If our participation in the dialogue is not an accommodation to the world, but rather the truth spoken in love, we need not fear that we will jeopardize or dilute the prophetic, countercultural message of the gospel. At the same time, we can anticipate that the conversation will lead us to a new and integral humanism which is thoroughly marked by the image of the new humanity manifested in the risen Lord.

In his 1986 World Day of Peace message, Pope John Paul II pointed out that dialogue can open many closed doors; it breaks down preconceived notions and artificial barriers. "Dialogue," he wrote, "is a means by which people discover one another and discover the good hopes and peaceful aspirations that too often lie hidden in their hearts."

In his 1987 encyclical, "On the Social Concern of the Church," the Holy Father echoed Vatican II in describing what the Church brings to dialogue with the world. As an "expert in humanity," the Church offers moral analysis and wisdom, not technical solutions or economic and political programs. The Church's social doctrine is not an ideology. It is an accurate formulation of the results of a careful reflection—in the light of faith and the Church's tradition—on the complex realities of human existence, in society and in the international order. As a partner in dialogue with the world, the Church's aim is to interpret these complex realities, evaluate them in the light of the gospel, and be a reliable guide for human behavior.

And what does the Church receive from its dialogue with the world? *Gaudium et spes* points out that the Church profits from the experience of past ages, from the progress of the sciences, and from the riches hidden in various cultures, through which greater light is thrown on the nature of man and new avenues to truth are opened up. . . . Whoever contributes to the development of the community of mankind on the level of family, culture, economic and social life, and national and international politics, according to the plan of God, is also contributing in no small way to the community of the Church insofar as it depends on things outside itself (44).

The council even acknowledged that the Church benefits from the opposition of its enemies and persecutors. They force the Church to focus its attention on the core of its mission and free it from illusions and superficialities.

Moreover, because the gospel is to be proclaimed effectively in every culture, the Church in every place must know that culture well—through direct experience and dialogue. (As you know, this has great significance for those of you who will minister in cross-cultural situations.) At the same time, while they are related, dialogue and evangelization are *distinct* realities. Dialogue is a process of searching and sharing so that the partners will come closer to the truth. The purpose of evangelization is to bring a non-Christian to faith in Jesus Christ and his message of salvation.

Each of these dimensions of dialogue between the Church and the world could profitably be explored in greater depth. But now let us consider the impact of this innovative dimension of ecclesial renewal on the Church and what remains to be done.

POSTCONCILIAR RESPONSE AND AGENDA FOR THE FUTURE

Gaudium et spes has perhaps had its greatest impact on the churches of the Third World. Especially in Latin America, the Church has made significant progress in applying the gospel and its values to daily life. In many countries the Church has become a prophetic advocate on behalf of the poor and other vulnerable members of their society. There has also been significant progress in acculturation—that is, adapting the proclamation of the gospel and religious practices to the respective cultural context.

The U.S. Catholic bishops have also responded to the call of Vatican II to dialogue with the world. Along with many others, they have engaged the world in a conversation on such critical issues as war and peace and the U.S. economy. They also based their Respect Life Program, from its very beginning, on the biblical truth that every human life is sacred because the human person is made in God's image and likeness. This concept is at the heart of the teaching of *Gaudium et spes*. In more recent years, as you know, I have made the theological basis of the Respect Life Program more explicit by calling for the development of a consistent ethic of life.

While these efforts have generated broad support, they have also received mixed reviews. While that may dishearten some, I personally read this fact as a sign that we are, indeed, learning to dialogue with the world. My concern is that we continue to learn this art of conversation.

One of the major criticisms of *Gaudium et spes* in the postconciliar period has been that it is too optimistic about the world. This criticism is not new; it was raised at the council during the development of the document itself. For example, while the German bishops objected to the fourth draft's alleged optimism and oversimplification of certain issues, the French and Belgian bishops defended the text. Nevertheless, the criticism was taken into account in the succeeding versions.

The debate continues today. The advocates of one approach attempt to correct a "too optimistic" view of the world by highlighting the presence of sin in the world, the reality of suffering and death, the need for redemption. The advocates of the other approach try to avoid a "too pessimistic" view of the world by emphasizing the goodness of creation, the implications of the incarnation, and the dominion of the risen Lord over the world and history.

The attempt to strike a balance between these opposing perspectives gave the final text of *Gaudium et spes* less homogeneity and greater complexity. Like most of the other conciliar documents, the Pastoral Constitution on the Church in the Modern World is a "compromise" document. I do not use that phrase in a disparaging way. Recognizing the tension between opposing, but complementary, views helps us avoid an oversimplified approach to complex matters and, in the context of *Gaudium et spes*, forces us to face the problems and difficulties involved in dialogue between the Church and the world.

At the same time, one cannot ignore the council's clear option for standing in solidarity with all our brothers and sisters in the human family. But this is not the result of a naive optimism about what this entails. The opening words of the pastoral constitution set the scene for all that follows: *Gaudium et spes, luctus et angor*—"The joy and hope, the grief and anguish of the men of our time . . ." The constitution acknowledges human grief and anguish but balances them with the biblical motifs of joy and hope, with those special gifts from God which enable the human family to survive in the midst of bone-crushing grief and anguish.

The pastoral constitution is a visionary document. It does not pretend to have all the answers to all contemporary questions. Neither does it exclude any topic or any person from the dialogue it has initiated. But it does point the way and challenges us to walk along its path.

That is the task which lies before us. Walking along its path means probing more deeply into its teaching about the dignity of the human person, the interdependence of the human family, the value of human activity, the role of the Church in the modern world. Walking along its path means continuing to solve the problems associated with marriage and family life, the development of culture, economic and social life, politics, and peace.

* * *

In a very real sense, we have only begun to implement the pastoral constitution. Its scope is so vast, and the world's crucial issues are so complex that we have a long way to go in understanding, integrating, and implementing its teaching. Some may choose to ignore *Gaudium et spes* or refuse to accept its normative teaching. But the impact it has already made on the Church is irreversible. Vatican II and the pastoral constitution are facts of history; they are now part of our prized tradition.

The pastoral constitution is addressed to everyone. This implies that every member of the Church has a responsibility to participate in this dimension of ecclesial renewal. But that will require a new perspective, a new way of looking at both the Church and the world, and, perhaps, even a new heart.

Preparation for ministry in the Church today must enable future ministers—priests, laity, religious—to acquire this new perspective. Formation must lead them to a new heart. I am confident that you are striving to do this at the Catholic Theological Union. Moreover, it is essential that theologians and bishops recover the sense of mutual respect and collaboration which made the Second Vatican Council possible. Please accept my presence and words this evening as encouragement and support for your own participation in the Church's renewal.

I am fully committed to the renewal begun by the council. More than most, I know the difficulties of renewal in the Church. I must confront them each day. I am not, however, discouraged by the slow process of renewal, and neither should you! In fact, I am greatly encouraged. And I am fully committed to the renewal begun by the Second Vatican Council!

I close with words of Pope John XXIII as he convoked the council:

> Distrustful souls see only darkness burdening the face of the earth. We, instead, like to reaffirm all our confidence in our Savior, who has not left the world which he redeemed. Indeed, we make our own the recommendation of Jesus that one should know how to distinguish the "signs of the times," and we seem to see, in the midst of so much darkness, a few indications which argue well for the fate of the Church and of humanity.

In this time of great challenge and potential, may we always keep in mind these sentiments of Pope John. The image we have of the Church and society may at times be distorted because we view them through the lens of the negative realities of the moment. This can and does discourage us. But, in faith, we know that Jesus, who is ever present among us through his Holy Spirit, is still Lord of the universe and head of the Church. We have the firm assurance that, if we persevere in our fidelity to him—a fidelity that calls for the best of which we are capable—in the end his will, his plan, will prevail. That assurance gives us hope that overcomes discouragement and calls us to greater things, even in the midst of adversity.

Address

"Catholic Identity: Resolving Conflicting Expectations"*

Fordham University, New York, New York

— April 20, 1991 ————————————————————————

It is good to be back at Fordham University which provided a forum in 1983 for my first in a series of addresses on the need for a consistent ethic of life. As I prepared that address, I was aware that I would be walking through a minefield. Somehow, I have that same uneasy feeling this afternoon as we discuss the Catholic identity of our institutional ministries in the future and, specifically, how to resolve conflicting expectations. I hasten to add, however, that I am sustained and encouraged by your good will in this endeavor.

I congratulate Fordham on this Sesquicentennial Project which is complex in its vision and scope and vital to the Church. I have a keen interest in the three dimensions of the Church's mission under discussion: higher education, health care, and social services. Besides this interest, I bring a quarter-century of episcopal experience and, naturally, some bias to this conference.

This afternoon I will focus my reflections on three areas: (1) the mixed model of sectarian/secular identity described in the Preliminary Report, (2) the underlying causes of tension and conflicting expectations, and (3) some practical ways of lessening this tension and resolving these conflicting expectations.

*Also published in *Origins*, vol. 21, no. 2, May 23, 1991, pp. 33–36.

THE MIXED MODEL OF IDENTITY

As the Preliminary Report indicates, a rather substantial majority of all who participated in the Delphi Process assume that the mixed model of identity will prevail in the future, not a strictly denominational or secular one. I fully agree. However, as we all know, despite the general agreement on what the future will look like, the task which lies before us will not be easy.

The history of our nation has many lessons for us. For the most part, the mainline Protestant churches established the first sectarian colleges and universities. There was considerable emphasis on moral rectitude and doctrinal orthodoxy—which led some of them to discriminate against Catholics. More recently, when academic excellence became the supreme value, and freedom of inquiry and expression a hallmark of higher education, the churches gradually ceded the religious identity of their schools. The strictly sectarian model eventually gave way to the secular. Today, those colleges and universities which retain their explicitly Protestant affiliation are largely sponsored by Evangelical and Fundamentalist groups who have chosen the sectarian model. However, to the extent that they do so, they risk losing their voice and credibility in the public forum because the sectarian model, by its very nature, tends to stand in defensive opposition to the world.

Catholic colleges and universities, health care institutions, and social service agencies already live with one foot firmly planted in the Catholic Church and the other in our pluralistic society. It should come as no surprise, then, when the competing vision and value systems of the "tectonic" plates on which they stand are in tension with one another, and shifts in the plates cause tremors which create anxiety and are, at times, seen as threats.

Catholic higher education, health care, and social services face a common dilemma. The bishop and diocese, at times, may consider them too secular, too influenced by government, too involved with business concepts. The public, on the other hand, often considers them too religious, too sectarian. As a result, they find themselves sandwiched between the Church and the public, trying to please both groups.

These *are* vital ministries, integral to the Church's mission. And this mission flows from the Church's identity. Understanding these three ministries as integral to the Church's overall mission, therefore, also helps shape their Catholic identity because both mission and identity are closely related and complement each other. So, our discussion of the Catholic identity and culture of these ministries will be enhanced by defining more precisely their relationship to the Church's mission.

The Preliminary Report indicates that large majorities of those who work in the three ministries are firmly committed to the Catholic identity of their institutions and view their work precisely as ministry. That accords with my experience as a pastor. I am often impressed by the spirituality and dedication of women and men religious, and of the growing numbers of laymen and laywomen who are assuming positions of leadership in these ministries.

At the same time, these three ministries of the Church are moving toward a mixed model of identity. The clients they serve, the contributors they approach, the staff and governing bodies they rely on include both Catholics and, increasingly, those who are not Catholic. They depend on federal, state, and local governments for such things as charters of incorporation, regulatory statutes, licensing, tax exemption status, and funding. They are also held accountable by government and the public, not only by the Church.

While some may decry the present circumstances and fear what the future holds as we move from a more sectarian to a mixed model of identity, there simply is no turning back now. For the most part, we can no longer effectively carry out the Church's mission by trying to isolate ourselves from the pluralistic society in which we live or impose our views on it. Indeed, the mixed model of identity should help us minister more effectively in the world.

The fathers of the Second Vatican Council clearly pointed out that the Church has to pay closer attention to the fact that it exists *in* the modern world. It does not go to the world, as though it were a fully separate entity. The Church is a community of Jesus' disciples in the midst of the human family. At the same time, the council acknowledged that there is a legitimate secularity in the political, social, and economic orders.

Something very significant happened to the council fathers during the course of Vatican II. A growing awareness developed that the Holy Spirit's influence extends well beyond the confines of the Christian flock to the entire world. This did not take away from the truth which the Church teaches, but it opened the Church to the possibility of discovering elements of the truth which others possess, even as it brings the message of the gospel to the world, even as it provides a moral and ethical framework in which societal issues can be evaluated and challenged.

The Pastoral Constitution on the Church in the Modern World states that the Church has much to learn from the world. The world is a possible partner for dialogue, a mutual exchange. While we may take this for granted, at least on a theological level, it was not always the thinking of the Church or its members; nor do we yet have sufficient experience or expertise to carry on such a dialogue in a way that will realize its full potential.

There are, of course, some dangers to be avoided in our dialogue with the world. To be faithful to the gospel, we cannot be satisfied with an uncritical acceptance of whatever the world offers. But neither should we be too quick to reject or distrust the world. If our participation in the dialogue is not an accommodation to the world but rather the truth spoken in love, we need not fear that dialogue will jeopardize or dilute the prophetic, countercultural message of the gospel. At the same time, we can anticipate that the conversation will lead us to a new and integral humanism which is thoroughly marked by the image of the new humanity manifested in the risen Lord.

Catholic educators, health care personnel, and social service providers work along the fault line of the Church's dialogue with the world. They are constantly in conversation with it. At times, it is less clear how they encounter the Church each day. Nevertheless, they are in a privileged position to learn from the world and to share that knowledge and insight with the rest of the community of faith. At the same time, they have the opportunity, and the responsibility, to speak the truth in love and to share the values of our Catholic tradition with others. The Holy Spirit works in the world, but there is much in the world that needs redemption, that needs to be challenged in light of the gospel, that needs healing.

Three especially effective pastors recently shared the secret of their success. One said that being an effective minister called for the ability to live with *ambiguity*. Another said it demanded the capacity to cope with *chaos*. And the third said it required the ability to manage the *"mess."*

Ambiguity, chaos, mess. Perhaps this is an apt way to describe what Catholic educators, health care personnel, and social service providers deal with each day. It also describes my own pastoral experience as a bishop, even though I do not encounter the world in quite the same way as others do in these three ministries.

The human context of our work causes many dilemmas and problems. As the Preliminary Report notes, "In a 'messy' world there are many instances of misunderstandings and bad behavior. Even more difficult are those instances in which caring people of faith disagree." That leads me to the second section of my presentation.

THE CAUSES OF CONFLICTING EXPECTATIONS

As I read the Preliminary Report, I made a list of the areas where there was disagreement—often between the bishops and those in the three fields—assuming that this would reveal where the conflicting expectations were to be found. I found twenty-eight instances of disagreement, ten each in only two categories: issues of control and behavioral issues.

Rather than examine these areas of disagreement in detail, it seems more appropriate to address the challenging key question posed in the report: "Are there ways in which the 'mixed' scenario can prevail in the future without the instances of rancor which seem to occur so very frequently at the present time to the detriment of both individuals, institutions, and the Church?" Before searching for solutions, it will be helpful to consider some of the underlying causes of the tensions that exist because of conflicting expectations.

First, I am a pastor, not a professor, health care expert, or social service professional. That is not an apology, simply a fact. Many of you are professors, health care experts, or social service professionals, not bishops. That is not an accusation, simply a fact. This means that I may not understand, in the same way as you, all your needs, dilemmas, questions, problems, dreams, presuppositions, or fears. Similarly, you may not understand mine in the same way I do. This, in itself, is a potential source of disagreement, conflict, and alienation. It is also an opportunity to transcend our respective roles and disciplines to learn more about one another.

A second important consideration is that of history. In the past, with the blessing of the local bishops, dedicated religious communities of men and women established, sponsored, and staffed most of the Catholic colleges and universities, as well as Catholic hospitals and other health care institutions in this country. Bishops were seldom involved in these endeavors other than as occasional commencement speakers and celebrants of liturgies to mark special anniversaries or bless new facilities. Bishops generally kept at a distance from religious communities, and vice versa.

Moreover, many of the Catholic social service agencies—Catholic Charities and the St. Vincent de Paul Society, to name only two—were initially established by lay people, with the approval of the local bishop. Again, he often played little or no role in these endeavors. And little, if anything, was expected of him.

More recently, however, there has been a change in the Church's understanding of bishops' responsibilities. The documents of the Second Vatican Council and postconciliar writings have consistently pointed out that the diocesan bishop is to serve all the people of the local church, including religious. When the Holy Father mandated a study of religious life in the U.S., we carried it out over a three-year period in the Archdiocese of Chicago. I attended many sessions during which the women and men religious and I discussed our hopes and fears about how I could better serve them while respecting their diverse charisms and internal authority.

This has implications for bishops' relations with Catholic institutions of higher education, health care, and social services today. While many bishops still play little or no role in the Catholic health care and/or social service institutions within their dioceses, the Preliminary Report suggests that many in these two ministries—both religious and lay—expect the local bishop to become more involved in their work. As the report also suggests, this is much *less* true of many Catholic educators!

Today, all three ministries are seen more clearly as ministries of the entire Church, not merely of the specific institutions themselves. This also implies that, as pastor of the local church, the bishop also has a role to play. The trick is to define that role more precisely and in a way that serves and supports the ministries while linking them with the local church. It must be a genuine, creative partnership that will give the bishop an opportunity to serve the people who engage in these ministries rather than merely react to problems which arise. It would also give the people in these ministries an opportunity to contribute more effectively to the Church's mission.

One of the primary tasks of a bishop is to teach. While this has always been so, it has taken on increasing importance in our fast-changing, pluralistic society. The crucial question for me is not *whether*, as a bishop, I should teach or even *what* I should teach. My basic concern is *how* I can pass on the Church's authentic teaching in the most effective, credible way. As you know, the best teachers are those who learn from their students. In fact, the best learning environment is often one in which teachers and students search together for the truth. That is my goal when I exercise my teaching office, especially in relation to Catholic higher education, health care, and social services.

As a pastor, I also have certain concerns. Let me give you some examples. Loyola University's teachers, students, and alumni are often members of the Archdiocese of Chicago. The university provides ministerial training for persons who either staff, or will staff in the future, many of our parishes and institutions. The Catholic staff and patients of Chicago's Mercy Hospital are also members of our local church; the same is true of Catholic Charities' staff, supporters, and clients. As archbishop, I have certain responsibilities in regard to the people I have been sent to serve. That is why I cannot ignore or disassociate myself from everything that happens at Loyola, Mercy, or Catholic Charities. The same is true of DePaul University and the other Catholic colleges, as well as the many health care institutions of the area.

But neither can I, nor should I try to, involve myself in *everything* that happens at these institutions. This means that I must be able to trust their administrators and staff to maintain the Catholic culture and identity required for fidelity to their mission. But when *should* I be involved in these institutions as the local bishop? The Preliminary Report shows considerable disagreement on this point, and I will not attempt to reconcile these differences here. However, in the third section of my presentation, I want to offer some recommendations as to how this issue may be resolved.

Let me give you a specific example of my concern as a pastor and a teacher. Last year, Father Matthew Lamb published an insightful article in *America* magazine, entitled, "Will There Be Catholic Theology in the

United States?" One of his basic theses was that, today, Catholic students at, and graduates of, non-Catholic divinity schools often lack an adequate background in Catholic theology and formation in the faith. This will have a serious long-term impact on their subsequent teaching, especially in Catholic institutions. Who will faithfully present the Church's teaching and tradition to the next generation of Catholic students? This is of great concern to the local church and the diocesan bishop. If I am to be faithful to my episcopal office, I must be aware of the potentially negative consequences of this turn of events. I hasten to add, of course, that the presidents and deans of Catholic colleges and universities share that responsibility.

While there are many other causes of the tension that arises from conflicting expectations, let me turn to my third set of reflections on how we might resolve conflicting expectations.

R ESOLVING CONFLICTING EXPECTATIONS

First, we must get to know and respect one another—as persons, as professionals.

I personally meet with the presidents of the Catholic colleges and universities in metropolitan Chicago each year at informal luncheons hosted by one of the presidents. In a relaxed atmosphere, usually without a formal agenda, we discuss issues of mutual concern. My experience suggests that, when educators get to know their bishop and vice versa, a climate of mutual respect, trust, and understanding usually develops. The presidents then feel free to contact the bishop about specific issues, and he feels the same, and this indeed happens throughout the year. Thorny problems can often be resolved before they are allowed to explode in public, causing rancor and eroding the public's confidence in the Church and its institutions.

Shortly after I came to Chicago, I called a meeting of the chief executive officers of all the Catholic hospitals in the archdiocese and representatives of the religious congregations which sponsor them. Unlike New York, the archdiocese does not own any of the twenty-two Catholic hospitals. We talked about mutual concerns—including their survival in a fiercely competitive environment—and, eventually, we formed the Catholic Health Alliance for Metropolitan Chicago. I meet with the fifteen representatives of the sponsoring communities three times a year. My personal representative sits on the Board of the Alliance which has twenty-three members. Again, we are getting to know and trust one another. Ongoing communication makes it less likely that disagreement over issues will divide us and spill over into public controversy.

I am also very involved with the Catholic Charities of the Archdiocese of Chicago, which is an integral part of our archdiocesan structure. I appoint its board of directors as my delegates to plan and monitor Charities' operations and the distribution of all its funds. It also has an advisory board of about three hundred members, who serve on nearly twenty committees. While I am, in effect, the chief executive officer and have the juridical authority to do so, in practice, I simply cannot make decisions on my own or chart Charities' course independently. The members of both boards are Catholic professionals, and I listen carefully to their counsel. Together, we have developed an agency which touches the lives of over 500,000 people each year.

I have used these personal examples simply to show that the approach I recommend is both feasible and effective. It works. But it takes a lot of determination and patience to make it work! However, the results are well worth the effort.

Second, besides getting to know and respect one another, bishops and people in the three ministries need to engage in honest dialogue about their mutual concerns. I am thinking, in particular, about some of the issues of control and behavior in the Preliminary Report, issues about the Church's juridical control of institutional ministries, the connection of these ministries with the local church, the tolerance of evil in these ministries.

There are many other important issues of mutual concern. For example, how do we maintain a Catholic culture in a pluralistic society? How do we infuse institutions with a Catholic culture, especially as they move toward a mixed model of identity? How far can we compromise in individual cases, especially when a conflict of values sets the parameters of the dilemma or dispute? As sponsorship of our institutions by religious congregations takes on new forms in the future, how can we maintain authorization by, and accountability to, the Church? How should the Church deal with modern ethical dilemmas in a pluralistic society? How can we arrive at a mutually acceptable understanding of academic freedom? How can bishops better serve Catholic colleges and universities, health care facilities, and social service agencies? How can these institutional ministries better serve the cause of justice in the world?

As I noted at the outset, the task before us is not easy. It may be helpful to recall that nearly a quarter century has passed since a group of twenty-six distinguished American Catholics, including my good friend and mentor, the late Archbishop Paul J. Hallinan, met at Land O'Lakes, Wisconsin, to redefine the Catholic identity of our institutions of higher learning in the wake of Vatican II. Today, we are still struggling with the same fundamental questions.

There are other things we can do to lessen the tension and resolve conflicting expectations.

It would be very helpful, for example, if five or six Catholic universities throughout the nation would offer seminars and similar academic programs to help new lay leaders of Catholic schools, hospitals, and social service agencies to understand in greater depth the basic components of Catholic culture, identity, and mission.

In the resolution of conflict, it would also be helpful to keep in mind the distinction which the U.S. bishops made in their pastoral letter on war and peace, where they distinguished between moral principles and their concrete application. The further one moves from principles into concrete application, the more likely it is that people of good faith will have different opinions. This may help explain why many bishops in Western Europe—for example, in France and Great Britain—often leave the concrete application of the principles to those engaged in higher education, health care, and social services.

Catholic institutions of higher learning could establish a chair or make other provisions to ensure that students have access to spiritual formation in addition to academic instruction. Catholic hospitals could work more closely with the parishes of the local church in reaching out to the surrounding community. Catholic social service agencies could work more closely with parishes and the local church to identify leaders, define goals, and deliver social services. In all three ministries, administrators' job descriptions could include an explicit acknowledgment of their responsibility to preserve the Catholic culture of their institutions.

The list of things we can do to lessen the tension and resolve conflicting expectations is limited only by our lack of creativity or resolve. I know we have the necessary creativity; I pray that we do not lack the needed resolve.

* * *

The challenges before us are real. They call us to find new ways to act in accord with our Catholic tradition. They call us to share our expertise and experience with one another. They invite us to embrace "the joy and hope, the grief and anguish" of the people of our day. They invite us to reach out to the world, willing to live with ambiguity, chaos, and "mess."

Let us proceed with a deep love for the people we serve, a heightened sensitivity for one another's needs, and renewed appreciation of what we can do for and with one another. Through this collaboration, your vital ministries will nurture their precious Catholic identity, and they, in turn, will invigorate the Church's mission. Toward that goal, let us proceed with willing hearts and diligent prayer.

Address

"The Catholic Church and U.S. Culture"

The Merton Lecture

Columbia University, New York, New York

— *November 10, 1993* ————————————————

INTRODUCTION

A few weeks ago, there was a *Firing Line* debate on PBS, centering around the following theme: whether the religious right poses a threat to the United States. The affirmative team argued passionately that the implicitly theocratic principles of the fundamentalist right represent a severe challenge both to the doctrine of separation of Church and state and to the essential freedoms enjoyed by Americans. Members of the team quoted extensively from the founding documents of our nation and from papers and speeches of the framers of the Constitution in order to support their position. Interestingly, the opposing team defended the religious right with what seemed to be an equal number of citations from the Founding Fathers, quotations which, this time, emphasized the indispensable importance of religion in the public and moral life of the United States.

This rather intriguing debate probably could proceed indefinitely, precisely because there is ample evidence for both positions in the thought of the founders and, indeed, in the public philosophy of this country. From the beginning, Americans have recognized the primal importance of religion, and they have reverenced the great secularist and rationalist ideals of the Enlightenment.

ENLIGHTENMENT HERITAGE

It is, indeed, the case that many of the leading personalities who gave shape to our country were profoundly marked by the élan and spirit of the Enlightenment. Freedom of inquiry, the rights and dignity of the individual, the primacy and inviolability of reason as an arbiter of truth were all principles that animated their thinking and action. Like many of their European confreres, our Founding Fathers were suspicious of the heteronomy and authoritarianism that characterized the religious heritage. Inspired by Immanuel Kant's adage, "dare to know," they felt that religious doctrine and dogma should be subjected to a process of intellectual purification. Only that which could be admitted confidently at the bar of reason would be accepted.

Our founders were also profoundly affected by the disastrous wars of religion that swept through Europe in the wake of the Reformation. Like many other eighteenth-century intellectuals, they felt that the only way to avoid such senseless carnage would be to encourage the development of a sort of "rational" religion, free of the taint of peculiar doctrine, and, above all, to foster toleration and mutual respect among diverse religious traditions.

These Enlightenment convictions were enshrined in the founding documents of our nation and, in time, gave shape to the culture of the United States. Thus, for example, the God invoked in the prologue to the Declaration of Independence is much more the God of Nature celebrated by rationalist Deists than the God and Father of Jesus Christ. Further, the "self-evident" principles that inspire respect for the individual and ground our government are much more those of seventeenth- and eighteenth-century philosophy than those of the biblical tradition.

The governmental system presented in our Constitution—one of elaborate checks and balances—is a reflection of Enlightenment skepticism and mistrust of authority. The process by which a bill becomes a law is determined, in large part, by the rationalist ideal of conversation as a model of the truth. And, perhaps most remarkably, the Constitution establishes the so-called wall of separation between Church and state. In the minds of the framers, at least many of them, the purpose of this separation was not to prohibit religion from having any voice in the public arena, but to guarantee that religious persecution and internecine religious warfare would never plague the United States.

One could argue that the great ideal of the Enlightenment was autonomy, self-rule, self-determination. For Kant, the Enlightenment represented the "coming of age" of the human race, the moment when human beings threw off the oppressive traditions and institutions that had enslaved them and assumed the dangerous but finally liberating responsibility of self-governance. The Enlightenment precept of autonomy, commonly assumed by our founders, has certainly had a profound impact on the cultural and social development of our nation.

Thus, there is a healthy sense of skepticism that marks many of our citizens, an instinctive suspicion of authorities, unquestioned traditions, *ipse dixits*. This, as I have often remarked, is only too evident in the dialogue between the Church's magisterium and U.S. culture. Americans tend not to be convinced simply by the dictate of authority; they want to hear persuasive arguments.

Further, our economic system is rooted in the ideal of autonomy. In the free market, one is able to buy and sell as one chooses. Many U.S. citizens are resistant to the efforts of government agencies to interfere inordinately in the subtle give-and-take of the market. And many feel that excessive taxation is an unwarranted and unwelcome meddling in the economic lives of free people.

We Americans are, furthermore, proud of our tradition of religious, ethnic, and cultural toleration. We reverence our principles of free speech, free assembly, and free artistic expression. We are convinced that no one perspective—be it religious, aesthetic, political, or cultural—ought necessarily to be imposed upon everyone.

In all of this celebration of diversity, rationality, individuality, and tolerance, we show ourselves to be the inheritors of the autonomous Enlightenment tradition bequeathed to us by the founders of the nation and the framers of the U.S. Constitution.

THE RELIGIOUS HERITAGE

As I intimated earlier, alongside this Enlightenment influence, there has been, from the beginning of this nation, an enormously powerful religious influence. Many of the first settlers came to these shores from England and Holland seeking religious liberty. They crossed the Atlantic as the Israelites crossed the Red Sea, leaving the sins of the Old World behind in the cleansing waters of the ocean. They established themselves in a geographically and spiritually "new" world, a place of hope and spiritual renewal, a sort of new Zion. The letters and diary entries of some of the first colonists reflect a profoundly Christian sensibility. The Great Awakening of the 1740s, led by Jonathan Edwards and other passionate preachers, fired the religious imagination and conscience of the thirteen colonies and inaugurated a long tradition of "revivalism" in both the social and the political life of the United States.

In his remarkable commentaries on the American national character just after the Revolutionary War, Alexis de Tocqueville speaks of the surprising religious vitality of the young United States of America. In the mid-nineteenth century, in his essay "On the Jewish Question," Karl Marx observes that the "official" atheism of the American state has by no means led to an eradication of the actual religiosity of the American people. Americans are, he laments, "among the most religious in the world."

And the largely Protestant religiosity of the United States was supplemented by the enormous influx of Catholic immigrants from the mid-nineteenth to the early twentieth century. The Irish, Germans, Italians, Poles, and other eastern Europeans who flooded to this land brought with them a richly textured and deeply felt Roman Catholic sensibility.

Even a cursory survey of U.S. history reveals the powerful impact that religious people and religious ideals have had on the shaping of our national life and imagination. The abolitionist movement, which led, in time, to the Civil War and the freeing of the slaves, was animated by profoundly spiritual values rooted in the Jewish and Christian ethical/religious tradition. The civil rights movement of the 1950s and 1960s was led largely by preachers whose minds and hearts were on fire with the ethical imperatives of the Bible and whose mouths were filled with the words of the Old Testament prophets, calling for justice and judgment. As Gary Wills and others have pointed out, religion continues to play a decisive role in today's political and social drama. Many of our passionate commitments to peace, serving the poor, protecting the unborn, working for economic justice, are fueled by more basic spiritual commitments.

And, as many statisticians indicate, Americans are among the most "church-going" people in the world. Even though there has been a decline in recent years, they are far more likely than their European counterparts to attend religious services, contribute financially to their churches and synagogues, and participate actively in the rhythm of church life. In the end, one cannot ignore or bracket the influence of religion in the social, political, and cultural life of the United States.

THE LIVELY TENSION

As became clear in the *Firing Line* debate that I described a few moments ago, our national life is characterized by the tension, the play, the conversation, between the Enlightenment tradition and the biblical/religious tradition. Any attempt to resolve the conflict by reducing one side to the other is doomed to failure. One could almost read the entire history of the United States from the perspective of this back-and-forth play between the autonomous ideals of the Enlightenment and the heteronomous ideals of the religious heritage.

At its best, this tension is creative and enlivening, indeed the animating force that makes our cultural life distinctive. A danger that I sense is not so much the play of opposition between autonomy and heteronomy, but rather the one-sided emphasis on one at the expense of the other.

The one-sided accenting of the autonomous and rationalist ideals of the Enlightenment has led to some of the great social and cultural problems that we confront today. When overstressed, the individualist ideal of the eighteenth century gives rise to a consumerist, materialist attitude and to a capitalism marked by ruthless competition and egotism. Much of what Marx and his colleagues criticized in mid-nineteenth-century capitalism was precisely this loss of community and shared responsibility. It could well be argued that much of the poverty, inequality, and lack of economic opportunity in our nation is a consequence of limitless autonomy, an uncritical acceptance of the individualism of the Enlightenment.

Similarly, when overemphasized, the rationalism and critical spirit of the eighteenth century can spawn a sort of fundamental skepticism, a sense of meaninglessness. When the insights of the religious heritage are simply forgotten, or perhaps dismissed as irrational or irrelevant, a debilitating loss of purpose and identity can result. Few can doubt that, at least in certain segments of U.S. society, there has been a breakdown in moral sensibility, a falling away from those convictions and principles that give structure and depth to human life. Many commentators have spoken of a "spiritual malaise," a sickness of the soul, that has gripped the United States. Again, I would argue that this sort of disease of the heart is the result of a setting-aside of the religious and spiritual dimension, the consequence of a too enthusiastic embrace of the skeptical spirit of the Enlightenment. It was to address this reality, on a global scale, that Pope John Paul II wrote his latest encyclical, *Veritatis splendor* (the Splendor of Truth), which articulates the basic principles underlying the Church's moral teaching, carefully showing how authentic freedom is directly and necessarily related to *truth*.

By the same token, when the heteronomous religious heritage is one-sidedly emphasized, we confront other national and cultural demons. When the churches perceive themselves as fortresses defending against the encroachments of a hostile culture; when they, as a result, embrace authoritarianism and uncritical traditionalism, they become, in the end, self-destructive and inimical to society. We have seen this in the various expressions of religious intolerance throughout our history. Even some of those colonists who fled from religious persecution in Europe became persecutors themselves in rather short order. In the nineteenth century, some fundamentalist Protestants turned viciously on Roman Catholicism, burning down convents and churches, attempting to exclude Catholics from the political process.

In our time, we can see certain signs of this excessively "heteronomous" spirit. The attempt by some fundamentalist Christians to require the teaching of "creation science" in public schools represents a clear violation of the canons of reasonableness legitimately established by the Enlightenment heritage. Similarly, the attempt to impose a narrowly conceived Christian political agenda, simply on the basis of biblical authority, is an act of intellectual and cultural aggression that is understandably resisted by a pluralistic society.

The inordinately heteronomous religion finally becomes destructive of the human spirit itself, denying to the mind and heart their legitimate freedom and expressiveness.

THE CATHOLIC VISION

It is my contention that the authentically Catholic vision of the relationship between God and the world allows us to push beyond the split between autonomy and heteronomy, to see that what is valuable in both can be preserved and that what is potentially dangerous in both can be checked.

At the heart of the Catholic sensibility is the person of Jesus Christ, the living union between the infinite and the finite, between God and what is not God. In the ever-fruitful language of the Council of Chalcedon, Jesus Christ is a divine nature and a human nature which are united hypostatically in one divine Person, united in such a way that there is no mixing or "confusion" of the natures. In other words, in Jesus Christ, God becomes a creature without ceasing to be God and without overwhelming the creature he becomes.

And thus what is disclosed in the event of the incarnation is that God is not simply a "thing in the world," not merely one being among many, a "supreme being" surely, but not over and against creation. Rather God is the sheer act of existence itself, in St. Thomas Aquinas's words, *"ipsum esse subsistens."* The God and Father of Jesus Christ cannot be a reality in competition with the world, but instead must be ground, support, continual sustainer, and creator of the world. What is revealed in the startling event of the incarnation is that proximity to the Creator does not threaten a creature but, on the contrary, enhances it. A creature becomes most itself when it is most given over to God.

The person of Christ discloses a truth about God's rapport with the whole of creation, but the hypostatic union is particularly illuminating with regard to the relation between the divine and the human. For the contemporary theologian Hans Urs von Balthasar, Jesus is the dramatic play between infinite and finite freedom. The Christ reveals that finite, human freedom comes to full flowering precisely when it is thoroughly rooted in divine freedom, precisely when it is transformed into radical obedience. Surrender to God is not the negation of human responsibility and autonomy, but rather their completion. For Balthasar, the kingdom of God is nothing but the "acting area" opened up by Jesus Christ, the "space" in which God's freedom and our freedom can coexist. The entire purpose of the Church is to draw people into the energy of the kingdom, to lure them into the acting area where real freedom and integrity are discovered in abandonment to the liberating will of God.

In light of the incarnation, one can more fully appreciate the parameters of sin. To sin is to refuse to enter into what Balthasar calls the "theo-drama," this salvific play between the infinite and the finite; to sin is to affirm one's freedom over and against God, to cling to oneself, and hence to see God as a rival, as a competitor. To sin, in the final analysis, is to refuse to be transformed by the paradoxical energy of the incarnation and thus to mistake slavery for authentic freedom.

This brief foray into incarnational theology and theological anthropology is, I think, a necessary background for understanding the Catholic vision of the complex rapport between Church and society. As the proclaimer of the incarnation, the Church speaks for neither autonomy nor heteronomy, but, rather, to borrow Paul Tillich's word, for "theonomy." In holding up the icon of Jesus Christ, God and man, the Church announces that our deepest freedom, individuality, and self-determination are paradoxically found in the most radical surrender in obedience to God—in short, that abandonment to rule by God is tantamount to the richest autonomy. The Church invites people out of the sinful illusion that the divine is either a threat that must be resisted, or a tyrant who must be feared.

This incarnational spirituality has allowed the Church to play its subtle and complex role in the world. On the one hand, as the bearer of theonomy, the Church has, from the beginning, been able to affirm and appreciate whatever is good, true, and beautiful in secular culture. Origen confidently employs the philosophical paradigms of Plato and Plotinus; Augustine can see anticipations of the *logos* who is Christ in all secular expressions of truth; Thomas Aquinas can articulate the radicality of the Christian vision in terms of Aristotelian science; John Henry Newman enters into dialogue with the epistemology of Locke and Hume precisely in his attempt to explore the "grammar" of the act of faith; John Courtney Murray celebrates the notions of freedom of conscience and religious liberty; Karl Rahner adapts Kant, Hegel, and Heidegger much as Aquinas had adapted Aristotle. All of these examples show that authentically Christian spirits embrace the goodness of the world, just as God embraced the world in Christ. Christian theologians bear a power that poses no threat to the integrity and "autonomy" of the world.

By the same token, the Catholic Church, throughout its history, has opposed overly "heteronomous" conceptions of religion. In the third century, Tertullian wondered, in his famous rhetorical question, "what Athens has to do with Jerusalem?" What does the revelation contained in Jesus Christ have to do with the findings of pagan philosophers; why, in short, should the faith of the Church subject itself to rational investigation? But, as the above-mentioned examples indicate, the mainstream of the Church's tradition has never sided with Tertullian. Our greatest saints, mystics, and scholars have implicitly recognized that the various truths of secular culture are embraced by the Truth disclosed in Jesus Christ and, thus, that the Church need not retreat into a defensive, authoritarian stance.

On the other hand, precisely as the bearer of theonomy, the Church is opposed to excessive expressions of autonomy. Filled with the spirit of Jesus Christ, the Church shows that our deepest freedom is tantamount, not to a puffing-up of the ego, but rather to a loving surrender to God. The selfishness, competitiveness, individualism, and meaninglessness, which, as we saw, plague Western society, flow from the ego's tendency to cling to itself. When human beings can abandon themselves to God, they find the freedom that is described in the Sermon on the Mount: a freedom to love radically, to trust, and to hope. The theonomous Christian view presupposes that the judgment of God is upon all one-sided autonomy and secularism and that the fundamental and irreducible transcendence of the divine must never be forgotten.

Thus, even in their embrace of the secular, neither Origen nor Augustine, neither Aquinas nor Newman, neither Murray nor Rahner ever succumbed to secularism; they never failed to emphasize the overwhelming transcendence of God which shakes, challenges, and converts the secular. Informed by the energy of the incarnation, the great Catholic spirits have always stubbornly refused to be drawn into the split between autonomy and heteronomy.

THE CATHOLIC CHURCH AND U.S. CULTURE

From all that has been said, it should be clear that the Catholic Church, as the bearer of the icon of Jesus Christ, as the advocate of theonomy, can play a uniquely helpful and healing role in the context of U.S. society. As the proclaimer of the God who became *human*, the Church can gratefully and enthusiastically celebrate all that is positive in the autonomous culture born of the Enlightenment: freedom of the individual, the dignity of the human person, the right to express oneself and seek one's own destiny. And, as the proclaimer of the *God* who became human, the Church can speak the word of judgment over all demonic distortions of autonomy; it can embody what is best in the heteronomous tradition that has shaped our nation. Standing, as it were, above the split between autonomy and heteronomy, the theonomous Church of Jesus Christ can serve as a uniquely powerful leaven to U.S. society.

I would like to explore this special role of the Church in society by examining the particular "case" of the Catholic intellectual in this nation. The Catholic thinker, I will argue, is the one who celebrates, cultivates, and practices theonomous reason, the one who is energized by the intellectual dynamism that flows from the incarnation. He or she is, therefore, the one who is intellectually attuned to a proper vision of the rapport between the sacred and the secular. Allow me to elucidate this point with the help of two great spokespersons for the Catholic imagination, John Henry Newman and Bernard Lonergan.

In his classic *The Idea of a University*, Newman maintains that the exclusion of theology from the circle of the sciences results in a skewing and diminishing of each particular discipline and the whole of knowledge. Theology speaks of the grounding and creating power of God and, hence, of that which lies at the root and fundament of what is studied by each science. Thus, physicists or chemists, who consider their subject independently of a sense of the Creator God, would communicate to their students a woefully incomplete, indeed finally incorrect, understanding of the physical world. Similarly, a professor of literature or psychology, who never takes into consideration the relationship between men and women and their Creator, would fail adequately to speak of the full richness of being human.

Indeed, says Newman, the exclusion of theology from the circle of university disciplines would allow other sciences to fill the vacuum left by divine science. Individual disciplines would assume the role and power of theology, arrogating to themselves the position of the all-grounding, all-embracing science. In short, the absence of the divine science would give rise to an excessive autonomy on the part of the secular sciences, permitting them to overstep their proper bounds.

By the same token, Newman insists that the science of God is in no position to dictate terms to another discipline within its own proper sphere. For example, the physicist, when going about particular research, is not obligated to make constant reference to the creative ground of being; and the theologian is not permitted to interfere in that physicist's technical and proper work. There is, says Newman, an altogether legitimate division of labor among the various intellectual disciplines. Each researcher, including the theologian, should be aware of his or her discipline's appropriate range and limitation. No heteronomous imposition of the theological upon the properly secular is to be permitted.

We find a similar description of the rapport between the sacred and the secular sciences in the writings of Bernard Lonergan. For the great Canadian Jesuit, each particular act of knowing is situated in the context of a general, overarching desire to know the fullness of reality. The dynamism of the human spirit, says Lonergan, is the "unrestricted desire to know," the orientation toward the Supreme Being. This is why Lonergan can affirm, with Aquinas, that the totality of existence is implicitly known in each individual act of knowing God.

The implication of this epistemology is that each science, each particular branch of knowledge, moves slowly but inevitably toward completion in a grasp of the fullness of reality. The energy that pushes the mind to understand any aspect of being eventually drives the mind in the direction of the Supreme Being. Thus, the mathematician—and Lonergan himself was an accomplished mathematician—precisely in grasping the truths of numeric relations, is compelled, by an inner dynamism of his consciousness, to see the rapport between those contingent truths and the Truth itself, God. As for Newman, so for Lonergan, the individual scientific and cultural disciplines are finally oriented toward, and intelligible in terms of, the grounding and all-embracing reality of which theology speaks. In short, the various particular sciences that are studied in the university naturally call out to theology as their proper end and fulfillment. And therefore, once more, the presence of divine science in the circle of academic disciplines challenges the unfortunate tendency of any secular discipline in the direction of excessive autonomy.

At the same time, for Lonergan, the ultimate orientation toward the horizon of all knowing by no means compromises the mind's capacity and desire to know the fullness of reality in its more particular modalities. Therefore, physicists, mathematicians, literary critics, philosophers, or astronomers can go about their work, following the canons of reasonableness proper to their individual disciplines. Though oriented implicitly to theology, secular researchers are not compelled to become theologians or to surrender to theologians a decisive role within their own field of study. Once again, no heteronomous dominance on the part of the divine science is called for or desirable.

But what is this strange science of God which both Newman and Lonergan describe, this intellectual discipline which concerns and grounds all other branches of knowledge without overwhelming them or compromising their inherent dignity and integrity? What is this discipline which seems to hover between heteronomy and autonomy? It can only be that science which speaks of the God disclosed in Jesus Christ, the God who grounds and transforms the finite without entering into competition with it, the God of the incarnation. In short, the theological vision that flows from the incarnation is theonomous; it encourages one to see and love and appreciate the world in all of its complexity. But it also compels one to look beyond to that infinite horizon which alone can give the fullness of meaning to the world.

As I hinted earlier, it is my conviction that Catholic intellectuals are the practitioners of theonomous thinking, whose worldview is informed by an incarnational sensibility. As such, they can be of enormous service to U.S. society which exists in the tension between the autonomy of the Enlightenment and the heteronomy of the various religious traditions. The Catholic thinker is the one who spells out and analyzes the cultural implications of the incarnation, who encourages the legitimate play between the sacred and the secular, who challenges the exaggerations of both autonomy and heteronomy. In their research and teaching, Catholic intellectuals honor the beauty, integrity, and freedom of the world in the context of that Other, namely God, in whom the world alone finds its fulfillment.

Thus, Catholic professors of economics can feel completely at home in the university milieu. They can confidently enter into their work, following the accepted norms of their discipline. But, in the theonomous spirit, they refuse to absolutize the economic realm. They communicate to their students a sense that the energies and movements of the market must be understood against the backdrop of one's basic moral obligations to foster a community of justice, love, and nonviolent cooperation.

Thus, Catholic professors of fine arts teach the great traditions of painting, sculpture, and architecture and instruct students in the techniques of those disciplines. But with an imagination fired by the incarnation, they stubbornly insist that whatever beauty we can discover or create through our own efforts is but a hint of the primal beauty of the Creator God. So, also, Catholic professors of psychology critically but unabashedly communicate all that Freud, Jung, Adler, or Skinner have taught concerning the dynamics of human consciousness and behavior. But reluctant to grant too much "autonomy" to their discipline, they allow the study of psychology to open their students' minds to the deepest and most provocative relationship that a human being can have, namely, that with the infinite God.

Mind you, I am not suggesting that the economist or the psychologist or the professor of fine arts use the classroom or the professional article as a place for propagandizing. In both contexts, the Catholic intellectual must be totally professional. Rather, I am suggesting that the Catholic values of the intellectual should radiate to others by the kind of person he or she is, by concerns shown for other people and their aspirations, their hopes and fears, and by an openness to the richness and implications of the Transcendent.

Catholic scholars, researchers, and teachers can thus uniquely enliven the intellectual life of this country. Speaking out of a tradition that transcends

both autonomy and heteronomy, the Catholic intellectual can be perfectly at home in a U.S. cultural milieu and can serve as a prophetic critic
of U.S. society. Catholic thinkers can share our country's Enlightenment
and religious assumptions *and* challenge them—in the name of the ever-
startling event of the incarnation.

While I have focused the latter part of this presentation on the specific
contributions which Catholic intellectuals can make to U.S. culture, as I
conclude, I return to what I said earlier about the broader relationship between the Catholic Church and U.S. society. In the light of the incarnation, we strive to preserve what is of value in both the autonomy of the
Enlightenment tradition and the heteronomy of this country's earlier religious heritage. We can also prophetically point out the limitations of both
traditions and the dangers of insisting on the principles and values of one
to the exclusion of those of the other. The Catholic Church is in a position to mediate the dispute between the two traditions, to bridge the gap
and heal the rift which a one-sided emphasis on either tradition causes.
May God give us, who are the Church, the wisdom, strength, and courage
to bring this about.

Address

"Tolerance in Society and Church"*

St. Mary's Cathedral, Sydney, New South Wales, Australia

— *February 21, 1995* ——————————————————

Tolerance may seem especially appealing when we consider its opposite: intolerance. However, we would not be celebrating an International Year of Tolerance if the concept were universally appealing or easy to acquire.

Alexander Chase has written that "the peak of tolerance is most readily achieved by those who are not burdened with convictions." Or, to put it in a more humorous way, using the words of Ogden Nash:

> Sometimes with secret pride I sigh
> To think how tolerant am I;
> Then wonder which is really mine:
> Tolerance, or a rubber spine?

So, some may reject or be uncomfortable with tolerance because they fear that their firm convictions might be diluted or their principles compromised. But is it true that only people without firm convictions or principles can be tolerant? I say no and base my response on my experience within the Church and in society. Let me briefly explore both realms with you this morning.

I come before you as a pastor of the Catholic Church in the United States. My experience has shaped what I will share with you this morning.

*Also published in *The Australasian Catholic Record*, vol. 72, no. 3, July 1995, pp. 365–69.

Nevertheless, what I say is a reflection and an extension of the concern of the teaching and practice of the Church throughout the world. Your reaction to my remarks will naturally be shaped by your own experience here in Australia. I trust that, *mutatis mutandis*, my reflection will be of some help to you.

TOLERANCE IN A PLURALISTIC SOCIETY

My reflections on tolerance in a pluralist society like the United States will specifically focus on the role of church, synagogue, mosque, and temple in the public policy debate.

Throughout its history as a nation, the themes of religion, morality, and politics are woven through the American experience. No single figure in U.S. history has had a greater impact on how Catholics conceive of the relationship between religion and politics than the late Jesuit Father John Courtney Murray. Murray's lasting contribution was that he provided the Catholic Church with a theological understanding of its role in a democracy and offered society a philosophical grounding for religious pluralism.

Murray was convinced that the Catholic tradition could learn from and contribute to life in the United States and, indeed, in every culture. To facilitate this exchange, he took on the task of being the "theologian of the First Amendment" to the U.S. Constitution, which states, in part, that "Congress shall make no law respecting an establishment of religion, or prohibiting the free exercise thereof; or abridging the freedom of speech." "Separation of Church and state" is the phrase often invoked to explain the relationship of religion to politics in the United States. Murray believed deeply in the political wisdom of the separation clause, but he resisted all efforts to transform the separation of Church and state into the division of religion and politics, as though neither related to the other.

The separation clause has a crucial but limited meaning: It holds that religious institutions are to expect neither favoritism nor discrimination in the exercise of their civic and religious responsibilities. The separation intended is that of the Church as an institution from the state as an institution. It was never intended to separate the Church from the wider society or religion from culture.

In the United States, as in Australia, civil discourse is structured by religious pluralism. The condition of pluralism, wrote Murray, is the coexistence in one society of groups holding divergent and incompatible views with regard to religious questions. The genius of American pluralism, in his view, was that it provided for the religious freedom of each citizen and every faith. However, it did not purchase tolerance at the price of expelling religious and moral values from the public life of the nation. The goal of the U.S. constitutional system is to provide space for religion in society but not a religious state.

A central theme in Murray's work is the imperative of providing a moral foundation for public policy, law, and the institutions of democracy. Religious tolerance cannot be purchased at the price of a moral vacuum. A society stands in need of a public consensus which "furnishes the premise of a people's action in history and defines the larger aims which that action seeks in internal affairs and in external relations" (*We Hold These Truths*, p. 10). Murray's writings ranged across the theory and practice of shaping a moral consensus in a pluralistic democracy—moving beyond tolerance to consensus.

From Murray, I have learned to respect the *complexity of public issues* and to recognize the legitimate *secularity* of the public debate.

The test of *complexity* is one we all must face; it is one the Religious Left in the U.S. has often failed and thereby paved the way for the Religious Right. From issues of defense policy through questions of medical ethics to issues of social policy, the moral dimensions of our public life are interwoven with empirical judgments where honest disagreement exists. I do not believe, however, that empirical complexity should silence or paralyze religious or moral analysis and advocacy of issues. But we owe the public a careful accounting of how we have come to our moral conclusions.

The *secularity* of the public debate poses a different test. I stand with Murray in attributing a public role to religion and morality in our national life. But I also stand with him in the conviction that religiously rooted positions must somehow be translated into language, arguments, and categories that a religiously pluralistic society can agree on as the moral foundation of key policy positions.

There is another lesson that I learned from Murray, and it is closely related to the concept of tolerance. He often spoke and wrote about the need for *civility*. We can keep our deepest convictions and still keep our civil courtesy. We can test others' arguments, but we should not question their motives. We can presume good will even when we strenuously disagree. We can hold firm beliefs and principles and still be tolerant of those who do not share them. We can relate the best of religion to the best of politics in the service of each other and the wider society, national and human, to which we are bound in hope and love.

Let us now turn to the role of tolerance within the Church.

TOLERANCE WITHIN THE CATHOLIC CHURCH

Rather than talk about general principles, I will focus on what has happened within the Catholic Church in the postconciliar era, the last three decades. Again, my experience is primarily of the United States and Western Europe.

What has been happening? There are some who feel that the conciliar teaching is depleted; that is, both the Church and society have moved beyond it. What is needed, they say, is *Vatican III,* and already their eyes are turned on what a new council might say or do. Indeed, some are already talking and acting in anticipation of a new council, presuming that they know what it would say and do. They look upon everyone else—including the hierarchy—as hopelessly fossilized.

There are others, however, who are committed to what has been labeled the "restoration." Their desire and intention is to restore things to what they were *before* the council. For them, the council was a well-intentioned effort that has not turned out too well. These Catholics are secure in their beliefs and theological opinions and do not hesitate to accuse anyone who disagrees with them—including bishops and cardinals—of heresy.

There are still others—the majority perhaps—for whom the Second Vatican Council is only a name. They do not fully understand the council's teaching and often fail to see its relevance to their daily lives. They shy away from both the innovators and the restorationists, whom they regard as extreme and intolerant.

Perhaps I have oversimplified matters. But I think all would agree that the two more extreme tendencies exist, and they create tensions within the Church.

It is my conviction that, as a community of faith, we do not fully understand all the implications of the council's teaching and, for that reason, have not adequately received and implemented it. While much has changed in the past thirty years, it takes more than a single generation to assimilate fully the teaching of an ecumenical council, especially one whose purpose was primarily pastoral and that addressed so many important topics and concerns.

One of the difficulties in this instance is that, in the conciliar documents, our traditional teaching is often presented alongside the newer theological and pastoral insights of recent decades. The great need now is to show how the two relate to each other, how the newer insights are a logical, legitimate—and, indeed, needed—development of our tradition. To fulfill this task, we must be faithful to the values of both the old and the new; one cannot be emphasized at the expense of the other. Such a comprehensive approach to the conciliar teaching, I believe, will prevent all of us from becoming preoccupied with single points in isolation from all the rest. It will enable us to see the full beauty and relevance of our heritage as it has developed under the influence of the Holy Spirit from the apostolic age to the present. It will also help us become more tolerant of one another.

This process will require the best efforts of our theologians working together with representatives of other disciplines. And they must, of course, pursue their efforts in partnership with the ecclesiastical magisterium, which has the ultimate responsibility for affirming the faith of the ecclesial community.

Unfortunately, a great deal of polarization exists within the Church. This has created a mood of suspicion, even acrimony. A candid discussion of important issues is often inhibited, so that we do not always come to grips with the problems that confront us.

There is nothing wrong *per se* with different visions of Catholicism. Such differences appear in the New Testament itself. Moreover, there were different schools of thought among the early Fathers of the Church and during the Middle Ages. But today the struggle is not always constructive. So what do we do?

The reality is that the extremes are often the most noisy. Those in the middle—the majority—are often quiet. So we must make a greater effort to engage those in the middle and, in the process, establish a common ground—a new space for dialogue—which will make it possible for us to reach those who are alienated or disillusioned for whatever reason.

To establish this common ground, this space for authentic dialogue, a broad range of the Church's leadership, both clerical and lay, must recommit themselves to the basic truths of our Catholic faith. The chief of those truths is that we must be accountable to our Catholic tradition and to the Spirit-filled, living Church that brings to us the revelation of God in Jesus. Jesus who is present in sacrament, word, and community is central to all we do. So our focus must constantly be on him, not on ourselves.

This rules out petty criticisms and jealousy, cynicism, sound-bite theology, unhistorical assertions, flippant dismissals. It rules out a narrow appeal to our individual or contemporary experience as if no other were valid. It acknowledges that our discussions must take place within boundaries because the Church, for all its humanness, is not merely a human organization. It is rather a chosen people, a mysterious communion, a foreshadowing of the kingdom, a spiritual family.

In sum, what we need in the Church today is a realization that there is room for considerable diversity among us. We should not, on the one hand, define orthodoxy too narrowly or, on the other, ignore or discard the notion altogether. Where there is a breakdown of civility, dialogue, trust, and tolerance, we must strive to build the unity of the one body of Christ. If we do not strive for such tolerance and unity in our search for truth, the Church's mission and ministries will suffer, and we will be a stumbling block to those we evangelize. The reign of God will appear to the extent that others can say: "See, how those Christians love one another!"

Address

Reception of the Medal of Freedom*

The White House, Washington, D.C.

— *September 9, 1996* ——————————————

I am indeed honored to receive the Medal of Freedom. I am grateful to President Clinton for naming me. The reception of such an honor is both humbling and challenging. Humbling, because you know that there are so many others who are deserving and, in many instances, more deserving of this honor. Challenging, because such an honor provides a strong motivation to work even harder to contribute to the justice, compassion, civility, and peace that should mark our society. For me, this challenge has special meaning because of the limited time I have left.

But I wish to move the focus from myself to what I believe my being honored symbolizes: the important role religion plays in our civil society.

In saying this, I am making a distinction that is fundamental to both U.S. constitutional theory and Catholic social thought—namely, that the state is not all of society. Civil society exists beyond the state and embraces the entire social fabric that includes realities such as the family and voluntary associations. Although our U.S. Constitution recognizes the legitimate separation of Church and state, it does not and should not call for a separation of religion and society. On the contrary, as I will repeat in an address this afternoon at Georgetown University, there should be a constructive engagement between religion and society.

Today, despite efforts to reverse this aspect of our American tradition, I reaffirm the value that religious vision and discourse have for the development of a public morality that should be the hallmark of a healthy society.

---

*Also published in *Origins*, vol. 26, no. 14, September 26, 1996, pp. 215–16.

I honor the essential contribution made by religious institutions to ensure that our society is one of compassion, care, and justice.

Whether it be the religious inspiration of a Thomas Jefferson or the biblical vision of a Martin Luther King, Jr., our society, our nation, is well served by its engagement with religiously motivated women and men and with both the intellectual analysis and thematic vision that emerge from the various religious traditions.

My fellow Roman Catholics and I are firmly committed to this engagement. We will continue to offer a vision of the inalienable dignity of human life as the foundational principle for a well-ordered society. And in that context we propose to our fellow citizens a consistent ethic of life that promotes all that enhances and nurtures life and rejects all that diminishes or destroys it. In particular, this ethic rejects the killing of the unborn and the legalization of euthanasia or assisted suicide.

As we strive to enhance and protect the dignity of individuals, we also speak of human solidarity—a solidarity that calls us to abandon no one in need, whether citizen or immigrant; a solidarity that compels us to look beyond our national self-interest to a sense of shared responsibility for the well-being of our sisters and brothers elsewhere who do not have the freedom or resources we enjoy.

I pray each day for the well-being of our nation as well as the entire human family. I pray that, as a nation, as a society, we will honor and protect all life, especially the unborn and the vulnerable, strive for justice, build communities that prize education and hard work as well as compassion and social responsibility, and work for freedom and peace throughout the world. Likewise, may we be able to model a form of human communication that, grounded in and formed by the truth, rises above pettiness and mean-spiritedness and fosters discourse marked by reconciliation and mutual respect. Today, I dedicate this honor to the realization of this prayer.

Health Care

Address

"The Consistent Ethic of Life and Health Care Systems"*

Foster McGaw Triennial Conference

Loyola University, Chicago, Illinois

——— *May 8, 1985* ———————————————————————

We meet on an auspicious day to explore more effective ways of preserving, protecting and fostering human life—the 40th anniversary of the end of the war in Europe which claimed millions of lives, both European and American. It was also a war in which, tragically, the word Holocaust will be forever emblazoned in history. We must never forget!

This anniversary is a day not only for remembering victory over the forces of oppression which led to this savage destruction of life but also for recommitting ourselves to preserving and nurturing all human life.

Daily we encounter news headlines which reflect the growing complexity of contemporary life, the rapid development of science and technology, the global competition for limited natural resources, and the violence which is so rampant in parts of our nation and world. The problems of contemporary humanity are enormously complex, increasingly global, and ominously threatening to human life and human society. Each of them has moral and religious dimensions because they all impact human life.

---

*Also published in *Health Progress* (1985); *Linacre Quarterly* (1985); *Consistent Ethic of Life* (Sheed & Ward, 1988); and *Celebrating the Ministry of Healing: Joseph Cardinal Bernardin's Reflections on Healthcare* (Catholic Health Association, 1999).

At times we may feel helpless and powerless as we confront these issues. It is crucial that we develop a method of moral analysis which will be comprehensive enough to recognize the linkages among the issues, while respecting the individual nature and uniqueness of each. During the past year and a half I have addressed this task through the development of a "consistent ethic of life"—popularly referred to as the "seamless garment" approach to the broad spectrum of life issues.

I come before you today as a *pastor*, not a health care professional or theoretician, not a philosopher, not a politician or a legal expert. As a pastor, I wish to share with you the teaching of the Catholic Church as it pertains to human life issues.

I am very grateful to Father Baumhart for the invitation to address you on "The Consistent Ethic of Life and Health Care Systems." I will first briefly describe the concept of a consistent ethic. Then I will explore the challenge it poses to health care systems both in terms of "classical" medical ethics questions and in regard to "contemporary" social justice issues.

THE CONSISTENT ETHIC OF LIFE

Although the consistent ethic of life needs to be finely tuned and carefully structured on the basis of values, principles, rules and applications to specific cases, this is not my task this afternoon. I will simply highlight some of its basic components so that I can devote adequate attention to its application to health care systems and the issues they face today.

Catholic social teaching is based on two truths about the human person: human life is both sacred and social. Because we esteem human life as sacred, we have a duty to protect and foster it at all stages of development, from conception to death, and in all circumstances. Because we acknowledge that human life is also social, we must develop the kind of societal environment that protects and fosters its development.

Precisely because life is sacred, the taking of even one human life is a momentous event. While the presumption of traditional Catholic teaching has always been against taking human life, it has allowed the taking of human life in particular situations by way of exception—for example, in self-defense and capital punishment. In recent decades, however, the presumptions against taking human life have been strengthened and the exceptions made ever more restrictive.

Fundamental to this shift in emphasis is a more acute perception of the multiple ways in which life is threatened today. Obviously such questions as war, aggression and capital punishment have been with us for centuries; they are not new. What is new is the *context* in which these ancient questions arise, and the way in which a new context shapes the *content* of our ethic of life.

One of the major cultural factors affecting human life today is technology. Because of nuclear weapons we now threaten life on a scale previously unimaginable—even after the horrible experience of World War II. Likewise, modern medical technology opens new opportunities for care, but it also poses potential new threats to the sanctity of life. Living, as we do, in an age of careening technological development means we face a qualitatively new range of moral problems.

The protection, defense and nurture of human life involve the whole spectrum of life from conception to death, cutting across such issues as genetics, abortion, capital punishment, modern warfare and the care of the terminally ill. Admittedly these are all distinct problems, enormously complex, and deserving individual treatment. No single answer and no simple response will solve them all. They cannot be collapsed into one problem, but they must be confronted as pieces of a *larger pattern*. The fact that we face new challenges in each of these areas reveals the need for a consistent ethic of life.

The precondition for sustaining a consistent ethic is a "respect life" attitude or atmosphere in society. Where human life is considered "cheap" and easily "wasted," eventually nothing is held as sacred and all lives are in jeopardy. The purpose of proposing a consistent ethic of life is to argue that success on any one of the issues threatening life requires a concern for the broader attitude in society about respect for life. Attitude is the place to root an ethic of life. Change of attitude, in turn, can lead to change of policies and practices in our society.

Besides rooting this ethic in societal attitude, I have demonstrated, in a number of recent addresses, that there is an inner relationship—a linkage—among the several issues at the more specific level of moral principle. It is not my intention to repeat these arguments today.

Nevertheless, I would like to examine briefly the relationship between "right to life" and "quality of life" issues. If one contends, as we do, that the right of every unborn child should be protected by civil law and supported by civil consensus, then our moral, political and economic responsibilities do not stop at the moment of birth! We must defend the *right to life* of the weakest among us; we must also be supportive of the *quality of life* of the powerless among us: the old and the young, the hungry and the homeless, the undocumented immigrant and the unemployed worker, the sick, the disabled and the dying. I contend that the viability and credibility of the "seamless garment" principle depends upon the consistency of its application.

Such a quality-of-life posture translates into specific political and economic positions—for example, on tax policy, generation of employment, welfare policy, nutrition and feeding programs and health care. Consistency means we cannot have it both ways: we cannot urge a compassionate society and vigorous public and private policy to protect the rights of the unborn and then argue that compassion and significant public and private programs on behalf of the needy undermine the moral fiber of society or that they are beyond the proper scope of governmental responsibility or that of the private sector. Neither can we do the opposite!

The inner relationship among the various life issues is far more intricate than I can sketch here this afternoon. I fully acknowledge this. My intention is merely to bring that basic linkage into focus so I can apply it to the issues facing health care systems today.

THE CONSISTENT ETHIC AND "CLASSICAL" MEDICAL ETHICS QUESTIONS

As I noted at the outset, the consistent ethic of life poses a challenge to two kinds of problems. The first are "classical" medical ethics questions which today include revolutionary techniques from genetics to the technologies of prolonging life. How do we define the problems and what does it mean to address them from a Catholic perspective?

The essential question in the technological challenge is this: In an age when we *can* do almost anything, how do we decide what we *should* do? The even more demanding question is: In a time when we can do anything *technologically*, how do we decide *morally* what we should *not* do? My basic thesis is this: Technology must not be allowed to hold the health of human beings as a hostage.

In an address in Toronto last September, Pope John Paul II outlined three temptations of pursuing technological development: (1) pursuing development for its own sake, as if it were an autonomous force with built-in imperatives for expansion, instead of seeing it as a resource to be placed at the service of the human family; (2) tying technological development to the logic of profit and constant economic expansion without due regard for the rights of workers or the needs of the poor and helpless; (3) linking technological development to the pursuit or maintenance of power instead of using it as an instrument of freedom.

The response to these temptations, as the Holy Father pointed out, is *not* to renounce the technological application of scientific discoveries. We need science and technology to help solve the problems of humanity. We also need to subject technological application to moral analysis.

One of the most recent and most critical ethical questions which impacts the quality of human life is that of genetics, genetic counseling and engineering. Perhaps no other discovery in medicine has the potential so radically to change the lives of individuals and, indeed, the human race itself.

As with most scientific achievements in medicine, there are advantages and disadvantages to the utilization of this theoretical knowledge and technological know-how. Many genetic diseases can now be diagnosed early, even *in utero*, and technology is also moving toward treatment *in utero*. Proper use of such information can serve to prepare parents for the arrival of a special infant or can allay the fears of the expectant parents if the delivery of a healthy infant can be anticipated. The accumulation of scientific data can lead to a better understanding of the marvels of creation and to the possible manipulation of genes to prevent disease or to effect a cure before the infant sustains a permanent disability.

On the other hand, people also use available diagnostic procedures to secure information for the sex selection of their children. Some may wish to use it to eliminate "undesirables" from society. Many believe that the provision of genetic information contributes to an increase in the number of abortions.

At the other end of life's spectrum is care of the elderly. Our marvelous progress in medical knowledge and technology has made it possible to preserve the lives of newborns who would have died of natural causes not too many years ago; to save the lives of children and adults who would formerly have succumbed to contagious diseases and traumatic injuries; to prolong the lives of the elderly as they experience the debilitating effects of chronic illness and old age. At the same time, some openly advocate euthanasia, implying that we have absolute dominion over life rather than stewardship. This directly attacks the sacredness of each human life.

Other new moral problems have been created by the extension of lives in Intensive Care Units and Intensive Neonatal Units as well as by surgical transplants and implants, artificial insemination and some forms of experimentation. Computers provide rapid, usually accurate, testing and treatment, but they also create problems of experimentation, confidentiality and dehumanization. Intense debate is being waged about the extension of lives solely through extraordinary—mechanical or technological—means.

The consistent ethic of life, by taking into consideration the impact of technology on the full spectrum of life issues, provides additional insight to the new challenges which "classical" medical ethics questions face today. It enables us to define the problems in terms of their impact on human life and to clarify what it means to address them from a Catholic perspective.

THE CONSISTENT ETHIC OF LIFE AND "CONTEMPORARY" SOCIAL JUSTICE ISSUES

The second challenge which the consistent ethic poses concerns "contemporary" social justice issues related to health care systems. The primary question is: How does the evangelical option for the poor shape health care today?

Some regard the problem as basically financial: How do we effectively allocate limited resources? A serious problem today is the fact that many persons are left without basic health care while large sums of money are invested in the treatment of a few by means of exceptional, expensive measures. While technology has provided the industry with many diagnostic and therapeutic tools, their inaccessibility, cost and sophistication often prevent their wide distribution and use.

Government regulations and restrictions, cut-backs in health programs, the maldistribution of personnel to provide adequate services are but a few of the factors which contribute to the reality that many persons do not and probably will not receive the kind of basic care that nurtures life—unless we change attitudes, policies and programs.

Public health endeavors such as home care, immunization programs, health education and other preventive measures to improve the environment and thus prevent disease, have all served as alternate means of providing care and improving the health of the poor and isolated populations. In the past, if patients from this sector of society needed hospitalization, institutions built with Hill-Burton funds were required to provide a designated amount of "charity care" to those in need.

In some instances, hospitals continue to follow this procedure. However, access to these alternate, less expensive types of health care is becoming more difficult. Cuts in government support for health programs for the poor, for persons receiving Medicare or Medicaid benefits, are making it increasingly more difficult for people who need health care to receive it.

Today we seem to have three tiers of care: standard care for the insured, partial care for Medicaid patients, and emergency care only for the 35 million Americans who are uninsured. Do we nurture and protect life when there appears to be an unjust distribution of the goods entrusted to our stewardship? How can Catholic hospitals continue both to survive and to implement a preferential option for the poor?

This is not merely a theological or pastoral issue. Access to standard health care is largely nonexistent for about half of the poor and very limited for the other half who are eligible for Medicaid or Medicare. The United States has the worst record on health care of any nation in the North Atlantic community and even worse than some underdeveloped nations.

Judith Feder and Jack Hadley, currently codirectors of the Center for Health Policy Studies at Georgetown University, have conducted research on uncompensated hospital care. Some of their findings are particularly disturbing. They concluded, for example, that *nonprofit* hospitals—

including Catholic facilities—do very little more for the poor than *for-profit* hospitals (which is very little, indeed). Free care provided by private, nonprofit hospitals averaged only 3.85 percent of all charges (gross revenues) in 1982. I am aware that some dispute the accuracy of these findings in regard to Catholic hospitals, but I have not yet seen data which shows that, overall, these institutions provide substantially more free care than their counterparts.

I must also affirm, of course, that there are some inner-city and other Catholic hospitals which do a great deal for the poor. Nonetheless, as the research seems to indicate, hospitals average less than 5 percent of patient charges for uncompensated care. Much of this is for deliveries to women who appear in heavy labor at our emergency rooms and the subsequent neonatal intensive care for their infants born with severe problems because of the lack of care given their mothers during pregnancy.

Our national resources are limited, but they are not scarce. As a nation we spend *more* per capita and a *higher* share of our Gross Domestic Product (GDP) on health than any other country in the world—nearly twice as much as Great Britain, for example. Yet our system still excludes at least half the poor. In 1982 the U.S. share of GDP devoted to health care was 10.6 percent against 5.9 percent within the United Kingdom, which has universal access to health care and a lower infant mortality rate than the U.S.

The basic problem of health care in the U.S. is managerial: the effective allocation and control of resources. The key is the underlying philosophy and sense of mission which motivates and informs managerial decisions.

As a nation, we spend enormous amounts of money to prolong the lives of newborns and the dying while millions of people don't see a doctor until they are too ill to benefit from medical care. We allow the poor to die in our hospitals, but we don't provide for their treatment in the early stages of illness—much less make preventive care available to them.

These facts are disturbing to anyone who espouses the sacredness and value of human life. The fundamental human right is to life—from the moment of conception until death. It is the source of all other rights, including the right to health care. The consistent ethic of life poses a series of questions to Catholic health care facilities. Let me enumerate just a few.

- Should a Catholic hospital transfer an indigent patient to another institution unless superior care is available there? Should a Catholic nursing home require large cash deposits from applicants?

- Should a Catholic nursing home transfer a patient to a state institution when his or her insurance runs out?

- Should a Catholic hospital give staff privileges to a physician who won't accept Medicaid or uninsured patients?

If Catholic hospitals and other institutions take the consistent ethic seriously, then a number of responses follow. All Catholic hospitals will have outpatient programs to serve the needs of the poor. Catholic hospitals and other Church institutions will document the need for comprehensive prenatal programs and lead legislative efforts to get them enacted by state and national government. Catholic medical schools will teach students that medical ethics includes care for the poor—not merely an occasional charity case, but a commitment to see that adequate care is available.

If they take the consistent ethic seriously, Catholic institutions will lead efforts for adequate Medicaid coverage and reimbursement policies. They will lobby for preventive health programs for the poor. They will pay their staffs a just wage. Their staffs will receive training and formation to see God "hiding in the poor" and treat them with dignity.

I trust that each of you has an opinion about the importance or viability of responses to these challenges. My point in raising them is not to suggest simplistic answers to complex and difficult questions. I am a realist, and I know the difficulties faced by our Catholic institutions. Nonetheless, I do suggest that these questions arise out of a consistent ethic of life and present serious challenges to health care in this nation—and specifically to Catholic health care systems.

Medical ethics must include not only the "classical" questions but also contemporary social justice issues which affect health care. In a 1983 address to the World Medical Association, Pope John Paul II pointed out that developing an effective medical ethics—including the social justice dimension—

> fundamentally depends on the concept one forms of medicine. It is a matter of learning definitely whether medicine truly is in service of the human person, his dignity, what he has of the unique and transcendent in him, or whether medicine is considered first of all as the agent of the collectivity, at the service of the interests of the healthy and well-off, to whom care for the sick is subordinated.

He went on to remind his listeners that the Hippocratic oath defines medical morality in terms of respect and protection of the human person.

* * *

The consistent ethic of life is primarily a theological concept, derived from biblical and ecclesial tradition about the sacredness of human life, about our responsibilities to protect, defend, nurture and enhance God's gift of life. It provides a framework for moral analysis of the diverse impact of cultural factors—such as technology and contemporary distribution of resources—upon human life, both individual and collective.

The context in which we face new health care agendas generated both by technology and by poverty is that the Catholic health care system today confronts issues both of survival and of purpose. How shall we survive? For what purpose? The consistent ethic of life enables us to answer these questions by its comprehensiveness and the credibility which derives from its consistent application to the full spectrum of life issues.

Address

"Spanning the Barriers:
Catholic Health Care in a World of Need"*

Catholic Health Association, San Diego, California
—*June 4, 1986* ——————————————————————

Health care has ever been and will always be an essential component of the Church's mission. Caring for the sick, both personally and collectively through Catholic health care facilities, is an integral element of the Church's ministry. I come before you today, as a pastor, to speak about this ministry. I come as one who subscribes wholeheartedly to the commitment made by the U.S. bishops in their pastoral letter, *Health and Health Care:*

> We pledge ourselves to the preservation and further development of the rich heritage that is embodied in the Church's formal health apostolate. . . . We commit ourselves to do our part in maintaining and developing a Catholic institutional presence within the health care field in our country.

What I wish to do this morning is reflect with you on the implications of that statement. If health care is an integral component of the Church's mission, how should the whole Church be involved in health care ministry? What roles should the various members of the Church—laity, religious, clergy, and bishops—play in such a ministry? How does a reading of the "signs of the times" tend to shape that ministry today?

*Also published in *Health Progress*, September 1986.

I would like to set the broader context for these reflections by briefly recalling the historical development of Catholic health care services in this country and the changes which are occurring today.

Historically, the Church has supported a health care ministry primarily through various health care facilities. The impetus for Catholic hospitals in this country often came from religious congregations. In many instances, they saw the need for health care in a specific geographical area or among a particular group of immigrants. To respond to this need, the religious sought the approval of the diocesan bishop to initiate a health care ministry within his diocese. Sometimes the bishop himself invited the religious to establish such a facility. Whatever their origin, most bishops thought—and still think—of Catholic hospitals as indispensable to the Church's mission of service.

Nonetheless, in the past, each health care facility operated more or less on its own. Its relationship with the local diocese, for example, usually consisted in adherence to Catholic moral principles, provision of chaplains, and an occasional visit from the bishop to celebrate a special occasion. This relationship seemed suitable at the time. Catholic hospitals flourished, and the entire Church is both proud of and grateful for the outstanding service which they have given to their patients—regardless of race, religion, or socioeconomic status.

However, the health care scene in this nation has changed dramatically in recent years. Undoubtedly, you have looked long and hard this week—as you do every working day—at the difficulties Catholic hospitals face today because of limited resources, lower patient census, DRGs, the expense of advanced technology, and myriad other problematic circumstances. Because of media exposure and marketing programs, the general public is very much aware that hospitals are vigorously competing for health care business.

Perhaps the core of the present crisis facing Catholic hospitals is the fact that health care is being identified more and more as a "growth industry" or an "investment opportunity." How will we be able to remain faithful to our concept of mission and service in such an environment? How will we be able to balance a commitment to providing health care for the poor with the need for cost containment? The impact of these significant changes in contemporary health care is articulated clearly and forcefully in the report of the CHA Task Force on Health Care of the Poor. I understand that you are reflecting on that document during this annual meeting.

Recently a prominent physician wrote to me in anticipation of this address. He pointed out that, even as we speak about the Church's mission and healing ministry,

> the hard financial issues faced by our institutions are forcing us to choose between ministry and economic pressure. The choice of money

over ministry will ultimately lead to either the loss of a sense of mission and ministry, or a significant perversion of the meaning of these terms.

He then reflected on the concomitant crisis in Catholic health care, its service to the poor:

When mission and ministry are subverted to technologic competitiveness and financial survival, it is this population [the poor] that falls through the cracks.

In short, Catholic health care is in crisis. The battle for its very soul is being waged. We are at a fork in the road, and we must make critical decisions.

I wish to make it very clear, however, that I look upon the current situation as an opportunity for new growth, as a challenge to realize more fully than ever the Church's healing mission. While I share your anxieties, I do not despair. In fact, I am quite optimistic. First, God has entrusted this mission to the Church, and he always gives us what we need to carry out our responsibility. I believe this with all my heart and soul! Second, we have incredibly valuable human resources within the Church. All we need is to tap our creative potential to solve problems. We must pool our creative resources and energies. We need to span the barriers. We must work together to do what we cannot accomplish alone!

COLLABORATION

Today, with a greater awareness of health care as a ministry of the entire Church and with the severe crisis threatening individual hospitals, my basic thesis is that *collaboration* rather than competition will make the difference between survival and demise. It will provide the catalyst that brings about new growth.

Collaboration is intimately related to gospel values; it is, indeed, implicit in those values. When Jesus prayed at the Last Supper for those who would be his future followers, he did not pray that they would be successful or even that they would be happy! Instead, he prayed that they might be *one*—united—so that the world might believe the gospel. Through collaborative efforts we can witness to the fact that we are a living community based on a common faith, common values, and a common mission.

Many hospitals have already begun to collaborate with others. There are new hospital systems, systems of hospital systems, joint ventures. These relationships tend to strengthen each partner's position, thus enabling it to fulfill its mission better and serve its people more effectively. Nevertheless, it is important that, when such choices and decisions are made, adequate consideration be given to the potential harm that may be caused to other facilities in the area which share the same ecclesial mission.

Collaboration, however, does not imply getting rid of all competition. Competition is healthy when it provides an incentive to be unsatisfied with oneself, to improve, to excel, to be the best one can be. Such competition can lead health care providers to excellence, and this benefits the people they serve. However, competition is morally unacceptable when it is dishonest or when its primary purpose is to eliminate or destroy others. The basic motivation, if we are to preserve our values and very purpose of existence, must be the health and well-being of those we serve.

Within the Catholic health care apostolate, diverse talents—as well as the differing vocations of the laity, the religious, and the ordained—provide an excellent opportunity to witness to the kind of Church Jesus prayed for. In other words, even if there were no particular crisis facing Catholic health care today, the time would still be ripe for collaboration because of the renewal of Church life and ministry inaugurated by the Second Vatican Council.

Let us now reflect upon some of the changes and challenges facing three actors in the Church's health ministry: the religious, the laity, and the pastors of the Church.

THE ROLE OF THE RELIGIOUS

As I noted earlier, the extensive system of Catholic hospitals owes its existence primarily to the religious institutes of women and men that founded them. Today most of the Catholic acute care hospitals remain under the sponsorship of religious congregations. These congregations have enriched the Church with their diversity, their number, and their dedicated service. It is impossible to imagine the Church in the United States without them!

Although the decline in numbers of religious is undeniable, it would be a tragic loss to the Church and to its health apostolate if the unique witness provided by religious completely disappeared. For the sake of the kingdom, religious have left everything to follow Christ, reminding the rest of us that there is something more than the "here and now." They show us how to glorify God through selfless service to the deepest needs of the human family.

The primary responsibility to provide long-term direction to Catholic health care facilities and to ensure their mission effectiveness belongs to the sponsoring body, which, in most cases, is a religious congregation. This sponsorship is the element that perdures over the years despite changes in personnel and administration. The continuing and deeper involvement of many sponsors in directing their health care facilities is an encouraging sign for the future of Catholic health care.

Nonetheless, the leaders of religious communities necessarily have multiple concerns. Their responsibilities often extend beyond the individual health care institution to include other ministries to which the congregation is committed. They cannot neglect the well-being of the entire religious institute and its individual members. On the other hand, hospitals' chief executive officers, whether religious or lay, necessarily focus their attention on the good of their particular institution, and rightly so.

While, at times, there may be differences or tensions because of the differing priorities of the sponsors and the administrators, open communication about the mission needs and the business exigencies of an institution can lead to a healthy balance between Christian ministry and financial viability.

Another hopeful sign for the future of Catholic health care is the increasing effort to promote intercongregational cooperation and collaboration. Religious congregations often have more in common than they may, at first, think. Even though each congregation is shaped by the special charism of its founder or foundress, all are firmly rooted in the one Christ. A Chinese proverb says: "One moon shows in every pool; in every pool the one moon." Although every pool, pond, and puddle is different, a single source of light is reflected many times over. Likewise, the one Christ is reflected in each of us, different though we are. No one of us, either individually or gathered in community, can fully or perfectly mirror the Lord. His gifts and charisms are not meant solely for us; they are to be shared with others. They are not in competition but are eminently complementary.

If we were to examine the mission statements of your hospitals, we would undoubtedly discover in most of them an expression of or allusion to the unique charism which motivates the sponsoring congregation. But we would also find much common ground in the stated purposes: for example, in such concepts as the healing mission of Jesus, the sacredness of life, care for the total person, adherence to Catholic ethical standards, a concern for social justice, a special love for the poor. What each Catholic hospital shares in common with all the others—its Catholic vision of mission and service—provides the basis and the motivation for taking steps toward working together more closely. With these elements as building blocks we can begin to erect bridges between and among religious communities.

THE ROLE OF THE LAITY

Along with the religious who play such a significant role in Catholic health care, we need also to affirm the legitimate and, indeed, necessary role of the laity.

Although a lay apostolate has existed in the Church since its beginning, it has been given new emphasis and importance by the Second Vatican Council. There are two arenas of apostolic activity for the layperson: the secular world and the Church. The world, the marketplace, if not the exclusive area of the laity, is certainly their primary responsibility. Nonetheless, they also have an indispensable role to play within Church institutions as well.

Although it is important that the laity participate in health care endeavors sponsored by other than Catholic institutions, bringing gospel values and the principles of ethics and social justice to these settings, I will concentrate my reflections on the lay role in Catholic health care facilities.

While the laity have always been associated with religious in Catholic hospitals, it is only more recently that they have assumed positions of leadership in administration and governance. Whatever the reasons for this development, Catholic health care ministry must clearly continue to be a collaborative endeavor with both lay and religious participation.

To put it briefly, the expertise and insight which the layperson alone can offer is indispensable for effective ministry and for a more perfect reflection of the whole Church. Sometimes people mistakenly think that the mission aspects of health care are the responsibility of the religious and the clergy, and the business aspects the responsibility of the laity. The integration of both aspects is essential for both religious and laity.

Continuing education and formation in spirituality, theology, and faith development, however, are required to make this an actuality. While religious have been afforded intensive Christian formation within their congregations, laypersons often have not had similar opportunities. Retreats, value-oriented seminars, and educational programs in the Catholic philosophy of health care can build bridges toward mutual understanding.

Organizations, such as the Academy of Catholic Health Care Leadership, can strengthen Catholic health care ministry through education and formation of their members. The CHA Task Force on Health Care of the Poor recommends that the CHA develop "a seminar on the spirituality, mission, and ethical concerns involved in service of the poor" for adaptation by sponsoring groups, systems, and local facilities. This would undoubtedly be a welcome help in the education and formation of board members and employees.

Catholic hospitals and other health care facilities will survive and even grow in number for service to future generations only if their leadership has a thorough understanding of the philosophy of Catholic health care and a personal commitment to it as a vital Church ministry. The formation of lay leadership becomes even more essential as we explore models of lay sponsorship as an alternative to more traditional means of sponsoring Catholic health facilities.

T HE ROLE OF THE CHURCH'S PASTORS

What role do the pastors of the Church play in regard to health care? Although I will primarily speak in terms of bishops, I wish to include all the clergy under the rubric of "pastors."

Because most Catholic hospitals are sponsored by religious communities, bishops are quite sensitive to their autonomy and particular responsibilities. At the same time, because they provide health care within the local churches, bishops, as shepherds of those communities, also have an important role to play in helping health care institutions carry out their individual missions.

The bishop is the leader, the spokesperson, the representative of the Church in his region. His responsibility, however, is not to control but "to foster the various aspects of the apostolate within his diocese and see to it that within the entire diocese or within its individual districts all the works of the apostolate are coordinated under his direction, with due regard for their distinctive character" (Revised Code of Canon Law, Can. 394).

While he may not interfere in the internal affairs of a religious institute or its institutions, he must be solicitous in those matters which pertain to works of the apostolate. In hospital planning and the expansion or curtailment of services, communication and consultation with the bishop can offer another perspective to meeting the needs of the community.

Because health care is so vital to the Church's overall mission, the bishop exercises a moral leadership when he facilitates a continued Catholic presence in the provision of quality health care for those who need it—including the poor. Especially where several Catholic hospitals are located in a city or metropolitan region, we must find ways to translate dreams and concerns about cooperation and collaboration into reality.

The report of your Task Force on Health Care for the Poor strikes me as a document of uncommon vision and realism. Detailing the increasingly difficult problems surrounding the accessibility to adequate health care for the indigent, the report recommends a plan of action which includes greater cooperation between health care providers, Church agencies, and government to assure all citizens the right to health care. Through efforts such as these, we are building bridges, consistent with and faithful to our mission.

To underline the fact that we can come up with creative solutions to the problems facing health care, I would like to share with you some of the initiatives being taken in the Archdiocese of Chicago. I do so not to suggest that we have all the answers but rather that many of the recommendations in your Task Force report are feasible.

This past Sunday I attended the dedication ceremonies of the Howard Area Center of St. Francis Hospital. This represents a collaborative venture of St. Francis Hospital, which is in Evanston, Illinois, and the Howard Area Community Center in Chicago. Its purpose is to provide health care and education for the many poor in the area, especially newly arrived Spanish-speaking immigrants.

Loyola University of Chicago recently sponsored a symposium on Limited Resources and Commitment to the Poor. It was a response to an address on "The Consistent Ethic of Life and Health Care Systems" which I delivered there at the Foster McGaw Triennial Conference last May. During the symposium the executive dean of the Stritch School of Medicine raised the possibility, among others, of Loyola's establishing a community-based primary care satellite clinic in Maywood, one of the poorer suburbs of the Chicago area.

In the past two years we have been developing an area ministry in Englewood, an inner-city neighborhood. Because poverty is widespread in the area, the ten Catholic parishes devote considerable resources to social services. In addition to a Catholic hospital within its boundaries, Englewood also has a clinic staffed by volunteers at St. Basil's parish and a primary health care center run by the Alexian Brothers at Our Lady of Solace parish. The St. Basil operation is two years old and has served between five and six thousand persons. The Our Lady of Solace center is less than a year old, but has served about five hundred people in the past three months.

Motivated by my own concern for the future viability of Catholic health care, over a year ago I called together the chief executive officers of the twenty-three Catholic hospitals in the archdiocese, along with representatives of the sixteen religious congregations that sponsor them. Our purpose was to discuss how joint effort and collaboration would strengthen our position, and hence our mission, in a highly competitive environment.

The participants agreed to undertake a professional study to ascertain the level of interest in joint action and to chart possible directions for the future. Based upon interviews with the CEOs, the provincials, archdiocesan officials, and several respected health care experts, the study advocated a change. It indicated that to continue a "business as usual" approach would bring far greater risks than the new model it was proposing. No change would weaken the competitive business position of surviving Catholic hospitals in the archdiocese and diminish their capacity overall to fulfill their mission. A number of them would be picked off—one by one, usually in the poorer sections of the city. To minimize these risks, the report recommended the development of several formalized structures for joint action which would support both the charitable and the business outreach of Catholic hospitals.

In effect, these structures will establish a new network involving the hospitals, the sponsors, and the archdiocese and making possible joint action aimed at improving the hospitals' *market-competitive positions*, promoting *governance continuity*, and *ensuring maximum mission effectiveness*.

While full acceptance of all the actions recommended by this study is not yet definitive, there is a consensus that the recommendations be pursued and steps taken toward implementation. With the number of people involved, understandably it will take some time to implement fully this collaborative effort. I personally have no intention of turning back, and I am confident that that is true of most of the others who are involved.

These are but a few examples of current efforts being undertaken in one local church. The task before us throughout this nation is enormous, but I am convinced that we have the motivation, the creativity, and the collective strength to see Catholic health care through this time of change and crisis. I also firmly believe that collaboration—difficult though it may be—is the key to both the survival and the growth of Catholic health care institutions. Collaboration strengthens the weaker institutions and benefits the entire health care apostolate of the Church.

No one of us has all the answers to the complex problems and challenges which health care providers face today. Now is the time for all those who have a stake in and a responsibility for Catholic health care—religious, laity, and pastors—to join together. We must face the challenges together if we are to strengthen and expand the compassionate healing work which we do in Jesus' name.

Address

"The Consistent Ethic of Life and Health Care Reform"*

National Press Club, Washington, D.C.
─── *May 26, 1994* ─────────────────────────────────

As many of you may know, in the last year I have experienced a significant amount of press coverage for reasons that are happily behind me.
There is a temptation in this prestigious forum to share some of my reactions and reflections based on that experience, but I am going to resist
that temptation. At another time and after more reflection on my part, I
might share some thoughts about what I learned about the news media
and related topics. But today I address a more important and more timely
topic—the moral dimensions of health care reform.

For the last decade as a pastor, a bishop, and a leader of our National Conference of Catholic Bishops, I have had the opportunity to address a series
of vital moral challenges. I chaired the committee that produced the pastoral letter on war and peace a decade ago. I have served as chair of our bishops' committees on pro-life matters and family-life concerns. As a bishop, I
have also seen the crime, injustice, and violence in our neighborhoods and
the loss of roots and responsibility in our cities, the loss of the sense of family and caring in our communities that is undermining millions of lives.

*Also published in *Origins*, vol. 24, no. 4, June 9, 1994, pp. 60–64; *A Moral
Vision for America* (Georgetown University Press, 1998); and *Celebrating the
Ministry of Healing: Joseph Cardinal Bernardin's Reflections on Healthcare*
(Catholic Health Association, 1999).

I believe that at the heart of so many of our problems—in Chicago and Washington, in Bosnia and Rwanda—there is a fundamental lack of respect for human life and human dignity. Over the past ten years I have articulated a "consistent ethic of life" as a moral framework to address the growing violence in our midst.

The purpose of the consistent life ethic is to provide a moral framework for analysis and motivation for action on a wide range of human life-issues with important ethical dimensions. The consistent life ethic, by design, provides for a public discourse that respects the separation of Church and state, and also recognizes the proper role of religious perspectives and ethical convictions in the public life of a pluralistic society.

Over the past years I have addressed many issues in the light of the consistent ethic. In addition to the central question of abortion, I have spoken about euthanasia and assisted suicide, capital punishment, the newer technologies used to assist human reproduction, and war and peace, to name a few. The foundation for all of these discussions is a deep conviction about the nature of human life, namely, that human life is sacred, which means that all human life has an inalienable dignity that must be protected and respected from conception to natural death. For the Christian believer and many others, the source of this dignity is the creative action of God in whose "image and likeness" we are made. Still others are aware that life is a precious gift which must be protected and nurtured.

For advocates of a consistent life ethic, the national debate about health care reform represents both an opportunity and a test. It is an *opportunity* to address issues and policies that are often matters of life and death, such as, who is covered and who is not; which services are included and which are not; will reform protect human life and enhance dignity, or will it threaten or undermine life and dignity? It is a *test* in the sense that we will be measured by the comprehensiveness of our concerns and the consistency of our principles in this area.

In this current debate, a consistent life ethic approach to health care requires us to stand up for both the unserved and the unborn, to insist on the inclusion of real universal coverage and the exclusion of abortion coverage, to support efforts to restrain rising health costs, and to oppose the denial of needed care to the poor and vulnerable. In standing with the unserved and the unborn, the uninsured and the undocumented, we bring together our pro-life and social justice values. They are the starting points for a consistent life agenda for health care reform.

In these remarks I speak as a pastor of a diverse local church. In Chicago we see both the strengths and the difficulties of our current system. We experience the remarkable dedication, professionalism, and caring of the *people* and the amazing contributions of the *institutions* that make up our health care system. I also see the children without care, the sick without options, the communities without adequate health services, the families and businesses strained and broken by health care costs. We see the hurts and pick up the pieces of a failing system—in our hospitals and clinics, our shelters and agencies, our parishes and schools. We look at health care reform from the bottom up, not who wins or loses politically, not how it impacts powerful institutions and professions, but how it touches the poor and vulnerable, the unserved and the unborn, the very young and the very old.

As I indicated earlier, I am also a member of the National Conference of Catholic Bishops, an organization deeply involved in this debate. Our principles and priorities are summarized in a resolution unanimously adopted by the conference last year. A unanimous vote of our bishops is an unusual accomplishment, as those of you who have ever seen us discuss holy days or liturgical texts can attest! But we found unity in embracing a consistent life ethic approach to health care reform.

The broader health care debate is driven by many factors. For the sake of time, I will list only five without discussing them at any length.

(1) The amount of money spent on health care is escalating at an unsustainable rate. It surpassed 14 percent of the gross domestic product (GDP) last year, and it is reasonable to assume that, without effective intervention, it could reach 18 percent of the GDP by the year 2000.

(2) This uncontrolled growth is creating economic hardships for many of our fellow citizens, especially working families.

(3) Private insurance programs are deteriorating through risk segmentation into programs that more and more serve those who have the least need for health insurance—the healthy.

(4) Cost shifting—that is, the passing on of unreimbursed expenses by health providers to employer premiums—has become a "hidden tax" that no longer is sustainable.

(5) Finally, and most significantly, the number of uninsured in the United States continues, now approaching nearly 40 million, a large portion of whom are people who work. Ten million are children. This lack of coverage touches African-American and Hispanic families most directly.

I join the many who have concluded that the United States needs profound systemic change in its health care system. We cannot rely on the system to correct itself. Without intervention, things are getting worse, not better.

I hasten to add that my advocacy is not partisan. Neither do I argue on behalf of any particular proposal before the Congress. I do, however, take exception with those who say that there is no serious systemic problem or that what we merely face is an insurance or a health care delivery problem. On the contrary, there *is* a fundamental health care problem in our nation today. I share this judgment with many leaders of the Catholic community whose outlook and convictions have been shaped

- by the experience of Catholic religious communities and dioceses that operate 600 hospitals and 300 long-term care facilities, constituting the largest nonprofit group of health care providers in the United States;

- by the experience of the Catholic Church in the United States, which purchases health coverage for hundreds of thousands of employees and their families;

- by the experience of Catholic Charities, the largest private deliverer of social services in the nation;

- by our experience as a community of faith, caring for those who "fall through the cracks" of our current system.

It is this broad range of experience that led the U.S. Catholic bishops to say last June:

> Now is the time for real health care reform. It is a matter of fundamental justice. For so many it is literally a matter of life and death, of lives cut short and dignity denied. We urge our national leaders to look beyond special interest claims and partisan differences to unite our nation in a new commitment to meet the health care needs of our people, especially the poor and the vulnerable. This is a major political task, a significant policy challenge and a moral imperative.

Before addressing some of the more specific issues associated with health care reform, it is important that we consider some even more profound issues. I say this because President Clinton's health care reform proposal and the alternatives to it, like any significant government initiatives that would reorder social relationships and responsibilities, have drawn us into a discussion of fundamental values and social convictions. Several important convictions, which serve as a kind of bedrock for the consistent life ethic, can assist us in this broader discussion. They are:

1. There are *basic goods and values* which we human beings share because we share the gift of human life; these goods and values serve as the common ground for a public morality that guides our actions as a nation and as a society.

2. Within the individual, these common goods and values express themselves in an inalienable human dignity, with consequent *rights* and *duties*.

3. One of the ways these rights and duties are expressed in the human community is through the recognition and *pursuit of the common good;* or, to say it differently, through a good that is to be pursued in common with all of society; a good that ultimately is more important than the good of any individual.

4. This common good is realized in the context of a *living community*, which is nurtured by the virtues and shared values of individuals. Such a community protects the basic rights of individuals.

5. As part of this community, both individuals and institutions (including government, business, education, labor, and other mediating structures) have an *obligation,* which is rooted in distributive justice, to *work to secure this common good;* this is how we go about meeting the reasonable claims of citizens striving to realize and experience their fundamental human dignity.

These convictions find their origin in a vision of the human person as someone who is grounded in community, and in an understanding of society and government as being largely responsible for the realization of the common good. As Catholics we share this vision with many others. It is consistent with fundamental American values, though grounded differently. For example, our Declaration of Independence and our Constitution reflect a profound insight that has guided the development of our nation; namely, that there are certain fundamental human rights that exist before the creation of any social contract (such as the constitution of a sovereign nation), and that these must be protected by society and government. There is an objective order to which we are held accountable and to which we, in turn, hold others accountable in our many relationships and activities. The Catholic tradition also affirms such rights but sees them emerging from the organic relationship between the individual and the community.

As a nation, we also have had a sense of a common good which is greater than the agenda of any individual. Alexis de Tocqueville noted this when he commented on the American penchant for volunteering. We also have been a nation of communities. Whether in the small towns of the Great Plains or the ethnic communities of the large cities, U.S. citizens had a sense of being bonded together and being mutually responsible. We also recognized that our individual and collective existence is best protected by virtuous living—balancing the demands of personhood and social responsibility. In more recent years, as our social order has become more complex, we have come to see that a proper sense of mutual responsibility requires a greater presence of the state in helping individuals to realize their human potential and social responsibility. Public education and social security are but two examples of this presence.

Without being overly pessimistic, I suggest that these fundamental convictions, which are essential both to a consistent life ethic and to our well-being as a nation and a society, are being challenged today. There is abroad a certain tendency which would suggest that law and public order are accountable only to the subjective convictions of individuals or pressure groups, not to any objective, albeit imperfectly perceived, moral order. Robert Bellah and his associates have convincingly shown how a sense of the common good, the role of community, and the value of virtuous living have been compromised, if not lost, in recent years. I am convinced that the violence that plagues our nation is a symptom of this loss of an overarching social order. We are a nation that is increasingly overly individualistic at the very time when the problems we face require greater common effort and collective responses.

All of this needs to be taken into consideration in any substantive discussion of health care reform. If we are not attentive to issues such as these, then our dialogues and debates will go nowhere because of disagreements—unknown and unacknowledged—on basic principles.

First, there is the issue of *universal access*. In the June 1993 statement I cited earlier, the U.S. Catholic bishops outlined key principles and priorities for initiating and executing reform. Our third principle was universal access to comprehensive health care for every person living in the United States.

We believe that health care—including preventive and primary care—is not only a commodity; it is an essential safeguard of human life and dignity. In 1981 the bishops spoke of health care as a "basic human right which flows from the sanctity of human life." In declaring this, the bishops were not saying that a person had a right to *health*, but that, since the common good is the sum of those conditions necessary to preserve human dignity, one must have a right of *access*, insofar as it is possible, to those goods and services which will allow a person to maintain or regain health. And if one views this right within the context of the convictions I have just discussed, then it is the responsibility of society as a whole and government to ensure that there is a common social order that makes the realization of this good possible. Whether we have health care should not depend on whom we work for, how much our parents earn, or where we live.

So far, so good. Most would agree, at least in theory. Where the disagreement comes is in regard to the last of the convictions I noted in discussing the consistent ethic. Allow me to rephrase it.

> Under the title of distributive justice, society has the obligation to meet the reasonable claims of its citizens so that they can realize and exercise their fundamental human rights.

When many of us Americans think of justice, we tend to think of what we can claim from one another. This is an individualistic understanding of justice. But there is another American instinct which has a broader understanding of justice. It has been summarized by Father Philip Keane, a moral theologian, who wrote: "justice shifts our thinking from what we claim from each other to what we *owe* to each other. Justice is about duties and responsibilities, about building the good community." In this perspective, distributive justice is the obligation which falls upon society to meet the reasonable expectations of its citizens so that they can realize and exercise their fundamental human rights. And, in this instance, the right is that of access to those goods and services that make it possible for persons to maintain their health and thus broaden health care beyond what is provided by a hospital, a clinic, or a physician.

So far I have argued that health care is an essential safeguard of human life and dignity and that there is an obligation for society to ensure that a person be able to realize this right. I now want to go a step further. I believe that the only way this obligation can be effectively met by society is for our nation to make *universal health care coverage* a reality. Universal *access* is not enough. We can no longer tolerate being the only Western nation that leaves millions of persons uncovered. For many, this will be a "hard saying." The cry of political expediency and the maneuvering of special interest groups already are working either to provide a program of access that maintains a two-tiered health care system (which marginalizes large portions of our society) or to limit coverage. When I speak of universal coverage, I do not mean a vague promise or a rhetorical preamble to legislation, but the *practical means* and *sufficient investment* to permit all to obtain decent health care on a regular basis.

If justice is a hallmark of our national community, then we must fulfill our obligations in justice to the poor and the unserved *first* and not last. Similarly, we cannot ignore the millions of undocumented immigrants. Even if the demands of justice were set aside, reasons of public health would necessitate their being included. The undocumented will continue to need medical assistance, and hospitals will continue to be required to provide medical care for those who present themselves for treatment. In a reformed system, which should contain, if not eliminate, the cost-shifting that previously had paid for their care, the medical expenses of the undocumented must be covered for both policy and moral reasons.

Unfortunately, as the national debate on health care reform has evolved, and as legislation has been proposed, an important fact has been lost; namely, that it is not enough simply to expand coverage. If real reform is to be achieved—that is, reform that will ensure quality and cost-effective care—then we must do what is necessary in order to ensure that our health care delivery system is person-centered and has a community focus. Health care cannot be successfully reformed if it is considered only an economic matter. This reform will be morally blighted if the nature of care—something profoundly human, not easily measured, yet that which,

far more than technology, remains the heart and breath of the art of healing—is not preserved and expanded along with health coverage itself. The
challenge is to provide universal coverage without seriously disrupting the
doctor/patient relationship which is so central to good medical care.

After a long period of research and discussion, the Catholic Health Association (CHA) developed a proposal for health care reform that seeks
to meet this and other challenges. It is called "Setting Relationships
Right." I hope that the values CHA has proposed and the strategies it has
developed in this regard will not be lost sight of. Our objective must be a
healthy nation where the mental and physical health of the individual is
addressed through collaborative efforts at the local level.

Let me summarize my major points so far. First, we need a profound systemic reform of our health care system. Second, justice and the common
good demand that this reform include universal coverage. Third, justice at
this time requires a program of effective universal coverage that is person-
centered and community-based. This leads us to two thorny questions:
How is the program to be funded, and how are costs to be contained?

As you know, these two questions are essentially interrelated. It is clear
that the rate of cost increases in health care cannot be sustained even if
there is no systemic reform. It also is clear that the demands of a more
fiscally responsible use of federal monies must be taken into account. We
cannot spend what we do not have.

Our episcopal conference has insisted that health care reform must
also include effective mechanisms to restrain rising health care costs.
Without cost containment, we cannot make health care affordable and direct scarce national resources to other pressing national problems. Containing costs is crucial if we are to avoid dangerous pressures toward the
kind of rationing that raises fundamental ethical and equity questions.
The poor, vulnerable, and uninsured persons cannot be denied needed
care because the health system refuses to eliminate waste, duplication,
and bureaucratic costs.

But we may also have to consider other steps to restrain costs and distribute health care more justly. For example, we may have to recognize
that basic and preventive care, and health care to preserve and protect life,
should be a higher priority than purely elective procedures. This raises the
often explosive concept of "rationing." I prefer a different word and a different concept—"stewardship." How do we best protect human life and
enhance human dignity in a situation of limited health resources? How do
we ensure that the lives and health of the poor and vulnerable are not less
valuable or less a priority than the lives and health of the rest of us?

This is not an abstract discussion. Rationing health care is a regular, if
unacknowledged, feature of our current health care system. Nearly 40
million are uninsured; 50 million more are underinsured. In 1992 nearly

10 million children were without medical coverage, 400,000 more than in 1991. In my own state of Illinois, 86,000 persons lose their health insurance each month. Being without insurance means being without care when you need it, delaying care until an illness or injury may require more costly intervention or be beyond any treatment.

We now have an insurance model that requires individuals to pay for the items and services which their health care needs require—some without limitations and others with enormous constraints. We have been rationing health care in recent years by squeezing people out of the system through insurance marketing techniques like medical underwriting, preexisting condition exclusion, and insurance red-lining. Actuarial pricing designed to protect insurance company assets pits one group against another—the old against the young, the sick against the healthy—thus undermining the solidarity of the whole community. We can see this tension playing itself out in the disturbing debates around this country about assisted suicide.

In light of these concerns, the nation must undertake a broad-based and inclusive consideration of how we will choose to allocate and share our health care dollars. We are stewards, not sole owners, of all our resources, human and material; thus, goods and services must be shared. This is not a task for government alone. Institutions and individuals must be involved in reaching a shared moral consensus, which will allow us to reassert the essential value of the person as an individual and as a member of the community. From that moral consensus must come a process of decision-making and resource allocation which preserves the dignity of all persons, in particular the most vulnerable. It is proper for society to establish limits on what it can reasonably provide in one area of the commonweal so that it can address other legitimate responsibilities to the community. But in establishing such limits, the inalienable life and dignity of every person, in particular the vulnerable, must be protected.

The Catholic Health Association has addressed the ethics of rationing and offered some moral criteria. These demand that any acceptable plan must meet a demonstrable need, be oriented to the common good, apply to all, result from an open and participatory process, give priority to disadvantaged persons, be free of wrongful discrimination, and be monitored in its social and economic effects.

This kind of framework offers far better guidance than the moral bankruptcy of assisted suicide and the ethically unacceptable withholding of care based on "quality of life" criteria. We will measure any cost containment initiative by two values: Does it distribute resources more justly? And does it protect the lives and dignity of the poor and vulnerable?

But the problem of rationed access to necessary medical care is only one aspect of the cost containment debate. What of the issue of *funding*? Obviously I cannot offer a detailed analysis of the specific proposals which are on the table. But I can say this: If systemic reform addresses in a substantive manner issues of quality care and cost effectiveness, then justice will demand that all sectors of our society contribute to the support of these efforts. And this support takes two forms. First, each individual must assume appropriate responsibility for the costs associated with health care and must assume responsibility to do all that is possible not to put his or her health at risk. Second, those segments of our economic order which have been able to avoid an appropriate level of responsibility for the health care of their employees must begin to assume their fair share, just as the rest of society must. In other words, we all must be willing to help meet this demand of justice. We must share the sacrifices that will have to be made.

Thus far, I have insisted that a consistent life ethic requires a commitment to genuine universal coverage, because lack of coverage threatens the lives and diminishes the dignity of millions of men, women, and children. I must also say clearly and emphatically that a consistent life ethic requires us to lift the burden of mandated abortion coverage from needed health care reform. I say this for several important reasons:

(1) It is morally wrong to coerce millions of people into paying for the destruction of unborn children against their consciences and convictions. How ironic it would be if advocates of "choice," as they call themselves, require me and millions like me to obtain and pay for abortion coverage, which we abhor. It is a denial of "choice," a violation of conscience, and a serious blow to the common good.

(2) It is politically destructive. Needed national health care reform must not be burdened by abortion coverage, which neither the country nor the Congress supports. Public opinion polls and recent congressional action clearly indicate that, whatever their views on the morality or legality of abortion, the American people and their representatives do not wish to coerce all citizens into paying for procedures that so divide our nation. A University of Cincinnati poll in January of this year indicated that only 30 percent favor the inclusion of abortion as a basic benefit even if it could be included at no cost at all. Only 14 percent wanted abortion coverage if it would add to the cost of health premiums.

(3) Abortion mandates would undermine the participation of Catholic and other religious providers of health care, who now provide essential care in many of the nation's most underserved communities. I fear our hospitals will be unable to fulfill their mission and meet their responsibilities in a system where abortion is a mandated benefit. Strong conscience clauses are necessary to deal with a vari-

ety of medical/moral issues, but are not sufficient to protect Catholic and other providers who find abortion morally objectionable. The only remedy is not to link needed reform to abortion mandates.

The sooner the burden of abortion mandates is lifted, the better for the cause of reform. We continue to insist that it would be a grave moral tragedy, a serious policy mistake, and a major political error to link health care reform to abortion. An insistence on abortion coverage will turn millions of advocates of reform into adversaries of health care legislation.

We cannot and will not support reform that fails to offer universal coverage or that insists on abortion mandates. While this offers moral consistency, it can place us in conflicting political alliances. For example, we concur with the position of the President and Mrs. Clinton in calling real universal coverage essential. We concur with Representative Henry Hyde and the pro-life caucus in insisting that abortion coverage must be abandoned. We concur with the Hispanic Caucus in our commitment that universal coverage must be truly "universal coverage."

This is our consistent ethic message to the White House, the Congress, and the country. We are advocates of these key principles and priorities, not any particular plan. We will not choose between our key priorities. We will work with the leaders of our land to pass health care reform, reform that reflects a true commitment to human life and human dignity. As I noted above, the polls indicate that most Americans join us in support for both authentic universal coverage and the exclusion of abortion coverage in health care reform. We will carry this message forward with civility and consistency. We offer our moral convictions and practical experience, not political contributions and endorsements. We have no "attack ads" or PAC funds. But we can be a valuable partner for reform, and we will work tirelessly for real reform without abortion mandates.

For defenders of human life, there is no more important or timely task than offering an ethical and effective contribution to the health care debate. The discussions and decisions over the next months will tell us a lot about what kind of society we are and will become. We must ask ourselves: What are the choices, investments, and sacrifices we are willing to make in order to protect and enhance the life and dignity of all, especially the poor and vulnerable? In the nation's Capitol, health care reform is seen primarily as a *political* challenge—the task of developing attractive and workable proposals, assembling supportive coalitions, and securing the votes needed to pass a bill. But fundamentally, health care reform is a *moral* challenge—finding the values and vision to reshape a major part of national life to protect better the life and dignity of all.

Ultimately, this debate is not simply about politics—about which party or interest group prevails. It is about *children*, who die because of the lack of prenatal care or the violence of abortion. About *people* who have no health care because of where they work or where they come from. About *communities* without care, and workers without coverage.

Health care reform is both a *political* task and a *moral* test. As a religious community with much at stake and much to contribute to this debate, we are working for health care reform that truly reaches out to the unserved, protects the unborn, and advances the common good.

Address

"Making the Case for Not-for-Profit Health Care"*

Harvard Business School Club of Chicago
Chicago, Illinois
—*January 12, 1995* ——————————————

Good afternoon. It is a privilege to address the Harvard Business School Club of Chicago on the critical, but often conflicted issue of health care. Because of its central importance to human dignity, to the quality of our community life, and to the Church's mission in the world, I have felt a special responsibility to devote a considerable amount of attention to health care at both the local and national levels.

In the last year, I have spoken at the National Press Club on the need to ensure access to adequate health care for all; I have issued a protocol to help ensure the future presence of a strong, institutional health care ministry in the Archdiocese of Chicago; and in order to be more in touch with ongoing developments in the field, I have joined the Board of Trustees of the Catholic Health Association of the United States—the national organization that represents more than 900 Catholic acute and long-term care facilities.

In the interest of full disclosure, I must warn you that this considerable activity does *not* qualify me as a health care expert. Health care policy is challenging and extraordinarily complicated, and in this area I am every bit

*Also published in *Origins*, vol. 24, no. 32, January 26, 1995, pp. 538–42; and *Celebrating the Ministry of Healing: Joseph Cardinal Bernardin's Reflections on Healthcare* (Catholic Health Association, 1999).

the layman. But because of its central importance in our lives—socially, economically, ethically and personally—we "nonexperts" avoid the health care challenge at our peril.

I come before you today in several capacities. First, as the Catholic archbishop of Chicago who has pastoral responsibility for numerous Catholic health care institutions in the archdiocese—though each is legally and financially independent. Second, as a community leader who cares deeply about the quality and availability of health care services throughout metropolitan Chicago and the United States. And third, as an individual who, like you, will undoubtedly one day become sick and vulnerable and require the services of competent and caring medical professionals and hospitals.

The Growing Threat to Not-for-Profit Health Care

In each role I am becoming increasingly concerned that our health care delivery system is rapidly commercializing itself, and in the process is abandoning core values that should always be at the heart of health care. These developments have potentially deleterious consequences for patients and society as a whole. This afternoon, I will focus on one important aspect of this problem: the future vitality and integrity of not-for-profit hospitals.

Not-for-profit hospitals constitute the overwhelming majority of Chicagoland hospitals. They represent more than three-quarters of the non-public acute-care general hospitals in the country. Not-for-profit hospitals are the core of this nation's private, voluntary health care delivery system, but are in jeopardy of becoming for-profit enterprises.

Not-for-profit hospitals began as philanthropic social institutions, with the primary purpose of serving the health care needs of their communities. In recent decades, they have become important nongovernmental "safety net" institutions, taking care of the growing numbers of uninsured and underinsured persons. Indeed, most not-for-profit hospitals regard the provision of community benefit as their principal mission. Unfortunately, this historic and still necessary role is being compromised by changing economic circumstances in health care, and by an ideological challenge to the very notion of not-for-profit health care.

Both an excess number of hospital beds and cost-conscious choices by employers, insurers and government have forced not-for-profits into new levels of competition for *paying* patients. They are competing with one another, with investor-owned hospitals, and with for-profit ambulatory facilities. In their struggle for economic survival, a growing number of not-for-profits are sacrificing altruistic concerns for the bottomline.

The not-for-profit presence in health care delivery is also threatened by a body of opinion that contends there is no fundamental distinction between medical care and a commodity exchanged for profit. It is argued that health care delivery is like other necessary economic goods such as food, clothing, and shelter and should be subject to unbridled market competition.

According to this view, economic competition in health care delivery is proposed as a welcome development with claims that it is the surest way to eliminate excess hospital and physician capacity, reduce health care prices, and assure the "industry's" long-term efficiency. Many proponents of this view question the need for not-for-profit hospitals since they believe investor-owned institutions operate more efficiently than their not-for-profit counterparts and can better attract needed capital. Thus, they attack the not-for-profit hospital tax-exemption as an archaic and unwarranted subsidy that distorts the health care market by providing exempt institutions an unfair competitive advantage.

This afternoon, I will make three arguments: first, that there is a fundamental difference between the provision of medical care and the production and distribution of commodities; second, that the not-for-profit structure is better aligned with the essential mission of health care delivery than is the investor-owned model; and third, that leaders in both the private and public sector have a responsibility to find ways to preserve and strengthen the not-for-profit hospital and health care delivery system in the United States. Before making these arguments I need to clarify an important point.

THE ADVANTAGES OF CAPITALISM AND FREE ENTERPRISE

In drawing the distinction between medical care and other commodities on the one hand, and not-for-profit and investor-owned institutions on the other, I am not expressing any general bias against capitalism or the American free enterprise system. We are all beneficiaries of the genius of that system. To paraphrase Pope John Paul II: If by capitalism is meant an economic system which recognizes the fundamental and positive role of business, the market, private property, and the resulting responsibility for the means of production—as well as free human creativity in the economic sector—then its contribution to American society has been most beneficial.

As a key element of the free enterprise system, the American business corporation has proved itself to be an efficient mechanism for encouraging and minimizing commercial risk. It has enabled individuals to engage in commercial activities which none of them could manage alone. In this regard, the purpose of the business corporation is specific: to earn a growing profit and a reasonable rate of return for the individuals who have created it. The essential element here is a *reasonable* rate of return, for without it the commercial corporation cannot exist.

SOCIETY'S NONECONOMIC GOODS

That being said, it is important to recognize that not all of society's institutions have as their essential purpose earning a reasonable rate of return on capital. For example, the purpose of the family is to provide a protective and nurturing environment in which to raise children. The purpose of education at all levels is to produce knowledgeable and productive citizens. And the primary purpose of social services is to produce shelter, counseling, food, and other programs for people and communities in need. Generally speaking, each of these organizations has as its essential purpose a noneconomic goal: the advancement of human dignity.

And this is as it should be. While economics is indeed important, most of us would agree that the value of human life and the quality of the human condition are seriously diminished when reduced to purely economic considerations. Again, to quote Pope John Paul II, the idea that the entirety of social life is to be determined by market exchanges is to run "the risk of an 'idolatry' of the market, an idolatry which ignores the existence of *goods which by their nature are not and cannot be mere commodities*" (emphasis added).

This understanding is consistent with the American experience. In the belief that the noneconomic ends of the family, social services and education are essential to the advancement of human dignity and to the quality of our social and economic life, we have treated them quite differently from most other goods and services. Specifically, we have not made their allocation dependent solely on a person's ability to afford them. For example, we recognize that individual human dignity is enhanced through a good education, and that we all benefit by having an educated society; so we make an elementary and secondary education available to everyone, and heavily subsidize it thereafter. By contrast, we think it quite appropriate that hair spray, compact discs, and automobiles be allocated entirely by their affordability.

HEALTH CARE: NOT SIMPLY A COMMODITY

Now it is my contention that health care delivery is one of those "goods which by their nature are not and cannot be mere commodities." I say this because health care involves one of the most intimate aspects of our lives—our bodies and, in many ways, our minds and spirits as well. The quality of our life, our capacity to participate in social and economic activities, and very often life itself are at stake in each serious encounter with the medical care system. This is why we expect health care delivery to be a competent *and* a caring response to the broken human condition—to human vulnerability.

To be sure, we expect our physician to earn a good living and our hospital to be economically viable, but when it comes to *our* case we do not expect them to be motivated mainly by economic self-interest. When it comes to *our* coronary by-pass or *our* hip replacement or *our* child's cancer treatment, we expect them to be professional in the original sense of that term—motivated primarily by patient need, not economic self-interest. We have no comparable expectation—nor should we—of General Motors or Wal-Mart. When we are sick, vulnerable and preoccupied with worry we depend on our physician to be our confidant, our advocate, our guide and agent in an environment that is bewildering for most of us, and where matters of great importance are at stake.

The availability of good health care is also vital to the character of community life. We would not think well of ourselves if we permitted health care institutions to let the uninsured sick and injured go untreated. We endeavor to take care of the poor and the sick as much for our benefit as for theirs. Accordingly, most Americans believe society should provide everyone access to adequate health care services just as it ensures that everyone have an education through grade twelve. There is a practical aspect to this aspiration as well because, like education, health care entails community-wide needs which it impacts in various ways: We all benefit from a healthy community; and we all suffer from a lack of health, especially with respect to communicable disease.

Finally, health care is particularly subject to what economists call *market failure*. Most health care "purchases" are not predictable, nor do medical services come in standardized packages and different grades suitable for comparison shopping and selection—most are specific to individual need. Moreover, it would be wrong to suggest that seriously ill patients defer their health care purchases while they shop around for the best price. Nor do we expect people to pay the full cost of catastrophic, financially devastating illnesses. This is why most developed nations spread the risk of these high-cost episodes through public and/or private health insurance. And due to the prevalence of health insurance, or third party payment, most of us do not pay for our health care at the time it is delivered. Thus, we are inclined to demand an infinite amount of the very best care available. In short, health care does not lend itself to market discipline in the same way as most other goods and services.

So health care—like the family, education, and social services—is *special*. It is fundamentally different from most other goods because it is essential to human dignity and the character of our communities. It is, to repeat, one of those "goods which by their nature are not and cannot be mere commodities." Given this special status, the primary end or essential purpose of medical care delivery should be a cured patient, a comforted patient, and a healthier community, *not* to earn a profit or a return on capital for shareholders. This understanding has long been a central ethical tenet of medicine. The International Code of the World Health Organization, for example, states that doctors must practice their profession "uninfluenced by motives of profit."

THE ADVANTAGES OF NOT-FOR-PROFIT INSTITUTIONS

This leads me to my second point, that the primary noneconomic ends of health care delivery are best advanced in a predominantly not-for-profit delivery system.

Before making this argument, however, I need to be very clear about what I am *not* saying: I am *not* saying that not-for-profit health care organizations and systems should be shielded from all competition. I believe properly structured competition is good for most not-for-profits. For example, I have long contended that the quality of elementary and secondary education would benefit greatly from the use of vouchers and expanded parental choice in the selection of schools; similarly, the Catholic Health Association's proposal for health care reform envisions organized, economically disciplined health care systems competing with one another for enrollees.

Second, I am *not* saying that all not-for-profit hospitals and health care systems act appropriately: some do not. But the answer to this problem is greater accountability in their governance and operation, not the extreme measure of abandoning the not-for-profit structure in health care.

What I *am* saying is that the not-for-profit structure is the preferred model for delivering health care services. This is so because the not-for-profit institution is uniquely designed to provide essential human services. Management expert Peter Drucker reminds us that the distinguishing feature of not-for-profit organizations is not that they are nonprofit, but that they do something very different from either business or government. He notes that a business has "discharged its task when the customer buys the product, pays for it, and is satisfied with it," and that government has done so when its "policies are effective." On the other hand, he writes:

> The "nonprofit" institution neither supplies goods or services nor controls (through regulation). Its "product" is neither a pair of shoes nor an

effective regulation. Its product is a changed human being. The non-profit institutions are human change agents. Their "product" is a cured patient, a child that learns, a young man or woman grown into a self-respecting adult; a changed human life altogether.

In other words, the purpose of not-for-profit organizations is to improve the human condition, i.e., to advance important noneconomic, nonregulatory functions that cannot be as well served by either the business corporation or government. Business corporations describe success as consistently providing shareholders with a reasonable return on equity. Not-for-profit organizations never properly define their success in terms of profit; those that do have lost their sense of purpose.

This difference between not-for-profits and businesses is most clearly seen in the organizations' different approaches to decision-making. The primary question in an investor-owned organization is: "How do we ensure a reasonable return to our shareholders?" Other questions may be asked about quality and the impact on the community, but always in the context of their effect on profit. A properly focused not-for-profit always begins with a different set of questions:

What is best for the person who is served?

What is best for the community?

How can the organization ensure a prudent use of resources for the whole community, as well as for its immediate customers?

HEALTH CARE'S ESSENTIAL CHARACTERISTICS

I believe there are four essential characteristics of health care delivery that are especially compatible with the not-for-profit structure, but much less likely to occur when health care decision-making is driven predominantly by the need to provide a return on equity. These four essential characteristics are:

(1) access

(2) medicine's patient-first ethic

(3) attention to community-wide needs, and

(4) volunteerism.

Let me discuss each.

First, there is the need for access. Given health care's essential relationship to human dignity, society should ensure everyone access to an adequate level of health care services. This is why the United States Catholic Conference and I argued strongly last year for universal insurance coverage. This element of health care reform remains a moral imperative.

But even if this nation had universal insurance, I would maintain that a strong not-for-profit sector is still critical to access. With primary accountability to shareholders, investor-owned organizations have a powerful incentive to avoid not only the uninsured and underinsured, but also vulnerable and hard-to-serve populations, high-cost populations, undesirable geographic areas, and many low-density rural areas. To be sure, not-for-profits also face pressure to avoid these groups, but *not* with the *added* requirement of generating a return on equity.

Second, not-for-profit health care organizations are better suited than their investor-owned counterparts to support the patient-first ethic in medicine. This is all the more important as society moves away from fee-for-service medicine and cost-based reimbursement toward *capitation*. (By "capitation" I mean paying providers in advance a fixed amount per person regardless of the services required by any specific individual.)

Whatever their economic disadvantages, fee-for-service medicine and cost-based reimbursement shielded the physician and the hospital from the economic consequences of patient treatment decisions and, thereby, provided strong economic support for a patient-first ethic in American medicine. Few insured patients were ever undertreated, though some were inevitably overtreated. Now we face a movement to a fully capitated health care system which shifts the financial risk in health care from the *payers of care* to the *providers*.

This development raises a critically important question: "When the provider is at financial risk for treatment decisions, who is the patient's advocate?" How can we continue to put the patient first in this new arrangement? This challenge will become especially daunting as we move into an intensely price competitive market where provider economic survival is on the line everyday. In such an environment the temptation to undertreat could be significant. Again, not-for-profits will face similar economic pressure but not with the added requirement of producing a reasonable return on shareholder equity. Part of the answer here, I believe, is to ensure that the nation not convert to a predominantly investor-owned delivery system.

Third, in health care there are a host of community-wide needs that are generally unprofitable, and therefore unlikely to be addressed by investor-owned organizations. In some cases, this entails particular services needed by the community but unlikely to earn a return on investment, such as expensive burn units, neonatal intensive care, or immunization programs for economically deprived populations. Also important are the teaching and research functions needed to renew and advance health care.

The community also has a need for continuity and stability of health services. Because the primary purpose of nonprofits is to serve patients and communities, they tend to be deeply rooted in the fabric of the community and are more likely to remain—if they are needed—during periods of economic stagnation and loss. Investor-owned organizations must, on the other hand, either leave the community or change their product line when return-on-equity becomes inadequate.

Fourth, volunteerism and philanthropy are important components of health care that thrive best in a not-for-profit setting. As Peter Drucker has noted, volunteerism in not-for-profit organizations is capable of generating a powerful countercurrent to the contemporary dissolution of families and loss of community values. At a time in our history when it is absolutely necessary to strengthen our sense of civic responsibility, volunteerism in health care is more important than ever. From the boards of trustees of our premier health care organizations to the hands-on-delivery of services, volunteers in health care can make a difference in peoples' lives and "forge new bonds to community, a new commitment to active citizenship, to social responsibility, to values."

ROLE OF MEDIATING INSTITUTIONS

In addition to my belief that the not-for-profit structure is especially well aligned with the central purpose of health care, let me suggest one more reason why each of us should be concerned that not-for-profits remain a vibrant part of the nation's health care delivery system: They are important *mediating institutions*.

The notion of mediating structures is deeply rooted in the American experience: On the one hand, these institutions stand between the individual and the state; on the other, they mediate against the rougher edges of capitalism's inclination toward excessive individualism. Mediating structures such as family, church, education and health care are the institutions closest to the control and aspirations of most Americans.

The need for mediating institutions in health care is great. Private sector failure to provide adequately for essential human services such as health care invites government intervention. While government has an obligation to ensure the availability of and access to essential services, it generally does a poor job of delivering them. Wherever possible we prefer that government work through and with institutions that are closer and more responsive to the people and communities being served. This role is best played by not-for-profit hospitals. Neither public nor private, they are the heart of the voluntary sector in health care.

Earlier, I identified several reasons why I believe investor-owned organizations are not well suited to meeting all of society's needs and expectations regarding health care. Should the investor-owned entity ever become the predominant form of health care delivery, I believe that our country will inevitably experience a sizeable and substantial growth in government intervention and control.

Until now, I have made two arguments: first, that health care is more than a commodity—it is a service essential to human dignity and to the quality of community life; and second, that the not-for-profit structure is best aligned with this understanding of health care's primary mission. My concluding argument is that private and public sector leaders have an urgent civic responsibility to preserve and strengthen our nation's predominantly not-for-profit health care delivery system.

This is a pressing obligation because the not-for-profit sector in health care may already be eroding as a result of today's extremely turbulent competitive environment in health care. The problem, let me be clear, is *not* competition per se, but the kind of competition that undermines health care's essential mission and violates the very character of the not-for-profit organization by encouraging it—even requiring it—to behave like a commercial enterprise.

Contemporary health care markets are characterized by hospital over-capacity and competition for scarce primary care physicians, but also and more ominously by shrinking health insurance coverage, and growing risk selection in private health insurance markets. These latter two features encourage health care providers to compete by becoming very efficient at avoiding the uninsured and high risk populations, and by reducing necessary but unprofitable community services—behavior that strikes at the heart of the not-for-profit mission in health care. Moreover, the environment leads some health care leaders to conclude that the best way to survive is to become for-profit or to create for-profit subsidiaries. The existence of not-for-profits is further threatened by the aggressive efforts of some investor-owned chains to expand their market share by purchasing not-for-profit hospitals and by publicly challenging the continuing need for not-for-profit organizations in health care.

ADVANCING THE NOT-FOR-PROFIT HEALTH CARE MISSION

Each of us and our communities have much to lose if we allow unstructured market forces to continue to erode the necessary and valuable presence of not-for-profit health care organizations. It is imperative, therefore, that we immediately begin to find ways to promote and strengthen them.

How can we do this? Without going into specifics, I believe it will require a combination of private sector and governmental initiatives. Voluntary hospital board members and executives must renew their institutions' commitment to the essential mission of not-for-profit health care. Simultaneously, government must reform health insurance markets to prevent "redlining" and ensure everyone reasonable access to adequate health care services. Finally, government should review its tax policies to ensure that existing laws and regulations are not putting not-for-profits at an inappropriate competitive disadvantage, but are holding them strictly accountable for their tax-exempt status.

Let me conclude by simply reiterating the thesis I made at the beginning of this talk. Health care is fundamentally different from most other goods and services. It is about the most human and intimate needs of people, their families, and communities. It is because of this critical difference that each of us should work to preserve the predominantly not-for-profit character of our health care delivery in Chicago and throughout the country.

BIBLIOGRAPHY

Bernardin, Joseph L., "The Consistent Ethic of Life and Health Care Reform," *Origins* 24 (June 9, 1994) 60–64.

Dougherty, Charles J., "The Costs of Commercial Medicine," *Theoretical Medicine* 11 (1990) 275–86.

John Paul II, "Centesimus Annus," *Origins* 21 (May 16, 1991) 3–24.

Relman, Arnold S., "What Market Values are Doing to Medicine," *The Atlantic Monthly* (March 1992) 99–106.

Address

"Renewing the Covenant with Patients and Society"*

AMA House of Delegates, Washington, D.C.

—— *December 5, 1995* ——————————————————

Thank you for your invitation to speak with you this afternoon. These are turbulent times for medicine and health care, especially for physicians, and Dr. Todd and Dr. Bristow may have felt that, as a pastor, I could give some comfort to you who daily navigate these powerful currents of change. I am not sure how much comfort I can offer, but I can offer some observations that may help guide your own conduct and that of the medical profession as the pace of change accelerates in the coming years.

Such an offer may sound presumptuous, coming as it does from a priest rather than a physician. So, before going further, let me share some of the experience that led me to this seemingly brash venture.

My many pastoral roles often intersect with doctors, institutions of health care, and health care policy. I am responsible, for example, for the spiritual care of the sick of the Archdiocese of Chicago. Within the diocese there are more than 100 health care agencies, including 20 hospitals and 28 nursing homes. As a member of the Administrative Committee of the National Conference of Catholic Bishops, I have helped to articulate the conference's views on national health policy and other social issues. I am also a member of the Board of the Catholic Health Association of the United States, which represents about 900 Catholic health care providers nationwide.

*Also published in *Celebrating the Ministry of Healing: Joseph Cardinal Bernardin's Reflections on Healthcare* (Catholic Health Association, 1999).

In these roles I have the opportunity to converse and consult with some of the best minds in medicine and health care administration. And I have had the chance to write and speak frequently on the nature of health care and its significance in human life, with a particular focus on the importance of not-for-profit institutions. In all of this I have seen access to health care as a fundamental human right and discussed the ethical dimensions of health care within the framework of the consistent ethic of life, which I have articulated and developed over the past twelve years.

I also stand before you as someone recently diagnosed and treated for pancreatic cancer. I am the beneficiary of the best care your profession has to offer. This experience has shaped and deepened my reflections on the challenges you face as individuals and as a profession.

Your profession and mine have much in common—the universal human need for healing and wholeness. What special qualities do ministry and medicine share?

First, we both are engaged in something more than a profession—a vocation. In its truest sense, it means a life to which we are called. In my own case I was called to both professions. As an undergraduate, I had decided to become a doctor and followed a premed curriculum. But long before I graduated, I heard a stronger call to the priesthood.

Second, we both are centered on promoting and restoring wholeness of life. The key words in our professions—heal, health, holy, and whole— share common roots in Old English.

Third, and most fundamentally, we both are engaged in a moral enterprise. We both respond to those who are in need, who ask us for help, who expose to us their vulnerabilities, and who place their trust in us.

As someone who has cared for others and who has been cared for by you and your colleagues, I hope you will allow me to speak frankly about the moral crisis that I believe currently grips the medical profession generally and physicians individually.

In speaking of a "moral crisis" I realize that I am assuming a position with which some within your profession would disagree. They would assert that the marketplace is the only valid reference point for evaluating medical practice. I respectfully, though forcefully, disagree with such an assertion. I believe that medicine, like other professions—such as teaching, law, and ministry—does have a moral center, even though this center is under attack. And I think you believe deep down as I do that such a moral center exists and that it must not be lost. Dr. Bristow's priority on medical standards as a hallmark of his administration reflects this concern.

What do I mean when I speak of a "moral crisis" in medicine? I mean that more and more members of the community of medicine no longer agree on the universal moral principles of medicine or on the appropriate means to realize those principles. Conscientious practitioners are often perplexed as to how they should act when they are caught up in a web of economics, politics, business practice, and social responsibility. The result is that the practice of medicine no longer has the surety of an accurate compass to guide it through these challenging and difficult times. In other words, medicine, along with other professions, including my own, is in need of a moral renewal.

My purpose today is not to dictate the details of medicine's moral renewal. Rather, it is to invite you to join me in a conversation that will lead to a restoration of medicine's first principles. I am convinced that, with good will and persistence, this process will benefit society, reinvigorate the medical profession, preserve its independence, and infuse your lives with a quality of meaning that has too often been missing.

How did we arrive at this situation? Medicine, like other professions, does not exist in a vacuum. The upheavals in our society, especially those of the past thirty years, have left their imprint on the practice and organization of medicine. Each of us has his or her own list of such upheavals. My list includes the shift from family and community to the individual as the primary unit of society, an overemphasis on individual self-interest to the neglect of the common good, the loss of a sense of personal responsibility and the unseemly flight to the refuge of "victimhood," the loss of confidence in established institutions, the decline in religious faith, the commercialization of our national existence, the growing reliance on the legal system to redress personal conflicts.

In addition to societal changes, there are causes specific to the medical enterprise that contribute to medicine's disconnection from its underlying moral foundation. For example, advances in medical science and technology have improved the prospect of cure but have deemphasized medicine's traditional caring function. Other contributors include the commercialization of medical practice, the growing preoccupation of some physicians with monetary concerns, and the loss of a sense of humility and humanity by certain practitioners.

None of this, I am sure, is news to you. In surveys, newspaper articles, and personal conversations, many physicians report that they are increasingly concerned with the condition and direction of medical practice.

What may surprise you, however, is my contention that, to reverse these trends, you, as individuals and as a profession, must accept a major share of the responsibility for where you are today. Physicians have too often succumbed to the siren songs of scientific triumph, financial success, and political power. In the process medicine has grown increasingly mechanistic, commercial, and soulless. The age-old covenants between doctors and patient, between the profession and society, have been ignored or violated.

This dire view is tempered by hope. If the present predicament is the product of choices—explicit and implicit—made by members of your profession, then it is possible that you can choose to change it.

The change I have in mind is "renewing the covenant with patients and society." That covenant is grounded in the moral obligations that arise from the nature of the doctor–patient relationship. They are moral obligations—as opposed to legal or contractual obligations—because they are based on fundamental human concepts of right and wrong. While, as I noted earlier, it is not currently fashionable to think of medicine in terms of morality, morality is, in fact, the core of the doctor–patient relationship and the foundation of the medical profession. Why do I insist on a moral model as opposed to the economic and contractual models now in vogue?

Allow me to describe four key aspects of medicine that give it a moral status and establish a covenantal relationship:

- First, the reliance of the patient on the doctor. Illness compels a patient to place his or her fate in the hands of a doctor. A patient relies, not only on the technical competence of a doctor, but also on his or her moral compass, on the doctor's commitment to put the interests of the patient first.

- Second, the holistic character of medical decisions. A physician is a scientist and a clinician, but as a doctor is and must be more. A doctor is and must be a caretaker of the patient's person, integrating medical realities into the whole of the patient's life. A patient looks to his or her doctor as a professional adviser, a guide through some of life's most difficult journeys.

- Third, the social investment in medicine. The power of modern medicine—of each and every doctor—is the result of centuries of science, clinical trials, and public and private investments. Above all, medical science has succeeded because of the faith of people in medicine and in doctors. This faith creates a social debt and is the basis of medicine's call—its vocation—to serve the common good.

- Fourth, the personal commitments of doctors. Relationship with a patient creates an immediate, personal, nontransferable fiduciary responsibility to protect that patient's best interests. Regardless of markets, government programs, or network managers, patients depend on doctors for a personal commitment and for advocacy through an increasingly complex and impersonal system.

This moral center of the doctor–patient relationship is the very essence of being a doctor. It also defines the outlines of the covenant that exists between physicians and their patients, their profession, and their society. The covenant is a promise that the profession makes—a solemn promise—that it is and will remain true to its moral center. In individual terms, the covenant is the basis on which patients trust their doctors. In social terms, the covenant is the grounds for the public's continued respect and reliance on the profession of medicine.

The first dimension of this covenant deals with the physician's responsibilities to his or her patients. They include:

- Placing the good of the patient over the interests—financial or otherwise—of the physician, insurance company, the hospital, or system of care. This issue is rarely overt; rather, it springs from a growing web of pressures and incentives to substitute someone else's judgment for your own.

- Ensuring that the use of advanced medical science and technology does not come at the expense of real caring. A recent study in the *Journal of the American Medical Association* documented a continuing compulsion to spare nothing for the dying patient, without regard for the patient's dignity, comfort, or peace of mind.

- Upholding the sanctity and dignity of life from conception to natural death. The consistent ethic of life calls on us to honor and respect life at every stage and in all its circumstances. As a society, we must not lose our shared commitment to protect our vulnerable members: the unborn, persons with disabilities, the aged, and the terminally ill. We must not allow the public debates over the right to life of the unborn person and legalized euthanasia to deter us from our commitment.

- Attending to your own spiritual needs as healers. As a priest or a physician, we can only give from what we have. We must take care to nurture our own personal moral center. This is the sustenance of caring.

The responsibilities I just noted are not new to the practice of medicine. Almost 2,500 years ago Plato summed up the differences between good and bad medicine in a way that illuminates many of the issues physicians face today in our increasingly bureaucratized medical system. In his description of bad medicine, which he called "slave medicine," Plato said,

> The physician never gives the slave any account of his problem, nor asks for any. He gives some empiric treatment with an air of knowledge in the brusque fashion of a dictator, and then rushes off to the next ailing slave.

Plato contrasted this bad medicine with the treatment of free men and women:

> [T]he physician treats the patient's disease by going into things thoroughly from the beginning in a scientific way and takes the patient and the family into confidence. In this way he learns something from the patient.

> The physician never gives prescriptions until he has won the patient's support, and when he has done so, he aims to produce complete restoration to health by persuading the patient to participate.

Similar ideas are reflected in the Hippocratic Oath attributed to an ancient Greek physician. This oath is still used at some medical school graduations. Its second section includes a pledge to use only beneficial treatments and procedures and not to harm or hurt a patient. It includes promises not to break confidentiality, not to engage in sexual relations with patients or to dispense deadly drugs. It specifically says: "I will never give a deadly drug to anybody if asked for it, nor will I make a suggestion to this effect."

There are plenty of pressures, some self-imposed and some externally imposed, that make it easy to practice bad medicine, just as there were two-and-one-half millennia ago. Sustaining your covenants requires a willingness to affirm and incorporate into your lives the ancient virtues of benevolence, compassion, competence, intellectual honesty, humility, and suspension of self-interest—virtues which many of you live quite admirably.

Let us move now from the covenantal obligations of the individual physician to the responsibilities of the profession. Medicine is a profession that has the freedom to accredit its educational institutions, set standards of practice, and determine who shall practice and who shall not. As such, it is a moral community subject to a set of moral obligations. First among these obligations is the requirement to enlist and train new members of the profession who befit the nature of the profession. Beyond intellectual ability, you must ask whether potential medical students have the potential to live up to the moral responsibilities of a physician, that is, will they be "good" doctors. In addition, those who teach and counsel medical students must be living models of the virtuous physician, living proof that the values we espouse are not romantic abstractions to be discarded when they enter the "real world" of medicine.

President Bristow has lamented the fact that one-fourth of our medical schools have no formal courses in medical ethics. Such courses should, of course, be required in every curriculum. Important as these courses are, however, they are not enough. Indeed, they run the risk of segregating these matters from the core of students' learning experience. If we do not infuse moral and ethical training into every class and practicum, in residencies, and in continuing education, we have not fulfilled our obligation to our students and the profession.

Finally, I would emphasize among medicine's professional obligations the setting and enforcing of the highest standards of behavior and competence. Although those who defraud government and private insurers, those who are incompetent or venal, those who look the other way at colleagues' wrongdoing are undoubtedly a minority, the profession is demeaned by them and must repudiate them. Your own Code of Medical Ethics speaks directly to this point.

Moreover, when physicians engage in sexual misconduct with patients, the "code of silence" that has protected physician and priest alike must be broken. I offer for your consideration what we have done in the Archdiocese of Chicago in matters of clerical sexual misconduct with minors. An independent review board, the majority of whom are not clerics, evaluates all allegations and presents to me recommendations for action. The participation of these dedicated individuals in this process has not diminished the priesthood, but enhanced it.

Failure to ground the profession in a strong set of moral values risks the loss of public respect and confidence, and with that the profession faces the further erosion of its independence. Society's stake in medical care is too great to sustain the present level of professional autonomy if confidence in the profession declines.

Although I am focusing on what I believe needs to be repaired, I do not overlook or take for granted the great and good works performed by physicians every day—the grueling work in hospital emergency rooms, the treatment of AIDS victims, the care for the poor and the homeless, the *pro bono* work—to name only a few.

Let me summarize my major points so far. First, the practice of medicine is by nature a moral endeavor that takes the form of a covenant. Second, that covenant involves moral obligations to patients, to the profession, and to society. Third, the moral compass that guides physicians in meeting those obligations needs to be fully restored so that the covenant can be renewed. I have discussed the covenantal obligations to patients and the profession and suggested some guideposts. I turn now to the obligations to society.

Physicians and the profession have a covenant with society to be an advocate for the health needs of their communities and the nation. This function is not as immediate or obvious as the others I have discussed, and in some respects its successful exercise depends on fulfilling those obligations that are more intimate to medical practice. The nature of these obligations may also be more controversial, but let me outline the primary elements of the social obligation.

• First, the establishment of health care as a basic human right. This right flows from the sanctity of life and is a necessary condition for the preservation of human dignity. Dr. Bristow has indicated that the opportunity for comprehensive reform of our health care system is "at least two administrations from now." I trust that the medical profession will take this prediction as a challenge, not as an inevitability.

- Second, the promotion of public health in the widest possible sense. In addition to the traditional public health agenda—clean water, sanitation, infectious diseases—we must include the health implications of inadequate nutrition, housing, and education. In addition, our public health horizons must include the "behavioral epidemics" engulfing our society—drug and alcohol abuse, violence, children raising children.

- Finally, leadership on the question of how best to protect human life and enhance human dignity in a situation of limited health resources. Although this issue is often framed in terms of rationing, I prefer a different word and a different concept: "stewardship." As a profession, you must take the lead in advising policy makers. This is a matter too important to be left to the government and the insurance companies.

If you sense an urgency in my voice today, it is because I believe we cannot afford to wait to renew the covenant with patients and society until some indefinite time in the future. The future is about to inundate us. If we do not reset the moral compass before the flood arrives, our opportunity may be washed away. Let me suggest only a few of the overarching issues we are already contending with: the aging of our society and of the industrialized world, the explosion of genetic knowledge and the potential for the manipulation of human life itself, the revolution in information and the attendant privacy issues. Confronting each of these issues will require our moral compass to be crystal clear and firmly set.

It is my hope that today will mark the beginning of a conversation among all of us concerned with the moral framework of health care in the United States, but especially among those of you within the medical profession. If current trends continue, the moral authority at the basis of medicine is in danger of being lost, perhaps irrevocably. You are closest to these issues, and, in the end, your choices will determine our course as a nation and community. Recommitting yourselves to medicine's inherent moral center will give you the strength and wisdom to renew the covenant and provide the leadership your patients, your profession, and your nation need and expect from you.

Catholic-Jewish Dialogue

Address

The Chicago Board of Rabbis and The Jewish Federation of Metropolitan Chicago*

Chicago, Illinois

—— *March 7, 1983* ——————————————————

My dear brothers and sisters of the Chicago Board of Rabbis and the Jewish Federation of Chicago!

I am grateful for your kind and thoughtful invitation. I am very happy to be with you this afternoon. From the very first moment that you invited me, I have looked forward to this encounter. My only regret is that because of the extraordinarily heavy schedule of my first six months in Chicago, it has taken so long to get together with you.

I wish first to address you very personally. I wish to greet you in the same way that I greeted my brother priests of the archdiocese on the evening before my official installation. I come to you as your brother, Joseph. I come to you as a friend, seeking the warmth, understanding and support of your friendship. I ask you to accept my presence among you as a sign of the great respect and affection I have for you, and as a pledge of my continued prayers and support for you in the future.

It is significant, I believe, that our first meeting should take place during the year marking the 20th anniversary of the beginning of the Second Vatican Council. From the Catholic perspective, the council was the turning point in Catholic-Jewish relations because from the council came

*Also published in *A Blessing to Each Other* (Liturgy Training Publications, 1996).

253

Nostra aetate. In that historic document, the council fathers reviewed the elements of our common heritage, called for a mutual understanding of and respect for our respective religious traditions, univocally stated that in no way could the Jewish people be held accountable for the death of Christ, and deplored "the hatred, persecutions and displays of anti-Semitism directed against the Jews at any time and from any source" (no. 4). The council gave impetus to a dialogue which has taken place at the local, national and international levels. In the United States, Catholics and Jews have worked together more than in any other country. There exists today a network of close, cooperative contacts between Jewish and Catholic representatives who can be called on in moments of crisis and need on both sides. Admittedly, this dialogue has not eliminated all tensions. Nonetheless, there have been continuing positive developments in Christian-Jewish relations and in the Catholic Church's appreciation of the Jewish tradition.

In November 1980, Pope John Paul II stressed the need for this dialogue in a talk he gave to the Jewish community at Mainz, Germany. "The depth and richness of our common heritage," he said, "are revealed to us particularly in friendly dialogue and trusting collaboration. . . . It is not just a question of correcting a false religious view of the Jewish people, which in the course of history was one of the causes that contributed to misunderstanding and persecution, but above all of the dialogue between the two religions which—with Islam—gave the world faith in the one, ineffable God who speaks to us, and which desire to serve him on behalf of the whole world."

A year and a half later—in March 1982—he returned to this theme when he addressed delegates of Episcopal Conferences and other experts concerning the Catholic Church's relations with Judaism who were meeting in Rome. On this occasion he also stressed the need for quality in our ongoing exchanges. "I am happy to know," he said, "that . . . you are making many efforts, by studying and praying together, to grasp better and to formulate more clearly the often difficult biblical and theological problems raised by the progress of Judeo-Christian dialogue. Imprecision and mediocrity in this field do enormous harm to such a dialogue. May God grant that Christians and Jews may hold more in-depth exchanges based on their own identities, without ever allowing either one or the other side to be obscured, but always seeking truly for the will of the God who revealed himself."

I wish to personally endorse the efforts to promote better Jewish-Christian relations and I pray that there might be a greater level of interaction here in the Chicago area. In line with the Holy Father's emphasis on the need for greater mutual understanding, I will encourage our educational institutions and programs of the archdiocese to enhance their treatment of Judaism and of Jewish-Christian relations as a way of eliminating any remaining vestiges of anti-Semitism and helping Catholics acquire a better understanding of the religious values of the Jewish tradition that were so central to the ministry and teaching of Jesus himself. In this connection, I am pleased to inform you that our Office of Divine Worship recently asked Father John Pawlikowski of Catholic Theological Union to write a series of articles in *Liturgy 80* on how Judaism might be presented during our key liturgical seasons.

I would like now to address briefly several areas of particular concern to the Jewish community.

The first, of course, is Israel and its relationship to all the Middle East. The volatile situation in the Middle East, constantly shifting and perennially complex, has created tensions for everyone. On this particular issue, we are united in many of our perspectives, but we also differ on some of them.

We both agree on the overriding need for peace. The NCCB, in its 1973 statement on the Middle East and again in November 1978, called unequivocally for the recognition of the State of Israel within secure and recognized boundaries as a basic element of any lasting and just peace. I believe that Catholics generally support Israel and have positive attitudes toward it. Catholics relate sympathetically to Israel as a democracy in an increasingly totalitarian world.

Moreover, Catholics are beginning to understand the religious and cultural factors which tie all Jews to the land of Israel. Whatever difficulties we as Christians may experience in sharing this view, we must strive to understand this link between land and people which has been a central element in the writings and worship of Jews for two millennia. In a 1975 statement commemorating the tenth anniversary of *Nostra aetate*, the American bishops affirmed the need for Catholics to be sensitive to this point, adding: "Appreciation of this link is not to give assent to any particular religious interpretation of this bond. Nor is this affirmation meant to deny the legitimate rights of other parties in the region, or to adopt any political stance in the controversies over the Middle East . . ."

In this connection, I would like to allude to the fact that some members of the Jewish community seem to be making the kind of support of Judaism and Israel found among certain evangelical groups the barometer for Jewish relations with mainline Christian churches, including the Catholic Church. This could create a problem for Catholic-Jewish relations. While Catholic theology has come to recognize clearly the permanence of the Jewish covenant, and while Catholics have grown in their appreciation of the Jewish land tradition as a result of Christian biblical scholarship, Israel will never play the kind of role in our theology that it does for some of these evangelical groups. Hence, while Catholics may retain a strong commitment to Israel, we cannot be expected to speak about this commitment in the same theological language as they.

It was because of this sensitivity to the link between land and people that we quickly expressed disapproval of the 1975 United Nations vote which sought to equate Zionism with racism. Speaking as the president of the NCCB, I stated at the time:

> The resolution is unjust. Because of its substantive inadequacy it both retards the necessary struggle against racism in the world and opens the door to harassment, discrimination and denial of basic rights to members of the Jewish community throughout the world (NC News Service, Nov. 11, 1975).

While there is agreement on many elements of the Middle East situation, nonetheless there also exist significant differences. This is why there is a great necessity for dialogue on the Middle East and on U.S. policy in the Middle East. We enter this dialogue not only as major religious traditions but also as citizens of the country with the most significant impact on the Middle East. The Catholic participation in this dialogue is based on the 1973 and 1978 statements to which I have alluded, as well as a series of statements dealing with Lebanon. Those statements call not only for a settlement in the Middle East based on the recognition of the right of Israel's secure existence, but also the right of Palestinians to a homeland. That is not all of our position because the issues themselves are so complex, but I am highlighting these two points to indicate that there are significant differences among us.

Other issues, for example, would include Israeli and other forces in Lebanon, as well as the status of occupied territories and this, of course, includes discussion of the question of Jerusalem. Obviously, the American bishops are much influenced on this latter point by the position of the Holy See. We have to discuss our differences among ourselves and at the same time cooperate to shape U.S. policy in the direction of a long-term, stable and just resolution of the Middle East situation. This dialogue will test both our religious vision and the moral vision we bring to the public debate in the U.S., but I am convinced that we serve religion and society best by actively participating in the public dialogue.

I take this occasion to commend the quality and sincerity of the official Israeli report on the Beirut camp massacres. In this connection, I cannot fail to mention that there was also Christian involvement in this tragedy since members of our faith community were the actual killers.

I am also sensitive to the displeasure of the Jewish community over the Holy Father's meeting with Yasir Arafat. We are faced here with differing perspectives on this visit in the Catholic and Jewish communities. The Catholic community generally sees such visits by the Holy Father as pastoral efforts at reconciliation. The Papacy has a tradition of talking with various world leaders. The popes have met with leaders of the Soviet Union and Poland; in recent days Pope John Paul II met with those of Nicaragua, El Salvador and Guatemala. Certainly such meetings in no way constitute an endorsement of their fundamental policies. Moreover, I have reason to believe that when the Pope did meet with Arafat he urged him to recognize Israel and to abandon terrorism.

I can understand, however, how Jews, in light of the PLO's past record of terrorism, might fear that this visit would be perceived as a toleration, if not acceptance of terrorism, even though this was certainly not the Holy See's intention. As a matter of fact, a number of Catholics communicated their reservations about the visit. At the same time, candor also prompts me to express some wonderment about statements made by a few Jewish leaders at the time of the visit. These statements, made at a time of great emotion, seemed to imply Church involvement in the Holocaust and were perceived by many as a personal attack on the Pope. Such comments deeply offended many Catholics and were not conducive to genuine dialogue.

Another area of concern of special importance to the Jewish community is proselytism. The many unjust practices, such as forced baptism, associated with the spread of the gospel throughout Christian history, have made this a particularly sensitive issue in our relations. Today the Church is clearly committed to the principles of religious liberty, a commitment which of itself necessitates the rejection of all unfair proselytizing which might have taken place in the past.

In a paper delivered in Venice at the 1977 meeting of the International Catholic-Jewish Liaison Committee, Professor Tommaso Federici, professor of biblical theology at Sant' Anselmo in Rome, set down clearly the principles to be followed in Christian evangelization. The mission to witness, he points out, is a vital necessity to the Christian; indeed, it is an essential aspect of Christian life. This is appropriate even in dialogue, for dialogue presumes that each side will articulate frankly and honestly what it believes in, and will respect the other's right to do so. We believe in Christ as the risen Lord and quite naturally invite all persons to join us in our community of faith. To deny or to hide this would destroy our integrity as committed Christians. As Professor Federici states, witness "is constitutive of the Church's very mission to the world and its peoples and is in accord with the concern which was to be heard in the very first days of the Church itself (cf. 1 Cor 9:16: 'Woe to me if I do not preach the Gospel!') and has never disappeared and has now been clearly restated by the Second Vatican Council" ("Mission and Witness of the Church," *Origins*, Oct. 19, 1978).

Witness, however, is to be distinguished from proselytism and is to be guided by the rules of justice and love. Federici thus excludes "any sort of witness which in any way constitutes a physical, moral, psychological or cultural constraint on the Jews, both individuals and communities, such as might in any way destroy or even simply reduce their personal judgment, free will and full autonomy of decision" (Ibid.).

Rather clear guidelines can be drawn from such principles which are particularly appropriate to a society such as ours in which one religion, Christianity, tends to dominate by sheer force of numbers.

A third area of concern is Soviet Jewry. In the past there have been many examples of close cooperation on this issue. Unfortunately, the situation has been rather bleak during the past year. I am familiar with the work of the National Interreligious Task Force on Soviet Jewry which is based here in Chicago and I recognize the role it fulfills. In this connection, I would like to voice my support for Anatoly Scharansky. I know his case has had special significance for the Jewish community.

I would like, at this time, to repeat a suggestion I have made several times in the past. Where possible, the protest should be broadened to include all people whose human rights are being violated, not only in Russia but elsewhere. I am thinking, for example, of the people of Lithuania who have suffered greatly because of their religious convictions since their annexation to Russia in the 1940s. There are also other groups in Russia and many other parts of the world as well whose human rights have been violated for religious and political reasons. We must remember all our brothers and sisters who need our help. Those of us who enjoy freedom must speak with one voice in condemnation of all persecution and oppression. Let it not be said that one segment of the human family suffered while another segment stood idly by, doing or saying nothing. Both the Hebrew and Christian Scriptures condemn this failure to stand up and be counted when the occasion demands forceful action.

So far, I have spoken about Jewish concerns and the Catholic response to them. There are also Catholic concerns about which we ask for more dialogue and understanding. The first is aid to children who attend church-related schools. This has long been a sore spot among American Catholics, especially parents. I suggest that, in the spirit that has marked our dialogue in other areas, we now sit down together to discuss this topic. The anguish and hurt felt by Catholics at the systematic economic discrimination against them in their efforts to maintain what they consider their right to "free" exercise of religion is very real and very deep. While there is still considerable opposition from the Jewish community, I am encouraged that some Jewish leaders have begun to call for a reassessment of the traditional line of opposition to any form of relief for parents who use their God-given and constitutional right to send their children to the school of their choice. I know, too, that the Union of Orthodox Jewish Congregations has dissented from the position of opposition assumed by other Jewish groups.

A second area of concern is respect for life and, in particular, abortion. Some maintain that this is simply a sectarian issue, but I reject that contention. While, admittedly, the Catholic Church is more concerned about it than any other institution, abortion—in my view—is basically a question of human rights, the right of an unborn infant to live. Because of the great debate about abortion, there is need for more dialogue so that we can avoid the misconceptions and stereotypes which plague us, so that we can develop greater understanding and sensitivity to deeply held convictions.

Happily, there exists a model of what can be done when our two communities commit themselves to authentic dialogue, even on such an emotion-laden issue as abortion. In September 1977, the Los Angeles priest-rabbi group (sponsored by the Los Angeles Chapter of the American Jewish Committee, the Board of Rabbis of Southern California and the Roman Catholic Archdiocese of Los Angeles) issued a joint statement on "Respect for Life—Jewish and Roman Catholic Reflections on Abortion and Related Issues." The differing Catholic and Jewish viewpoints were presented separately, along with an indication of the areas of considerable mutual concern and convergence. While no consensus was reached on certain points, ground rules for future dialogues and cooperation were set forth in a concluding "Joint Expression of Goals." After stating what might be done to reduce tensions in the abortion controversy, to encourage religious groups to teach respect for life in their individual communities in accordance with their sacred traditions, to eliminate coercion by government agencies, to advocate positive alternatives to abortion and to promote social situations which will encourage the responsible bearing and rearing of children, the group concluded: "While Roman Catholics and Jews may not agree to make the prohibition of all abortions American law, nonetheless we should work together to make respect for life, and particularly the joyful celebration of new life, an American ideal." This significant effort in Los Angeles proves that even the most volatile subject matter can be faced positively and creatively if properly approached in dialogue.

I would like now to conclude with an appeal for a greater degree of interreligious cooperation on various social issues which are affecting both our nation and our city. The current economic crisis is playing havoc with so many of our people. Even though there are signs of an impending recovery, it will be a long time before the present crisis, with all its human suffering, is resolved. While we are not economists, we do have the obligation, I believe, to help make sure that the voices of the poor and disadvantaged are heard in the national debate about the allocation of resources and the development of policies which affect the well-being of our society.

There is another concern which we must address in some way. The political changes presently underway in our city have given rise to many fears and prejudices. Our united voice should be heard on behalf of justice, decency and fairness. We already have a structure, of course, which makes it possible for us to come together, as Jews, Protestants, Orthodox and Catholics, to address the important social issues of our day. I am referring to the Chicago Conference on Religion and Race. Let us use this and other structures to full advantage.

I also invite you to join us Catholic bishops in our search for peace. As you know, the bishops of this country are involved in the development of a major document (called a pastoral letter) on war and peace, with special emphasis on the nuclear arms race and the need to find alternatives to warfare, both nuclear and conventional. This pastoral has two purposes: to help form the consciences of our own constituents on war and peace issues and to make our contribution to the public debate on these topics. As expected, the document has been both praised and damned. The important thing, however, is that it has been noticed and, indeed, taken seriously, both in our own country and abroad. The document we are preparing, when completed, will not be the last word. It is really only the beginning of our reflection on the necessity of turning the ever-upward spiral of the arms race downward and how we might go about that. I invite you to join us in this reflection. I know, of course, that the organized Jewish community has also been concerned about peace as evidenced by the fact that the General Assembly of the Council of Jewish Federations endorsed the nuclear freeze. I recognize and understand, too, certain Jewish difficulties in this area because of their deep concern for Israel's security. Still, it would be useful to have you join us in our reflection on the use of power and the circumstances under which that use is legitimate. It would also be helpful to get your perspective of war and peace in the Hebrew Scriptures as we develop a theology of peace, based on both the Hebrew and the Christian Scriptures.

As Pope John Paul II told the Jewish community at Mainz: "Jews and Christians, as children of Abraham, are called to be a blessing for the world (cf. Gen 12:2ff.), committing themselves together for peace and justice among all men and peoples, with the fullness and depth that God himself intended us to have, and with all the readiness for sacrifices that this high goal may demand. The more our meeting is imprinted with this sacred duty, the more it becomes a blessing also for ourselves."

My dear brothers and sisters, dialogue and collaboration are not options for us. They are a necessity. Never again can we permit ourselves to be alienated from each other; never again can we let our minds and our hearts be misshaped by the prejudices and hatreds of the past. Never again can we allow a climate which could produce another Holocaust.

We have so much in common. But ultimately it is our faith in God, who created us in his image and likeness, that unites us. So may we always celebrate that unity, while respecting our different traditions, and working with each other, in love, for the betterment of ourselves and the entire human family.

Today, I pledge to you my love, my support, my determination to work with you on all the matters that concern us as Jews and Catholics, as citizens, but most of all, as caring friends.

Address

Twentieth Anniversary Celebration of *Nostra Aetate**

Mundelein College, Chicago, Illinois

— *October 27, 1985* ─────────────────────────

My brothers and sisters, I greet you today in the spirit of *shalom,* for "peace" captures very well the theme of our celebration of the twentieth anniversary of *Nostra aetate.* This Vatican II Declaration on the Church and the Jewish People marked a turning point in Jewish-Christian relations. It called for a mutual understanding of and respect for our respective religious traditions, and deplored "the hatred, persecutions and displays of anti-Semitism directed against the Jews at any time and from any source" (no. 4).

This evening we give thanks to the God of Abraham and Sarah, of Jesus and Mary, for the two decades of enhanced understanding and reconciliation which have marked the relationship between our two religious communities since the council.

Peace, *shalom,* is increasingly becoming characteristic of our encounters after centuries of mutual hostility caused in large part by some Christians' misguided belief that it was permissible to punish Jews as so-called "Christ killers." The Second Vatican Council made it clear that such actions cannot be considered as consonant with the teaching of the New Testament.

On a number of occasions in the past three years I have had the opportunity to address the Jewish community on the subject of Christian-Jewish

*Also published in *A Blessing to Each Other* (Liturgy Training Publications, 1996).

relations. This evening I welcome the opportunity to address my remarks on this important topic primarily to the Catholic community of
the archdiocese.

Nostra aetate has given Catholics a threefold responsibility. Our first
task is to ensure that all vestiges of anti-Semitism are removed from our
teaching, liturgy and preaching. For this goal to be fully realized, we must
begin to acknowledge and proclaim—far more extensively than we have
thus far—the profoundly positive impact which the Old or First Testament and Second Temple Judaism had on the religious perspective and
values of Jesus and the early Church. The Gospel of Matthew states clearly
that Jesus came—not to reject or abolish the Law and the Prophets but—
to fulfill them.

In recently released catechetical *Notes* on the proper presentation of
Judaism by Catholics, the Holy See has emphasized:

> Because of the unique relations that exist between Christianity and
> Judaism—"linked together at the very level of their identity" (Pope
> John Paul II, March 6, 1982)— . . . the Jews and Judaism should not oc-
> cupy an occasional and marginal place in catechesis: Their presence
> there is essential and should be organically integrated (I:2).

I urge archdiocesan educators, preachers and liturgists to make this ecclesial perspective their own in their ministry. Any presentation of Jesus'
message which fails to note its indebtedness to the Jewish biblical heritage and the Judaism of his time fails to present the gospel in its fullness
and integrity. Jewish tradition was integral to the piety, preaching and
ministry of the Lord.

Our second responsibility in light of *Nostra aetate* is authentic dialogue
with members of the Jewish community. While study of the Jewish tradition is vital, it can never be a substitute for face-to-face encounters with
our Jewish sisters and brothers. I'm very pleased that a number of local
dialogue groups already exist in the archdiocese, one going back as far as
1969. I encourage our pastors and people to cooperate with our Office of
Human Relations and Ecumenism in supporting the efforts of existing
groups and in establishing additional dialogues.

In these groups, Catholics and Jews have the opportunity to share their
religious and moral perspectives. They come to understand better the va-
rieties of Jewish and Catholic expression, the ways in which we define
our existence as religious communities. In doing this we will move beyond dealing with one another as caricatures, as has too often been the
case in the past. In this regard, the Holy See's 1975 Guidelines for the
implementation of *Nostra aetate* specifically remind Catholics that coming to know the Jewish people "as they define themselves" is indispensable for authentic dialogue.

My experience has been that Catholics who enter into dialogue with our Jewish friends come away with a new appreciation—not only of the richness of the Jewish tradition, but also of how much it has contributed to the development of the Christian faith. They also learn how pivotal both the experience of the Nazi Holocaust and the rebirth of the State of Israel are to Jewish self-identity in our day. I have, as you know, spoken about this on a number of occasions and will continue to listen and to reflect on these and other matters which are so central to Jewish contemporary identity.

Interfaith dialogue is essential if we are to experience *shalom*, but dialogue is not an easy process. It requires mutual respect and trust. Each party must strive to understand the ideas and feelings, the dreams and values of the other. Dialogue, in other words, is a two-way street. Eventually, we must be able to discuss our differences, no matter how painful that may be, no matter how sensitive the issues might be. As we grow in the awareness that we are brothers and sisters, children of the same God, we will find both the wisdom and the courage to deepen our commitment to the dialogical process.

Through dialogue Catholics and Jews will also come to experience a new sense of bondedness, a new spirit of *shalom*, which is so necessary for the cooperative efforts we need to transform our national ethos from a proclivity for war to a burning passion for peace.

This brings us to the third responsibility which *Nostra aetate* outlines for Catholics: the pursuit of peace with justice. If our study and dialogue fail to develop within us a new commitment to work with one another towards the elimination of economic and political injustice, it will ultimately have failed.

I welcome the Jewish input into the U.S. Catholic bishops' pastoral letter on the economy. I also welcome the joint publication by the Union of American Hebrew Congregations and the National Conference of Catholic Bishops of a common study guide on the bishops' pastoral letter on war and peace: *The Challenge of Shalom for Catholics and Jews* (edited by Annette Daum and Eugene Fisher). I urge archdiocesan educators to use this valuable resource. We also need to intensify our combined efforts on behalf of freedom and dignity for Catholics and Jews in the Soviet Union and other parts of Eastern Europe.

Closer to home, we are all residents of this metropolitan area where human suffering is on the increase. In my address to the annual meeting of the Jewish Community Centers of Chicago last year, I spoke of the impressions of human suffering which I received as I visited a West side housing project. If the spirit of *shalom* generated by our dialogue is to meet the full test of both Torah and Gospel, we must reconcile ourselves with those in our midst who increasingly lack the basic requirements of food and shelter.

Before closing, I would like to mention a project which is presently being considered here in Chicago. This project, I am convinced, will have special meaning for Chicago which is home to so many Eastern Europeans.

We believe that a deeper understanding of the past will help us to understand better the present. In particular, we believe that a deepened study—by scholars, clergy and teachers—of the past eight hundred years of Eastern European Judaism and Catholicism will greatly enhance our understanding of this important period and ambiance of our history. But even more important, such a study will contribute to a greater appreciation of the bonds which have united our two religious communities both in the past and at the present.

It is with that conviction that Chicago's Spertus College of Judaica has announced its intention to establish a Center for the Study of Polish and Eastern European Jewry. My name will be associated with the center. I consider this a great honor and will do all I can to make what is presently a dream become a reality.

My prayer is that this weekend of commemoration and celebration will begin a new phase in the history of Catholic-Jewish relations in Chicago. We have the opportunity to become a shining example to the nation of interreligious reconciliation that results in deep social commitment.

We will probably never agree on all the theological issues which lie before us, nor are we likely to achieve consensus on every public policy question. But we can seek and find a unity of heart whose enriching power will sustain us despite our differences until God's reign appears in its full glory. May God strengthen us in this resolve.

Address

Center for Jewish and Christian Learning*

College of St. Thomas, St. Paul, Minnesota

—— *September 28, 1988* ————————————————

I am very grateful for your kind invitation to address this ongoing forum on Christian-Jewish relations. I commend the College of St. Thomas for its long-standing efforts to explore the profound links that exist between Jews and Christians. In particular, I commend the Center for Jewish and Christian Learning for promoting Christian-Jewish dialogue. You have clearly helped to make the Twin Cities area one of the principal regions in the U.S. for the promotion of Christian-Jewish dialogue. This was quite evident to all when St. Paul-Minneapolis hosted the last National Workshop on Christian-Jewish Relations.

I am happy to say that Chicago will have the pleasure of welcoming the 1990 National Workshop. We will commemorate the twenty-fifth anniversary of the historic Vatican II statement on the Catholic Church's relationship with the Jewish people, the ecclesial document which gave birth to many significant interfaith endeavors.

The very allusion to *Nostra aetate*, which describes Catholicism's enduring bonds with the People Israel, makes us aware of how far we have come since that monumental day in 1965 when, pursuing the vision of Pope John XXIII, the Second Vatican Council, after careful deliberation, gave final approval to that document.

*Also published in *Journal of Ecumenical Studies*, vol. 26, no. 3, Summer 1989; *1989 Lecture Series of Center of Jewish-Christian Learning*, College of St. Thomas; and *A Blessing to Each Other* (Liturgy Training Publications, 1996).

As you know, the experience of U.S. Catholicism, as well as the leadership of the U.S. bishops, played an important role in its eventual passage. We can truly say that *Nostra aetate* represents one of the most important contributions of the Church in the United States to the ecumenical council. That is why we Americans have a particular responsibility to protect and develop its basic understanding and intent. And that, in turn, points to the importance of the work of the College of St. Thomas on Christian-Jewish relations. My hope is that many more Catholic institutions will follow your leadership.

This evening I would like to share with you my own vision of developments during the last quarter century and to raise some issues that call for additional reflection. I will focus my reflections on four areas: (1) the role of the Hebrew Scriptures or Old Testament in the Catholic Church; (2) the growing appreciation of Jesus' profound ties to the Jewish tradition; (3) the sense of a special, deep bonding between the Church and the Jewish People; and (4) the significance of the *Shoah* or Holocaust about which some tension remains in our relationship.

THE HEBREW SCRIPTURES AND THE CATHOLIC CHURCH

Even before the Second Vatican Council, Catholic attitudes towards the Old Testament—or the "Prior Testament" as the Pontifical Biblical Commission has called it more recently—had begun to change. A growing number of Catholic exegetes had come to a better understanding of the richness of the first part of the Bible and a deeper appreciation of how these writings had positively influenced the teachings of Jesus and early Christianity.

That process has greatly accelerated since the appearance of *Nostra aetate*. There has been a gradual, but persistent, shift in emphasis away from the viewpoint that regarded the Hebrew Scriptures simply as background material for understanding the New Testament. In its place has come an emerging sense that the books of the Hebrew Bible are worth studying in their own right, apart from whatever legitimate insights they may offer us into the meaning of Jesus' life and mission. These documents are no longer seen as mere "prelude" or "foil" for the teachings of Jesus in the New Testament. Rather, we are recognizing, however slowly, that, without deep immersion into the spirit and texts of the Hebrew Scriptures, Christians experience an emaciated version of Christian spirituality and know but a very truncated version of Jesus' full religious vision.

While we have made great strides in this regard, we still have a considerable way to travel in order to accord the Hebrew Bible its rightful place in Christian life and spirituality. These inspired books in their entirety—and not only the prophetic and wisdom sections—must be accorded their rightful status as essential, not merely peripheral, resources for Christian retreats, preaching, religious education, liturgy, and theology.

This is being done throughout the Catholic Church. When the U.S. bishops wrote their pastoral letter on war and peace, for example, they began with an examination of the relationship between peace and fidelity to God's covenant with Israel. Likewise, in their pastoral letter on the U.S. economy, they drew significantly upon the book of Genesis for insights in regard to human co-creatorship with God in economic decision-making today. Both pastoral letters implicitly acknowledge the importance for Christians to complement the insights of the New Testament with those of the Hebrew Scriptures for a comprehensive biblical spirituality. This same approach is clearly present in Pope John Paul II's first social encyclical, *Laborem exercens*.

Legitimate questions certainly remain for Jewish and Christian scholars to pursue in regard to the interpretation of the texts of the first part of the Bible. But, as such reflection and study continue, we Christians may draw far more deeply than we have in the past from this spiritual well.

JESUS AND JEWISH TRADITION

Since the Second Vatican Council, the Christian dialogue with Jews and Judaism has begun to demonstrate even greater impact on our understanding of the New Testament, especially in terms of Jesus' links to the Judaism of his day. We are witnessing a genuine revolution in New Testament scholarship, made possible by a much greater understanding of Hebrew and Aramaic and an enhanced reliance upon and availability of Jewish materials from the Second Temple or so-called "intertestamental" period. We are seeing, for example, a rapid end to the dominant hold of that form of biblical interpretation which stressed the almost exclusively Hellenistic background of Pauline Christianity. Such exegesis of the New Testament seriously eroded Jesus' concrete ties with Second Temple Judaism. This, in turn, tended to produce an excessively "universalistic" interpretation of Jesus' message which contained fertile ground for theological anti-Judaism.

In the last two decades, a dramatic shift in New Testament scholarship has begun to restore Jesus and his message to its original Jewish milieu. This is not to say that complete agreement now exists among scholars regarding the exact form of Judaism that most directly impacted Jesus' teaching. Far from it. In 1985 the Holy See's Commission for Religious Relations with the Jews issued its *Notes on the Correct Way to Present*

Jews and Judaism in the Preaching and Catechesis of the Roman Catholic Church. These *Notes* regard Jesus as closer in perspective to Pharisaism than to any other Jewish movement of the period, but leave the question open for further research and discussion.

Despite the remaining ambiguity, which is likely to continue for some time, there is a growing overall consensus that makes the state of New Testament scholarship today far different with respect to the fundamental vision of Jesus' relationship with Judaism than was the case even a decade ago. That consensus involves a number of central conclusions:

(1) The movement begun by Jesus—which grew into the Christian Church—can best be described as a reform movement *within* Judaism during his own lifetime. There is little evidence during this formative period that Jesus and his disciples wished to break away from their Jewish context.

(2) The missionary movement launched by Paul, as Paul himself understood it, was essentially a Jewish mission which intended to include the Gentiles as an integral part of the divine summons to the People Israel.

(3) At the same time, there were conflicts between Jesus and certain Jews. Moreover, the majority of the Jewish people and their leaders did not believe in Jesus, and this strained their relationship with his disciples.

(4) Nevertheless, Church and synagogue began gradually to walk their separate ways only after the conclusion of the first Jewish war with the Romans (70 C.E.). Prior to that, Jesus' disciples did not demonstrate a self-understanding of themselves as members of a religious community standing over against Judaism. And upon closer examination, even the later writings of the New Testament, although they manifest signs of the movement toward separation, continue to demonstrate some form of dialogue with the Church's original Jewish matrix. Moreover, the inevitable rupture between Judaism and the early Church did not and does not eradicate the spiritual "bond" to which *Nostra aetate* refers.

This recent transformation in New Testament scholarship regarding Jesus' ties with Judaism carries far-reaching implications not only for biblical interpretation, but also for contemporary theology, religious education, spirituality, and worship. In the past, for example, when we listened to the narrative of the so-called Council of Jerusalem in the book of the Acts of the Apostles, our tendency was to identify fully with the Apostle Paul in his dispute with Peter, James, and the Jewish-spirited Jerusalem

Church. But the enhanced appreciation of Jesus' positive Jewish ties now prompts us to take a second look at the passage and its historical context.

From the new perspective, it now appears that Peter and James were trying to hold on to something very important, however inadequately they made their case. Insofar as the fundamental decision recorded in this story played a role in the subsequent severing of all constructive links with Judaism, it also had the effect of deadening an important dimension of the Church's soul.

It is this buried heritage that Pope John Paul has brought to our attention on numerous occasions during his pontificate. Nevertheless, this profound shift in Christian exegesis of the New Testament will not have its full impact until it begins to influence all other aspects of church life. We have much work to do in the Church to incorporate this new perspective on Jesus and Judaism into our theological statements; our education of clergy, seminarians, and lay people; our preaching; and our worship.

Again, this is being addressed in the Church. For example, to provide additional help and guidelines to Catholic preachers in regard to the presentation of Jews and Judaism, the Bishops' Committee on the Liturgy of the National Conference of Catholic Bishops issued an important statement earlier this month. It includes such topics as the Jewish roots of the Christian liturgy, the relationship between the readings taken from the Hebrew Scriptures and the New Testament during Advent and Lent, and suggestions for pastoral activities during Holy Week and Easter. While the Episcopal Conference will undoubtedly continue to address such matters, the Church will also need the assistance of centers, such as yours here at the College of St. Thomas, for these efforts to be fully effective.

We humbly acknowledge that, regrettably, there has been widespread theological anti-Judaism in the history of Christianity, and it has infected every dimension of ecclesial life. Vatican II gave us a historic mandate to change that tragic legacy. Recent exegesis has, in turn, provided us with the scriptural resources for carrying out this mandate. We must maintain our commitment to this endeavor in the years ahead, for it involves our very faith identity as Christians. If anything, we need to accelerate the work undertaken thus far and give this mandate a renewed priority in the Church's life.

THE CHURCH AND JUDAISM

Our renewed appreciation of the thoroughly Jewish context of Jesus' preaching and ministry has inevitably led the Church to a reconsideration of how it expresses theologically its relationship with Judaism. It is no secret that many of our past formulations have seriously distorted the role of the Jewish People in human salvation. These distortions undoubtedly played a role in the persecutions borne by Jewish communities in so many parts of the world and tragically helped provide a seedbed for Christian collaboration with the fundamentally antireligious philosophy of Nazism.

Now all that is beginning to change as individual Christian theologians, Church leaders, and official ecclesial documents increasingly challenge this long-standing theology of total Jewish displacement from the process of salvation after the coming of Jesus. The prevalent "supercessionist" approach to Judaism on the part of much of classical Christian theology is being replaced by a theology of covenantal partnership.

No one has given greater impetus to this new theological understanding of the Jewish-Christian relationship than Pope John Paul II. In recognition of his contribution, the United States Catholic Conference, in collaboration with the Anti-Defamation League of B'nai B'rith, published a collection of his addresses on the topic between 1979 and 1986 (cf. *Pope John Paul II on Jews and Judaism, 1979–1986*, edited with introduction and commentary by Eugene J. Fisher and Leon Klenicki). Several themes emerge in the book as cornerstones of the developing theology of covenantal partnership.

The first theme is that of a "spiritual bond" which links the Church to the People Israel. This was a notion central to *Nostra aetate*. Pope John Paul made it a prominent part of his very first statement on the subject as Pontiff in March 1979 when he spoke to an international group of Jewish leaders in Rome. On that occasion he interpreted the conciliar phrase "spiritual bond" to mean "that our two religious communities are connected and closely related at the very level of their respective identities" and affirmed the need for "fraternal dialogue" between them.

Such language makes it clear that the Pope wishes to underscore the fact that the Jewish-Christian relationship could not be interpreted as merely marginal for the Church's identity. The Holy See's *Notes* of 1985, which build upon the Pope's own statements, insist that this relationship reaches to the very essence of the Christian faith. Hence to cover over or deny its reality is, in effect, to sacrifice something at the very core of Christian existence, something *integral* to the Church's authentic proclamation of its faith (cf. *Notes*, 1.2).

Earlier that same year, in an address at a twentieth anniversary commemoration of *Nostra aetate* in Rome, the Holy Father insisted that the spiritual bond between Christians and Jews must be viewed as a "sacred one, stemming as it does from the mysterious will of God." And during his historic visit to Rome's synagogue in 1986, he further intensified this theme of "spiritual bonding" with the following words:

> The Church of Christ discovers her "bond" with Judaism by "searching into her own mystery" (*Nostra aetate*, 4). The Jewish religion is not

"extrinsic" to us, but in a certain way is "intrinsic" to our religion. With Judaism, therefore, we have a relationship which we do not have with any other religion. You are dearly beloved brothers and, in a certain way, it could be said that you are our elder brothers.

The second major theme of Pope John Paul's newly emerging theology of the Christian-Jewish relationship focuses on the "living heritage" of Judaism in which Christians share by reason of their inherent bond with the Jewish people. The Holy Father treads very cautiously here, as well he must, for there is a deep-seated tradition in Christianity that would argue that, by rejecting Jesus as the Messiah, Jews forfeited their patrimony which then became the sole possession of the Church.

Pope John Paul, following in the footsteps of St. Paul in his letter to the Romans, will have no part of any "theology of abrogation." During his pastoral visit to the Federal Republic of Germany in 1980, he strongly emphasized that this was a *living* heritage in which Christians shared. At the Rome synagogue he called upon Jews and Christians to witness together in an assertive way to this common patrimony.

In proclaiming the Jewish heritage a "living patrimony" for Christians the Pope is reminding us of an important reality also stressed in the 1985 *Notes* of the Holy See, namely, that this heritage includes far more than the Hebrew Scriptures. The Jewish People have continued to reinterpret their covenantal relationship with God throughout the centuries after the close of the biblical canon. These reinterpretations are to be found in the Talmud and in the writings of Jewish mystics and philosophers, past and present. This literature, too, has great religious value. As Pope John Paul has pointed out, it is important for Christians to know "the faith and religious life of the Jewish people as they are professed and practiced still today" (March 6, 1982). He adds that this body of Jewish literature "can greatly help us to understand better certain aspects of the Church."

There is an additional implication to these first two central themes of Pope John Paul's emerging theology of the Jewish-Christian relationship. If we are prepared to integrate the themes of "bonding" and "shared patrimony" into our spirituality as Christians, as the Holy Father urges upon us, then we must recognize the impossibility of discussing critical contemporary questions in theology and ethics without explicit reference to the ways various Jewish scholars have interpreted covenantal responsibility throughout the ages, including the present day. Hence contemporary Jewish reflections on the meaning of such basic religious issues as the significance of the God of the covenant today, or Jewish deliberations on such pressing ethical issues as peace, power, and economic equality assume a very important status.

Let me be clear on this point. There is no question here of incorporating such reflections simply out of interreligious sensitivity, or because of a general commitment to pluralism, as important as such sensitivity and commitment might be. Rather, in light of the renewed theology of the Christian-Jewish relationship rooted in a sense of spiritual bonding and a shared patrimony with Jews, such reflections now are seen to be integral to the Christian community, not merely as extra resources from a parallel community to be used in a peripheral way.

The third critical theme in the developing Catholic theology of the Jewish-Christian relationship, as articulated by Pope John Paul II, is one to which I have previously alluded: his constant insistence on the permanent validity of the original divine covenant with Israel. On numerous occasions he has made explicit what was already present, though still in somewhat embryonic form, in the documents of Vatican II, particularly in *Nostra aetate* and the Dogmatic Constitution on the Church, *Lumen gentium*.

On a 1980 pastoral visit to Mainz, in the Federal Republic of Germany, the Pope, citing Romans 11:29, told a group of Jewish leaders that the original Jewish covenant has never been revoked by God. And, in 1982, meeting with representatives of episcopal conferences and ecumenical leaders in Rome, he underscored the present tense of Romans 9:4-5 concerning the Jews, calling them a people "who have the adoption as sons, and the glory and the covenants and the legislation and the worship and the promises." This theme reached a remarkable climax while Pope John Paul was visiting Australia in 1986 when he said that:

> The Catholic faith is rooted in the eternal truths of the Hebrew Scriptures and in the irrevocable covenant made with Abraham. We, too, gratefully hold these same truths of our Jewish heritage and look upon you as our brothers and sisters in the Lord.

Taken together, the three themes which I have just outlined offer us a framework for understanding the Christian-Jewish relationship in a theological context quite unlike what we have known for centuries in the Church. Upon further reflection, this framework, as the Holy Father has pointed out, is at its heart deeply based in the Scriptures. The challenge for all of us in the Church today—and I lay that challenge in a special way upon all theologians, religious educators, and pastors in the audience this evening—is to begin to incorporate this new theology into every aspect of our life as Christian communities. Our theological writings, our liturgical and catechetical volumes, and our preaching must begin to reflect these themes in a consistent and thorough way.

Theologians will continue to pursue better ways of expressing this developing understanding of the Christian-Jewish link. Certainly the Pope himself would be the first to acknowledge that not all issues have been fully clarified. But the ongoing discussions should never serve to cloud over the emerging consensus around the three basic themes articulated by Pope John Paul throughout his pontificate.

THE HOLOCAUST

During the last decade, we have witnessed important developments within Christianity in understanding the centrality of the Holocaust for the ongoing life of the Jewish People, in coming to grips with the role that theological and popular anti-Semitism played in undergirding what was at root a militantly antireligious philosophy, and in beginning to incorporate the Holocaust as a significant experience for Christian theological interpretation in our day. All three dimensions of the Holocaust are crucial for continued Christian existence. Reflection upon them should continue in earnest and, as far as possible, in tandem with one another.

The primary goal which led to the Holocaust was an attempt to shape a totally "new person," a "super being," in a social milieu in which growing technological competence combined with bureaucratic proficiency and the gradual erosion of traditional moral restraints to swing open the gates to the virtually unlimited use of human power. The Nazis were convinced that it was now possible to reshape human society, perhaps humanity itself, to a degree never deemed imaginable in the past.

To accomplish this, they were determined to exterminate or subjugate those whom they regarded as inherently inferior. Their calculated plan for "renewing" humankind included Gypsies, homosexuals, the mentally and/or physically incapacitated, and the Slavs, especially the Polish nation. First and foremost, they targeted the Jewish People whom they classified as "vermin," although it has become evident recently that their attack against Gypsies had similar features.

Scholars have now demonstrated that, in a significant way, the centuries of Christian degradation of the Jewish image contributed to this Nazi classification of the Jews. Pope John Paul II has summoned Christians to a forthright confrontation with this anti-Semitic tradition. I applaud those scholars who have taken up the challenge in a responsible and thorough manner. Christian theological and institutional collaboration with Nazism must be pursued in depth for the Church's moral integrity. In his address in Miami during last year's papal visit to the United States, the Holy Father announced the establishment of an international project in which Catholic and Jewish experts would probe the significance of the Holocaust in preparation for an eventual statement by the Holy See.

The Holocaust challenges the Church today on many theological fronts as well. Most importantly, it raises serious questions about how we might understand God's relationship to creation in our time. In this regard, our new awareness of the deep bonding between Christianity and Judaism assumes great importance. In dialogue with Jewish thinkers, we must pursue the question of God's relationship to the world after the Holocaust. We must also be prepared to turn to the Jewish tradition to discover possible pathways to answer the question.

The Holocaust has also raised profound ethical questions, for its aim was nothing less than the total transformation of human values. How do we anchor moral responsibility in public society in a technological and bureaucratic age in which the basic sensitivity to human life seems to be rapidly eroding at all levels? How do we harness the newly available forms of power for the promotion of good rather than massive destruction? How do we recover an adequate sense of the importance of history as a locus of salvation? How do we make theology more "subject-centered"? Again, Christians need to confront these issues in dialogue with Jews. Above all, we must come to recognize that the face of the Holocaust affects Christian theology as a whole, and not merely the more limited area of Christian-Jewish relations.

This evening, I would like to raise two final issues regarding the Holocaust. The *first* is the feeling among some within the Jewish community that the Catholic Church—and Pope John Paul, in particular—is "universalizing" the Holocaust or trying to take away its Jewish specificity. This concern has been raised by several prominent Jewish leaders long committed to dialogue and by Nobel Prize recipient Elie Wiesel. So they deserve a response—not a superficial apologetic on behalf of the Pope, but simply a review of his actual record.

In his 1979 visit to Auschwitz, the Pope singled out the Hebrew inscription honoring the Jewish victims in that camp. He recalled this event during his address at the Rome synagogue in 1986. His 1987 presentation to the Jews of Warsaw acknowledged both the priority and the uniqueness of Jewish suffering in the *Shoah*. And in a well-publicized letter to Archbishop John May of St. Louis, president of the National Conference of Catholic Bishops, the Holy Father emphasized that any "authentic" approach to the Holocaust must first grapple with the specific Jewish reality of the event. And only then may other considerations be added.

Those who express concern about the Holy Father's direction should be relieved by examining the full range of papal statements these last several years. Taken together, they provide the Church with a powerful mandate to countenance no compromise on the question of acknowledging the Jews as the Holocaust's primary victims.

The *second* issue is the concern of some within the Jewish community that the Catholic Church is trying to "appropriate" the Holocaust, to turn it into a monument to Catholic martyrdom. Their concern is based upon the facts that the Church, in recent years, has highlighted certain non-Jewish victims of the Holocaust, pointed out the fundamental anti-Christian nature of Nazism, and beatified Edith Stein.

These actions might be interpreted as attempts to place Christians exclusively within the *victim* category, glossing over collaboration by Church members and officials. I assure you that I stand ready to repudiate any such effort, were it to arise within the Church. But I am convinced that it has not.

Rather, with all due respect for its Jewish uniqueness, the Church is trying to grapple with the Holocaust in its own unique way. And we must do this because, unlike the Jewish community, baptized Catholics were not only among its victims but also prominent among its perpetrators. The Church unquestionably has the responsibility to bring these other issues to the forefront of its consciousness—and before the world—because they bear a special relevance for contemporary ecclesial and civic life. At the same time, in reflecting upon the Holocaust, the Church must preserve the primacy of Jewish victimhood. And it has done so.

* * *

My sisters and brothers, as I compliment you on your past achievements, permit me also to challenge you to pursue with intensified seriousness some of the critical issues I have just laid before you. In so doing, you truly will bring *tikkun,* "healing," to our world.

Dialogue and collaboration are not options for us. They are a necessity. Never again can Jews and Christians permit themselves to be alienated from one another. Never again can we let our minds and hearts be misshaped by the prejudices and hatreds of the past. Never again can we allow a climate which could produce another Holocaust.

We have so much in common. But ultimately, it is our faith in God, who created us in his image and likeness, that unites us. We need to celebrate that unity always, even while we respect our different traditions.

I trust that my presence among you this evening is a sign of my deep respect and affection for you. This evening I pledge to you my love, my support, and my determination to work with you and others on all the matters that concern us as Jews and Christians, as citizens, but most of all, as caring friends.

Reception of Tree of Life Award, The Jewish National Fund

Chicago, Illinois
——*June 28, 1994* —————————————————————————

I am grateful to the Jewish National Fund for honoring me with its Tree of Life Award. An award like this has a great symbolic value—for me as an individual and for all of us as a community of people committed to the religious values and moral principles of our Jewish and Christian heritage. It will serve as an impetus for me to do even more in the future. It also will be a reminder to all of us of our God-given responsibility to reach out to our brothers and sisters regardless of who they might be or what their needs are.

We represent communities which are diverse in their religious beliefs and traditions, but united in their common goal of respecting the dignity of the human person and of protecting the rights which flow from that dignity. So, we must stay in close touch with one another. Such dialogue is needed to clarify and resolve, where possible, differences which, left unattended, might become troublesome. Such communication is also essential to support and strengthen our common vision and goals. Fortunately, this dialogue, especially between Jews and Christians, has increased and matured significantly over the past quarter century. I applaud and support this development which has accomplished so much good for our faith communities and for the human family as a whole.

Allow me to give an example of such productive dialogue. On May 31, the International Catholic-Jewish Liaison Committee published a joint statement at the Vatican, affirming "the sacred value of stable marriage and the family as intrinsically good." The statement said that churches and synagogues, separately and together, can make important, positive contributions to discussions about the family during this United Nations-designated International Year of the Family. The Jewish and Catholic representatives pointed out that families are in a unique position to teach and hand on the cultural, ethical, social, and spiritual values essential for the well-being of both individuals and society as a whole.

There is a growing concern in our country about the eclipse of such values and the concomitant rise and increase of many social problems, including the violence on our streets, as well as in our schools and playgrounds. My friends, our churches and synagogues have inherited a valuable legacy of wisdom and insight into human nature based on our respective religious beliefs and values. We dare not hoard this teaching for ourselves or fail to pass it on to the next generation. Our society desperately needs to hear about basic human values, and we are in a unique position to share our collective wisdom with all persons of good will.

Even as we face the future, we cannot forget the past. The persistence of anti-Semitic outbreaks in several parts of the world, including metropolitan Chicago, troubles me greatly. I have twice visited Auschwitz. Actually, one cannot simply *visit* Auschwitz. Standing there, we are strongly challenged to face squarely the capacity of humanity for organized mass destruction. We recognize that we have no alternative but to take a firm stand against such irrational prejudice directed against anyone or any group that differs from us in race, religion, or political outlook.

My experiences at Auschwitz have deepened my commitment to take very seriously any and all manifestations of anti-Semitism—no matter how inconsequential they may appear at first glance. The rapid rise of Nazism earlier this century showed us how quickly an apparently insignificant movement can assume control over a society.

As you know, on April 7, Pope John Paul II hosted an unprecedented symphonic concert in the Vatican's audience hall to commemorate the Holocaust, the *Shoah*. The Holy Father sat with the chief rabbi of Rome and the president of Italy. The conductor was Gilbert Levine whose mother-in-law survived Auschwitz. During the concert the U.S. actor, Richard Dreyfuss, recited the *Kaddish*, a Jewish prayer for the dead.

After the concert the Holy Father addressed the audience which included some of the survivors of the Holocaust. He said,

> We would risk causing the victims of the most atrocious deaths to die again if we do not have an ardent desire for justice, if we do not commit ourselves, each according to his capacities, to ensure that evil does not prevail over good as it did for millions of the children of the Jewish nation. We must therefore redouble our efforts to free man from the specter of racism, exclusion, alienation, slavery and xenophobia; to up-

root these evils which are creeping into society and undermining the foundations of peaceful coexistence.

He concluded his remarks by asking everyone present to observe a moment of silence to pray and, he said, "to hear once more the plea [of the Holocaust's victims], 'Do not forget us.'"

Keeping Holocaust memories alive has helped to bring about two recent, significant events: the Israel–PLO peace accord and the establishment of diplomatic relations between Israel and the Holy See.

In 1989 the U.S. Catholic bishops had stated that true peace in the Middle East would only come through dialogue. They pointed out that "the key to successful political dialogue will be Palestinians willing to discuss secure boundaries and stable political relations with Israel, and Israelis willing to discuss territory and sovereignty with Palestinians." In 1989 such a dialogue seemed quite impossible to most observers. Today, we see that this kind of dialogue is *difficult*, but not impossible!

Last November, at our annual bishops' meeting, we called the interim agreement between Israel and the PLO "a historic opening to a new era for which the whole world has been longing for many years." On May 4, the human family's hopes for peace in the Middle East were raised a notch higher, when the Israel–PLO accord was signed in Cairo. None of this would have been possible without the courage, imagination, and spirit of compromise of leaders on both sides of the long-festering conflict. Nevertheless, enormous obstacles remain to be overcome: extremism on the part of some on both sides of the conflict; the complex relations among the various nations of the Middle East; the extremely difficult social, economic, and political conditions of Gaza and the West Bank during the past twenty-five years. Let us pray that justice will take firm hold in that area and that its fruit will be true peace for all concerned.

If one were to rely only on media reports about religion in the Middle East in general, and the Holy Land in particular, one might conclude that the problems there involve only Jews and Muslims. However, there are over 2 million baptized Catholics [2,147,000]—not counting large numbers of Orthodox and other Christians—in Israel and the Arab lands of the Middle East (Statistical Yearbook of the Church, 1991). That is one of the reasons why the Catholic Church has taken an intense interest in what happens in the region.

Progress in relations between Israelis and Palestinians undoubtedly helped to accelerate the developing relationship between Israel and the Holy See (or the Vatican, as it is more popularly known). As a result, Israel and the Holy See established full diplomatic relations on June 16. Following the practice of all countries, including the United States—with the sole exceptions of Costa Rica and El Salvador—the Holy See's embassy will not be in Jerusalem, but, rather, in Jaffa, near Tel Aviv.

This fact acknowledges that there is still considerable unfinished business between Israel and the Holy See, including the legal and financial status of the Catholic Church in the Holy Land.

On June 13, I attended a meeting in Rome of the world's cardinals with the Holy Father. He told us that the new relationship between Israel and the Holy See is one of the most important recent accomplishments of Vatican diplomacy. He also pointed out that a similar relationship is being established with Jordan and that a "significant development of dialogue with the Palestine Liberation Organization" has also taken place.

The Church's new relationship with Israel offers a special channel of dialogue between the two parties for the promotion of the values of peace, freedom, and justice. The accord is especially important because it will provide greater confidence and security to the communities of the Catholic faithful who live in Israel and the West Bank.

The Holy See has also made it clear that, while it has paid particular attention to the sensitivities of the other Christian communities in the Holy Land—those that are not in full communion with the Catholic Church—it has avoided giving the least impression that it was negotiating in their name. At the same time, it kept them informed of the progress of the negotiations.

Some commentators, noting that Jerusalem is not mentioned in the agreement between the Holy See and Israel, concluded that the Vatican has pulled back from its long-standing insistence that the special status of the Holy City of Jerusalem be protected by international guarantees. This is not the case. The Holy See's position on these matters has not at all changed. However, the bilateral agreement between the Holy See and Israel could not resolve this issue because of its international and multilateral dimensions. The Vatican issued a statement after the accord was announced, stating that

> The Holy See, in solidarity with the followers of all three monotheistic religions and with so many people of good will, always hopes for the day when the Holy City of Jerusalem may become truly the . . . crossroads of peace, a privileged place for the meeting of people, cultures, and civilizations.

Both the government of Israel and the Holy See see this new relationship as much more than the routine business of diplomacy. It also impacts the relationship of Catholics and Jews throughout the world. It is a new chapter in a long, sad history between our two communities. The Holy See is convinced that dialogue and respectful cooperation between Catholics and Jews will now be given new impetus and energy, both in Israel and throughout the world. I pray that that will, indeed, occur, especially here in metropolitan Chicago.

* * *

My dear friends, while we differ in many respects, we have so much in common. Ultimately, it is our faith in God, who created us in his "image and likeness," that unites us more than anything else. May we always celebrate that unity, while respecting our different traditions, and working with each other, in love, for the betterment of our respective communities and the entire human family. Please accept my presence among you this evening as a sign of the great respect and affection I have for you, as well as a reaffirmation of my commitment to dialogue and work with you.

May the Lord bless you and keep you!
May his face shine upon you, and be gracious to you!
May he look upon you with kindness,
and give you peace!

"Anti-Semitism: The Historical Legacy and the Continuing Challenge for Christians"

Hebrew University of Jerusalem, Israel

— March 23, 1995 ——————————————————

Ladies and gentlemen, I am greatly honored by your conferral upon me of the Honorary Fellowship of the Hebrew University of Jerusalem. It is a humbling experience, indeed, to receive such an honor from this distinguished scholarly community. I am also very grateful for this opportunity to address you on the subject of anti-Semitism from a Catholic point of view.

In recent years the Catholic Church has undertaken important efforts to acknowledge guilt for the legacy of anti-Semitism and to repudiate as *sinful* any remaining vestiges of that legacy in its contemporary teaching and practice. In 1989, the Pontifical Commission for Peace and Justice issued a strong declaration on racism, which had an international impact. The document, entitled *The Church and Racism: Towards a More Fraternal Society,* insisted that "Harboring racist thoughts and entertaining racist attitudes is a sin" (no. 24).[1] And it clearly included anti-Semitism on its list of continuing manifestations of racist ideologies that are to be regarded as sinful. In point of fact, *The Church and Racism* calls anti-Semitism "the most tragic form that racist ideology has assumed in our

---

[1] Pontifical Commission, *Justitia et Pax: The Church and Racism: Towards a More Fraternal Society* (Washington, D.C.: U.S. Catholic Conference, 1988) 34 (no. 24).

century" and warns that certain forms of anti-Zionism, while not of the same order, often serve as a screen for anti-Semitism, feeding on it and leading to it (no. 15).[2]

Pope John Paul II has taken up the challenge to anti-Semitism put forth by the Pontifical Commission on several occasions in recent years. During a visit to Hungary in 1991, conscious of the post-Communist era resurgence of anti-Semitism in certain parts of Central and Eastern Europe, the Pope spoke of the urgent task of repentance and reconciliation:

> In face of a risk of a resurgence and spread of anti-Semitic feelings, attitudes, and initiatives, of which certain disquieting signs are to be seen today and of which we have experienced the most frightful results in the past, we must teach consciences to consider anti-Semitism, and all forms of racism, as sins against God and humanity.[3]

And in his current book, *Crossing the Threshold of Hope*, the Holy Father repeats this theme as he calls anti-Semitism "a great sin against humanity."[4]

In my address this afternoon I will reflect on how we can work to eradicate the evil of anti-Semitism from our midst. This is not an easy task; it is one to which I have been dedicated for many years. My reflections will have four parts: (1) the roots of anti-Semitism in Christian history; (2) contemporary developments in Catholic theology; (3) thoughts on the relationship between anti-Semitism and Nazism; and (4) actions that can be taken to ensure that anti-Semitism is not part of the future.

ORIGINS OF ANTI-SEMITISM

Allow me to explore briefly some of the reasons why anti-Semitism has been part of Christian life. It is important that we do this because anti-Semitism has deep roots in Christian history, which go back to the earliest days of the Church. In fact, as Father Edward Flannery has shown in his classic work on anti-Semitism, *The Anguish of the Jews*,[5] the early Christian community inherited a cultural tradition from the Greco-Roman civilization that included a prejudicial outlook towards Jews. Jews were

---

[2] *The Church and Racism*, 23 (no. 15).

[3] Pope John Paul II, "The Sinfulness of Antisemitism," *Origins* 23 (13) (September 5, 1991) 204.

[4] Pope John Paul II, *Crossing the Threshold*, ed. Vittorio Messori (New York: Alfred A. Knopf, 1994) 96.

[5] Edward Flannery, *The Anguish of the Jews*, rev. ed. (New York/Mahweh: Paulist Press, 1985).

disliked in pre-Christian Greece and Rome for their general unwillingness to conform to prevailing social mores. It is regrettable that this long history of anti-Semitism in a Christian context has been virtually eliminated from our history texts and other educational materials. Inclusion of this history, as painful as it is for us to hear today, is a necessary requirement for authentic reconciliation between Christians and Jews in our time.

In addition, there were many other factors that likely contributed to the growth of anti-Jewish feelings among Christians in the first centuries of the Church's existence. For one, the overwhelming number of early Christians came from Greco-Roman communities with little personal acquaintance with Jews and Judaism. We now know from scholars dealing with early Christianity, such as Robert Wilken[6] and Anthony Saldarini,[7] that the final break between Judaism and Christianity was a far more gradual process than we once imagined, extending into the third and fourth centuries in some areas of the East. Nevertheless, the *formative* influence of Jewish Christianity upon the Church as a whole declined rapidly after the pivotal decision reached by Paul and the representatives of the Jerusalem Church at what is often called the Council of Jerusalem. This resulted in the loss of any countervailing positive identification with Jews and their religious heritage that could overcome the new converts' inbred cultural prejudices. This tendency towards separation from anything Jewish was further enhanced by the desire to avoid any linkage between the Church and the Jewish community after the disastrous Jewish revolt against the Roman imperial authorities (66–70 C.E.) which, besides the destruction of the Temple in Jerusalem, generated continued postwar pressure and retribution by Rome against the Jewish community.

Another factor contributing to the emergence of anti-Semitism in early Christianity may be the image of Jews that emerges from the New Testament itself. There are texts that remain open to anti-Judaic interpretation, and there is ample evidence that such interpretations emerged in the first centuries of Christian history.

Negative attitudes towards Jews in the New Testament were only the beginning of difficulties for the Jewish community. Unfortunately, there soon developed within the teachings of the early Fathers of the Church a strong tendency to regard Jews as entirely displaced from the covenantal

---

[6] Wayne A. Meeks and Robert L. Wilken, *Jews and Christians in Antioch in the First Four Centuries* (Missoula, Mont.: Scholars Press, 1978); Robert Wilken, *John Chrysostom and the Jews: Rhetoric and Reality in the Late 4th Century* (Berkeley: University of California Press, 1983).

[7] Anthony J. Saldarini, "Jews and Christians in the First Two Centuries: The Changing Paradigm," *Shofar* 10 (1992) 34.

relationship because of their unwillingness to accept Jesus as the Messiah, despite the clear teaching to the contrary on the part of St. Paul in Romans 9–11, which served as a basis for the Second Vatican Council's renewed constructive theology of the Christian-Jewish relationship.

This belief, that the Jews had been totally rejected by God and replaced in the convenantal relationship by the "New Israel," led to the emergence of another widespread doctrine in patristic writings. I have in mind the so-called "perpetual wandering" theology which consigned Jews to a condition of permanent statelessness as a consequence of their displacement from the covenant as a punishment for murdering the Messiah. This condition of being permanently displaced persons was meant as an enduring sign of Jewish sinfulness and as a warning to others of what they could expect if they too failed to accept Christ. This theology became so deep-seated in popular culture that even a familiar houseplant—the "wandering Jew"—took on its name.

We can illustrate this theology of "perpetual wandering" with references from certain central figures in the patristic era. Eusebius of Caesarea (ca. 265–339 C.E.), for example, speaks of how the royal metropolis of the Jews would be destroyed by fire and the city would become inhabited no longer by Jews, "but by races of other stock, while they (i.e., the Jews) would be dispersed among the Gentiles throughout the whole world with never a hope of any cessation of evil or breathing space from troubles."[8] St. Cyprian of Carthage (ca. 210–258 C.E.), relying on various prophetic texts, which suggest desolation and exile as a consequence of sin, envisioned Israel as having entered its final state of desolation and exile. Following in the same vein, St. Hippolytus of Rome, who was born around 170 C.E., insisted that, unlike the exilic experiences suffered by the Jews at the hands of the Egyptians and the Babylonians in earlier times, the postbiblical exile would continue throughout the course of human history. In the East, St. John Chrysostom (344–407 C.E.) clearly linked the now permanent exilic condition of the Jews with the "killing of Christ." And St. Augustine of Hippo (354–430 C.E.) in his classic work, *City of God*, speaks several times of the Jews as having "their back bend down always."

While the patristic writings were far more than an extended anti-Jewish treatise, Christians cannot ignore this "shadow side" of patristic theology, which in other aspects remains a continuing source of profound spiritual enrichment. Jews are very well aware of the "shadow side" of this theology; unfortunately, Christians generally are not. It has been omitted from basic Christian texts far too often. Yet, we cannot understand the treatment of Jews in subsequent centuries without some grasp of this theology.

---

[8] *Demonstration of the Gospel* I, I.

The history to which it gave rise is replete with persistent forms of social and religious discrimination and persecution, which brought upon the Jewish community continual humiliation as well as political and civil inequality. On occasion, this further degenerated into outright physical suffering and even death, especially in such periods as that of the Crusades.

This legacy of anti-Semitism, with its profoundly negative social consequences for Jews as individuals and for the Jewish community as a whole, remained the dominant social pattern in Western Christian lands until the twentieth century. While we can point to some notable breaks in this pattern in such countries as Spain and Poland, as well as for individual Jews in the liberal democracies created in parts of Europe and North America, the respite was sometimes short-lived and, as in the case of Spain, followed by even more flagrant forms of attack on the Jewish community.

At the dawn of the twentieth century the theology of perpetual divine judgment upon Jewish people did not vanish overnight. Rather, it continued to exercise a decisive role in shaping Catholicism's initial reactions, for example, to the proposal for restoring a Jewish national homeland in Palestine. It also was of central importance in shaping popular Christian attitudes towards the Nazis and their stated goal of eliminating all Jews from Europe and beyond through deliberate extermination. While I will return to this question of classical anti-Semitism and its role during that period, there is little doubt that this persistent tradition provided an indispensable seedbed for the Nazis' ability to succeed as far as they did in their master plan. They would not have secured the popular support they enjoyed were it not for the continuing influence of traditional Christian anti-Semitism on the masses of baptized believers in Europe.

Both Father Edward Flannery and the late Professor Uriel Tal have emphasized the significant impact of classical Christian anti-Semitism upon the development of Nazism, despite their shared conviction that the philosophy of the Third Reich resulted primarily from distinctly modern forces. Flannery argues that the architects of the *Shoah* found their Jewish targets well primed for the formulation of their racist theories:

> The degraded state of the Jews, brought about by centuries of opprobrium and oppression, gave support to the invidious comparisons with which the racists built their theories. And in their evil design, they were able to draw moral support from traditional views of Jews and Judaism.[9]

Professor Tal offered an analysis very similar to that of Father Flannery's in this regard. He insisted that Nazi racial anti-Semitism was not totally

---

[9] Edward Flannery, "Anti-Zionism and the Christian Psyche," *Journal of Ecumenical Studies* 6 (2) (Spring 1969) 174–75.

original when subjected to careful scrutiny. Rather, traditional Christian stereotypes of Jews and Judaism were clothed in new pseudoscientific jargon and applied to specific historical realities of the period. Tal insisted that

> racial antisemitism and the subsequent Nazi movement were not the result of mass hysteria or the work of single propagandists. The racial anti-semites, despite their antagonism toward traditional Christianity, learned much from it, and succeeded in producing a well-prepared, systematic ideology with a logic of its own that reached its culmination in the Third Reich.[10]

CONTEMPORARY DEVELOPMENTS

Having traced the development of anti-Semitism within Christianity, we can turn to contemporary developments. In the three decades or so since the beginning of the Second Vatican Council, the negative theology of the Jewish people has lost its theological foundations. In chapter four of *Nostra aetate*, the council clearly asserted that there never existed a valid basis either for the charge of collective guilt against the Jewish community for supposedly "murdering the Messiah" or for the consequent theology of permanent Jewish suffering and displacement. With its positive affirmation of continued covenantal inclusion on the part of the Jewish People after the coming of Christ Jesus, following St. Paul in Romans 9–11, the council permanently removed all basis for the long-held "perpetual wandering" theology and the social deprivation and suffering that flowed from it.

The Second Vatican Council's removal of the classical "displacement/perpetual wandering" theology from contemporary Catholic catechesis has been enhanced in subsequent documents from the Holy See and Pope John Paul II. The Holy See's 1985 *Notes on the Correct Way to Present the Jews and Judaism in Preaching and Catechesis in the Roman Catholic Church*, issued to commemorate the twentieth anniversary of *Nostra aetate*, make two very important constructive affirmations, especially when these are set over against the history of Catholicism's traditional approach to the question of Jewish existence. Both occur in paragraph no. 25 where the *Notes* maintain that "the history of Israel did not end in 70 A.D. (i.e., with the destruction of the Jerusalem Temple by the Romans). . . . It continued, especially in a numerous Diaspora which allowed Israel to carry to the whole world a witness . . . while preserving

---

[10] Uriel Tal, *Christians and Jews in Germany: Religion, Politics and Ideology in the Second Reich, 1870–1914* (Ithaca, N.Y.: Cornell University Press, 1975) 305.

the memory of the land of their forefathers at the heart of their hope" and, subsequently, that "the permanence of Israel (while so many ancient peoples have disappeared without a trace) is a historic fact and a sign to be interpreted within God's design." Both these statements clearly repudiate a "displacement" theology.

Pope John Paul II, who has contributed significantly to the development of the Church's new theological outlook on Jews and Judaism,[11] wrote the following in his 1984 statement *Redemptionis anno:*

> For the Jewish people who live in the State of Israel and who preserve in that land such precious testimonies of their history and their faith, we must ask for the desired security and due tranquility that is the prerogative of every nation and condition of life and of progress of every society.[12]

This statement clearly exhibits on the part of the Holy Father a sense of the deep intertwining of faith and continued attachment to the land on the part of the Jewish people, a sense that further draws out the profound implications of the renewed theology of the Christian-Jewish relationship put forth by the Second Vatican Council.

Two recent documents of the Holy See further seal the coffin of the biblically unfounded "displacement" theology. The first is the text of the new *Catechism of the Catholic Church*, which reaffirms the two major points on which the council built its new theological approach to the Jewish people. In paragraph no. 597 the catechism rejects any idea that all Jews then or now can be charged with the responsibility for Jesus' death. It reminds Christians that their sins were largely the reason why Jesus died on the cross. And paragraph no. 849 speaks of the distinctiveness of Jewish faith as an authentic response to God's original revelation and underlines the permanence of the divine promise made to the people Israel.[13]

The second document is the Holy See–Israeli Accords. While this is fundamentally a political document that develops a framework for dealing with concrete issues, it has an underlying theological significance as well. Mindful of the longstanding theological approach to Jewish political sovereignty on the part of the Catholic tradition, the Preamble to the Accords has set this essentially political document within the overall context of the process of Catholic-Jewish reconciliation underway in the Church since the Second Vatican Council:

---

[11] Cf. Eugene J. Fisher and Leon Klenicki, eds., *John Paul II on Jews and Judaism* (Washington, D.C.: U.S. Catholic Conference, 1987).

[12] Cf. *The Pope Speaks* 29 (3) (1984) 219–20.

[13] Cf. *Catechism of the Catholic Church* (Collegeville, Minn.: The Liturgical Press, 1994) no. 597; no. 839.

[A]ware of the unique nature of the relationship between the Catholic Church and the Jewish people, and the historic process of reconciliation and growth in mutual understanding and friendship between Catholics and Jews . . .

So reads the opening part of the Accords.

It is also well to note that article no. 2 of the Accords contains a very strong and unequivocal condemnation by the Holy See of "hatred, persecution, and all manifestations of anti-Semitism directed against the Jewish people and individual Jews . . ." I welcome this forthright statement as well as the accompanying pledge by the Holy See and the State of Israel to cooperate in every possible way

> in combating all forms of anti-Semitism and all kinds of racism and of religious intolerance, and in promoting mutual understanding among nations, tolerance among communities, and respect for human life and dignity (no. 1).

This statement makes concrete the renewed theological vision of the Christian-Jewish relationship developed at the Second Vatican Council. It also solidifies the notion that forms of racism, including anti-Semitism, are fundamentally sinful as the 1989 Holy See document and the papal statements I cited earlier make clear.

The Holy See's action in formally recognizing Israel through the Accords represents a final seal on the process begun at the Second Vatican Council to rid Catholicism of all vestiges of "displacement theology" and the implied notion of perpetual Jewish homelessness. The Accords represent the Catholic Church's full and final acknowledgment of Jews as a *people*, not merely as individuals. I recognize that for the vast majority of Jews, Israel signifies their ultimate tie to Jewish peoplehood, their central point of self-identity. And, as the Holy See's 1974 Guidelines on Catholic-Jewish relations pointed out, authentic dialogue requires that all partners come to understand and respect one another as they define themselves. As Arthur Hertzberg has shown very well in his classic work *The French Enlightenment and the Jews*,[14] even democratic societies that were prepared to grant Jews a measure of personal freedom and political rights were unable to accept the idea of Jewish peoplehood.

Until now I have been speaking of developments that have already occurred. As we all know, much more needs to be done. In particular, there is need for continued scholarship and theological reflection, especially with regard to what many consider to be problematic New Testament

[14] Arthur Hertzberg, *The French Enlightenment and the Jews: The Origins of Modern Antisemitism* (New York: Schocken, 1968).

texts. While it is not certain that any of these texts themselves can be legitimately termed "anti-Semitic," or even "anti-Judaic," scholars differ significantly on this point and will likely do so for the foreseeable future. I am aware that some scholars doing important research on this topic, including people here in Jerusalem such as Malcolm Lowe, believe the problem is essentially one of mistranslation. Others interpret it primarily as an internal Jewish polemic, which was not an uncommon phenomenon in the period, as we know from certain Jewish documents, the Talmud included.[15] Retranslation (where scholarly consensus can be achieved) and reinterpretation certainly are to be included among the goals we pursue in the effort at eradicating anti-Semitism. But at this point, the requisite scholarly consensus on the especially problematic passages appears a long way off.

In the interim, as we await a scholarly resolution of the question of anti-Semitism in the New Testament, I would strongly urge that the Church adopt a pastoral approach. Father Raymond Brown, a renowned Catholic scholar on the Gospel of John, has suggested the basis of such a pastoral approach, at least with respect to the Fourth Gospel, which is generally considered among the most problematic of all New Testament books in its outlook towards Jews and Judaism. In commenting on John's use of the term, "the Jews," Brown expresses his conviction that, by deliberately using this generic term (where other gospel writers refer to the Jewish authorities or the various Second Temple Jewish parties), John meant to extend to the synagogue of his own day blame that an earlier tradition had attributed to the Jewish authorities. Although John was not the first to engage in such extension, he is the most insistent New Testament author in this regard. Brown attributes this process in John to the persecution that Christians were experiencing during that time at the hands of the synagogue authorities. Jews who professed Jesus to be the Messiah had been officially expelled from Judaism, thus making them vulnerable to Roman investigation and punishment. Jews were tolerated by Rome, but who were these Christians whom the Jews disclaimed?

Father Brown maintains that this teaching of John about the Jews, which resulted from the historical conflict between Church and synagogue in the latter part of the first century C.E., can no longer be taught as authentic doctrine or used as catechesis by contemporary Christianity. This is the key pastoral point. Christians today must come to see that such teachings, while an acknowledged part of their biblical heritage, can no longer be regarded as definitive teaching in light of our improved understanding of developments in the relationship between early Christianity

---

[15] Cf. John T. Pawlikowski, "New Testament Antisemitism: Fact or Fable?" *Antisemitism in the Contemporary World*, ed. Michael Curtis (Boulder and London: Westview Press, 1986) 107–27.

and the Jewish community of the time. As Brown says in his book, *The Community of the Beloved Disciple,* "It would be incredible for a twentieth-century Christian to share or justify the Johannine contention that 'the Jews' are the children of the Devil, an affirmation which is placed on the lips of Jesus (John 8:44)."[16]

Negative passages such as these must be reevaluated in light of the Second Vatican Council's strong affirmation in its Declaration on the Relation of the Church to Non-Christian Religions *(Nostra aetate)* that Jews remain a covenanted people, revered by God. The teaching of recent popes has also emphasized this. Pope John Paul II, in particular, has often highlighted the intimate bond that exists between Jews and Christians who are united in one ongoing covenant.

Nazism and Anti-Semitism

I would now like to return to the issue of Nazism and anti-Semitism, which continues to elicit considerable discussion today. I know it remains an important area of concern for this university, especially the Sassoon International Center for the Study of Anti-Semitism directed by Professor Yehuda Bauer. I am likewise aware of the many outstanding contributions made to our understanding of the *Shoah* by other members of your faculty, including Professors Israel Gutman and Emil Fackenheim.

During the past several decades, scholars throughout the world have advanced various perspectives on the relationship between the rise of Nazism and classical Christian hatred of the Jews. Some draw virtually a straight line from classical Christian thought regarding the Jewish People to the emergence of the *Shoah.* They point, for example, to Hitler's often-quoted remark to Church leaders, who came to see him to protest his treatment of Jews, that he was merely putting into practice what the Christian churches had preached for nearly two thousand years. These perspectives also highlight the close similarity between much of Nazi anti-Jewish legislation and laws against Jews in earlier Christian-dominated societies.

As I have already pointed out, relying on the research of Father Flannery and the late Professor Tal, there is little doubt that classical Christian presentations of Jews and Judaism were a central factor in generating popular support for the Nazi endeavor, along with economic greed, religious and political nationalism, and ordinary human fear. For many baptized Chris-

---

[16] Raymond Brown, *The Community of the Beloved Disciple* (New York: Paulist Press, 1979) 41–42. Cf. also, "The Passion According to John: Chapters 18 and 19," *Worship* 49 (March 1975) 130–31.

tians, traditional Christian beliefs about Jews and Judaism constituted the primary motivation for their support, active or tacit, of the Nazi movement. Some even went so far as to define the Nazi struggle against the Jews in explicitly religious and theological terms. In the Church today, we must not minimize the extent of Christian collaboration with Hitler and his associates. It remains a profound moral challenge that we must continue to confront for our own integrity as a religious community.

Nevertheless, in the final analysis, I must side with the perspective of those scholars such as Yosef Yerushalmi who have insisted that "the Holocaust was the work of a thoroughly modern, neopagan state," not merely a "transformed" medieval anti-Semitism rooted in Christian teachings.[17] The *Shoah* cannot be seen as simply the final and most gruesome chapter in the long history of Christian anti-Semitism. Rather, it was a plan for the mass destruction of human lives, supposedly undertaken in the name of "healing" humanity, as the psychologist Robert J. Lifton has put it, rooted in modern theories of inherent biological and racial inferiority, coupled with the escalation of bureaucratic and technological capacities. At its depths, it was profoundly as anti-Christian as it was anti-Jewish, evidenced by the fact that at least one of its theoreticians attempted to rewrite the New Testament totally based on Nazi concepts. It coalesced several important modern strains of thought into its master plan for human extermination.

To bring this plan to realization required, as the Nazis envisioned it, the elimination of the "dregs" of society. These they defined as first and foremost the Jewish people, but the category also was extended to embrace the disabled, Gypsies, the Polish leadership, homosexuals, and certain other designated groups. Proper distinctions need to be maintained between the wholesale attack on the Jewish people, for whom there was absolutely no escape from Nazi fury, and the others subjected to systematic Nazi attack. But there is also a linkage with the victimization of these other groups whose suffering and death were integral, not peripheral, to the overall Nazi plan. This is what makes the Holocaust *sui generis*, even though the fate of its primary victims, the Jews, had important ties to classical Christian teachings.

FUTURE POSSIBILITIES

Let us turn now from the horrors of the past to the possibilities of the future. Confronting the legacy of anti-Semitism will not prove easy, but confront it we must. Allow me to discuss several ways in which this can be done.

---

[17] Yosef Hayim Yerushalmi, "Response to Rosemary Ruether," *Auschwitz: Beginning of a New Era?*, ed. Eva Fleischner (New York: Ktav, the Cathedral Church of St. John the Divine and the Anti-Defamation League, 1977) 103.

1. The history of anti-Semitism and of anti-Judaic theology must be restored to our Catholic teaching materials. Innocence or ignorance is not a pathway to authentic virtue in this regard; courageous honesty is. In our religious education programs we should be prepared to tell the full story of the Church's treatment of Jews over the centuries, ending with a rejection of the shadow side of that history and theology at the Second Vatican Council. We can and should highlight moments of relative tranquility and constructive interaction when they occurred in such countries as Poland, Spain, and the United States, but these stories should never obscure the more pronounced history of hostility and subjection.

2. We also need an integral understanding of the Holocaust. In developing such an understanding, we have a responsibility to speak against unwarranted and generalized accusations directed at the Church and Church leaders. We need to reemphasize the protest statements and oppositional actions of Christian leaders and grassroots groups and individuals. The Fulda Declaration of the German Catholic Bishops, the Barmen Declaration of the Confessing Church (Lutheran) in Germany, the encyclical letter *Mit Brennender Sorge* issued in German by Pope Pius XI, the efforts of Archbishops Angelo Roncalli and Angelo Rotta, the *Zegota* movement in Poland, the many Catholic women religious whose communities hid Jews, the men and women of Le Chambon in France, Jan Karski of the Polish government-in-exile, the Austrian peasant Franz Jägerstätter—I could go on. To be sure, there were not enough. But these Christians preserved a measure of moral integrity in the Church during these years of Nazi darkness.

Nevertheless, the witness of these courageous Christian leaders, groups, and individuals should never be used to argue against the need for a full scrutiny of Church activities by reputable scholars. We must be prepared to deal honestly and candidly with the genuine failures of some in the Christian churches during that critical period. To that end, I would repeat what I first said in my keynote address to those attending the meeting of the International Catholic-Jewish Liaison Committee held in Baltimore in May 1992. The Catholic Church must be prepared to submit its World War II record to a thorough scrutiny by respected scholars. The detailed investigation of diocesan records from the Nazi era undertaken that same year in Lyons, France, with the support of the cardinal archbishop is a fine example of what I have in mind.

Such efforts should avoid broad generalizations, but instead focus in depth on specific geographic regions, as do, for example, the recent work on Poland by Dr. Ronald Modras[18] here at this university and the sympo-

---

[18] Cf. Ronald Modras, *The Catholic Church and Antisemitism in Poland, 1933–1939* (Chur, Switzerland: Harwood Academic Publishers, 1994).

sium papers collected by Professors Otto Dov Kulka and Paul Mendes-Flohr in the volume *Judaism and Christianity Under the Impact of National Socialism.*[19]

3. Education about the Holocaust should become a prominent feature in Catholic education at every level. To assist in realizing this goal, Seton Hill College near Pittsburgh has established a program explicitly designed for Catholic teachers that works closely with both *Yad Vashem* and the U.S. Holocaust Memorial Museum. And in Chicago, I have instructed the arch-diocesan school system to comply with the state mandate on Holocaust education even though it does not technically apply to our institutions.

4. But we must go beyond merely teaching the failures of the past, as crucial as that task remains. *Nostra aetate* and subsequent documents from the Holy See, as well as Pope John Paul II, have not merely removed the classical prejudices against Jews and Judaism from Catholic teaching. They have laid out the basis for a positive theology of reconciliation and bonding. This, too, must become part of our current effort in education.

In fact, several studies on Catholic religion materials undertaken by Sister Rose Thering at St. Louis University,[20] Dr. Eugene J. Fisher at New York University,[21] and most recently, Dr. Philip Cunningham at Boston College,[22] have shown a steady development in the presentation of the Christian-Jewish relationship, from one marked by classical stereotypes to one focused on the bonding of Christians and Jews within the one covenanted family. Not all problems have been resolved, but the progress has been remarkable. In this connection, I wish to add that it is my hope that, at the same time as we seek to develop a positive Christian under-standing, Jewish educators will also be able to rethink the Jewish com-munity's understanding of its relationship with the Church.

5. Liturgy and preaching are additional areas that require continued attention by the Church. In 1988, the U.S. Bishops' Committee on the

[19] Otto Dov Kulka and Paul R. Mendes-Flohr, eds., *Judaism and Christianity Under the Impact of National Socialism* (Jerusalem: The Historical Society of Is-rael and the Zalman Shazar Center for Jewish History, 1987).

[20] For a description and analysis of the Thering study, see John T. Pawlikowski, O.S.M., *Catechetics and Prejudice: How Catholic Teaching Materials View Jews, Protestants and Racial Minorities* (New York/Paramus/Toronto: Paulist Press, 1973).

[21] Eugene J. Fisher, *Faith Without Prejudice: Rebuilding Christian Attitudes Toward Judaism*, rev. and exp. ed. (New York: The American Interfaith Institute and Crossroad, 1993).

[22] Philip A. Cunningham, *Education for Shalom: Religion Textbooks and the En-hancement of the Catholic and Jewish Relationship* (Collegeville, Minn.: The Litur-gical Press, 1995).

Liturgy released a set of guidelines for the presentation of Jews and Judaism in Catholic preaching.[23] They offer directions for implementing the vision of *Nostra aetate* and subsequent documents of the Holy See in the Church's ministry of the word during the various liturgical seasons. Especially highlighted are the seasons of Lent/Holy Week and Easter, whose texts can serve to reinforce classical Christian stereotypes of Jews and Judaism if not interpreted carefully. The great challenge of these liturgical seasons is that they become times of reconciliation between Jews and Christians rather than conflict and division, as they were in past centuries. Christians need to recognize their profound bonds with the Jewish people during these central periods of the Liturgical Year in accord with the vision expressed by the Second Vatican Council and Pope John Paul II.

6. But education and preaching will not prove completely effective unless we also have women and men of vision and reconciliation who embody the new spirit of Jewish-Christian bonding. I especially honor all those Christians in this land who have embodied *Nostra aetate* in their lives and work for many years. In a particular way, I would like to congratulate Father Marcel Dubois of the Dominican community on this his seventy-fifth birthday. Through his many years of service as a member of the faculty here at Hebrew University, and through his painstaking efforts as a consultant to the Holy See's Commission for Religious Relations with the Jews, he has helped to shape the face of contemporary Catholic-Jewish relations.

7. Above all, in light of the history of anti-Semitism and the Holocaust, the Church needs to engage in public repentance. As I remembered the six million Jewish victims of the *Shoah* this morning at *Yad Vashem*, I was reminded of the Holy Father's call upon the Christian community, in preparation for the celebration of the third millennium of Christianity, to foster a genuine spirit of repentance for "the acquiescence given, especially in certain centuries, to intolerance and even the use of violence in the service of truth." The Church, he added, bears an obligation "to express profound regret for the weaknesses of so many of her sons and daughters who sullied her face, preventing her from fully mirroring the image of her crucified Lord, the supreme witness of patient love and of humble meekness."[24]

It is in this spirit that my brother bishops in Germany, on the occasion of the fiftieth anniversary of the liberation of Auschwitz–Birkenau, issued

---

[23] U.S. Catholic Bishops' Committee on the Liturgy, *God's Mercy Endures Forever: Guidelines on the Presentation of Jews and Judaism in Catholic Preaching* (Washington, D.C.: U.S. Catholic Conference, 1988).

[24] Pope John Paul II, Apostolic Letter, "As the Third Millennium Draws Near," *Origins* 24 (24) (November 24, 1994) 411.

a statement in which they took responsibility for the failure of the Catholic community during the *Shoah*. While mindful of the exemplary behavior of certain individuals and groups, some of whom I have already named, the German bishops acknowledge that "Christians did not offer due resistance to racial anti-Semitism. Many times there was failure and guilt among Catholics." And they go on to add a point with which I wholeheartedly concur: "The practical sincerity of our will of renewal is also linked to the confession of this guilt and the willingness to painfully learn from this history of guilt. . . ."[25]

* * *

My friends, as I draw these reflections to a close, I cannot help but reflect on the fact that I have spoken to an often tragic past in the history of Christian-Jewish relations here in this city of Jerusalem, which both of our religious traditions have always envisioned as ultimately a city of peace. In this context, let me lift up the powerful words of the Nobel Prize winners, including Elie Wiesel, who gathered with President Lech Walesa of Poland at the fiftieth anniversary commemoration of Auschwitz–Birkenau. "To the victims of this crime, we owe a commitment to the memory both of their death and their life," they proclaimed in their *Appeal to the Nations of the World*.

> Their heritage must help mankind to build faith in a future free from racism, hatred and antisemitism. . . . In equal measure, we owe a duty to the living to safeguard peace, tolerance, and fundamental human rights. . . . Let instruments of governance be created which will guarantee the peaceful resolution of all conflicts.

As we reflect today on the legacy of anti-Semitism, Jews and Christians need to recommit themselves to counter its disturbing resurgence in North America, Latin America, and Europe, together with other forms of racism and intergroup violence. Here in Jerusalem, where the vision of peace may seem very far off at times, there is need to find ways to cooperate for the development of a genuine peace among Christians, Jews, and Muslims, Arabs and Israelis, that includes living faith communities with full opportunity for economic justice. Jerusalem, my brothers and sisters, cannot become a mere monument to peace. It must be a true city of living communities of peace, a true *Neve Shalom*. That is my prayer. That is my hope. That is my dream!

---

[25] "Statement of the German Bishops on the Occasion of the 50th Anniversary of the Liberation of the Extermination Camp of Auschwitz," January 27, 1995, 1–2.

Jewish Federation of Chicago

Chicago, Illinois

— *September 7, 1995* —————————————————————

As you can imagine, I have had to curtail my public schedule a great deal recently, and I will continue to do so well into 1996. But I was eager to honor my commitment to be with you, my friends of the Jewish Federation of Chicago. I am happy to be with you.

The last three months have been quite difficult, but I am happy to report that I am doing quite well now that the nearly six weeks of radiation and chemotherapy are over. My doctors are pleased with my progress to date, and we are very hopeful about the future. During this ordeal my morale has been greatly uplifted by the thousands of messages of prayerful support, including so many from members of the various Jewish communities. I am grateful to all of you for your expressions of respect, concern, and solicitude.

Today, I will offer brief reflections on my visit to Israel, the West Bank, and Gaza last March, my address at Hebrew University during that trip, and a situation that continues to haunt all people of good will: the terrible carnage and suffering that have been going on in the former Yugoslavia, specifically in Bosnia.

My visit to Israel with a delegation representing the Jewish-Catholic dialogue of metropolitan Chicago had a certain symbolic value. The joint delegation was the fruit of our interfaith dialogue over the years. Our visit to the land that is holy to both of us—a visit marked by mutual respect, understanding, and love—clearly showed how far we have already come in our interfaith efforts. While it has not always been easy to understand

301

each other, we have worked hard to develop mutual trust and respect as we seek to learn more about each other. We have found that we have much in common. At the same time, while we continue to have different views on many issues, we have learned the importance of making a sincere effort to understand each other's positions, and the reasons—the basis—for those positions.

Precisely to deepen our mutual understanding of each other's traditions and practices, we went together to Israel, the West Bank, and Gaza. We visited the Church of the Holy Sepulchre and gathered at the Western Wall to welcome the Sabbath. We attended a *Shabbat* service at Hebrew Union College and gathered with Christians at St. Savior Church in the Old City. Especially moving for me was the visit we made on the very first day to Yad VaShem. It brought home to me—in a way I had never experienced so deeply before—the horror of the Holocaust. Also moving for me was the respect and warmth with which my Jewish friends walked with me the traditional Way of the Cross.

Because interfaith dialogue with Muslims in metropolitan Chicago is still in its infancy, including them in the delegation seemed to be premature. However, because of our respect for this great monotheistic religion for which Jerusalem is also holy, we did visit the Dome of the Rock on the Temple Mount. It is my intention to do what I can to nurture our dialogue with the Muslims of our metropolitan area.

My visit enabled me to learn firsthand about both the prospects for peace in the Middle East and the serious obstacles facing the peace process. It was a valuable learning experience as our delegation, representing the Chicago Catholic-Jewish Dialogue, met with and listened to people of diverse backgrounds. It is one thing to read or hear about these matters in the media. It is another to listen personally and directly to the lived experience of the people in Israel, the West Bank, and Gaza. During meetings with various civic and religious leaders, I urged them to hold firm to their commitment to the peace process. They have exhibited a bold vision for peace in the Middle East, and I admire the courage with which they have entered into dialogue and negotiations with their opponents.

I pointed out to both sides that authentic peace can come only when the security needs of both Israelis and Palestinians are respected and secured by both peoples. Acts of terrorism feed the tragic cycles of violence that have been so much a part of the history of the State of Israel. As we know so well, violence does not resolve disputes; it only exacerbates them. And both the Israelis and the Palestinians continue to suffer. Moreover, as we have seen again in recent weeks, violence and recrimination engender a cynicism that seriously erodes the hope so essential for the achievement of peace. Civic and religious harmony and peace require that both peoples respect the human dignity and rights of one another. I am encouraged that, even though some tragic incidents have occurred since our visit, the leaders of both sides have continued the negotiations. We must give them our full support, because in the long term there is no other viable solution. I heard many people say this during our visit.

Like my fellow Christians, I continue to watch carefully what is happening in Jerusalem, a unique city, a holy city in the eyes of Jews, Christians, and Muslims. When I met with the mayor of Jerusalem, I disavowed any competence to address the political issues involving the Holy City, which remain to be resolved through the peace process. But I pointed out that, as a churchman, along with other Christian churches, as well as our Jewish and Muslim brothers and sisters, I do have an interest in the *religious* status of Jerusalem. Jerusalem is a spiritual home to Jews, Christians and Muslims. The resolution of the *religious* status of Jerusalem, therefore, is necessarily multilateral. Moreover, not only the concerns of the relatively small Christian community in Jerusalem must be taken into consideration in this regard, but also those of Christians throughout the world.

In a sense, my address on the roots of anti-Semitism, which I delivered at Hebrew University, also had symbolic value. First, it was delivered on Mount Scopus, overlooking the Old City, which was shared by the early Christians and their Jewish brothers and sisters, the very city where the divisions between Christians and Jews first began. Second, my address was made possible by the interfaith dialogue and research of the last 25 to 30 years. Consequently, it was important to me that this address be given at Hebrew University in the company of my Jewish friends from Chicagoland. On the historic Mount Scopus I spoke as a bishop and cardinal of the Catholic Church. I acknowledged that anti-Semitism has been a sad historical legacy and continues to be a challenge for Christians. I discussed the controversial fact that Christian anti-Semitism helped shape popular attitudes toward the Nazis who launched the *Shoah*.

I also pointed out that very important developments in Catholic theology are moving the Church beyond anti-Semitism, especially the official removal of the classical "displacement/perpetual wandering" theology from contemporary Catholic catechesis. I also recommended several actions that will help to ensure that anti-Semitism is not part of our future. I would like to add parenthetically that, while most of the reaction to my address was positive, after returning to Chicago I received some letters which indicate that anti-Semitism is not a dead issue.

I am happy to say that the address attracted considerable attention in the media and among Jewish and Catholic scholars. It will soon be published by Sacred Heart University in Fairfield, Connecticut. There was overwhelming support for what I said and the way I said it. Nonetheless, a small minority in the Catholic community, primarily among the very conservative, have alleged that I have not been faithful to Catholic teaching.

I am disappointed that these persons are not conversant with the developments that have occurred in Catholic theology since the publication of *Nostra aetate* of the Second Vatican Council and subsequent postconciliar documents, as well as a number of significant statements by Pope John Paul II. My friends, I assure you that what I said in that address was fully in accord with the current teaching of the Catholic Church.

This is important to know because the issues of anti-Semitism and of how present-day Christians and Jews understand and teach about each other are very important to the Catholic/Jewish dialogue. In the light of my address at the Hebrew University and my subsequent reflection on that experience, I have concluded that more work needs to be done by both of our communities on these questions. To help foster that work, I have decided to establish an annual lecture held near the anniversary of my Hebrew University address. This lecture, which I hope will be a collaborative project of the archdiocese with our several Jewish partner organizations, will bring to Chicago world-class scholars, both Christian and Jewish, in order to continue the exploration of these topics. In this way, what we shared in our dialogue on Mount Scopus can continue and grow.

As my visit to the Holy Land and my address at the Hebrew University also demonstrate, we can take positive steps to resolve the conflict and alienation of the past, especially through dialogue, the development of mutual respect, and careful study. The resolution of long-standing conflict and division is never easy, but neither is it impossible.

However, some conflicts seem to bear no promise of an early resolution. I am thinking especially of the Balkans. We are obviously at a critical moment in the tortured narrative of that area of the world. After four years of brutal violence a series of factors have converged to create a moment for fundamental decisions. The changing dynamic in the war highlighted by events in Croatia, the more vigorous use of air strikes by NATO, and the renewed diplomatic efforts led by the United States shape the possibility of moving from war to peace in the Balkans. A possibility is never a sure thing, and in this complex part of the world grasping possibilities takes an extraordinary combination of intelligence, skill, courage, and luck.

It is difficult, therefore, at this time of flux and change to say much definitively about tactical choices in the Balkans for the United States or any other party. But it is possible, after watching four years of this tragic conflict, to make some general comments about the situation.

First, the kind of war ravaging the states and peoples of the former Yugoslavia is not an isolated event. Since the collapse of the Cold War, the cosmic fear of a catastrophic war, which defined much of international relations for fifty years, has been replaced by a multiplicity of real wars, local in scope, complex in character, and threatening not cosmic destruction but an atmosphere of chaos in world politics. These shooting wars were often contained *within* a state (although this is not the case in Bosnia), and they have erupted in Central Africa, in the Balkans, and in the former Soviet Union. The roots of the conflict often are a mixture of political, economic, ethnic, nationalist, and religious factors. The proportion of each element varies in different cases. These are very different kinds of problems from those that absorbed most of the intellectual and political attention of states and international institutions during the Cold War. Hence, we are in short supply of wisdom and experience in addressing these bloody and brutal wars. But my first reflection is that they will not go away. We need to think through not only the roots of these local wars, but also how the policies of other states as well as regional and international institutions ought to respond to them.

Second, religion is a persistent element in such conflicts, and, more generally, in the contemporary pattern of world politics in our day. This is a topic that needs much more attention than it has received thus far in several quarters. For a very long time, the standard model of studying world politics and making foreign policy has presumed a strictly secular context in which religion was treated, at best, as a purely private force with little or no public or policy significance. Events have been challenging this model for the past twenty years in regions as different as Latin America, Central Europe, and South Africa. But the secularist vision has resisted the evidence. Today, it is a risky and short-sighted conception of the world that continues to deny the *public* role of religion. There is a twofold need: first, to establish a consensus in the study and practice of world politics that religion is both a public and private force in human affairs, and second, to develop models for integrating the religious factor with political, economic, and strategic issues, which are the normal categories for considering policy choices.

Third, while there is an urgent need *to understand* the secular and religious roots of contemporary conflicts, it is equally necessary *to respond*, even with limited knowledge, to the crisis presently engulfing whole communities. In cases as different as the Sudan, Rwanda, and Bosnia, the international community has shown itself unprepared to act with sufficient speed, purpose, and resources to address either the human or political needs.

I do not underestimate the complexity of the choices facing states and other institutions. But, my Jewish friends, you and I are uniquely aware of the solemn pledge reiterated often in the last half-century: "Never again!"—there can never be another Holocaust. We have tried to convince ourselves that a repetition of that terrible event is unthinkable. But is it really unthinkable? The root causes of the Holocaust are still with us: deep-seated hatreds, claims of ethnic and racial superiority that allegedly give rise to an immoral means of establishing or maintaining that superiority, a reluctance to expose or hold accountable those who use those means to achieve their goals. We have had documented genocide that ran its course in Rwanda, and we have witnessed "ethnic cleansing" on a repeated basis in Bosnia.

Like so many of you, I have been horrified at the suffering and death inflicted on so many, and dismayed by the reluctance of people in positions of power to take effective action to stop these atrocities. But shock and horror are not enough. The need is to press public officials, private agencies, and others with the capacity to contribute to effective policy toward more adequate responses. As I said earlier, I do not think Bosnia represents a unique case. The dynamic of world politics in this last decade of a bloody century promises more situations like Bosnia and Rwanda. One need only look to Liberia and Burundi to see other examples.

Effective policy, in my view, will have to be a mix of international action and initiatives by leading states in the world. Here I can do no better than to reiterate President Vaclav Havel's call for U.S. leadership in the world, made during his commencement address at Harvard University this June. It is not that the U.S. has all the answers or all the responsibility; but the absence of a strong U.S. role leaves a vacuum and often a statement among other key actors. Effective action will require the coordination of humanitarian aid, political negotiation, and the credible threat of force if all else fails.

Humanitarian aid and disaster relief are always in need in large-scale conflicts; it may be the simplest of the three requirements I am listing here. It should be noted that the role of private relief agencies, often supported by religious communities, is an increasingly significant part of world politics today.

Political leadership, involving a vision of what is possible in resolving a conflict, and the skill to translate vision into a practical negotiating strategy, is *the* essential element in all these cases. Aid does not get to the political root of problems, and force by itself lacks purpose. While the conflicts that confront us today have multiple roots, politics must be the way forward to an acceptable settlement. In international affairs, however, politics sometimes requires the supporting arm of military force. I say this with regret, and I do not intend to provide a broad license to anyone to resort easily to coercive violence. But Bosnia illustrates that the absence of a credible threat of force does not preserve peace. It simply leaves the world at the mercy of those who have no scruples about using force as an instrument of repression.

As chairman of the committee that drafted the U.S. Catholic bishops' pastoral letter, *The Challenge of Peace*, I spent a good part of the 1980s trying to enunciate principles that, if followed, would help to restrain resort to war in world politics. I remain convinced this must be the primary message of religious leaders addressing the political process. But there are moments when all other measures have been exhausted, and the threats to human life and human dignity are so great that force becomes the last resort and, therefore, the morally justified course of action. I believe that moment has long been present in Bosnia, and the selective, limited use of air power is an appropriate action for NATO and the United Nations to employ.

To say this is to acknowledge a failure. Ultimately, a political resolution is the only long-term answer to Bosnia and the other conflicts I have spoken of today. One lesson of Bosnia is that force may sometimes be necessary. The larger lesson is the need for early, preventative diplomacy, seeking to head off the Bosnia-, Rwanda-, Somalia-kind of conflict before they reach the state of open war. It is to this political and moral task that the international community, and our own nation particularly, is called by the politics of the 1990s.

My dear friends, we have been engaged, as Christians and Jews, in an interfaith dialogue that seeks to bring about greater mutual understanding, an understanding that will never permit such tragedies as the Holocaust to occur again. It is this kind of dialogue that is urgently needed on a universal basis, involving all peoples, to prevent the violence, carnage, and, indeed, genocide affecting so many parts of the world today. In other words, our endeavors are not merely an academic exercise; they constitute a model desperately needed today. May God give us the courage and strength to prevail in our efforts so that the words "Never again!" will be not only a hope but also a reality.

Catholic Common Ground Initiative

Remarks
Catholic Common Ground
News Conference
Chicago, Illinois
— *August 12, 1996* ————————————————————

Thank you for coming today! I am very grateful that Mr. Thomas Donnelly, Sister Doris Gottemoeller, Monsignor Philip Murnion, and Professor James Kelly (secretary) are with me as I announce this new endeavor.

As many of you know, I have been a Roman Catholic bishop for over thirty years. My episcopal service began shortly after the Second Vatican Council ended. In large measure my pastoral ministry has been concerned with implementing the teaching and pastoral directives of that ecumenical council, which, I believe, was truly the work of God's Holy Spirit.

In carrying out my pastoral responsibilities, I have been sustained by the example of two great churchmen who served as my mentors: John Cardinal Dearden of Detroit and Archbishop Paul Hallinan of Atlanta. I learned a great deal from them—for example, to trust that, through open and honest dialogue, differences can be resolved and the integrity of the gospel proclaimed. I have tried to do this throughout my ministry as archbishop of Cincinnati and, now, of Chicago; as general secretary and, later, as president of the National Conference of Catholic Bishops (NCCB), as chairperson of several NCCB committees, and in recent years as senior active cardinal in the United States.

More recently, however, I have been troubled that an increasing polarization within the Church and, at times, a mean-spiritedness have hindered the kind of dialogue that helps us address our mission and concerns. As a result, the unity of the Church is threatened, the great gift of the

Second Vatican Council is in danger of being seriously undermined, the faithful members of the Church are weary, and our witness to government, society, and culture is compromised.

While these are not new realities, in the past year I have come to see them in a new light. As I have said on several occasions, when one comes face to face with the reality of death in a very profound way as a cancer patient, one's perspective on life is altered dramatically. What seemed so important before, now is seen as trivial, and what is truly important invites new commitment and a realignment of priorities.

It is in this context that I am pleased to announce today the inauguration of what is being called the Catholic Common Ground Project. This endeavor is inspired by a statement I am making public today, a statement that emerged from a series of discussions in which I participated. These discussions began more than three years ago. The paper is entitled *Called to Be Catholic: Church in a Time of Peril*. It decries the growing polarization in the Church, which hinders our addressing important pastoral concerns, and calls for a new kind of dialogue that will engage people of diverse viewpoints in the Church. I am releasing this statement today with the invitation and the hope that other Catholic individuals and groups will study it carefully and consider its implications for the way in which they carry out their responsibilities in Church life.

The Catholic Common Ground Project that the committee and I are undertaking is one response to this statement. Using the teaching of the Second Vatican Council as its basis for dialogue, this project will sponsor conferences that bring together persons of diverse perspectives in search of a "Catholic common ground." Working within the boundaries of authentic Church teaching, these conferences will address with fidelity and creativity the myriad challenges that we face as a Church and as a society. With this approach we should find ways to enhance our common worship, our religious education efforts, and our outreach to those in need. Our tentative plans call for a conference in early 1997 on the relationship between the Church and U.S. culture, developed in the context of the Pastoral Constitution on the Church in the Modern World of Vatican II *(Gaudium et spes)*. The conference will address such questions as: In what ways can we bring the gospel to bear on our culture? In what ways are we positively or negatively affected by our culture?

I am very grateful that seven bishops and sixteen other prominent Catholic leaders have agreed to join me in overseeing the project's initiatives. The diversity among my colleagues demonstrates that there is a desire in all parts of the Church to pursue the goals of this project.

I am also very grateful to Monsignor Philip Murnion and the National Pastoral Life Center for agreeing to serve as staff for the project. I look forward to working with Professor James Kelly who will serve as secretary of the project. Father Michael Place will serve as my liaison to the project.

Let me conclude by speaking directly to my sisters and brothers in the Lord here in Chicago and throughout this great land:

Our faith and our common life as members of the community of faith, which is the Church, are indeed great and precious gifts. Let us together leave behind whatever brings discord. Let us recommit ourselves to our great heritage of faith. Let us walk in communion with, and in loyalty to, our Holy Father in order to restore and strengthen the unity that has been fractured or diminished. And may our service to the Lord God and to our world be enhanced by our efforts to reclaim the "Catholic common ground" that can support renewed and revitalized lives of faith as we enter the third millennium of Christianity.

Response

Catholic Common Ground Project*

Question-and-Answer Format

Chicago, Illinois

— *August 29, 1996* ————————————————————

On August 12, I announced an initiative aimed at getting beyond the entrenched positions and polarization that I believe are blocking critically needed fresh thinking about the challenges facing the Catholic Church in the United States. There have been many strong reactions to the announcement of the formation of the Catholic Common Ground Project, much of it very favorable, some of it decidedly critical. I thought it would be helpful to respond, with gratitude, to the positive reactions and address in greater detail the issues that seem to be the cause of several of the principal criticisms. A question/answer format seems best suited for this purpose.

Why did you hold the August 12 press conference?

First, to release a statement I was involved in developing: "Called to Be Catholic: Church in a Time of Peril." The statement identifies some of the pastoral issues we need to address and calls for a new kind of discussion. Second, as one response to this call, I announced the formation of the Catholic Common Ground Project.

*Also published in *Origins*, vol. 26, no. 13, September 12, 1996, pp. 204–06, and by the National Pastoral Life Center in *Video and Leader's Guide: Called to Be Catholic and Principles of Dialogue.*

316 The Life of Society

What positive reactions have you received?

We have received calls and letters from bishops, parishioners, pastors, women and men religious, professors, and individuals working in diocesan offices. With rare exceptions, they thanked us for spelling out fears and hopes about the Church that they have long entertained. Furthermore, many of them wanted to know what they can do in their own communities. I was particularly gratified by the support of Bishop Anthony Pilla, president of the National Conference of Catholic Bishops.

What are the criticisms?

Some of these have been sharp indeed. To some extent, they confirm the need for this initiative. Even a carefully framed appeal for dialogue coming from an archbishop and seconded by a broad range of distinguished advisors was met with immediate suspicion.

Of course, we anticipated criticisms from some groups on the right or left who are convinced that anything not explicitly committed to their respective agenda will only strengthen their adversaries or legitimate the status quo. They simply do not see the situation as we do.

More troubling is the criticism that mixes arguable points with what I believe are grave misunderstandings.

A lot of criticism focused on the statement "Called to Be Catholic." Let's start with that. What is the statement's origin?

About four years ago, I had a conversation about parish life with Monsignor Philip Murnion of the National Pastoral Life Center. We discussed how conflicts between certain camps in the Church were hindering efforts to address serious pastoral challenges. It occurred to us that further discussion of this problem might be helpful. Over the ensuing years, the center held a number of consultations with clergy, religious, and laity in a variety of positions in the Church. I participated in a number of these discussions. Some of us thought that a statement describing the situation and calling for pastoral discussion, which would take into account a variety of perspectives, might encourage others. The statement was developed by the center from the contributions of a number of people. I was in touch with this effort, and in no way do I wish to be distanced from the statement.

What, then, is the advisory committee's relationship to the statement?

First, it was not our intention to ask anyone to sign the statement; that would have given it too much importance and suggested that it must be accepted in its entirety. When I decided that an effort should be made to foster the kind of dialogue called for by the statement, I felt the need for an advisory committee that would represent diverse positions and responsibilities in the Church. In inviting people to serve on this committee, I asked if they could accept the statement as a good starting point for the effort, even if not every phrase or point was to their liking. This is what they agreed to. Perhaps the best way of describing their relationship is Archbishop Oscar Lipscomb's reply that he could accept about ninety percent of the statement, which is better than usual in the present environment within the Church.

What are the main criticisms of the statement, and how do you respond to them?

As I see it, three major criticisms have been made about the statement. First, that it does not adequately acknowledge Scripture and tradition as the actual common ground of the Catholic Church and reduces the magisterium to just one more voice in a chorus of debate. Second, that it places dissent on the same level as truth and seems ready to accept compromise of the truth. Third, that it insufficiently acknowledges the centrality of Jesus.

My response to the first criticism is that Scripture and tradition *are* the foundational sources of Church teaching and, therefore, the basis for the "common ground." The primacy of Scripture and tradition is fully recognized in the statement. The statement also clearly calls for accountability to the Catholic tradition and rejects any approach that would ignore the "living magisterium of the Church exercised by the bishops and the chair of Peter."

In regard to the second criticism, the statement's call to dialogue within the Church no more legitimates dissent than does dialogue with other faith traditions. In fact, the question of dissent in the Church and whether it is ever justified is a complicated and theologically technical one, and our statement did not pursue it.

The premise of our statement is that many serious disagreements among Catholics—for example, about the state of the liturgy or religious education or the role of women in the Church—do not necessarily involve dissent in the sense of a clear departure from authentic teaching. But the statement also shows full awareness that such departures do exist. The statement recognizes the legitimacy, even the value, of disagreements, but it also insists that dialogue about them must be accountable to Catholic tradition and the Church's teaching authority. Likewise, the statement insists that "discussion about the Catholic Church take place within boundaries" and "defining limits." It explicitly challenges two of the most

318 The Life of Society

popular reasons for dismissing tradition or boundaries, the appeals to "experience" and to "inclusivity."

In a few paragraphs the statement tries to capture both the demands and the dynamism of orthodoxy. It is willing to consider the new but insists that it be accountable to tradition and the magisterium. This clearly is not establishing truth by compromise or accommodation.

In regard to the third criticism, the statement begins by asserting that the very first condition for addressing our differences constructively must be "a common ground centered on faith in Jesus." Moreover, in the statement's section proposing a solution it again begins with the profession: "Jesus Christ, present in Scripture and sacrament, is central to all we do. He must always be the measure and not what is measured."

I am convinced that a careful reading of the text ought to reassure those who expressed these concerns.

But hasn't the very idea of dialogue become questionable? Isn't it a slogan to elude or erode Church teaching or to prevent closure on a subject? Is it sufficient to resolve all issues?

There are some legitimate fears in this area. Yes, the idea of dialogue has sometimes been cheapened by turning it into a tool of single-minded advocacy. It is also true that dialogue is not in every case or at every moment the universal solution to all conflicts.

Nevertheless, I am convinced that, in the United States today, dialogue is a critical need. The Church is built up, not brought down, by genuine dialogue anchored in our fundamental teachings. While millions of Catholics of good will cannot deny their concerns and dissatisfactions, they do not want to be drawn into some basically hostile posture toward the Church and its teaching. It is essential that we offer these faithful people guidelines and models of dialogue. We do not seek "least common denominator Catholicism." Rather, we seek to help the faithful move beyond the often unnecessary and unhelpful polarization in our community and to refocus on the fundamental principles and pastoral needs of the Church.

To move from the statement to the Catholic Common Ground Project, how would you describe its purpose? What activities will be involved?

It should be clear that our focus is pastoral, not doctrinal. We are not trying to change the Church's teachings by some method of consensus or polling. We are primarily concerned with building up the Church's unity by addressing many serious questions where Catholics may understandably disagree among themselves. These questions are not directly doctrinal, but they do require consideration of any doctrinal implications.

It is absolutely essential to understand that no one is equating the Catholic Common Ground Project with the Church itself, nor are we equating the "revitalized common ground" we seek with the faith.

The project will sponsor conferences and other reflections in which we will seek, as the opening paragraph states, "conditions for addressing our differences constructively," or as the statement later states, "a way" to understand and articulate discipleship in our time and place. We do not see ourselves as having a monopoly on this effort or even necessarily reaching collective positions. But, if the latter happens, we would not claim any special status for them.

Who will be involved in this effort?

First, I hope that many individuals and groups within the Church will consider the statement to see if it suggests anything for their own work. Actually, this is already happening. Many have told us that they wish to take this effort into consideration in their parishes, colleges, deaneries, religious congregations, and other forums. We will have to consider how to help them do this.

In regard to the conferences or consultations sponsored by the project, the advisory committee will be involved to the extent that their calendars and interest in the particular topics allow. We also hope to bring together many other people of diverse backgrounds and perspectives that will contribute to examination of the particular subject of each conference.

What will be discussed? Do you expect to discuss the issues that the media finds most divisive, such as abortion and women's ordination to the priesthood?

"Called to Be Catholic" lists a number of pastoral issues: changing roles of women, religious education, parish liturgy, human sexuality, the strain on dwindling numbers of priests, adequate formation for the increased number of lay persons in Church leadership, the Church in political life, the responsibility of theology to authoritative ecclesial teaching, and other issues. This list is a good place to start. These pastoral matters, regarding which the local church has responsibility, will be the object of our discussion. Present plans for the first conference focus on the Church and U.S. culture.

As a realist, I expect that some participants will come to conferences holding positions at variance with ecclesial teaching or discipline regarding ordination, capital punishment, or any number of issues. But the role of authentic Church teaching will always be clear and will be upheld.

Will the very fact of the conferences suggest that certain authoritative teachings are open to negotiation?

We cannot control how people interpret our effort, but the entire approach will be different from those efforts at mediation whose goal is simply compromise and false harmony.

What do you hope will be accomplished at the conferences?

Our hope is threefold. We hope that people of faith and leadership, whose divergent viewpoints have prevented them from listening adequately to one another, will have an opportunity to deepen and broaden their understanding of pastoral matters. Second, we hope that whatever emerges from these conferences in the way of publications will contribute to discussion in the larger Church. Third, we hope to offer an example of how to engage in mutually respectful and constructive dialogue from which others might learn. As you can see, our goals are focused and modest.

How is this related to the National Conference of Catholic Bishops, and why wasn't the conference the forum for such an effort?

In the Church there are numerous unofficial initiatives to address Catholic concerns. For example, there has been a recent and ongoing effort involving Catholic bishops and other individuals who issued a statement a few years ago that was intended to foster cooperation between Catholics and Evangelicals on matters of public policy. Moreover, the Catholic Campaign for America is an organization of prominent Catholics, which has the support of members of the hierarchy, but it is a public policy advocacy group independent of the official efforts of the bishops' conference. Pax Christi also brings together bishops and other Catholics in the effort to promote peace in the world. These are but three of a vast array of independent associations concerned about Catholic life. Our project is only another effort like these. The bishops' conference, on the other hand, is the official teaching and policy body of the Catholic Church in the United States.

Is it possible that the media can misuse this project to deepen divisions in the Church or to suggest that the Church should be guided by fluctuations in popular opinion?

Of course, this is true of all such projects. We are neither responsible for this result nor exempt from it, but we are trying to move beyond such manipulation by the way we drafted the statement and by the creation of forums where we can hear more clearly what is really being said.

What is the National Pastoral Life Center, and why is it involved?

The center is dedicated to serving our parishes and other forms of pastoral ministry through its publications, conferences, and research. It was begun thirteen years ago with the encouragement of the Administrative Committee of the U.S. Bishops' Conference and has served us well since. As I mentioned, the National Pastoral Life Center was involved from the beginning in the discussions that led to the statement and the project. The center's entire work has been to stimulate sound reflection and responsible action in parishes and dioceses in carrying out the Church's pastoral mission. A majority of the bishops of our country have supported its work over the years, and I am confident they will continue to do so in coming years.

* * *

In conclusion, I assure you that I remain fully committed to this project. As I said at my press conference on August 12, "Our faith and our common life as members of the community of faith, which is the Church, are indeed great and precious gifts. Let us together leave behind whatever brings discord. Let us recommit ourselves to this great heritage of faith."

I firmly believe that the ultimate test of this new initiative will be the one that Scripture proposes: if it is of God, it will bear fruit.

"Faithful and Hopeful:
The Catholic Common Ground Project"*

Chicago, Illinois
— *October 24, 1996* ————————————————————

Two and a half months ago, I announced an initiative called the Catholic Common Ground Project. My aim was to help Catholics address, creatively and faithfully, questions that are vital if the Church in the United States is to flourish as we enter the next millennium. At every level, we needed, I felt, to move beyond the distrust, the polarization, and the entrenched positions that have hampered our responses.

At the same time, I released a statement, *Called to Be Catholic: Church in a Time of Peril.* Its very first paragraph summed up what this initiative was about: "Will the Catholic Church in the United States enter the new millennium as a Church of promise," it asked, or as "a Church on the defensive"? The outcome, it proposed, depended on "whether American Catholicism can confront an array of challenges with honesty and imagination." "American Catholics," it stated, "must reconstitute the conditions for addressing our differences constructively." This can happen if we find a common ground. But not just any common ground. It has to be, as the statement said, "a common ground centered on faith in Jesus, marked by accountability to the living Catholic tradition, and ruled by a renewed spirit of civility, dialogue, generosity, and broad and serious consultation."

*Also published in *Origins*, vol. 26, no. 22, November 14, 1996, pp. 353–58; *A Moral Vision for America;* and *Video and Leader's Guide: Called to Be Catholic and Principles of Dialogue.*

At that time, I also announced that I had assembled a committee of outstanding Catholics to join me in this project—seven other bishops, including a fellow cardinal, five priests, three women religious, and eight lay men and women. They come from across the country, from diverse backgrounds in public service, intellectual life, business, and labor—and from a range of viewpoints regarding the needs of the Church.

Although I felt that the statement *Called to Be Catholic* was an excellent description of our situation today, I did not ask these advisors to endorse its every word. I regret that some press reports mistakenly reported that committee members had signed the statement. My conviction, in fact, was that the words were not enough. The idea behind the Catholic Common Ground Project was to demonstrate how this call for a civil and generous dialogue, Christ-centered and accountable to the Church's living tradition and teaching of the authentic magisterium, could be put into action.

To do that will take time, and at the end of August, as you well know, I discovered how little time remains for me personally. Earlier today, I met with the committee so that my role in this venture can be passed to others, and this evening I am sharing these reflections with you in the hope that you too, in your own ways, will take up this task.

My thoughts this evening will cover several areas: the response to the project; the reality of differences in the Church; the relationship of the project to doctrine and dissent; what is meant by the word "dialogue"; and, finally, my hopes for the future of the project.

R̲ESPONSE

The importance of our task has been reinforced by the response that the announcement of the Catholic Common Ground Project has generated. I am not thinking so much of the public statements, for and against, that were widely reported in the media, although those, too, were welcome and valuable, even when unanticipated.

Rather, I am thinking of the outpouring of personal letters that have been sent to me and to the National Pastoral Life Center in New York—letters filled with words like "grateful," "heartening," "timely," "common sense," and even "joy." Priests and parishioners, women and men, recounted their frustrations and their fears that hope for the Church was fading into deadlock or acrimony. Their letters also offered ideas, energy, institutional support. They reported discussions already being organized around *Called to Be Catholic*. The letters were charged with the sense that something bottled up had been released, that something grown dormant was being reawakened.

Most of the letters avoided any note of triumphalism. They called, instead, for humility and prayerful reflection. Among the letter writers were some identifying themselves as conservatives and others calling themselves liberals, but both confessing that they had felt the acids of polarization, anger, and overreaction at work in their own souls.

There were, however, exceptions. A few people welcomed the project, it seemed, as offering a new front or a promising arena in what they clearly viewed as little more than an ongoing battle within the Church. But most, I am happy to say, seemed truly to feel the need to apply to themselves as well as to others the statement's call that we examine our situation with fresh eyes, open minds, and changed hearts.

If there was any frequent misunderstanding of the Catholic Common Ground Project, both among its supporters and its critics, it only reflected the Church's current state of nervous anxiety. Some people hoped, and others feared, that this initiative would aim ambitiously at resolving all the Church's major conflicts in our nation. Some seemed to imagine that the project planned to bring contending sides, like labor–management negotiators, to a bargaining table and somehow hammer out a new consensus on contentious issues within the Church. In this misconception, the Common Ground Project's conferences would culminate in quasi-official reports or recommendations that had the potential to challenge or supplant the authority of diocesan bishops.

I apologize if any of my statements contributed to this impression. Precisely because this effort is so important to the hopes of so many, we need to be clear about the limits of this effort. Our aim is *not* to resolve all our differences or to establish a new ecclesial structure. Rather, it is, first of all, to learn how to make our differences fruitful. Agreements *may* emerge—all the better. But our first step is closer to what John Courtney Murray called the hard task of achieving genuine disagreement.

Common ground, in this sense, is not a new set of conclusions. It is a way of exploring our differences. It is a common spirit and ethic of dialogue. It is a space of trust set within boundaries. It is a place of respect where we can explore our differences, assured in the understanding that neither is everything "cut-and-dried" nor is everything "up for grabs."

DIFFERENCES

As we know, differences have always existed in the Church. St. Paul's letters and the Acts of the Apostles and the fact that there are four gospel accounts rather than one all tell us that Christian unity has always co-existed with Christian differences. Differences are the natural reflection of our diversity, a diversity that comes with catholicity. Differences are the natural consequence of our grappling with a divine mystery that always remains beyond our complete comprehension. And differences, it must be added, can also spring from human sinfulness.

In the Church's history, differences have often been the seedbeds of our most profound understanding of God and salvation. Differences and dissatisfaction have spurred extraordinary institutional creativity. And differences too often have provoked unnecessary, wasteful, and sometimes terrible division.

What about today? By most historical standards the Catholic Church is not racked by overt divisions. Quite the contrary. No other global movement or body—political, religious, ideological—begins to approach the unity demonstrated time and again in the travels of the Holy Father whose remarkable pastoral leadership as shepherd and teacher has prepared us well for the new millennium and can be a helpful basis for the dialogue about which I will speak later. Our oneness in Spirit, our gathering from east to west at the eucharistic banquet, has never been rendered so visible to the human eye.

Yet, we have learned that in modern societies the greatest dangers may not manifest themselves so much in schism and rebellion as in hemorrhage and lassitude, complacency, the insidious draining of vitality, the haughty retreat into isolation, the dispiriting pressure of retrenchment. Secularization has triumphed where the Church defaulted.

Are the differences among U.S. Catholics generating reflection, exchange, debate, ideas, initiative, decisiveness? Or are they producing distrust, polemics, weariness, withdrawal, inertia, deadlock?

No one can answer these questions definitively. But I and many others representing a range of theological outlooks feel that, in far too many cases, the brave new sparks and steady flame of vitality in the Church are being smothered by the camps and distractions of our quarrels. The statement *Called to Be Catholic* described the situation realistically. "For three decades," it noted, "the Church has been divided by different responses to the Second Vatican Council and to the tumultuous years that followed."

Despite the emergence of new generations with new questions, experiences, and needs, the statement continued, "party lines have hardened. A mood of suspicion and acrimony hangs over many of those most active in the Church's life. . . . One consequence is that many of us are refusing to acknowledge disquieting realities, perhaps fearing that they may reflect poorly on our past efforts or arm our critics. . . . Candid discussion is inhibited. . . . Ideas, journals, and leaders are pressed to align themselves with preexisting camps."

One could expand on that analysis. Rather than listen to an idea, we look for its "worst-case" extension; we suspect a hidden agenda. Anticipating attack, we avoid self-criticism and fear frank evaluation. We silence our doubts. We list the events of ecclesial life in parallel columns as wins or losses in a kind of zero-sum game.

I am almost embarrassed to give examples—first, because some of them are so painfully obvious and, second, because it is difficult to do so without inviting this process of testing for partisanship and hidden agendas. But let me mention only the very first item among the statement's examples of urgent questions that the Church needs to address openly and honestly: "the changing roles of women." That would seem to be a rather obvious topic for examination, since the Holy Father has himself drawn our attention to it. Yet in the public responses to the statement, the fact that this question was listed first was enough to render our undertaking suspect by some, while the fact that it did not stipulate anything about ordination was a cause for rejection by others.

I believe that we long for a climate where a question as basic as this could be brought to the table in a mood of good will and with a readiness to learn from one another. We long to exchange ideas, informed by Church teaching and witness, with a confidence that our heartfelt concerns for living the gospel faithfully will be heard and not slighted or betrayed.

CATHOLIC DOCTRINE

Do the differences on topics like this have to do with Catholic doctrine, an area that is obviously less subject to change than pastoral practice? The question is significant. Some of the harshest criticisms of the Catholic Common Ground Project have arisen from anxiety that the exploration of differences could compromise the truth of Catholic doctrine. Such doctrine, it is said, already constitutes more than sufficient common ground, if only it were proclaimed without trepidation.

The answer to this question is twofold. First, many of the controversial differences among U.S. Catholics are not strictly doctrinal but, indeed, pastoral. The collaboration between clergy and laity in parish life, the effectiveness of religious education, the quality of liturgical celebration, the means of coping with a declining number of priests and sisters—all the crucial areas pose numerous questions for which neither the *Catechism of the Catholic Church* nor the documents of Vatican II nor other magisterial sources provide precise and authoritative answers.

For example, in what sequence, and with what mixture of the affective and the conceptual, should the truths of the faith be introduced to children? How should religious education be structured around family life, sacramental preparation, classroom activities, the liturgy and its cycles? How should resources be distributed among Catholic schools, other forms of religious education, the family teaching moments of baptism, First Communion, marriage, and death? How should religious educators be formed, and programs realistically suited to volunteer teachers with high turnover rates? How can qualified lay professionals be identified, selected, sustained, and assured of respect and recompense in team ministries? What can be done to make the quality of homilies and congregational singing genuine assets in building a parish community?

To no small extent, the future vitality of the Church hangs on such issues, and for concrete solutions we will not be able to rely solely on magisterial documents but will, instead, have to use our collective wisdom, knowledge, prudence, and sense of priorities.

But that is not the complete answer. There are doctrinal aspects to even the most pastoral of these questions, and these doctrinal aspects generate anxiety. It is both justified and imperative to ask what are the implications for doctrine of pastoral proposals or the implications for pastoral proposals of doctrine.

To ask such questions is more than an obligation. It is also an opportunity. Catholic doctrine provides enduring truths about divine and human reality. It should enlighten our minds, guide our daily actions, inform our spiritual striving. As we know, doctrine is often refined and nuanced, and is expressed as a carefully articulated structure rather than as an undifferentiated block. There also exists, as the Second Vatican Council stated, and the catechism repeats, a "hierarchy" of truths varying in their relation to the foundation of Christian faith. And Catholic belief is not static. Assisted by the Holy Spirit, the Church is able to grow in its understanding of the heritage of faith. The *Catechism of the Catholic Church* is a gift to the Church because it is a compendium of this rich doctrinal heritage as it has developed over the centuries.

What is the practical import of this interlacing of the pastoral and the doctrinal? On the one hand, as *Called to Be Catholic* urges, "We should not rush to interpret disagreements as conflicts of starkly opposing principles rather than as differences in degree or in prudential pastoral judgments about the relevant facts." On the other hand, we must also "detect the valid insights and worries" embedded in our differing arguments. That being said, ultimately, our reflections and deliberations must be accountable to Scripture and tradition authentically interpreted—or in the words of the statement, to "the cloud of witnesses over the centuries or the living magisterium of the Church exercised by the bishops and the Chair of Peter." On this point let there be no uncertainty!

DISSENT

You may have noticed that so far I have spoken about differences without using the word "dissent." Some people have objected that the Catholic Common Ground Project will legitimate dissent, and others, perhaps, have hoped that it will. In part, I have addressed this concern by noting the range of differences among U.S. Catholics that are not strictly or primarily doctrinal. But dissent, in addition, is a complicated term. I mean neither to avoid it nor to pretend to address all the issues surrounding it.

One can find, however, some major points of consensus about dissent.

On the one hand, consider the view that all public disagreement or criticism of Church teaching is illegitimate. Such an unqualified understanding is unfounded and would be a disservice to the Church. "Room must be made for responsible dissent in the Church," writes Father Avery Dulles, whom no one can accuse of being radical or reckless in his views. "Theology always stands under correction."

"Dissent should neither be glorified nor be vilified," Father Dulles adds. It inevitably risks weakening the Church as a sign of unity, but it can nonetheless be justified, and to suppress it would be harmful. "The good health of the Church demands continual revitalization by new ideas," Father Dulles says, adding that "nearly every creative theologian has at one time or another been suspected of corrupting the faith." In fact, according to Dulles, theologians ought to alert Church authorities to the shortcomings of its teachings.

Similarly, in *Veritatis splendor* Pope John Paul II distinguished between "limited and occasional dissent" and "an overall and systematic calling into question of traditional moral doctrine." I would argue that dissent ceases to be legitimate when it takes the form of aggressive public campaigns against Church teachings that undermine the authority of the magisterium itself.

No one can deny that such campaigns exist. But I would go further. The problem of dissent today is not so much the voicing of serious criticism but the popularity of dismissive, demagogic, "cute" commentary, dwelling on alleged motives, exploiting stereotypes, creating stock villains, employing reliable "laugh lines." The kind of responsible disagreement of which I speak must not include "caricatures" that "undermine the Church as a community of faith" by assuming Church authorities to be "generally ignorant, self-serving, and narrow-minded." It takes no more than a cursory reading of the more militant segments of the Catholic press, on both ends of the theological and ideological spectrum, to reveal how widespread, and how corrosive, such caricatures have become.

This is why the Catholic Common Ground Project, while affirming "legitimate debate, discussion, and diversity," specifically targets "pop scholarship, sound-bite theology, unhistorical assertions, and flippant dismissals." Moreover, it aims at giving Catholics another model for exploring our differences. Before speaking of that model I want to make it clear that, in speaking of a "common ground," this project does not aim at the lowest common denominator. Nor when it speaks of dialogue does it imply compromise. Rather, in both instances its goal is the fullest possible understanding of and internalization of the truth.

Dialogue

The project's model is dialogue. But we have done more than merely invoke that word. Unfortunately, the call for dialogue has too often become routine, a gambit in the wars of image-making, a tactic in reopening or prolonging bureaucratic negotiations. Nonetheless, the recognition and highlighting of dialogue remains one of the glories of the Second Vatican Council and of the papacies that nurtured and followed it. In dialogue we affirm, examine, deepen, and rectify our own defining beliefs in relationship to another person. That relationship involves opposition but also sincere respect, trust, and expectation of mutual enrichment.

The statement *Called to Be Catholic* proposes conditions for a renewed and successful dialogue among U.S. Catholics. Let us remind ourselves of a few of them:

1. that Jesus Christ, present in Scripture and sacrament, be central to all that we do;

2. that we reaffirm basic truths and stand accountable to Scripture and Catholic tradition, witnessed and conveyed to us by the Spirit-filled, living Church and its magisterium exercised by the bishops and the chair of Peter;

3. that the complexity and richness of this tradition not be reduced or ignored by fundamentalist appeals to a text or a decree and/or by narrow appeals to individual or contemporary experience;

4. that the Church be treated not as a merely human organization but as a communion, a spiritual family, requiring that a hermeneutic of suspicion be balanced by a hermeneutic of love and retrieval, and that Catholic leadership embrace wide and serious consultation;

5. that our discussions assume the need for boundaries, distinctions, and defining limits, even where these may be open to reexamination;

6. that we recognize no single group as possessing a monopoly on solutions to the Church's problems or the right to spurn the mass of Catholics and their leaders as unfaithful;

7. that we test proposals for pastoral realism;

8. that we presume those with whom we differ to be in good faith and put the best possible construction on their positions;

9. that, above all, we keep the liturgy, our common worship, from becoming a battleground for confrontation and polarization.

Hopes

I trust that these reflections have been of some help in our coming to a better understanding of the project and its direction. Now allow me some personal thoughts.

Shortly after the project was announced, a friend asked me, "Joe, why at this time in your life did you take on this project?" My friend was referring to the stress of the last three years, in particular the stress of a false accusation and then of being a cancer patient. It was a good question. It prompted me to reflect more deeply about my many life experiences and my own spiritual journey.

I thought immediately of the lessons I had learned from my mentors, Archbishop Paul Hallinan of Atlanta and John Cardinal Dearden of Detroit: to trust that, through open and honest dialogue, differences could be resolved and the gospel proclaimed in its integrity. Over the years I learned from you and so many other of our sisters and brothers the correctness of what these two great churchmen taught me. I have been impressed and humbled by the willingness of so many to rise above differences in search for the truth that can bind us together. I have been nurtured by the peace and joy of communities that have worked hard for reconciliation and peace.

This same insight prompted me to move beyond the family of faith and speak to our society about a consistent ethic of life. In asking opponents of abortion and opponents of capital punishment and nuclear war to perceive a whole spectrum of life issues not in identical terms but, rather, in relationship to one another, I have been moved by the conviction that the Church's understanding of the gospel defies conventional political and ideological lines. By juxtaposing positions that are conventionally set apart and by searching for the common thread, we enrich our own understanding and open others to persuasion.

Similarly, the Catholic Common Ground Project offers the promise of our rising above hardened party lines and finding renewal in the splendor of the truth revealed in the person of Jesus who is our Lord and our savior.

This evening, I assure you that, having entered the final phase of my life's journey, I am even more committed than before to this central conviction. A dying person does not have time for the peripheral or the accidental. He or she is drawn to the essential, the important—yes, the eternal. And what is important, my friends, is that we find that unity with the Lord and within the community of faith for which Jesus prayed so fervently on the night before he died. To say it quite boldly, it is wrong to waste the precious gift of the time given to us, as God's chosen servants, on acrimony and division.

And so, in that spirit I hand on to you the gift that was given to me—a vision of the Church that trusts in the power of the Spirit so much that it can risk authentic dialogue. I hand that gift on to you without fear or trepidation. I say this because I know that it is a gift you already prize and cherish. I ask you, without waiting and on your own, to strengthen the common ground, to examine our situation with fresh eyes, open minds, and changed hearts, and to confront our challenges with honesty and imagination. Guided by the Holy Spirit, together, we can more effectively respond to the challenges of our times as we carry forward the mission that the Lord Jesus gave to us, his disciples. It is to promote that mission that the constructive dialogue we seek is so important.

In addition, I ask you to read carefully *Called to Be Catholic*. Like some of the committee, you may not agree with every sentence or paragraph. But ask yourself carefully where and why you agree or disagree. Discuss it in your families, your parishes, your schools. Make it the occasion for a serious examination of conscience and not for further contention.

Then, I ask you to go a step further. Whether you are guided by this statement or similar principles, please decide how it might modify the conduct or the tone of whatever group efforts engage you in the Church—your parish council, your prayer group, your Catholic grade school or high school faculty, your academic department or professional organization if these deal with religious issues. Are these the principles—the centrality of Jesus, the serious accountability to Church tradition and authentic teaching, the spirit of dialogue and consultation—that govern the Catholic periodicals you read, the television programs you watch, the organizations to which you belong, or the conferences you attend? If not, make your preferences known.

As you do this, return to the teachings of the Second Vatican Council, which I believe with all my being was the work of God's Holy Spirit. While there is so much in conciliar teaching that can guide these efforts, you might find inspiration in a passage at the close of *Gaudium et spes*, the Pastoral Constitution on the Church in the Modern World. This passage calls on the Church to become a sign of sincere dialogue as part of its mission to enlighten the world with the gospel's message and unite all people in the one Spirit. I close with the inspiring words of that passage: "Such a mission," the council fathers instructed, "requires us first of all to create in the Church itself mutual esteem, reverence and harmony, and acknowledge all legitimate diversity; in this way all who constitute the one people of God will be able to engage in ever more fruitful dialogue, whether they are pastors or other members of the faithful. For the ties which unite the faithful together are stronger than those which separate them: let there be unity in what is necessary, freedom in what is doubtful, and charity in everything."

Part Two

THE LIFE OF THE CHURCH

Introduction to Part Two:
The Life of the Church

Joseph Cardinal Bernardin was a recognized leader among the U.S. Catholic bishops throughout his episcopal ministry. He was an extraordinary person in many ways. For example, some people are gifted with broad vision but lack the ability to translate it into action. Others are gifted with an ability to act but lack a broad vision to give their thoughts coherence and their actions consistency. Cardinal Bernardin had both vision and the capacity to translate it into action. His attention to details is legendary among his staff, but I doubt that many people walked away from an encounter with him without feeling themselves stretched by his vision of the Church, the world, the human person. As Francis Cardinal George said at his initial press conference upon being named Cardinal Bernardin's successor, "After Cardinal Bernardin spoke, there seemed to be more room in the discussion."

Cardinal Bernardin was a pastor, not an intellectual or a professional theologian. He brought Catholic teaching to bear on the pastoral situations and cultural circumstances he encountered. He was also able to listen attentively to many sides of an argument or various approaches to a problem and appreciate elements of truth and wisdom on all sides. As a result, he often was able to bring people to a *consensus*, at times to a *compromise* that did not dilute basic beliefs or principles, more often to a *common ground* that focused more on the essentials that united people rather than the details on which they were divided. He was fully committed to dialogue as a means to resolving conflicts and differences. He never assumed that he had all the answers!

When Cardinal Bernardin spoke about certain issues affecting both the Catholic Church and the broader society, he often attracted considerable attention, especially from the media. He is widely known for his views on peacemaking, the consistent ethic of life, religion and society, health care, Catholic-Jewish dialogue, and the Catholic Common Ground Initiative. Selected works on these topics appear in Part One, The Life of Society, in this volume.

However, he spoke even more frequently about other issues of vital interest to the life of the Church. These presentations received less media attention, even from Church media, but they remain of abiding value to Catholics and other people of good will. This second part contains talks on six topics: ecclesial vision and mission, evangelization, education, religion and spirituality, pastoral ministry, and pastoral outreach. This is only a representative sampling of his many addresses in these six areas, and there are other areas that also deserve attention. As I noted in the Preface to this collection, about 450 addresses by Cardinal Bernardin are extant as well as nearly 500 of his weekly columns in the archdiocesan newspaper, *The New World*. The selection presented here is, therefore, quite limited, and future researchers will undoubtedly detect deficiencies in my method of selection. However, my choices reflect, I hope, many of Cardinal Bernardin's deepest convictions and most valuable insights as archbishop of Chicago.

ECCLESIAL VISION AND MISSION

Cardinal Bernardin's entire episcopal ministry occurred in the shadow of the Second Vatican Council. He was thoroughly familiar with its teachings and fully committed to the Church's renewal called for by the council. He paid close attention to the Church's self-understanding as a communion, the collegiality among the bishops with the pope, and the shared responsibility of all the baptized for the Church's mission and ministry. Such conciliar concepts helped to shape his participative style of episcopal leadership.

In 1985, Pope John Paul II called an Extraordinary Synod of Bishops to commemorate the 20th anniversary of the closing of the Second Vatican Council and issued an invitation for all of the faithful to reflect upon and evaluate what had occurred in the two postconciliar decades. This was the only Synod of Bishops that Cardinal Bernardin did not attend; except for the presidents of episcopal colleges, it was by invitation only. Nonetheless, he decided to deliver an address at The Catholic University of America (November 1985) in which he articulated his basic understanding of the council and the postconciliar process. He pointed out that the Church had renewed its theology and style of leadership, changed its self-perception, and adopted a more positive posture toward the world. He also noted his ongoing concerns about collegiality, social ministry, and the role of theology and theologians in the Church.

E VANGELIZATION

Evangelization was the first priority and underlying goal of Cardinal Bernardin's ministry as archbishop of Chicago. As noted in the Preface, at his installation he said simply that he had come to Chicago "with only one desire: to do all in my power to proclaim the Lord Jesus and his Gospel in word and deed."

Because he saw evangelization as the integrating focus of all ministry, his commitment to evangelization remained constant throughout his ministry in metropolitan Chicago. In November 1988, when he announced four priorities for the Archdiocese of Chicago (including vocations to the priesthood and religious life, racial harmony, and stewardship of ecclesial resources), he identified evangelization as the first and overarching goal. In 1993, he initiated *Decisions*, a five-year strategic pastoral planning process, which focused everyone's attention on two areas: evangelization/education and ministerial personnel. Unfortunately, he did not live to see the process completed.

Cardinal Bernardin's views on evangelization were influenced, in part, by the 1974 synod on evangelization, which he attended, and by *Evangelii nuntiandi*, Pope Paul VI's Apostolic Exhortation on Evangelization in the Modern World (1975). At the 1974 synod, Cardinal Bernardin pointed out that the synodal fathers at the 1971 synod, which he had also attended, conceived of justice as a constitutive dimension of the Church's ministry, and he, among others, urged the 1974 synod to relate the consideration of justice in the world to its reflection on evangelization. In other words, one cannot faithfully or effectively proclaim the gospel without also working for social justice. At the same time, he immediately acknowledged that this linkage involves a complex and profound theological problem that requires continuing reflection.

E DUCATION

Education, especially Catholic education of all kinds, was a subject dear to Cardinal Bernardin's heart. He had earned a master's degree in education at The Catholic University of America before he was ordained a priest and taught high school part-time as a young priest in the Diocese of Charleston. As a bishop, he was firmly convinced of the necessity of a good education in today's world and the enduring value of Catholic education at all levels, which he frequently described as a vital ministry of the Church. Although he reluctantly closed some Catholic elementary and secondary schools in the Archdiocese of Chicago, he did so only when he was convinced that it was the only realistic choice he had. Even then the decisions bothered him a great deal.

He understood well and spoke clearly about the contemporary challenges of religious education programs as well as Catholic primary, secondary, and college/university education, bringing both vision and inspiration to educators even as he spoke about such issues as rising costs, diminishing resources, changing roles, and new needs of students. He also placed great emphasis on value education in all schools, public and private, often highlighting the need for future employees and citizens to have acquired Judeo-Christian values if they are eventually to take their rightful place in society and the workplace and be able to help develop a moral vision for this nation commensurate with the global challenges of the day.

RELIGION AND SPIRITUALITY

Cardinal Bernardin knew that, in order to be an effective evangelizer, he had to be a man of faith, understanding, love, mercy, and compassion—hence, a man of prayer. He often spoke about the importance of spirituality and frequently called other evangelizers—clerical, religious, and lay—to a deeper faith, a more intense prayer life.

At the very core of his being Cardinal Bernardin was a man of deep faith. He invested precious time each day in prayer in order to nurture his spiritual life and deepen his relationship with the Lord Jesus. Daily, he integrated his spirituality with his ministry and was eager to share with others the benefits of an authentic spiritual life whatever one's vocation. He was a humble, honest man, aware of his defects and weaknesses; he had an uncommon ability to share these with his audiences, giving them the strength and courage to take an honest look at their own shortcomings. Like St. Paul, he also found God-given strength in his weaknesses.

In retrospect, Cardinal Bernardin's enduring legacy and ongoing popularity may be due less to what he said and did as archbishop of Chicago—as important as these were—than to his deep spirituality, especially evident in the severe trials he faced during the last three years of his life. As a good pastor after the model of the Good Shepherd, when there was nothing more he could do, he showed us how to embrace death as a friend and die a truly Christian death.

PASTORAL MINISTRY

Cardinal Bernardin carefully presented clearly and accurately the Catholic Church's teaching and discipline whenever the situation called for this. At the same time he was a very compassionate person, sensitive to people's dilemmas, suffering, and circumstances. This dual approach is seen, for example, in his 1983 address to those who ministered to persons who are separated, divorced, and/or remarried as well as his 1989 address to Catholic campus ministers.

Sunday Masses in the Archdiocese of Chicago are officially celebrated in twenty languages (over 40 parishes in Polish, over 100 in Spanish). Cardinal Bernardin was very sensitive to the needs of immigrant Catholics, especially newcomers from such places as Mexico, Poland, and the Philippines. For example, under his leadership the Archdiocese of Chicago developed a mission partnership with the Diocese of Chilapa-Chilpancingo in Mexico (he visited there three times) in order to be more responsive to the needs of Mexican Catholic immigrants in metropolitan Chicago. He made a two-week pastoral visit to Poland in 1984 to show the solidarity of people in Chicagoland with the people in Poland and to learn how to minister more effectively to Polish immigrants. He made three visits to the Philippines, and his 1990 address to those who minister to Filipino Catholic immigrants reflects his awareness of cultural differences and the needs of immigrants from Asia.

Cardinal Bernardin's concern for families drew upon his own experience; he kept in regular contact until his death with his many relatives in northern Italy from where his mother and father had emigrated to the United States. His concerns also derived from the many serious new challenges that affected family life in recent years. From 1990 to 1993 Cardinal Bernardin served as chairperson of the U.S. bishops' Committee on Marriage and Family Life, one of the three episcopal committees that issued *Putting Families and Children First* in 1992. Subsequently, he gave several talks on this program in Chicago and elsewhere, including the United Nations in New York at the outset of the International Year of the Family.

PASTORAL OUTREACH

Although he was more widely known for his contributions to the Catholic-Jewish dialogue, Cardinal Bernardin was also very involved in ecumenical affairs. Early in his tenure as archbishop of Chicago he revived an ecumenical-interfaith group that had ceased to meet, now called the Council of Religious Leaders of Metropolitan Chicago. He encouraged ecumenical and interfaith cooperation on a broad range of issues, including promoting racial harmony and building affordable housing. Under his leadership the Archdiocese of Chicago entered into covenants with the Episcopal Diocese of Chicago (1986) and the Metropolitan Synod of the Evangelical Lutheran Church in America (1989).

Unfortunately, metropolitan Chicago has had a long history of racial disharmony, some of it overt, much of it subtle. As archbishop of Chicago, Cardinal Bernardin addressed the issues of racism and civic harmony "in season and out of season." Racial harmony was one of his four archdiocesan priorities announced in 1988, and it remained a personal priority until his death. He made many efforts to strengthen bonds with African-American and other minority Catholics and to ensure that they took their rightful place in the Church, sharing their unique gifts with their fellow Catholics.

While I have included only one address by Cardinal Bernardin about child abuse in this collection, he devoted enormous amounts of his time to this difficult topic, especially when allegations of clerical sexual misconduct with minors arose in the archdiocese.

As general secretary of the Episcopal Conference (1968–1972), Bishop Bernardin played an important role in the founding of the U.S. bishops' Campaign for Human Development, which celebrated its 25th anniversary in 1995. Its genius was to help local communities help themselves. In its first year U.S. Catholics contributed $8 million to this new program, and CHD had received 1,000 requests for grants. It has been one of the more successful programs established by the bishops in this nation. CHD seed monies have generated billions of dollars' worth of resources for underprivileged communities, and Cardinal Bernardin was especially proud of the program.

Alphonse P. Spilly, C.PP.S.

Ecclesial Vision and Mission

"The Church's New Self-Understanding"

Symposium on the 20ᵗʰ Anniversary of Vatican II
Loyola University, Chicago, Illinois
── *March 21, 1983* ─────────────────────────

Twenty years in the life of an individual person is a time span which encompasses a tremendous variety of change and growth. In its first days the newborn learns to focus its eyes and to take nourishment. It is a big day when the baby can lift its head or roll over. Then come the momentous signs of progress such as sitting up, standing erect, learning to crawl, learning to walk and talk, and, of course, that day when one gains freedom from diapers. As the years pass, the milestones continue. Most of us can recall the thrill, and in some cases the pain, of our first day at school. We learned to spell, to count, to multiply and divide. We left grade school, entered high school with its challenges and opportunities. Before we knew it, we had earned that wonderful piece of paper called a driver's license. With each sunrise and sunset, to borrow an image from *Fiddler on the Roof,* we had unfolded the powers and talents that had been given us at birth. And then we were twenty, at the borderline between adolescence and adulthood.

If the Vatican Council were an individual person, it would have passed through all those stages. We are here this week to reflect upon the somewhat similar process of growth and development—the unfolding and blossoming of its potential, if you will—which has taken place in the body of Christ, the Church, during these past twenty years. I think the analogy is important because, in the ultimate analysis, the Second Vatican Council is not a collection of documents, or an accumulation of dates and names, debates and decisions, photographs and memorabilia. It has been, and continues to be, a stream of a spirit-filled vitality in the ongoing story of the pilgrim People of God. As one of those who have shared that pilgrimage, I am very happy to be with you today.

A few moments ago I referred to the first days of a newborn infant. When a baby comes home from the hospital, everyone scrutinizes it for signs of the future. Who does it look like? Is its personality calm or high strung? Will it sleep through the night without awakening us at odd hours? The same questions arose in those opening days of the Vatican Council. People were looking for signs. Those signs came quickly. Most of the bishops arriving in Rome had come with the desire to find more effective ways of explaining and proclaiming the ageless message of the Gospels to the modern world. They wanted the council's statements to be rooted in the Scriptures, in touch with the realities of human life as experienced by ordinary people, and available not just to Catholics but accessible to all people of good will. So, as many of you will recall, in those days the first drafts of the central council documents which had been written by the Preparatory Commissions were criticized for failing to meet those criteria.

For instance, on October 21, 1963, an American bishop criticized the draft of chapter two of the proposed document on the Church for its lack of realism. He argued that "before we describe the Church as being without stain or wrinkle," there should be a paragraph emphasizing that the Church is a home for the weak and the struggling. He reminded the council fathers that Jesus had said, "I have not come to summon the just, but sinners."

On October 5, 1964, that same American churchman pointed out inadequacies in the draft of the document on divine revelation. He wanted the document to emphasize that inspiration is "a personal communication to men of the Word of God which goes beyond merely manifesting concepts to one another." He submitted that the neoscholastic character of the draft obscured the true nature of divine inspiration.

Fifteen days later, this same bishop expressed the view that the schema of the Constitution of the Church in the Modern World was vitiated by a fear of contamination by the world. There was, in his view, far too little stress on the theology of salvation and on the links which "redemption had established between God and man."

This American bishop was, of course, my predecessor as archbishop of Chicago, the beloved and highly respected Albert Cardinal Meyer. He became an important figure in the process of ending the dominance of the "classicist" mentality in the Church. The Church, at its highest level, was moving beyond the notion that there is a single non-native culture which always and everywhere furnishes the best means for planting and nurturing the seed of the gospel. Instead, it affirmed "from the beginning of her history, (the Church) has learned to express the message of Christ with the help of the ideas and terminology of various peoples, and has tried to clarify it with the wisdom of philosophers, too. Her purpose has been to adapt the gospel to the grasp of all as well as to the needs of the learned. . . . Indeed, this accommodated preaching of the revealed Word ought to remain the law of all evangelization. For thus each nation develops the ability to express Christ's message in its own way. At the same time, a living exchange is fostered between the Church and the diverse cultures of people." That quotation is from *Gaudium et spes,* section 44.

Allow me a personal reflection on that phrase, "to adapt the gospel to the grasp of all as well as to the needs of the learned . . ." I still continue to be amazed at the number of people who recall my invocation of that popular figure from the movies, E.T., on the occasion of my installation Mass in Holy Name Cathedral. It may be a trivial matter, but some things like that seem to open the doors of people's minds, and hopefully their hearts, so they can begin to hear the message of Jesus through our words. In his opening address to the council, Pope John XXIII expressed that theme when he stated, "The substance of the ancient doctrine of the deposit of faith is one thing, and the way in which it is presented is another." Perhaps today, as we celebrate the twentieth birthday of Vatican II, that has become a commonplace insight, but in those days of infancy it was a momentous declaration.

In this, as in so many of its key teachings, the council was picking up important threads from the past. To continue the analogy with the development of a child, the unfolding qualities of an individual reveal his inheritance. "It's all in the genes," we sometimes say. For example, in the Gospel of Mark we hear Jesus say to his first followers, "Go forth to every part of the world, and proclaim the good news to the whole creation." And in the opening scene of the Acts of the Apostles, we read the charge, "You will bear witness for me in Jerusalem, and all over Judea and Samaria, and away to the ends of the earth." These commissioning accounts show that the Lord wanted his Church to be universal, to be about his work in all places and to be at home among all peoples, no matter where they are found: in the teeming cities of India, in the rain forests of Southeast Asia, in the deserts of North Africa, in the villages and plains of Russia, along the rivers and mountains of South America, on the streets of Chicago.

The council fathers realized that if the Church is not truly universal— if it is not truly at home all over the earth—then the Good News of the Lord Jesus which the Church serves and proclaims will be distorted. But it has not been easy to do this. The Church has never abandoned Christ's mandate of universality. However, history tells us that we have not always understood the practical implications of the command of Jesus to make all nations his disciples.

346   *The Life of the Church*

At times, the Church has unwittingly erected barriers between the gospel and the people. At times, the graced wisdom, values, and traditions of non-European cultures have been insufficiently respected. Fortunately, the Second Vatican Council began to see the urgency of this matter. We have made a good beginning, but as I mentioned in my comparison with the development of a twenty-year-old person, we stand on the threshold between adolescence and adulthood in implementation. I agree with Karl Rahner when he says, "The Second Vatican Council is, in a rudimentary form still groping for identity, the Church's first official self-actualization as a world church."

Rahner argues that there have been three epochs in the history of the Church. The first epoch was relatively brief, that of Jewish Christianity. It comprises that brief span of time when the gospel was proclaimed primarily to the people of Israel. The languages of preaching and catechesis were Jewish. The young Church's rituals and symbols had their roots in the temple and synagogue. The mission to the Gentiles was peripheral. There were, as you know, bitter arguments between the dominant Judaizers and the innovative Hellenists. Only the fall of Jerusalem in 70 A.D. terminated the dispute.

The apostle Paul was, of course, the leading spirit in the transition to the second epoch of Church history, in Rahner's scheme, "The period of the Church in a distinct cultural region . . . that of Hellenism and of European culture and civilization." This period lasted from the end of the first century up to the Second Vatican Council and its effects are still very much with us. (One can recall, for example, the jarring effect during the television coverage of the Vietnam War when one would see a Gothic church that would look much more at home in the French countryside than in a Southeast Asian city.) That long period is characterized by a Christianity which understands and interprets itself in the languages and categories and structures of thought inherited from classical Greece and imperial Rome. They are part of our tradition which we treasure; they have served us well. The task which now lies before us is to help bring new manifestations or "inculturations" of Christianity into being and nurture them to maturity. And the challenge is to do this in a way that will enhance, not undermine, the unity which is part of the Church's nature and so essential to its well-being.

Here again we pick up threads from the past. For example, Francesco Ingoli was the first Secretary of the Propaganda Fidei, founded by Pope Gregory XV in 1622. These words of his would have fitted beautifully into the deliberations of Vatican II:

> Do not regard it as your task, and do not bring any pressure to bear on the peoples, to change their manners, customs and uses, unless they are evi-

dently contrary to religion and sound morals. What could be more absurd than to transplant France, Spain, Italy or some other European country to China? Do not introduce all that to them but only the faith, which does not despise or destroy the manners and customs of any people, always supposing they are not evil, but rather wishes to see them preserved unharmed. . . . It is the nature of men to love and treasure above everything else their own country and that which belongs to it. . . . Do not draw invidious contrasts between the customs of the peoples and those of Europe; do your utmost to adapt yourselves to them.

How did the Second Vatican Council actually implement these ideals? First of all, the council itself was truly universal in its membership. For the first time in the history of the Church, the fathers of a council came from around the world. They did not come to Vatican II as Americans or Europeans who served as missionary bishops in foreign territories. They came as native Christians from their own cultures who had now become shepherds of their local churches. Names like Doi, Rugambwa, Roguchi, and Rakotomalala and dioceses like Saigon, Toyko, Tampico and Noseng bespeak a council truly universal in its membership.

Secondly, besides being universal in its membership, the council sought to be universal in its outreach. Following the lead of Pope John XXIII who addressed his great encyclical *Pacem in terris* to all people of good will, the council fathers began their deliberations with an address to all of humankind. They said, "We take great pleasure in sending to all peoples and nations a message concerning that well-being, love, and peace which were brought into the world by Christ Jesus, the Son of the Living God, and entrusted to the Church." So too, the opening paragraphs of its constitutions on the Church and on the Church in the modern world *(Lumen gentium and Gaudium et spes)* eloquently attest to the council's desire to proclaim the Good News to all the peoples of the earth.

Thirdly, the bishops of Vatican II called for new structures in the Church to provide for an ongoing actualization of the universality which they themselves experienced so powerfully. They wanted this new experience to continue and develop after the council ended. Let me discuss three of these new structures.

First, while recognizing the great services performed over the years by the Roman Curia, they determined that henceforth its membership should be drawn from all regions of the world. They were convinced that this would enhance the effectiveness of the Curia. The basic principle behind this decision has been followed by Popes Paul VI and John Paul II in "internationalizing" the College of Cardinals. Thus, it is not surprising that the newest cardinals in the Church—my own group—come from all over the world, from places like Latvia, Lebanon, New Zealand, Venezuela, Thailand, the Ivory Coast—and the United States. Moreover, Pope John Paul II is now using the College of Cardinals more frequently as a body of advisors so that the wisdom, needs and priorities of the entire Church might be tapped in confronting a number of issues facing the Church today.

Second, Pope Paul VI, who as Cardinal Montini had been a bishop of Vatican II, established the Synod of Bishops on September 15, 1965. In the document which established the synod, the Pope said that it was especially during the sessions of the council that he became profoundly convinced of the importance and the necessity of a broader use of the bishops for the welfare of the universal Church. He went on to make it clear that the synod would represent the entire body of Catholic bishops and that one of its specific aims would be "to insure that direct and real information is provided on questions and situations touching upon the internal action of the Church and its necessary activity in the world of today." A short time later, in its Decree on the Pastoral Office of Bishops, the council itself affirmed the establishment of the synod.

My own experience as a participant in the Synod of Bishops has shown the wisdom of the Pope and the council in establishing it. It has indeed stimulated the development of authentic universality in the Church, enabling the richness of individual churches to be shared by the rest.

It has been my privilege to attend three synods—on evangelization in 1974, catechesis in 1977, and marriage and the family in 1980. I am also serving my third term as a member of the Council of the Synod Secretariat which has the responsibility of preparing for the synods. In October, I will participate in another synod which will deal with penance and reconciliation in the Church.

For me, these synods have been real eye-openers. In the general sessions, but even more so in the small group discussions, one comes face to face with the Church as it is incarnated in the diverse lands and cultures of the world. Both the diversity and unity of the Church stand out in bold relief. These sessions have given me an understanding and a vision of the Church which I would not have had otherwise. Such an experience, I believe, is important if the Church is to respond realistically and effectively to the challenges and problems of the contemporary world.

My only wish is that the synod could be structured in such a way that it could be used to advise the Holy Father on a wide variety of important issues as they arise within the Church. At the present time, each synod addresses a topic which is selected, after consultation with the local churches, over two years before the synod is actually held. While the topic may indeed be important, given the rapidity of developments in today's world, it may have been superseded in importance by some other concern before the synod actually begins.

Last, but not least, the council fathers also urged the establishment of national conferences of bishops wherever they did not already exist. The passages in *Lumen gentium* and *Christus Dominus* which discuss such conferences insist that they are not merely an innovation for the purpose of bureaucratic convenience, but rather an important instrument in the service of the gospel. Such conferences are clearly intended to stimulate and empower the Church's mission to the world by promoting the specific identity and role of the regional and local churches, with all their diversity, as well as their communion with one another and with the See of Rome.

Again, this was not a totally new innovation, but a development that had its origins prior to the council. As I have noted earlier, it is similar to the growing child whose characteristics are manifestations of his inheritance. For example, the prototype of a national conference of bishops is the Latin American Episcopal Conference established in 1899. After World War I, the bishops of France, Spain and the United States also formed national conferences. These were established as permanent, ongoing organizations. Of course, periodic councils of bishops in a particular region have been part of the Church's life from its earliest years.

For instance, here in the United States the influential plenary councils of Baltimore in 1852, 1866 and 1884 have had a profound effect on our life as Catholics in this country, especially during some of the most challenging years of our existence.

Reflecting upon this prior experience, the council fathers noted that, "Nowadays especially, bishops are frequently unable to fulfill their office suitably and fruitfully unless they work more harmoniously and closely every day with other bishops. Episcopal conferences, already established in many nations, have furnished outstanding proofs of a more fruitful apostolate. Therefore, this most sacred synod considers it supremely opportune everywhere that bishops belonging to the same nation or region form an association and meet together at fixed times."

Thus, after Vatican II, the bishops of the United States organized the National Conference of Catholic Bishops to be the successor to the Annual Meeting of Bishops of the United States which had started in 1919. The NCCB was organized specifically to operate according to Vatican II's Decree on the Pastoral Office of Bishops. In addition to the NCCB, which is the canonical entity, there is also the United States Catholic Conference, the civil corporation, which provides an organizational structure and the resources needed to insure coordination, cooperation and assistance in the public, educational and social concerns of the Church at the national or interdiocesan level. As most of you know, I have served both the NCCB and the USCC as their general secretary from 1968 to 1972 and as their elected president from 1974 to 1977.

The two conferences, NCCB and USCC, have played an important role in the life and ministry of the Church in the United States since Vatican II. In such diverse areas as liturgy, doctrine, canon law, ecumenism,

Catholic schools, vocations, priestly formation, catechetics, health care, social concerns, right-to-life issues, evangelization, and countless others, the conferences have made it possible for the local churches in this country to work together for the common good. The conferences have enabled the local churches to take advantage of their rich diversity while maintaining unity among themselves as well as with the local churches of other countries and the Holy See.

An important by-product of these national and regional episcopal conferences is the manner in which they stimulate, support, and challenge one another. Let me give you two examples. Not long ago, we bishops of the United States held an extended meeting—it was really more of a retreat—at Collegeville in Minnesota. We gathered not to issue statements or vote on documents or make policy decisions. Rather, we gathered to learn from one another, to support one another, to pray with and for one another, and to discern where the Lord was calling us. As many of you know, Cardinal Hume of England served us as spiritual guide or facilitator. In addition, much of the inspiration grew out of the experience which several of our bishops had when they attended the meeting of the Latin American Bishops' Council (CELAM)—a regional conference of bishops—in Puebla, Mexico. As observers at Puebla, they were so impressed with the process and the results of this gathering of our brother bishops to the south that, upon their return, they proposed a somewhat similar meeting for us here in North America. Thus, while the Collegeville meeting was quite different from that at Puebla in purpose and scope, we profited from the inspiring example of another episcopal conference. That is the kind of organic growth and deepening which prompted me to begin this talk by comparing the twenty years of the Vatican Council to the twenty years of an individual person. The Holy Spirit planted the seed and the Holy Spirit has fostered its growth, sometimes in directions we did not expect.

Another example. This past January, Archbishop John Roach, our current president, Monsignor Daniel Hoye, Father Bryan Hehir and I met with bishops of Europe about our forthcoming pastoral document on war and peace. Our conversations were open, intense and extremely beneficial for all of us. Before long, the bishops of several European countries, including Germany, will issue similar statements on war and peace. Of course, I cannot say how our conversations in Rome will affect the final version of these documents. But I am confident that their statements will be influenced by our discussions together, just as I am confident that the statement of the United States bishops which will be considered at our May meeting will benefit because of these conversations. In other words, we have served and helped one another better to meet our responsibilities as teachers and pastors in the Church.

The fact that our meeting was held in Rome, and that we were assisted in our efforts by some of the Pope's closest advisors underscores the vision of the bishops of Vatican II who saw the Holy Father as "a permanent and visible source and foundation of unity of faith and fellowship." In this instance, those words were translated into reality for us. The Pope promoted unity and harmony among us not by imposing a false unity which would paper over disagreements or obliterate genuine differences. Rather, through the service of his associates, he gave us guidance from his perspective of the universal Church, and he enabled us to share and sharpen our own particular insights for the ultimate benefit of all in the Church and in the world. Our local churches and our national conferences need such an expanded vision if we are to achieve our true and authentic mission.

Speaking of the NCCB, the National Conference of Catholic Bishops, I must honestly confess that I am proud of the forthcoming pastoral statement on war and peace. I have seen this referred to as the statement of the Bernardin Committee. Our committee is certainly not the Bernardin Committee, nor does the statement belong to the five bishops who serve on the committee. In a sense, it is not even the statement of the American bishops alone. Rather, we have tried to make it truly a statement of the Church in the United States. Many hours of study, discussion, listening, dialogue, and consultation have gone into its formation. Whether or not you will agree with the document in all its particulars when the final text is ready, the collaborative process of its development marks a kind of watershed in the history of the Church in the United States. It is a sign of the humble self-confidence and spiritual and intellectual maturity of the Catholic Church in our nation. It reflects a Church more sure of itself because it is more trustful of the gifts which have been given it, and therefore is more able to understand and assume a responsibility for the entire world. From my viewpoint, both this collaborative process and this deeper spirituality are part of our inheritance from the Second Vatican Council.

Tonight and all this week here at Loyola, you will be considering the Second Vatican Council from the perspective of twenty years. As we look back on the journey we have taken during that time, we are like the disciples who traveled on the road to Emmaus. The road was not always smooth. Our hearts were sometimes heavy. And the stranger with whom we traveled sometimes chided us as "Foolish people, so slow to believe." But as we take a deep breath and prepare to continue the pilgrimage, perhaps we, too, can say, "Did not our hearts burn within us as he talked to us on the road and explained the Scriptures to us?" Thank you.

Address

"Changing Styles of Episcopal Leadership"

Centennial Conference of the Third Plenary Council of Baltimore

Baltimore, Maryland

— *November 10, 1984* ─────────────────────

I am happy to be with you this evening as we mark the centenary of the Third Plenary Council of Baltimore. I am especially grateful to Archbishop Borders and the planning committee for their kind invitation and this opportunity to address you.

As I previewed Msgr. John Tracy Ellis's article, "Episcopal Vision in 1884 and Thereafter," in preparation for my address, two things struck me: how similar the Church of 1884 is to our own—and how dissimilar! Let me be more specific. Regarding religion and politics, the bishops of 1884 warned against clerics engaging in partisan politics. That, of course, is the current official position of the National Conference of Catholic Bishops. Although the debate of the relationship between Church and state may have been conducted in a more defensive manner in 1884 than in our own day, we share their appreciation of the liberty we enjoy in this land.

In 1884 the bishops tended to resolve problems of immigration by advocating full assimilation into American culture. Today, however, we appreciate the importance of retaining cultural identity and heritage as immigrants become assimilated into our society.

The 1884 concern for catechesis continues in the contemporary Church, but today it is complemented by a new surge of interest in evangelization. Our recognition of the contribution of black culture to the Church has been long overdue, as Msgr. Ellis points out. But we have moved well beyond the timid approach of the Third Plenary Council. The recent pastoral letter of our ten black bishops demonstrates that we live in a new era, even though we still have a distance to travel in this regard.

Concerning social questions, we are less concerned about secret societies than the bishops of III Baltimore. We are more directly engaged in public policy discussions. One last point—whether we have moved from what Msgr. Ellis identifies as a nineteenth-century "authoritarian episcopal temper" to an actual consultative model, I will leave to your own judgment! My mother has advised me to steer clear of such verdicts!

The key influence on the episcopacy in this century has surely been the Second Vatican Council. I was trained for the priesthood and exercised my priestly ministry in the preconciliar Church. I was appointed auxiliary bishop of Atlanta only three months after the conclusion of the council. So all my ministry as a bishop has been exercised within the context of Vatican II. I have tried to bridge the old and the new within the Church, both at the local and national levels. As you have probably also experienced, these eighteen years have been a time of great expectation, growth, and even exhilaration.

But they have also been marked by anxiety, frustration and conflict.

Using Vatican II as a point of departure, I will focus my reflections on where we find ourselves today. My assigned topic is "Changing Styles in Episcopal Leadership." I will develop the theme in this fashion: I will first examine the impact of contemporary christology, ecclesiology, and ethics on the episcopacy and then draw from these the challenges of episcopal style today.

CHRISTOLOGY AND THE EPISCOPACY

The Second Vatican Council is known largely for its emphasis on the Church. This is understandable, since the nature and mission of the Church have been dominant themes in theological circles throughout this century, both inside Roman Catholicism and outside. We are all familiar with *Lumen gentium* which dealt with the inner nature of the Church as established by Christ and *Gaudium et spes* which spoke of how the Church should address the challenges and problems of the concrete external situation in which it finds itself.

If the Church has been the dominant theme of theology in this century up to now, the study of Christ is replacing it on center stage. This is logical, perhaps inevitable, for not only was the Church founded by Christ—it is also the body of Christ, Christ present in the world today. Reflection upon the Church leads naturally to reflection upon him. Indeed, our response to the person of Jesus shapes and informs our approach not only to God and the Church but also life generally.

From the very beginning, Jesus emphasized the communitarian dimension of his mission. While there was a deep personal relationship between him and each of the disciples, he was also related to them as to a community whose common bond was their faith and commitment to him. The gospel tells us how he brought this community together, how he taught and challenged its members, how he encouraged and even corrected them when necessary.

Before returning to his Father, Jesus laid the groundwork needed for the continued stability of the community of his followers. Even during the awesome events of Good Friday, when they were so frightened and despondent, they did not lose their identity and unity as believers in the Lord. After the resurrection, when the Holy Spirit came to them, they emerged as a courageous and determined group, ready and indeed eager to begin proclaiming Jesus and his gospel to a hostile world.

The Church, then, is not simply an organization. It is a community of faith over which the risen Lord presides and through which all the baptized make their pilgrim way to the Father.

This renewed emphasis on the centrality of Jesus is having a significant impact on our ministry. It demands, for example, that we minister in a way that does not suggest a dichotomy between Jesus and the Church but instead makes it clear that the Church is a sacrament of Christ's presence in history.

Let me hasten to add that this is not always easily achieved. Someone recently told me the story of a priest who was explaining to his bishop what had happened at a communal anointing service. The priest had observed an old man—who was not Catholic—approaching the sanctuary to be anointed. The priest pointed out the dilemma: the man was not Catholic but he was so intent on being anointed! The priest went on to explain that he had resolved the matter by asking himself, "Now what would Jesus have done in this situation?" The bishop immediately blurted out "You didn't!!"

As I noted, this centrality of Jesus in the Church has profound implications for the way we minister: the basis and meaning of our ministry are the person of Jesus. Without in any way minimizing the importance of the principle of *ex opere operato*, our ministry will fall short of its desired effect unless we are faith-filled people; unless, in our own lives and ministry, we reflect the Lord and all his lovable qualities. People must see in us his love and mercy, his understanding and compassion. Otherwise they will perceive us as mere functionaries and the Church we represent as an impersonal, faceless institution. As people who have been redeemed by Jesus, it is our task to continue his redemptive mission in the world.

In everything we do, therefore, we must witness to the fact that Jesus is not a myth, or an abstraction, or a mere memory of someone who lived long ago and who has no relevance to our lives now. Jesus is alive and close to all of us—now, at this very moment. He is brother, he is lover, he is friend. He cares about us, about our well-being and our needs, about our joys and sorrows. As ministers, we need to be filled with faith, living in close union with Jesus, reflecting his qualities in our own lives.

ECCLESIOLOGY AND EPISCOPACY

As I noted earlier, the theme of the Church was the organizing concept of Vatican II. In the nineteen years since the council, this ecclesiological focus has remained a central reality around which many other topics were articulated.

In an address to the episcopal conference five years ago, I noted that three ecclesiological themes have a direct bearing on our work—individually and collectively—as bishops: community, historicity, and the local church.

1. Community

At the heart of the conciliar and postconciliar conception of the Church is the theology of *Lumen gentium*. Central to this document, which Pope John Paul II has called the "magna carta" of Vatican II, is the idea of the Church as a community.

Because the Church is the whole community of the baptized, we can no longer understand the role of the episcopacy apart from the total community of the Church on both the universal and the local levels.

Our ecclesial community is structured and hierarchical, and these characteristics have crucial practical consequences. Within the total community of the Church, there exists the communion of bishops, in union with the pope, bound together by the principle of collegiality. The communion of episcopacy exists for the rest of the Church; but it is a community which also must be understood and fostered as a distinct communion with a distinct ministry of service within the Church.

2. Historicity

The distinct ecclesiological contribution of *Gaudium et spes* is to situate the Church in history. It is concrete, specific, historical, and oriented toward action in the name of the gospel. In a key sentence, reaffirmed by *Redemptor hominis*, the conciliar text states that the Church should stand in society as the sign and safeguard of the dignity of the person.

The human person—at all stages of development and in all circumstances—is the key to the social ministry of the Church and, hence, to episcopal service.

3. The Local Church

The theology of *Lumen gentium* stimulated a renewal of theological and pastoral interest in the local church. For example, the concept played a particularly important role in the 1974 synod on evangelization. In his apostolic letter *Octogesima adveniens*, Pope Paul VI called upon "local Christian communities" to specify and discern the concrete implications of the Chu·ch's teaching in each place. This invitation gives the local church the active and creative role of incarnating the demands of the gospel in diverse cultural, social, and geographical situations. The church in each locality must read the signs of the times and make specific choices in light of this process of discernment.

Although the upsurge of interest in the local church and its relationships is a relatively recent phenomenon, even a preconciliar ecclesiology stressed that in the Church as a whole, and in the church of each locality, the bishops are called to a role of leadership. This is the way Christ ordered the Church. In the postconciliar years both the context and the content of this leadership have changed to some degree; but the intrinsic bond between leadership and episcopacy remains constant. We are called to a more collegial style of leadership—consultative as well as directive—as we are called to attend to many voices in the ongoing life of the Church. Yet the episcopal role has an irreducible quality of leadership.

The role of the bishop in the local church is often misunderstood by many people. Bishop Kenneth Untener's recent article in *America* summarizes well the problem and the theology involved. He explains: "A bishop in an individual diocese does what he thinks is best for that local church. He tries to implement his best pastoral judgment in consultation with others, lay and ordained." Bishop Untener suggests, and I agree, that many Catholics see bishops as mere branch managers with the significant authority and leadership in Rome. That is why some bypass the local bishop or even the episcopal conference in sending letters to the Pro-Nuncio or directly to the Holy See. While they surely have the right to do this, this practice often belies a faulty ecclesiology. Whereas the lines of authority are clear and each bishop is directly subject to the Holy Father, the danger remains that this mentality can reduce both the efficiency and the legitimate authority of the local bishop.

It is easier to point to the leadership role of bishops than to define its content. Indeed, one result of Vatican II is that expectations for leadership in the Church have been intensified on all fronts. Both the style and substance of leadership are often debated. And this is healthy, inasmuch as good leadership requires good ideas which at some point must be transformed into living patterns of leadership. Episcopal conferences exist in part so that bishops do not have to struggle with the question of leadership in isolation. They can share with and learn from one another even as they support one another.

ETHICS AND EPISCOPACY

A third theological development which has helped shape the episcopacy in our time derives, in part, from *Gaudium et spes*. As the Church situates itself in the world, it faces an increasingly complex series of ethical issues. The development of the U.S. bishops' pastoral letter on war and peace is an example of how an ethical issue influenced the episcopal role as well as the way we work together as bishops. The letter on the economy which we will work on during the coming year will be another example.

Our motivation in writing *The Challenge of Peace* was due to a convergence of several forces of long-term significance which created a basic consensus of opinion among the bishops. In my view, three distinct forces were important in the 1980 decision to proceed with a pastoral letter. First, the U.S. bishops have been profoundly influenced by the teaching of recent popes, particularly Pope John Paul II, on the issues of war and peace. This influence has been rooted in two characteristics: first, the intrinsic religious and moral power of the teaching itself; and second, the particular pastoral responsibility we feel in the United States to make the papal teaching applicable to the policies of one of the two nuclear superpowers.

A second motivating force for our episcopacy has been the experience we have had in opposing abortion in the United States. No institution in our country has been as vocal, as visible, or as persistent in its opposition to abortion as the Catholic Church. As bishops, we have diligently and consistently worked for the maximum legal protection possible for the unborn. The experience of the abortion debate also had a double effect on us: on the one hand, we have experienced sustained involvement in a public policy debate at the center of American political life; on the other hand, we have always seen a direct parallel between the protection of human life in the womb and the preservation of human life in the face of the nuclear threat. In both cases we believe we have a pastoral responsibility to stand for the sanctity of life in the face of two menacing "signs of the times."

The third motivating force was a sense among many of the bishops that the nuclear arms race in particular was heading in an ever more dangerous direction, quantitatively and qualitatively, as we entered the 1980s. We were faced, on the one side, by the urgent papal pleas for a redirection of global resources away from instruments of destruction and towards the satisfaction of the basic human needs of the poor. On the other side, we encountered proposals to expand the nuclear arsenals of both superpowers. The U.S. bishops became convinced by 1980 that a clear moral voice was needed in our country calling for a drastic change in our definition of security.

As bishops enter public policy debates, they should expect neither favoritism nor discrimination in the exercise of their religious and civic functions. They are free to participate in any dimension of the public debate, but they must earn the right to be heard by the quality of their arguments.

The nuclear issue—like many ethical issues we face, including our forthcoming study of the economy in the light of Catholic social teaching—is very complex. The process we used in developing the pastoral letter reflected this: it was based on broad and intensive consultation, which attempted to examine all relevant aspects of the issue. Bishops shared and listened with one another and with experts in a variety of related fields. Three years of consultation and discussion led to an impressive consensus among the bishops so that we could speak virtually with one moral voice. The statement we issued was very long, but, given the nature of the issue we addressed, we could not afford to be less than comprehensive and nuanced in presentation.

In short, addressing ethical issues has been changing episcopal style—individually and collectively.

E PISCOPAL STYLE IN THE 1980S

I would like to specify some implications for episcopal style which derive from the theological and ethical developments I have described. These provide criteria appropriate to our time and place for the selection of new bishops.

Because a bishop's primary role is to proclaim the Lord Jesus and his gospel, he must be a man of faith, understanding, love, mercy, and compassion. For this to be a consistent way of life and ministry, it means that a bishop must be a man of prayer. Reflection on Scripture, discourse with the Lord, and discernment through the Spirit have to be deeply rooted in one's daily life.

Secondly, a bishop exercises leadership in the local Christian community. His ministry is akin to that of a shepherd, caring for others, nourishing them, guiding them, defending them when their rights or lives are threatened or diminished.

Episcopal authority is God-given, irreplaceable. But it must be exercised with the prudence and latitude which would be expected of a good shepherd who knows how to judge times and persons, potentials and limitations, frailty and talent. At times, it is exercised more through caring presence than through formal counsel and directives—a presence which demonstrates a love and concern for people even when there is no immediate solution for their problems.

There is another important dimension of episcopal leadership. The bishop, together with his priests, has a serious responsibility to help all the members of the community discover, develop and use their God-given talents and charisms for the well-being of the Church and society. This is not so much a practical necessity imposed by a shortage of priests today. It is a consequence of the rights and obligations of every baptized member of the Church. The Church is poorer whenever any of its members fail to use their gifts. A successful shepherd, therefore, is one who not only uses his own gifts, but also knows how to help others use theirs. St. Paul confirmed this in his letter to the Romans where he wrote of the one body having many members, each with its own proper function. The well-being of the whole depends on the contribution made by each member.

Thirdly, there is a prophetic dimension to the episcopacy which has come more to the forefront in recent years as we have addressed ethical issues in our society. I do not foresee that changing in the latter part of this decade except perhaps to become even more intensified.

Like all prophets, bishops who exercise such an office can expect opposition and even rejection. This makes the task very challenging. I acknowledge that, like many other bishops, I pay attention to what I read about myself in the media and in my mail. I would very much like to bring people together, to establish effective dialogue, to bridge gaps, to reconcile. But sometimes this simply is not possible, and it is painful to admit this fact. Prophetic ministry is supported by God's gifts of courage and prudence, perseverance and fidelity.

Another problem that bishops face is their personal limitations as they attempt to address the moral dimension of any issue. I am simply Joseph Bernardin—nothing less, nothing more. I have my own blind spots. I have my own doubts. At times I lack the courage to set forth my convictions clearly and without hesitation. Sometimes I simply do not know what to do. I suspect I am not unique in these limitations.

A key solution is to engage in frequent dialogue with others—with experts in various fields, with respected colleagues, with trusted advisors, with the public at large. The pastoral letter on peace and war was conceived and brought to full term in a process of dialogue. While this was not the first time the bishops have consulted with others in preparing a pastoral statement, none has involved such an open, broad, interdisciplinary exchange. Through our participation in dialogue we share our competencies and God-given personal resources while compensating for our weaknesses and personal limitations. Our collaboration helps ensure the quality of a moral vision for this nation and makes it both credible and worthy of implementation.

I would like to address one other issue related to a bishop's participation in public policy debates about ethical issues. Bishops constantly encounter pressure from special interest groups. I have great respect for people who commit their talents and energies to specific projects which impact in significant ways on public policy discussions. But a bishop must keep within his perspective the whole range of issues that affect the quality of human life. Although he may focus his personal resources from time to time on a particular area, he must also keep the whole spectrum of issues in broad perspective. He must choose prudently and wisely which ones to address at a particular time. When I attempt to do this, I find the task stretches me. At the same time, it can disappoint those who expect a bishop to agree with them on every idea and strategy or who expect a religious leader to be available full time for a particular project.

How should a bishop exercise leadership in the local church? This question is easily disputed. Sometimes, it seems that some people think a bishop should simply affirm what his priests and people do; that he should not involve himself too much or ask many questions. In other words, the bishop should preside over a congregational-type church where each entity is more or less on its own. Then there are those who think a bishop is not exercising leadership unless he calls all the shots—or, at least, most of them. "Tell us what you want; tell us what to do, and we will do it." These are extremes, of course—almost caricatures. But they help us understand better that good episcopal leadership lies somewhere in between.

I believe in a style of leadership which is "participative." Leadership is truly effective, I believe, only when it succeeds in involving many other people. Such leadership does not hesitate to make decisions, to cut new ground, to take stands which may sometimes be unpopular. But it does not want to stand alone. It seeks guidance; it needs support. Generally its goal is to find workable alternatives. So before it acts, it consults. It challenges people to use their own energy, talents and creativity in analyzing a situation and coming up with solutions. It seeks to create a broad base of support if not a consensus. Moreover, it tries at all times to be charitable, respectful. It deals with people as they are rather than as they should be or one would like for them to be—even when they do not respond in this way.

This kind of leadership takes time; it requires persistence and patience. Admittedly, to some it may seem to be a sign of indecision or a lack of will. I would also like to add that this kind of leadership does not assume all the blame when something goes wrong—if indeed many people have taken part in the decision-making process. But neither does it take all the credit when things turn out well. Participative leadership is consonant, I believe, with current developments within the Church both christologically and ecclesiologically. It is also well suited to the prophetic role bishops assume when engaging in public policy discussions about ethical issues.

* * *

What I have said about episcopal style is realistic and challenging. At times, in the midst of a hectic schedule and controversy, I wonder to myself, "When will it all end?" That kind of question arises when I am tired, vulnerable—when my head, my heart, and my stomach seem to be going in different directions. Humanly speaking, I wonder if Jesus did not ask himself the same question at times. But he also provided a model for episcopal leadership: a Good Shepherd who is willing to lay down his life for his flock.

At the same time, exercising episcopal leadership is a most worthwhile service to perform in the Church. When a bishop gets a glimpse of the kingdom of God in the midst of his people, when he sees people come alive in the presence of the Lord, when he see ministers caring for the poor, the sick and the marginalized—he knows that it is good to be alive and a part of the Church's mission in the world. What I find ultimately reassuring is that it is God's Church—not mine!

I am grateful that God has called me to this service with my brother bishops at this time and in this place. We must look to the Father's redemptive plan for the world, to Jesus' witness to God's love for all his people, and to the Spirit who guides, consoles, and challenges us. We need not fear for the future of God's Church!

"Satisfying the Hungers of the World's Children: Eucharist: Call to Unity and Peace"

Eucharistic Congress, Nairobi, Kenya

—— *August 14, 1985* ————————————————————

My brothers and sisters in Christ Jesus:

A few months ago a U.S. magazine published a dramatic, poignant portrait of a mother with her child. The setting was clearly hunger and famine. The mother's sunken eyes were filled with tears. The child in her arms was holding a piece of bread, the only food the mother had at the moment. She had given it to the most vulnerable, the weakest, the neediest member of her family because she desired to continue to give life to her child, who was a sign of hope and the future.

The children of the world represent the most vulnerable among us. Today with access to global travel and instant communication, we are more aware than ever of the diverse hungers they experience. Like the mother in the picture, we, too, must nourish the children of the world, for these members of the one human family are signs of hope and our future.

I come before you today as a pastor, as a believer. I come as one committed to the Lord, as one who struggles—like you, I am sure—to walk faithfully in his footsteps. It is that commitment which makes me eager to share with you some deeply held convictions about human life—the life God has entrusted to us, the life God expects us to cherish and protect. The diversity of participants in this Eucharistic Congress adds a sense of urgency to my reflections while our unity in faith around God's altar reflects the realism of this vision for the future.

I wish to explore with you some of the human hungers found in our world today and then reflect upon the Eucharist as God's gracious action and upon our response to this gift. All of us can identify hungers within our own hearts. In faith we know that God will graciously nourish us just as a mother feeds her child. The difference is that God's gifts are neither scarce nor limited. This, in turn, prompts us to respond in love—toward God and all our sisters and brothers. It challenges us to satisfy the hungers of the world's children.

HUMAN HUNGERS OF THE WORLD'S CHILDREN

Daily we encounter news headlines which reflect the growing complexity of contemporary life, the rapid development of science and technology, the global competition for limited natural resources, and the violence rampant in parts of our world. The problems of contemporary humanity are enormously complex, increasingly global, and clearly threatening to human life and human society. Each of them has a moral and religious dimension because they all directly and indirectly impact human lives.

There are many, diverse threats to human life and dignity in our world, each of which gives rise to the hungers of the world's children. As I identify some of these hungers, I do not mean to imply that each is the exclusive experience of the specific children I name. Most of the experiences are widespread rather than territorial. In fact, to some extent, all of us experience each of these hungers. I am simply locating specific examples to demonstrate the poignant reality of the individual hungers.

In Ethiopia and the Sudan children face the numbing effects of famine. They hunger for basic nourishment to sustain life. Children in North America and Western Europe live in an atmosphere of materialism and secularism. They hunger for something deeper, a *vision* which will sustain and nourish them, a *mission* to which they can commit their lives and energies.

The black children of South Africa daily face the indignities of apartheid and discrimination. They hunger for justice and the recognition of the human dignity which is their God-given right. The children of Central America and the Middle East are daily confronted by violence, war and violation of human rights. They yearn for peace and harmony. The children of Southeast Asia experience homelessness and abandonment. They long for a place to call home where they can live in peace and security.

The children of Eastern Europe experience discrimination and persecution because of their religious beliefs. They long for freedom to live in accordance with their beliefs and values. This is evident from the throngs of pilgrims at Velehrad, Czechoslovakia, last month celebrating the 1100th anniversary of St. Methodius's death and by the great multitudes gathering this very day at Czestochowa, Poland, to honor Our Lady of Jasna Gora.

The children of India and South America confront disease, illiteracy, and inadequate housing. They hunger for medical services, education, and the warmth of a family home.

All the children of the world are held hostage by the great sums of money spent each year on the worldwide arms race. They also live under the threat of nuclear warfare. They know the truth of the Kikuyu proverb: When elephants fight, it is the grass that suffers. The children of the world hunger for peace!

The list of the hungers of the human heart is virtually endless. Each example bespeaks threats to human life and dignity—threats which can cut off the future not only of a particular people but the entire world. The hungers and the starvation to which they give rise will not be satisfied easily or quickly. We will need all the God-given resources and creativity at our disposal.

Despite the diversity of the threats to human life and dignity, there are certain underlying common denominators: in the face of the multiple threats to human life and dignity, the people of the world—especially the most vulnerable among us—cry out for justice! Their deepest hunger is for peace!

To satisfy these basic hungers, we will need to bring unity and harmony to our diversity—whether it is social or political, economic or religious. We will have to do so on a scale previously unimaginable. The task is enormous and dazzlingly complex. But we can accomplish whatever God's will is for us because he gives us all we need to carry out our mission. One of his greatest gifts is the *Eucharist*, which is the paradigm of unity and the basic source of our nourishment, guidance, and strength.

THE EUCHARIST: GOD'S GRACIOUS ACTION

As a loving Father, God nourishes his hungry children with a great abundance of gifts. He does so freely and with great compassion. His son Jesus especially understands the hungers of the human heart because he was "like us in all things but sin."

Encountering oppression, injustice and suffering, Jesus, too, hungered for justice. Seeing the ill effects of *bad news* on human lives, he preached the *Good News* of redemption and reconciliation. He was sent by his Father to bring healing and compassionate love to those in need. His vision of the human family extended well beyond the frontiers of his own land, and his embrace on the cross reached out to the whole world. With his friends—and often with those whom others considered outcasts—he sat at table in peace and fellowship, sharing food and drink.

On the night before he died, he nourished his disciples with the One Bread and the One Cup. He did so, not with saints so much as with sinners, not with those who stood courageously and confidently at his side but with those who shortly would scatter in fear and confusion like sheep without a shepherd. In his apostles he found weak, vulnerable brothers. He shared the peace and love of the Eucharist with an incomprehensible Philip, a doubting Thomas, an impulsive Peter and, perhaps, even with Judas who betrayed him. He also gave us a striking example of service, teaching us how to wash one another's feet, how to care for the weak and vulnerable in our midst.

In the Eucharist Jesus gives us food and drink and wisdom which can heal our personal and collective woundedness, which can make us whole and build us into one community, which can satisfy the deepest hungers of the human family.

In the eucharistic assembly, God's Word both comforts and challenges us. It prompts our conversion and helps reconcile us. It develops our Christian vision and teaches us gospel values. We learn the necessity—and, therefore, also the possibility—of living in right relationships: with our environment, with one another, with ourselves, and, especially, with God. The Word of God assures us that true peace, real *shalom*, can be achieved only when we live justly and rightly in our world.

It is, above all, at the Lord's own table that we learn that he wants all people to partake of his wisdom and nourishment. It is at God's altar that we discover that we are all brothers and sisters, children of the same Father—that we are diverse members of one human family. It is then that we begin to identify more closely with all the children of the world, that we come to recognize that their hungers are fundamentally the same as our own.

THE EUCHARIST: OUR RESPONSE

The Eucharist, rightly understood and received, demands that we respond. Having received forgiveness and reconciliation, we are prompted to forgive others, to be reconciled with them. Having experienced the peace and fellowship of the Lord's Table, we are compelled to work for justice and harmony in the world. Having experienced the unity of the One Table, we are enabled and mobilized to work for peace, harmony, and unity among all God's children. In fact, in the Beatitudes the title "God's children" is especially reserved for peacemakers.

The Scriptures repeatedly underline the fact that peace is ultimately *God's work*, his gift, his promise. Nonetheless, he does not impose peace upon us. The Scriptures also make it clear that peace does not come about without *human efforts*—sometimes in the simple exchanges of daily life, sometimes in the heroic giving of one's life for one's friends, always through living in right and just relationships with one another.

The task of living justly, of making peace, is awesome and arduous. But it is also a possible mission to carry out because God gives us all the resources we need. Jesus shares his Spirit with us, empowering us to continue his mission and ministry of setting things right, of making peace. The Church has a long tradition of moral analysis and discernment. Our heritage and the teaching ministries of the Holy Father and bishops provide essential guidance for our contemporary efforts in regard to justice and peace.

Despite the complexity of contemporary life, the basic principles which govern our Christian behavior are quite simple. Catholic social teaching is based on two truths about the human person: human life is both sacred and social. Because we esteem human life as *sacred*, we have a duty to protect and foster it at all stages of development, from conception to death, and in all circumstances. Because we acknowledge that human life is also *social*, society must protect and foster it. We are living at a special moment in human history. For the first time we have the opportunity as well as the challenge to collaborate on a *global* scale in protecting and fostering human life.

Because of such contemporary realities as travel, trade, technology, monetary policy, and communications, the world is rapidly becoming a global village in which all of us are increasingly interdependent. A farmer in Kenya is petrochemically dependent on foreign oil-producers if he uses fertilizers to enhance the growth of his crops. His family's lifestyle is also dependent on the grain exchange in such a faraway place as Chicago. The same world market affects the economies of both Nairobi and Chicago, significantly affecting the lives of the people of both cities.

It is because of our growing interdependence that Pope John Paul II has pointed out that the approach of the next century—the next millennium—requires that problems among peoples and nations be resolved on a worldwide scale.

As citizens of the world, we need to face these facts in our decision-making. No private individual, no corporation or institution, and no government can afford to live in isolation. Global resources are limited. Individuals, institutions and governments will continue to make decisions in the next decade and into the next century about such matters as the equitable distribution of the earth's resources, scientific research, and technological application. What is at stake is how we use and invest our resources to solve the diverse problems impacting human lives.

Increasingly, voices reflecting the concepts of philosophers and the concerns of ordinary people say that the distinctive mark of human genius is to order every aspect of contemporary life in light of a moral vision. A moral vision seeks to direct the resources of politics, economics, science and technology to the welfare of the human person and the human community.

As Christians, we are intensely aware that there are important moral and religious dimensions to each of the problems facing the world community—dimensions which must be taken into consideration in the development of civilization and culture.

Moreover, as Christians, we are heirs to a long tradition of moral analysis. As Catholics, nourished daily at the Eucharist, we must take our rightful place in our world as peacemakers. The Eucharist impels us to bring our moral principles and analyses with us as we participate in the development of private, corporate, and public policies which affect human lives.

Allow me to elaborate upon the challenge which lies before us. Tragically, at present, more resources are being committed to the destruction of human life than to saving it. In 1981, the nations of the world spent more than $558 billion on military appropriations. This figure represents only what nations *reported* as military budgets; the actual figure is not known. In 1982, they spent about $650 billion, of which approximately $100 billion was for nuclear weapons. A recent report indicates that the developing nations are currently spending more than $190 billion per year on military expenditures.

The specter of nuclear holocaust will not fade away as more nations develop nuclear capabilities and those with well-stocked nuclear arsenals continue to develop and deploy these weapons. The large-scale purchase of non-nuclear military hardware continues to siphon off financial resources which are sorely needed to combat serious social problems which significantly impact human lives.

It is surely the right and obligation of the state to protect and defend its citizens. However, the development of military capabilities in many areas of the world are not merely defensive in nature. Some are offensive, while others are directed primarily against their own citizens.

A former U.S. general of the army, Omar Bradley, summarized our current global situation many years ago:

> We have grasped the mystery of the atom and rejected the Sermon on the Mount. The world has achieved brilliance without conscience. Ours is a world of nuclear giants and ethical infants. We know more about war than we do about peace. We know more about killing than we do about living (Address on Armistice Day, 1948).

Let me put some of our global human problems in clearer perspective.

A 1970 United Nations study noted that 1.1 billion units of housing would be needed in the world by the end of this century. By 1976 only 14 million units were being built each year—and more than one half of these were being constructed in the developed world which had only one-eighth of the global need. The United Nations predicts that 1 billion people will die early because of inadequate housing!

One half of the world's people do not have safe drinking water. This, of course, causes serious disease and many deaths. It has been estimated that this problem could be solved within a decade if the nations of the world together invested $30 billion a year—a mere 5 percent of total military budgets!

It has also been estimated that three million children could be immunized with vaccines for the price of *one* modern fighter plane ($20 million). This could have a dramatic impact on the spread of such crippling and sometimes fatal diseases as polio, tuberculosis, diphtheria and tetanus.

It is estimated that 800 million people suffer from malaria throughout the world. Each year one million children die of the disease in Africa alone. The diversion of half a day's global military expenditures would finance the whole malaria control program of the World Health Organization.

To build and preserve peace in our world, the key moral question is how we relate politics, economics and ethics to shape our *material* interdependence in the direction of *moral* interdependence, and to bring the technology of the arms race to its appropriate subordinate role. To accomplish this, as I intimated earlier, a moral vision is needed. But only people possess moral vision. Our hope is rooted in people who can express such a vision and in those who are willing to implement it.

Pope John Paul II, effectively addressing the whole world at Flatrock, Newfoundland, last September combined such moral vision with practical recommendations for implementing it. In part, he noted that:

> In a world of growing interdependence, the responsible stewardship of all the earth's resources, and especially food, requires long-range planning at the different levels of government, in cooperation with industry and workers. It also requires effective international agreements on trade. It must take into account the problem of food aid and aid to development, and be responsible to those in need.

* * *

These are the challenges which lie before those who work for peace and justice in our contemporary world. We live in an age of danger but also of opportunity, a time of worry but also of hope for the future. For those who believe in justice and peace, for those who are nourished by the word of God and the Eucharist, there will be adequate energy, creativity and wisdom to transform the world.

The Eucharist looks forward to the eschatological banquet at which *all* nations and peoples will sit in fellowship as friends and children of God and brothers and sisters of one another. The Eucharist is both a sign of the unity and harmony which we already experience, as well as a source of the unity and harmony which we still lack. Whenever we celebrate it, we look forward to the harmony, peace and unity which are yet to come.

Because, as human beings, we continue to be vulnerable—and sinful—we need the ongoing experience of the Eucharist. God graciously shares it with us each day. Moreover, we anticipate the eschatological banquet whenever we come together in faith and unity—despite our diversity—to praise and thank God, to listen to his word and to receive his nourishment. The Eucharist also helps us to transform our lives so that we might become the people God has called us to be—his loving children.

Nourished and guided by the loving God, we must, in turn, look into the eyes of the children of the world to find our own innocence, vulnerability, and the hungers of our hearts. We must hold the children of the world in our arms and share whatever bread we have with them for they are signs of hope and the future. We must hold them close to our hearts because they are our brothers and sisters.

Address

The Catholic University of America

Washington, D.C.

── *November 6, 1985* ─────────────────────────────

This is not my first lecture at The Catholic University, but it is the first since I was elected chairman of the Board of Trustees. It gives me the opportunity to say a word about the life and significance of this university. In all honesty, I did not need another assignment, but, when I was approached about the position of chairman of the board, I did not hesitate. The reason is the importance of this university for the life of the Church in the United States.

In the Catholic tradition the life of faith and the life of the mind are complementary. Faith goes beyond reason, but it never contradicts it. This relationship of faith and reason exists in the personal life of every believer, but it also must take on institutional form. The Catholic University exists to provide living witness to the complementary character of faith and reason. It also exists to provide a living example of how the Church seeks to engage the modern world in dialogue about the major social and intellectual questions of the day.

I use the opening lines of this lecture to express my appreciation of the multiple ministries which are pursued on this campus, to promise my support, and to say how pleased I am to be able to work with Archbishop Hickey, the chancellor, and Fr. William Byron, S.J., the president of The Catholic University.

The framework of my address this evening is set by two actions of Pope John Paul II. First, his calling of the Extraordinary Synod of Bishops (November 24–December 8) to commemorate the closing of the Second Vatican Council (1962–1965) is an invitation for the whole Church to

371

reflect upon and evaluate the last twenty years. Second, in his first encyclical, *Redemptor hominis*, the Holy Father encouraged the Church, in preparing for the future, to think in terms of the year 2000 and beyond—the third millennium.

We are now nearer to the year 2000 than we are to the close of the council. My address will examine the period from the council to the synod, indicating specifically how the synod needs to point us toward the year 2000. My plan is to offer, first, an interpretation of the conciliar event; second, an evaluation of the postconciliar process; and third, a perspective on the promise and potential of the synod.

VATICAN II: AN INTERPRETATION OF THE EVENT

Ecumenical councils are powerful events in the life of the Church. In the Church's two-thousand-year history only a few generations of Christians have experienced the event of a council, but every generation has been shaped by the twenty ecumenical councils. With the privilege of being a conciliar generation comes the responsibility to appropriate its meaning, interpret its content, and share its significance with future generations. The calling of the synod helps to focus attention on the last twenty-five years since Pope John XXIII called us to a profound renewal of Christian life and witness for the world.

In the postconciliar period, a voluminous corpus of commentary on Vatican II has appeared. Quite appropriately, most commentaries have focused upon one aspect or document of the council and sought to explain its meaning and press forward its implications. In recent years there has appeared another kind of commentary which is particularly helpful in evaluating any single aspect of Vatican II and in preparing for the synod. It is an assessment which seeks to interpret the conciliar event in its *totality*, to evaluate its place in the historical and theological development of the Church.

Two examples of this kind of analysis are Karl Rahner's essay, "Toward a Fundamental Interpretation of Vatican II" (*Theological Studies*, 1979) and John W. O'Malley's essay, "Developments, Reforms and Two Great Reformations: Toward an Historical Assessment of Vatican II" (*Theological Studies*, 1983).

It is neither my purpose nor my role to elaborate on these extensive articles, much less to offer a systematic interpretation of my own. I cite them because they provide the kind of broad framework we need to connect the conciliar and postconciliar periods of Catholic life and ministry. Such a perspective helps us to dispel the popular notion that the council suddenly dropped from heaven (or emerged from Hades!) in finished form.

Interpreting the conciliar event means identifying its historical roots, evaluating its theological content, and recognizing that the implementation of the council has been complex and even a bit untidy, but still a blessing. On several occasions recently the Holy Father has referred to the council as a positive event in the life of the Church.

By examining the event of the council we can show that it follows the law of development in Catholic thought—that is, the dynamic which Father John Courtney Murray used to call "the growing edge of tradition." The Catholic style admits of change—indeed, requires change—but it is *change rooted in continuity*. Anyone familiar with the Church's recent history knows that Vatican II was a surprise but not an aberration from the law of development.

In areas as diverse as liturgy, ecumenism, and social thought a basic pattern is visible in the council. Everything said in the conciliar documents had a history in nineteenth- and twentieth-century Catholic authors and movements, but both the authors and movements had been relegated to the edge of the Church's life. The movements (in the fields of liturgy, ecumenism, and social action) and the authors (Congar, de Lubac, Chenu, Murray, and Rahner) had been in the Church but not at the center of attention. They had lived on the *growing edge*, saying and doing things which fascinated some but made others uncomfortable or even hostile. These reactions flow from the dynamic of a growing community and institution with its attendant tensions.

In light of the history of these movements and authors, Vatican II's significance is not that it said entirely new things, but that it took these ideas from the edge of the Church's life and located them in the *center*. In the process the council gave new legitimacy to the growing edge of the Catholic tradition and also added its own content to the ideas and movements. The council both authenticated many of these ideas and contributed its own as well.

Precisely because it followed the law of continuity and change, Vatican II was an event which summarized a previous process of development, becoming at the same time the starting point for a new process of growth. Once the growing edge had been taken into the center of Catholic thought, it was time for new growth at the edge.

In his *Theological Studies* article, Father John O'Malley argues that both continuity and change are evident in Vatican II, but the emphasis should be placed upon the *degree* of change introduced by the conciliar event. To use his words: "I know of no other such assembly in history that undertook such a bold reshaping of the institution it represented, and did it with more fairness, serenity and courage."

The teaching of Vatican II did not break with Catholic tradition, but it has profoundly reshaped Catholic thinking and practice, as well as the

Church's relationships with other institutions and communities. In particular, it has affected three dimensions of Church life: its polity, its self-perception, and, significantly, its posture in the world.

Catholic *polity*—the internal governance of the Church—has been most decisively affected by the principle and practice of collegiality. In the strict sense, of course, the principle applies to the role of the episcopal college in the Church, and particularly to the relationship of the pope and the bishops in their responsibility for the universal Church. But the collegial principle has had a ripple effect since Vatican II: a "collegial style" of ministry now influences national episcopal conferences, dioceses and parishes.

The collegial style has several distinct consequences in Catholic polity: It involves a decentralization of decision-making, an engagement of a wider circle of people—bishops, clergy, religious, and laity—in positions of responsibility in the Church, and a recognition of the diverse charisms needed to carry out the Church's ministry. To understand the scope and significance of the collegial principle, therefore, requires not only a reading of The Constitution on the Church, but also The Decree on the Laity, and The Decree on the Pastoral Office of Bishops. In describing the collegial style of polity, I am presently exploring its elements; the question of what success we have had in implementing the potential of collegiality will be addressed later in my presentation.

A second consequence of the council has been a shift in the way the Church *perceives itself*, again, a shift of degree within a predefined Catholic framework. It involves the use of metaphors which have been part of our tradition but were not at the center of Catholic thinking at the Councils of Trent or Vatican I. The Vatican II shift of perspective is perhaps best illustrated in the now famous example of placing the chapter on "The People of God" before the chapter on "The Hierarchy" in The Constitution on the Church. But other examples complement this basic move. For example, the description of the Church as a "pilgrim people," with its implied notion of the need for ecclesial change and reform, also contributed to the shift in perception.

The reemergence of these themes was critically important because they provided a basis for other steps the Church would take at the council in its relationship with Protestant churches, with the other faith communities, and with the world. The acceptance of shared responsibility for the events leading to the Reformation, the concept of a Church which both learns from and teaches the world, and the explicit acknowledgment of God's saving action in other ecclesial and faith communities all testify to the impact of the council on the self-perception of the Church.

Both changes in polity and perception are consequences of the council which primarily affect the internal life of the Church. A third result has been the *posture* of the Church in the world. In terms of theological *prin-*

ciples, Catholicism has always affirmed a positive relationship between the Church and the world. But much of the post-Reformation and post-Enlightenment ecclesial *policy* placed the Church in direct opposition to major currents of change.

The historical context of ecclesial policy in the seventeenth through the nineteenth centuries provides an understanding of why Catholicism reacted as it did, but Vatican II did not engage in a historical assessment of the past. Instead, in its Pastoral Constitution on the Church in the Modern World, it established a position for the Church in the world which has had striking consequences in the last twenty years.

The council opened a new chapter of dialogue between the Church and contemporary culture, and it ascribed to the whole Church the task of protecting human dignity, promoting human rights, and fostering the spirit and substance of peace in the nuclear age. The involvement of the Catholic Church today from Washington to Warsaw, from Soweto to Sao Paulo, in precisely these questions is impossible to explain apart from the posture set for the Church by Vatican II.

Nevertheless, as I indicated earlier, these developments—of a renewed theology and style of leadership, an altered self-understanding, and a more positive approach to the world—were changes rooted in continuity with the past. Vatican II adapted Church thinking and practice to contemporary needs while remaining faithful to our heritage.

THE POSTCONCILIAR PROCESS: AN EVALUATION

Interpreting the meaning of Vatican II is never a simple or settled process, but the resources available for examining the council itself far outstrip those available for evaluating the process of *implementing* the council. Not only are we too close in time to the process to gain a balanced perspective; we are, of course, intimately and intensely involved in what we are evaluating.

Having acknowledged the difficulty, let me, nevertheless, offer an assessment of the postconciliar period. I will use two models which were set forth at the time of the council itself to describe the postconciliar challenge. Each model tells us something about what has occurred since 1965, but neither explains everything. As I intimated, we have, as yet, no comprehensive explanation of this complex period.

The first description of the postconciliar period was that of Pope Paul VI in his closing address to the council. Essentially, the address predicted a process of *orderly change* in the Church.

The dynamic of the model would be to share with the Church as a whole the spirit and substance of what occurred in the council. In a sense it was a "trickle-down" description of change.

Six months after the council ended, Father John Courtney Murray proposed a more complex description of the postconciliar process. The themes of the council, said Murray, were "renewal and reform," but our understanding of these terms is often too simple. *Renewal* is an intellectual notion; it means designing and projecting a vision for the Church, the kind of design reflected in the conciliar documents. *Reform*, in contrast, refers to changing institutions. Its atmosphere is less serene than that surrounding renewal. The dynamic of the postconciliar reform, argued Murray, will be the *tension* between renewal and reform. The tension will exist because our vision of renewal will inevitably be larger, and clearer, than our ability to reshape institutions to meet the design of a renewed theology.

Both orderly change and the tension between renewal and reform have been present in the postconciliar period. The liturgical changes, for example, fit the notion of orderly change. This is not to say that the renewal of liturgical practice has always been peaceful or devoid of disagreement. But there *has* been a comprehensive reshaping of our sacramental practice and a substantial broadening of access to liturgical ministry for both men and women. The most recent statistics indicate overwhelming support for the liturgical changes by U.S. Catholics.

There are other examples of orderly change, but the more interesting ones are the examples which fit Murray's model. They are interesting in the sense that they remain as challenges yet to be fully faced. Two examples are the *role of the laity* in the Church and the *renewal of religious life*.

The *lay role* in the Church received its strongest theological affirmation at Vatican II. It's a fascinating exercise to pick up Yves Congar's work, *Lay People in the Church*, and to see how both The Constitution on the Church and The Decree on the Laity reflect—perhaps even surpass—Congar's hopes of the 1940s. I do not believe we have as yet created the structures within the Church, nationally or even at the diocesan level, to meet the potential which full-scale lay involvement holds for the Church. This is especially true with regard to the contribution of women.

Neither have we yet provided a framework and support system to realize the potential of lay Catholic witness in the larger society. While vigorously fostering and supporting the ministries of lay people, we must at the same time give greater visibility to the truth that all members of the Church have an authentic vocation to the apostolate. All are called and empowered to carry on the mission of Jesus and to spread the Good News according to their circumstances. Catholics live out their vocations, professions and occupations in the world, but we are not yet the kind of constituency which our numbers, and our civic maturity in this country, should make us. We are on the way, but the potential of renewal lies ahead of us. Reform of our institutions is not the sole problem, but it is one of them.

The *renewal of religious life* in the United States has been one of the most visible realities of the postconciliar era. Most religious communities have systematically undertaken and enthusiastically pursued the efforts at renewal and reform. As I indicated earlier, part of the Church's challenge during these two decades has been the struggle to adapt established institutions to new ways of meeting the vision of renewal. The meetings of bishops and religious, which have been occurring in the past two years as a consequence of the Study of Religious Life initiated by the Holy See, have given me and other bishops a more specific sense of how much has been done in this regard by religious men and women. Many of you present this evening have been a part of this effort.

The dialogue currently taking place represents a new dimension in the relationship between bishops and religious. My brother bishops and I welcome this opportunity to be of pastoral service to religious. The dialogue promises to be mutually beneficial and can have an important impact on the Church's ministry and service to the larger society.

Now that the constitutions of many religious communities have been reshaped as a result of the processes of renewal and reform, the challenge of the moment is to evaluate what has been accomplished, to determine what has truly contributed to the renewal of religious life, and to arrive at a consensus in the broader Church as to the wisdom of the changes made. The current dialogue between religious and bishops provides an appropriate forum in which the positive experience which the renewal of religious life has been for the Church in our country can be brought into clearer focus, as well as those elements which may continue to be problematic. This, in turn, must also be communicated to the universal Church.

Neither of these examples is a finished story; each of them will continue to develop. But the mix of orderly change and the unfinished work of renewal which awaits reform provides a snapshot of the implementation of the council in the United States.

THE SYNOD: ITS PROMISE AND POTENTIAL

The synods which have been held since the council are both a reflection of the change introduced by Vatican II in Catholic polity and an example of Murray's theme of renewal and reform. The synods are a direct expression of the teaching on collegiality. They are a consultative means of collaboration between the Holy Father and the bishops of the world. The synods also exemplify the tension of renewal and reform. Many have argued that the institution of the synod could be used more effectively, should be given more than consultative status, and should play a larger role in setting the direction of Church policy.

This Extraordinary Synod comes at a particularly significant moment in the postconciliar period. To use Toynbee's distinction between critical and organic moments of history, it could be argued that a synod meeting twenty years after Vatican II and fifteen years before the twenty-first century begins is a critical event in history.

It is also critical because of its subject matter. Precisely because the conciliar texts made very important advances in Catholic teaching, but also left key questions unresolved, the postconciliar period has witnessed major differences over what constitutes both the substance and the spirit of Vatican II. The Extraordinary Synod is meeting for too short a time to become a court of last resort for these differing interpretations of the council. But the synod will set a tone, establish themes, and, undoubtedly, influence how we will move as a Church in the last fifteen years of this century.

In light of the original vision of the council discussed earlier in this address, and in light of the U.S. experience since Vatican II, I will comment on three issues which will undoubtedly arise in the synod. On each of these issues I have had direct, personal involvement as a bishop in the postconciliar era, and I will speak to them from that perspective.

The first is the *future of collegiality* as a principle and a style of leadership in the Church. One crucial dimension of this topic will be the status and function of episcopal conferences as an expression of collegiality. It is impossible in this brief address to offer a general review of the role of episcopal conferences since Vatican II, but I can speak with conviction and concrete data about the significance of the episcopal conference in the United States. It serves to enhance the pastoral role of each bishop precisely because it provides a framework and a forum for us to share ideas, set a pastoral direction and project policy positions on major issues of the day in our society.

I understand the legitimate concerns of some that a conference structure could inhibit creative initiatives, but I fear much more what would be lost if the capability to project a unified voice on both pastoral and policy questions were diminished. In my view both the theology and the practice of the postconciliar period point toward an enhanced role of episcopal conferences precisely as a means of implementing the collegial principle in the Church. Such collegiality or shared authority is not a power struggle but a proven means of effective service to the Church and society. That is why I hope the synod provides new impetus and direction for the future of episcopal conferences.

Second, a particular dimension of ministry which convinces me of the indispensable role of the episcopal conference is *social ministry*. My direct involvement as chairman of both the Committee on War and Peace and the Committee for Pro-Life Activities has convinced me of the immediate and necessary connection between an active, engaged social ministry and the work of evangelization in the Church. Especially in a society like the United States, the social witness of the Church is an integral element in its pastoral credibility.

In the face of the nuclear threat to all life, the assault upon human life by abortion, or the impact on the lives of others which U.S. policy has in Central America, silence or passivity on the part of the Church and its leadership comes very close to pastoral scandal. The council provides renewed impetus to social ministry, and I hope the synod will reaffirm that direction.

Both theology and pastoral necessity call the U.S. Church to continue what we have begun in social teaching and witness.

Third, the synod will undoubtedly address the question of the *role of theology and theologians* in the life of the Church. The starting point for this reflection should be the experience of Vatican II. In the end, Catholic faith tells us an ecumenical council is the work of the Holy Spirit, but human collaboration mightily determines the quality of a council's work.

The beneficial impact of Vatican II was in great measure the result of the theological work which preceded it. This fact points up the indispensable role of theological research and writing. It also highlights one of the perennial complexities of Catholic polity. Research requires an atmosphere of freedom, for freedom is the natural habitat where the exchange of ideas keeps the "growing edge" of Catholic tradition alive and productive of creative insight. At the growing edge mistakes are sometimes made, but it is also there that truth is found.

Theologians and other scholars are the primary agents of the growing edge. Nonetheless, bishops have a distinct but complementary function. They must have a concern for the public order of the Church's life, for pastoral guidance, and for the quality of Catholic teaching and preaching in the community of faith. They must assure that work at the growing edge of the tradition ultimately enriches the center and will not erode its substance.

The requirements of public order and the necessity of free inquiry are sometimes in tension, but it is an essential tension for the Church. The relationship between bishops and theologians has always been found to be somewhat problematic. The task before us today is to find a proper balance. At the present moment those areas which need most attention by both theologians and bishops are ecclesiology and moral theology because these are fields which are experiencing the most conflict.

Precisely because the truth which sustains faith is of such transcendent importance, there is usually an inclination in the Church to stress the needs of public order. Too much freedom seems more risky than too much order. The inclination is understandable, but it also needs to be tempered. We live in an age of explosion of knowledge and in a culture which prizes an educated citizenry. The life of faith needs to be presented as an enhancement of all that we know—not in isolation from the frontiers of human knowledge and creativity. Theological research is a requirement of evangelization in our culture.

It is for this reason that I welcome the opportunity I have to serve this university. It is essential that we be absolutely faithful to the center of Catholic tradition and attentive to the need for a creative growing edge within the tradition.

The joining of reason and faith is a permanent element of the Church's ministry in the world. Another perennial responsibility is that the Church, as a community and an institution, in its worship, witness and words, be a sign of hope in the world.

This is, in my view, the great test for the synod: to carry on its deliberations and to shape its conclusions *in a way which gives hope* to members of the Church in their daily lives and to the wider society as it confronts its daily decisions and dilemmas.

In my review of the past twenty years, I have emphasized the positive. I have stressed the potential before us as a Church in regard to the problems which confront us. I might be described as naive, but I fear that charge less than the judgment that I failed as a pastor and a teacher to be a sign and a source of hope for the Church and world. It is my prayer that the synod will be just such a sign of hope.

I also pray that each of us will cultivate loyalty to the Church. I am not suggesting that we embrace a kind of mindless ideology or, worse, a stultifying romanticism about the Church. No, I'm thinking of something quite different. By loyalty I mean a thoughtful, persevering, costly attachment to the Church, an attachment which is also critical, creative, and—above all—loving, that is, forgiving.

Being both loyal and creative will enable us to receive the future Church as a gift, enable us to build the future Church as our committed task, and enable us to pass on to future generations a dream that is more alive than ever!

Address

"The Church in the Third Millennium: Age-Old Values and New Challenges"

The Eugene M. Burke, C.S.P.,
Lectureship in Religion and Society

University of California, San Diego, California

── *October 28, 1986* ──────────────────────

I am deeply honored to be invited to speak to you as the Fourth Burke Lecturer. This Lectureship is a great tribute to Father Burke who touched so many lives in such wonderful ways during his seven years of service to this university community. I am delighted to have this opportunity to participate in the series.

Although the scope of the lectureship spans both Church and society, I have chosen to focus my presentation this evening primarily upon the Church, alluding to its present and potential impact on society. One of the topics initially suggested for my consideration was "The Second Vatican Council in 1986." Although I will not comment directly about the current status of conciliar teaching and implementation, what I say about the Church is rooted in the work of that great council (Roman Catholic perspective).

I come before you as a pastor. Beyond the theological concepts that I will share with you, my intent is to convey to you my *love* and *hope* for the Church. I firmly believe that, while the Church's future is ultimately in God's hands, it will also be shaped to a large extent by the love and hope of its members.

As I speak of this hope and love, I assure you that I am not a "Pollyanna." I am well aware that the Church's history since the Second Vatican Council has been marked by tension and turmoil as well as growth and development. Recent ecclesial events have made us more aware of this fact. As a pastor, I admit that I am embarrassed, at times, by the human imperfection and sin which also mark and mar the Church.

However, today, I will not address this negative dimension of our community of faith. Rather, I wish to dream with you about the future. Although this will not diminish our present responsibilities, it will offer us a context in which we can understand and assess the current situation. It will also provide us with the strength and motivation necessary to work for the future.

What I want to say clearly to you is that I *love* the Church, and I do have great *hope* for it. It is the assembly of God's holy people, stretching and growing and slowly becoming the sign of the coming of the reign of God. And I believe that, with God's help, we can begin to build that future.

I propose to speak about the Church in the third millennium in this fashion. If we want to anticipate the Church's future, then we must understand the complex and dynamic reality that is at its heart. We must understand the Church in at least three different ways. First, the Church is something *given:* a grace from God received humbly and gratefully. Second, the Church is something to be *done:* an involvement that demands commitment and work. Finally, the Church is something to be *handed on:* a tradition. Let me hasten to add that I think of tradition in a dynamic sense: much more a library than an ancient museum. Tradition is not merely a piece of the past brought into the present, but rather the dreams and hopes of both past and present brought into the future.

When we understand the Church in these three different but complementary ways—as gift, as task, as tradition to be handed on—then we can begin to uncover the future shape of the Church. Then we will be able to "read" the picture of the future, as we try to understand what God is giving us, what we must do, what we hope to pass on to future generations.

I propose to offer a picture of the future Church as gift, task, and tradition by sketching *ten* elements which give a certain shape to the Church. Five of them spring almost spontaneously from the hearts and souls which have been touched and formed by the teaching and spirit of the Second Vatican Council. The other five also find their origin in Vatican II but are perhaps more subtly implied in the process of renewal. Finally, I would like to indicate some qualities which I believe must be cultivated within Church members if the Church is to take root in the hearts of young people.

A YOUNG CHURCH IN THE SPIRIT OF VATICAN II

I enjoy spending time with young people, partly because they have vivid dreams and dramatic vision. The dreams and vision of most young Catholics have been nourished by the Second Vatican Council, which was and continues to be a great gift from God. They have been sharpened and refined by the struggles of understanding and adaptation during the past twenty years. But, most remarkably, they are still alive and, in fact, growing all the time.

As I listen to their dreams and vision, I frankly take them quite seriously.

In their vision, many young Catholics see a certain kind of Church. It is not simply a sociological aggregate, some sort of "religious crowd." No, this Church is a *community*, a place where people are called by name, a place of belonging, a home.

This community can be described in five different ways. Let me share them with you.

1. This Church community *responds to human needs*. Because we have recovered a deeper sense of the incarnation and its implications for the human family, because we believe that God has touched all aspects of being human, we want and expect the Church to embrace all the needs of humanity. In very practical ways, we want the Church to deal with the pains of injustice, aimlessness, and lack of purpose and meaning in individuals and in society.

We want the Church to be responsive to the multitude of human needs, spiritual and material alike, recognizing that those to whom it ministers are themselves unique composites of matter and spirit. A Church that responds to these needs is a sensitive community, listening intently, moving swiftly, and, sometimes, courageously to heal the human hurts, to bind the divided into one.

2. Second, this Church is a community that gives a clear and transparent *witness to a life of justice, peace, equality and holiness*. The Second Vatican Council and the postconciliar developments have convincingly shown us that words do matter, but a life of witness is even more important. When preaching and practice match each other—when we, in other words, not only speak a message but also embody it—then the attractiveness and power of the gospel take hold of people's lives. Many young people today want to build a Church which is authentic and faithful to its own word.

3. Third, this Church is a community of *celebration*. For too long we had allowed our faith and religious practices to become drab and uninspiring—punctuating them with severity, guilt, somber notes of struggle—and all of this in the context of a pessimistic view of human nature. This is not the stuff of laughter and dreams. It might be well to recall the words of the poet, Langston Hughes:

> What happens to a dream deferred?
> Does it dry up
> like a raisin in the sun? . . .
> Or does it explode? *(Harlem)*

Deferred dreams lead to a dreary and joyless diet of the religious masochist. They also lead to a shattering of the dreams themselves.

Instead, the Church is called to be a community of celebration because we remember and recall what God has done in Jesus Christ by the power of the Holy Spirit. We celebrate because the story is not finished, but simply unfolding to its dramatic and saving conclusion. The Second Vatican Council recovered and renewed our sense of the *full* paschal mystery—death, resurrection, ascension, and sending of the Spirit. The new rites for the sacraments are meant to embody with greater clarity and noble simplicity the cause of our celebration.

Many young people today want a Church which is a community of celebration. They will work strenuously to enhance its worship. They know that, even before we begin to devise our own plans or weave the designs of what *we* are to do, we must recognize and celebrate what *God* has done and is doing.

4. Fourth, this Church is a *compassionate* community. Why is it that an elderly nun, who does little in a structural or systemic way for the poor and the dying, electrifies the world? But that is precisely what Mother Teresa of Calcutta does. The fact is that mercy is not all that plentiful in today's world; the possibilities of experiencing a compassionate encounter seem to grow more remote. We have more technology each day to extend life, yet we tend to forget that, ultimately, we do not live by the latest technological advance but by simple mercy, by loving compassion. Many young people today know this. They hunger for it. They know that many people share their hunger for compassion. Compassion allows us to walk in the other person's moccasins. When the Church is experienced as compassionate, it becomes attractive. Moreover, it is then being faithful to the mission of Jesus, the compassionate shepherd.

5. Fifth, this Church is a *truly welcoming* community, a place that people can call *home*. In a world of many transitions and migrations, people feel unanchored, uprooted. They need a place to land. Hospitality characterized the ministry of Jesus, who continues to invite people: "Come to me all you who labor and are burdened." The Second Vatican Council helped us to understand how the Church comes alive and is realized in the local community. People like Father Burke have worked and will work very hard to make people feel at home or, rather, to help them recognize that the Church *is* their home, that they belong there.

These, then, are five dimensions of the kind of Church that many young people want and are willing to build—and that, I believe, they have been trying to build: a community responsive to human needs; a community that witnesses in its own life to justice, peace, equality, and holiness; a community of celebration; a compassionate community, a welcoming community in which people feel at home.

I want to affirm and support their vision. I hope that I have portrayed it accurately. It is, may I add, my vision also. We have been steeped in the renewal of Vatican II for the past twenty years. We have heard the word of God proclaimed in our own language. We have experienced community in an enriching and, perhaps at times, dramatic way through our active participation in the liturgy. We have grown to know—and be convinced—in our hearts that the Church cannot simply be concerned with internal matters. Working for justice, for example, is an integral part of the proclamation of the gospel.

So, we are a people committed to the renewal of the Church. We have received that renewal as a gift, as a task, as a tradition to be handed on. And the renewal affects us as we bring into focus our vision of the Church in the twenty-first century.

My hope is that these developments will take deep root in the Church's life and ministry.

A BOLD CHURCH IN THE SPIRIT OF VATICAN II

I have tried, as best as I can on the basis of what so many young people have told me, to represent their ecclesial concerns and hopes. As I have already intimated, I support them and share them. But now, I want to *expand* them.

I want to highlight five other dimensions that help to shape the contemporary and future Church. They are just as essential as the five I have already noted. Yet, they may pose a difficulty, for they may not seem so appealing—at least some of them. They do not necessarily flow from our contemporary American culture. In fact, in some instances, they are starkly countercultural.

I have entitled this section of my talk "A Bold Church in the Spirit of Vatican II." By this I imply that these aspects of the Church put it in a more assertive posture. St. Paul used the Greek word *parrhesia*, meaning "boldness or forthright speaking," to characterize his apostolic ministry. He recognized the imperative to preach the gospel at all costs and without reserve. And so must the Church today.

What are the five additional dimensions of the Church?

1. First, the Church is called to be a community of *conscience* in the world, a people of firm principle. We are the holy Church of God, not, of course, because we are personally holy, but because we stand for the Holy One in whom we live and move and have our very being. As God's holy people, we need to stand as a community of conscience, a people of principle.

We do not do this in a finger-wagging way, self-righteously judging the defects of others. No, we do it humbly because we know that we are a community of sinners just as we are a communion of saints.

We need to speak out when armaments take food out of the mouths of children, when abortion kills unborn life, when uncommited sexual pursuits trivialize human love, when the poor are pushed down lower rather than raised higher, when farm people are unjustly dispossessed of their land, when victims of oppression and poverty are denied entrance to or refuge in this land of opportunity. These are—at least, some of them—hard sayings. Who can stand them? As a community of conscience, we must speak to the divided hearts of so many people. We must integrate the personal and the social, that which is prudent and that which is gospel-centered. Decisions made in this perspective foster the kingdom of God.

2. Second, the Church must continue to grow so that it will become a community of *great linkage*, a community that understands the concept of interdependence and lives in solidarity with all people. The Church is the *ecclesia catholica*, the universal Church. The ministry and mission of Jesus linked rich and poor, men and women, Samaritans and Jews, the powerful and the humble. The early Church, especially through the heroic efforts of St. Paul, continued the linkage: In Christ Jesus all are one; no longer is there male or female, Jew or Gentile, free or slave.

Today's Church—and tomorrow's—must continue to link all people together. This is a task of reconciliation and education. It is also an extremely bold and costly enterprise.

What divides us must be subsumed into a greater unity. Where there are wounds of division, there is need for healing. We also need to know about each other and share our concerns. We know about the situation in South Africa, Lithuania, and Chile. We need to know and feel our links with the people of El Salvador, the Philippines, and Lebanon.

Within our own country, the Church must help bring together black and white and brown and red and yellow. We must, with the experience of Pentecost, come to know that those who speak different languages, in fact, speak a common language in the Spirit. We must find ways for people to preserve and celebrate their cultural heritage.

It is not easy to be a truly "catholic" Church. Catholicity is something given, a grace. But it is also something to be achieved in the future. It is both a tradition and a dream to be handed on. It has demanded and will continue to require great and bold efforts and sacrifice.

3. Third, the Church is a community of *history*, of *tradition*. It is built on the foundation of Jesus and the apostles. We live in an instantaneous culture. Our sense of history may sometimes extend to last week, if we're lucky. With such a fast pace, with such intense forms of secular existentialism, it strains our imagination to consider ourselves a community of history and tradition.

Yet it is crucial, as the Second Vatican Council pointed out, that members of the Church remember their origins, for only then will they know who they are. To lose the memory of our past is really to lose ourselves, our identity, our hope. Loss of memory denies the past just as loss of imagination blinds us to the future. Both losses are connected and tragically costly.

The Church draws its beliefs and teaching from the earliest witnesses to the event of Jesus Christ. It holds to doctrine which, although subject to development, keeps drawing its members back to the central truths of our historical tradition. We unite ourselves with the pope, who, together with the college of bishops, ensures, protects, confirms, and enriches our fidelity to our history.

In an existentialist age it is bold to be historically conscious, but it is vital to the Church's future.

4. Fourth, the Church is a community not only of celebration but also of *struggle*. In a very real sense, the Church's mission is to follow the example of Jesus who united himself with suffering and sinful humanity. He suffered for our sake and took on our sin so that we might become the very holiness of God. Jesus, the risen Lord but also the crucified one, embraces our human struggle. The cross remains a central message on our human journey.

Although the Church extends mercy and compassion, concretizing it in many specific ways, it also renders a silent kind of service. It is wordless; it may also be actionless. It is bold and full of risk. It is simply the association and sense of solidarity with suffering people throughout the world.

To take on pain and suffering is neither glamorous nor attractive. Still, members of the Church are challenged and, indeed, committed by the Second Vatican Council not to isolate themselves from the world but to take within themselves—as Christ did within his own body—all that needs healing and redemption.

It is the suffering Church—for example, the Church in Central America, Poland, South Africa, China—that will give the universal Church great vitality. This is not so much because of any specific accomplishments but rather because the Church in these places follows closely in the footsteps of Jesus. Through their experience of death will come resurrection and new life.

5. Fifth, the Church must be a community of *learning and teaching*. Discipleship—and the root of that word means "learner"—must mark the lives of its members. "Faith seeking understanding" was St. Anselm's definition of theology. In that sense, we need to become a deeply theological Church, for there are so many things that we need to learn, so many things we need to teach.

We need to know how to make technology serve humanity. And once we learn that, we must teach it. We need to know how to protect the most helpless and vulnerable among us—the unborn, the sick, the aged—and to teach that. We need to find a way to develop a more equitable economic order and to teach that. We need to support a political order that respects the dignity of the individual person in light of the common good, and we need to teach that also.

Of course, for all of these issues, there are experts in various fields of secular learning and there are diverse strategies. They must be listened to and considered. But beneath all these human efforts lies the question of *value*. Ultimately, we must come to grips with the question of value in light of the mystery of God. So, solutions will not emerge simply from the cleverness of our own ingenuity or our creativity. A process of careful and close discernment in faith is also needed.

Nationally and internationally, who will give shape to the view of the world we want to build? Will it be a materialistic philosophy which is simply insufficient for the human spirit? Will it be a kind of crass secular humanism that limits human efforts in the same moment that it claims absolute freedom from religious ties and values? Or will it be, on the other hand, a demagogic religiosity that slides perilously into the idolatry of raising human interpretation to the level of God's sovereign word?

I hope it will be none of these. I firmly believe that the Church's tradition which is profoundly human in its respect for critical reason and profoundly faithful in its attachment to the word of God, has much to offer our nation and our world in terms of future direction. It will be a bold Church that will dare to learn and to teach, a theological Church alert to human dilemmas and suffused by the intelligence of faith.

These, then, are five perspectives of the Church—not in contradiction to the first five and certainly not in opposition to the movements of renewal since the council. No, these five derive from both the council and the Church's tradition, and they speak in a complementary way to the images and concerns about the future of the Church that might be more spontaneously our own.

Conclusion

If the Church is to move into the third Christian millennium in the fashion I have described this evening, then its members will need to cultivate three qualities that will enable them to receive the future Church as a gift, to build the future Church as their committed task, and to pass on to future generations a dream that is more alive than ever.

First, they will have to cultivate *loyalty* to the Church. I am not suggesting a kind of mindless ideology or, worse, a stultifying romanticism about the Church. No, I am thinking of something quite different. By loyalty I mean a thoughtful, persevering, costly attachment to the Church, an attachment which is also critical, creative, and, above all, loving—that is, forgiving.

Second, they will have to cultivate *creativity* within the Church. We are living in a time of transition—culturally, religiously, and in so many other ways. We must apply our intelligence to the situations in which we find ourselves. We must be creative, take the initiative, doing so in the context of a community in which we submit our ideas and our hopes. In other words, we exercise our creativity humbly, but we *exercise* it because it's needed. And may I add that we must—we *must*—respect the gift of intelligence that God has given us. If we do not cultivate it, we simply will not be creative. The Church of the third millennium will emerge strong and vibrant in good measure if we exercise a ministry of study and reflection.

Finally, there is often a tension between loyalty and creativity, between receiving gratefully what is handed down and integrating what is new. This tension is somewhat resolved when we cultivate a *spirit of centering*, when we nourish the life of contemplation. Prayer is essential if we are to remain committed to what we are about in the Church. Key to our spirituality will be recollection, gathering ourselves together in order to go out of ourselves in prayer and then in action. Without that, we lose our focus. It is so easy to be sidetracked. We need to be anchored in faith. We need to develop a habitual stance of centering, of returning to the core—which, of course, is the Lord.

Concrete, specific events and experiences in the life of the Church readily distract us from the larger perspective of what the Church is, where it is going, and where it should go. At times, there may appear to be setbacks, and we become discouraged. But we must hold on to our dreams and the vision of the Church which we have inherited from the Second Vatican Council. We must remain a people of hope, willing to commit ourselves to building up the Church of the next millennium!

"The Assembly: Basis for Liturgical Renewal"

Southwest Liturgical Conference

Corpus Christi, Texas

—January 18, 1988 ———————————————————

When I celebrated my first Mass nearly thirty-six years ago, I did so in Latin, with my back to the people. Servers stammered through the Latin responses, and the choir sang mightily. For the most part, the congregation was silent, its participation limited to kneeling, standing, and sitting at the appropriate times. At that time, many people received Communion only occasionally, kneeling at the altar railing with great devotion, awaiting the moment when the host would be placed on their tongues.

Next December will mark the twenty-fifth anniversary of the promulgation of the Second Vatican Council's Constitution on the Sacred Liturgy. Those of you who, like me, have been around for awhile may well marvel at how far we have come liturgically in the past quarter century. Those of you who were born more recently may ask yourselves, "If some marvel at what we see now, just what did we miss in the former liturgical rites?"

While we dare not take for granted the great progress we have made in liturgical renewal, it is correct to say, I believe, that the vast majority of Catholics seem to feel quite positive generally about the reform of the liturgy. The Notre Dame Study of the American Parish has recently confirmed this welcome reaction.

While nostalgia may prompt some to want to experience a Latin Mass "at least one more time," few want to return to a regular and exclusive Latin liturgy. Most congregations today are accustomed to lay readers, cantors, and extraordinary ministers of the Eucharist. They have adjusted well to the revised order of Mass including the nine Eucharistic Prayers, and to the revisions of all the other sacraments.

The election of catechumens at the cathedral, the initiation of adults at the Easter Vigil, the reception of Communion under both forms, the celebration of Christian burial imbued with the spirit of Easter—these are all positive signs both of a reformed liturgy and a Church renewing and implementing its understanding of its identity and mission.

When I was ordained a bishop nearly twenty-two years ago, I had the wonderful privilege of serving as an auxiliary to Archbishop Hallinan of Atlanta, who played a significant role in the development of the Constitution on the Sacred Liturgy. I learned a great deal from him about many dimensions of Church life, in particular the many implications of the Second Vatican Council for the contemporary local church. In regard to the renewal of the liturgy, he pointed out at the 1964 National Liturgical Conference that:

> If the liturgy is to be restored, if man is to be sanctified and God praised, if we are to become truly "one in holiness," then it must be done by the whole Church, not only by the bishops, priests, and leaders among the faithful. It will either be accomplished by the gradual joining in of all God's people, the eager and the apathetic, the anxious and the confident, the favorable and the hostile—or it will not be done rightly at all.

This wisdom underlines the importance of the theme of your conference this week—"The Assembly: Becoming One Body"—and provides a point of departure for the rest of my address on "The Assembly: Basis for Liturgical Renewal."

The reformed liturgical rites say a great deal about *us*—about who we are as God's people. If we examine them carefully, we will learn what it means to be an assembly. They remind us that none of us stands alone. We are not saved as private individuals, but as a people in covenant with the Lord and one another. The Church's rites make effective use of many wonderful signs and symbols. They also reveal that we ourselves are a primary sign of the risen Christ. They presume that it is a *people of faith* who celebrate them and give life to the music, words, and gestures.

The Church's rites are composed for faithful pilgrims—not for a perfected people who have already reached the Promised Land! The rites welcome people who are broken, vulnerable, and wounded—yet never despairing, because they know that they bear the Cross of Jesus which is life-giving. The rites admit the sinful who are called to holiness and are bonded to one another through baptism. Baptism itself frees the holy assembly of any distinction based on class, color, gender, or nationalism. Even ordination or a call to a special ministry does not break this essential solidarity that is rooted in our common baptism. The liturgy welcomes people who are frightened by the thought of a nuclear holocaust and already scarred by violence and war. It also welcomes the complacent and offers them a challenge. It offers hope, peace, and a glimpse of the kingdom.

The Church's liturgy does not inspire hope by ignoring the reality of pain and suffering. Rather, it takes our humanity and transforms our brokenness in the light of the Cross. It also accepts our successes and joys, which we might arrogantly attribute entirely to our own merits and hard work, and shows us the hand of God in all of life.

While you may be nodding your head in agreement with me—at least on a theoretical level—your own experience of the assembly back home may be somewhat less than what I have just described. You may work very hard to refine the music, redesign the sanctuary, implement new liturgical norms, and earnestly try to be creative about seasons and feasts. Nevertheless, after twenty-five years of such commitment and dedicated labor, we must admit that there is still very much that needs to be done. This does not imply that efforts to provide good music, art, and environment—to prepare effective lectors, preachers, and presiders; to prepare and rehearse rituals carefully—have not succeeded or are totally unequal to the task.

It's simply a fact that, even when all these many dimensions of liturgical preparation are well attended to, they still may not be able to fulfill completely, within a given time span, the vision of the Constitution on the Sacred Liturgy which said:

> The Church earnestly desires that all the faithful be led to that full, conscious, and active participation in liturgical celebrations called for by the very nature of the liturgy (no. 14).

In my pastoral letter on the liturgy, which I issued in Chicago nearly four years ago, I stated that it would take an *ongoing,* dedicated commitment to see the council's vision become a reality:

> The commitment I envision must be in our Catholic bones: the need to assemble each Sunday, to make common prayer in song, to hear the scriptures and reflect on them, to intercede for all the world, to gather at the holy table and give God thanks and praise over the bread and wine which are for us the body and blood of our Lord Jesus Christ, and finally to go from that room to our separate worlds—but now carrying the tune we have heard, murmuring the words we have made ours, nourished by the sacred banquet, ready in so many ways to make all God's creation and all the work of human hands into the Kingdom we have glimpsed in the liturgy (*Our Communion, Our Peace, Our Promise,* 6).

The commitment to this vision of the liturgy and the assembly begins with those who are responsible for liturgical preparation in each parish.

Nonetheless, to achieve the kind of worship we long for, the whole community must share in this commitment. If we do not appreciate or understand our vocation, rooted in baptism, we will not get very far. If we do not believe with all our heart and soul that, together, we are the Church and that we need one another in liturgy, mission, and ministry, we will not see much progress in liturgical or Church renewal.

The words flow easily enough today. No one is startled in your parish when you tell them that they, too, are the Church, the body of Christ. But carrying out the implications of the words does *not* come easily. Our assemblies may more accurately resemble a convenient grouping of a number of people ready to say their own prayers and leave. They may feel little or no connection to anyone else.

That may help explain why some people fail to see a reason why they should sit through someone else's baptism, exorcisms, or renewal of marriage vows. In fact, they may regard these rites as an intrusion into their private prayer. Or, if they are celebrating the rites themselves, they may consider the participation of others an intrusion into their privacy. Many people seem not to have even imagined that they could draw inspiration from the liturgy for their private prayer. Many simply have not understood that the liturgy is meant to be *their* prayer. The tragic overemphasis on individualism in our society does not help our cause. Rather, it pushes us deeper into a private world that disconnects us from others.

Some also have the unfortunate misunderstanding that, when we come to church, we are expected to leave at home our worries and anxieties, our achievements and failures—as if they will get in the way of our common prayer. In reality, however, the Church invites us to bring these human experiences and emotions with us to public prayer to be transformed—to be the very stuff which gives our common prayer a heartbeat. At the same time, the assembly's prayer is a more inclusive gathering of the universal Church's agenda and prayer, not merely a collection of the particular community's concerns.

There is considerable evidence to support the thesis that, even when all the right liturgical pieces seem to be in place, a spirituality in which all baptized members of Christ's body take seriously their roles at worship is not yet planted deeply enough. Failing to recognize this fact, we may too quickly conclude that the liturgy itself has failed. Rather than looking at ourselves—that is, the assembly—as the problem, we may be quick to judge that the Church's rites are deficient.

This, in turn, may lead to hasty, homemade revisions of liturgical texts which may tend more toward entertainment or the performance of prose and poetry of questionable value, not to mention doubtful orthodoxy at times. Let me hasten to add that the rites themselves are not perfect; official revisions of the Church's liturgy continue to be made. However, I often wonder whether we truly understand them as they are, and whether we really use them as they were intended to be used.

In other words, when we feel we've done all we can to make the rites work, but sense that something is still missing, then we need to ask ourselves honestly whether the rites themselves have failed or whether we— that is, the assembly—are not yet fully ready to worship with Christ and one another.

At the same time, as important as liturgy is, it isn't everything! Our worship in common is to reflect all that we do together as a Catholic community. It is, indeed, the source and summit of the Church's life, but "the liturgy does not exhaust the entire activity of the Church" (Constitution on the Sacred Liturgy, no. 9). Intimate bonds connect our activities at home, in the workplace, and the public arena with what we do when we gather in the name of the Father, Son, and Holy Spirit.

This has important implications for our responsibilities as the Lord's disciples. I put it this way in my pastoral letter on the liturgy:

> [P]articipation in liturgy does not exhaust our duties as Christians. We shall be judged for attending to justice and giving witness to the truth, for hungry people fed and prisoners visited. Liturgy itself does not do these things. Yet good liturgy makes us a people whose hearts are set on such deeds.

As a bishop, I have visited literally hundreds of parishes in the past two decades. My overall impression is that, when the liturgy has been celebrated well—that is, prayerfully, with style and grace—it is due to more than a good liturgical coordinator. It reflects a community that knows itself to be an integral part of the Church, exercises a discipleship beyond the time and place of worship, and has learned to make connections between liturgy and the rest of life.

How does this come about? How does a parish become such an assembly? Many factors undoubtedly have to be taken into account, but *pastoral leadership* is crucial. The pastor and his pastoral staff need to have a comprehensive and integrated vision of the parish. Then they will commit themselves both to good liturgy, to the formation of the faithful in the liturgy's spirit, and to making the necessary connections between every aspect of the parish's life and its liturgy.

You may have noticed that the same paragraph in the Constitution on the Sacred Liturgy that calls for "full, conscious, and active participation" of the faithful also makes an urgent appeal to pastors:

> [I]t would be futile to entertain any hopes of realizing this unless, in the first place, the pastors themselves become thoroughly imbued with the spirit and power of the liturgy and make themselves its teachers (no. 14).

This is a very great challenge, for the constitution does not simply prescribe that pastors be better educated. It calls for them to be *"thoroughly imbued* with the spirit and power of the liturgy." This implies that the pastors' spirituality is to be rooted in the liturgy, and that this liturgy-formed spirituality is to give life and meaning to all their other activities. It also means that the liturgy is not merely one more task of pastors on a long list of parochial duties. The liturgy is like a home for them; that is, a place where they draw together the lives of their people. And, without forgetting that they themselves are one with them, they lead their people in prayer and motivate them to continue their service for the sake of the kingdom.

In more concrete terms, what does this mean for pastors? It implies that their prayer of praise and thanksgiving underlies and pervades all other activities. It makes breaking bread at the altar the paradigm for all other forms of service; it inspires them to break the bread of their own lives for others. It also means listening attentively to the word of God and making it the foundation of all teaching. It includes understanding the liturgy in its fullness and becoming so comfortable with its rites, words, and gestures, that the pastors truly identify with what they pray and ritualize. In sum, pastors "imbued with the spirit and power of the liturgy" will be hard-pressed to distinguish where the liturgy begins and ends, and where all other pastoral obligations commence and cease.

While the constitution forthrightly challenges pastors as spiritual leaders, it does not leave the rest of the assembly "off the hook!" Anyone who accepts a role in the preparation or celebration of parish worship must likewise be "thoroughly imbued with the spirit and power of the liturgy."

What all of this leads to is something very basic, but quite difficult to achieve. The bottom line in our understanding of the assembly is *conversion*. In the final analysis, we cannot expect people to worship fully and consciously without undergoing a change of heart. We must first move from being isolated individuals to becoming a people in covenant with the Lord and with one another. We cannot expect congregations to appreciate their active role in the liturgy if they do not yet comprehend the depth of the mystery of being baptized into Christ Jesus, of sharing in his death and resurrection, his mission, his priesthood.

This process of conversion begins with *us*, those committed to the liturgical apostolate. As I have noted, *we* have to be "thoroughly imbued with the spirit and power of the liturgy." We must reflect more deeply on the radical nature of *our* baptism and the implications of *our* being in covenant together.

Again, admittedly, the words come easily, but the work is difficult. The reality requires years of spiritual therapy. God knows we have already tried to address the challenge of conversion. You may have been intimately involved in such programs as RENEW, Christ Renews His Parish, the Cursillo, and Teens Encounter Christ. You may have formed an evangelization committee in your parish. You may have written well-composed bulletin articles and preached eloquent homilies about conversion. You have convened wonderful liturgical conferences, such as this. You may also have caught a glimpse of conversion at work in the catechumenate which gives birth to neophytes who know they are called to be active members of the Church, who know that conversion has its price and risks as it forces us to change our ideas, values, and behavior.

So, what more can we do to foster the conversion of our assemblies and lead them to that "full, conscious, and active participation" for which the Second Vatican Council called?

As you may suspect, we have now arrived at a crucial moment in my address. Although I have not come here with complete answers or magical potions, I suspect you will not let me out of Corpus Christi unless I give you something more to take home with you! And so, I offer you seven recommendations that will both console and challenge you, as they do me. I urge you, however, not to let their simplicity distract you from their validity and potential.

1. Continue all the good work you are already doing. Do not give way to discouragement in the face of the awesome challenge that lies before us. The renewal of our liturgical assemblies has only begun and will take many years to sink deep roots. When I remember the 1960s and the dreams and enthusiasm of good people like Archbishop Hallinan, I am encouraged by how far we have already come. This historical perspective will help us to persevere in our task, to continue to work toward good music and environment and effective proclamation of the word.

2. Take the challenge of conversion seriously. Begin with yourselves. Start with the sacraments of initiation and be "thoroughly imbued" with the spirit of those liturgies.

See and hear in all liturgy the challenge to conform our lives to Jesus' life and way. Avoid the trap of judging liturgy good because it made you feel good. While, indeed, we draw hope and consolation from the liturgy, we also encounter a gospel which tells us to love our enemies, to forgive others seventy times seven times, and to leave all we have for the sake of the kingdom. We take the cup into our hands only to hear Jesus say, "Are you willing to drink of the cup I will drink?" And we also hear, "Do this in memory of me," knowing full well that Jesus implies more repetition of the ritual.

We must begin to see the primary source of our ongoing conversion in the liturgy. As we pray the texts, sing the psalms, listen to the prophets, and break the bread, the liturgy helps reshape our lives. Trust the process, but also be aware of the consequences. When the challenge of conversion is unmistakably confronted, not everyone will respond "Amen!" Some will walk away, disheartened. Others will resist because they are not yet ready or willing to change. But they remain our brothers and sisters in the Lord. We must never abandon or walk away from them!

3. Remember that conversion compels us to renew our vigor and solidarity as an assembly and also to reach out in mission to the world. The Church's mission extends beyond the boundaries of the parish.

Good pastoral leadership is essential in this regard. Someone needs to lead the community beyond itself by drawing out of the liturgy the implications for the neighborhood or town or region and the global village. A parish that creates one renewal program after another sooner or later will grow in upon itself because of its narcissism. Eventually, it will wither on the vine and bear no fruit. On the other hand, the more catholic or universal a parish is in the understanding of its mission, the more it will be able to enter into the true spirit of the liturgy and help renew the face of the earth.

It may be helpful to think of the liturgy as the soil for the seeds of the U.S. bishops' pastoral letters on peace and the economy. Those who say that the bishops should stay in their pulpits and talk only of "spiritual" things do not understand the necessary connection between worship and working for justice. They have not yet heard the consistent prophetic message of the Scriptures: that a community's worship will ultimately be judged in light of its work on behalf of justice and peace.

This has many implications for the Christian community. As I pointed out in my pastoral letter on the liturgy:

> At [the Lord's] table we put aside every worldly separation based on culture, class, or other differences. Baptized, we no longer admit to distinctions based on age or sex or race or wealth. This communion is why all prejudice, all racism, all sexism, all deference to wealth and power must be banished from our parishes, our homes, and our lives. This communion is why we will not call enemies those who are human beings like ourselves. This communion is why we will not commit the world's resources to an escalating arms race while the poor die. We cannot. Not when we have feasted here on the "body broken" and "blood poured out" for the life of the world.

4. In all of your work and effort to renew the assembly, remember that we Christians live *in the world*. The very liturgy we celebrate takes place in the world. And the world often does not support or affirm what we celebrate at the altar. The contrary values and attitudes of our society pose significant obstacles to our struggle to form vigorous worshiping assemblies.

Individualism, for example, undermines our efforts to be an authentic worshiping community. When the emphasis is on *my* needs, *my* feelings, *my* priorities, *my* prayers—how can *we* ever become one people who put on the mind of Christ? When *I* can do anything I please, have it my way, and do it by myself, how can *we* celebrate sacraments which, by their nature, always require at least two believers?

Consumerism, too, is a serious obstacle to an assembly's worship. In a culture where possessions and production are more valuable than existence itself, what value can there be in liturgy which seemingly produces nothing, but simply enjoys being in God's presence, offering praise and thanksgiving, finding peace in sacred silence?

These and many other attitudes, values, and idols—so pervasive in our contemporary society—demonstrate why conversion is necessary. And let us be honest with ourselves. We are all affected by our cultural milieu. We may even adopt some of its values, at times, unreflectively accepting them as Christian.

I raise these issues simply to indicate that we cannot pretend to create good liturgy and form holy assemblies without taking into account the real world in which we live. And when we have done all we can to prepare the assembly and the liturgy, and still fall short, we need not accept it as a failure. It provides us an opportunity to acknowledge that Christ's mission—which he has entrusted to us—is far greater and more important than we may have imagined.

5. Review your formational and catechetical programs, if you want to form a Christian assembly that worships fully and consciously and recognizes the liturgy as the indispensable source of the true Christian spirit.

If, indeed, worship is a primary obligation of every baptized Catholic, then we will have to rethink how we train, form, catechize, and initiate persons into the Church. We may already have learned much from our experience of the catechumenate, especially in our use of the lectionary as the Church's basic catechism.

We may no longer simply assume that the members of the assembly know how to pray the liturgy, how to make it their personal prayer, how to join their hearts and voices with one another in a harmonious choir of praise. An amazing number of books, pamphlets, and cassette tapes on prayer are readily available, but how many of them help us pray the Church's public prayer?

Even some of the best and most extensive catechisms or catechetical programs lack the solid grounding in the liturgy which we will need if future generations of Catholics are to make the liturgy the source and summit of their lives. Often these currently available resources simply mention the liturgy as an example or as background to a particular point rather than presenting the liturgy as the wellspring of our faith *(lex orandi, lex credendi)*.

If we want the assembly to be fully conscious and active in its worship, then we will have to help its members see that the liturgy holds a great treasure—that the signs and symbols, words and gestures are not foreign to our experience, that the liturgy takes the faith, suffering, and joy of real people into its heart. We can hardly do this unless we begin, even with young children, to open up the beauty and power of the sacred liturgy to explore, to taste, to make one's own.

6. Evaluate your worship environment. Just as the Church's revised liturgical rites tell us a great deal about who we are as an assembly, so does the space or environment in which we worship. Liturgical space is important because it provides the environment in which the assembly consciously or unconsciously learns who they are by their position at the table, their ability to see one another, or to gather before and after the liturgy. When we put new wine into old wineskins, we sometimes expect the revised rites to work in a space that simply cannot accommodate them.

This is a difficult challenge because it implies investing money into renovation at a time when we may increasingly find our coffers low or empty. Yet, good stewardship implies a wise, effective use of our available resources in light of our priorities. Because this dimension of liturgical reform affects the assembly's attitude about itself, and its ability to celebrate the revised rites as intended, we must take it into serious consideration when we set our pastoral priorities.

7. My last recommendation is a personal plea for patience and love. You and I know better today than we did twenty or twenty-five years ago what it means to be the Lord's assembly. Our enthusiasm for the liturgy, our acquired knowledge and insights must not be allowed to breed contempt for our brothers and sisters who do not yet share our vision or enthusiasm. We have received many blessings—the benefits of liturgical education, conferences like this, and a variety of experiences which have taught us a lot. And yet, even with all our insights, we frankly do not fully understand the liturgy. We cannot pretend to comprehend fully all its mystery.

Our sisters and brothers, whom we try to animate and lead to that "full and conscious participation," have been incredibly faithful to God and the Church in spite of what we may judge to be their lack of liturgical insight or spirit. Our assemblies have been steadfast in faith and have gathered each Sabbath in spite of poor preaching, poor music, poor liturgical planning.

Their loyalty alone is admirable, a wonderful image of the assembly of the Lord. Many have learned to love the liturgy from their childhood, even though they never enjoyed the opportunity to be led to a deeper understanding of it. Our assemblies have been as loyal as old friends who never studied psychology or communication arts but can touch our hearts with an innocence and love we would never want to lose.

There is no room for contempt for others in any attempt to build up or nurture a Christian assembly. In the past, most Catholics were taught to be rather passive. Beyond passing the collection basket, they were not expected to understand the language of the liturgy or exercise any special role in it. They learned that the action of the liturgy belonged to the priests, and, unfortunately, they may have learned that too well!

Yet, they still belong to the Lord's holy assembly. Their dignity as a priestly people does not depend upon their deeper knowledge or greater activity. Beautiful music and polished ceremonies will not bestow upon them the grace and privilege of being members of the assembly. God has already done that for them! He planted the seed. We can only water the soil and nurture lovingly the fragile, growing seedlings. Without such loving care and patience, our liturgical ministry will be empty and fruitless.

* * *

I wish I could offer you a magical formula or give you a mysterious potion with which you could return home to your parishes and other communities to help form your brothers and sisters into model assemblies of the Lord.

But pastors do not have that power, as you well know. However, I wish to assure you that my brother bishops and I share your fond hope that, in every parish, we will one day find the kind of assembly envisioned by the Second Vatican Council and by the liturgical rites themselves.

As I intimated earlier, I make many parish visitations and celebrate many liturgies in various languages, styles, and forms. On some occasions, I go away from the liturgy inspired and challenged. At other times, I am disappointed and wonder where I would begin to reshape the assembly if I were the pastor of the parish.

These experiences become a collective memory for me of a people still on the march as faithful pilgrims. I often pray for pastoral ministers who daily walk with their brothers and sisters, pray with them, and challenge themselves and the others to become "a living sacrifice of praise."

That, too, is my prayer for you, and I trust that it will be your prayer for me as well.

Address

"A Pastor's Vision"
Parish Vitality Day
Mundelein, Illinois
— *February 10, 1989* ————————————————

With great pleasure I welcome all of you to this Parish Vitality Day. Fathers Roache and Prist have already explained the rationale for our gathering. Because we are partners in serving the people of the archdiocese, this is an important moment. I trust that you will leave this day more aware of some newly available resources designed to assist you in promoting and nourishing the life of our parishes.

Our being together is important for still another reason. This is the first time that the pastoral ministers of our parishes, together with their priests and deacons, have gathered as one body. It is also the first time that I have been with all of you in one place. Consequently, this is the first opportunity that I have had to affirm you, as a group, in your ministry and to tell you how important you are to the people of this metropolitan area and to me personally.

Our collective presence is a powerful witness to the multiplicity of gifts and charisms which the Spirit has given in such abundance to this particular Church. This gathering also reminds us of the many challenges we face as we work together for the good of our faith community.

Recently, I shared with you the archdiocesan priorities which I have established for the next two years. I chose these priorities after more than six years of consultation with the vicars and deans, the Presbyteral Senate, the Archdiocesan Pastoral Council, and my staff. I hope that, by focusing on these priorities, and slowing our pace a bit, we will be better prepared, as a Church, to enter into the Third Millennium of Christianity.

Today, however, we will not discuss the priorities themselves. Rather, we will review three factors which are essential to the vitality of parish life. Such vitality, of course, is a necessary prerequisite for the effective implementation of the priorities and for creative planning in the future.

What I will say about these dimensions of parish life is itself the result of several years of consultation in which all of you have been involved in various ways. I am confident that our time together will underscore the importance of that consultation and the seriousness with which it was undertaken.

A PASTOR'S DREAM

Others will explain in greater detail these three areas of concern. My specific task this morning—one which I relish—is to offer a vision of parish life which will serve as the *context* for our reflections on this Parish Vitality Day. Although I will describe my vision or dream in images taken from my own experience, I can summarize it in a few words.

My dream of the parish, quite simply, is that it be a *spring-like community of new life* that *feeds*, *welcomes*, and *incorporates* persons in the Church. Let's explore each of these concepts.

A spring-like community of new life: Before I came to the archdiocese, I was aware, as were many others across the country, of the great good that had been accomplished here. The priests and the people of this great archdiocese have made significant contributions to the rest of the Church, in the United States and elsewhere. And the vibrancy of the life of our parishes was a primary source of all this.

More recently, however, some have questioned whether changes in the times, as well as the impact of external factors beyond our control, have diminished our potential for making such contributions in the future. In fact, some question whether our parishes themselves will even be able to be vital communities of faith in the future.

I wish to state emphatically that this is *not* my perspective. As I travel from the Wisconsin to the Indiana border, as I go from the Lake to the Tri-State Tollway, I encounter a people of great faith. Together with those who serve them in ministry, they are building up the Church in a quiet and, at times, painstaking way. And as I talk, work, and pray with all of you, I am convinced that we are at a turning point.

With the Lord's help, it is quite possible and necessary for us to leave behind some of the winter doldrums that have touched our lives and ministry so we can experience a "second spring" in our parishes. This spring of which I speak will not be created by the world around us or by the forces of nature. Rather, it will come from within *ourselves* when we trust the Spirit and our own good instincts and ability enough to dream great dreams.

It will not be the springtime of adolescence, a season of unbridled enthusiasm and naive expectations, but the mellow springtime of midlife, a springtime that is realistic about our limitations but also has the maturity, the experience, and the determination to make dreams come true.

When I think of this new, second spring, I see the biblical imagery of the Word going forth like the rain, being received by an expectant earth, and sprouting new life. This imagery becomes a reality when we prepare young families for baptism, when we touch youthful minds and hearts with the Good News, when we walk the journey of faith with others in the RCIA, when young adults participate in "Theology on Tap," when the sick and aged are comforted by weekly visits of caring priests and parishioners and by communal celebrations of the sacrament of the sick that give the promise of an eternal spring.

Yes, in my vision, my dream, I see the parish as a specific gathering of the faith community where a new spring is ushered in so that new life can burst forth.

A community that feeds: Last fall I took some time off, some time to recreate—something I do too little of. Because my objective was to take that word "re-create" seriously, I decided to visit my family in northern Italy, to return to my parents' birthplace to find nourishment and strength. While there, as you can well imagine, there were many family *festas* to celebrate my presence. The food was plentiful, the courses many, the wine generous; and ever present was the invitation, given more as a command, to eat more—*mangia, mangia.* All of this was done in the context of a familial love that sought to bring together as many family members as possible in this time of celebration so as to feed, as abundantly as possible, the spiritual and physical hunger of those present.

As I flew home afterwards, I reflected on that happy time. And it struck me that parish life should be somewhat similar to our family celebration. The parish should be a place where people turn to be re-created in the Lord. It should be a community that is centered around the Table of the Lord where the Bread of Life is plentiful. In the mutual support of parishioner for parishioner, and in the many services that a parish provides, people should find the hungers of our age satisfied: the hunger for a sense of transcendence, for a purpose that is greater than personal narcissism, for that solidarity which overpowers loneliness and alienation.

My dream, then, is that, when people think of a parish or experience parish life, their mind's eye should see a friendly Italian aunt saying "Come, eat more! It's good for you! *Mangia, mangia!*"

A community of welcome: All of you, I'm sure, carry special memories of certain gifted moments in your life of ministry. For me, one of those special moments was "The Picnic in the Park," the Mass and public reception that climaxed the week of celebration marking my arrival as your bishop. What a marvelous scene it was! People from all parts of the archdiocese gathered together in the scenic setting of Grant Park—people of different colors, national origins and ethnic backgrounds, social and economic levels. All came as one family to greet me and, more importantly, to celebrate, in the Eucharist, the death and resurrection of the Lord and the sending of the Spirit.

As I stood at the altar that day, I thought of another scene, some sixteen years earlier, in that same park: the demonstrations and violence during and after the 1968 Democratic National Convention. What a contrast! In '68, the crowds came to protest; in '82, they came to celebrate. In '68, there were barriers to keep people apart; in '82, the only barriers were the contours of chairs and picnic tablecloths, and these were not guarded but shared. In '68, convictions brought division; in '82, faith brought unity. In a word, '68 was a tragedy that caused alienation and hostility; '82 was a celebration of welcome and hospitality.

So, when I think of parish life and vitality, I think, not of 1968, but of the "Picnic in the Park." I envision a parish as a place where barriers are dismantled and life is shared; where honest differences are discussed and reconciled in a faith-filled spirit of charity that promotes authentic unity; where all people of good will experience welcome and hospitality.

A community of incorporation: One of the great treasures of the archdiocese is our University of St. Mary of the Lake with its two components—Mundelein Seminary and the Center for Development in Ministry—and the land on which they are situated. A little over seventy years ago, that land was undeveloped acreage surrounding a small lake. Through the energetic leadership of Cardinal Mundelein and the ceaseless efforts of Willy O'Carroll, that undefined acreage was turned into a place of natural beauty. But as time passed, changing priorities and the forces of nature took their toll. The previous beauty was marred by overgrowth and fallen timber.

But now, a change has occurred. With patience and good stewardship, a plan has been developed to rejuvenate the campus. The formal gardens of old have not been restored, but dead branches have been pruned, the overgrowth trimmed, and fallen timber removed. To my mind, the university grounds have a new and, perhaps, more natural beauty. It is the awesome beauty of a tall, stately oak tree, proudly trimmed, standing next to a younger pine whose growth had been hindered for lack of light but now is free to grow towards the heavens. It is the simple beauty of wild crocuses popping up each spring through the mulch of the decaying leaves of the previous fall. It is the ordered beauty of newly planted flowers complementing a vast lawn that had cried out for a finishing touch.

Perhaps you already know what I am going to say. Isn't the image I just described a parable of parish life? I think so. The story of Mundelein's acreage contains the key to my vision, my dream, of vital parish life. Parishes can and will thrive

- when their natural beauty is allowed to emerge;

- when, with limited resources, they develop a thoughtful, realistic plan for renewal;

- when the ancient ministry of the priest is truly understood and appreciated and stands in natural harmony with the newer ministries that seek the heavens;

- when the new and unexpected gifts of the Spirit are given space to grow by allowing the nonessential accretions of the past to die;

- when the vast treasure of the tradition handed on to us is complemented by the genius of today's creativity.

This vision which I have shared with you is, for me, like a powerful dream that urges me on and gives me hope. This is what I meant when I described the parish as a spring-like community of new life that feeds, welcomes, and incorporates.

A PASTOR'S CONCERNS

I am confident that all of you are here today because, in some way, your vision of parish is similar to mine. But do you at times lie awake at night or come to prayer concerned about whether your vision will ever be realized? I surely do. And after nearly thirty-seven years of priestly ministry, I have learned that, unless we acknowledge our concerns and address them creatively and effectively, they can work against the realization of our dream. Let me share with you some of my concerns.

In nature, spring is a gift from God. The ancient religions acknowledged this, and, each year, the people asked the Supreme Being whom they worshiped to bless them again with the gift of spring. As people of faith, we know that, in the death and resurrection of Christ Jesus, we have been given an *eternal* spring. Our gift will never be taken away. But a gift need not be accepted. That is left to our free choice. My fear is that the complexity of Church life today might be so overwhelming that we will miss the opportunity to celebrate a new spring; that the possibility of a second spring will not be recognized and, therefore, cast aside as allegedly is done with many of the letters from the Pastoral Center!

When I think of the nourishing water of God's Word, I am concerned that it may never be delivered or spread as widely as it could be because of our fear of what might happen if, suddenly, people took their faith more seriously. Similarly, because parts of our community have experienced a spiritual drought, the earth might be so dry and cracked because of hardened routine or deep-rooted anger, that the flowing waters will simply run off and never soak in deep enough to bring forth new life.

As I remember the Lord's Table that should nourish, I also remember a nephew who, as a child, was a finicky eater. And I worry that preconceived attitudes as to what we can and cannot eat will keep us from partaking of the truly nourishing food. Similarly, I remember a neighbor who was offended when invited to a friend's home because the table was not set as she thought proper. She was so focused on form that she could not taste the excellent cooking of a simple, uneducated person.

The newspapers I read each day cause me to wonder about hospitality and welcome in our society. The rise of new forms of racism and bigotry alongside the old concerns me greatly. Our fear of the stranger, of things different and unknown, as well as an inordinate determination to exclude anyone who does not belong to one's ethnic or racial group, will ultimately close in on us and cut us off from accepting a welcome offered. And in so doing, our life, individually and collectively, will be that much poorer.

Finally, as I walk the grounds of St. Mary of the Lake University on a hot summer day and see those parts of the grounds that have yet to be reclaimed, I note the muted and stunted growth that remains because of the unwitting dominance of unpruned trees and shrubs. There is a crying need for gardeners who come, not to dominate nature, but to free it so that its gifts can flourish; to assist the natural order so that true beauty can be seen. There is need for gardeners who can work in the heat of summer and the cold of winter to ensure the fruitfulness of a new spring.

To be honest, on some days these concerns become almost overpowering. They can enervate me, sap my energy and my drive. They can turn me in on myself and cause me to indulge in self-pity.

When that happens, the morning hour I spend with the Lord, and my moments with both the young and the old faith-filled people of your parishes, become so important. For, it is then that I am reminded, as I must be continually, that spring and new life are ultimately gifts of grace, the gift of God's love. We cannot do it on our own. Our dream will never be realized until we let go and trust in the Lord, until we taste the bread of life and experience the eternal welcome that incorporates all. For, in the end, it is not *our* vision that we are seeking to bring alive in our parishes but *God's* promise of the kingdom.

A PASTOR'S SUGGESTIONS

If there is one message that I would like to leave with you today, it is my conviction, rooted deeply in faith, that we *can* work together to achieve our dream, our vision, of vital parish life. For that to happen, however, we must bring our dream to bear on the concrete issues which confront the life and ministry of our parishes. And that is why we have gathered this day.

I would now like to relate my vision of the parish to the three areas under consideration today.

First, *parish governance*. A parish is not a thing. It is a community gathered to proclaim the Word, celebrate the Eucharist, and offer service to God's people. For a parish to be vital, it must have a sense of mission, a purpose. And for that mission to be effective, it must reflect the needs and desires of the entire community of faith. Within that community, there are *two* gifts: the charisms of the baptized *faithful* and the ordering ministry of the *priest*. These gifts serve a single purpose: the proclamation of the kingdom of God. And that purpose will be best achieved when all parties work together in a complementary, not a conflictual, manner.

I am convinced that the parish pastoral council, as envisaged in our new norms, is a vehicle that will assist in bringing about this complementarity. Resources have been prepared to assist you in implementing those norms. As a planning body that serves the entire parish community and incorporates the diversity and complementarity of God-given gifts, effective parish councils will help focus the energies and dreams necessary to renew and strengthen parish life.

Second, *staff collaboration*. The many ministries or services provided by the parish staff are essential to a parish's vitality. The parish staff, however, is not the parish. Rather, gathered together by the ordering ministry of the pastor, the staff is to assist the entire parish community as it implements its mission and priorities. To do this well, several things are necessary.

First, it is not the responsibility of the staff to do everything itself. On the contrary, its ministry is to empower the community to carry out the parish's mission.

Second, the manner in which staff members relate to one another significantly influences the life of the parish. This is why we have invested over four years in preparing the handbook which will be discussed today. It is a guide that can assist parish staff members to relate to one another in a way that will be healthy and nurturing for them and also serve as a model for the rest of parish life. For this to happen, there will be need of conversion—a conversion that causes us to think in terms of ecclesial *service* rather than of job or career, one that replaces a spirit of *dependence* with that of *mutuality*.

Finally, the goal of a parish staff must go beyond simply getting people involved in ministry. The ultimate test of our ministry is whether we are instrumental in getting people to see themselves as agents of the gospel in the marketplace, as well as the other dimensions of their daily lives. The parish staff serves a community of faith in order that that community, individually and collectively, might become the leaven that will transform our world into the image of the eternal Word.

In this context of staff collaboration, I want to highlight the need for encouraging more young people to consider whether God is calling them to priesthood or religious life. We are blessed with so many wonderful lay ministers and deacons. But the well-being of the faith community also needs the witness of priests, sisters and brothers who embrace a state in life which is precious and enriching for the whole community. This is why the encouragement and promotion of such vocations has been given a high priority in the archdiocese.

Third, *stewardship*. In light of the fiscal realities which the archdiocese and its parishes are experiencing, it is imperative that we expand our base of financial support. Not to do so would be irresponsible. To continue our mission and our ministry, we must invite our people to share not just their *time* and *talent* but also their *treasure* with the community of faith.

But, as I said several years ago when I first discussed this matter, if we are really serious about our responsibilities as a Church, it is not enough to ask for stopgap contributions. We need to develop and propose a spirituality of stewardship that is both inviting and compelling, a spirituality that will properly motivate people to help provide for the many needs of our faith community. Grounded in the richness of the theological principles of solidarity, co-creatorship, and co-discipleship, we must propose a spirituality that begins with an appreciation of our own *giftedness* and of our *inner need to give* in response to all our loving God has given *us*—an inner need that models divine giving and is joyful, generous, and done in a manner commensurate with our capability. We must witness this spirituality in our own lives as we invite the Christian faithful to be accountable for all the gifts that God has given us.

FINAL THOUGHTS

I hope that these reflections on the three areas of concern, and the vision of parish presented earlier, will provide a helpful context for the presentations that will follow. During the rest of the day, please keep in mind what we all know—that we are not here as members of an organization or the staff of a corporation. Rather, we are here as a community of faith, believers who share in the life of a great mystery, the mystery of the Triune God. Although mystery will always remain, we can grow in our awareness and understanding of God who is the source of life, love and faithful relationships. Our challenge is prayerfully to use what we learn to engender a spirit of creativity. But realistically, such a spirit will never enjoy the security or luxury of a neatly packaged plan—one that will fully achieve either our vision or what we hope to accomplish through governance, collaboration, and stewardship.

As I noted at the beginning, some may question whether we are capable of this creativity. Others may be afraid. If you have those questions or fears, you are not alone. I, too, have concerns and fears. For example, I worry that consultative governance processes may become so complex that it will be difficult, if not impossible, to make needed decisions in a timely fashion. I have seen that failures in attempts to collaborate often lead to two unfortunate results: (1) a diminishment of the distinctiveness and importance of priestly ministry and (2) the discouragement and anger of others who, filled with good will, also want to serve the community of faith but are unsupported or feel frustrated in their efforts. And I worry that our efforts at stewardship will not be fully successful, forcing us to make serious and painful choices about our future.

But, my sisters and brothers, as I look out at all of you, I know that it would be wrong to give in to those concerns, to be paralyzed by those fears. For, what do I see as I gaze across this room? First of all, I see your talent, your giftedness, and your dedication. And if that were all we had, we would still have reason to hope.

But I see much more than that. I also see *you* who, in so many ways, are experiencing the life-giving love of God the Father and Creator, the self-giving love of Jesus the Savior, and the seductive, empowering love of the Spirit. It is this generous life-giving, empowering love that will make the difference!

As you have blessed me so abundantly, so may you be blessed!

"A Vision of Church: Local Church and Universal Church"

The University of Mary, Bismarck, North Dakota

— *August 17, 1992* ————————————————————————————

My entire ministry as a bishop has occurred in the shadow of the Second Vatican Council. I was ordained a bishop a few months after the council ended, and I have endeavored to implement its teaching and insights to the best of my ability. So, in addressing the topic which I was asked to present—the relationship of the local church and the universal Church—I will do so both from the perspective of the teaching of Vatican II and my own experience of the past twenty-six years.

Ecumenical councils are powerful events in the life of the Church. In our two-thousand-year history only a few generations of Christians have experienced the actual event of a council, but every generation has been shaped by the twenty which have occurred. With the privilege of being a conciliar generation comes the responsibility to interpret its content, appropriate its meaning, and share its significance with future generations. Interpreting the meaning of the Second Vatican Council is not a simple or settled process. Nevertheless, the resources available for examining the council and what it actually meant far outstrip those available for evaluating the process of *implementing* the council.

The first description of the postconciliar period was that of Pope Paul VI in his closing address to the council. Essentially, that address predicted a process of *orderly change* in the Church. The dynamic of the model would be to

413

share with the Church as a whole the spirit and substance of what occurred at the council. In a sense it was a "trickle-down" description of change.

Six months after the council ended, Father John Courtney Murray proposed a more complex model for the postconciliar process. The themes of the council, said Murray, were "renewal and reform," but our understanding of these terms is often too simple. *Renewal* is an intellectual notion; it means designing and projecting a vision for the Church, the kind of vision or design reflected in the conciliar documents. *Reform*, in contrast, refers to changing institutions. Its atmosphere is less serene than that surrounding renewal. The dynamic of the postconciliar reform, argued Murray, will be the *tension* between renewal and reform. The tension will exist because our vision of renewal will inevitably be larger, and clearer, than our ability to reshape institutions to meet the design of a renewed theology and ecclesiology.

Both orderly change and the tension between renewal and reform have been present in the postconciliar period. The liturgical changes, for example, fit the notion of orderly change. This is not to say that the renewal of liturgical practice has always been peaceful or devoid of disagreement. But recent statistics indicate overwhelming support for the liturgical changes by U.S. Catholics.

There are other examples of orderly change, but more interesting are the examples that fit Murray's model which envisions tension. They are interesting in the sense that they remain as challenges yet to be fully faced. Among these are *collegiality*, the *role of the laity* in the Church, the Church's *dialogue with the modern world*, and the *relationship between the local church and the universal Church*. You have asked me to focus on the last. In the process, however, I will also touch on collegiality.

More specifically, I will do three things this morning. First, I will examine Vatican II's vision of the Church in terms of the relationship between the local and universal Church. Then, I will reflect on some aspects of our experience of the implementation of this vision during the postconciliar period. Finally, I will offer some reflections on how we can build up ecclesial unity amid the diversity within the Church.

THE VISION OF THE CHURCH: LOCAL AND UNIVERSAL

The Church's self-understanding was one of the major themes of the council. While two of its documents—*Lumen gentium* and *Gaudium et spes*—deal very explicitly with this theme, the council's ecclesiological insights are found scattered through virtually all the conciliar documents. I will concentrate on its key concepts which directly affect the relationship between local church and universal Church.

The concept of *communio* is of primary importance. It sheds light on all else that is said about the Church in conciliar teaching. In 1987, when the U.S. bishops met with Pope John Paul II in Los Angeles, I was asked to address the relationship between the universal and particular churches. I began by acknowledging:

> Your presence among us today, Holy Father, brings into clear focus the nature of the church as a *communio:* a communion of particular churches in which and from which exists the one and unique Catholic Church; a communion which is not fully the church unless united with the bishop of Rome. This communion over which you preside as Peter's successor brings together the strength of our unity in faith and the richness of our diversity as a world church rooted in every region and culture of the earth.

In his response on that occasion, the Holy Father agreed that "the extremely important reality of *communio* . . . is the best framework for our conversation." He went on to point out that

> Since, as the extraordinary session of the Synod of Bishops in 1985 indicated, "the ecclesiology of communion is the central and fundamental idea of the council's documents," it follows that we must return time and again to those same documents in order to be imbued with the profound theological vision of the church which the Holy Spirit has placed before us and which constitutes the basis of all pastoral ministry in the church's pilgrimage through human history.

The very first paragraph of *Lumen gentium* highlights the concept by asserting that "the Church, in Christ, is in the nature of sacrament—a sign and instrument, that is, of communion with God and of unity among all men" (no. 1). Elsewhere the council fathers point out that there is, first of all, a spiritual or invisible communion of all the faithful which derives from a common baptism, is created by the Holy Spirit, and is nurtured by the Eucharist. From our communion with God flows our spiritual communion with all other members of the Church.

However, because of the Church's sacramental nature, a visible communion must complement this spiritual or invisible communion: that is, *ecclesial* communion among all the local churches in which the universal Church is manifest, and *hierarchical* communion among all the bishops with their head, the Supreme Pontiff.

In the context of the Church as a communion, *Lumen gentium* describes the relationship between the local church and the universal Church. It should be noted that, with one exception (*Presbyterorum ordinis*, no. 6d), the conciliar documents refer to a diocese when they use the terms "particular church" and "local church." A parish is called a "local assembly" or "local community." This is what *Lumen gentium* says about particular or local churches:

> Holding a rightful place in the communion of the Church there are also particular churches that retain their own traditions, without prejudice to the Chair of Peter which presides over the whole assembly in charity, and protects their legitimate variety while at the same time taking care that these differences do not hinder unity, but rather contribute to it (no. 13).

This single sentence articulates the crucial issue that affects the Church as a communion: the built-in tension between its overall unity and the legitimate diversity of its local churches. As is also clear from the text, the Petrine ministry has a special responsibility for preserving communion by protecting legitimate diversity and ensuring that differences do not hinder unity, but contribute to it. The pontiff, however, is not exclusively responsible for this; bishops also share this responsibility.

As with any living organism which values both its unity and diversity, there are bound to be misunderstandings and tensions at times. Tension in itself need not be debilitating or destructive. Often it is a sign of growth. We know that in the apostolic church reflected in the New Testament and in the young church described by the fathers there were disagreements and conflicting points of view.

It was largely for this reason that the Lord gave the Church the ministry of *episkopoi*, or overseers, to provide for the unity of the particular churches and protect the unity of the universal Church. Thus, the Church was provided with those who would have authority to make the decisions necessary for the Church to remain one. The Holy Spirit, present in the Church and working in a particular way through the college of bishops in union with Peter and his successors, has successfully guided the Church through twenty centuries marked by both harmony and strife.

The Second Vatican Council gave expression to this fact by further developing the principle of *collegiality*. Again, let us listen to what *Lumen gentium* itself says about this:

> Together with their head, the Supreme Pontiff, and never apart from him, [the bishops] have supreme and full authority over the universal Church; but this power cannot be exercised without the agreement of the Roman Pontiff (no. 22).

While the college of bishops, with the Holy Father, exercises this collegiality in a solemn way in an ecumenical council, *Lumen gentium* also points out that

> Collegiate unity is also apparent in the mutual relations of each bishop to individual dioceses and with the universal Church. The Roman Pon-

tiff . . . is the perpetual and visible source and foundation of the unity both of the bishops and of the whole company of the faithful. The individual bishops are the visible source and foundation of unity in their particular Churches, which are constituted after the model of the universal Church; it is in these and formed out of them that the one and unique Catholic Church exists (no. 23).

The bishops, then, have a special responsibility to be the visible source and foundation of unity in their dioceses. They also share responsibility with the Roman Pontiff for the universal Church.

In the strict sense, of course, the principle of collegiality applies only to the role of the episcopal college in the Church, and particularly to the relationship of the pope and the bishops in their responsibility for the universal Church. But the collegial principle has also had a ripple effect since Vatican II: A "collegial style" of ministry now influences national episcopal conferences, dioceses, and parishes.

The collegial style has several distinct consequences. It involves a decentralization of decision-making, an engagement of a wider circle of people in positions of responsibility in the Church, and a recognition of the diverse charisms needed to carry out the Church's ministry. Such collegiality or shared authority is not to be a power struggle but a means of effective service to the Church and society. It is bishops, clergy, religious and laity working with *each other*, working *together* for the well-being of the Church.

The Church's hierarchical communion also extends to the parish level. The priest is in communion with his bishop and makes him present in the parish. The priest participates in the bishop's pastoral ministry to the particular church. This means that the universal Church is truly present in the local parish community, as it is in the particular church or diocese.

In summary, the Church's nature as a communion is the focal point for understanding the relationship between local church and universal Church. The Petrine ministry and that of every bishop is, first and foremost, to preserve the unity of the Church which enjoys great diversity throughout the world. And the practice of collegiality is an effective means to do precisely this.

As I noted earlier, while renewal of vision, a renewal of the Church's self-understanding, was an important legacy of the Second Vatican Council, it is also important to translate the insights of a renewed vision into our ecclesial structures and processes. Visibility and structural integrity are an essential part of our Catholic identity, which is based upon a profound sense of sacramentality; that is, an understanding that spiritual realities find both *symbolic* and *real* expression in our life together as a community of faith. So if we are to take up the task of ecclesial renewal, and if we are to be faithful to the renewed teaching and spirit of the Second

Vatican Council, we must reform our Church structures. This requires a correct understanding of the purpose of such structures and how they need to be reshaped in order to fulfill their purpose in today's world. This, in turn, requires a great deal of openness and patience.

Let us now reflect on some aspects of our experience of the relationship between the local church and the universal Church since the Second Vatican Council.

EXPERIENCE OF THE LOCAL AND UNIVERSAL CHURCH

Generally speaking, our experience of belonging to the universal Church has three dimensions—*geographical, cultural,* and *historical.* We belong to a community of faith which extends throughout the world and, potentially, embraces all people. Universality also means that the Church crosses cultural boundaries. The Church respects and cultivates particular cultures, linking them together in the mystery of Christ, purifying them of elements which are contrary to the gospel. We are, moreover, aware that we are only the latest members of a historical people of faith, whose traditions and customs, some essential and others peripheral, are part of our religious inheritance.

The universal Church is not remote from our local experience, for, when we come together for worship, services, and mission, we ourselves are its realization and manifestation. This is true also of other particular churches, all united by bonds of common faith, sacraments, charity, mission, and authority. While retaining their particularity, they are in communion with one another. They form a communion of communities which manifests the universal Church.

More specifically, several factors give us an ongoing experience of the Church's universality. For example, many of our local churches continue to incorporate immigrants from all parts of the world. This has important implications for our ecclesial life, worship, and ministry. In the Archdiocese of Chicago, for example, the Sunday Eucharist is currently offered in 20 languages besides English, including Polish in 40 parishes, Spanish in nearly 100 (99), and Vietnamese in 1. Another factor that reminds us of our communion with the larger Church is the generous response of many U.S. Catholics to requests for spiritual and financial support of such things as Peter's Pence, the Propagation of the Faith, Catholic Relief Services, and various missionary endeavors.

Belonging to this great communion of particular churches means we are accountable to a community larger than our own. We have a responsibility for handing on the faith we have received. Perhaps we question the

pace or the direction of change in some other local churches. In our country we tend at times to overemphasize our own experience, not always
giving adequate recognition to the insights and experiences of others. As
Americans, whose history goes back only a little more than 200 years, we
tend to lose sight of the 2,000-year history and tradition of the universal
Church. To belong to the universal Church, in other words, means both
sharing our gifts with others and putting aside excessively narrow perceptions limited to our own experience.

While we have provided various forms of assistance to other local
churches, we also have much to learn from them. That is why the Archdiocese of Chicago has developed a Partnership in Mission with the Diocese of Chilpancingo-Chilapa in Mexico. This enables us to experience in
a special way the communion between our two local churches. The basic
agreement is that we send a ministerial team to Chilpancingo-Chilapa
to minister and learn from the people there, and that the Diocese of
Chilpancingo-Chilapa send a priest to Chicago to minister to our Mexican-
Americans and learn from our local ecclesial life and ministry. The commitment of each exchange is for three to five years. I have just returned
from my second pastoral visit to our mission in Quechultenango where I
presented new members of our ministerial team to Bishop Ramos. The
new priest who will serve the church in Chicago was also presented to me
on this occasion. Bishop Ramos also hopes to send a married couple to
Chicago in the not-too-distant future. I am pleased to say that the relationship is on a firm foundation, and we look forward to its future mutual
benefits.

We U.S. Catholics also have much to learn from the suffering Church
that will give the universal Church great vitality—for example, in El
Salvador, Haiti, Croatia, Bosnia-Herzegovina, Lebanon, and the People's
Republic of China. This is not so much because of any specific accomplishments as it is the fact that the Church, in these places, follows
closely in Jesus' footsteps. Through their experience of suffering and
death will come resurrection and new life. Recently, we have seen the
truth of this in such nations as Poland, Lithuania, and Ukraine.

There is an added advantage today in belonging to a universal Church.
Considering its traditions, its commitments, and its universality, the
Catholic Church now has an opportunity enjoyed by no other community
or organization in the world. It is the opportunity to influence for the better the values, attitudes, and structures of the whole human family. Even
though they may disagree on specific points, Pope John Paul II is recognized today as the premier religious leader by all people and religious
groups. Communications, economics, and even the threat of global nuclear or chemical holocaust make the peoples of the world increasingly
interdependent. As the earth continues to "shrink" and becomes a "global

village," the Church has an important role to play, bringing the message of Jesus Christ to bear upon a new era in human history.

By now, you will undoubtedly have noticed I have highlighted only good or potentially valuable experiences of the relationship between the local church and the universal Church. But there are also many problems and tensions. The practical question that must be addressed today, as before, is how to maintain our unity while affirming the diversity in the local realizations of the Church; how to discern a proper balance between freedom and order.

The Second Vatican Council invited us to engage in a discernment which identifies and confirms the elements of truth and grace found in our respective cultures, purifying them of what is evil and elevating them by restoring them to Christ. Faithful to this invitation, we in the United States have confronted the realities of our modern age: instant worldwide communication, the desire of people to exercise more control over their lives and destiny, the rising expectations of both men and women, and the insistence that their rights be respected, a heightened national consciousness among peoples even as the world becomes more of a global village.

Facing these realities of our time has helped shape the particularity of the local churches in the United States. And this in turn has led to (a) a strain, at times, in our relationship with the Holy See and (b) a polarization within our local churches.

(a) Our centralized Roman administration, the Holy See, often undergoes serious critique. Some criticize the seemingly ever-increasing centralization of administration in the Roman Curia because they feel it inhibits local initiatives. Others censure the central offices for what they perceive as ineffectiveness in "stabilizing" the Church in this turbulent time of change and transition. In all candor, the same criticisms are made about our dioceses—"downtown" as the central offices are called.

While there may be some validity to these criticisms, it is important to recall some of the positive values of the Petrine ministry as it is exercised in the Church as well as the extension of that ministry in the various offices of the Holy See.

First, the process of ecclesial renewal, incomplete as it is, has truly made giant strides in most parts of the world. This is particularly evident, for example, in the liturgical renewal and the Church's willingness to address the more urgent social issues of our times. We must give due credit to Popes Paul VI and John Paul II for serving the unity of the Church during a time of considerable change and potential danger. We need the Petrine ministry to confirm us as brothers and sisters in faith, even as we move in renewed directions.

More recently, the Church—through the Holy Father and parts of the Roman Curia—has been able to address the momentous changes currently taking place in the world political order. Indeed, the Holy See's longstanding policy of *Ostpolitik*—being willing to dialogue with communist governments in Eastern Europe and the former Soviet Union—while opposed by some within the Church, has proven its value in the rapid improvement of the Church's status in several of these countries in the last three years. The Holy Father's convocation of a synod of European bishops last December to chart the course of the Church's development in Europe into the third millennium is another important exercise of the Petrine ministry which allows our vast and diverse community of faith to speak with a clear voice when addressing significant world issues. A similar synod has been called for Africa. In a word, the Petrine ministry—with its central services—allows us Catholics to speak globally, from our 2,000-year tradition, with a world that is ever more interconnected and interdependent.

Nevertheless, tensions remain. It is painful for us, the shepherds of our local churches, when we are cast in an adversarial position with the Holy See or with certain groups within our own dioceses. Sometimes this is done by persons who do not understand us or the positions we have taken; sometimes, however, by people at either extreme who simply oppose some of the teaching of the Second Vatican Council or the way its insights have been and are being implemented in the postconciliar local church.

In this context we can appreciate two unfortunate tendencies which affect the relationship between the universal Church and the particular churches of our country. As I said in my address to the Holy Father in Los Angeles, when the Holy See reaffirms a teaching which has been part of our heritage for centuries or applies it to today's new realities, it is sometimes accused of retrogression or making new and unreasonable impositions on people. In like manner, when someone questions how a truth might be better articulated or lived today, he or she is sometimes accused of rejecting the truth itself or portrayed as being in conflict with the Church's teaching authority. As a result, both sides are sometimes locked into what seem to be adversarial positions. Genuine dialogue becomes almost impossible.

(b) At the same time, the conflict is by no means found only between local churches or some of their members and the Holy See. It also permeates our local churches. In the May 2, 1992, issue of *America* magazine Margaret O'Brien Steinfels, the editor of *Commonweal*, published a very insightful article under the provocative title, "The Unholy Alliance Between the Right and the Left in the Catholic Church." Her underlying premise is that the *vitality* of the Church in every time and place does matter. It has a great impact on the present generation, as well as on the next. Her basic thesis is that "the present and future vitality of the Church is being put at risk by an unholy and usually unwitting alliance between Right and Left in their attitude and conduct toward one another and toward the Church." In the article she describes nine ways in which this collusion, by making authentic dialogue almost impossible, brings serious harm to the Church.

The polarization of the present moment strikes at the very heart of the Church as a communion. It has an enormous, deleterious effect on the relationships among members of a local church, the relationships among local churches, and between them and the universal Church. We cannot afford to allow the vitality of the Church to be further sapped, nor can we stand idly by when the extremes—on both the right and the left—try to set partisan parameters, or lay down unreasonable conditions, for future discussion.

BUILDING UNITY AMID DIVERSITY

What are we to do in order to move beyond the present impasse and help build ecclesial unity amid the diversity of our particular churches? I do not presume to have a complete answer to this problem, and neither does Ms. Steinfels. But some brief reflections might help us. They are basically the same suggestions I made in Los Angeles during the Holy Father's visit in 1987.

First, there has to be in the whole body of the Church a much greater trust in the promise of the risen Christ to be present with his Church and in the living action of the Holy Spirit. We are part of a mystery, a unique convergence of the divine and human. For this reason, we cannot rely only on secular models—although we can surely learn from them.

Second, we must be able to speak with one another in complete candor, without fear. This applies to our exchanges with the Holy See as well as among ourselves as bishops and priests, and with our people. Even if our exchange is characterized by some as confrontational, we must remain calm and not become the captives of those who would use us to accomplish their own ends.

Third, we must break down the barriers of hostility and mutual distrust in order to restore a sense of civility and Christian charity in our discourse so that we can, once again, sit down to dialogue with one another, with mutual respect, trust, and concern for the common good.

Fourth, in such a mutual exchange—conducted with objectivity, honesty, and openness—we can discern what will truly enhance the Church's unity and what will weaken or destroy it. Sometimes the outcome of our endeavors will not be immediately evident, but this in itself should not deter us because we must allow for growth and development in certain areas of the Church's life and ministry.

Fifth, we must affirm and continue to grow in our appreciation of the conciliar vision of collegiality as both a *principle* and a *style of leadership*

in the Church. Here in the United States our national episcopal conference has been a visible expression of that collegiality. It has served to enhance the pastoral role of each bishop precisely because it provides a
framework and a forum for us to share ideas, to teach and elucidate
sound Catholic doctrine, set pastoral directions and develop policy positions on contemporary social issues. I believe that we are learning how to
balance this dimension of collegiality with the collegiality of the bishops
of the universal Church, in union with the Roman Pontiff as head of the
episcopal college.

Finally, I pray that each of us will cultivate loyalty to the Church. I am
not suggesting that we embrace a kind of mindless ideology or, worse, a
stultifying romanticism about the Church. No, I'm thinking of something
quite different. By loyalty I mean a thoughtful, persevering, costly attachment to the Church, an attachment which is also critical, creative,
and—above all—loving, that is, forgiving. As St. Paul reminded the Corinthians, we are nothing if we have not love.

* * *

I personally know the difficulties of Church renewal and reform. Like
you, I face them every day. What I want you to know, above all, is that I
am not discouraged by the slow process of change and occasional setbacks—and neither should you! Rather, I am full of hope.

I close with the words of Pope John XXIII as he convoked the Second
Vatican Council. He said:

> Distrustful souls see only darkness burdening the face of the earth. We,
> instead, like to reaffirm all our confidence in our Savior, who has not left
> the world which he redeemed. Indeed, we make our own the recom-
> mendation of Jesus that one should know how to distinguish the "signs of
> the times," and we seem to see, in the midst of so much darkness, a few
> indications which argue well for the fate of the Church and of humanity.

Evangelization

Address

"A Day in His Name"

The Chicago Catholic Evangelization Program

St. Viator High School, Chicago, Illinois

— *October 16, 1982* ————————————————

I have always been fascinated by an incident which Luke describes in the ninth chapter of his gospel. "One day," Luke tells us, "while Jesus was praying in seclusion and his disciples were with him, he put the question to them, 'Who do the crowds say that I am?' 'John the Baptizer,' they replied, 'and some say Elijah, while others claim that one of the prophets of old has returned from the dead.' 'But you—who do you say that I am?' he asked them. Peter said in reply, 'The Messiah of God'" (Luke 9:18-20).

On another occasion, when some of the Lord's followers began to walk away because they found it difficult to accept his teaching, Jesus turned to Peter and said: "'Do you want to leave me too?' Simon Peter answered him, 'Lord, to whom shall we go? You have the words of eternal life. We have come to believe; we are convinced that you are God's holy one'" (John 5:67-69).

Peter, then, was a believer. It is true that once, because of a fear that stemmed from human weakness, he denied he knew the Lord. But he immediately repented. After the ascension, as we know from the Acts of the Apostles, he fearlessly proclaimed the gospel and ultimately gave his life for his beloved Jesus.

Today, my brothers and sisters, I come to you as a believer. Like Peter, in your presence and with your encouragement and affirmation, I profess my faith in Jesus and his Lordship over us. I believe in him and I love him with all my mind and heart and soul. So much do I love Jesus that I find it difficult both to express adequately and to contain my feelings about him.

427

And yet, I experience a profound sense of inadequacy when I compare his love with mine which is so conditioned by my own weakness and failures.

I know that you also believe in the Lord and love him. Your presence today testifies to that. And so, together, we celebrate our common faith in Jesus and we do so within the context of our Catholic tradition which means so much to us, and to which we are deeply committed. To him be honor and glory forever!

I was anxious to join you today so that, together with you, I could recommit myself to our most important task as Christians. It is not enough that we believe in the Lord personally. We must also proclaim Jesus and his gospel to others so that the whole world will come to know him and accept him as Savior. This is the work of evangelization, which always aims at conversion, and it is the first and most important work of the Church.

There are many reasons why this is so. Perhaps the most significant is that we live in a world dominated by secular and material values. Many people no longer perceive their lives as having a dimension of transcendence. As a result, more and more people have shown signs of apathy and indifference, alienation and hostility—even to the point of no longer practicing their religion and falling away altogether from the faith.

At the same time, many others—even though they go to church less often and sometimes challenge religious authority—retain a religious orientation. Surveys show that they yearn for a closer relationship with God and that they pray frequently.

Fortunately, there are also many people who are truly committed to the Lord. They are totally dedicated, very much involved in the life of the Church and they give a marvelous witness to God's love and mercy in their daily lives. These good people, who often go unnoticed, are more aware than ever of the need to make the Lord known to those who have turned away from him and those who are searching for him; to show in a concrete and credible way that the Christian faith is as relevant as it ever was; that, without faith in the Lord, even the greatest of human accomplishments will have little lasting value.

Committed Christians have come to the realization that, in the face of this great need for evangelization, they cannot simply sit back and do nothing. While the grace of faith and conversion surely comes from God, we are the human instruments he uses to draw people closer to himself.

The great need, then, is to evangelize. It is not really a new need because it has existed since the Lord first called us to believe in him and accept him. However, as I have already indicated, it has a special urgency today. Fortunately, the Church has addressed it.

In 1974, the Synod of Bishops met in Rome to discuss humanity's spiritual needs, the need of a renewal of evangelization in the Catholic Church, and some of the roadblocks that increasing secularization creates for the evangelizing Church. The next year the late Pope Paul VI continued this emphasis on evangelization, calling the Church to see in evangelization its central mission and ministry as we prepare for the third millennium of Christianity. His apostolic letter *Evangelii nuntiandi* has given a new impetus and direction to our evangelizing efforts. In this document, the Holy Father described evangelization in a beautiful and all-embracing way. Evangelization, he said, is introducing or reintroducing people to the Lord Jesus. It is proclaiming his Good News which gives us a radically new and uplifting vision of life. It is pointing out, as Jesus himself did, the reality of the kingdom of God—and all that he meant by that rich term. It is helping with and facilitating the conversion process of turning away from what is self-serving, trivial or evil and instead turning to the Lord, the Good News, and the kingdom.

Through the power of the Holy Spirit, the Good News of Jesus is proclaimed and lived, transforming individuals as well as communities and their structures, liberating them from sin and all that oppresses. This communication of the gospel—by witness of life, by the ministry of word and sacrament, and by service for justice and peace—initiates or deepens commitment to Jesus and active membership in the community of believers.

Evangelization in this sense is surely directed to the unchurched, of whom there are over seventy million in our country. But it also addresses those who may have had some religious affiliation at one time but no longer work at it. Even though such persons may still have faith and may retain nominal affiliation with the Church, functionally they are similar to the unchurched. Finally, evangelization is also directed to us who are active, committed Church members; to you and to me! Some years ago, I startled some of the bishops when—in my last address as president of the Episcopal Conference—I challenged them to be evangelized themselves. The reason we all need evangelization is simple: no matter how committed we may be, there is always room for growth. Conversion to the Lord is a lifelong process which is never really completed. Both the Hebrew and Christian Scriptures make it abundantly clear that life is like a pilgrimage, a journey, which constantly brings us closer to the Lord. In this world the journey is never completed. There is never a time when we can say that we have no further need of growth, that we are totally without personal sin and imperfection, that our spiritual potential has been realized to the fullest.

Fortunately, evangelization is a concept and a reality whose time has come. Because of the impetus given by the 1974 synod and Pope Paul's apostolic letter on evangelization the following year, a high priority has been given to evangelization; everyone wants to "do" it. That is why here in Chicago, happily, we established a special office for evangelization in 1980.

In light of the description I have given, however, I hasten to point out that evangelization is basically a work of the Spirit active within God's people, and not primarily a technique or a specific program. It is true that frequently we use various techniques or programs to proclaim the Good News and we do so with some success. For example, we use radio and television to put the message across; we organize parish visitation programs for the same purpose, etc. But in the final analysis, the most powerful witness to God's love are the lives of those in whom the love of God is evident and whose love for one another is equally evident. This is why the greatest need at this time, for each of us as individuals and for all of us as a community of faith, is to live out our faith in our daily lives. To put it another way, our lives must be so gospel-oriented that people will be convinced that we are believers—even without our saying so.

Books of the New Testament like the Acts of the Apostles and the epistles tell us a great deal about the early Christians, those who lived at a time when personal witnesses to Jesus and his ministry were still alive. The most evident phenomenon is the radical change that took place in their lives after they converted to the Lord and were baptized. And more than what they said, it was that change—in the way they lived, the way they incarnated in their day-to-day lives the teaching of Jesus—that impressed their neighbors. "See how those Christians love one another." This became the distinctive mark of the early faith community. This is what caused others to sit up and take notice and ultimately join the community themselves.

Evangelization, then, is not an office, or a program, or a technique. It is a way of life. It is a matter of waking up, stirring up, challenging. To evangelize is to be in a constant state of spiritual growth and renewal. This has many implications for our parishes and our ministry in its many forms. It means proclaiming the gospel and ministering in such a way that we help people take the radical stands of the kingdom which stand in stark contrast to the cultural values of our time. It means transforming the parishes so that they become true communities of faith, communities alive with the Spirit, communities that truly understand the demands of discipleship, communities that are not turned in on themselves but have adopted the cosmic vision of crucified and risen Christ. It means that business can no longer go on as usual but must be refashioned so that the riches of the gospel can been seen and appreciated.

Before concluding, I would like to address one particular dimension of evangelization which needs to be kept in correct perspective. I refer to the area of social justice. Sometimes the impression is given that evangelization and the promotion of justice are, at best, minimally related and, at worst, almost hostile to each other. Nothing could be further from the truth.

The Second Vatican Council said that Christians should "contribute to a just appreciation of the dignity of the human person, the promotion of the blessings of peace, the application of gospel principles to social life, and the advancement of the arts and sciences in a Christian spirit. Christians should also work together in the use of every possible means to relieve the afflictions of our times, such as famine and natural disasters, illiteracy and poverty, lack of housing, and the unequal distribution of wealth" (Decree on Ecumenism, no. 12).

Seven years later, the bishops at the 1971 synod said that the promotion of social justice appeared to them to be a constitutive dimension of the Church's mission. Quite simply, this means that work on behalf of justice is so much a part of the Church's mission that the one may not be separated from the other if we are to be faithful to the Church's mission. In 1979 Pope John Paul II, in his talk to the bishops of Latin America meeting in Puebla, Mexico, elaborated on this idea. Some of the early secular commentators mistakenly gave the impression that the Holy Father had backed away from the Church's commitment to social justice. Pursuing this mistaken analysis and taking statements out of context, certain people in our country began saying, with obvious satisfaction, that the Pope had said the Church should return to its business of "saving souls," that the pulpit is no place for anything that might be considered social or "political" in nature.

I am afraid that these people do not know what the Holy Father said or that they have grossly misunderstood his message. Listen to the actual words of Pope John Paul to the bishops in Puebla: "If the Church makes herself present in the defense of or in the advancement of man, she does so in line with her mission, which although it is religious and not social or political, cannot fail to consider man in the entirety of his being. The Lord outlines in the parable of the Good Samaritan the model of attention to all human needs, and he said that in the final analysis he will identify himself with the disinherited—the sick, the imprisoned, the hungry, the lonely—who have been given a helping hand."

Then, alluding to the statement of the bishops at the 1971 synod, the Holy Father went on to point out that there is an essential link between evangelization and the work of justice—a work for which the Church "does not need to have recourse to ideological systems in order to love, defend and collaborate in the liberation of man."

The Holy Father, in effect, made it very clear that the Church must defend the dignity of the human person; it must use its influence to protect the rights of the poor and the oppressed. In doing so, however, the Church must not become identified with any political system or any ideology, especially any ideology—like Marxism—which has a perverted vision of man and his destiny. Rather, the Church must remain independent; it must have at all times the freedom to evaluate and to criticize the philosophy, the decisions and the programs of any secular authority or society. Moreover, the Church's method of overcoming error is not through violence, but through persuasion. The Church's way is the way of the gospel which is the way of truth. As Jesus told us: "If you live according to my teaching, you are truly my disciples; then you will know the truth, and the truth will set you free" (John 8:30). This effectively depoliticizes the Church, without at all removing it from the world of sociopolitical concerns.

Perhaps one of the greatest contributions which you, as lay people, can make to the work of evangelization is to convince people that there is a connection between what Jesus said and what is happening in the real world. But if those of you who represent the business and industrial world say it, perhaps it will make an impression. One of the greatest needs today is to convince people that there is a moral dimension to so many of the issues we face in our contemporary society. It may well be that, even in the light of the Church's moral teaching, there may be more than one morally acceptable solution. Still, the point is that there is a moral dimension to most problems, and the Church has not only a right but an obligation to make its voice heard.

My dear brothers and sisters in the Lord! How happy I am to be with you this afternoon. I appreciate very much this opportunity to share with you some personal reflections on how, together, we should go about the task of proclaiming Jesus and his Good News to the community in which we live.

I am very convinced that this is a privileged moment for all of us. The extraordinarily warm welcome I have received since coming to Chicago is a sign of a deep spiritual hunger which is present in Chicagoland. While there is perhaps a personal dimension to it all, in the final analysis people are not so much interested in me as in him whom I represent. They are searching for meaning in their lives; they are looking for spiritual strength and stability. They are looking for the Transcendent; they are looking for God.

In his day, Jesus asked the people: "Who do the crowds say that I am?" He asks that same question of the people of our day. It is our task to help them see the Lord with eyes of faith so that, like Peter, they will recognize Jesus and say, "You are the Messiah of God."

May our personal interests, no matter how legitimate they may be, never become obstacles to our witness to the Lord Jesus. May what we do, be done "in his name." May we always reflect his goodness, his love and mercy, his understanding and compassion, his healing power. Only then will people come to know who Jesus really is. Only then will they experience conversion. Only then will they reach out to him so that he can embrace them and shower upon them his love.

"Evangelization:
Integrating Focus of All Ministry"

Catholic Evangelization Association

Chicago, Illinois

——*June 12, 1983* ———————————————————————————

Perhaps you occasionally read the Peanuts comic strip. In one a couple of months ago, Charlie Brown and his sister Sally were having a conversation. Sally reported that she had just converted to her own religion the boy who sat behind her at school. "I would have made a good evangelist," she said with pride. "How did you convince him?" Charlie asked. "I hit him with my lunch box," said Sally. (Sounds more like Lucy!)

Evangelization: what has been happening to that word in the years since Pope Paul VI's *Evangelii nuntiandi?* For many, it is a buzzword that describes anything from a parish's social affairs to its outreach to the unchurched. For some, it remains a somewhat disturbing or frightening word, one that does not belong to Catholics. So often, evangelization seems to have the connotation of hitting people over the head, or asking them questions, in a coercive way, about the quality of their spiritual lives. For others, it has become a kind of automatic, mechanistic way of achieving a "born again" experience. Such approaches to evangelization leave a bad taste in our mouths. We know life's ambiguities and the mysterious nature of things. We know how faith often involves risk, surrender, trust in the face of that ambiguity and mystery. Evangelization efforts that smack of superficiality, coercion, easy answers or cheap grace—that is, evangelizing that is not rooted in the human experience and does not

433

try, through faith, to make sense out of daily living—will ultimately turn people off to the whole notion of evangelization.

"Evangelization" must not become just another term in our ministerial jargon, one whose meaning is diffuse. Neither can it be, in the Catholic perspective, a ministerial strategy that plays on people's vulnerabilities, offering them a world of easy answers, a world of black and white, one that is mystery-free. And it certainly is not a continuation of the evangelization of Jesus if it reinforces some of the values present in our culture. By that I mean ministry or evangelizing styles that allow godless people to pursue godless ways, all the while feeling religious about it.

WHAT IS EVANGELIZATION?

So as not to spend all my time explaining what evangelization is *not*, allow me to make a few positive statements about what I believe it to be. In the Scriptures, Jesus never evangelized through coercion. Rather, he did it by *invitation*. Jesus evangelized by inviting people to embrace several realities—all of which are connected and interrelated.

1. First, Jesus invited people to the kingdom of God. This is the essence of his evangelization. What did he mean by this term, the kingdom of God, which he uses so often in the Scriptures—sometimes referring also to the reign of God? The kingdom or reign that Jesus preached was at once a new *vision* of life and a *task* or responsibility for his followers to achieve. The kingdom was and is a *vision* or a *dream*, a reality yet to be fully realized. Jesus knew that the human heart hungers and thirsts for something beyond itself. He also knew the human tendency to try to satisfy our growling spirits with illusions, with what I would call spiritual junk food. In inviting people to the kingdom, Jesus was revealing the reality—and the only one—that satisfies the heart's deepest hunger and thirst, namely, *the presence and love of God in our lives*. The evangelizing of Jesus offered people a new foundation for their lives, a new filter through which life can be experienced. So Jesus' encouragement and invitation to the kingdom is a beckoning: (1) to build our lives on God's love; (2) to live in a spirit of trust and surrender; (3) to believe in the paschal nature of daily living; (4) to hope in his promise of eternal life; (5) to relate to each other as brothers and sisters who have a common Father; (6) to redeem society and culture. The kingdom is both a new consciousness and a task, a quest.

2. Second, Jesus invited people to *conversion*. Conversion is the rite of passage into the kingdom. Conversion now, as then, is a turning, a turning *from* something *to* something else. Generally, conversion is a turning from sin to grace. To use our previous terminology, conversion is a turning from illusions about life to the kingdom, that is, the truth about life. As we try

to continue the conversion ministry of Jesus, his evangelizing, we need to be more and more attuned to the thresholds for conversion in people's lives.

The life cycle itself is a threshold for conversion. As we grow older, the life questions we thought we had already answered satisfactorily present themselves to us again. "Who am I? What is life about? Why do people suffer? What will become of me after death?" These are the conversion questions, asked ever more deeply as we advance in years. As Christian ministers, we must invite people to a deeper identification with Jesus and the kingdom as they wrestle with life.

Like Jesus, we need also to be present to people in the difficult moments of life, that is, when life surprises them, especially with hurts and disappointments. In these moments, people tend to ask the same question as Job, "Why?" While we do not have clearcut answers to this question, we do have a loving God, an abiding presence, a promise of resurrection, a hope that we can use to nurture them.

Sometimes people simply awaken to their deep spiritual searching; they suddenly become aware that they are seeking something beyond themselves. Such a time is a third kind of threshold for conversion. The psychotherapist Alfred Adler used to speak of the phenomenon of "catching one's self." It is only when we "catch ourselves," or see ourselves as we are—as compared with what or who we could be—that we feel the impulse to change, to turn from where we are to something else.

Evangelization is an invitation to conversion. Like Jesus, we must be sensitive to the thresholds or opportunities in people's lives when the potential for conversion is most alive.

3. Third, the evangelizing of Jesus was also an invitation to discipleship. In a recent book, *A Church to Believe In*, Father Avery Dulles encouraged us to begin seeing the Church in the way Pope John Paul II saw it in his encyclical *Redemptor hominis*. In that letter, the Holy Father referred to the Church as a community of disciples. When Jesus evangelized, he invited people to develop a consciousness of the kingdom which calls us to a totally new vision and way of life. The process of growing in this new consciousness is discipleship.

The Scriptures tell us a great deal about disciples. Disciples are on a journey, the journey of life. On that journey they are following the teacher, the rabbi, Jesus. Most important in the discipling process is the personal relationship they have with the Master. As that relationship grows, *they* grow, however imperfectly, in appreciation of his vision, his values. Finally, this new vision or consciousness is shared with others. Conversion and discipleship flow into ministry. What is received as gift is given as gift. Christian discipleship is the experience of a transforming relationship with Jesus the Master. Evangelization is an invitation to that relationship.

Let me summarize. Evangelization is always an invitation—to the kingdom, to conversion, to discipleship. Jesus evangelized through word and deed. At times, his very presence evangelized. When Jesus evangelized, he offered people *meaning* for their lives. As he offered meaning to people, he joined words of meaning to gestures of healing. For so many people today, the most effective evangelizing can be done through ministries of caring, healing, and helping. Evangelization is not just a piece of the Church's educational ministries. It is surely that, but it is more, much more. It is the integrating force and thrust of all the Church's ministries. The Church exists to teach the Lord's *meaning* and extend his *healing*.

EVANGELIZATION IN CULTURAL AND ECCLESIAL CONTEXTS

One of the dangers in talking about evangelization and conversion in this way is the tendency to think in overly narrow categories, or to focus too much on personal salvation. In the Catholic tradition evangelization is also an invitation to become part of that community of believers we call the Church. There can be no closet Christians. Our call to conversion is to become part of a redeemed people. In the body of Christ, believers become agents of conversion for one another. We become sacraments of God's presence for one another. The kingdom happens for us in relationship, dialogically. We are a converting Church, and the Church (whether the parish or some other ecclesial body) is the organism that nurtures the ongoing conversion of its members.

Along the same relational line, evangelization must involve a confrontation with the values of the culture around us. In *Evangelii nuntiandi*, Pope Paul VI spoke of evangelization as the transformation of culture. The loudest and most effective evangelizing force in our midst today is the media. Movies, television, and radio speak to our people's hungers and thirsts, our collective search for meaning, but the gospel they preach does not touch the mind and heart; their gospel is about things. There are things outside of you; only if you achieve them, they say, will you be happy. *Things* are offered as satisfaction for our need for love, belonging, and meaning. In its proclamation of truth and meaning, evangelization must address this *consumer culture*, in which human beings and human nature are treated as commodities.

Paul VI also stated in *Evangelii nuntiandi* that authentic evangelization leads to the development of people. Our evangelization, in other words, must lead us toward justice and peace. While the bishops' pastoral letter on nuclear arms addressed one demonic force in our day—the threat of a nuclear holocaust—there are many more that cry out for attention and evangelizing. Poverty, racism, sexism—indeed all the paralyzing "isms" of institutionalized living—are in need of the Good News. Our evangelizing efforts will not be authentic if they do not create a greater awareness of and a more intense determination to promote justice and peace in every sphere of life.

*E*VANGELII NUNTIANDI:
A BLUEPRINT FOR THE EVANGELIZING CHURCH

In *Evangelii nuntiandi* Pope Paul VI weaves a beautiful description of evangelization. He also issues a challenge: that evangelization indeed be seen as the central mission of the Church in the third millennium of Christianity. He attaches to that challenge a hint about the future of ministry in the Church. He speaks of the beneficiaries or the target groups for our evangelizing.

1. First, we need to concern ourselves with the evangelization or re-evangelization of so-called active Catholics. Realizing that so many active Catholics are actually quite uninvolved, we must make this one of our chief evangelizing concerns. While programs for parochial self-evangelization abound, the answer is ultimately not in programs, but rather in priorities. Parish staffs and leaders must make evangelization, conversion, and the needs of the people in the parish their filters for ministering. This is what parish renewal is all about.

2. Second, we need to engage in ministries of reconciliation for alienated or inactive Catholics. The alienated are in need of evangelists to invite them home, to listen to them, to allow them to ventilate, to help them reflect on the meaning of faith for their lives now, and to reintegrate them into the mainstream of parish life. We need to sensitize ourselves to their thresholds for conversion: their children's sacramental plateaus, their interaction with active Catholics and their own inner search.

3. Third, I feel we have yet to tap the full richness and power of the Rite of Christian Initiation of Adults in our outreach to the unchurched. The fact is that the RCIA is a paradigm for the formation of the entire parish, whether this is done through sacramental or other programs. Relative to the unchurched, the parish needs to be in a continual state of pre-catechumenate evangelization, or hospitality, welcoming those with no formal religious affiliation to the Catholic community. As ministers, we need a better feel for the dynamics of evangelization, catechesis, election, enlightenment, initiation, and mystagogia as the ministry and ritual that mark the conversion process of catechumens and the entire community of disciples.

4. The adolescent and young adult also cry out for evangelizing. Pope Paul VI gave them special mention in his encyclical. There are some

systemic difficulties in the way we do youth ministry. Some parishes are divorced from their young people when they leave the eighth grade, abandoning them in one of the most critical periods of life. Adolescence and young adulthood, searching times as they are, are opportune times to evangelize, to present the person and the value system of Jesus, to help the young sort out the many cultural realities and enticements they face in the light of the spirituality of the kingdom. Again, the RCIA rhythm and a reconsideration of the power of sacramental moments in adolescence and young adulthood could greatly facilitate our efforts.

5. Finally, Pope Paul VI reminded us that true evangelization is *ecumenical* in spirit. Much can be done in the cause of Christian unity by fellow believers of different denominations cooperating in evangelistic ministry that tends to heal the wounds and address the needs of their communities.

In sum, Pope Paul VI's blueprint for an evangelizing Church calls us to evangelize the churched, the unchurched, the alienated, the young, and to join hands with our Protestant brothers and sisters.

MINISTRY OF THE WORD OR ENERGIZING CENTER OF ALL MINISTRIES

As I conclude, I would like to emphasize again the point I have tried to make in this presentation. The popular understanding of evangelization as the primary step in the process of the ministry of the word, followed by catechesis and theology, is indeed a proper understanding of the term. But the term is broader than that. Evangelization is the meeting ground where the ministries of the word, worship, youth, pastoral care, and other areas of the Church's work all converge. The Church's central mission is to evangelize, that is, to invite everyone to the kingdom, to conversion, to discipleship. The Church's central mission is to evangelize, that is, to proclaim the Lord's meaning of life, offer and extend his healing, transform culture, promote justice and peace. The Church's central mission is to have an expansive notion of evangelizing, one that includes the many kinds of people hungering and thirsting for the kingdom. For such an expanded notion of evangelization, the Church needs a broad range of strategies and skills if it is to minister successfully in a culturally pluralistic society.

CONCLUSION

I would like to close by again encouraging us, as ministers, to open ourselves to the wisdom and richness of the Rite of Christian Initiation of Adults. In the third century, the golden age of the catechumenate, evan-

gelization always had two characteristics: (1) it was not so much program-
matic as it was relational; the Lord, his vision, and his kingdom lifestyle
were transmitted initially through primary relationships in which people
witnessed by word and deed to their newfound life; (2) it was not so
much cerebral as it was experiential; the kerygma became a life-changing
event. In other words, conversion was always involved. In the fourth and
fifth centuries, however, the relational, experiential tone of evangelization began to be minimized.

To be effective, Catholic evangelists need to recapture that earlier,
twofold approach. An ecclesial conversion needs to take place, wherein
Catholics sense the power and responsibility invested in them through the
sacraments of initiation. No longer can the cleric or the religious be looked
on as the ones entrusted with the mission to evangelize. All are called to
evangelize by who they are, what they say, how they live. All are called to give
witness to that transforming relationship present in their lives.

My fellow evangelists, to evangelize we need not hit anyone over the
head with anything. We need only to speak the Lord's word of meaning
and extend his healing touch. Then we will change lives and transform
hearts.

Keynote Address

"Lay Ministry and Evangelization: Sent to Be a Blessing and Blessing the Ones Sent"

Archdiocesan Conference on Religious Education

Los Angeles, California

—— *March 13, 1987* ——————————————————————

My sisters and brothers, the grace of our Lord Jesus Christ, the love of God the Father, and the communion of the Holy Spirit be with all of you!

Thank you very much for inviting me to participate in this locally based, but nationally significant, conference on religious education. It is a privilege and an honor to speak with you.

I am both delighted and challenged. I am also somewhat hesitant—if cardinals are permitted such emotions or, perhaps, more precisely, allowed to express them! I am not frightened by you, for I have been told that you are a "speaker-friendly" audience. No, I am awed by the staggering importance of the topic I am to address: lay ministry and evangelization.

The theme is quite simple and yet very profound: the People of God carrying the Good News into the world. In treating this topic, we begin to touch our deepest identity as a Church and as a believing people.

Pope Paul VI in his visionary apostolic exhortation *Evangelii nuntiandi* expressed it in this way:

> Evangelizing is in fact the grace and vocation proper to the Church, her deepest identity. She exists in order to evangelize, that is to say in order to preach and teach, to be the channel of the gift of grace, to reconcile sinners with God, and to perpetuate Christ's sacrifice in the Mass, which is the memorial of his death and glorious Resurrection (no. 14).

441

Yes, we are reflecting upon important matters. This evening, we will consider the true sense of *tradition*—handing on the faith. As religious educators, we may rightly say with Paul, "I hand on to you what I myself received." We are at that privileged and responsible point of intersection between the living past and the hope-filled future.

As a pastor, I face many issues and have many cares for the Church. Since you are a captive, collective shoulder on which I can lean for a moment, let me name a few: finances, buildings, personnel, relationships with other local churches and the universal Church, world peace, the economy, sexuality, the challenge of harmonizing diverse ethnic and racial groups, the relationship between men and women in society and in the Church. These are issues that are external to me personally. I also face my own spiritual journey. I must come to grips with my inner self, with my gifts and limitations, which become more evident as I grow older—at least, the limitations!

However, the invitation to speak to you on the topic of lay ministry and evangelization helped me shake off the hypnotic quality of all these other concerns. It prompted me to return to the heart of the Church's mission: the proclamation of Jesus Christ to the world.

I have many things to say and a limited time in which to say them. So, permit me to strike a deal with you, my "speaker-friendly" audience. Allow me simply to name some important dimensions of our topic. I will share with you five *realities*, five *hopes*, five *obstacles*, and five *suggestions* concerning lay ministry and evangelization. I invite you to think about them as we proceed through each series. You need not focus your attention on all twenty issues. But listen for the ones that particularly strike you. Fill them out from your own experience. Talk about them with others afterwards. You need not agree with me. But I ask you to consider these points, because, as a pastor and a fellow believer, I am convinced that they are very important.

FIVE REALITIES

The *first reality* is that we are recovering a sense of the common priesthood of the baptized and our shared responsibility for the proclamation of God's word. We have not yet arrived at a full understanding, but we are moving in that direction. That is why I say we "are recovering," not we "have recovered."

Some of the difficulty and slowness in making this recovery may be theological hesitation, but some of it may also be due to our social or cultural understandings. "Lay" or nonprofessional practitioners in our society are often substitutes for the real thing in many areas of life.

Paramedics, for example, substitute for physicians; paralegals for real attorneys. But we do not have "parapriests" in the Church, because all the baptized form a true priestly people who are called in a direct and responsible way to proclaim the word of God in the world. The difference between laity and clergy is not one of degree, as if lay people were a "watered-down" clergy. Rather, they are different in kind, although totally necessary and complementary to each other. The priestly vocation is to build up the Church, the lay vocation to consecrate the world. I will develop this at greater length later.

The *second reality* of our time is the critical need of the world for God's word. At the beginning of St. Paul's letter to the Romans, he explains how the world has fallen "under the wrath of God"—how, in other words, the world needs Jesus Christ. For us, the daily newspaper signals the need of the redeemer and his redemption. We find this need in the various stories of violence, war, hunger, disease, family disintegration, child and spouse abuse, abortion, materialistic extravagance, drugs, and death.

Because the world desperately needs God's word, evangelization is of critical importance—indeed, a matter of life and death.

A *third reality* today involves competition within the Church's ministry. Although we are not proud of this, its presence in the Church's life, nonetheless, is quite understandable. For many years, ministry was narrowly conceived and lived as *ordained* ministry. In most people's understanding, ordained priests alone ministered, and only they *could* minister.

A great blessing in the contemporary Church is the recovery of a sense of the apostolate of all the baptized and the call of many to ministry, whether they are ordained or not. But such recoveries are not made easily. History is at times a great burden. We are a limited and sinful people, subject to insecurity when confronted with rapid change, impatience when numbed by slow transformation, and pride when faced with the possibility of someone else "doing the job better" than ourselves.

So, there are, quite honestly, some tensions in ministry as it has come to be shared. They will not disappear quickly. We do, however, have to be committed to transforming competition, which sometimes has negative connotations, into collaboration. The stakes are high. We simply cannot afford to trip over each other as we seek to serve what seems to be, at times, a world on the verge of collapse.

A *fourth reality* is really a deeper insight into the power of God's word proclaimed in the world: the word of God is linked to the whole of life. It has implications for all the dimensions of human endeavor, including, for example, our economy, the provision of health services, the manufacture of goods, the delivery of various human services. As the 1971 World Synod of Bishops pointed out, working for justice is a constitutive element of proclaiming the gospel.

We have become more sharply attuned to our belief that the incarnation means that the Eternal Word assumed, in an integral way, the whole of human existence, in all its dimensions. This insight in faith, of course, has numerous implications for lay ministry and evangelization, for the precise task of the laity is the *consecratio mundi*, the consecration of the world.

The *fifth reality* needs honest expression: we all fear the future—at least, to a degree. In the past, people may have been afraid, but they were perhaps more excited about, than fearful of, the future. Today, with good reason, we readily encounter or easily develop a catastrophic mentality. We live in fear of global nuclear war, worldwide economic disaster, widespread incurable disease.

Lay ministry and evangelization in this world beset by fear of the future must be especially attuned to the "great hope to which we are called." The twin foundations of evangelization in such a situation are a *sober realism* rooted in an honest knowledge of the world and a *hope anchored* in a faith made firm by God's promises.

FIVE HOPES

Let me now shift to a second series, the hopes related to lay ministry and evangelization. The premise of these hopes is that dimensions sometimes thought of as separate will be seen as complementary and necessary ingredients for evangelization.

My *first hope* is that ordained priests and those who share in the priesthood of all the baptized will come to recognize with great clarity their reciprocal and mutual interdependence. Earlier, I spoke of competitiveness. Now, I want to share my vision, my hope, of how people might work together more effectively.

Ordained priests serve God's priestly people who carry on a mission of proclamation and consecration in the world. This is certainly not a new thesis, yet its full implications are still to be unfolded. The functions of ordained priests in this framework need to be refocused as formation, encouragement, and support for those who exercise their ministry in the world. It makes a difference whether a priest preaches to his people for their own information and edification, or whether he proclaims the word in such a way that they can carry it into a larger context—namely, the world.

My *second hope* is that lay evangelization in the world will be rooted in prayer. In effect, my hope is for contemplatively based efforts of evangelization. St. Thomas Aquinas's understanding of preaching, adopted as the motto of the Order of Preachers, is also an appropriate standard for lay efforts of evangelization: *contemplata aliis tradere*, to hand on to others what we ourselves have contemplated.

There is an inextricable link between prayer and proclamation. If the link is broken, we are at best clever salespersons without heart, without the word being rooted deep within us. My hope is that the link will be forged and held tightly.

My *third hope* is that fidelity and creativity will be seen, not as competing, but as complementary values. We are called to be *faithful* to the traditions of our Church, its doctrines, its discipline. We are a Catholic Church which, by God's grace, links its faith to its foundations with the apostles and which, also by God's grace, unites its faith in a worldwide communion. To proclaim the word, to bear the Good News, we must be faithful to what has been given to us.

At the same time, we are called to *creativity*. God's word needs to be proclaimed afresh to varied groups of people, in different circumstances. The inspired authors of the New Testament give witness to ways in which the perennial truth of Jesus Christ can be embodied in creative ways and adapted for diverse communities. The double imperative of fidelity and creativity provides balance and enthusiasm for our efforts to proclaim the word.

A *fourth hope* for the future of lay ministry and evangelization is that our vision will be both expansive and focused. If we take seriously the task of evangelization, proclamation to the whole world, then our vision must be continuously *expansive*. We need to include ever wider ranges of human life in our circle of concern. Our problem is a tendency to be consumed with our own in-house concerns, forgetting that the Church is for the world and not for itself.

At the same time, we need to maintain a clear *focus* on our message, the proclamation of Jesus Christ and his saving mysteries. We need to keep returning to the center, re-anchoring ourselves in the heart of the matter. We tend to allow ourselves to be pulled away, off center, by countless forces at work in our lives. This reflects the centrifugal side of being human. We need centering, focus.

Taken together as complementary visions, expanding and focusing provide us with both a horizon and a channel for efforts at evangelization.

A *fifth hope* is that we will combine bold critique of our world with great compassion. A vision of life that is filled with faith and rooted in hope can offer an honest *critique* of a world burdened and clouded with many assumptions about human relationships, the use of material things, the fate of our planet. Lay evangelization of the world needs to direct the light of faith into the shadows of life. This can and ought to be done without apology—boldly, honestly, directly.

At the same time, the world sorely needs a *compassionate* presence. It needs human and tender voices that acknowledge sin but offer a possibility of forgiveness, that recognize woundedness but indicate ways of healing, that honestly note human divisions but invite people together.

My hope is that we will develop a style and content which combines bold critique and great compassion. I cannot imagine anything more powerful or more gentle, for this combination mirrors in an unequivocal way the biblical patterns of the ways God deals with us.

FIVE OBSTACLES

So far, I have offered five realities and five hopes. Now I wish to offer you a list of five obstacles that hinder effective lay ministry and evangelization.

Let me state the *first obstacle* quite frankly. We have squabbles within the Church, and these internal divisions hurt our efforts to proclaim the Good News to the world. For, our proclamation is to be not merely a matter of words, but a witness of life. If the unity we proclaim is not a living reality, the credibility of our message is severely undercut.

Somehow, without glossing over very real difficulties, we need to return anew to the enduring gospel that brings us together in the first place and sheds light on our relatively short-lived problems with each other. Furthermore, we need to establish some pattern of civil, courteous, and—yes, even—charitable dialogue which will keep the conversation going even if not every bit and piece of disagreement finds resolution. Our squabbles within the Church are a major obstacle to proclamation of the Good News.

A *second obstacle* is a bit more complex, because it involves a mix of perception and reality. In the minds of many, what matters most are moral restrictions about such issues as abortion, sexuality, and divorce. Then, in second place, and only perhaps, comes the proclamation of Jesus Christ and his saving mysteries. The perception is first the moral demands, then maybe the Good News. The perception may be partially rooted in older patterns of moral insistence that overshadowed the core of our faith.

In fact, what comes first is, of course, Jesus Christ and his saving mysteries. Moral demands make sense *in light of Jesus*, not the other way around. To the extent that this is truly an obstacle and a misunderstanding, we need to correct this.

It should be said of us, "Those people truly believe in Jesus Christ, and, because of their faith, they live differently."

A *third obstacle* is the paralyzing and immobilizing complexity of our lives and world. Earlier, I spoke of a catastrophic mentality formed, in part, by the many tragic stories we encounter daily and, in part, by the wide range of issues we face both inside and outside the Church. All this may lead us to wonder if we truly can change things or transform human life and the world. Might it not be better to pray and hope and let things evolve as they may? Moreover, all these issues and concerns sap our energy. Can we invest ourselves in everything that is transpiring in this messy world?

Paralysis, immobility, and their underlying foundation in discouragement are obviously not God's work. They are the fruits of darkness. God, through the incarnate Word made flesh with all its limitations, moves in limited and ultimately redeeming ways. Our own steps may be halting and limited, but they are nonetheless movement forward. In the face of discouragement, paralysis, and immobility, we need to reaffirm that God moves, and moves through us, in limited but effective ways.

A *fourth obstacle* to evangelization is an ignorance of history, especially Church history. We would have a clearer sense of the urgency, the possibilities, and the patience that is necessarily connected with efforts at evangelization in the world, if we had a sharper sense of the history of our tradition. How much we could learn from Francis of Assisi with his insistence on proclaiming the humanity of Christ, or from Vincent de Paul who combined preaching with practical charity, or Frances Xavier Cabrini who deciphered the special needs of immigrants and developed creative responses.

A sense of history would help and encourage us and also engender some new thinking about our evangelizing efforts.

A *fifth* and final *obstacle* is an ingrained attitude that must be changed: a "traditional" Catholic shyness about sharing the faith. The roots of this attitude lie in the past. Perhaps, in part, it derives from people who belonged to an immigrant Church, people who never quite felt like "insiders" in this country. Perhaps it is because faith and religion became very privatized in our tradition and in our pluralistic society. Whatever the causes, this shyness about speaking of the things of faith greatly hinders our efforts at evangelization.

This attitude stands in sharp contrast to Paul's understanding of his ministry of proclamation as marked by what he called *parrhesia*, bold and forthright speaking. We need to adopt Paul's attitude as our own.

Five suggestions

The final series is a set of five suggestions. I will mention them briefly, not because they are unimportant, but simply because they require much more development and expansion by others in the Church.

My *first suggestion* concerning lay ministry and evangelization is that we focus special efforts, energy, time, and money in proclaiming the Good News to the *poor*. This is at the heart of our tradition. It is also a sign of the coming of God's kingdom.

Who are the poor? The ones the world regards as worthless and hopeless. They might be young, rich, and beautiful—but also drug dependent. They are black, Hispanic, Native American, and Asian women who often bear the harsh burden of racial, cultural, and sexist prejudice as well as great material poverty. They are homosexual men and drug-users and children dying of AIDS. What all the poor share is a negative assessment by the larger society where they are written off and viewed as hopeless.

When we invest hope in those whom our society considers lost or in the people it abandons, then we truly become light in the world. The critical test of evangelization is not simply unlocking the human potential of the upwardly mobile or the well established. It is nothing less than offering God's immeasurable and unaccountable love in places that seem frozen out by sin, hopelessness, and death.

When we evangelize the poor, we witness to the larger world the depth of our hope and the extent of God's grace.

A *second suggestion* is that we build into our current liturgical practices a sending forth for mission. If our liturgies, especially those that are carefully planned and beautifully executed, are celebrations that only turn us inward, we have failed.

Liturgy can and should be a comfort. In a world beset by many storms, it is to provide a consoling haven, a reassuring touch. Liturgy can and should be aesthetically pleasing. In its noble simplicity, a beautiful liturgy alerts us to the larger harmony of God's reconciling love. But beyond comfort and beauty lie challenge and empowerment.

The men and women who hear the word and share the bread of life, who allow the death and the resurrection of the Lord to wash over them, must leave not only comforted and pleased but also haunted by the deep urgency to share the saving mysteries of Christ. The liturgy is destined to lead us outward to the celebration of all that the baptized can and must do in the world. *Ite, missa est.* Go, the Mass is ended.

My suggestion to liturgists and liturgy planners is simple: let us creatively use the available options to shape the present liturgy in such a way that its *com-missioning* aspect is highlighted. This could have a great impact on fostering a greater and more urgent sense of lay evangelization.

A *third suggestion* is that we pay special attention to our Catholic identity. Of course, this means fidelity to our heritage and loyalty to the Holy Father and the bishops. It also implies an ongoing awareness that we belong to a worldwide communion of faith, hope, and love. We have not fully appreciated the implications for evangelization which are found in the powerful witness of such a world-embracing Church, a place that can be home to all God's children.

Our preaching, textbooks, prayer services, parish bulletins, and diocesan papers need to underscore the catholicity of our Church. When it becomes quite clear to us that the Church is a home for everyone—all colors, all cultures, all persuasions, all economic classes, all levels of education, all languages, all heights, all widths—then it will become very clear in our proclamation and appeal to everyone.

We need a heightened and deepened consciousness of our catholicity. This will fuel our efforts at evangelization, for we will be aware of the breadth of God's embrace. It will also make our efforts more effective, for we will be more transparent witnesses to God's universal invitation.

A *fourth suggestion* is that we need more research and publications about ministry of the word. There is a certain body of literature, some of it very erudite, concerning the ministry of the word and ordained priests. However, we seem to lack adequate reflections on the ministry of the word as exercised by all the priestly People of God.

This is the responsibility of theologians, religious educators, and pastors—people with the gift and training to reflect on our experience as believers. Their task will be to examine the lived experience of parents, workers, professional people, lay ministers, and others who exercise a ministry of the word. Writings that both underscore our experience and relate it to biblical patterns will inspire us to support and encourage efforts at lay ministry and evangelization.

A *final suggestion:* We need to find ways of acknowledging, celebrating, and supporting the efforts of lay ministry in evangelization. We need to develop appropriate rituals and symbols that celebrate and support lay ministry, because the Catholic tradition relies on rituals and symbols.

In various ways, bishops, priests, deacons, religious, and laity need to remember always and celebrate often the gift of lay ministry in evangelization. Symbols and rituals have been powerful ways of remembering key elements of our Catholic identity. The liturgy, for example, offers a wide range of supportive expressions. Perhaps there are other means which we also ought to explore. The point is simply this: it is not enough for us to gather and agree on the importance of lay ministry and evangelization. We need to keep this value alive before us well beyond this assembly. Again, it is a matter of creativity and imagination. We need to discover or design new ways of remembering these values.

* * *

I have offered you five realities, five hopes, five obstacles, and five suggestions. I hope the net effect has been stimulating, not overwhelming or boring!

Let me close with three pictures. The first is of a grandmother holding the tiny hands of her granddaughter and tracing the Sign of the Cross over her. The second is a teenage boy who, at considerable personal cost, visits patients in an AIDS hospice. The third is a husband, wife, and young child in Africa where they do medical-missionary work. I see, and I remember.

This is what we proclaim to you:

> what was from the beginning,
> what we have heard,
> what we have seen with our eyes,
> what we have looked upon
> and our hands have touched—
> we speak of the word of life.

1 John 1:1

Address

"Evangelizing the Active Catholic"

Pentecost 1987, A National Satellite Celebration of Catholic Evangelization

Washington, D.C.

——*June 6, 1987* ————————————————————————

Ours has been called the "Age of Anxiety." More than half of the visits to doctors' offices and emergency rooms are estimated to be stress-related. The most used legal drug in the United States is the tranquilizer Valium. Over forty million Americans suffer from hypertension. A growing body of research reports the alarming amount of anxiety and stress being experienced by children and adolescents.

Recently, David Elkind has highlighted a growing phenomenon: young people are losing the "markers" or "signposts" that would help them along the journey of life. Two of these important markers are the family and the Church.

There is clearly some truth to his analysis. One out of two marriages today ends in divorce. And many young people end their formal relationship with their parish after elementary school.

Moreover, each year over 250,000 young people attempt to take their own lives. A suicide note found in the pocket of a Houston youth contained this heart-rending message: "The only thing with roots around here is the tree that I'm hanging from."

Could it be that many of us in contemporary society have lost *our* markers or roots? Is this at least one of the causes of the "Age of Anxiety"?

Children and teens often reflect the values and expectations of the adult world. Many people in this country have either lost their markers and roots or are using illusory or false ones. This shouldn't surprise us because our contemporary, secular society often propagates false markers and roots. In many ways it does so in a louder voice than our Christian evangelizing.

What do I mean? I am referring to the prevailing voices of materialism and consumerism. With evangelical zeal, these forces exhort adults and young people to live their lives in pursuit of fantasies and possessions that are reputed to be able to satisfy the deepest longings of the human heart. This consumer "spirituality" advocates individualism, excessive competition, aggression, and success at any cost. While many people cannot afford the financial costs this implies, others flaunt conspicuous consumption.

What are the results? People are treated as though they were inanimate objects or exist merely for self-gratification. Human sexuality deteriorates from I-Thou relationships to I-It exploitation. Multiple contacts are emotionally safer than loving commitment to one person. Ethics—instead of being a consistent, integral system of morality and responsibility—is reduced to a smorgasbord of alternatives from which one can pick whatever is comfortable. On a global scale, resources that could be used for human liberation or development are channeled, instead, into the proliferation of weapons that make the world a more perilous place, not a safer one.

Is it any wonder that ours is the "Age of Anxiety"?

The brassy voice of consumerism threatens to drown out God's Word, incarnated in the person of Jesus, and in God's ongoing self-revelation made manifest in individual lives and the Church. Is it surprising that so many people are motivated by the "spirituality" of consumerism?

Unfortunately, too many Christians are "lukewarm." They allow the toxic vision that I just spoke of to shape them, their children, and their world. We are called, instead, to a holiness that is countercultural. The world cannot afford to have the body of Christ be in collusion with the idolatry, agnosticism, and atheism of the consumer vision.

Our parishes, united with the local and the universal Church, must become communities of *solidarity* and *resistance* to materialism and consumerism. We must resist the false wisdom of the age. We must stand in solidarity with one another and with Jesus. We must live in accordance with the values and lifestyle he has challenged us to practice.

Our parishes and other Church institutions need to move beyond merely reactive evangelizing. More than ever, we need a proactive proclamation of the gospel. This is not manipulative proselytizing. That approach, in fact, has led many people to a negative view of the word "evangelization." Rather, I am urging bishops, priests, deacons, religious, and lay people not to be satisfied with waiting for people to come to our programs, ministries, and services. We must also begin to take bold, creative steps to proclaim the Good News.

Jesus does not tell us to wait for people to come to us. He has given us the mission of making disciples of all nations. Perhaps we need to learn how to do this from our Evangelical brothers and sisters. They know that, often, the most important evangelizing is done in the marketplace and public forum, not in church buildings.

George Gallup recently referred to the Catholic Church as the "evangelical sleeping giant." He's right on target! We have all the right pieces—word, ritual, community, leadership, institutions of learning and care. But for too long we have been doing reactive evangelizing rather than boldly proclaiming the gospel. Too many of us are doing "maintenance work." Not enough are doing mission work.

The very word "evangelization" implies dynamism, movement, action. This may frighten the complacent. Nevertheless, more of us need to embrace the challenge of proactive evangelization.

In a recent interview, Martin Marty, the Lutheran theologian and Church historian, encouraged all mainline Churches to become more "inviting" in their attitudes and ministries. He predicted that those Churches which fail to become hospitable communities would run the risk of becoming dying, decaying Churches.

Many people today, realizing the emptiness of the consumerist vision, experience a deep hunger and thirst for Jesus, prayer, Scripture, and community. Evangelical churches are seeking to minister to these people—some of them unchurched, some of them alienated from their Church of origin, some of them crossing denominational lines to embrace the new meaning for life they have found in Jesus.

The challenge that faces all of us is this: let us create faith communities in the Catholic tradition where the active, the inactive, the unchurched, the young, the middle-aged, and the old will find life-transforming experiences of Jesus in prayer and the sacraments, in Scripture and community. We may well begin with the three generations of active Catholics in the Church.

The first group are older Catholics, perhaps like my mother or some of your parents and grandparents. Their faith is firm. They worship regularly, some of them daily. They support ecclesial efforts—whatever the circumstances. They will probably remain active in the Church as long as the breath of life is in them. They represent a solid foundation on which to build.

The second group, for the most part, is somewhat younger. Like many of us involved in this event, they have lived through and benefited from the Church renewal initiated by the Second Vatican Council. After they experienced and understood various aspects of this renewal, many of them welcomed these developments and are quite active in the Church.

Nevertheless, some of them have difficulty accepting some of the Church's teaching and, at times, experience a tension between that teaching and their own consciences, inclinations, or desires. Many are also looking for effective ways to satisfy the deepest hungers of their hearts.

The third group consists primarily, but not exclusively, of the youngest generation. Although they have been baptized, many of them have, at best, a tenuous relationship with the Church. They tend to be suspicious, and sometimes hostile, toward structures and institutions. They are and will be our greatest evangelical challenge. Like every other human being, they have a deep spiritual hunger, whether or not they identify it as such. I am convinced that Jesus-centered, Scripture-oriented, prayerful communities of warmth and intimacy will alone satisfy these young people. It is our task to awaken to their spiritual hunger and to offer them the kind of faith community which will appeal to them.

At the same time, in our evangelizing, it is necessary to avoid reductionism or operating out of impoverished, minimalist understandings of God's word. There is far more to evangelizing than maintaining Church structures or building up membership rolls. To evangelize is to invite people, through a variety of human experiences—some of them joyful, others painful—to discover Jesus as Lord. In this personal acceptance of Jesus as the foundation of their lives, they are led to experience a new reality which Jesus called the "kingdom of God."

To live in this kingdom is to see others, self, and the world with Jesus' eyes. To live in the kingdom is to live as Jesus did—in prayer, trust, compassion, love, forgiveness, justice, and peace—to live our lives centered on Abba, our Father.

The prerequisite for entering and remaining in the kingdom is conversion, a spiritual rebirth which leads to profound changes in the way we live. The Church, our parishes and institutions, all exist to build up the kingdom. And that implies, as Pope Paul VI once pointed out, that the kingdom is the transformation of our world from within. Three realities, then, keep our evangelization in proper balance and perspective: the Church, the kingdom, and the world.

What can we do to take bold initiatives in evangelizing? How can we move away from merely reactive proclamation of the word?

First, we might learn from the Church's experience in Central and South America and parts of Africa. There evangelical zeal and enthusiasm are an important part of "basic Christian communities." In the U.S., many of our parishes are quite large and, consequently, may exhibit anonymity more than community. In such settings, it is often difficult for effective evangelization to take place.

A possible solution is to restructure the parish as a community of communities. In such a vision and structure, Catholics gather in small groups determined by neighborhood, family, needs, interests, or a common ministry in order to pray, read Scripture, and share. Authentic community is vital to effective evangelization. It nurtures believers. If Catholics experience community on a smaller scale, they may form and experience more of a community when they gather for the parish Eucharist on the weekend.

Second, good Bible study in our parishes and institutions is an essential foundation for evangelization. Catholics need help in learning how to interpret Scripture. Without such aid, they may drift into fundamentalist Bible groups that often lack the proper background and tools for interpretation. There are already many fine programs available within the Catholic Church; such as, the Little Rock Scripture Study, Share the Word, the Word program, and Adult Biblical Interdependent Learning (or A.B.I.L.). They deserve support at all levels of the Church.

Third, we must renew the active members of our parishes through such means as parish retreats and missions, or programs like Christ Renews His Parish and RENEW. In our religious education, we have wonderful opportunities to teach children, teens, and adults different styles of prayer, meditation, and spiritual growth. We can also help them identify their gifts, which are the building blocks of community and the means by which we bring the presence of the risen Lord to the world.

It is important that all baptized Catholics become aware that they are called to be active participants—not mere observers—in the Church's mission. They are to use their gifts both in the Church and in the public arena.

In the cause of justice, our preaching and teaching seek to lead believers to a deeper awareness of the need for justice in our world so that we all may work for equality, justice, and peace.

All of this implies that we must evangelize active adult members. As I intimated earlier, children and teens will have faith to the extent that they belong to communities in which adult faith is strong. Going to church on Sunday will make more sense to young people to the extent that they experience the Church in their own family life.

We must also reach out to the sixteen million Catholics who no longer actively practice their faith—some because they have been hurt and are alienated from the Church, others for different reasons. As disciples of Christ, the Good Shepherd, we must search for ways to reconcile them.

We have the RCIA for the evangelization of the unchurched. Would it not be helpful to develop a similar process for returning Catholics? Can we not find a way to enable them to capture some of the mood of true reconciliation with the Church as they reenter the community of faith?

Perhaps it would be useful to retrieve the former ministry of "the fisher." This was part of the original Confraternity of Christian Doctrine developed by St. Charles Borromeo centuries ago in Italy and other parts of Europe. The "fisher" visited Catholics at home, inviting some, reconciling with others. This or a similar ministry would offer a remedy for those who feel that we neglect or abandon them.

* * *

The rabbis of old used to tell a wonderful story that goes like this.

Rabbi Joshua Ben Levi encountered the prophet Elijah one day and asked him when the Messiah would come. Elijah responded, "Go, ask the Messiah this question yourself." "But, where is he?" Ben Levi inquired. Elijah replied, "Sitting at the gates of the city."

"How shall I recognize him?" Ben Levi asked. "He is sitting among the poor," the prophet said, "himself covered with wounds. And he binds his wounds and all their wounds, one by one and all together, saying to himself, 'Perhaps I shall be needed, and if so, I must always be ready so as not to delay for a moment.'"

That captures Jesus' evangelizing style: his words were intimately joined with gestures of love and healing.

That is to be our style as well. The world is waiting—not for another program but—for us! As individuals and communities, we must not delay in binding up its wounds!

Address

"A Vision of Evangelization As We Approach a New Millennium"

Congress 1988—An Ecumenical Festival of Evangelism

Rosemont, Illinois

── *August 4, 1988* ──────────────────

My sisters and brothers in Jesus Christ, on behalf of the millions of Roman Catholics in this local church and throughout the United States, I bring you greetings and blessings. It is truly good for us to be here, sharing a common life in the Spirit and the firm conviction that "Jesus Christ is Lord!" We are his disciples, and it is through us that Jesus continues his mission to the world.

A TV COMMERCIAL

My work habits do not allow for much television viewing. But recently, I saw a striking commercial. What impressed me first was the starkness of the scene. A young man, in his mid-twenties, sat on a chair and stared into the camera.

He said simply: "I believe in fast cars." There was a cut-away to a sports car traveling at a fast speed. Then the young man said, "I believe in racquetball." The scene cut away to a hotly contested game of racquetball. He continued, "And I believe in my girlfriend." The next scene, of course, was an attractive young woman. What struck me the most was this: throughout all the scenes, the only emotion or feeling the young man showed was when he held up a can of beer! He looked at the can with the kind of wonder or awe that evokes images of Rudolf Otto's description of an encounter with the sacred. The young man then delivered the bottom line: "And I believe in Old Style." The scene faded to a script: "Old Style—a beer you can believe in."

My point in telling you about this TV commercial is simply this: it seems to me that its producers had an intuitive sense of what it means to evangelize. In thirty-five seconds or so, they offer some dominant images to the human imagination. In effect, the young man says, I *believe* in fast, expensive cars. I *believe* in the competitive nature of sports. I *believe* in an intimate relationship with my girlfriend. I *believe* in substances that alter consciousness and help relieve the anxiety, pressure, and stress of the age in which we live.

Notice the word which the advertisers use to present their dominant images: "I believe"—*credo*. As you undoubtedly know, before *credo* took on a predominantly intellectual or theological tone in the Church, it primarily meant, "I give my heart to [God] . . ." My friends, we are in serious trouble today if we have nothing more to give our hearts to than cars, sports, sex, and beer. But the world offers these as dominant images to animate and energize us.

THE WORLD IN WHICH WE LIVE

Consumerism, not the Bible, is the loudest voice in our society. The secular world preaches its own kind of gospel, suggesting to its hearers that "There is *something* that you do not yet have. Go for it! Then you'll be happy. It will bring you inner peace, great courage, sexual attractiveness, and satisfying intimacy."

What happens to people who believe this distorted message? They become increasingly frustrated because, the more possessions they acquire, the more their sense of meaning and purpose in life is diminished. They tend to shrink and wither as persons. Eventually, they feel devalued and discounted. They also seem to have less concern for those who have little or nothing. At the same time, the poor and the needy are led to believe, from the constant bombardment of advertising and the blatant example of others, that they, too, will find authentic salvation and liberation in acquiring more *things*.

Is it any wonder that anxiety, despair, drug dependency, alcohol abuse, and suicide abound in this country?

We are, indeed, living in a time of spiritual crisis, an era of increased individualism and narcissism. Witness, for example, the manifestation within the U.S. of a growing self-centeredness, a preoccupation with looking youthful and fit, and a fascination with casual sex. All of this is taking place in the context of the breakdown of family life and what some call "spiritual bleeding."

At the same time, many people in our society would readily wear the word "Christian" on their tee shirts. But what does this mean to them? To some, but surely not to all, it may imply regular participation in public worship. But would it go so far as to include an incorporation of the values of the gospel into their daily lives and work?

The truth is that we live in an increasingly secular culture. Secularization is manifest in declining attendance records at public worship. It is also seen in the lives of people who create a dichotomy between religion and daily life; people who leave the vision and values of the gospel in church rather than take them into their home, the marketplace, the workplace, the world; people for whom "the reign of God" is a quaint phrase from the past rather than a dynamic reality which should shape our lives here and now.

J ESUS, THE GREAT EVANGELIZER

This prompts us to ask: What *does* it mean to be Christian today? As always, to answer this question, we must look first to Christ himself, the world's greatest evangelizer. He, and he alone, is our model.

In his life, death, and resurrection, Jesus revealed the extent of his Father's great *love* and the *wisdom* of his plan for the human family. He constantly taught his followers about his Father and what he expected of them. As we know from the Gospels, he taught in a very simple, down-to-earth way, frequently in parables. So compelling was his personality that people were eager to hear what he had to say, even though he called them to a way of life not always to their liking.

To those sorely tempted by the craving to acquire countless possessions in the search for true inner peace, Jesus counsels poverty of spirit. To those who are infatuated by an exaggerated individualism or controlled by the blind obedience of totalitarian systems, he counsels obedience to God's will. To those seduced by the allurement of constant pleasure-seeking, he counsels chaste love, an intimacy that reflects the inner life of the triune God.

To those who hunger for something more in life, he proclaims, "I am the Bread of Life." To those who stumble around in the darkness, he affirms, "I am the Light of the World." To those who founder and lose their way, who are vulnerable to attack and need tender loving care, he says reassuringly, "I am the Good Shepherd." To those who stand fearful before the domain of death, he asserts, "I am the resurrection and the life." To those who have shared the psalmist's experience of being like the earth, "parched, lifeless, and without water," he says with outstretched arms, "I am the Vine . . . you are the branches."

Jesus, the great evangelizer, announces the Good News of God's enduring love, the imminence of God's reign, and the importance of repentance, bringing one's behavior into accord with the gospel. His wisdom often differs from that of the prevailing culture, just as his loving service of his brothers and sisters sets him apart from the predominant popular role models. We believe and we affirm with all our being that he alone is the savior of the human family; he alone can give us the peace and harmony for which we hunger within our own souls and with all our sisters and brothers.

THE RISEN LORD'S ABIDING PRESENCE IN THE CHURCH

We know, of course, that Jesus' mission and ministry of evangelization did not end with his public ministry. As he himself said, he would not leave us orphans. He promised to send the Holy Spirit who would instruct his disciples in everything. Moreover, he himself remains with the community of faith. When he gave his disciples the Great Commission to "go . . . and make disciples of all the nations," he immediately added, "And know that I am with you always until the end of the world!" (Matt 28:19-20).

His disciples undoubtedly understood the significance of the continuing presence of the risen Lord in the community since they had already experienced that presence on several significant occasions after the resurrection.

Recall, for example, this incident of Jesus' presence among his disciples—a paradigm instructive for our own day. I am referring to the Emmaus story as told to us by Luke. Two of the disciples are walking from Jerusalem to Emmaus, puzzled and distraught over the events of the previous week. Suddenly, Jesus begins to walk with them—although they did not recognize him. Their incorrect interpretation of the events that had just taken place in Jerusalem reveals their distorted expectations of him and prevents them from seeing him as one who *lives and walks with them.* Moreover, despite early morning reports about the empty tomb, their hearts are slow to believe.

Then Jesus takes the initiative and, in effect, begins to tell his own story. Exposing their lack of understanding and faith, his main point is a rhetorical question: "Did not the Messiah have to undergo all this so as to enter into his glory?" He reviews the Old Testament Scriptures with them. It's all there in the tradition. The picture Jesus paints of the Jerusalem events is radically different from that of the disciples. His version ends, not with failure, but with triumph over death, with glory!

When Jesus seems intent on going beyond Emmaus, the disciples earnestly invite him to spend the evening with them. He has shared his story with them, so they offer him hospitality. They open their hearts to him in love, and, when they are seated at table, Jesus responds in love. The guest becomes the host!

And in their table fellowship, the two disciples recognize that the stranger is, in fact, a dear friend. Their eyes are opened in the breaking of the bread. Jesus immediately vanishes from their sight—but not from their hearts! He disappears physically, but he remains present in their midst—in the word and in the fellowship of his table.

They immediately acknowledge that their hearts were *burning* as he proclaimed and explained the Scriptures to them. The fire had not altogether been extinguished by the disillusioning events of the previous week. Jesus has fanned the fragile spark into a strong burning flame—a flame of new life and love.

And now they have a *new* story to tell. They not only see Jesus differently, they also see *themselves* in a new way. They are not ex-followers of a dead prophet, but disciples of the risen Lord. That is why their second response to this encounter is to return to Jerusalem, despite the late hour, to give witness about their experience. At that moment they become evangelizers! They share the fire in their hearts with the eleven and the others assembled in the upper room.

This encounter with the risen Lord and their initial sharing of the experience with the other disciples prepares all of them for the wonderful gift of the Spirit on Pentecost. The flame of the Holy Spirit empowers them, as disciples of the risen Lord, to proclaim the Good News, to share with all others the flame of new life and love which was in their hearts. They had finally found someone to whom to give their hearts—totally, without any reservations. Now, as evangelists, they call others to believe in the same risen Lord Jesus.

CHRISTIAN EVANGELIZATION

The journey to Jerusalem—the pilgrimage to the site of the cross *and* the resurrection—remains essential to the Christian life. It cannot be avoided. To be an *authentic* Christian, one cannot walk away from Jerusalem and abandon hope—no matter how difficult things may become, no matter how opposed the world may be to the gospel. As Jesus' disciples, we must stand at the foot of the cross and learn its meaning. We must also believe—with all our being—in the risen Lord. The empty tomb must be forever etched in our memory. Then, when we have done both of these tasks, and have also received the gift of God's Spirit, we are ready to fulfill the mission given us of telling Jesus' story "to the ends of the earth."

Evangelization leads to personal conversion, an experience that may include one or more life-changing events and is usually a painstaking, lifelong process. But, while it establishes an intimate relationship between the believer and the risen Lord, between the Christian and Christ himself, it is *not* an exclusively personal matter.

If we examine the Christian tradition—from the table fellowship of Jesus with both friends and enemies, to the vast crowds he taught, to the small groups of apostles and disciples in whom he invested so much time, to the early Christian household churches, to our Sunday assemblies and worldwide ecclesial communities—personal conversion always demands affiliation, community, Church. Christians come to recognize the Lord both in the word and in the breaking of bread—in the proclamation of the gospel and in table fellowship. And these are actions of the community.

Within the Roman Catholic tradition, as it undoubtedly is in many others, to evangelize is to invite people both to Jesus and to responsible Church membership. It is true that affiliation or membership in the Church *without* personal transformation means little. Nevertheless, it is also true that personal conversion *without* the comfort and challenge of the community of faith may be merely a form of spiritual narcissism. Conversion is nurtured and deepened in ecclesial communities of faith where the evangelizing mission of Jesus is continued.

In our contemporary society of technology and individualism, evangelization has a great capacity to help people discover that they need help, that they need others, that they need community. It helps them understand the significance and importance of the incarnation—that the Spirit of the living God and the risen Lord are alive in faith-filled relationships within a community, a Church.

This implies that one of the great tasks we face as evangelizers is to join the comfort of identifying Jesus as "*my* personal savior" with the challenge of naming him as "*our* savior."

* * *

My brothers and sisters in the Lord, I am here, and you are here, because we know that we have much to learn from one another. In the mystery of life, Jesus has called each of us by name. He has called us to faith. And he has called us to evangelize so that we might share that faith with others. He has also prayed for our unity as his disciples. When we are divisive, argumentative, or negatively critical, we undermine the very power that we have received in abundance from God—the power to bring about, in the Spirit, "new heavens and a new earth where, according to his promise, the justice of God will reside" (2 Pet 3:13).

There is truth, beauty, goodness, and the presence of the Spirit in each of our ways of following the Teacher. As his disciples, let us meet with one another, pray with one another, pray for one another, and learn from one another. Let us talk of the One to whom we have given our hearts.

Praised be Jesus Christ, now and forever. And glory to God, his loving Father. Send forth your Holy Spirit, and we shall be reborn. And with you we can renew the face of the earth! Amen!

Education/Catholic Education

Loyola University

Chicago, Illinois

——*January 15, 1983* ——————————————————

Father Baumhart, Honored Guests, Distinguished Members of the Faculty and Administration of Loyola University, My Dear Students, Parents, Family and Friends:

Congratulations!

This is a common expression of praise, but I mean it in an uncommon way. I mean it for all of you—students, faculty and family—for what we celebrate today is not an isolated event but the culmination of the effort and love of many people.

Can you feel it? What this ceremony tells us, what our presence here means to each other? That we need each other and that, with each other, great things are possible?

To the faculty and administration, then, for their generosity and wisdom; to the graduates, for their persistence and work; to the family and friends of this class, for their affection and support—to all of you, congratulations . . . and thank you.

"Thank you" is also a common expression, but I wish to thank you today for a special reason. Our education begins the day that someone loves us, or perhaps we should say, the moment that we *know* that someone loves us. It is our first leg up, so to speak, the motivation we must have, then and now, to use our minds, to search for the truth, to leave the darkness and reach for the light.

And as we grow, we begin to see the complexities of the love we receive; we see that love not only comforts but challenges; that love meets

467

our demands only to make its own; that love seems to draw away at times, not to desert us, but that we might follow.

Love eventually lets go altogether, that it may be rediscovered by the learner in the learner's own way, over and over, time and again.

It is difficult for a university, especially a large one, to duplicate such an atmosphere of learning. It is much easier to develop a kind of compartmentalized society in which each discipline pursues its own agenda, without a sense of sharing with the campus at large. It is easier, in other words, to create a university which may well be competent, but which has no soul. The principles of each discipline may be clear, but not the philosophy which binds them together.

That philosophy must address the question that rises from the heart of every human being: "Why do I exist?" Is there something, is there someone, for whom I am made? Every other question is secondary.

For that reason, because of that question, I am grateful to you today, I thank you. As a university, as faculty and students, you have wrestled with that deeply human question, and have helped all of us who know you to become wiser, more thoughtful human beings. Loyola University is more than an institution, it is a presence in our city, to share and confront with us the dilemmas of modern life, to support and challenge us.

The question of our existence is addressed in Loyola's general policy statement. The policy reads in part:

> The goal of Jesuit higher education is men and women who are intellectually mature, whose lives express the values which they embrace, who spend themselves in service to others, and who view their work as a contribution to the glory of God.

That single statement may be expressed this way:

"Why do I exist?" Because I am loved, loved by the One Who is Meaning itself. There *I* have meaning; I have dignity which nothing and no one can take from me.

"Why do I exist?" To live as he lives, Who has named himself Love. Therefore I am most alive when I love as he loves, most unfulfilled when I do not.

"Why do I exist?" To express in my society what Christ Jesus declared before the powers of his time, for it is true about both of us: "For this I was born, for this I came into the world, to give witness to the truth."

These three "creeds," then, make up a general policy statement about human life: I believe in my dignity as a human being, a child of God; I believe in the dignity of my fellow human beings, made as I am in his image; I believe in the dignity of my mind, my body, my talents, my mission, which is to bear witness to his truth in every conceivable way.

This is why I exist, this is what every development of my mind and body must further express.

But it is also true that any creed remains on paper as an ethical abstraction until it is lived. Only then do we know how worthwhile it is.

And how well some people have lived their beliefs! I would like to share with you today the thoughts of a group I will call "January's People," for this is the month that commemorates their lives.

Anything good about January may be hard to believe, because January is not usually considered a memorable month in the Midwest. There is usually too much snow or not enough. Last January it was so cold that many Die-Hard batteries did. I hear Bears' fans say that January is totally forgettable because Chicago is never in the Super Bowl. Last year, Cincinnati *was* in the Super Bowl—we played San Francisco—and let me tell you, January is still totally forgettable!

But surprisingly, January does afford us glimpses of people whose lives were extraordinary, and more than that, eloquent. They have something to tell us that is powerful and lasting.

An unforgettable man was born in January in 1915, a thinker, a poet, a dreamer whose premature death in 1968 stunned the world. His name was Thomas Merton, and with his lectures, his books, his poetry, most of all with his engaging wit and honesty, he took us along on a constant rediscovery of our humanity and our faith.

Where he began was where we all must begin.

"I *am* the world," he cried, "just as you are! Where am I going to look for the world first of all if not in myself?"

He was a Trappist monk, and yet he knew that he was part of humanity, and humanity part of him despite his life of seclusion. He knew that the worst sin is to exploit or ignore what we were born to serve.

"We must *choose* the world," he said. "To *choose* the world is not merely a pious admission that the world is acceptable because it comes from the hand of God. . . . To choose the world is to choose the work I am capable of doing, in collaboration with my brothers and sisters, to make the world better, more free, more just, more livable, more human. Rejection of the world or contempt for the world, for whatever reason, is in fact not a choice but the evasion of choice."

Merton's opinions about the role of Christians were often controversial, and inevitably aroused anger and irritation both from those outside the Church who are always enraged when Christians try to act on their beliefs, and those inside who prefer to use their beliefs as a defense against the horrors of the world. But Merton believed, as did Thomas More, that we are gifted people, meant to serve the Lord "in the wit and tangle of the mind."

For this reason, Thomas Merton had a horror of passivity in Christians. Without the dialogue of faith, reason, and politics, he felt the world lost what he called "measure," a contemplative stance, a wholeness of perspective. Without some such measure, the sense of the unimportance of our egos in comparison to the true center on which they should be rightly focused, there was a total disharmony in individuals and societies, a loss of all true happiness, and a corresponding attempt to fill the void in ways that were destructive and suicidal.

He told a little story once that was typically Merton, poetic and ironic. He was sitting on a plank by an old barn in the pasture near the monastery's enclosure wall, meditating with a book, when he spied two hunters and a dog in the orchard beyond the wall. After watching them for some time he came to understand that the hunt was an act, that neither the men nor the dog really wanted to find a rabbit, and that the barking and loud talking, the jumping upon the wall to wait for rabbits to run by, and the aiming of the gun were all part of the act. When the "hunters" became aware of the "monk" watching them, Merton began to ask himself whether he should act out his own part by sitting still, appearing to have good will toward the world but unwilling to get involved in it, as a good monk. Or should he shake his fist at them to get off his wall!

He decided to sit still. He mused: "So there we stay. He stands on top of the wall 'hunting' and I sit on a board, 'meditating.' I have a book with me. He has a gun. Both are factors in a disguise. And that leaves me in the presence of an immense difficulty—the task of asking myself if I am a monk in the same way as he is a hunter, and if so, if this should be a cause for alarm."

And we, he asks us, are we in the same difficulty? Are we Christians with a baptismal certificate, a sacramental life, a theology training, like the hunter with his gun, and the monk with his book? Are they indications of reality, or factors in a disguise?

Merton concluded that sooner or later, if there is to be any progress in faith, every Christian must know two movements of the soul: the exodus and the passover. We must first experience the exodus, the liberation from despair that Christ has won for us, the freedom from all that draws us toward the self-destructive and the suicidal. But after the exodus, the freedom *from*, there must be the freedom *for*, a direction to my giving of self, and this means a continuous involvement in the death and resurrection of Christ. St. Paul spoke of it in his famous analogy of the race:

> All I want to know is Christ and the power of his resurrection, and to share his sufferings by reproducing the pattern of his death. . . . I am still running, trying to capture the prize for which Christ Jesus captured me.

The pattern of Christ's death and resurrection is reproduced in us through the changes in our lives, the growth of our minds, the testing of our hearts. Always there must be this dying, this death in us, that we may break through into new life.

Because he had experienced this hunger and this necessity of life in Christ, St. Paul was able to say: "Let us go forward on the road that has brought us to where we are."

In the town of Pisa in Italy, in 1803, Elizabeth Seton faced the tragedy that was the turning point of her life. This American woman, who was then visiting in Italy, lost the one human being she loved most in the world. Her husband, William, died in her arms. She was overwhelmed by grief. Life suddenly seemed to make no sense to her, for her life had been planned with and around her husband. She felt alone as never before in her life, as if she had never known what the word "alone" meant.

After her return to the United States, looking for answers, for some light and peace, she pursued her questions of faith, and in doing so, lost her relatives and friends to their prejudices. They could not accept her, her new faith, what she had become, and most of all, they could not accept the new family she was gathering about her. For she was gathering the destitute, the wretched, the ignorant, into her orphanages and schools. She was gathering those who also knew what it was to be alone.

Those who had never known that feeling could never understand. She, in her loneliness, had been grasped by Christ, and now she would be the one to reach out and embrace.

She had died, she had risen. It happened many times in her life, but all the while the magnificent person that was Elizabeth Seton was being discovered by the world—and by Elizabeth herself.

What T. S. Eliot says so beautifully in *Four Quartets* might be descriptive as well about such a human discovery:

> We shall not cease from exploration,
> And the end of all our exploring
> Will be to arrive where we started
> And know the place for the first time.

In St. Luke's Gospel, Jesus dies between two thieves, with the world's outcasts. He dies there because he had lived there, with the poor whom he would not abandon. His death is of a piece with his life.

On January 31, 1948, Mahatma Gandhi was assassinated, and the world lost its most eloquent voice of reason and compassion. But Gandhi knew he would die such a death because his life's work against injustice prophesied it. Such a unified man in body and spirit, he knew his death would be one with his life, a final gift to the dispossessed, final testimony to the futility of violence.

His love of his people has had incalculable influence.

In a recent interview, actor Martin Sheen described that influence on his own life. He was working in India on the new film of Gandhi's life, and moved by the story of the man, he had decided to donate his salary to charity. Suddenly one day, Sheen and his son were confronted with the overwhelming truth about poverty. As Martin Sheen himself describes it:

> One day several groups of beggars from a temple surrounded us; one was a little girl with one arm who presented herself to us: "No mommy, no daddy, need food." We said yes, yes, and threw a few coins. We got into a cab and drove off. When I looked back, she was hanging on the bumper in heavy traffic. She was risking her life. That's when it sparked in me, a kind of surrender. We put them inside the cab; we took them wherever we went.

> They were covered with lice, they were filthy all over, skinny, starving, rotten teeth, eyes bloodshot. Then I began to see my own children in these babies. They *were* my children. That was really the start of it, the physical level. You just surrendered.

There was another who knew such an experience, more than once. And he also surrendered to it. Dr. Tom Dooley, friend, doctor and advocate of the people of Laos. He died in January of 1961, and as with Gandhi, it was his death that was his last and greatest gift to humanity. But also, and again, it was because, as with Merton and Seton and Gandhi, Dr. Dooley's life was integral. What he believed, he ritualized, what he ritualized, he lived, each element returning to enrich the others. The ritual of faith becomes life, and life is faith's most beautiful ritual.

One night, as Dr. Dooley recovered from his first operation for cancer, he dreamed of his people in Laos burning away the jungle growth of a mountain so that they could plant new seedlings into the burnt soil.

May, he remembered, is a time when the season is driest there. Those are the nights that they burn the mountain.

And this is the rest of his reflection:

> The mountain in my dream was burned, and now they were planting the new life into the near dead soil. I dreamed this clearly and when the blue turquoise of morning came, though perhaps neither ear could hear nor tongue could tell, I knew the meaning of my dream.

> From my hospital bed in New York, with the same white light of revelation I had known years before, I saw what I must do. After Communion that morning, Tuesday, the first of September, my God and my dream commanded me. I must, into the burnt soil of my personal mountain of sadness, plant the new seedlings of my life—I must continue to live. I must cultivate my fields of food, to feed those who cannot feed themselves.

> The concept came to me as strongly and as powerfully as if a peal of bronze bells proclaimed it. There was no more self-sadness, no darkness deep inside: no gritty annoyance at anyone or anything. No anger at God for my cancer, no hostility to anyone. I was out of the fog of confusion standing under the clear light of duty.

The jagged, ugly scar went no deeper than my flesh. There was no cancer in my spirit. The Lord saw to that. I would keep my appetite for fruitful activity and for a high quality of life. Whatever time was left, whether it was a year or a decade, would be more than just a duration. I would continue to help the clots and clusters of withered and wretched in Asia to the utmost of my ability.

And maybe I could now be tender in a better way. I was a member of the fellowship of those who know the mark of pain. What Dr. Schweitzer told me years before became more vivid to me: "I do not know what your destiny will ever be, but this I do know. . . . You will always have happiness if you seek and find: how to serve."

There is one last witness from January to speak to us. Dr. Dooley and Mahatma Gandhi had a brother, a man whose life and death, beliefs and actions were of one cloth; and we celebrate his birthday today: Dr. Martin Luther King, Jr. His death in 1968 brought tears, rage, and new hope of reform. But as he himself so often told us, the reform will not happen, nor the cure for racism and other oppressive injustices be found, unless *we* make the reform happen, unless *we* find the cure.

At the height of the bus boycott in Montgomery, Alabama, Dr. King said this to his congregation, something he could well say to all of us here:

We so often ask, "What will happen to my job, my prestige, or my status if I take a stand on this issue?" The good man always reverses the question: what will happen if I don't take a stand? What will happen to others if I don't take action to help them?

True altruism is more than the capacity to pity; it is the capacity to sympathize. Pity may represent little more than the impersonal concern which prompts the mailing of a check, but true sympathy is the personal concern which demands the giving of one's soul. It is fellow feeling for the person in need—his pain, his agony, his burdens.

For the ultimate measure of any one of us is not where we stand in moments of comfort and convenience, but where we stand at times of challenge and controversy.

My brothers and sisters, these are January's people: Thomas Merton, Elizabeth Seton, Tom Dooley, Mahatma Gandhi, Martin Luther King, Jr. But they are with the Lord. Their gifts to us will perish and their eloquence be muted if there do not follow the kind of people that they were, the kind of human beings this university has pledged itself to develop: men and women who are intellectually mature, whose lives express the values which they embrace, who spend their lives in service to others, and who view their work as a contribution to the glory of God.

My dear graduates, it is you who are now January's people. With our love and prayers, go now and do your work. Be afraid of nothing, not of your weaknesses, or your pain, or whatever obstacles the world may present to you, not of those small deaths we must all die. You have been grasped by the Lord and he will not let go, nor let you perish.

In the midst of winter, may I look forward to the springtime of your lives with a little prayer that Tom Dooley used to love: "O Lord of light and love, give my roots rain."

Address

Catholic Principals' Association

McCormick Place, Chicago, Illinois

── *February 15, 1983* ─────────────────────────────

Fifty years ago, when the little children came out of the back streets of
the city, heads bent against the wintry west wind, and entered their
parish school, they stood on the fateful frontier between the warm and
understanding world of the family, and that other, more authoritative and
awe-inspiring world. Crossing the threshold, the children entered the
overwhelming grandeur of the parochial school: the sudden silence, the
sisters each standing at her classroom door, like a medieval saint in its
niche. This atmosphere, all seriousness and quiet, sprinkled with prayer
and punctuated with exemplary stories of the saints, fostered a learning
environment in which the elementary skills of modern life were, through
repetition and drill, acquired to the point of near-mastery; at the same
time, these skills were caught up in the larger movement of the child's
becoming an adult Christian. Like the darkened, candle-flickering church
of childhood, the parish school had a mystique all its own.

As the church of yesteryear has given way to the modern assembly in
which darkness has been replaced by quiet, even bright, lighting and as silence has been replaced by the friendliness of neighbors coming together
to celebrate their faith in the Lord, so the parochial school of fifty years
ago has undergone similar changes. The education of the child more
clearly than ever begins in the home and progresses through the efforts of
parents and the media, so that entry into school is more like passing from
one room to another than from one world to another. The teachers look
and act like parents, though many of them are religious. The quiet of the

classroom is like the busy quiet of a well-run home. The activities, in many cases, are indistinguishable from the activities of children in the home. In a sense, the children in a parish school are at home and feel at home.

This turn has indeed been successfully negotiated. Thus it gives me great pleasure to acknowledge the health and vitality of our Catholic schools today. Like me, you are aware of the great changes that have occurred in school governance, school financing, and school membership in recent years. Yet these changes have been accomplished without losing continuity with the past or contact with those who send their children to our schools. And for this we are grateful.

It is generally acknowledged that Catholic schools are viable and thriving alternatives to the public schools and to other private schools. More than mere alternatives, they are often seen as models and trailblazers in America's quest for excellence in education. Our schools continue to be strong in the traditional areas of the 3 R's. Our students continue to be well disciplined. And our schools are open to the innovative. Religion is stressed with great seriousness. For all these splendid accomplishments we ought to be grateful and give thanks to God—and to you.

What makes these accomplishments especially noteworthy is that they take place in institutions that honestly strive to be true communities of persons. In an age of computerization, our schools foster a personal approach. Pope John Paul II often speaks of the dignity, uniqueness, and holiness of the person who is both king and priest. In his encyclical *Redemptor hominis*, the Holy Father writes:

> The essential meaning of this "kingship" and "dominion" of the human person over the visible world, which the Creator Himself gave man for his task, consists in the priority of ethics over technology, in the primacy of the person over things, and in the superiority of spirit over matter (no. 49).

It is one of the glories of our schools that we unceasingly strive to treat each child, parent, teacher, and administrator as a person, created in God's image and redeemed by his Son. "Individual help" and "regard for each other" are not empty phrases. It is true that no school can take the place of a family. But in the spirit of the family, our schools see themselves as existing for the sole purpose of the making of persons, persons with the dual destiny of transforming the world and of living with God and his family forever. For your accomplishments in helping bring about this atmosphere of growth, the Catholic community of the archdiocese cannot be too profuse in its praise, nor can I. We all thank you for your labors as an indispensable part of the Church's work on earth.

I appreciate the fact that, splendid as your accomplishments are, you are very conscious of the problems that you must face every day. There is an old Spanish proverb: *El amor y la luna se parecen; menguan cuando no crecen:* "Love and the moon are alike; they diminish when they do not grow." So your relations with all of your publics can flourish and grow; when they do not, however, they can become frayed. Together, let us look at some of these relationships.

As principals, you work closely with your pastors. It is frequently said that the bottom line is: the pastor is in charge. Thus, if the relationship is good, everything goes well; if it is not, life becomes very difficult. How can you foster a vital relationship with the pastor, the associate pastors, and the parish team? I would like to emphasize that your relationship is not simply one of educational leader to spiritual leader. For you, too, have a role in the ministry of the parish. You are the managerial and instructional leader of the faculty. But you exercise a certain spiritual leadership as well. In ministering to the non-Catholics in the parish, you play the primary and, indeed, an extremely vital role in leading these people to full participation in the life of the parish. Inevitably a certain anxiety and apprehension are felt in exercising this ministerial role. I do appreciate how anxiety affects your lives and not only in relation to the pastor and the Church. Every principal, I suspect, feels somewhat uneasy before the school board election not because the new members will not be helpful but because changes—the need to establish new relationships—are frequently traumatic. Will we have the psychic energy for another new beginning? I know the feeling. In the past year, I have had to face a new beginning. But my experience tells me that new beginnings are not as bad as they are thought to be!

At times these anxieties and uncertainties reveal resentments. Lay principals sometimes feel that religious principals are given *carte blanche* and are, from the beginning, trusted while they themselves are evaluated more stringently and watched more closely. Religious principals sometimes feel that they are being used because they do not receive the same pay and benefits that lay people receive. These feelings are never wholly without foundation. But the real question is: How do we move forward beyond old inequities? How do we heal the past? We know what the ancient Greek poet knew:

> One thing alone is denied even to gods (even more to humans): to make undone the deeds which have been done.

Even though we may know intellectually that times have changed and the new realities demand new responses, it is not always easy simply to let go of the past. The past is often a burden which is difficult to shake, one which impedes our creativity and ability to look ahead.

Your relations with parents are also in need of continuous strengthening. Fifty years ago, parents of our students were not, in general, as well educated as were the teachers and principals. Today, it is not uncommon for them to be as well educated as, or even more highly educated than, school personnel. Educated parents can put school personnel on the defensive in what is meant to be a common and cooperative enterprise.

"Consumerism" has also changed the relationship of parents to school. With a freedom unavailable to them in previous times, parents pick and choose the school their children will attend, and that freedom can be perceived as a threat rather than as one of many factors, all of which together constitute the very grounds of a fruitful relationship.

Then there are the people "downtown": the School Office of the Archdiocese of Chicago and the archdiocese itself. How often principals find themselves saying, "I stay as far away as I can!" And the resources available, the expertise, can remain untapped. A school is built on the supposition that little children cannot grow without the help of others, and yet we find it difficult to seek the help of others ourselves.

Now all these fears and anxieties are understandable. And they will be allayed and our problems solved not by my coming up with "the" answer, but by all of us cooperatively addressing them forthrightly in a spirit of mutual respect, understanding, and love. I am confident that, if we cooperate with each other, we can bring about even better relations among all of these publics.

What is more difficult is finding the time and energy to be educators as well as managers. The days go by so quickly. It is not uncommon for you even in February to realize that you have not visited all the classes in the school. Or you visit the first grade and realize that those who were kindergartners the year before are known by name but not those who entered school this year. What eats up your time? Paper work mounts higher and higher. Trying to keep up with changes in state requirements and in the law seems to take more and more time. School buildings and equipment demand your attention. Yet you see yourselves as educators who ought to be spending much of your prime time in educational thinking and planning. You want to stay abreast of the latest educational developments. You want to encourage your teachers to update themselves. Who would have thought ten years ago that schools would be as deeply involved in computers—for faculty, for students, even for students who have not yet learned to read—as they are today? Like every administrator, you, like me, must cope with the immediate crisis, while trying to find time to reflect on the truly essential matters that will affect our schools for better or worse in the future.

May I share with you one essential problem that faces all educators and one that is of special concern to those who profess to be following in the footsteps of Jesus Christ: the education of the handicapped. More than four years ago, the bishops of this country issued a statement on handicapped people. Understandably, the main focus of the document was on the need to welcome the handicapped and their families into the mainstream of community worship in our parishes. For, as the bishops wrote, "The Church finds its true identity when it fully integrates itself with these 'marginal' people, including those who suffer from physical and psychological disabilities." In addition to offering a compassionate justification for this integration, the bishops wished to be practical. For example, they encouraged parishes to take steps to make the churches physically accessible to the handicapped. Then, near the end of the statement, the bishops turned their attention to education. Let me quote them directly:

> Dioceses might make their most valuable contribution in the area of education. They should encourage and support training for all clergy, religious, seminarians and lay ministers, focusing special attention on those actually serving handicapped individuals, whether in parishes or some other setting. Religious education personnel could profit from guidance in adapting their curricula to the needs of handicapped learners, and Catholic elementary and secondary school teachers could be provided in-service training in how best to integrate handicapped students into programs of regular education. The diocesan office might also offer institutes for diocesan administrators who direct programs with an impact on handicapped persons.

> The coordination of educational services within the dioceses should supplement the provision of direct educational aids. It is important to establish liaisons between facilities for handicapped people operating under Catholic auspices (special, residential and day schools; psychological services and the like) and usual Catholic school programs. Only in this way can the structural basis be laid for the integration, where feasible, of handicapped students into programs for the non-handicapped. Moreover, in order to ensure handicapped individuals the widest possible range of educational opportunities, Catholic facilities should be encouraged to develop working relationships both among themselves and with private and public agencies serving the same population.

I apologize for the length of the quotation, but I am asking your help in addressing this mandate. Its implementation is by no means simple, nor the ways to implement it clear. Should your school accept handicapped children? Should it mainstream them? Should several schools cooperate so that these children can be placed in schools with special equipment and specially trained teachers? Should our efforts be focused on cooperating with public agencies? I suspect that no single answer will be the right one. Learning difficulties are varied in nature. No one situation is optimal for all children with disabilities. The very enormity of the problem calls for cooperation. No one school can solve the problems it encounters even within its own boundaries. How can we genuinely assist these "members of the community to do the Lord's work in the world, according to their God-given talents and capacity"?

I ask your help in this area of very special concern for all of us. Yet I am not unmindful that you have other concerns, that your concerns are multiple and complex. Let us, therefore, at least briefly look at some of these other concerns.

Education is the most expensive part of archdiocesan activities. How can we make our publics aware of how necessary their continuing support is? I said "continuing support," but I really should have said "increasing support." All of us are aware of how costs have escalated as we made the transition from schools exclusively staffed by religious to schools involving the full cooperation of large numbers of lay people, and we are aware that this transition has occurred in a period of inflation accentuated by skyrocketing energy costs. (I am sure you have all been grateful for the comparatively mild winter we have been experiencing.)

Many of you are concerned with problems of inequality. Better schools in better neighborhoods frequently have better educational programs and charge less tuition than schools in poorer neighborhoods. How can we make it easier for parents with lower incomes to place their children in our schools?

Many of you are concerned about problems of stability, turnaround, and burnout. I am told that, as principals, you last, on the average, about five to seven years. When you change, the direction of the school and the membership of the faculty tend to change. Fifty years ago, the character of a school was fairly stable, because its character was set by the religious order whose members constituted the faculty, rather than by the principal. Now, though there are many nuns teaching in our schools, they may come from a variety of religious communities and traditions. When teachers are lay people, they come from a variety of traditions and do not represent, or perhaps feel comfortable in, the tradition they find operative in the school. I believe that, as a result, the character of the school today depends much more on the principal and on the parish priests than ever before. You set the tone and the aims, and you are aware of the enormous responsibility you bear in so doing.

I want you to know that I am concerned about your lives as principals. Americans have been brought up to respond to the cry: go higher, go higher. It is almost unAmerican to be satisfied with what you are doing. Yet principals, like pastors, are, in the main, in terminal positions. Very few pastors become bishops. Very few principals of Catholic schools become superintendents. Unlike the public schools, Catholic schools do not have a large number of positions above that of principal to which the principal can aspire. You cannot see your jobs, as can many Americans in business and industry, as mere stepping stones to something more responsible, better paid, more respected and applauded. Like the lady from Boston who was asked why she did not travel, principals have to respond, "because we're there." You have to see your work as permanent and so intrinsically worthwhile that you would not want to "go higher." I worry about this because changeovers are frequent, because in the increasing complexity of schooling you find yourselves wearing more and more hats. The pace of life of the principal has quickened enormously over the past fifty years. How can we prevent burnout and the loss of experienced and capable people who have given their all and now feel enervated? I ask myself: How can we make the position of principal more attractive over a long period of time? I ask: Are the jobs principals are taking when they cease being principals bringing them greater satisfaction than the satisfaction they are receiving now? How can I be of help?

It is with this last question that I will stop. We are joined in continuing the work of Jesus Christ in bringing a fallen but redeemed humanity to the Father, a humanity capable of participating in the work of transforming the world into a place marked by peace and justice, love and joy. As the pastor of this local church, I pledge to you today my full support and cooperation. As I indicated earlier, I cannot personally resolve all the problems you face. What I can do is continue serving as an instrument of the Lord, reflecting his love and understanding, his compassion and healing power. In this way, I can perhaps be instrumental in helping you grow spiritually, in nourishing your faith and strengthening your commitment, in supporting and affirming you, in providing the motivation we both need to go about our respective tasks with conviction, creativity and enthusiasm.

Newman Centennial

Cleveland, Ohio

—— *February 24, 1983* ——————————————————

I am honored to be with you today for this celebration of the Centennial Anniversary of the Newman Movement. From its founding in 1883 until today, your apostolic work in the area of campus ministry has been important to the Church's mission. I know it has not always been easy. But you and your predecessors have accumulated a wealth of experience during the sometimes painful process by which the Newman Movement's identity has evolved during the past one hundred years. Those who performed this special ministry before you were masters of adaptability. They were patient and trusting in the face of bewildering conflicts and frustrations. My prayer today is that you will be blessed with those same qualities as you continue to discern the signs of the times and adjust to the changing circumstances of your challenging and exhilarating apostolate.

Your namesake, John Henry Newman—Cardinal Newman, was a penetrating thinker. In his book, *The Idea of a University*, he describes authentic education as a lifelong process of enlarging our ideas by constantly interconnecting our experiences. Let me quote his own words:

> It is a digestion of what we receive, into the substance of our previous state of thought; and without this no enlargement is said to follow. There is no enlargement unless there be a comparison of ideas one with another, as they come before the mind, and a systematizing of them. We feel our minds growing and expanding then, when we not only learn, but refer what we learn to what we know already. It is not the mere addition to our knowledge that is the illumination; but the locomotion, the

movement onwards of that mental center to which both what we know
and what we are learning gravitate. And therefore a truly great intellect
. . . is one which takes *a connected view* of old and new, past and present, far and near, and which has an insight into the influence of all these
one on another; without which there is no whole and no center. It possesses the knowledge not only of things, but also of their mutual and
true relations.

What a tightly written and carefully reasoned paragraph that is. We're
not often accustomed today to think that way. Unfortunately, Cardinal
Newman's beautiful ideal of a university bears little resemblance to the
educational processes we see today in most major institutions of higher
learning in the United States. In their efforts to develop programs for the
dissemination of useful knowledge, universities often omit the reflective
efforts so important for the integration of what we accumulate through
the learning process. Perhaps the decision of *Time* magazine to select a ma-
chine—the computer—as its "Man of the Year" last January is a symptom
of the current situation. Today's emphasis on experimental methods of research and the development of computer technology have seriously altered the mission of higher education. These modern developments can be
excellent tools for learning. But they are only tools. Newman's words remind us that the core of education lies in the development of that "connected view" of the bits and pieces of reality which come within our grasp.

That is where you come in. The Newman Movement, through its centers, helps to restore to the life of today's universities some of the important interpersonal elements which are so necessary to that integrating
process which leads to the enlargement of our ideas.

With that in mind, I'd like to go back to one of Newman's sentences
from the longer paragraph I quoted a minute ago from *The Idea of a University*. He said, "There is no enlargement (of our thought) unless there
be a comparison of ideas one with another as they come before the mind,
and a systematizing of them." With your kind permission, I'd like to become engaged with you now in that kind of process. What I propose is
this: I'd like to focus on six brief quotations from Cardinal Newman's
writings and attempt to connect them with six particular aspects of the
challenging opportunity which, I believe, faces you in your apostolate at
modern American universities. Whether we succeed or not, you must
judge for yourselves at the end of my remarks. But, at least, in the spirit
of Cardinal Newman, let us give it a try.

First, in 1873 Newman wrote, "It is almost a definition of a gentleman
to say he is one who never inflicts pain." I think it is accurate to say that
many persons view a Newman Center as a place where a privileged type
of dialogue and human interaction can occur. You provide a focal point or
forum where persons involved in the intellectual quest for truth can en-

gage in mutually enriching dialogues with people who represent the theological and faith perspectives of the Church. This involves a disciplined respect for truth from the parties involved in the exchange. It's never been easy to do this well. Since both the Church and the university are changing, this task of integrating faith and culture can seem today an overwhelming challenge. We strive to maintain a dialogue which respects the university's need for institutional autonomy and academic freedom in its pursuit of truth, on the one hand; on the other we recall that it is the teaching mission of the Church to bring the revealed Word of God to bear when discussing the nature of the world, the human race, and the way for all of us to live appropriately in this world. Keeping this delicate balance without inflicting pain is that admirable skill of those whom Newman defines as gentle persons.

Your task of facilitating such dialogue requires that you maintain a balanced outlook in representing, reconciling, and integrating the missions of Church and university and their different perspectives. Sometimes this can seem like a thankless task, particularly when you feel caught in the crossfire in times of controversy. However, I believe that your role in promoting such dialogue has never been more important for the well-being of both institutions, Church and university.

My second point begins with one of the most familiar and beloved quotes from Newman's writings: "Lead, kindly Light, amid the encircling gloom, lead thou me on. The night is dark, and I am far from home; lead thou me on! Keep thou my feet; I do not ask to see the distant scene; one step is enough for me." A key feature of today's educational efforts is to prepare young people to survive in, and eventually assume leadership roles in a world where human life and work are organized in large institutions and corporations. The task of helping students develop a sense of direction and a healthy sense of self is complicated by the increased use of high technology and the fact that ability to communicate with computers is becoming a basic language skill in the academic and business worlds. As the Church and the university combine their resources in the educational venture of preparing students for leadership in the world, it is imperative that the job be done well despite its bewildering complexity. The pressures can be enormous. Competition is fierce. Just keeping up with ever escalating technological innovation can be a source of immense stress. Discovering the "kindly light" which provides a personal compass for this challenging journey of life is a precious possession for any student. You are often the ones who assist them in doing this.

In 1868 Cardinal Newman wrote these words: "Living Nature, not dull Art shall plan my ways and rule my heart." Let's take a closer look at the raw material of today's student body. What rules their hearts? Most of the students entering our colleges and universities have been subjected to a very powerful educational influence outside the hours spent in school. Recent studies indicate that a typical college student may have invested as much as 20,000 hours of his or her life in viewing TV or movies. We have to surmise that such extensive exposure to these media is having a serious impact on the personality development of many of these highly impressionable viewers.

Generalizations about the exact long-range benefits or destructiveness of this media impact would be hazardous. Researchers have not reached any consensus. However, one source of concern is that the dramatizations involved in many prime-time TV shows and movies provide high-level emotional stimulation for children and young adults, while at the same time the usual domestic or social surroundings in which these programs are viewed requires containment or repression of this intense emotional excitement. The result can be a pattern of undesirable passivity in a young person's development. It seems to reverse Newman's dictum, to the effect that "dull Art or artificiality is planning the ways and ruling the hearts" of many of our young people raised in our modern electronic village.

Furthermore, commercial advertising during some television shows seems designed to break the action in a program precisely at a point when viewers are caught up by the drama, and are feeling some response to what is dramatized.

Thus a viewer's reaction is distracted away from a caring response to the individuals involved in the story, and refocused on representations of some form of pleasurable or need-fulfilling product or experience presented by the advertiser. What effect does this process have on the students who come to our universities for formal education? Is it harmless or formative? Does the repetition of this pattern develop a type of apathy or perhaps the substitution of some form of compensatory self-gratification in place of a caring response to people and their problems? As I said, the research is inconclusive. But the question needs to be asked since, as Cardinal Newman observed so aptly, it touches upon the ruling of our hearts.

My fourth point in this listing of challenges which face you in your work today is based upon another quotation from *The Idea of a University*. Cardinal Newman says, "A great memory does not make a philosopher, any more than a dictionary can be called a grammar." We are all acquainted with students of limited abilities who achieve high grades due to hard work and excellent memories. Conversely, there are very gifted students who don't achieve their potential. Sometimes in elementary and secondary schools there are necessary economy measures which dictate unduly large class rolls and overburdened teachers. As a result our brighter students can become understimulated and experience intellectual frustration in the classroom. The potential negative effects of some level of emotional repression occasioned by viewing media—informal education—coupled with the intellectual frustration involved in the classroom—formal education—can combine to create an obstacle to personality development. This social scenario can leave university personnel with more than a few students who come onto campus, and into your Newman Centers, with an inadequately developed sense of identity and perhaps an underdeveloped "sense of responsibility" or ability to make permanent commitments with confidence.

Let me add another element to this effort we are engaged in together here today . . . this effort to understand the challenges of the modern Newman apostolate. In a work called "Flowers Without Fruit" Cardinal Newman makes this observation:

> Who lets his feelings run
> In soft luxurious flow,
> Shrinks when hard service must be done
> And faints at every woe.

Jesus challenges us to hard service when he says, "Whatsoever you do to the least of my brethren, you do unto me." We all struggle with the implications of those words. And yet we live in a society where many people simply do not wish to get involved. We have read stories similar to that famous incident some years ago in New York City where a woman named Kitty Genevese lay dying near a large apartment complex. Her cries for help went unheeded. In less dramatic ways, many of the young people who come to our campuses have experienced examples of looking the other way rather than responding. Sometimes they have witnessed repeated instances of noninvolvement by their own parents in real-life distress situations. Having learned through massive doses of exposure to television and movies to repress one's personal reactions, it is relatively easy to fall into the parental pattern of nonresponse and prefer not to get involved in situations which compromise comfort or convenience, or occasion personal risk. To paraphrase Newman's words, the challenge which you and I face in working with young people is to "reverse that soft luxurious flow and gradually introduce them to the hard service which must be done" in our modern world.

Finally, in his powerful poem "Dream of Gerontius" Newman has a line which states:

> It is the very energy of thought
> Which keeps thee from thy God.

The United States Catholic Conference recently commissioned a study entitled "Dropouts, Returnees, Converts" which probes the notable tendency in young Catholics to lapse in official Church membership. According to the findings of that study, a large number of young adults go through a rather prolonged period of spiritual drifting. Often this is accompanied by some hostile reaction to authority. Young adults, perhaps due in part to the repressive conditioning I have described, seem to feel the need to be free of supervisory comment while they experiment with values and test themselves and their emerging capabilities in a variety of new experiences. Being the Church's contact person on campus with young adults who have been affected by even some of the influences which I have cited can constitute a perplexing challenge for the apostolic work of Newman Centers. Often the seeds which you plant in the lives of these young men and women will not blossom until much later. Often you will never see the result of your good work. But you deal with them at a crucial time in their lives when many complex factors are conspiring to keep them from their God.

The previous six points have focused on problems and challenges which face all of us, but especially those of you who work on college campuses. I'd like to look at some of the unique opportunities which are yours. One of the "signs of the times" emerges in Pope John Paul's encyclical "On Human Work" wherein he underlines the increasingly important role of the laity in bringing Christ and his message to the world. The reduced number of priestly and religious vocations also underscores the need for vigorous and well-trained laity who will exert an active role in the pastoral mission of the Church. Leaders in today's corporate world wield immense power for good or for evil. Business leaders and directors of the mass media exert an especially powerful influence in shaping the values which dominate our society. It is in educating potential lay leaders for the morally responsible use of this corporate power that Christians today may best be able to promote the kingdom of God. You occupy a pivotal point in that process, for you are able to bring the best insights and resources of Catholic tradition as interpreted by Vatican II into the university community. And conversely, you can bring the best of the wisdom and experience of the intellectual community into the life of the Church. You are called to be mediators and bridge-builders for both traditions and both communities.

What are people looking for when they approach a Newman Center? What is going on within the depths of their spirits? I suspect that they sense, at least vaguely, that something more is needed in their lives, something is missing, some important dimension of their life is not quite properly attended to. I wonder if many of them might not be experiencing a kind of desert experience in their own personal developmental history. The story of John Henry Newman chronicles this same kind of spiritual odyssey. The history of the Newman Movement reflects a similar quest and search and desert wandering. By virtue of the knowledge and compassion acquired in your own previous struggles as human beings and as Christian believers, you may have been prepared in God's providence to be trusted guides to whom young people can turn. Truly happy lives today will be far more frequent if our students can learn to deepen their union with God through the sometimes confusing and frustrating variety of seemingly negative human experiences through which the Lord alerts us to the danger of his absence from our lives.

In the opening quote which I presented from the writings of Cardinal Newman, he described the truly great intellect and the truly magnanimous religious person as one who "takes a connected view of old and new, past and present, far and near; and which has an insight into the influence of all these one on another; without which there is no whole (w-h-o-l-e) and center."

This wholeness and this centeredness are what we strive to find in our own lives and, having begun to find it for ourselves, move into the role of assisting young people to begin that same discovery not only out of the accumulated wisdom of the past, but in the accumulated experiences of their own personal lives. Thus your work may very well be moving from what has been a marginal apostolic role on the fringes of our institutions of higher learning towards being the cutting edge by which the Church prepares its laity for entry into important leadership positions and effective Christian presence in the world. You can identify the graces of God's "negative presence" in these experiences and help young adults transform restlessness, confusion, aloneness, and ambiguity into occasions for spiritual growth and a deepening awareness of the Lord's presence as one who comforts the troubled and troubles the comfortable.

It is the kind of work which is worth a lifetime of effort. I sincerely congratulate those of you who are committed to doing it.

We Catholics are accustomed to beginning and ending our prayers with the Sign of the Cross. Let me conclude these remarks with a lovely little poem which John Henry Newman wrote as a young man of thirty-one. The year was 1832 and the title is simply, "The Sign of the Cross." It goes like this:

> Whene're across this sinful flesh of mine
> I draw this holy sign,
> All good thoughts stir within me, and renew
> Their slumbering strength divine;
> Till there springs up a courage high and true
> To suffer and to do.
> And who shall say, but hateful spirits around,
> For their brief hour unbound,
> Shudder to see, and wail their overthrow?
> While on far heathen ground
> Some lonely Saint hails the fresh odor, though
> Its source he cannot know.

That poem says to me that we are all in this together—you as campus ministers, the young people whom you seek to serve, I as an archbishop, John Henry Newman as a great spirit who lives on through his writings and his example, and, most of all, the Lord who surrounds us all with his love.

Thank you.

Address

High School Principals' Luncheon

Chicago, Illinois

— *May 1, 1986* ─────────────────────────────────

A couple of weeks ago I witnessed the wedding of my nephew Jimmy and his wife Marianne. Many thoughts and feelings coursed through my mind and heart that day. For example, as I saw Jimmy all dressed up for the special occasion, I suddenly realized that he has truly grown up. "Little" Jimmy is now a husband with adult responsibilities. Where have the years gone, I wondered.

High school proms are similar. As we watch the young people in this rite of passage, we suddenly realize that they *have* grown and developed during the previous four or more years even though, at times, it might have seemed to occur at a snail's pace! The early teen years are so special—yet filled with paradox!

Young teens often dream dreams that far exceed the capacity of the human condition. They reach for the stars without seeming to be able to reach the shelves in their closets—leaving clothes and other paraphernalia scattered around their rooms like cosmic matter and space junk! They readily rebel against older authority while being oblivious, by and large, to the tyranny of their peer group which dictates—more rigidly than their parents would ever attempt—how they will talk, what they will wear, and what music they will listen to! They laugh and "party" at a given signal while, on the inside, many of them already have deep emotional scars which slowly bleed in their souls and may lead them to contemplate suicide.

For young teens, the earlier presumed innocence of elementary school is history. But they do not yet have to shoulder adult responsibilities—unless they are poor, unless they belong to one-parent families, unless they are aware of the specter of nuclear warfare and the implications of a rapidly changing world economy. Teen years have always been a delight and a challenge, but today, perhaps more than ever before, young people need mentors who can help them cross the minefield of early adolescence, who can help them believe in themselves in realistic ways, who can prepare them to take their rightful place in society and in the Church.

High schools, of course, play a major role in the formation of these young people. As young teens move beyond the pale of parental influence—some more rapidly than others—they are not yet ready to make it on their own. Their reliance on peers for support and advice trades insecurity for inexperience. Secondary educational institutions provide a vitally needed structure and a catalyst for helping youth face the particular tasks and challenges of their age group. High schools prepare the next generation of citizens and disciples.

This morning I wish to offer you some reflections on the role of high schools in this local church. I will discuss briefly the role of high school teachers in Catholic education, the new challenges of some significant changes in Catholic education, and the need for collaboration among Catholic high schools and between the high schools and the archdiocese.

Catholic schools *are* different from public schools. In its educational ministry the Church promotes both academic achievement and value or religious formation. In other words, we are concerned with the minds of high school students, and also with their hearts and spirits. We want them to learn the arts and sciences as well as a faith and values that will provide nourishment and guidance for their lives. We want them to develop a disposition for service. We want to spark within them a passion for justice. We want to evoke their commitment to creating and building community.

There are many vehicles for carrying out this mission, but none is as essential as the individual teachers—and, of course, the principals. The U.S. bishops affirmed this in a 1976 statement entitled *Teach Them:*

> The integration of religious truth and values with the rest of life . . . is expressed above all in the lives of teachers in Catholic schools whose daily witness to the meaning of mature faith and Christian living has a profound impact upon the education and formation of their pupils (8).

This morning I wish to offer you—and your teachers—my heartfelt gratitude for the dedicated services which you and they provide your students. I also pledge my support to help you provide your teachers with the formational resources they need to carry out the Church's mission in secondary education. Your heritage is glorious, and you are rightly proud of it. Nevertheless, we must face today's new challenges. Our future depends on it.

What are some of the new challenges? A number of significant changes have affected Catholic secondary education in recent years, perhaps the most important being the increasing involvement of lay women and men as teachers and administrators and the concurrent decreasing number of religious in these roles. In 1962, 30 percent of the teachers in Catholic high schools were lay and 69 percent religious. In 1985, 77 percent of the teachers in Catholic high schools are lay—a significant change in two decades! The trend undoubtedly will continue.

I applaud and support the integration of laity into teaching and administrative positions. At the same time, this change gives rise to further challenges. Traditionally, most of the Catholic high schools in the archdiocese have been sponsored by religious communities who still provide support and governance. These religious institutes now face the new challenge of integrating lay persons into the actual governance of these institutions.

In the light of these changes, people ask important questions about what has been happening to Catholic secondary education in the Chicago metropolitan area. They ask, for example: "Is the quality of religious education as high as it was in the past when more priests and religious taught the religion courses?" "Are young Catholics being taught what they need to know to continue the exercise of their faith?" "Is the Church losing the next generation of Catholics?" "How shall we ensure that Catholic faith and values are being effectively passed on to the next generation?"

Such questions represent the serious concerns of parents, grandparents—and pastors! Naturally, many of them have opinions about these matters, often based on individual experiences. But, how do we move beyond mere opinion to actual fact? How do we situate individual experiences within their larger context?

It is interesting to note that the Notre Dame Study of Catholic Parish Life found that education of teenagers ranked highest among the activities to which the parish should devote attention; such education was perceived as the most compelling need.

Today sociologists regularly assess the depth of faith and values of young Catholics and others, comparing them with previous generations. Recent studies indicate that young people today are not much different from other generations in this regard. That may not, in itself, be reassuring news, but it seems to indicate that, for the present at least, we are not losing ground!

But this, in turn, raises another set of questions: What impact do teachers in Catholic high schools have on their students in regard to religious formation? Where do these teachers stand on issues of Catholic faith and values? Are there any noteworthy trends? What new challenges do we face today?

Recently, the National Catholic Educational Association conducted some significant research projects to assess the effectiveness of Catholic high schools in a variety of settings. Its 1985 report, *Sharing the Faith: The*

Beliefs and Values of Catholic High School Teachers, reflects such a project. Early in 1984, a total of 1,062 full-time teachers from a national sample of 45 Catholic high schools responded to a 260-question survey about their personal beliefs and values. The survey revealed that, on a general index of religious commitment, teachers in Catholic high schools are *more* committed than U.S. Catholics in general or the U.S. public at large.

It further revealed that the vast majority of high school teachers place a high value on religion in their own lives. Nearly 90 percent claim church membership and nearly three-fourths attend church weekly. One of the report's conclusions is that "A student in a contemporary . . . Catholic high school will be surrounded by teachers who care about the faith." This is, indeed, good news.

However, there is another side of the coin. One of every six teachers in Catholic high schools is not Catholic. Moreover, of those teachers who are Catholic, only about half have attended a Catholic college or university. This might indicate that, for some, at least, their own last formal religious education was at the high school level.

The report noted that, although the non-Catholic teachers who participated in the survey are not hostile to the religious identity of the Catholic schools in which they teach, neither are they enthusiastic supporters of Catholic teaching in a number of areas. The challenge before such schools is how to balance respect for the conscience and competence of its non-Catholic teachers—many of whom are unquestionably people of faith and good will—with institutional commitments to a specifically Catholic religious formation for their students.

Some may point out that it makes a difference whether a non-Catholic teacher is a member of a Religious Education or a Mathematics Department. This observation has some validity, of course. Nevertheless, students learn a great deal from their teachers, and not all of what they learn is academic content. Whether they intend to be or not, whether they do so consciously or not, teachers are role models, mentors, and communicators of values. The NCEA report indicates: "Their convictions—strong or weak, orthodox or unorthodox, shared or hidden—become known to students and are influential in students' efforts to sort out and build their own positions on matters of faith and values."

You and I face a complex, common challenge as we teach moral norms in a pluralistic society. To meet the challenge we must alert teachers to their impact on the religious and moral development of their students. It also involves helping teachers in an ongoing development in a mature faith and a deeper understanding of the Church's teaching about faith and values.

In this connection, I want to tell you about a project I am working on in consultation with a number of other people. Within the last year, I happened to meet informally with some high school religion teachers in the archdiocese. They shared with me their dilemmas and frustration, as well as their commitment and great desire to communicate the treasury of our faith to their students. As a result of that discussion, I decided to prepare some reflections which might be of help to all who teach religion to young people. The document, which is now in its fifth draft, is entitled "The Challenges We Face Together." The tasks which lie before us are, indeed, *shared* challenges. It is my hope that, when completed, these reflections will be helpful to you and your colleagues.

There are other factors which also call for greater collaboration between Catholic high schools and the local church.

One of the hallmarks of Catholic secondary schools is their high morale, *esprit de corps*, sense of community. I trust that each of you is dedicated to the institution which you represent and that your teachers are likewise imbued with a school spirit which is readily communicated to their students. Moreover, since our Catholic high schools are also sponsored by religious communities, there is often a further identification with and loyalty to the values and characteristics of these institutes.

Nevertheless, no school is an island. As a Catholic institution, each is part of a larger Church which itself has a mission to youth. Collaboration and cooperation among all the Catholic providers of youth services is essential if young people are to be served in a way that will respond to their needs—and, indeed, as this era and its challenges demand.

What are some of the implications of this? What, for example, should shape the relationship between the individual Catholic high school and the parishes which send their students to it? How can an ongoing, healthy relationship be established and nurtured—by both the high school and the parishes?

In providing appropriate spiritual and character formation for their students, Catholic high schools often develop faith communities which are, in effect, mini-churches. The school provides welcome opportunities for students to pray together, to share faith experiences and convictions, to engage in service activities, to study justice issues. The provision of these opportunities is part of the school's mission. But it can also unwittingly alienate the students from their parishes, making reentry or integration into parochial life and activities difficult.

How can parishes and high schools work together in a more collaborative manner so as to facilitate the necessary transitions rather than foster competing structures or programs? How can this local church help the high schools to ensure that their teachers receive ongoing formation in their own faith and value development? What can all of us do together to serve youth better?

By now it is evident that I have raised more questions than I have answered. The reason for that is quite simple: I don't have the answers! But that does not prevent me from raising these questions because I firmly believe that, in our collaboration as members of this local church, we can meet the challenges which lie before us; we can find suitable answers to the many questions we must ask.

My sisters and brothers, I have great faith in you, in your teachers, in your students. I respect and esteem your work which—like other Christian ministries—has its moments of agony as well as ecstasy. This archdiocese must stand by its young people, especially those in the early teen years—embracing them when they need a hug, holding their hands when they are afraid, being willing to let go of them when they need to walk alone a bit, always providing the kind of hospitable space into which they can enter, be themselves, and rest awhile, knowing that someone loves them.

You provide an indispensable service to this community and to this Church. As pastor of this local church, I assure you that you are not alone. Collaborating with one another—and with our students—we can realize some of their dreams and ours—dreams which too often seem unrealizable when we are left to our own rather limited resources.

Address

"Catholic Education—Alive and Well"

Malcolm Sharp Memorial Lecture

Rosary College, River Forest, Illinois

— *October 3, 1989* —————————————————————

I am honored by the invitation to deliver this address in honor of the late Dr. Malcolm Sharp. While I did not have the privilege of knowing him personally, I have been told that he was an extraordinary man, a thoughtful champion of liberal causes, an educator who found personal enrichment here at Rosary College after retirement from the University of Chicago Law School.

I have been asked to address the vast topic of Catholic education this evening. I will share some reflections, first, about education in our contemporary society; then, the role of values in the curriculum; and, finally, the specific contribution of Catholic education to our society. While my reflections are specifically addressed to Catholic higher education, they apply as well to elementary, secondary, and adult education.

EDUCATION IN OUR CONTEMPORARY SOCIETY

One of the crucial questions before us, as a society, is this: How shall we educate our students so that graduates are well prepared for their future responsibilities?

Epictetus, the Greek Stoic philosopher, said it clearly: "Only the educated are free." The founders of this nation knew that a strong educational system is essential to the success of our American experiment in freedom and democracy. Throughout our history, education has been the principal foundation of U.S. prosperity, security, and civility. A Gallup Poll several years ago suggested that many people still subscribe to this view. They reported that education was considered more important than the best industrial system or the strongest military force, because neither industry nor defense will long endure without education.

We live in an enormously complex, fast-paced world. As U.S. citizens, we take rightful pride in our pluralistic society and in our commitment to preserving individual freedom. Nevertheless, to compete effectively in world markets, to engage wisely in foreign affairs, and to foster a common culture of our own, we must be able to reach some shared understandings on the major issues confronting us. Education is an indispensable vehicle for helping us form such understandings.

In light of this, let me rephrase the question before us today: How shall we educate students to continue to be a free people—to enjoy prosperity, preserve security, and exercise civility? This immediately raises several related questions. What will the future be like? What do students need to learn for the future? How shall we teach them what they need to learn? Our answers to these important questions will have a vital impact on the future itself.

As we approach the third millennium of Christianity, certain global trends stand out which demand our attention because of the way they can impact both the present and the future. I will highlight five in particular.

First, the world's population is growing at an extraordinary rate, and, increasingly, it is shifting from rural to urban settings. In particular, Third World cities are growing faster than predicted. The United Nations now estimates that, by the year 2000, 17 of the world's 20 largest cities will be in the Third World. The implications of this rapid growth of *population* and *urbanization*, and their impact on the effective distribution and use of limited global resources, are staggering.

Second, because of contemporary travel, trade, technology, monetary policy, and communications, the world has become a global village in which all members of the human family are increasingly *interdependent*. We experience this every time we buy raspberries from Chile, a new car from Sweden, or a new computer from Japan—and every time we hear news about the financial markets in New York, Chicago, Tokyo, Hong Kong, Sidney, Bonn, Zurich, and London.

I might add, parenthetically, that this interdependence in the social sphere has a profound influence on the Church. While by its very nature the Church is a world community of faith, the implications of this universality are much clearer and more demanding now than ever before. This becomes especially evident at international gatherings of Church representatives, such as the Synod of Bishops which normally meets every three years.

Third, despite a factual global interdependence, there are also considerable forces of *fragmentation* within many societies throughout the world. For example, there are nationalistic movements within the six republics of the single nation of Yugoslavia and among the many republics in the USSR. There is civil war in Lebanon, parts of Central America, and Southeast Asia. There is tribalism and apartheid in South Africa, and the *intifadah* in the Holy Land. This fragmentation, which often results in violence, draws attention and resources away from building a fair, effective, equitable world order. Rather than lessening global interdependence, moreover, it tends to increase it by drawing other societies into the conflict.

Fourth, while the major geopolitical challenge of the last forty years has been the *East-West* ideological rivalry, increasingly as we approach the 21st century, the more serious challenge confronting the world is the widening gap between the *North* and the *South*. Many nations of the Southern Hemisphere suffer from the numbing effects of *underdevelopment:* poverty, illiteracy, unemployment, inadequate housing, poor health care. Many nations of the North, on the other hand, suffer from the heady effects of *superdevelopment:* materialism, consumerism, and exaggerated individualism.

Fifth, *science, technology,* and the *explosion of knowledge* and information in virtually every field are transforming individual human lives and society on a scale unimaginable only thirty years ago. Our ability to develop and control atomic energy and lasers has had a tremendous impact on many fields of human endeavor from medicine to the development of weaponry, from life-giving and life-sustaining advances to life-taking and life-threatening regressions. Moreover, in a society which prizes information, knowledge readily translates into power, and those without adequate education find themselves on the fringe of the community, ever more powerless and less able to contribute to the common good.

While I am speaking of the global implications of inadequate education, I see its tragic effects in Chicago where a permanent, deprived underclass of people has emerged. Two years ago, for example, private businesses made available several thousand summer jobs for poor inner-city youth. The tragedy is that only *half* of these jobs were filled, even though many thousands applied. The reason was that the majority of the applicants did not have the basic skills needed, such as the ability to read and write.

THE IMPORTANCE OF VALUES IN CONTEMPORARY LIFE AND EDUCATION

Because all these trends (and many more which I do not have time to deal with) directly involve human lives, each of them has important religious and moral dimensions that must be taken into consideration in the development of civilization and culture.

Rapid growth of population, global interdependence, and competition for scarce resources raise questions about justice, equity, and fairness—about the ways we exercise wise stewardship over the earth's resources and respect the rights of others.

The underdevelopment of the South and the superdevelopment of the North also raise serious ethical concerns. In his encyclical entitled "On the Social Concern of the Church," Pope John Paul II said that development demands a spirit of initiative on the part of the underdeveloped countries and their solidarity with one another. But he notes rather emphatically that other nations also have a responsibility for seeing to the equitable distribution of the earth's blessings among all members of the human family.

The development of new knowledge and technology progresses more rapidly than our capacity to use them responsibly. This raises fundamental questions which must be addressed: In an age when we *can* do almost anything, how do we decide what we *should* do? In a time when we can do anything *technologically*, how do we decide *morally* what we should not do?

To achieve an international order conducive to building and preserving right order and peace, the key moral question is how to relate politics, economics, and ethics so as to shape our *material* interdependence in the direction of *moral* interdependence and to bring technology to its appropriate subordinate role. To accomplish this, we need a *moral* vision.

What does this imply for education? Several implications immediately come to mind. An educational curriculum which does not help students to read, write, or compute condemns them to a bleak future. A curriculum which does not enable them to develop skills of comprehension, analysis, problem solving, and drawing conclusions ill prepares them for the future. And a curriculum which does not assist them to integrate important moral values into their lives and to develop a moral vision adequate to the challenges of contemporary society jeopardizes the future of our nation and the world community.

Although the development of technical and occupational skills is a vital component of an effective curriculum, the arts and humanities are also essential to enrich daily life, to preserve civility in our society, and to develop a sense of community and culture. In seeking the development of the whole person, I acknowledge I am looking back to some extent toward an earlier model of education which aimed at producing people of broad learning and wisdom, which enabled students to become more fully developed citizens of a free society.

While developing the whole person and a sense of community are important objectives, many forces in contemporary society tend to pit us against one another. They inhibit the development of common approaches and solutions to the problems we all face. This evening I would like to single out two of these forces: *radical individualism* and *specialization*.

One of the most disturbing social forces at work in our society has been the growing tendency toward *radical individualism*. Robert Bellah and his associates describe it in part as the belief that persons may do anything they like without ethical or moral qualms. When people begin thinking and acting this way, they readily neglect or forget the common good. Ultimately, they see no compelling reason not to separate themselves from the lives and concerns of others.

This is why an exaggerated individualism and isolationism go hand in hand. Traceable to the European continent and the dawn of the so-called Age of Enlightenment, it has been part of our background for centuries. In previous years, however, it was tempered by a religious and cultural heritage that provided coherence to life and supported the concept of the interdependence of individuals and their mutual responsibilities. Today, this is no longer the case, and this change affects each of us personally as well as the quality of life in our communities.

Nevertheless, as I listen to people, I sense a growing dissatisfaction with the isolation and concomitant lack of meaning associated with an exaggerated individualism. The difficulty, as Bellah points out, is that this dissatisfaction often remains a prisoner within the narrow confines of individualism. In other words, because our cultural patterns have become so imbued with individualism, attempts to break out into the world of interdependence and meaning are frustrated or short-changed.

This means that we must find ways to offer people the opportunity to take on a new perspective, one that builds upon the best of an earlier vision of human personhood. If education, for example, becomes a mere instrument for individual careerism, then it is no longer an effective vehicle to enable students either to develop a deeper sense of personal meaning or to understand themselves as participants in and contributors to the Church and civic culture. We must help students see themselves and their roles in the world in a new way—one which better prepares them both to cope with and to contribute to contemporary life.

As I noted earlier, another force which tends to inhibit our working together to develop common approaches and solutions to contemporary needs and problems is *specialization*. Developments in many fields of knowledge have required and produced a new class of professionals, specialists who provide important services to their profession and the human family.

But specialization also carries within it the risk of neglecting the social sphere of human activity. By focusing on a particular area of concern—however important and necessary it may be—it tends to obscure the broader picture or context in which the speciality should be seen and understood. Coupled with exaggerated individualism, specialization can unwittingly feed the tragic vortex of isolation and alienation which ultimately lead to the loss of personal meaning and erode the very foundations of a free society.

In sum, the factors impacting contemporary life have essential moral and ethical dimensions. But two tendencies within our society tend to discount or ignore important ethical questions—an exaggerated individualism and a specialization which can become myopic. We must resist and overcome these tendencies if we are to develop a moral vision which is capable of seeing beyond the concerns of individuals or special interest groups, one which embraces the hopes, aspirations, and concerns of the entire human family.

THE CONTRIBUTION OF CATHOLIC EDUCATION TO SOCIETY

Catholic education makes a significant contribution to society in several regards.

At the elementary and secondary levels, we strive to provide as good an education as possible for all who choose to come to our schools. As you undoubtedly know, this implies a considerable investment of financial resources and personnel today. Because I am convinced that our Catholic schools often mean the difference between future success and failure—especially for poor youths in the inner city—I have established the Big Shoulders Fund with several prominent lay leaders in order to help secure the survival and growth of our inner-city elementary and secondary schools. Those who have supported the Big Shoulders represent a broad diversity of religious, racial, and ethnic backgrounds. Together, we want to ensure that considerably more applicants will be equipped for future jobs. The future of metropolitan Chicago depends on it. So does the future of these young people.

At the same time, our schools include faith and value formation as integral components in their curriculum. In other words, we are interested both in future competent workers and effective citizens and disciples.

High schools, in particular, play a major role in the formation of young people. As teens move beyond the pale of parental influence—some more rapidly than others—they are not yet ready to make it on their own. Their reliance on peers for support and advice trades insecurity for inexperience. Catholic high schools provide a vitally needed structure and a catalyst for helping youth face the particular tasks and challenges of their age group.

Catholic schools are different from public schools. In its educational ministry the Church promotes both solid academic achievement and value or religious formation. We are concerned with the minds of our students, and also with their hearts and spirits. We want them to learn the arts and science as well as a faith and values that will provide nourishment and guidance for their lives. We want them to develop a disposition for service. We want to spark within them a passion for justice. We want to evoke their commitment to creating and building community.

We rely, above all, on Catholic higher education to help us form the kind of moral vision needed in our world today. As the beneficiaries and trustees of the Judeo-Christian heritage, we are called to demonstrate how the values of that tradition and wisdom throw light on all fields of human study and endeavor. The specific role of Catholic higher education is to enable students to think and act within a vision of life that includes the religious and moral values of our distinctive Catholic tradition.

Our institutions of higher education have the obligation to study and teach the moral and ethical dimensions of every discipline so that their graduates may fulfill their obligations in society. They do this by developing an integral moral vision and implementing it in personal and corporate or collective decision-making as well as in expressions of public opinion that seek to promote just legislation and public policies. In short, Catholic institutions should offer a curriculum that enables faculty and students to develop a personal synthesis between faith and culture that will enable them to witness to their faith before the whole world.

As the Second Vatican Council, the 1987 Synod of Bishops, and Pope John Paul's recent Apostolic Exhortation on the Vocation and Mission of the Laity in the Church and in the World have pointed out, the specific vocation and mission of the laity is to be salt, light, and leaven in the world. They are to take the message and values of the gospel, which they have interiorized in their own lives, into the workplace, the marketplace, the public arena, the home. Catholic education is the primary vehicle for helping them carry out this vital responsibility.

Just as importantly, Catholic colleges and universities must give credible witness to gospel values in their own policies and experience of authentic community. This implies that they will frequently examine their policies, programs, and practices to ensure that neither their behavior nor their language bespeaks—even subtly—the kind of exaggerated individualism or intellectual and professional myopia that undermines or belittles the common good.

It also implies that Catholic colleges and universities will foster the kind of interdisciplinary dialogue which allows scientists to talk with ethicians and philosophers, and enables all members of the community to share their individual expertise, values, and moral vision with one another.

We need to encourage an honest and mutually respectful interchange which helps us arrive at common understandings and enables us to cope with the complex realities of today's and tomorrow's world.

Finally, it implies that Catholic institutions of higher learning will sponsor and support programs and activities that allow people to experience authentic community. By that I mean a community of faith over which the risen Lord truly presides; a community which continues to incarnate, in our contemporary context, the life and ministry of the members of the first Christian community. It is a community in which all members witness to Christ's saving deeds before the entire world and work for the emergence of the kingdom he proclaimed. It is a community whose designated ministers—laity, religious, deacons, priests, and bishops—understand and accept their uniquely different but complementary and necessary roles, working together for the good of all.

It is a community whose faith in Jesus is far more compelling than any human consideration; one which honors truth more than idle speculation and bias; a community in which respect for persons rules out pettiness, unfairness, and mean-spiritedness, promoting instead dialogue, reconciliation, and unity. It is a community in which Jesus' love and mercy, his justice, his compassion and healing power are powerfully evident each day.

When Catholic educational institutions model such a Christian community and integrate gospel values into the curriculum, they help prepare their students well for the future. Because I am confident that we are, indeed, striving to do this here in the archdiocese and elsewhere, I conclude that Catholic education today is alive and well, which leads me to some final thoughts.

* * *

To prepare themselves for the future, students must know the enormous challenge of the world's needs and its problems, including those of metropolitan Chicago. They also have to be realistic about the limitations of the earth's resources and the constraints on human activities, rooted in events of the past and the realities of the present. But they also need to learn that nothing can suppress the God-given potential of human intelligence, individually or collectively, to shape a better tomorrow.

At times of great change and challenge like this, we need hope above all. Hope helps us face problems that are larger than life. It gives us courage and constancy in the face of frightening realities. Hope must be rooted in the deep conviction that we do not face the challenge of building a just and peaceful world alone.

Ultimately, for people of religious faith, our hope is based upon the belief that God is at our side, sustaining and enhancing our efforts. That makes all the difference in the world. It is the beginning and solid foundation of our hope.

We have gathered this evening in the last few months of the Eighties, in the shadow of the Nineties and, beyond them, the third millennium of Christianity. H. G. Wells was an extraordinary human being who was able to interpret the signs of the times and the trends of his world and show others what was looming on the horizon. As you know, despite the scornful criticism which it earned him, he predicted the development of tanks, air warfare, and the atomic bomb. Perhaps we should pay close attention to his words even today: "Human history becomes more and more a race between education and catastrophe."

Catholic education is well equipped to help win that race for the sake of the common good.

Religion and Spirituality

Archdiocesan Council of Catholic Men and Holy Name Societies

Chicago, Illinois

——— *May 5, 1984* ———————————————————————

May the peace of Christ, the strength of God, and the wisdom of the Spirit be with you and your families today. The Church in its prudence and loving enthusiasm invests six weeks in the celebration of Easter. I think that it is appropriate for me then to wish you a Happy Easter. My prayer is that we always know that Christ is truly risen and that we become faithful witnesses to his resurrection in all we think, say, and do.

I cannot begin to tell you how much I personally appreciate you and all that you do for God and his people. As a man I can appreciate the struggles, the pressures, the lack of support or appreciation, the loneliness sometimes that you face in your lives. And yet, faith and ministry call upon us to persevere in our work with good humor, fraternity, creativity, and enthusiasm. I suspect that, if you are like other men, you are not accustomed to reflecting on the good that you do, perhaps at times not even being aware of the impact that you are having on someone's life.

Let me explain what I mean by telling you what I experienced a few weeks ago while presiding at a Eucharist on the South Side. While I was distributing the Eucharist, a man came up with his son to receive Communion. He seemed to be a tradesman, big and brawny, with hands as rough and large as a catcher's mit. His son, who was not yet old enough to receive Communion, stood by his side watching with eyes as big as silver dollars. Since they were last in line, I was able to watch the following scenario unfold. They both went back to their pew, and the father knelt down and buried his face in his hands to pray. The son watched and watched, absolutely fascinated. He didn't know to whom his dad was talking. He couldn't figure out what was in that little white host that stopped his big, strong Dad in his tracks and moved him deeply into prayer. The little son began pulling on his dad's big arm, hoping to pry apart those hands to see what was happening inside. He was unsuccessful and finally decided, I suppose, "if you can't beat Dad, join him." He buried his face in his little hands, and they knelt there together—father and son, deep in prayer.

My brothers, that is the kind of thing you do for us so often, perhaps without knowing it. Your faith, your personal example helps so many of us to believe more deeply, to follow Christ more closely. You minister to other men in so many ways—through prayer and support groups, retreats for the unemployed, participation in Christ Renews His Parish, and in all the other parish events and ministries. Your own struggles to live out Christian values in your homes and places of employment are powerful witnesses with effects that you often do not see. In the name of God and his holy people here in Chicago, I thank you for all you have been, all you are, and all that you will, I am sure, continue to be.

There are many words that describe contemporary life in our rapidly changing and fast-paced world, but a key term certainly is *pressure*. Our lives so often seem like clusters of pressure points, areas of conflict. I am not implying that our lives are not good, but that they are complex and demanding. Certain areas and issues in life stand out in particularly stark relief. I would like this morning to reflect on these pressure points from the perspective of our faith.

My brothers, God is always talking to us. His call to a deeper life in him and with each other is constant and unavoidable. Even though at times we may try to ignore or shut out the message, God's call continues to call us to deeper life and faith. This call and how we respond to it can make an important difference in how we cope with the pressure points in our lives. We can understand these pressure points as God-given opportunities to choose between life-denying and life-enriching patterns of behavior in our lives. Our pressure points are the arenas in which our movements into sin or into grace are played out. Our pressure points are one of God's ways of engaging us in a choice between a deeper life in him and deepening patterns of paralysis and spiritual decay. When we face and probe our pressure points, we become more aware of how they are God-given opportunities for our growth. This morning I would like to (1) explore with you some of these pressure points, (2) recommend some responses that we can make as men of faith, and (3) suggest some practical strategies that will foster your spiritual development.

First, what are our pressure points, our internal concerns and struggles? One of them is intimacy. This means how we live a life of love. Do we express affection and support towards those we love? Do we know how to communicate beyond superficialities with members of our families, our neighbors and friends? Are you working at developing a more loving relationship with your wife? Is there someone with whom you can relax and be yourself, someone with whom you can share your struggles, values, concerns, and dreams? As men, do we confuse strength with silence, manliness with machismo?

My brothers, the First Epistle of John tells us that God is love, and he who abides in love abides in God and God in him. Our intimacy pressure points—the struggles we have in the areas of love, communication and closeness—are God's ways of helping us decide between patterns of isolation and patterns of connection, between sin and grace.

Another personal pressure point is the issue of self-worth and identity. Perhaps you are middle-aged and questioning whether your dreams about being the head of a corporation are a young man's fantasies and nothing more. Perhaps you are balder on the top and wider in the middle than you used to be. Perhaps you are realizing that you seem to be more vulnerable than you once thought you were. Perhaps you are in your thirties and are not the only breadwinner in the family or are finding that the bread you are earning is not enough. Perhaps you are torn between being the aggressive, competitive tough male that others seem to be and being the loving, caring, sensitive husband and father at home that your wife and family appreciate. Perhaps you are unemployed or in danger of losing your job.

What is the function of your work in your life? Are you more than your job? Who are you without work? Who are you without the material possessions you work so hard for? Each of us, my brothers, has been created as a son of God. We are precious in his eyes, unique and special. The concerns we have and the tensions we feel regarding our self-worth and identity are opportunities from God to become aware of how we are in his eyes—how we will act when we accept how much he loves us.

I have been speaking about pressure points within us. But there are also pressure points that arise in the world around us. Perhaps the most public thing we do is work. How are we being affected by our work? Let me give some examples. How does the businessman respond when pressed for the quarterly profit or the tradesman when pushed to cut material costs and building time? How does a policeman face a seemingly endless stream of violence and crime or the man in social services cope with escalating public needs and decreasing resources? On the other hand, how do we affect our fellow workers by our values, ideals and faith? Do we practice justice, truth, and love in the competitive world in which we work? That is the challenge of the gospel that engages us in our work.

Being a member of a human community creates other pressure points. The challenge is finding the time and energy to work on the issues we encounter in this human community without neglecting our families, our homes, and our jobs. On the other hand, it is difficult to avoid many of these community problems. They include the disintegration of the family unit, discrimination and racism, joblessness, world disarmament and peace, the need for a just society, Third World hunger and poverty. Although many of these problems are clearly enormous, something that we cannot solve by ourselves, that does not absolve us from facing these pressure points and coping with them in a realistic way. It is in such pressure points as these that we can find God calling us to cooperate with him in building up his kingdom of justice and peace, a place where all can live in harmony and unity.

There are also pressure points in our spiritual lives. From time to time we are called to evaluate whether there has been growth in our relationships with God and our church community. It is easy for us to separate religion from our daily lives or to reserve only Sundays and special occasions for religious or spiritual matters. It is not hard for us to allow our spiritual life to develop as an exclusive affair between ourselves and God without taking into consideration the larger community to which we belong as believers.

At the same time, each of us longs for greater meaning, feeling and depth in our prayer and worship, in our understanding and living out of faith. In these stirrings in our hearts and in the pressure points in our spiritual lives, we encounter God's invitation to deepen our Christian commitment.

Questions of intimacy, self-worth and identity, family life and jobs, social problems and our own spirituality involve pressure points in our lives. I would like to turn now to some recommendations about how we can respond to them as men of faith.

First, we need not fear them. They do not have to involve ulcer-causing worry or move our blood pressure up a few more points. The alternative is to see them as opportunities for growth. We can probe them and come to understand the struggle that they involve—the struggle between patterns of sin and grace that causes the pressure. We can learn to listen to our God who calls us to deeper life from the heart of conflict and tension. We can learn to trust these pressure points and recognize in them the agenda for growth in our life with God. In other words, we can look at them with the eyes of faith.

Secondly, as men of faith, we can share our experience of these pressure points with one another. You can make the understanding, sharing, and resolving of these pressure points the focus for your work in your various parish organizations. The Holy Name Society came to Chicago seventy years ago. Throughout its history in Chicago it has adapted itself to the ever-changing needs of the Church. Today the Holy Name Society is facing its own pressure point as it searches for its identity and task. The pressure points we are reflecting upon this morning might provide ample and appropriate agenda for your societies.

Let me suggest some practical strategies that you might adopt to develop this new agenda. Holy Name Societies have always built community among men in our parishes through poker games, smokers, softball leagues, and parish picnics. But you probably find, as so many have found, that our need for community goes deeper than these traditional means can fulfill. We are not meant to move through life alone. Your Holy Name Societies can be the forum that brings men together to minister to one another in important ways, especially by sharing and working together to cope with common pressure points and thereby grow together as Christians and as Catholics.

Holy Name Societies have always been involved in the spiritual development of their members through such means as father-son Communion breakfasts, special retreats, and Holy Hours. But again, you may find as so many have found that your spiritual needs go even deeper than these means can fulfill. Your Holy Name Societies can be the setting for individual and parish spiritual renewal. The Church is in such need of great men of faith and spirituality! Holy Name Societies can be the shapers and formers of those men.

Holy Name Societies have always addressed themselves to the social and ethical problems of their day through the Big Brother Movement, the lay apostolate, as well as parish food and clothing drives. But again our need to work for the betterment of our human community goes beyond these means, valuable though they are in themselves. Your Holy Name Societies can minister to the real areas of hurt and need in your parishes and communities. Your members have so many talents and experience. I am sure that they also have the requisite generosity to share these gifts if you enable them to serve the larger community.

This morning I wish to bless and endorse strongly all the efforts you have undertaken along these lines during the past five years. Men's Ministry to Men, Christ Renews His Parish, support groups for the unemployed, sharing groups concerned about bringing gospel values into the workplace—all of these ministries have developed as responses to pressure points. They have drawn all of you together in deeper faith and community. Through them you have done God's work in grace-filled and creative ways. My prayer is that you will continue to expand the scope of your ministry to one another.

Finally, I ask you to embrace your vocation as Catholic laymen. It is crucial for yourselves and for the Church that you do so. It is essential for you to be aware of this aspect of your life as a Christian, so that you can carry out your mission and ministry as a Christian. It is especially important for the Church at this time because of the diminishing number of

514 The Life of the Church

priests in the American Church. At its zenith in 1970, the diocesan priesthood in the United States numbered about 37,000 ordained men. By the year 2000, it is estimated that this population will only be 16,000–17,000. This would represent a decline of about 54 percent.

Equally disturbing is the trend occurring in the age distribution of the clergy. By the year 2000, those who are in the 56–75 age bracket will account for almost half of the diocesan priesthood. Another way of describing this phenomenon is to foresee that in the year 2000 we will have roughly the same number of priests as we had in 1925, but the number of Catholics will have quadrupled in the same time frame. This is certainly a pressure point for the Church! But what is God's plan in all this? What is the movement of his grace in this pressure point? What is the opportunity for growth that we face in this situation?

The answer is not entirely clear at this point, but certainly part of the answer will have to be shared by you. In the years to come the Catholic layman is going to be called to greater and deeper involvement in the ministry of the Church. The future of the Church is bound up with the exercise and expansion of your lay vocation. What the Church will be in the future will depend increasingly on you and how you grow into your ministry.

* * *

The gospel being proclaimed at our Eucharists this weekend is St. Luke's beautiful Emmaus story. It tells how two men recognize Jesus in the breaking of the bread. My prayer for all of you is that you continually recognize the Lord and grow together in him in all the ways that you break bread together in his name—in your Eucharists, in Christ Renews His Parish weekends, in your support and sharing groups, in your social functions and fundraisers. Whenever you gather, may you recognize the Lord in your midst and the great tasks of ministry to which he calls you.

I want you to know that I believe in you and I love you. My prayers and my love will go with you as you struggle as I do to go with God.

Spiritual Convocation of Priests of the Archdiocese of Newark

Newark, New Jersey
—*June 18, 1984* ————————————————

I thank Archbishop Gerety and I thank all of you, the priests of Newark, for the invitation to speak to you this evening. I have known, respected, and worked with Archbishop Gerety for a long time. And I have some very close friends among the Newark presbyterate. Two of my classmates are from this archdiocese: Mike Fitzpatrick and Frank McNulty. Then there are several colleagues with whom I worked at our Episcopal Conference in Washington. But I do not know most of you. And yet, the priesthood is the common bond that unites us; we are not strangers. So I do not hesitate to come among you this evening—as your brother, Joseph—to share with you some of the things I have learned and some of the experiences I have had during my thirty-two years of priesthood. What I say this afternoon will flow in a very special way from my experiences during the past twelve years with two truly wonderful groups of priests—those of Cincinnati where I served as ordinary for nearly ten years and, since August of 1982, the priests of Chicago.

I would like to communicate three very important, indeed essential, ideas while I am with you this evening.

First, I want you to know that I understand what you are facing in your priestly ministry, whether you are in a parish or in some special work. The day when the bishop might have lived in isolation—if indeed it ever existed—is gone. Like you, I am very much in touch with and bewildered by the structural, societal, ecclesial and personal issues that take up so much of our time and energy, and draw on our deepest reservoirs of hope. I plan to name some of these issues more specifically in a few moments.

Second, I want you to know that I do not pretend to have all the answers to the issues and questions confronting us. Like you, I am a priest because I have high ideals; because I would like to bind every wound; because I have dreams which I want to fulfill—even the impossible ones! But I repeat: I do not have all the answers. Like you and with you, I am a struggling and sometimes stumbling pilgrim. The answers we are seeking will come only after much prayerful reflection, study, and experience—all carried on in openness to the Spirit. They will come—even the partial answers—only after we have worked together collaboratively.

Third, I want you to know that I am with you. I want to be present to you, accompany you, and share with you in the search for spiritual renewal which is being celebrated here these days. This search is very much part of my own personal life and I want you to know that I stand in solidarity with you.

Overall, I hope that we might leave this place with a sense of peace and a sense of confidence in our humanity with all its fragility. For it was just in such human and fragile flesh that the Word of life came among us. Overall, I hope that we might be renewed in spirit, remembering and celebrating more clearly who we are and the greatness to which we are called.

THE ISSUES

When scholastic philosophers or theologians attacked a problem (and the word "attacked" is used deliberately), they would begin their argumentation with the *status questionis,* "the state of the question" literally but, in fact, a listing of relevant issues to be considered.

What are the issues we face as a Church? More specifically, what concerns do we encounter each day as ordained ministers? What are the issues that become the primary focus of our work day in and day out?

I will name a number of such issues, not in any particular order, nor with any pretension that it is a complete list. My purpose, rather, is to bring into focus the kinds of concerns we face, the kinds that demand our energy and attention and, at times, leave us perplexed, weary, discouraged.

Some of these issues are societal in nature. Others are also societal but they have a more direct impact on the life and ministry of the Church. Still others are rooted more in the internal life and teaching or discipline of the Church.

The Church in the United States faces issues which are part of our national shame, issues which threaten to block our path to greatness as a nation, issues which contradict the intent of the Founding Fathers of our country who held the values of life, freedom, and the pursuit of happiness so dear. I want to single out two such issues.

The first is racism which is a fundamental contradiction of our national ideals. Racism is not only a sin but a heresy because it is in fundamental contradiction to the most basic doctrines of Christianity. It is an attack on Christianity at its roots because it is a denial of the essential equality of all human beings, based on their relationship to God as their Creator and to Jesus as their Redeemer. Moreover, racism—by reducing classes of human beings to one dimension of their existence—diminishes us all.

The other is the 1973 Supreme Court decisions which, under the guise of promoting freedom and privacy, have licensed the death of countless unborn children. The mentality bred by ready access to and use of abortions diminishes all of us. For it generates a thoughtlessness about the gift of life; it encourages a self-serving ethic of convenience; and it contradicts the gospel's call to self-giving and self-sacrificing love.

As a Church we must also face, of course, the question of our planet's survival, our own survival—in the context of global conflicts and tensions. It is a massive problem, complex and seemingly insoluble. At times, it appears to be abstract and remote. But deep in our hearts, we know the issue is close to us, as close as a finger is to a button. The years ahead will demand much of us both in terms of keeping the peace and building the peace in our interdependent world.

The Church in the United States must likewise deal with a diversity which is not known in many other countries. In a very special way, it must face a growing Hispanic population. In my own archdiocese, for example, we anticipate that by the end of the century, one-half of our Catholic population will be of Hispanic origin. I do not know Newark's statistics or projections, but I believe you are experiencing something similar. The Hispanic presence is clearly not simply another wave of immigration which, of course, has been the foundation of the Church in the United States. The numbers and the continuance of cultural and language ties with the countries of origin make this a different sort of situation. The politicians are already alert to the implications of what is happening. We ought to be also. Just as numbers of American Catholics are achieving more solidly established social, educational, and economic positions in the United States, a very large group of Catholics appears and begins to grow rapidly, a group which seems to be disadvantaged in our society—socially, educationally, and economically. The Church will find itself challenged and tested to see if its reach and its embrace are wide enough to include very diverse people who all contribute to its nature as *catholica*, universal.

The Church in our country must also address issues surrounding family life and sexuality. Family life is a very fragile reality. As parish priests, we may be more aware of that fact than any other group in the nation. We know the pain and brokenness in the children of alcoholic parents. We know the agony of parents who watch helplessly as their children are drawn more and more deeply into the dead-end tunnel of drug addiction. We know the pain of husbands and wives who are unable to communicate. We know, too, the pain of separation, divorce and remarriage, all of which are complex problems that do not always have simple solutions. The solutions must be sought within the framework of the Church's teaching concerning the permanence and indissolubility of marriage. At the same time, we must minister to the separated, divorced and remarried with compassion and in the spirit of Jesus. So often we get caught in the middle, trying to balance the teaching of the gospel with human cries for understanding and help.

We know also the pain of men and women who have come to an awareness of their homosexual orientation, a pain rooted in a complex mix of convictions and emotions, ranging—sometimes in the same person—from joy and militancy to self-hatred and despair. How do we minister to them both with integrity and compassion?

Another critical issue facing the Church is that of women. As a Church we are always walking a course that is partly shaped by social forces, for ours is not a disincarnated Church. It is very much a Church of the here and now. Today there is a growing consciousness that women have been diminished, their potential not allowed to be realized, their dreams cut short by cultural biases and expectations. We have come to know that women deserve a full slice of the human pie. We still struggle to figure out how that will happen, how we might change our own consciousness so that it will mirror the gospel's plea for justice and dignity for all.

Making the issue more difficult and complicated for us is our tradition which does not permit us to admit women to the priesthood. The Church does not see this as a justice issue but one that is related to the way Christ structured the Church. The normative character of our position, however, is not accepted by many. It has become a neuralgic issue which frequently destroys the credibility of our efforts to promote the equality of women in other ways, and engages us in an adversarial rather than a collaborative relationship with many women.

As a Church we face—and this must be said frankly even if we are hesitant about articulating it—our own internal ecclesial pain and woundedness. Some of this stems from living in our time and culture. Such, for example, is the question of women who want their rightful place not only in society but also in the Church which they love. Sometimes our internal ecclesial difficulties are rooted in a lag between the momentum of the Second Vatican Council, completed nearly twenty years ago, and our lumbering way of moving toward renewal. We need to take a look at how we deal with power, authority, service, compassion, and vision in effective ways.

Related to this is the priesthood itself and, in particular, the effect that the decline in numbers is having on priests and their ministry. There are fewer active priests today and there will undoubtedly be even fewer in the years immediately ahead. The median age is rising, as are the workload and expectations which people have of priests today. We all have likewise experienced unrelenting attacks from ultraconservative as well as left-wing individuals and groups; both can be equally punishing. The ultimate issue is not conservatism or liberalism, but cruelty, manipulation, and coercion. The result of all this is that priests are tired; they are more prone to illness; often they are discouraged.

Recently, the Archdiocese of Chicago participated in a NCCB survey of pastors; some one hundred fifty-seven responded. Many were joyful and full of hope. As one said, "It is by far the most rewarding role that God could give to a human being, not only in the Church, but in life . . ."

Others, however, revealed anger, hurt, and frustration. "A pastor," one said, "gets caught in the middle of old expectations and new ones. As a result he feels guilty and gets complaints from both sides. It's an impossible role. It's hard to discern, set priorities, say 'no' without offending people." As to what might be done to help support pastors more effectively, the recommendations were as numerous as those responding; sometimes they were contradictory.

Perhaps when all the issues are laid out in this way, they become tiresome, unsettling. We know the issues of justice and peace, the growing Hispanic presence, racism, abortion, family life, sexuality, women, Church life itself. Since we know them, some may think that it is simply an exercise in discouragement to repeat them. I do not think so, however. If the point of this convocation is spiritual renewal, such renewal does not happen abstractly. It occurs, as did the incarnation, in the midst of life and especially at its most problematic and vulnerable points.

THE CHALLENGES

Let me continue with our reflection. As I do, however, I want to make a very important, decisive distinction. I want to distinguish between the *issues* we face, some of which I have listed to provide a context for my presentation, and the *challenges* which confront us. The basic challenge for us is not simply to go after the issues and resolve them. We have already admitted that we do not have all the answers. The challenges, in contrast to the issues, are *how* we face the issues—the convictions and qualities we bring as believers and as ministers of the gospel. So when we talk of challenges, we are really talking about ourselves and our response, made in faith and trust.

With this understanding, I would like to share with you four challenges. I spoke of these challenges recently to our newly ordained priests and I included them in a letter I am sending to all our priests on the feast of Corpus Christi. I believe that if we accept these challenges, they will move us beyond the particular issues and begin to locate us in the framework of faith which is, of course, the heart of the matter.

SUFFERING

The first challenge is to suffer with our people. We love as Jesus loved when we suffer with our people, for that is what he did. Like Jesus, you and I are not a cool and detached group of professional people with well-delineated parameters for our work and human involvement. The issues we have enumerated, which we face now and will continue to confront in the years ahead, speak of suffering. Like Jesus, we have to walk with our people in the valley of darkness. There is no fear in the valley, because the shepherd goes with the sheep. We need to walk the dark valley of moral dilemmas; the valley of sickness, both physical and spiritual; the dark valley of injustice and oppressive structures.

But understanding and accepting the redemptive, life-giving value of suffering in our own lives and in the lives of those we serve does not happen automatically. A precondition is that we must be intimately united with the Lord. I have been ordained thirty-two years and it took me nearly twenty-five years to realize, in the deepest part of my being, that, if I wanted to be a truly successful priest and bishop—one who could walk with my people in the valley of darkness—I had to put Jesus first in my life, not merely in theory but also in practice.

It was seven years ago—with the help of some priests, most younger and holier than I—that I learned how to pray; that I made the determination to find the time each day to devote to prayer. It was then that I let go of myself and grabbed onto the Lord. And since that time everything has changed!

Do not misunderstand: the human condition which I share with you and everyone else has not disappeared. Externally, my responsibilities—the pressures—have increased. Internally, I confront the same difficulties as before. I must come to grips with my sexuality and what it means for me as one who has committed himself to celibacy for the sake of the kingdom. I experience loneliness at times, despite a life crowded with people and events. I experience anxieties caused by a fear that I will not live up to others' expectations. My feelings are hurt when others misunderstand or criticize what I do. I am frustrated when my best efforts seem to accomplish little or nothing. I feel keenly the hurts, the alienation, the apathy of the people whom I love and serve. I am personally plagued at times by a certain spiritual dryness or aridity, a sense of abandonment—even when I am desperately searching for the Lord in prayer. I suffer a loss of morale when people seem not to notice what I am doing; when they take me for granted.

So the human condition has not changed. I experience the same difficulties as before. Suffering has not disappeared.

But something has changed! What has changed is the fact that I can deal with them better. Now it is no longer I, alone. It is the Lord and I, together. Indeed, it is my weakness and vulnerability that have become my strength because I no longer pretend that it is I who am calling the shots, or am in control, but the Lord Jesus. It is then that I understand Jesus' suffering; it is then that I understand and accept my own suffering and that of my people, a suffering that is redemptive, a suffering that has meaning, a suffering that gives life.

CELEBRATION

The second challenge we face is celebration. Together with our people, we must stop the merry-go-round on which we find ourselves. We need a *vacatio* from the many problems and issues. We have to learn how to draw on the deep memory that lies both beneath and ahead of the present moment. We ourselves need to learn how to celebrate, and we must learn how to lead others in the celebration of the Father's great "yes," spoken to us in his Son Jesus, who is the "amen" to all his promises. And when we have celebrated with our people—from the inside, that is, in spirit and in truth—we will have moved them through and beyond the particular issues. As they celebrate the ordinary and extraordinary moments of their lives in word and sacrament, particularly in the Eucharist, they will be renewed in hope, because they know that they are loved. Our leadership in celebration will become an act of saving memory for our people. For when they know that they are loved, they can continue to live and grow in life.

When we gather at the Lord's table with our people, the meaning and importance of our ministry, and all our pastoral activities, come into clear focus. In the celebration of the sacred mysteries, we see our life experiences and those of our people transformed by the death and resurrection of Jesus. That is why we bring all our hopes and joys, frustrations and sufferings to the eucharistic celebration.

As priests, we are expected to do more than simply say the words and preside over the actions of the ritual. We are called to be effective signs of Christ who is present to the people with whom we celebrate. The greater our love for the Lord and for our people, the more genuine will be our prayer, the more evident will be Christ's presence. The more aware we are of our own need for redemption and the more sensitive we are to the joys and sufferings of our people, the more profound will be our prayer of praise and thanksgiving and the more effective will be our preaching.

In the Eucharist, the Church learns what it means to be a self-giving servant. Each time we celebrate the Eucharist, we are sent forth as a "living sacrifice of praise," "to proclaim the glorious works of him who called us out of darkness into his marvelous light." This essential dimension of the Eucharist has special meaning for us as priests. For if our outreach to others becomes disconnected from the Church's sacramental life, it will lose its unique, compelling character. Our ministry will soon lose its spark, its inner dynamism, its capability continually to renew itself, unless we ourselves become the bread broken and the wine poured out for the life of the world. This is why the liturgy, particularly the Eucharist, must always be at the heart of our life and ministry. There is simply no other way.

CREATIVITY

Another great challenge "on the inside" of the issues we noted earlier is that of creativity. "Behold, I do a new thing!" the Lord says through the prophet Isaiah. The complexities of the issues can never let us lose sight of the fact that Jesus is the Lord of history, drawing all things to himself. It is truly a new thing that we are involved in. If this is so, then we cannot merely repeat conventional wisdom or hand out cliches. On the inside, we are called to the strenuous exercise of creativity, so that the power of the gospel can come alive and support people who will live in a new world.

An example of this kind of creativity, I believe, is the way our theology can be used to link the various "life" issues, some of which I mentioned earlier. Last December, in a lecture I gave at Fordham University, I stressed the need for a consistent ethic of life for our Church and our society. The idea was not really new because our Episcopal Conference has linked these issues in its Respect Life Program for a number of years. But coming in the wake of the pastoral on war and peace, my call for a consistent ethic of life captured the imagination of people. I asked for a public debate on the theme, and I got it!

I introduced this theme last December and have developed it since then in a number of talks because I am convinced that demonstrating the linkage between abortion and other issues is both morally correct and tactically necessary for the pro-life position. The convergence of themes concerning civil rights, human rights and family life with the abortion issue is simply an indication of deeper bonds which exist along the full range of pro-life issues. The proposals I have made on the linkage of issues are, I submit, a systematic attempt to state the vision which has always been implicit in a Catholic conception of "pro-life."

It is necessary to cultivate within society an attitude of respect for life on a series of issues, if the actions of individuals or groups are to reflect respect for life in specific cases. The linkage is designed to highlight the common interest and reciprocal need which exist among groups interested in specific issues—peace, abortion, civil rights, justice for the dispossessed or disabled, etc.—each of which depends upon a basic attitude of respect for life. The consistent ethic seeks to build a bridge of common interest and insight on a wide range of social and moral judgments.

This "seamless garment" approach, as it is now more popularly known, will not solve all the life issues, each of which presents a unique moral problem and requires its own moral analysis. But it will, I believe, engage the moral imagination and political insight of diverse groups and begin to build a network of mutual concern for the defense of life at every stage in the policies and practices of our society; it will, I am convinced, bring us beyond the point where we are now.

I have brought up the consistent ethic theme only as an example of the kind of creativity needed today in our ministry. Parenthetically, I am pleased to say that there has been a great deal of support for the idea. But there has also been a significant vocal opposition from some groups who either do not understand what I have been saying or simply do not want to be associated with the Church on some of the life issues other than abortion.

HEALING RECONCILIATION

The final challenge is that of continuing our ministry of healing reconciliation in all the circumstances in which we find ourselves. For all the issues have, as their common root, the sort of brokenness that we are born into when we come into the world. We desperately need the healing touch of the Lord Jesus. To the extent that we have felt in ourselves the reconciliation of our own inner conflicts and wounds—not necessarily their perfect resolution, we will succeed in mediating the healing and reconciliation which Jesus wants his people to experience, even in the midst of confusion, heartaches, and near-despair.

Since I began my ministry in Chicago, I have experienced two marvelous instances of reconciliation which I would like to share with you. They emphasize my basic point: that while healing reconciliation may not resolve all the difficulties, it gives us a new spirit and courage to carry on.

The first occurred the evening before my formal installation when I had my first encounter with the priests. I was very mindful of the fact that before my arrival there had been a considerable amount of tension and unrest. Some of it was directed against my predecessor, Cardinal Cody. Some of it had resulted in strained relationships among the priests themselves. After putting the matter in perspective and pointing out the many good things the cardinal had done for the church in Chicago, I said: "If any hard feelings, bitterness, or anger—toward the cardinal or among yourselves—remain in your hearts for any reason, tonight is the night to cast off the burden and purify your hearts. Let us continue to pray for Cardinal Cody. May he be with God even as we speak." This had an electrifying effect, accentuated by a thunderstorm that developed just as we were leaving the cathedral; it was just what the priests needed. It immediately changed the climate, though it surely did not solve all the problems, as I quickly found out! To this day, the priests talk about the powerful, purifying effect of that extraordinary evening.

The other experience was the televised mission I conducted during Holy Week, whose theme was forgiveness and reconciliation. In preparation for the mission, I asked people to send me their own experiences of reconciliation. I received more than seven hundred letters, most of them beautiful testimonies to the grace of healing and reconciliation at work in their lives. Then I received many letters after the mission. They convinced me that, even though the dilemmas of the human condition have not disappeared, people do understand that the Lord loves them and they want to be reconciled with him and with their brothers and sisters. This experience is uplifting; it gives people a new vision and direction.

SYNTHESIS: PRESENCE

The issues are many. They are complex, beyond our capacity for analysis, much less our resolution. The challenges on the "inside" of those issues also seem to be many and, at times, out of reach. But I am convinced that what our people want of us—and it is a desire, I am convinced, planted in their hearts by God—is really far simpler than what we imagine it to be. They want us to be present to them: present to them in faith, hope and love; present to them in such a way that they know that God cares and will deliver them safely home; present in a way that discloses the One in whom we live and move and have our very being.

CONCLUSION

Now I must conclude. I will do so by elaborating a little on what I said when I talked about what we must do to meet the challenges of suffering in our own lives and in those of our people.

When all is said and done, the most important thing of all—the thing that will make sense of all we are and do, or rob our lives and ministry of their meaning and vitality; the thing that will make it possible for us to suffer with and for our people, to celebrate with them, to be creative in ministry and to be healers and reconcilers—is our relationship with the Lord. In the end, the real challenge is inside ourselves: the challenge to be intimate with the Lord. My plea is that you accept this challenge. Remain close to Jesus through personal prayer and the Liturgy of the Hours, through the celebration of the Eucharist and the sacrament of reconciliation, through good spiritual reading and direction, through days of recollection and an annual retreat. Admittedly, this is old-fashioned advice. However, although some of the forms may have been different, in substance it really is not any different from that given by the Lord to his disciples.

To do all these things well, of course, requires time and rest. It demands, above all, a willingness to let go so that the Lord can take over; so that he can love us and we can love him in return. For, as Carlo Carretto asks in his wonderful little book, *Letters from the Desert,* what is the use of saying the Divine Office well, of sharing the Eucharist, if one is not impelled by love? What is the use of giving up so many things which, humanly speaking, we have every right to expect, if only to resist love? In the final analysis, we will be judged according to whether we have loved, but the ability to love will never become operative if we have not first experienced the Lord's love for us.

My plea that you give first priority to growth in intimacy with the Lord stems from deep convictions—convictions that I have developed from discussions with fellow priests over the years but, even more, from my own personal struggle each day. I can tell you that, without the Lord who is brother and lover to us all, I could not survive. And neither can you.

But growing spiritually—finding the time it takes to be truly intimate with Jesus—is very difficult, as you well know. It is so easy to become discouraged and to give up because frequently, despite our best efforts, we find nothing but a barren desert when we had our hearts set on something far more satisfying and fulfilling.

We have to develop such a hunger for Jesus that we will never give up the effort, no matter how often that effort meets with frustration because of physical or emotional fatigue, because of spiritual dryness, because of human frailty and sinfulness, because of ungodly thoughts which so often fill our minds, distracting us from the godly realities for which we are searching.

It is only when we are willing to renounce the desire to satisfy the senses that our prayer becomes strong, real, and persistent. The reason, quite simply, as Carlo Carretto reminds us, is that we meet God beyond the senses, beyond the imagination, beyond nature. But, I repeat, the struggle is not easy, because nature will try to get back its own, get its dose of enjoyment. And union with Jesus crucified, the intimacy we long to have with him, is something so different.

My brothers, if after your years together as the Newark presbyterate— whether they be few or many—you can say one thing: that you held each other accountable spiritually; that you helped each other grow in intimacy with the Lord—that will be enough. Then you will have met the challenge successfully because it is a deep spirituality—and that alone— that gives meaning and power to your life and your ministry.

Address

"The Spirituality of the Priest"

The Presbyteral Senate, Mundelein, Illinois

── *September 9, 1986* ───────────────────

"It was the best of times, it was the worst of times, it was the age of wisdom, it was the age of foolishness, it was the epoch of belief, it was the epoch of incredulity, it was the season of Light, it was the season of Darkness, it was the spring of hope, it was the winter of despair, we had everything before us, we had nothing before us, we were all going direct to Heaven, we were all going direct the other way . . ." So spoke Charles Dickens in *A Tale of Two Cities*.

Like you, I could speak about these times as the best of all, I could speak at length about the constructive and creative developments within the archdiocese and elsewhere that give us a sense of satisfaction and well-being, as well as hope for the future. I have done so in the past and will do so in the future. But life is not composed merely of hope. We must deal with reality in all its complexity.

In this context, let me tell you what is really pressing in on me. We confront difficulties and challenges today that directly affect our morale and the effectiveness of our ministry. I am concerned that we are buffeted daily by a culture that is becoming increasingly more detached from the Judeo-Christian values which shaped our society and its institutions in the past. Every day I become increasingly aware that the community of faith to which we belong has become a countercultural reality; we have become a minority. We cannot assume that values that traditionally have given meaning and credibility to our ministry and lifestyle are still operative; indeed, they are questioned and sometimes ridiculed. Gentlemen, we are at a critical stage in our priesthood.

527

It was in this context that I spoke to you on May 20 about the need to develop a deeper, more mature spirituality for priesthood. I emphasized the need for bringing into clear focus our identity as priests. Who are we? What is our role, our responsibility? And when we understand who we are, how do we respond to our personal needs as celibate men ministering in a society that is becoming increasingly secularized? I am not suggesting an exercise in narcissism, but I am saying that unless we come to grips with our own selves—unless we are able to develop as healthy human beings—our ministry will be adversely affected. There is really no dichotomy between life and ministry. The two are so intimately related that the well-being of one impacts the well-being of the other.

I told you last May that I do not have total answers to these troublesome questions. Like you, and with you, I am searching for them. Already I have spent two days with several priests of the archdiocese exploring the possibilities.

Today I would like simply to highlight certain points that must be taken into account as we pursue the matter. These realities, I believe, provide the context in which our future reflections and planning should take place. They are *trust, self-image,* need for *support and affirmation,* and the need to intensify our *prayer and spiritual life.* Each of these can be merely a pious abstraction or a source of general revitalization.

TRUST

There is a great need for deepening our faith at the practical level so that we can live more trustful lives. As I indicated a moment ago, we have all been affected by the times in which we live. The secular values that shape our modern culture have taken their toll whether we realize it or not. The mystery that forms the core of the Church and its priesthood— that marvelous intermingling of the divine and the human whose depths we will never be able to fathom totally in this life—has been obscured to the point where the Transcendent no longer gives meaning and purpose to much of what we are called to be and do.

This weakens our faith; it diminishes our trust in the Lord. We are no longer willing to "let go" because we are no longer convinced that, despite our daily trials and tribulations, the Lord is still in charge, that he loves us and has called each of us by name, and that he will never abandon us. Because we don't trust enough to let go, we do not experience his presence and power in our lives and ministry.

Lest you think that I am preaching at *you,* I'd like to share with you my own experience. Quite frankly, I must struggle each day to let go, to put total trust in the Lord. One reason, I guess, is personal pride. I am concerned that, if things don't go well, that will reflect badly on me. And this I want to avoid.

Some of it is professional or institutional pride: I love the archdiocese so much that, for the sake of our priests and people, I don't want anything to go wrong. Pride causes me to put too much emphasis on what *I* do and too little on the Lord. Pride leads me to want to "control" things so that I can make sure that everything will turn out all right. When we control things, as you know, we don't have to worry about what might happen; we simply arrange for the right thing to happen!

This lack of trust in the Lord (and, I might add, in the goodness and integrity of those around me) creates tension for me and, if the truth were known, for others. The reason is simple: There is no way in which I can or should control everything. There is no way in which I can dot all the i's and cross all the t's to my satisfaction. Our inability to control naturally causes disappointment and tension. It surely does for me and, I suspect, for you also. How foolish, then, to put so much trust in ourselves. If our predecessors had done this, much of what we take for granted today would never have happened.

Today we may be focusing too much on the human sciences in our evaluations and planning. The sociological and psychological instruments so much in vogue today must certainly be used, and we do use them. It would be foolish not to do so. But we must avoid the temptation to put all our trust in them. We must also trust in the Lord, as well as in ourselves and in others. We must leave room for Jesus' power and strength; we must be open to the movement of his Spirit. We must allow for the possibility of a change of mind and heart, for conversion.

SELF-IMAGE

Putting our total trust in the Lord does not mean that we must cultivate a poor self-image, that we must constantly demean ourselves. Quite the opposite. Since we are created in God's image and all our gifts are from him, we must acknowledge the good that is in us, even as we place ourselves totally in his hands.

In all candor, however, we must acknowledge that in recent years we have witnessed serious assaults on the image of the priest. This has quite understandably created doubts; it has, at times, caused us to lose nerve. When we should have been on the front line fearlessly witnessing to the values so dear to us, we have sometimes stayed behind, too timid to share with others the riches that are ours. Perhaps this has also made us tentative in openly encouraging others to consider the priesthood as a vocation. Sometimes priests not only feel bad about themselves, but they lose heart about the priesthood as well. As our self-image goes, so goes our sense of self-worth, our ability to witness and to recruit those who will follow us.

These assaults are sometimes made by angry people who are upset with what is happening in the Church. For them the priest becomes a lightning rod for everything that is perceived as wrong in the Church. You meet these people in your parishes and on the streets; you read their letters, whether to you personally or to the editor of the local paper, everyday.

The assaults are also made at times under the guise of combating clericalism. This in itself, of course, is legitimate because an overclericalized Church is not healthy. In reality, however, it sometimes turns out to be nothing more than an effort to diminish the value of the priesthood and priestly ministry. To overcome clericalism it is not necessary to become anticlerical. We can and should be co-responsible; we can and must welcome and encourage laity and religious, without undermining the value and importance of the priesthood. The emphasis must be on collaboration, not extinction!

It is also important to remember that these assaults are not only personal. As I intimated earlier, our secular culture does not value the priesthood because it does not measure up to the criteria for success. Our culture does not see priesthood or priestly ministry as money-making, upwardly mobile, pleasure-seeking, or sexually gratifying. Indeed, the priesthood is not and should not be oriented toward such values. Nonetheless, there is a personal cost in moving against widely held values.

So, we feel these assaults. We become defensive. We are put on the run because we feel bad about ourselves. If people tell us that we are not worthwhile long enough, we will eventually believe it. We must recognize these assaults for what they are—in effect, a kind of brainwashing—and not become entrapped by them.

In the face of a shaky image, we must recall that we are truly important—not on the level of personal grandiosity but as individuals loved by God and entrusted by the Church with a special ministry. In our personal uniqueness and in our sacramental ministry, we offer something of irreplaceable value to the world. If we don't really believe this, then why bother with the struggles of priesthood, why return to service among our people?

Let us renew and share with one another our deepest aspirations. Let us encourage and support one another in our priesthood. Such a climate will contribute to our personal fulfillment and satisfaction as priests, as well as our continued commitment to the priesthood. It will move us to celebration.

I know that many of you are positive and hopeful about the priesthood and your own ministry as priests. We need to share and celebrate that more—among ourselves and with our people.

In this connection, I wish to name and reflect briefly on two particular problems that we must see in correct perspective.

The first is that, during the course of this year, we have seen an increase in the number of priests who have requested a leave of absence. Quite understandably, this is being talked about with some alarm and considerable disappointment. I have met with each one of them, and each has his own story. Sometimes, unfortunately, the story is distorted in the gossip that seems to flourish extraordinarily well in our presbyterate, both as to the number who have gone on leave and their reasons for doing so. It is important to remember that today, more so than in the past, people go on leave for a variety of reasons—not simply as the first step toward leaving the active ministry permanently. In any case, we stay in touch with those who go on leave, and we help them in every way possible. Some will return, and, indeed, some are in the process of returning. Some will not.

However sad this phenomenon is, we must not permit it to discourage us or distract us from the overarching value and importance of priestly ministry. The departure of priests has waned in recent years, and hopefully the present increase will be only temporary. As important and serious as such departures are, they are only one piece of a much larger picture. The worst mistake we could make would be to let our focus become so locked on this particular piece that we fail to see the larger picture and lose heart. In fact a number of priests I meet are enthusiastic and positive about their ministry and find great satisfaction in what they do.

The second thing I wish to speak about is our seminaries. I do not have to remind you that, like most of the rest of the Western world, the number of men ordained in recent years is much smaller than previously. This year, however, we ordained the largest number of priests of any diocese in the United States—21. Next year, it will be 7, and the following two years the number will be up to 14 or 15.

The number of first theologians from Chicago at Mundelein this year is 8. (With the one we have in Rome, that makes a total of 9.) But this year we have begun a pretheology course of a full year's duration. Six men who, in previous years, would have entered first theology are in the new pretheology course, that is, a year of preparation in philosophy and religious studies.

This year, at the very time we are upgrading the facility, only three of the Niles' graduating class entered theology: two to Mundelein and one to Rome.

Because it has become a regional seminary, the overall number of seminarians at Mundelein this year is 149, which makes it one of the largest seminaries in the United States. However, the number of Chicago students is 53, and it should be double that.

The numbers at the Quigleys have remained fairly constant over the last few years. Both schools continue to attract a substantial number of minority students. It is still too early to tell how many of these students will persevere to ordination.

These realities have caused some to question our seminary system, that is, whether the number being ordained justifies the expense involved in keeping all four seminaries open—especially in view of the fact that approximately half of those currently in the theology program come from outside the system.

This is a legitimate question. I would like to make several observations which I hope will help to put the matter in perspective. There are a number of positive developments that should give us encouragement and hope.

First, I appointed a Task Force to design a process that will evaluate what we have at present and indicate what directions we should go in the future. In the terminology used by academic institutions, this is called "strategic planning." Such planning is aimed at using limited resources in the most productive way possible to accomplish the goal of the system: to ordain more priests for the archdiocese each year. The Task Force has completed its work, and I will present its recommendations for the development of a strategic plan to the Board of Trustees of the seminaries at their meeting later this month. I am confident that the board will approve it, at least in principle, since it was the board itself that emphasized in a previous meeting the need for such planning.

Second, a number of other initiatives have been undertaken to ensure that we put our best foot forward in the future. The program at Niles, for example, has been refocused, with the unanimous approval of the faculty, which we are confident will bode well for the future. The recent visitation of the seminary by the Pontifical Commission was very helpful, providing us with both the occasion and the motivation to make changes that will emphasize to a greater degree the seminary character of the college and place more emphasis on spiritual growth and development. (At this point we have not received the final report and recommendations from the Holy See; the changes we have undertaken are the result of our own convictions in the matter.) Fifty-one students have entered Niles. Thirty-nine of these went through the Quigleys. The senior class numbers 42, and the prospects for Mundelein at this point are good. The total enrollment is 178.

Our program to encourage and attract men for theology who have not gone through our system continues and, indeed, has been intensified. In the past year contacts have been made, through the ministry weekends and parish priests, with a number of excellent candidates, a number of whom will enter Mundelein in the next year or two.

Finally, our vocation office is developing a new program for the archdiocese which will be more parish-based than in the past. While the central office can provide many helpful materials and services, in the final analysis vocation awareness and recruitment must take place at the local level where the young people actually are. Part of the new program will be to encourage and motivate parish ministers, especially priests, to become more active in vocation awareness and recruitment. It will take a year or two to develop the full program, but we are very enthusiastic about it and confident that it will give a new impetus to our vocation efforts. The role of each of you and the priests that you represent is critical to the development of this program. I cannot emphasize enough the responsibility each of us must bear for fostering vocations to the priesthood.

NEED FOR SUPPORT AND AFFIRMATION

Each one of us needs support and affirmation, whether we admit it or not. Moreover, a number of priests have told me, and I am inclined to agree, that we need a better system of supporting and affirming each other.

The difficulty is that too often we tend to think that giving affirmation is someone else's responsibility. But if we all look to someone else, no one will ever do it. The solution, quite simply, is that each of us must be willing to support and affirm one another.

One problem may simply be that we are too bashful or we feel too awkward to do it. Sometimes we may be afraid that our sincerity will be questioned. Whatever the obstacle, we need to talk about it more; we need to learn how to give affirmation and support in a relaxed, credible way.

Two weeks ago a young priest told me this story. He had attended the funeral of Jack Sweeney. In my brief remarks before the commendation and farewell, I had encouraged the people to love and affirm their priests. He said that, when he returned home later in the day, it suddenly occurred to him that, although I was speaking to the laity, what I said applied also to priests. So that night he called all his friends to tell them that he cared for them and wanted to support them. Half of the ones he called, he said, asked whether he was drinking or whether he had flipped. Despite this initial reaction, he sensed the men appreciated the call. In any case, he told me that the calls did him a lot of good!

This reluctance to affirm and support people is not confined to the priesthood. Many marriages go sour and ultimately break up, for example, because of a lack of communication and affirmation. In the United States, our culture and our upbringing have made it difficult especially for men to engage in mutual affirmation and support. It is not in keeping with the "macho" image that we sometimes feel obligated to maintain.

As I was reflecting on this, it occurred to me that, like so many other people, we seem to be very adept at gossip within our own ranks. Are we more prone to spread bad news than good news about our brother priests? That's not only hurtful but also strange, since, as priests, we are expected to proclaim the gospel, the *Good* News.

I personally am not reluctant to admit that I need affirmation. I am happy to say that many of you have given it to me, and for this I am deeply grateful. I want also to affirm and support you. I do try. Sometimes, however, I get caught up in the press of things and fail to do it. It's difficult when you are on the "fast track," as we all are.

Perhaps the best thing we could all do is slow down, relax a little. Then we would have the time and energy to become reacquainted with each other, the time to share our joys and sorrows, our doubts and frustrations. Then out of that deeper, more intimate relationship would emerge the understanding and support that we all need so much.

THE NEED TO INTENSIFY OUR PRAYER/SPIRITUAL LIFE

As priests, we are called to a ministry of prayer. We are expected to lead people in public prayer and engage in personal prayer ourselves. The Church expects this of us, and our people want it. Not to be, or not to be perceived as, men of prayer greatly diminishes the effectiveness of our ministry.

Seen in this light, prayer is not merely a matter of personal luxury. It is not simply private time, time taken *away* from our ministry. Quite the opposite: it is indeed an indispensable part of our ministry. As one priest told me recently, "When I pray, the meter is on because I *am* ministering when I pray."

How do we encourage the development of our prayer life? How do we intensify our spiritual growth in a culture that places so much emphasis on the quick fix, the tangible, the attraction and indispensability of material things? Let me mention several ways.

First, a good annual retreat is essential for spiritual growth. Some priests have told me that they do not need to withdraw from their ministry to recoup their focus and spiritual energy. That is simply not true; they are fooling themselves. If Jesus retreated from his public ministry to restore his spiritual strength, so must we.

There are many opportunities available to us now. I particularly want to commend Bob Ferrigan for the great work he has done at our diocesan retreat house. Just the other day he wrote a note to tell me about a directed retreat which was made by eighteen of our priests. He said that it was a marvelous experience. Later one of the priests who made the retreat told me the same thing.

We must hold each other accountable in this regard. To put it another way, we must challenge each other to take a spiritually productive retreat, at least once a year. I personally have given a high priority to the Cardinal Stritch Retreat House for this very reason.

Second, spiritual direction on a continuing basis is essential to spiritual growth. We need the insights and the objectivity of someone other than ourselves. The difficulty is that often we are not inclined to give spiritual direction to each other, although we have no difficulty giving it to lay people. While I support priests obtaining formal training in spiritual direction (and many have done so in recent years), such training is not the only avenue to brotherly assistance. What is needed is a greater willingness to help each other in this regard, a greater willingness to give each other time to listen with care and compassion, to reflect with honesty and trust, and to encourage one another's best instincts.

Finally, we cannot talk about spirituality without taking into account our sexuality. Is sexuality a problem? A challenge? A joy? A mess? In my experience, it is all of the above! Its many facets in our lives are anchored in the reality that sexuality is an important and integral part of our identity and our lives.

We are men—men who experience all the phases of human growth and personal integration: men who profess a central commitment to the Lord and who, for that very reason, are invited and trusted to share many of the deeper moments of others' lives. We are celibate *and* relational, and both are dynamic realities we grapple with and grow into day by day. We cannot turn away from this challenge—whether we find it problematic or joyful or messy. And it will be all of these at various times in our lives.

Unfortunately, the focus in the public forum is on the discovered breach of priestly, celibate commitment, especially the more dramatic and tragic instances. Such occasions dishearten us anew; they further erode respect for the priesthood; they feed suspicions—in our sexually drenched culture—that no celibates are faithful. But these instances also warn us of the necessity of integrating our sexuality and our spirituality. To suppress or pretend or ignore this dimension of our lives can invite later tragedy.

We are not, of course, the first generation of priests to discover our sexuality, although sometimes we—and others—talk that way. Nonetheless, we must address the question in the context of *today's* world with all its pressures and countervalues. And we must do so from a spiritual perspective, not only from a psychological one.

It is my intention, during the coming year—after the current overnights with priests are over—to call you together again, in similar sessions, to reflect on our spirituality in its many dimensions including our sexuality. I know of nothing more important for our well-being, and I intend to give it a high priority.

* * *

My dear brothers, I recently came across a prayer for priests which made such an impression on me that I have used it everyday since. May I offer this prayer for you?

> Risen Lord Jesus, you love us with all your priestly heart.
> Hear my heartfelt prayer for my brother priests.
> I pray for faithful and fervent priests,
>> for unfaithful and tepid priests,
>> for priests who labor at home and abroad,
>> for tempted priests,
>> for lonely and desolate priests,
>> for young priests, old priests, sick priests,
>> for dying priests, and
>> for the souls of priests in purgatory.
> Merciful Jesus, remember that we are but weak and frail human beings.
>> Give us a deep faith, a bright and firm hope,
>> and a burning love.
> I ask that,
>> in our loneliness, you comfort us;
>> in our sorrow, you strengthen us;
>> in our frustrations, you show us that it is through suffering that
>> the soul is purified.
> Eternal high priest,
>> keep us close to your heart,
>> and bless us abundantly,
>> in time and in eternity.
>>> Amen.

Priests of the Diocese of Fort Wayne–South Bend

Warsaw, Indiana

— *March 7, 1990* ————————————————

I thank Bishop D'Arcy for this opportunity to speak to you this morning. I am delighted to be here. I have come both to encourage you and to be encouraged by you.

You are dedicated priests, servants of the gospel of our Lord Jesus Christ. You proclaim God's word in the pulpit, in the sick room, in the classroom, in the office. You give the Bread of Life to children for the first time, and to the dying for the last time as their viaticum. You nourish your people with the Eucharist each Sunday. In a broken world, divided by sin and injustice, you are ministers of reconciliation. You celebrate God's loving forgiveness sacramentally. And you extend that reconciliation as you counsel families, work for community harmony, and sensitize people to the need to work for justice and peace. In the Liturgy of the Hours you are united with ordained ministers and many religious and lay people throughout the world, fulfilling the Lord's precept to pray without ceasing, at once offering to God the praise of the entire community of faith and interceding for the salvation of the world.

You are called "Father," and rightly so, because you generate and protect life. Through the sacraments of initiation you introduce people to new life in Christ. You anoint the sick and bring healing of soul and spirit to the ill. You defend life by supporting the rights of the unborn, the young, the abused, the handicapped, the sick, the elderly, and the dying.

I could go on, but, for now, I will stop. Simply to enumerate—in a very incomplete way—what you do is itself very impressive and even immeasurable by ordinary human standards. But it is, indeed, more awesome to consider *whom you and I represent*: the Lord himself. For although we are involved in many particular activities, one thread unites them all and gives them a unique character. That thread is Jesus, for it is in him, whose priesthood we share, that we discover our own specific identity as priests of the New Covenant. Like Jesus, we are chosen, anointed, and sent forth to proclaim the Good News of salvation.

We are instruments who minister *in persona Christi*. We are like Paul who identified himself as an ambassador of Christ. And precisely because we represent the risen Lord, we are representatives of the Church which continues his mission and makes him present and accessible in word, sacrament, and service.

In the midst of our busy lives, our struggles and questions, as well as the stress and strain of pastoral ministry, we need to pause regularly to grasp more deeply *what* we are about and *whom* we represent. We need to know and reaffirm that what we do and who we are is of immense significance to a broken world—at times, all the sadder and more broken because it does not recognize its own sad plight.

At a time of ecclesial renewal with its attendant turmoil and questioning, at a time when we might entertain self-doubts unimaginable a mere twenty years ago, we need to spend some precious moments reflecting and reaffirming who we are and what we do.

This gathering of priests is a celebration of God's continuing provident care of the world through the ministry of his priests. My brothers, recognize and acknowledge this. Rejoice in it. Be grateful for it.

It is sometimes said that when priests and other ministers gather today, "seldom is heard an encouraging word." I want to break that pattern clearly and definitively. And I do that by affirming, with great conviction, that you *are* important, that what you do has great and even eternal significance for this world of ours.

But what do we priests need to sustain us? What carries us through hard times, unrewarding moments, trying situations? The answer is clear, but not simple. *Our spiritual lives sustain us.* When we consciously walk by God's Spirit; when our hopes are fixed on God's grace, not our own efforts; when our lives and ministry end in surrender, not in attempts to control them—then we are living "spiritual lives."

As you know so well, there are many approaches to the spiritual life. This morning I will focus on a particular dimension which has special relevance for us priests: the need for *inner balance*.

The ancients spoke of *aurea mediocritas*, which is literally but incorrectly translated as "golden mediocrity." The real sense of the phrase is a "golden balance," that is, an enriching and complex attitude and spirit about life that keeps us poised and reflective even when we are in motion. Inner balance is necessary for the outer balance of a gymnast on a crossbar, for example, who traverses confined space with incredible ease and grace. Golden or inner balance is the gyroscope of our hearts that keeps us poised and reflective—in conflict, in hardship, in struggle, and even in success!

As I explore this concept with you in greater depth, I assure you that it is not a detached discourse, a merely theoretical exercise. No, I personally struggle daily to learn the art and style of inner balance, so that I may serve my people well, with ease and grace. The categories which I will describe are windows to my soul. But in the end, you and I are, I'm sure, more alike than unalike, so these are windows to your souls as well.

THE INNER BALANCE OF SHAMAN AND PRIEST

In his wide-ranging interviews with Bill Moyers, Joseph Campbell spoke of many things concerning religion. At one point, he made a distinction which is well-known in the study of comparative religions—that between a shaman and a priest.

A *shaman* is a person who has had an intense and often ecstatic—even mystical—religious experience. This experience is completely personal and, at the same time, the foundation for the shaman's future role in the community. For, on the basis of this intense personal religious experience, the shaman exercises a role of religious leadership and guidance for others.

The *priest*, on the other hand, is a person who hands on the received tradition. The priest is responsible for the proper exercise of prescribed rituals, making sure that all is correct and in conformity with the tradition. The priest hands on what is given, is immersed in his people's timeless rituals, and thereby is a source of continuity within the community.

If we were to translate the categories of shaman and priest into scholastic categories, we might say that the shaman functions *ex opere operantis* and the priest does so *ex opere operato*.

In the history of other religions, one was *either* a priest *or* a shaman. But the ordained or hierarchical priesthood of Jesus Christ in the Catholic tradition is unique because *both* dimensions are combined in our priestly ministry. We serve as both shaman and priest. We serve from the profound religious and spiritual experiences which are deeply personal, while, at the same time, we also serve as vehicles of our tradition, handing on what we ourselves have received.

From another perspective, we are called to *creativity* and *routine*. Yes, we must be creative in adapting to new circumstances and developing our vision of pastoral ministry in light of our spiritual experience. We exercise this creativity when we guide a parish or school or serve in a chaplaincy. But we also serve in the midst of routine—not routine in a bad or boring sense, but in the repetition of rituals, the return to basics in our proclamation of God's word, the faithful following of the Christian life cycle of birth, growth, reconciliation, marriage, aging, sickness, and death.

We are called to an inner balance of our roles as shaman and priest, drawing from our personal spiritual experiences *(ex opere operantis)* and drawing from the perennial and assured presence of God in our traditions of faith and sacrament *(ex opere operato)*. A failure to maintain such a balance can jeopardize the effectiveness of our ministry.

THE INNER BALANCE OF BEING COMMUNITY BUILDERS AND SOLITARIES

There has been considerable discussion of the particular charism of the diocesan priest. What marks us as special or unique? From a theological point of view, our collaboration with the diocesan bishop in the care of people within a given geographical area may be the center of our "charism," or, at least, this seems to be indicated in Vatican II's Decree on the Ministry and Life of Priests. Yet, from an experiential perspective, the more immediate and, at times, overwhelming sense of diocesan priesthood is our immersion in the lives of our people. We are with people of all kinds, ages, sizes, shapes, racial and ethnic backgrounds—in sickness and health, in poverty and prosperity, until death do us part.

As pastors, we are particularly concerned about building and nurturing a parish community. It is in our ministerial bones to know that the people around us are not simply a randomly assembled mass, nor are they merely a functional unit of some sort. No, the people we serve are called to be a community, a living organism of knowledge and love. This is my deepest experience of the Church: people gathered together with a rich heritage of the past, with present struggles and celebration, with a future hope. It is a community and a way of life which depends totally on God's grace and our free human response. That is how the Church represents the presence of the body of Christ in the world.

So many of our pastoral efforts center on bringing people together. So many of our satisfactions rest in the ways that is achieved. So many of our frustrations stem from the difficulties of binding a disparate community together. In short, so much of our outer life and inner concern focuses on people and the building of community.

But there is also another side to us. Because of our celibate commitment and our unique form of religious leadership, we also stand alone. So, at the same time, we are community-builders *and* solitaries.

At its best, our solitude has little or nothing to do with a stultifying loneliness that is perceived as imposed and draining. As one writer has recently said, our solitude is a return to self. I would add, it is a return to self *in God*. This solitude is a powerful source of our pastoral energy and creativity, for in this solitude we are in touch with God who is power and life.

Attention to, and cultivation of, the inner balance between community and solitude is no simple matter. We may feel a bit odd about ourselves at times. We *are* odd, at least different. Most people do not share our experiences of the radical shifts between being immersed in community and in solitude. We struggle with our balance between the two. Our commitment to our people often seems to pull us away from deep and real solitude. We feel guilty for the time "stolen away" from them. Yet, when the balance is broken—or, even more fundamentally, not dealt with—our lives and our ministry are diminished.

THE INNER BALANCE OF BEING HEARER AND PROCLAIMER OF THE WORD

The ideal male in the U.S.—according to the tradition developed in Western movies—is an independent individualist. The Lone Ranger does not need help and support from the outside. He can rely on himself. He is active, not passive. He moves forward with little or no reflection, because he is so sure of what he is doing.

For us priests, it must be different. We are both active and passive. We are *doers*, but also *receivers*. It is necessarily so because we are *hearers* of the word just as we are *proclaimers* of the word.

I frequently return to Thomas Aquinas's definition of preaching which is also the motto of the Dominicans: *contemplata aliis tradere*—to hand on to others what we ourselves have contemplated. Proclamation, according to Thomas, is clearly an action. It is a handing on of the word. At the same time, it is rooted in the prayerful, contemplative reception of that same word.

In order to cultivate an inner balance of receiving and giving, we have to break cleanly with cultural biases which prize independent action and depreciate or discount reflection.

The inner balance of hearing and proclaiming the word can also be expressed in another way. We are to listen and celebrate. Learning to listen attentively is no simple matter, as we well know. It takes work—the fatigue that follows counseling sessions attests to this fact. Our fundamental listening is tuned to the word of God in the Scriptures, the Church's doctrinal and spiritual and ethical tradition, and the experience of our people. In all of these listening places, we perceive and receive what we are to proclaim. We celebrate the word we have received. We help people to notice and identify God's word, to accept it gratefully, to rejoice in it.

Inner balance involves learning how to receive and proclaim faithfully the very word of God.

THE INNER BALANCE OF BEING A MAN OF GOD AND A MAN OF THE PEOPLE

There is a wonderful, but frightening scene in the book of Numbers. God resolves to destroy the people of Israel because of their infidelity. But Moses bargains with God. Moses argues the people's case. Remember that this is the same Moses who slammed down the tablets of the Law in anger at the idolatrous infidelity of the same people. In this instance, however, God relents, and Moses returns to lead his rebellious, unruly people.

Moses' example symbolizes both the inner balance—and tension—of being both a man of God and man of the people. Often we may feel that we walk the intercessory razor's edge between God and people.

We are men of God. We proclaim his kingdom, uphold his justice, issue his invitation, recite his praises. We are walking, breathing symbols of the presence of transcendent mystery in this world. The Curé of Ars once said, "Oh, the priest is something great; if he knew it all, he would die!" Surely we know better than anyone else that we are earthen vessels, chipped and marred, but we hold a precious treasure nonetheless, and it is the Lord.

Spiritually and psychologically, this means that we have been swept up by a mystery infinitely greater than ourselves. We are not simply our own person. We have claimed the Lord as our inheritance, or, better, he has claimed us as his inheritance. Ecclesially, this means that we are called not only to do the things that priests do but also to live a life of consistent witness to the transcendent mystery of God for whom we speak and whose praise we lead in the assembly. This witness has many ramifications for our lifestyle: how we speak, what we wear, how we deal with money, how we treat people—the list is endless.

The other side of this balance is that we are also men of the people. We are brothers to the men and women we serve. We come from them. We return to them in service. Our human condition is clear and evident. Furthermore, we do not render priestly service apart from our own humanity. Our model and pattern are found in the incarnation. God could have chosen to save the human family from without. Instead, with mysterious wisdom and love, he decided to redeem humanity from within: "And the Word was made flesh and dwelt among us." This is our model of priestly life and service. It can never be an evasion of the human condition or experience. It must always be an authentic immersion in all that is human. We serve, as Jesus served, in solidarity with our brothers and sisters in the human family.

If this is so, there are many implications for us. Such a vision of service means, for example, that clericalism—a distancing and privilege-seeking style of life—is utterly incompatible with the gospel model of service. To serve from within the human family, to be truly a man of the people, implies that we are not only curious about the human condition, but willing to explore its intricacies, grasp and identify with its questions and pain.

Moreover, to serve from within the human family, to be truly a man of the people, requires a style of ministry which can only be described as collaborative. Although the word "collaboration" is so overused that it tends to become mere ministerial jargon, it has deep theological underpinnings. Ministry is not simply the execution of a task or function; it is also directed toward greater communion with God and one another in God. It follows, therefore, that collaboration and the building of wholesome relationships belong to the very essence of ministry; it is not simply an optional touch of frosting.

It is a challenge of inner balance to be both men of God and men of the people. The two are not in conflict, but they do express polarities of our ministerial lives which must be reconciled, in harmony with each other.

THE INNER BALANCE OF BEING A PROPHET AND A RECONCILER

People tell me that one of my contributions to the Church is that, by nature, I am a good *reconciler*. That is, indeed, one of the great hopes of my pastoral ministry. I do try to bring people together. But, while this is a particularly important dimension of my ministry, I am certainly not unique in this regard.

Contrasted to this ministry of reconciliation is *prophecy*. The reconciler brings people together and facilitates healing when that is necessary and possible. The prophet, however, stands clearly for the truth which he proclaims boldly. An authentic prophet or teacher preaches God's message, not his own. As ministers of the word, we too must remember that it is the Lord's gospel we preach, not our own. Certainly we must use all our talents to present the message entrusted to us in the most creative, compelling manner possible. But in doing so, we must be careful not to distort this message in any way. This requires intellectual honesty and humility. It also demands fidelity to the teaching authority of the Church, which has from Christ the responsibility of handing on his message in all its richness and without error. Preaching the gospel in its full integrity is not always easy. The gospel challenges people's complacency; frequently it upsets their consciences. A prophet's words, often sharp and incisive, are often more like a knife than a soothing ointment. The prophet calls people to decision and, therefore, sometimes divides them.

Reconciler or *prophet*, which is it to be? While our nature or personality may lead us in one direction or the other, the two are not contradictory; neither are they optional alternatives. Our priestly ministry involves both. We are both healers who reconcile and prophets whose message sometimes divides.

There are times when both are in play. For me, this has been the case with the various life issues and my commitment to develop what I have called a consistent ethic of life.

I feel strongly—indeed, passionately—about the precious worth and inviolability of every human life from the moment of conception to natural death. Abortion is a terrible evil that multiplies its effects in the diminishment of respect for life and the rending of the social fabric of this nation. I am firmly convinced that we must speak the truth about the right to life, especially the right to life of those who are most vulnerable and least protected: the unborn, infants, the poor, the elderly, the developmentally disabled, and the dying. Our prophetic responsibility is to speak to the evils of this age, to expose them, to proclaim the truth in an integral, responsible way. If that proclamation divides us from people who make a choice against life, if they feel they must walk away from us, that is their choice and responsibility.

Nevertheless, I also want to bring people together on the life issues. I am convinced that people of good will can find in our natural law tradition and the consistent ethic of life guides for protecting and nurturing all human life. My dream in this pluralistic society is that we will recover a deep sense of the first right, the right to life.

So, just as I am clear about our convictions in regard to life—convictions that are rooted in both faith and reason—I also invite others to a mutually respectful dialogue—not to diminish or water down the truth, but to give it greater exposure—to inspire others to join us in working for legislation that will defend and enhance human life. In short, I will state the truth *and* I will do everything possible to keep the conversation going.

To be both prophet and reconciler is, I can attest, a soul-wrenching enterprise. It requires an inner balance of the two. And from that inner balance will emerge the appropriate responses at the right times, in the right circumstances—the responses of clear teaching and honest dialogue.

THE INNER BALANCE OF BEING SERIOUS AND LIGHTHEARTED

Recently, I heard of someone who had to undergo some surgery and delicate medical treatments in Chicago. When the patient heard that his attending physician was a Hindu, he panicked. Why? Because he knew of the

Hindu belief in reincarnation. He thought to himself that the doctor might not take his case too seriously. If the doctor failed and his patient died, the doctor would simply assume that the patient would be reincarnated in some other person or form. The patient began to think that it would be better to have an atheist physician who believed that all we have is this life! Then he would apply himself more diligently to saving the patient's life.

This story illustrates the need for another kind of inner balance. We certainly need to take ourselves, one another, and, of course, God seriously. Life is not merely a game. Our belief about human freedom places great responsibility in our hands. Our ministry as priests is very significant, even decisive for many people. There ought to be alive in our hearts a deep appreciation for the greatness of the task to which we have been called. There is no room for flippancy or waffling commitments. Priestly ministry is a matter of the whole mind, the whole heart, the whole soul.

At the same time, there is a heaviness that comes from a misplaced sense of responsibility, as if we were *ultimately* responsible for the salvation of people. Such misplaced responsibility is really a manifestation of exaggerated self-importance and, sometimes, willful control over people and situations.

The fact is that our lives and ministry are quite serious and significant and, at the same time, completely in God's hands. We are not only called to do certain things; we are also the gifted recipients of God's favor. From that stems another inner attitude of heart and soul: confident joy which manifests itself in a lightheartedness. This has nothing to do with bland superficiality. Rather, it is quiet confidence that allows us to laugh at ourselves, to sleep at night, to enjoy our ministry. This was the secret of many of our saints.

The balance of seriousness and lightheartedness is not easy to achieve, but it is essential. In a practical way, it demonstrates how we live our doctrinal convictions about the interplay of divine grace and human freedom.

THE INNER BALANCE OF RAISING QUESTIONS AND OFFERING ANSWERS

Sometimes the greatest service we can provide our people is simply to raise questions. Must people be content to live with anger? Do nations have to wage war against one another? Is sexual activity really necessary for human happiness? Why do we have poor, homeless, hungry people in a nation with such great abundance? Can anyone find fulfillment apart from God?

These questions are at the heart of a ministry that cares for people and is not content to leave them alone in their assumptions and in the pervasive convictions of our culture. We are countercultural when we turn over the biases and presuppositions of our culture with our questions.

We ourselves need questioning minds and hearts before we can raise questions for others. We can take nothing for granted. In prayer and our study of God's word, we confront the truly important questions: Who is God? What is life about? What is our future? How ought we to act toward one another?

At the same time, we have answers. We hold truth. We see a future hope. We walk a clear path. There is no arrogance in our approach to providing answers to people. Our own limitations and continuing questions spare us from that. But the clarity of our tradition and our conviction of the presence of the guiding Holy Spirit impel us to speak.

Raising questions and providing answers begins within each of us. It begins with the inner balance of searching and finding, raising questions and offering answers.

* * *

There are so many things to say about priestly life and ministry. This morning I have limited my reflections to the need for various kinds of inner balance.

When we begin to see and accept the polarities of our inner life, when we engage them in dialogue with one another, then there will be integrity and wholeness to our ministry. We will be even more faithful, because we will follow the example of Jesus himself: creative shaman and fulfiller of the law, community builder and solitary, listener of the Father and speaker of the word, Son of God and Son of Man, reconciler and prophet, someone who was serious in purpose and joyful in hope, asker of questions and one who offered great answers. In him is the pattern and the fulfillment of our priesthood.

Address

Second Monday Club of O'Hare

Chicago, Illinois

—— May 14, 1990 ————————————————————

I am very happy to be with you this afternoon, and to have this opportunity to share some reflections with you. I will speak to you from the heart, out of my own experience as a pastoral leader. As you will see, I share many of the same pressures, problems, and concerns that you experience each day. I trust that my reflections will be pertinent to your own lives.

Allow me to begin by acknowledging that I lead a hectic, demanding, fast-paced life. You will have no problem identifying with this. While metropolitan living often involves running in the "fast lane," the pace noticeably accelerates and the pressures escalate in the O'Hare community.

What's it like in the "fast lane"? We rush from one project to another, from one fire to another, from one meeting to another, and, often, through appointments and phone calls at a dizzying rate. We have instant access to diverse modes of communication: car phones, FAX machines, electronic mailboxes, and the ever-present xerox machines. We can keep track of traffic patterns and obstacles and stay in contact with our office or home while we drive along the freeways, competing with others for the even faster lanes.

Last Thursday morning I witnessed a small symptom of our preoccupation with speed. Radio news reporters were covering the aftermath of Wednesday night's significant rainfall. More specifically, they were primarily reporting on its effects on traffic patterns. One report, in particular, started me thinking. It involved a fairly detailed coverage of a pothole that had seemingly been greatly enlarged by the storm. The reporter eventually concluded that the obstacle was probably lengthening the travel time of many people by a whopping four and a half to five minutes. I wondered what people in the developing nations or in Eastern Europe would think of such a detailed analysis of a fairly insignificant fact! On the other hand, I also mused about how many commuters might have decided to take an alternate route to avoid "wasting" five minutes out of the 1,440 minutes of that day.

What happens in our fast-paced lives? Too often, I find myself thinking that there simply is not sufficient time to think through, in an adequate way, all the options that deserve consideration in coming to an important decision. Too often, I find myself lacking the energy to treat each individual who comes into my office, or each phone call that summons me, or each letter that crosses my desk, with the personal care and time each deserves. It isn't that I don't want to invest myself; and it isn't that I don't try, for I do. It's simply a characteristic of life in the "fast lane" that seems to exclude some of the behavior I most value.

Another consequence of a busy life is that there is seldom what I would call "recovery time" built into my schedule. That is, time to relish a project well done; time to digest a tough decision made; time to analyze and learn from a mistake. There isn't time to break away from the crush of day-to-day responsibilities in order to get a firmer grasp on the larger picture, the overall direction. There isn't time simply to be with my thoughts and feelings, to let them develop at their own pace. Always, there is the next project, the next decision, the next crisis, the next presentation to deal with.

A third deficit in a busy life is the scarcity of opportunities simply to sit with trusted friends—quietly over dinner, or through a relaxed evening— to share our stories; to compare our struggles; to rediscover our common values, hopes, and dreams, in a way that would give us all greater strength, firmer resolve, and renewed enthusiasm for days to come.

I do not mean to imply that such occasions are totally missing from my life. If that were true, I would long ago have ceased to be able to function effectively. Nor do I want to give the impression that what I am describing is somehow the result of my particular vocation to the priesthood, or to my celibate lifestyle. I do not believe that to be true. Rather, I suspect the experience I have described is part of the reality of life in the "fast lane" in any field. It may well be part of the experience of many of you here this afternoon, regardless of your vocation or lifestyle.

Still, we manage. Somehow, we are able to put aside our frustrations and attend to the matter at hand. Somehow, we are able to juggle multiple concerns, and handle them all with some expertise. Somehow, we are able to go from detail to detail with only a sketchy sense of the bigger picture, and still remain true to the values or goals which underline and shape our life's work. Somehow, we manage to be fairly successful—by whatever standards our individual professions use to judge us.

If we had more time together this afternoon—time to compare notes and swap life stories—we would probably learn how much we have in common with one another. Such experience would strengthen us in our particular roles and create a greater sensitivity for those who, in one way or another, are influenced by our lives and work.

Unfortunately, as I mentioned, it is just that sort of heart-to-heart sharing that seems characteristically absent in the executive lifestyle. In the Catholic Church in Chicago, that need has been recognized in the last several years by many individuals who have sought out opportunities to gather regularly with others like themselves to probe the values by which they function. For some men and women, these opportunities are the first real chance to unburden themselves of pressures that have built up for years; the first chance to hear the supportive words of others who share their struggle—to live worthwhile lives, to find the fairest compromise, to be faithful to deeply held convictions.

As a result, there is a growing conviction that such opportunities for sharing should be at the top of the list of those demands which leadership must assume in the years to come. Rather than seeing such sharing as an occasional luxury, in a complex world such as ours it must be a regular feature of any busy person's life, especially of any leader who intends to survive.

While such sharing with others in like positions of leadership is becoming quite essential, it is also important to seek out and ensure adequate contact, on a regular basis, with many different groups. There are too many artificial distinctions of race, nationality, and socioeconomic standing in our society. One of the great pitfalls of leadership is to become isolated from those who are or appear to be different, to allow an image or stereotype to blind us to the essential bonds we have in common, to allow our position or status to become a barrier between ourselves and those who do not have a similar position.

Another unique demand on anyone who wants to do more than merely survive in a fast-paced lifestyle is a commitment to investing time—significant amounts of time—for personal reflection. Whether one views this demand from a religious perspective, and speaks in terms of the upsurge of interest in prayer and meditation—or views it from a secular perspective, and simply identifies it as a need for solitude or reflection—there seems to be an ever greater need for time away from a busy schedule; time to gain perspective, refocus energy, rekindle drive.

About thirteen years ago, I came to understand that the pace of my life and the direction of my activity were unfocused, indeed uncentered in a significant way. I am not talking simply about the organization of time and energy for efficient work. The issues were really problems of the spirit, that is, I found myself anxious, fragmented, and in need of inner healing. Through the assistance of others who had already passed through this kind of personal journey toward healing, wholeness, and inner peace, I came to understand that I, too, had to make some important changes in my lifestyle.

It would be difficult for me to elaborate on the full set of changes in this context. So many elements—in fact, the most important ones—are tied to my religious faith and beliefs. Let me say this much, however. I found that the way to inner healing, peace, and wholeness—the key to more than survival in the "fast lane"—meant that I had to have a more centered, focused life. I needed a renewal of prayer in my life.

When I mention prayer, it may evoke an image of "saying" prayers, of reciting formulas. I mean something quite different. When I speak of the renewal of prayer in my life, I am referring to uniting myself with the larger mystery of life and expressing my common existence with other people. This certainly involves a certain kind of discipline in the use of time. It requires, too, some ability to focus or center our thoughts around a particular theme. But the essential ingredient is a contemplative stance toward life—an attitude of openness that is ready to receive what the larger mystery we call God has to offer us by way of insight, perspective, feelings, inspiration, or a sense of values.

I have discovered that this is a remarkably rich, even if not always easy, path toward healing, wholeness, and a more peaceful way of life. I have also found myself called to be a contemplator in the widest and the narrowest sense of that word: one who gazes and looks beyond the surface, or, rather, one who allows the deep dimensions of life to surface. I am not an expert at this. I am clearly no guru. I am a learner, and I dialogue in a process we call spiritual direction about my prayer. The point I want to make is simply this: to survive in a fast-paced lifestyle, it is important to reflect regularly on the deepest dimensions of one's life.

This might be done in the cool quiet of a church or the O'Hare chapel, in the privacy of one's home or office, or sitting under a tree in the park. At first, many of us will feel a bit guilty because it may seem that we are wasting, rather than investing, valuable time. But, with patience and perseverance, the guilty feelings will give way to a renewed sense of purpose, vision, and enthusiasm for life and work. Believe me, it's time well invested!

Moreover, I sorely miss the inner peace and harmony, the enthusiasm for life and work, when I do not invest an hour in prayer and reflection each day. When I do not make that spiritual investment, I find myself on a treadmill, not a pilgrimage. My work tends to dominate me; I do not manage it. I become distracted in my thoughts, isolated from my associates, and out of touch with my deeper—authentic—self.

I suspect that I've not told you anything you do not already know. I did not accept the invitation to address you because I had all the answers to questions raised by life in the "fast lane." I did not come here to offer you new insights or great revelations. Rather, I simply wanted to be with you and let you know that I share your pressures, your problems, and your concerns. I also wanted to affirm the growing need for sharing with others and personally reflecting on our busy lives.

Some time ago I read an article which referred to an apparent lack of any new frontiers to be conquered in the world today. I respectfully suggest that just the opposite is true! As a matter of fact, the greatest frontier of all remains barely explored, infrequently challenged, far from conquered. That is the frontier of the human heart.

That frontier stands, for example, between the young and vibrant members of our society and those who are aged and infirm. It separates the privileged and the wealthy from those who are poor, homeless, or imprisoned. It isolates those of us who are fortunate to live in peace and freedom from those who know only terrorism and violence. That frontier keeps those of us who are blessed with opportunities for education, travel, and new experiences—all those things which fill our lives with hope—from those who know only the despair of a given lot in life.

We have only to hear the shocking statistics on infant mortality in the poorer neighborhoods of metropolitan Chicago, or witness the troubling cutbacks in public funding for social programs, or observe the number of homeless who sleep in airport lounges or under viaducts, or watch the violence on our television screens—to be reminded again and again that there truly is a great frontier still to be conquered in our time. And only our hearts can conquer that frontier.

It is up to you and me to commit ourselves to conquering that frontier. It is up to you and me to recognize the bonds which establish our solidarity with one another and the entire human family. It is up to you and me to reach out to one another in human compassion, remembering how much our common hopes and dreams make us one family.

Accepting the challenge of conquering this important frontier may well keep most of us in the "fast lane." At stake, however, is the very quality of our lives and the effectiveness of our work. My hope is that I've persuaded you this afternoon that it's possible to do more than merely survive a busy life—and that the Church stands ready to help you because we share your experience as well as your hopes and dreams for happiness.

Priests of the Diocese of Charleston

Charleston, South Carolina

—— *October 17, 1991* ————————————————

My brothers in the priesthood of Jesus Christ: It is good to be home! It is wonderful to be so graciously honored by you, the presbyterate that first received me thirty-nine years ago and nourished and supported me during my early years. From the heart, I thank you for all that I have received through you and through the diocese which in many ways is still home to me.

I remember well Msgr. Martin Murphy, pastor of St. Peter's, my home parish in Columbia. Together with several associates and the Ursuline Sisters, he was very instrumental in shaping my spiritual life through sacramental preparation, catechesis, and service as an altar boy. It was also Msgr. Murphy who sent me to the seminary in 1945. Later, when we moved to St. Joseph's parish, Msgr. Alfred Kamler became both a friend and mentor. There were also many other priests, some here today and some deceased, who in many ways supported and helped me as I began my priestly ministry in Charleston, first at Bishop England High School and St. Joseph's parish on Anson Street, and then at the chancery and the cathedral. So the faces and memories of the Charleston diocese are very real for me. Indeed, they continue to shape and affect me in so many ways.

Today, I would like to reflect on some of the things that concern me now, which may give you some insight into my growth and development. My comments will center on two concerns of great importance to me: the *Church* and *spirituality*. I hope that these reflections might be an expression of my gratitude to you and, perhaps, also a way for you to know what is on my mind and in my heart these days.

You and I serve in vastly different settings, so, undoubtedly, our daily routines differ in various ways. Still, our service is marked by common, deep bonds. Above all, our ministry as bishops and priests is quite complex. We are to offer guidance and leadership to our people through our words and counsel and sacramental celebration. We often try to unify communities, bring about healing and reconciliation, promote, through our lives and our work, the great prayer of Jesus "that they may be one." No matter what we are specifically involved in, we certainly want to inspire and affirm, to offer spiritual sustenance for our pilgrim people who make their journey to God. And at times, what we must do is difficult— we must offer challenge and correction so that we and our people may be more open, more pliable to God's ways.

With all the complexity we face, we need to return often to some of the underlying convictions and beliefs that give us energy and direction. That is precisely what I would like to sketch out for you this afternoon, as I speak about *personal spirituality, apostolic spirituality, priestly spirituality*, and *ecclesial spirituality*.

Personal spirituality

I begin my reflection on personal spirituality with a clear and evident fact. For most people living at the end of the twentieth century in the United States, life is very fragmented. There is much talk about burnout. Generally, people equate burnout with overwork. But hard work, even difficult work, doesn't necessarily result in burnout. It is more closely related to a fragmented life. When the center doesn't hold, when the pieces are simply pieces, when our endeavor doesn't seem to go anywhere, then we find ourselves burned out, unwilling and unable to keep going.

Unfortunately, fragmentation and a dispersive way of life are not limited to "the world out there." They also affect us in the Church and, more particularly, those of us in ministry.

If personal spirituality means anything at all, it begins with a continual return to the center of our lives. It means that we hold before ourselves what really matters, what really counts. It means claiming and reclaiming, over and over again until it finally sinks in, that our fundamental identity is simply this: We are disciples of Jesus Christ and partakers of his destiny.

I readily admit that it is not enough simply to identify ourselves as Jesus' disciples; merely calling on him in a superficial way can become a kind of sloganeering. That alone will not heal our fragmentation and bring wholeness to our lives. Something much deeper is needed. We must face with great candor and honesty, and perhaps some struggle, the crisis of our fragmented lives and the haunting sense of moving in circles. Only then will we come to the realization that the only real answer is Jesus. He is our only hope for he is the *unum necessarium*, the only one who can give us the wisdom and strength to gain control over the continual ebb and flow of our daily lives; the only one who makes it possible for us to achieve a certain integrity of life, a true wholeness of existence, rather than the fragmentation that causes us to become disconnected from the center, to lose focus. It is to Jesus, then, that we must make a total and unequivocal commitment. "Now I live, not I, but Christ Jesus lives in me," says St. Paul.

The *fact*, then, is fragmentation. The *hope* is an integrity of life and the means is a return to the center in Jesus Christ. It sounds simple. But, as we all know, it isn't. A recent article in *America*, which you may have seen, described a Catholic's disenchantment with Catholicism and his movement into evangelical Christianity, where, he felt, he really heard Christ proclaimed. Our immediate reaction may easily be defensive. But perhaps we need to listen more deeply; perhaps we need to change. Jesus lost in the details, lost in the myriad programs, lost in the endless committee meetings, lost in the planning, lost in the problems, lost in the finances—*that risen Lord needs to be reclaimed as the center of our lives.*

Personal spirituality means embracing the *unum necessarium*, reclaiming the one important thing, recognizing Christ at the center. When that happens, we begin to experience a breakthrough in our fragmentation and a certain wholeness.

Apostolic Spirituality

Apostolic spirituality. What does this mean? Let us begin again with a *fact*. Along with many others in the Church, we tend to be ecclesial introverts. By that I mean that we who minister full-time often find ourselves preoccupied, consumed with ecclesial concerns. They burn brightly before our eyes, so brightly indeed that at times they blind us to other realities *beyond* the Church, the very world that the Church is called to serve.

One of the great gifts of the Second Vatican Council was a renewed sense of the Church and, more particularly, the Church *in the world*. The Church is to be leaven and salt, a creative force and an agent of transformation. The Church is to inspire imaginations that will devise new ways of solving the riddles of war and conflict, poverty and injustice. The Church is to work as salt works and as leavening agents work: quietly, *within* the world.

And what is the principal means by which the Church works *in* and *for* the world? What is the means by which the Church is an agent of transformation? The answer is clear and startlingly simple. But first we must exclude some means, which although good in themselves, are not appropriate ways for the Church to fulfill its mission. It is *not* principally through the hierarchy, nor principally through the letters of national conferences of bishops. Neither is it principally through political or institutional clout (what there is of it!) and certainly not principally through in-house programs.

The principal means by which the Church works for the transformation of the world is through the exercise of the *priestly ministry of the baptized*. This holy nation, this royal priesthood, this people set apart are indeed living sacrifices, ambassadors of Christ, healers, reconcilers, prophets, and visionaries.

Ironically and sadly, the greatest obstacle to unleashing the priestly and transforming power of the baptized has been a confusion about "ministry." So much talk about ministry, lay ministries, and the development of ministries in the Church has to do with in-house concerns. Considerable effort has been expended to involve lay people more in the Church, to give them a greater sense of ownership for the life of the Church, to help them participate more fully in the various dimensions of Church and ministry. I applaud and support these efforts. In my own archdiocese, I have consistently tried to support and encourage the development of a wide range of ministries in the Church. A significant amount of resources, both material and personnel, has been invested in these efforts. I know you can say the same in the Diocese of Charleston.

Unfortunately, however, one of the by-products of our concern and investment of energy and resources in ministries has been a blunting of the apostolic and priestly task of baptized people in the world. In other words, our emphasis on ecclesial roles and service has dulled our sense of mission to the world, a mission that is exercised primarily through the priesthood of the baptized.

Let me cite some examples from our experience in Chicago to illustrate what I mean. We are experiencing an all-time high murder rate, especially in the African-American community. We are experiencing an extraordinarily high drop-out rate from the public high schools; this is especially notable in the Hispanic community. We continue to experience inequities in education, housing and employment for people of different races and ethnic backgrounds. Women are not dealt with fairly in many circumstances. The delivery of health care and educational services seems to be in perpetual crisis.

These are issues of justice, peace, reconciliation. They are issues that beg for transformation through imagination, creativity, hard work, and, in no small measure, the presence of grace. The bishops and priests of Chicago are not going to solve these problems. The situation calls for the exercise of the apostolic mandate, the mission, of God's priestly people, whose gifts, expertise, and response in faith will lead us forward and break open a path for the emergence of the kingdom of God.

Documents from the Holy See have raised the warning about clericalizing the laity. This warning has not always been well received, but I believe it is well founded. If we are so absorbed with ecclesial services and roles for the laity, we have in effect clericalized the laity and deflected them from the authentic exercise of their priesthood in the world.

An apostolic spirituality, a heightened sense of the priestly mission of the baptized in the world, is essential for the Church today.

PRIESTLY SPIRITUALITY

My comments on priestly spirituality are intimately related to what I have just said about the apostolic spirituality of the baptized. For I believe what the Second Vatican Council said so clearly about the priesthood of the baptized and the ministerial or hierarchical priesthood. Most often quoted is the essential distinction of the two. Most often neglected is the council's affirmation that they are ordered to each other. Ordained priests are to encourage and support the priestly people of God in their mission in the world. In turn, the priestly people and their service reveal for the ordained God's presence and action in the Church and in the world.

Let me explore this further in terms of a specific function of ordained ministry, namely, preaching. Often, an underlying assumption of our preaching is that we, the ordained, have something to give the unordained which they do not have. In fact, preaching at its best works differently. The priest—listening both to the Word of God and to the experience of his people—draws both unto himself, contemplates on both, and then returns the graced experience of his contemplation, illumined by the word of God, to the people. This indeed is how St. Thomas Aquinas described preaching: *contemplata aliis tradere,* to hand on to others those things on which we ourselves have contemplated.

For example, often the people in our parishes most deeply and intensely involved in prayer are the chronically ill and the dying. The priest receives their experience of prayer; indeed, they teach him about prayer, perhaps not explicitly, but effectively nonetheless. He takes that experience and the gospel teaching on prayer and draws both unto himself, contemplates on it, and then returns it to the people in his preaching and teaching. A similar thing happens when the priest deals with new parents and their children. He draws together within himself the experience of those parents, as well as his own, and the word of God. He is then able to celebrate and proclaim the gift of life, its frailty, its hope, and its destiny. Similarly, from the experience of people who grapple with sin, broken- ness, and alienated relationships, and from the experience of the gospel call to reconciliation, the priest is able to proclaim a gospel of forgiveness, a possibility for living life in a reconciled way. From people with addic- tions, he can learn to proclaim the workings of grace.

My point is simply this: in preaching and in other functions of ordained ministry, there is a circuitous process. We draw from the experiences of the priestly people of God. We draw from the word of God. We bring all this into ourselves through contemplation. And then, we proclaim and celebrate both word and sacrament.

Underlying all of this is an assumption that God is already at work, that our ordained priestly service is to uncover, to discover, to reveal the workings of divine grace. We are not so much constructing a better world, as laying bare the reality of God's movement, alive and at work in our lives. Obviously, this means that our spirituality as ordained priests must strive constantly to be alert to God's action in life.

There is a world of difference between *our* being responsible for "mak- ing things alright," and our acknowledging that God's reign is, in fact, al- ready beginning to break into human history, independently of ourselves. If the latter is true, then we need to ask ourselves why are we working so hard at what God is already doing.

Priestly spirituality, as I understand it, is living in a world of grace. It is, first of all, being sensitive and alert to the grace at work in our people. It is the faithful reception of God's word. It involves, in the midst of our busyness, the spirit and practice of contemplation. Its fruit is the com- munication and celebration among our people of what God has already done for them. And from that comes their response in prayer, faith, and action.

ECCLESIAL SPIRITUALITY

Ecclesial spirituality is the Church's response to the promptings of the Holy Spirit. The Church, of course, can never willfully plot its own course. It is always docile to the Spirit who leads and guides.

A brief, very brief, recap of Church history may serve to help you under- stand what I mean by ecclesial spirituality today.

During the first several centuries of the Church, being a Christian en- tailed making a significant personal commitment that might lead to death. An example of one who died for the faith is the saint whose feast we celebrate today—St. Ignatius of Antioch. Martyrdom was constantly on the horizon of Church life. The life of the Church, although certainly not without problems, was embedded in the courageous commitment of those who were incorporated into it.

With Constantine and the conversion of the barbarian hordes, from whom many of us are descended, a major shift occurred. The chief was baptized, and all others followed. So, the Church experienced a rapid growth of membership. If, in the early years, the emphasis was on commitment, now the emphasis shifted to inclusion. There was a great desire to bring everyone into the Church.

Throughout Church history, we have been an untidy lot. God has raised up individuals and movements for the renewal of the Church: Benedict and monasticism, the mendicant orders, the apostolic spirituality of Ignatius of Loyola, the charitable efforts of Vincent de Paul.

Now we are in a *new* moment in the Church's life. The Second Vatican Council and, more specifically, the Apostolic Exhortation of Pope Paul VI, *Evangelii nuntiandi*, have mandated us to be as inclusive as Jesus was inclusive, to preach the gospel to all creation, to draw all people to Jesus. At the same time, through the pattern set in the RCIA and other processes of sacramental preparation and initiation, we are asking for firm commitments. It is not sufficient merely to call oneself Catholic. This has caused considerable tension, especially for priests who are trying to balance both inclusiveness and commitment.

We are far from resolving the tension, but there is a direction to follow. As a Church, the Spirit calls us today to issue an open invitation to everyone to follow the Lord Jesus. The invitation must be genuine, human, realistic, and—above all—inclusive. At the same time, it is an invitation to make a firm choice, to make a commitment to be his disciple.

Our ecclesial spirituality, the Spirit prompting the Church today, leads us to uncompromising patterns of inclusion and commitment.

SUMMARY AND CONCLUSION

In the area of spirituality, we could and should consider many things: for example, prayer, discernment, spiritual direction, liturgy, devotional life, the sacraments, faith, and works of justice. In considering the state of the Catholic Church today, again, there are many things to consider: for example, the specifically Catholic slants to the Christian tradition, sacramentality, community, living tradition and historical continuity, and authority. But of all the possible issues and concerns, I have selected what I have come to consider central to the others, namely, the way we grapple with the unity of life in personal spirituality; the way we grapple with a sense of mission in the world for all the baptized in an apostolic spirituality; the way we grapple with the relationship of ordained ministry and service of the baptized in an authentic sense of priestly spirituality; the way we grapple with the Spirit-prompted directions for the Church today, in an ecclesial spirituality.

My reflections express concerns that are part of my mind, heart, and ministry today—all of which were born and formed in this community of faith in South Carolina. It is with deep personal gratitude and hope that I am with you here today.

Address

"Whoever Is in Christ, Is a New Creation"

Young Adult Catechesis, World Youth Day '93

Denver, Colorado

— August 12, 1993 ——————————————————————

What would you say if I told you that these are among the most religious years of your life, a time of great significance? What would your friends or coworkers say if you told them that *they* are living out some of the most religious years of their lives?

You are in transition from youth to full adulthood. Many of you are in your first major job. Many of you are looking for a partner in marriage, making the choice for a single life, or considering a vocation to priesthood or religious life. Recently, for the first time, you may have experienced a serious illness, become aware of a troubling weakness, or experienced a personal loss. You are also becoming more aware that life is not always fair. Some people appear to have it easy. But, for others, life seems to be a curse. All of these are significant experiences with profoundly religious dimensions.

Who are you? Where do you live? What is your life like? What issues are you facing? What makes you happy? What do you worry about? What are you passionate about?

Clearly, there is not time for me to speak with each of you personally in order to learn more about you. Instead, I will rely on how some of the young adults, whom I know personally, describe their lives and those of their friends.

Many young adults enthusiastically embrace life with all its opportunities and possibilities. Many are well educated and generous with their

561

time and talent. They are determined to protect and preserve the environment. They are willing to volunteer to help when someone is in need. They're like the thousands of young people who have helped in the backbreaking task of sandbagging during the past several weeks of flooding in ten Midwestern states.

Many young adults are also interested in how their faith relates to the rest of their lives. Isn't this the reason why you yourselves are in Denver, participating in World Youth Day '93? At times, you face an enormous challenge in matching what you believe—both in terms of faith and morality—with the requirements of your job or the lifestyle of your friends.

At the same time, while you are young, bright, and energetic, you don't have everything under control. Many young adults experience great insecurity. They report that they are often anxious and depressed. One young woman recently remarked that she lives her life between Prozac—a capsule taken for depression—and Zanax—one taken for anxiety. The most common emotions among many young adults today, I am told, are fear and loneliness. As a result, panic attacks and obsessive-compulsive behavior are not uncommon.

This is understandable. Because of a worldwide recession, yours is the first generation which faces the prospect of not earning more money than your parents. Many of you are well educated but lack high-paying or meaningful jobs. Someone recently told me that some young adults who, earlier in life, were attracted by the prospects of a successful career in corporate law are now eager to get out of it and into something more meaningful to them—like advocacy work.

On the whole, your generation approaches marriage ever so cautiously. You, too, search for love and meaningful relationships, but many young adults are the children of failed marriages or grew up in families virtually destroyed by drug or alcohol abuse. As the years roll by, many young adults question whether they will ever find a suitable partner to marry or even close friends with whom to share life's meaning. That is where the fear and loneliness hit the hardest.

You have grown up with many more available life choices than previous generations. But you may find it harder to make decisions, especially major ones—for example, in terms of employment and career as well as of marriage, single life, priesthood, or religious life. There's so much from which to choose. If you choose one thing or commit yourself to one person or vocation, you automatically exclude other options. Fear of making a mistake can paralyze us when we are faced with multiple choices.

Contemporary culture also has an enormous influence on our lives. There is an erosion of respect for human life, including the unborn, the elderly, and the disabled. Where human life is considered disposable, it is difficult to develop a clear sense of one's inherent human dignity and worth. Moreover, the exaggerated individualism of our culture constantly bombards us with the false message that we are responsible only for our own lives—that we are laws unto ourselves. But an exaggerated individualism leads to self-centeredness, loneliness, isolation, and alienation from others, our true selves, and God.

My dear sisters and brothers, if some of what I have said finds an echo in your life, I assure you that there is an alternative to the superficial, materialistic culture in which we live. That alternative way of life is to be found through faith. Faith is a fully new way of looking at our lives. The gospel, which helps us to see how faith should be lived, runs against the popular currents in our culture. It helps us see things, events, and persons—including ourselves—in new ways, with new eyes. It's not a question of getting new glasses or having tinted lenses. It's a matter of seeing reality as God sees it.

Our theme this morning gives us a new way of looking at our lives: "Whoever is in Christ, is a new creation." A new creation! A radically changed order where God's enduring love, revealed to us through his Son Jesus, guides the way we look at our lives and the world around us!

It is not a question, of course, of our re-creating ourselves. The new creation is *God's* work, and it has already been accomplished in Jesus' death and resurrection. Through baptism, we receive the Holy Spirit who makes us a new creation.

When we think of the waters of our baptism, we often imagine a gentle, brief trickle of a little water. Let me suggest another image for our reflection this morning: the mighty Mississippi River! Shelby Foote, a writer who lives near the river, was quoted recently as saying: "I don't mean to be irreverent, but the Mississippi has a presence in life. When I think of it, I think about God almighty . . ."

Let us focus on that analogy for a moment: God's love and grace working in the world like the power of a mighty river. This may seem somewhat overwhelming at first. We may fear that it will harm or even destroy us. But God's redemptive love does just the opposite—it makes us a "new creation." It surrounds us with the embrace of God's healing, lifegiving love.

That may be true, but it's still a bit frightening. Conventional wisdom has claimed that we must build dams and levees to control the Mississippi River. For the past fifty years, we've invested considerable effort and money to do precisely that. When the dams and levees cannot control the floodwaters, many communities build the levees higher and higher with millions of bags of sand—at times, to no avail. Last week the people of Prairie du Rocher in southern Illinois came to the painful conclusion that the only way to protect their historic town was to break through a nearby levee and allow the river to flood more farmland. It worked! Elsewhere, too, questions are being raised about the wisdom of trying to control the mighty Mississippi with dams, levees, and sandbagging.

But can we control God?! Yes, to some extent. God does not force love or impose salvation upon us. We can—and, at times, do—build dams and levees and pile up sandbags to keep God out of our lives. For example, we may try to control our own lives and destiny without seeking God's help or striving to do God's will. We may become arrogant and selfish in our relationships with others, discounting them and using them for our own ends. The conventional worldly wisdom is that we should protect ourselves, look out for ourselves, always give ourselves the benefit of the doubt. But when we build barriers to keep God and others out of our lives, we sin. Sin is not a popular concept in today's world. But it exists, and if we deny that we are sinners, we are simply deluding ourselves. We hold back a part of our lives that needs God's healing touch, the Church's ministry of reconciliation for which Jesus gave us the wonderful sacrament of penance.

As St. Paul points out, Jesus reconciled us to God through his death and resurrection. In effect, this means that he enables us to remove the sandbags around our besieged lives and allow God's healing, forgiving love to wash over us. When it does so, it gives us a refreshing humility and the courage and strength to live again as a new creation.

In the Scripture passage we heard a few moments ago, St. Paul passionately urged us to be reconciled with God. Why hesitate? Why hold back? I know that it is somewhat awkward for some people to celebrate the sacrament of penance. Some of you may have had an unfortunate experience in confession—leading to more sandbagging—but please do not let that stop you from receiving the sacrament.

I can tell you, on a very personal note, that the sacrament of penance means a great deal to me. I have found it to be very helpful in dealing with my personal and ministerial struggles. I don't know what I would do without it. Believe me, you will also find it helpful and spiritually refreshing. So, if you have not already done so, I invite you to use the opportunity to go to confession during these days. God's saving love can penetrate the most hidden, darkest, disordered part of our human experience. The Lord is waiting to embrace us with his healing, forgiving love.

Being reconciled with God—removing the sandbags which keep us from experiencing God's love—is an ongoing, lifelong process of discernment and conversion. When we allow the floodwaters of God's forgiveness to wash over us, we may first experience some pain. It is not easy to transform our lives so that we are, indeed, a new creation. It may mean letting go of comfortable but harmful habits. But think of what happens when the floodwaters recede and the sun comes out, and we discover that our lives have been greatly enriched by God's forgiving, healing love!

When we remove the obstacles that keep God's love from us, we must also remove the sandbags which keep us from being reconciled with one another. As we know from elsewhere in the New Testament, we cannot claim to be reconciled with God unless we are also reconciled with one another.

St. Paul also reminds us that we have received a ministry of reconciliation, that we are to be ambassadors for Christ. What does that mean? As you know, ambassadors work in an alien culture. They promote the best interests of their countries in a foreign land.

As ambassadors for Christ, we are called to be spokespersons for the reign of God. We do not speak simply for ourselves. By our actions we are to give witness to the power of God's love in the world. We are to proclaim Jesus' gospel and continue his ministry, especially to the most vulnerable in our society. As Jesus' disciples, we know that we cannot measure the new creation by how much money one has, or how much power one has, or how one satisfies every desire for pleasure. This is not the way of the gospel. We are called to promote the gospel values of justice, peace, harmony, and unity in an unjust, violent, divided world.

My friends, I charge you to start a quiet revolution in your life, your circle of friends, your culture. Once you begin to remove the obstacles in your life that keep you from being immersed in God's love, you are in a better position to help others to begin removing the dams, levees, and sandbags in their lives. This is what it means to be ambassadors for Christ.

We will inspire others to accept God's forgiving love when we, too, forgive them. We will also motivate others to receive Christ's reconciliation by our own enduring commitment to personal reconciliation with God by sincere contrition for our sins and participation in confession and penitential acts. Tomorrow, as you know, will be a day of penance at World Youth Day. We will be asked to fast and give alms for the poor. Fasting and almsgiving are very powerful ways of removing the obstacles which keep us from God's love and from one another. There are many ways to fast—for example, abstaining from watching television or from alcoholic beverages one day a week. Fasting has a powerful impact on our lives. Combined with almsgiving, it also benefits others: We fast in order that others may eat.

My brothers and sisters, you and I are called to be open to the unexpected. We are invited by God to embrace new possibilities of life and love. We are called to be more than we are at present.

Admittedly, the call to be a new creation involves risk. It will cost us something. At times, it seems much safer, much easier to remain within our comfort zones, even if we are not totally happy with ourselves. To change, to take risks, and to experience new life is, at times, frightening.

But if you remove the sandbags, if you tear down the levees which isolate you from God's love—and your neighbor—the power of God's love will overcome you, and you will begin to realize that you are a new creation. It will give you freedom where there is routine. It will offer you hope where there is despair. It will show you compassion where there is indifference. It will offer you forgiveness where there is resentment. And it will offer you love that lasts forever.

So, have courage. Start that quiet revolution. Begin to remove the sandbags. Tear down the levees. Open yourself to God's almighty, all-embracing love. Become a new creation and help build up the reign of God! The Lord Jesus needs you! The Church needs you!

Pastoral Ministry

"Pastoral Care of the Separated, Divorced and Remarried in Light of the Catholic Theology of Marriage"

Diocesan Directors' Conference,
Ministry for Separated and Divorced Catholics

Chicago, Illinois

——*July 18, 1983* ——————————————————————

Let me begin by saying how pleased I am that this conference is taking place, and how delighted I am at your presence here. There is little doubt about the importance of your ministry to the many members of our community who suffer the effects of separation and divorce and who struggle with the issue of remarriage. I commend you for your dedication to this important work.

I am well aware that you will spend much of this conference developing plans and strategies for this ministry of yours. In my presentation this afternoon, I have no intention of trying to take over that task. There are practitioners of this ministry among you who know far more than I about the specifics of programming, advertising, organization, psychological approaches and the like. I urge you to take full advantage of the expertise among you; indeed, I rejoice in the fact that this conference brings together men and women with such a wealth of experience to share. I will not pretend to be the source of such concrete advice.

Nor do I intend to preempt the work of professional theologians today. Many of you are aware of the theological discussions pertinent to your ministry that are going on today. And there can be little doubt of the importance of the questions being raised. I cannot resolve these matters by a simple statement of my own; and I do not see this as the proper occasion for me to enter the theological conversation with my own thoughts and opinions.

No, I wish to use my time with you to do something quite different but, I believe, quite important. I wish to speak to you as a bishop, as a pastor of the Church. I wish to recall to your minds, and to my own, some of the central truths and convictions of our Christian faith. I wish to reflect with you about the implications of these core convictions, about the agenda they give us and the obligations they place upon us. My title is "Pastoral Care of the Separated, Divorced, and Remarried in the Light of the Catholic Theology of Marriage." Very well, then. Let us look to our tradition; let us highlight pivotal themes about each: about pastoral care and about marriage. And let us notice together the light these themes provide to the important task that is yours.

I

I start where this conference starts: with the issue of pastoral care. That is to say, I start with persons, with our care of and responsibility for persons. For that is where our Christian faith begins. As the New Testament repeatedly reminds us, Jesus came that we might have life and have it more abundantly, that we might be one even as he and his Father are one, that we might be free and whole and at peace. Jesus came, he lived, and he died in order to bring about the kingdom of his heavenly Father, to allow us to enter that kingdom and, indeed, to be that kingdom both now and in the age to come. And the rising of Jesus to new life confirmed his victory in this task.

So Jesus began with persons. All else follows from this. The very existence of the Church presupposes the need on the part of men and women for a community of faith, to support them and challenge them, to give them direction, to provide them with nourishment and solace and strength in their arduous journey to the kingdom. We know that in the world to come the Church, as we now experience it, will not exist. In the fullness of the kingdom it will not be needed. But for now, human persons need the social structure of a faith community. And so Jesus calls together followers, he develops a ministry of leadership, he gifts the community with his abiding presence, he challenges it to continue his own teaching and his ministry of care in time and space. And thus what we call Church is born.

This same priority of persons exists in the case of the sacraments. The old theological textbooks said it clearly: "*Sacramenta propter homines*"—sacraments are for persons. It is because we, who are the Church, still need to experience in a concrete and human way the presence of Jesus and his love that sacraments exist. They are the signs of his promised presence, the pledges of his proffered love. In the sacraments we experience what we profess and celebrate: that Jesus is near, that he is for us, and that in his strength we can be who we are called to be. In this experience we are nourished and strengthened so that we can see and notice and appreciate his presence everywhere. And we are mandated and empowered to share this Good News of the kingdom with those we meet, with the persons we are called to serve.

And so it is persons that concern us, first and last. It is the pastoral care of God's people and our own that is our vocation. All else must be understood in light of this.

But in highlighting the priority of persons I am not only proclaiming a truth of our faith. I am also adverting to a historical fact that is significant for your specific ministry. It is this: the Church's first involvement in the phenomenon of marriage was under the rubric of pastoral care. In the early centuries of our existence we did not have a canon law of marriage; the administration of the details of marriage was supervised by civil authorities. We did not have a wedding liturgy or, indeed, any ritual of marriage; men and women exchanged marital consent by means of ceremonies dictated by local custom.

What we did have was a process of pastoral care. We had a community of faith concerned about the healthiness and holiness of its members, reaching out to them in care and concern. And since most members of the Church, throughout history, have been married, this solicitude naturally embraced the state of life in which they found themselves. When they succeeded in the challenge of faithful and loving and fruitful marriage, the community rejoiced and praised the Lord. When they failed in that challenge, the community exhorted, forgave, supported, and invited them to conversion and renewed commitment. When they were victimized by the failure of others, the community consoled, compensated, and provided opportunities for new life, new beginnings and the hope of a new tomorrow. In all these human moments, the men and women who comprised the Church acted as the disciples and, indeed, the embodiment of Jesus. And they offered pastoral care to their brothers and sisters in need.

So let no one speak disparagingly of the ministry you exercise. You are no latter-day addition to the Church's ministry to marriage. No, you hold pride of first place in that work. For the very first form of the Church's ministry to marriage was the simple but challenging, faith-motivated and love-filled work of pastoral care for those seeking to live rightly that challenging state of life.

But allow me to pursue this historical reflection a bit further. Scholars tell us that very soon a second ministerial element joined this work of pastoral care. And that new element was formalized prayer. Christians are, after all, followers of Jesus. Their concern for their sisters and brothers is not solely a project of human compassion. It is also the expression of deep-rooted faith. We believe in the loving presence of God in Jesus to the struggles that are ours. And thus, when Christians struggle with the difficulties of human life, they inevitably feel inclined to make prayer a part of their plan. They cannot help but carry these human concerns to the Lord in their times of personal prayer. They wish to ask the Lord to come in aid to those so deeply in need. And ultimately they want to share this prayerful sentiment with the very ones who are its beneficiaries. They want to pray with those needy ones, to pray for them while in their presence and to invite them to shared prayer on behalf of the need deeply felt.

And so the formalized practice of prayer for married people, especially on the occasion of the wedding, became increasingly common. There eventually emerged what we now know as the nuptial blessing. And from that followed the first of a long succession of marital liturgies within the life of the Church.

For our purposes, however, I wish to emphasize the underlying faith-instinct. If our pastoral care is authentic, if it is in tune with the earliest beliefs and life of the Church, then it will express itself both in concrete action and in prayer. Not one or the other; but both together out of love for our fellow travelers to the kingdom. That is what the history of our community teaches; that is what faith confirms. And that, I hope, is what our own style of action increasingly exemplifies.

II

Thus far, I have reflected on the life of the early Church and on the commitment of its members to pastoral care. As the centuries passed, the size of the Church grew amazingly. The role the Church exercised in the civil community also expanded. And the time eventually came when, precisely because pastoral care required it, the leaders of the Church assumed some responsibility for administering the details of the marriage contract. A canon law of marriage thus developed, not for its own sake but for the sake of the reality of marriage itself as well as the members of the community. Because of those unmet needs of the people, there finally emerged stipulated wedding ceremonies, requirements of witnesses, documents and the like, legal definitions of marriage, and indeed, marriage tribunals for the interpretation and application of this evolving law. All of this occurred as a specification of the Christian call to pastoral care.

And in this regard may I say a word of commendation for those who today provide the service of applying the Church's law in the area of marriage. I know that you will have other occasions to discuss the canon law of marriage during this conference. I simply want to express my admiration for those who do this work. It is clear to me that they are in continuity with this ancient tradition which I have been describing. The men and women who work in chanceries and marriage tribunals clearly see themselves as Christians seeking to exercise pastoral care. Theirs is not an exercise of domination; it is a ministry of service. They see the agencies in which they work, and the law itself, as the Church's sincere attempt to institutionalize pastoral care of married people in order to make it more effective. These officials are under no illusion about the imperfections of the law. Nor am I. But we all know that in a community the size of ours, structure is humanly unavoidable. And inasmuch as it does serve the real needs of people, this structure is to be appreciated and applauded. So I commend those who pursue this difficult and sometimes unrewarding ministry. I praise them for their commitment to pastoral care, and I assure them of my prayers for their continuing and increasing success in that endeavor.

But if the centuries saw the Church's increased involvement in the administration of the institution of marriage, they also saw a deepening appreciation on the part of the Church for the spiritual significance of the marital state. The community of faith came to realize that marriage among the disciples of the Lord is not merely a good thing, it is truly and profoundly sacramental. And so there developed a genuine theology of marriage, an appreciation of marriage as an occasion of grace and a privileged locus of the presence of Jesus Christ. It is in this context that our teaching about the permanence and indissolubility of marriage can be better understood and appreciated.

What a powerful insight this is; how guided by the Spirit must the Church have been in realizing that Jesus Christ has established the human experience of marital love as a sacred and sacramental event.

How shall we understand this? Once again, I do not wish to enter the detailed discussions of the professional theologian. Instead let me reflect on the fitness of the sacramentality of marriage in light of yet more central truths of our faith.

I have mentioned that Jesus' concern was for persons. He incarnated his Father's abiding and unequivocal love for all of us, in all the moments of our lives. In Jesus, God dwells with us; he walks with us and his Spirit guides us in the movements of our life's progression. Again and again we are told, especially in the Acts of the Apostles, that the disciples experienced the presence of Jesus. They knew he had not abandoned them. He remained with them, though in mystery and obscurity. His Spirit enlightened them and empowered them and guided them; this was their faith conviction.

And in this experience of the presence of Jesus and of his Spirit, they knew the presence of God his Father. God had not abandoned them. He cared for them still. He lived out ahead, where Jesus had gone; and as he had called them into being, so now he called them forward to the kingdom of everlasting light.

These disciples knew, then, that they were loved and called by God. They had a calling, a vocation, to which it was their privilege to respond. They discerned the movements of God in the events of their lives, both good and ill. They sought to understand and implement the will of God in their own decisions and acts. And through it all they had a sense of the importance of their lives. Their vocation made them different; not isolated from the world or haughtily standing over it. But still different, special, blessed for the sake of the world. They had a vocation: a common vocation as disciples of Jesus. And particular vocations, discerned as each one shaped his or her life. God was active in those vocations; and conversely, those concrete and diverse vocations were the arena in which God acted and made his presence known.

In recent years, as you know, we have retrieved this rich theology of vocation. We now appreciate how the term should never be reserved just to those in religious life. No, it describes each of us as we listen to the Lord and shape our lives in response to his loving call. And it invites a sort of reverence as we contemplate the concreteness of those lives. For here, in the nooks and crannies of our very ordinary existence, here is where God is at work today.

But what do we see when we contemplate our lives as vocations? What do we notice when we seek to understand our lives in the light of the model of Jesus and his life? We see a pattern, I believe; and we notice certain factors that invite our attention. Let me name just four.

We see the need for truth, integrity. It is always the vision, the teaching of Jesus we must keep in clear focus. As Paul told the Corinthians: "It is not ourselves we preach but Christ Jesus as Lord, and ourselves as your servants for Jesus' sake." A way of life that is not rooted in the truth is not authentic just as pastoral care that is not shaped by truth is ultimately harmful.

We see our relatedness. None of us is self-sufficient. No one of us can bring himself or herself to complete fulfillment. We are in the world together. And it is our vocation to relate one to another, to attend to one another's needs, to live in mutuality and in sincere concern.

We see also our need for fidelity. There is so much that changes in our lives. Every one of us asks: Will life be true? Will the one I trust be worthy of that trust? Can I really depend on the other to remain, to be committed to me and my needs? In turn we realize that we owe one another that gift of fidelity. You need to know you can depend on me, that I will be here tomorrow for you, that I am trustworthy.

Finally we see the sad fact of sin. We share the common reality of frailty. Our dreams exceed our capacity for fulfillment, our expectations go beyond what our effort can achieve. There is brokenness and failure, isolation and misunderstanding, disappointment and betrayal. And so there is no escaping our need for forgiveness and a second chance. We need to be renewed, to be helped to conversion, and to be given the gift of new hope. For while we reach for the kingdom, we are surely not dwelling there yet.

I am sure that there is more that could be said about our lives as vocation. But I will settle for just these four factors: truth, relatedness, fidelity and sin. For they are enough to impress me with how appropriate it is that married life is a sacrament of Jesus Christ and of his Church.

Is there any state of life that so totally expresses the truth of God's love and the way that love is incarnated in two people whose covenantal union brings into existence a total, permanent sharing of life? Is there any state of life which brings into such clear focus the fact of our relatedness in human life? Is there any relationship that highlights so strikingly our need for fidelity in love and in mutual concern? Is there any life experience that so easily forces us to a humble admission of our weakness, our need to grow, our failure to achieve the good for which we seek? No. There is something special and pointed about marriage. There is a sense in which it is a microcosm and model of all the rest of human life.

But we assert, in faith, that our lives are a vocation, that God is present, in the midst of those very human moments of our existence. It follows then, that, in a specially pointed and focused way, we can claim to find God and his actions in the interweaving textures of married life.

How much sense it makes, then, that marriage among believers should be a sacrament. We claim that sacraments are promised signs of God's abiding and transforming love, signs that truly make that love present through the loving action of Jesus Christ. At the same time we claim that sacraments are not magic. They touch us and transform us only inasmuch as we are ready and receptive to their gift. That is what we claim about sacraments. That is also what we assert about marriage. This paradigm of human living, when it is embraced by believers in their embracing of each other, is just such a privileged sign of God's abiding and transforming love. It reveals God's love for the couple and for all the human family. It offers transformation to them and, through them, to us all. At the same time, this marital sacrament is no feat of magic. Sin remains, and all the frailty to which the sons and daughters of Adam are prone. And so the element of struggle, the fact of failure and the need for renewal, still remain. Indeed, it always will until the Lord comes again in his glory.

III

I have spoken about the historical fonts of our Christian concern for married people, about the project of pastoral care and about the priority of persons. I have then reflected with you about the great beauty to be found in our theology of marriage, about its roots in our sense of vocation, and the power with which its sacramentality speaks to the need for integrity, to our relatedness, our need for fidelity, our sin. Let me conclude with some brief comments on your own ministry of pastoral care to those brothers and sisters who have experienced failure in their effort to live marital life.

Let me begin with a small comment upon the law. You are well aware that in November of 1977, in response to a request made by the National Conference of Catholic Bishops, Pope Paul VI removed the law which imposed automatic excommunication upon those who attempt marriage invalidly. To some, this act of the Holy Father appeared merely symbolic; and its symbolism of affection and care was certainly evident. But it was more than merely symbolic. For in lifting this automatic excommunication, Pope Paul VI was removing any doubt about the status of these men and women. They are members of the Church. And as such, they have as much right to the pastoral services of the Church as any other member. Indeed, given the pain they so often experience, one can argue that they most especially deserve those services.

I think this point is worth emphasizing. One occasionally hears complaints when, for example, a diocesan office for the divorced is established. "What right do these people have to such pastoral care?" it is asked. I hope you can see the clear answer: they have every right. For they are our brothers and sisters, fellow members of the Church, the People of God. Whatever else we may say, this we must say first of all.

So your ministry of pastoral care to the divorced is genuine and authentic. For that very reason, I hope it will have several other qualities as well.

First, let it be truthful and prudent. We are not fair to people when we are ambiguous about the true nature of marriage as this is understood by the Church. We do them a disservice when we suggest that complex problems have simple solutions. They do not. The problem of marital failure, both in the individual instance and as a cultural phenomenon, is glaringly complex. It does not involve just two individuals; it involves children, extended families, friends, a community of faith, social institutions, and long-cherished structures of civilization. These other individuals require our attention because of the human dignity which they, too, possess. The various social and legal structures also need protection, not, of course, for their own sakes, but because of the human persons they are designed to serve. I do not recommend a ministry that is cowardly, or locked in blind conformity to convention. But I do recommend a ministry that is real, and that expresses that reality with integrity and in genuine Christian prudence.

Let it also be compassionate. The reality of faithful and lifelong marital commitment is not only a demand and challenge of Christian faith. It is also a dream of all good women and men. Those who have not achieved that dream experience a most poignant sort of pain. They need our very special care and solicitude. They need us to act in the spirit of Jesus. So, like Jesus, within the context of our teaching on marriage, let us search always for ways to affirm rather than to reject, to assist rather than to criticize, to include rather than to exclude. In all you do—even when you cannot resolve a person's problem or regularize his or her situation—let your ministry be compassionate.

Finally, let your ministry be hopeful. St. Paul, in his first letter to the Corinthians, contrasts the present age with the age to come by saying that "Now we see indistinctly, as in a mirror, then we shall see face to face" (13:12). How true that is. I would not be so foolish as to suggest that I know how best to serve all those who have experienced marital failure. Even less do I know how to bring about in every case a fuller incarnation of the beautiful theology of marriage I described earlier. And I must say that I suspect you do not know either. All of us are struggling together to find ways of being the disciples we are called to be, to follow the lights we are given, however dim they may be, in caring for our brothers and sisters. We are frustrated by the indistinctness with which we see. We yearn for the ability to see clearly, as if face to face, in this important work. But that gift is not yet ours.

You act in faith; act also in hope. In you God is doing a great deed. In your ministry he is reaching out to those in need; he is healing, supporting, challenging, guiding. In you he is embracing the brokenhearted, raising them up and making them new. So be hopeful in your ministry. Know that, even in the darkness, you are walking with the Lord and he is walking with you.

When Paul offered his comparison of the present and the age to come, he was concluding his great hymn about the excellence of love. It is a text that is often used at weddings. But it speaks a truth for all of us. It speaks a truth no less for those who struggle with the experience of marital failure. And it speaks a very special truth, I feel sure, for you who give yourselves to them in the ministry of pastoral care.

"There are in the end," said Paul, "three things that last: faith, hope, and love, and the greatest of these is love."

Address

National Convention of Catholic Campus Ministry Association*

New Orleans, Louisiana

── *January 8, 1989* ──────────────────────

I am delighted to have this opportunity to address you—the members of the Catholic Campus Ministry Association. I congratulate you on twenty years of faithful collaboration and service. I am enthusiastic about speaking with you because your ministry plays such an important role in helping to shape the future Church in the United States. I trust that my words will reflect my esteem and respect for you and offer you encouragement, support—and challenge.

As you know, I am not a campus minister or a university professor, although in the early years of my priesthood I did serve as the Catholic chaplain at the Citadel, the Military College of South Carolina. I come to you simply as a pastor, as one who loves the Church and recognizes that this is a critical time of ecclesial renewal.

Many different voices speak in the Church today, and they will continue to do so for the foreseeable future. Some lament the lack of "real" renewal and change. Others mourn the loss of "orthodox" faith and practice. Some belittle or ridicule official Church teaching about sexual morality or social justice. Still others take up a single issue of Church life—indeed, an issue which might be quite important in itself—but focus their full attention exclusively upon that single issue, and nothing else. As a result, these different

*Also published in *Origins*, vol. 15, no. 34, February 2, 1989, pp. 553–56.

voices seem, at times, to drown out efforts to promote and strengthen Church unity. Yes, there are many pushes and pulls in the Church today. You and I must face them, feel them, deal with them every day.

It is sometimes said that, where two or three professional Church ministers are gathered, you will hear discouraging words, especially about the future of the Church. Frankly, I do not share such pessimism. While I am realistic about the difficulties which confront us, I am convinced that there are great possibilities ahead. I base this assessment on what I see and hear at the heart of the Church—that is, the hearts of believers—and on my faith in God who remains faithful and abides with us.

I will do four things in my address this morning. First, I will briefly sketch certain key features of the Church of the future, the Church that will belong to the students you now serve. Then I will outline five formational objectives to help prepare them for their future life in the Church and the world. A third consideration will be attitudes that all of us—including both students and campus ministers—need to cultivate. Finally, I will raise two additional issues for your consideration, significant issues for all who are concerned about the future of the Church.

THE CHURCH OF THE FUTURE

A number of sociological studies have projected a profile of the Church of the future in the United States. *My* observations about the future are based more on my own day-to-day experience as a bishop. In several ways, however, the conclusions of the sociologists and my own impressions converge. I will summarize four of them as features of the Church of the future.

(a) First, the Church in the United States will remain quite similar to the Church of today, but it will experience even greater diversity. It will be a community of considerable racial, ethnic, socioeconomic, cultural, and religious diversity. Catholics, especially college graduates, are and will be among the more economically advantaged people in this country. But the new Catholic immigrants from Asia and Latin America will be among the poorest.

Catholics will continue to adopt a diversity of religious styles. Some will continue to hold to forms of "popular religion." Others will find themselves at home in traditional U.S. Catholic patterns. Some will look for new forms of religious expression and spirituality. Still others will borrow eclectically from various types of religious experience.

(b) Second, U.S. Catholics will continue to grapple with a sense of ecclesial identity. The change in the way we have begun to talk about the Church reflects a change in our hearts. Gradually, we are learning not to say "the Church this," or "the Church that," as if the Church were separate from ourselves. *We* are the Church, and we are learning to say so.

At the same time, the number of people who belong to the Church—*really* belong, not simply in a nominal or perfunctory way—will probably be fewer in the future. But those who do belong will be more deliberate, more intentional in their decision. They will grapple with the meaning of *being* the Church, not merely *belonging* to it.

(c) Third, the Church in the future will more and more find itself by losing itself. The gospel mandate applies not only to individuals but also to the Church. Although we will always need to pay attention to our life as a community of faith, we are coming close to a saturation point of intra-ecclesial, intramural discussion. The Church is most truly faithful to its mission when it focuses its attention on Christ and the world; when it sets aside its own self-concerns and embraces the example of the Lord Jesus, immersing itself in a world awaiting healing and redemption.

(d) Fourth, the Church of the future in this country will not be able to rely on general social support, the structures of popular culture, or the kind of civic leverage formerly wielded by priests in Bing Crosby movies. As a Church, we will rely much more on resources *within* our community than those outside it. Local churches will grow to the extent that they have cultivated their inner resources of graced commitment and surrender.

While this is only a brief sketch of the Church of the future in the U.S., I trust that it has given you a sense of my projections of what lies ahead.

A FORMATIONAL AGENDA FOR CAMPUS MINISTRY

If, indeed, the Church of the future will resemble what I have just described, how can campus ministry best serve students who are preparing to meet and live the future? I suggest that the following five areas are worthy of your best efforts: (a) a sense of ecclesial identity, (b) the habit of worship, (c) the cultivation of personal spirituality, (d) the development of critical consciousness; and (e) the awareness of mission in and to the world.

(a) *A Sense of Ecclesial Identity.* As I have intimated, we are gradually changing our language to reflect the fact that we not only belong to the Church, we *are* the Church. The Church is not something outside of us. Neither is it opposed to our experience and hope. In other words, there must be a real sense of ownership.

Campus ministry faces the great challenge of drawing people into and sustaining them in the communal life of the Church. But beyond this, and perhaps even more challenging, it also has the responsibility of giving them a sense of the Church's true identity, and their ownership of it. Such ownership does not mean, of course, that we can make the Church whatever *we* want it to be. We must be faithful to the Scriptures, our tradition, and the promptings of the Holy Spirit. But within these theological and pastoral boundaries, there is a wide range of opportunities for ecclesial understanding and growth.

When people take initiatives to pray, discuss, and develop programs for justice, peace, and charity; when they share in the administrative, organizational, and financial dimensions of Church life—they will develop a healthy sense of ecclesial identity, an awareness of being the Church. Campus life—usually the first time that students are away from home—offers a unique opportunity for them not only to "go to Church" passively or, perhaps, reluctantly, but to *be* the Church really and truly. By establishing a climate of welcome and a forum for sharing, you will help prepare them to be the faithful Church of the future.

(b) *The Habit of Worship.* Campus ministers have a wonderful opportunity to develop a habit of worship in the students they serve. The Eucharist is the central act of worship, but the Liturgy of the Hours and other forms of communal worship are also very important. By "habit" I do not mean a pattern of automatic or routine response, but, rather, an integrated rhythm of life that regularly turns to God in shared worship.

Worship must be a primary concern of campus ministers. But to develop a life of worship that draws people into a habit of prayer requires an investment of time, creativity, money, energy, and personnel. Moreover, if the habit of worship is to be sustained beyond the students' college years, the pattern of campus worship must have a connection and continuity with the liturgy of our parishes, our history, and our liturgical books. We need the regularity and the predictability of ritual that gently repeats itself year in and year out. Within these boundaries, there is considerable room for creative, prayerful efforts which seek to be an authentic expression of *this* community at *this* moment.

The habit of worship is decisive. In the earlier years of this century, Romano Guardini recognized this in his work with German students. His intuition was rooted in an accurate reading of human nature. There rests in each of us, he said, an instinct for worship. It is as strong as our instinct to survive and to propagate. It is a need which will not go unmet. If people do not worship in Spirit and in truth, they will worship false gods. If they do not praise God, they will end up praising themselves, as Isaac Bashevis Singer has noted. If they do not surrender in thanksgiving to God, they will surrender to money, power, pleasure, status, chemicals, glamour, or any number of other things.

The habit of worship, then, is much more than getting people to go to Mass on Sunday, although that *is* included. It is the sensitive heart that renders worship in Spirit and truth, and thereby finds a life path that leads to justice and peace.

(c) *The Cultivation of Personal Spirituality*. Believers, even those who cling closely to a faith community and its worship, will continue to find themselves more and more alone. To cope with this, they need to cultivate a personal spirituality. In other words, they need to learn how to prize solitude, silence, meditative and contemplative prayer. Above all, people, especially our young people, must learn not to fear being mystics.

When their spiritual journey is on the right path, and they actively cultivate their personal spirituality, people will find within themselves the resources of love. They will not focus their attention simply on their own perfectibility, as some suggest. Rather, by concentrating on the Lord Jesus and union with him, they will be in touch with the sustaining forces of hope and courage. These stem from love and enable people to see the story of God inscribed in the very heart of their lives.

You know better than I that there is a serious quest for spirituality among young people. For some, the vaporous movements and techniques of various forms of "new age" spirituality are an unfortunate detour. For nearly two millennia we Christians have had the rich experience of encountering women and men who have lived and breathed by the Spirit. Campus ministers need to prepare people to cultivate a personal spirituality that builds upon this tradition.

(d) *The Development of a Critical Consciousness*. In Scripture, and in the rest of our tradition, the "world" is created by God and loved by God. It is also a broken world, marked by sin, in need of healing and redemption. Sometimes, it stands opposed to God, against God.

Campus ministry can serve students well by helping them to learn not to take things for granted, not to live simply by the assumptions of our age and culture. Through worship, formal and informal teaching, and dialogue within the college or university community, campus ministry can help students develop a critical eye. That will enable them to discern both now and later what they should embrace, celebrate, and promote as well as what they ought to confront, combat, and transform.

Pope John Paul II and our own National Conference of Catholic Bishops have offered some helpful perspectives in this regard. Critical consciousness looks carefully at all areas of contemporary life, such as work, the right to life, the economy, peace, race relations, and sexism.

Sadly, some young people want to "buy into the system," and they do this blindly. Others want to make more authentic commitments based on what they have sorted out in a critical, thoughtful fashion. Campus ministry offers a valuable service when it helps prepare people to evaluate the various dimensions of contemporary life by the standards of the gospel.

(e) *Consciousness of Mission*. By their baptism, confirmation, and participation in the Eucharist, Catholic Christians are destined to be a leaven in the world, a transforming agent that allows the power of the reign of God to be unleashed in the world.

For many people in the Church, the past decade has been the decade of ministry. It's been the "in" thing. This reflects, of course, a wonderful recovery of the concept and practice of special service rendered in the Church's name. But often, ministry has meant limited perspectives, narrowly understanding its scope to be limited to the Church or ecclesiastical affairs.

As I noted earlier, the Church exists, not for itself, but for the Lord and for the world. As members of the Church, we are not to search simply for a particular role to play within the faith community. We are *sent* into the world—that place of profound divine love and distressing human brokenness. The great priesthood of the baptized celebrates God's love in the world and serves as a balm, a healing presence to human hurt, injustice, and pain.

Campus ministry, then, can prepare people for the future by cultivating in them a sense of mission. Each person has a unique task in the world. When people appreciate their own mission, they have a sense of their true importance; they appreciate the call to greatness which is given to them.

These five formational objectives represent significant areas of concern for me as a pastor who must anticipate the need for solidly developed Christians in the Church of the future. To have a sense of ecclesial identity, to acquire a habit of worship, to cultivate personal spirituality, to develop a critical consciousness about the world, to grow in a consciousness of our mission to the world—all these form a substantial and necessary formational agenda for campus ministers.

ATTITUDES

Now I will briefly describe certain attitudes which need to be cultivated by campus ministers and those whom they serve. These attitudes will help create an environment which allows for the unfolding of the formational agenda which I have just outlined.

The first is *loyalty to the Church*. For some, this phrase has a quaint ring of a bygone day. Others react strongly against it, understanding loyalty to be a kind of blind submission to a triumphalistic Church. Still others feel so hurt by some position taken by the Church or some ecclesial experience that they simply cannot entertain the idea of cultivating "loyalty" to the Church.

When I say that we need to develop an attitude of loyalty to the Church, I am not advocating a nostalgic return to days long past; neither am I suggesting that we glorify blind submission to what we do not understand.

Loyalty, for me, is shaped by a sense of familiarity or family. Everyone knows that families endure great pressures and face many difficulties. Sometimes they are places of profound suffering and deep alienation. But in the best of times, and often even in the worst, the family provides a homing point. It is, as Robert Frost described "home" in *The Death of the Hired Hand*, "the place where, when you have to go there, they have to take you in."

Without a fundamental commitment to this kind of loyalty to the Church, how can we help prepare people for a future in it?

Another attitude to cultivate is *excitement and passion*. There must be a conviction that what we proclaim and aim for, as Catholic Christians, is important. It is not directed toward decline or failure, even though it may be countercultural. Our message and our ministry are truly significant. When we have that conviction, we will be excited and passionate in a contagious way. No one has ever moved constructively into the future without excitement and passion.

Again, a particular danger for professional ministers is to focus excessively on the number of difficulties and painful situations we face each day. But simply to allow ourselves to be absorbed by these issues, and to be blinded to the larger vision and so forget the deeper hopes, is to miss the point and to face the future with depressing and self-defeating attitudes. Realism, yes, but realism must include hope, excitement, and passion.

Another essential attitude to cultivate is *inclusiveness*. There needs to be a largeness of heart in us, a generosity of spirit in imitation of Jesus. All are called to the Church, and all are to be welcomed. We can both retain and develop our unique Catholic identity precisely as we interact with people in an ecumenical, interfaith, or secular context. Offering hospitality and fellowship, being inclusive, does not imply watering down our Catholic identity or betraying our Catholic faith. Rather, it reflects a posture of welcome and sharing, precisely as Catholic people who share Christian faith with many, the covenant faith of Israel with others, the search for transcendence with some, and human values with still others.

A fourth attitude to develop is *trust*. Hope, confidence, and trust underpin everything else. If we do not believe that we are in God's hands, if we do not believe that the Spirit still guides us, if we cannot rely on God's promise and one another, our ministry will be unproductive and our future bleak.

TWO FINAL ISSUES

I would like finally to raise two additional issues. I do not have specific answers or a concrete program in mind. In fact, I am not quite certain what to do about these two issues. However, I think that they are quite important for developing the kind of campus ministry which effectively prepares people for the Church in the future. These issues are religious literacy and vocational discernment.

(a) *Religious Literacy*. As you know, there is considerable discussion in higher education circles about cultural literacy. Educators ask: What do people need to know so that they can communicate with one another, learn from their past, and build for their future?

Within the Church we need to debate a similar question: What do responsible Catholic Christians need to know so that they can communicate in faith with one another, learn from their tradition, and build for the future?

I am not speaking about the kind of Catholic "trivial pursuit" information that appears regularly in plays, humor books, and even some board games. Rather, my concern is this: What constitutes basic catechesis in the faith for responsible adults who need to believe with understanding and to understand with faith; people who need a sound foundation in a larger wisdom for making moral decisions in a complex age; people who are called to make a difference in the world?

Such catechesis clearly includes knowledge of God as ineffable mystery, as community of persons, as graciously involved in human history, as revealed definitively in Jesus Christ who reconciles us to God and one another, whose mission continues in the Church, who is met in the sacraments, who gives us his Spirit—a Spirit of wisdom and understanding, binding, uniting, healing, bringing all things and all people to fulfillment.

Please understand me correctly. I do not think that everyone must be a theologian or conversant in all kinds of theological subtlety in order to be saved. No, I mean a basic grasp of the great mysteries that enables people of faith to stand in awe before the great love of God and encourages them to probe more deeply to discover how God is alive and at work in their lives.

Certainly, campus ministry cannot be fully or exclusively responsible for religious literacy. What I am suggesting is that young people involved in higher education are in a sense "vulnerable" to learning. They are "ripe" for such catechesis. We cannot ignore this critical moment. Again, I present this for your consideration.

(b) Another issue for your ongoing reflection and discussion—and I know that you have already considered it in various ways—is *vocational discernment*. Ordinarily, the pattern of the discovery of a special calling to live out the Christian life in a more intense way or in a particular form of public ministry or witness begins with an invitation from someone. I am talking about religious life, lay ministry, missionary outreach either in religious or lay life or as an ordained minister, diocesan priesthood, the diaconate, and secular institutes.

At this time in our history, it might seem foolhardy to some, and outrageous to others, that I propose, for example, that women working in campus ministry invite young men whom they esteem to think about the possibility of diocesan priesthood. But that *is* part of what I am suggesting. I am also recommending that campus ministers invite and encourage young men and women to consider religious life and other Christian lifestyles and ministries.

The choice before us is clear. We can live with the Church we have, and love it and seek to build it up from within, even as we work for renewal and conversion. Or, we can retreat from it and let it decline or be directed by voices other than our own.

Admittedly, the primary focus of campus ministry is not discernment of vocations to the priesthood, religious life, and other forms of ministry and Christian witness. However, you have an important role to play in the process of awakening and inviting people to these possible vocations.

Conclusion

I wish to close with a word of gratitude. Thank you for your dedicated, generous service.

You and I live in an age, and in a Church, which are quite complex. As members of the Church, we continue the process of personal and ecclesial renewal, perhaps in its most delicate and decisive phase. It is not a question of basic principles; they have already been articulated in our tradition. The real edge of renewal is in its unfolding implications *in the course of ministry itself*.

This is where you and I are today. Frankly, it is often not an easy place to be. I affirm your courage, and I encourage you to continue your wonderful ministry in hope and trust.

May God bless you, your ministry, and the students you serve.

Keynote Address

"Pastoral Care of Immigrants in the United States"

First National Convention on Filipino Ministry

San Francisco, California

—*January 13, 1990* ———————————————

Mabuhay! Less than a month ago, I celebrated the second night of Simbang Gabi with members of the Filipino community in the Archdiocese of Chicago. I had also participated in the celebration two years ago, and both events impressed me very much. They and my other contacts with Filipinos in Chicago allowed me to see their deep faith firsthand and to get a glimpse of their struggles as immigrants.

In some ways, this reminds me of the difficulties my own mother and father experienced when they emigrated from northern Italy to the United States, and of the importance of their deep faith and the welcome of the local church in South Carolina. I trust that most of you have similar stories to tell—of yourselves, your parents, or your grandparents.

This evening my reflections on the pastoral care of immigrants in the United States will highlight the special gifts, characteristics, and needs of Filipino immigrants. While I will talk about the Church in the United States, I will also, at times, make my reflections more concrete by referring to what we are doing or need to do in the Archdiocese of Chicago.

THE IMMIGRANT EXPERIENCE AND THE CHURCH'S RESPONSE

In 1986, the Administrative Committee of the National Conference of Catholic Bishops issued a pastoral statement on migrants and refugees, entitled "Together, A New People." At the outset, it noted that "the loving concern of the Church for immigrants and refugees is a thread that ties together more than three centuries of its history in the United States." The statement also acknowledged that the Church here has faced a great ongoing challenge: to incorporate into one community of faith peoples from a hundred or more diverse cultures and to lead "this new People of God" to take its rightful place in our pluralistic society.

Immigration has substantially shaped our national and ecclesial life. Waves of European immigrants came to these shores in the last century and the early part of this one. The Church faithfully and generously extended its pastoral care to the newcomers—by educating their children, setting up parishes for various language groups, forming immigrant associations, helping immigrants understand and accept their responsibilities as citizens. It also offered its collective voice in the advocacy of fair immigration laws and shared its resources in assistance, relief, and social services. In these endeavors, the Church's pastoral response was facilitated by the fact that many of these groups brought their own priests with them to serve their special needs.

Although European immigration has now subsided, and the children and grandchildren of those who came from the Old Country are now well established here, immigration itself continues, especially from Asia and Latin America. A new immigration policy in 1965 made it possible for Asian and Pacific Isles immigrants to come here, and they have done so in great numbers. For example, in 1985, 47 percent of all the 570,000 immigrants who came to the United States emigrated from Asia and the Pacific Isles. As a result, the Filipino American population has grown from 780,000 in 1980 to an estimated 1.4 million today and may number more than 2,000,000 by the year 2000. The majority of these immigrants have settled in seven states, in this order: California, Hawaii, Illinois, New York, Texas, New Jersey, and Washington. This has great significance for the Church in these areas because 90 percent of Filipino immigrants are Catholic.

Why do they come to the United States? For the same basic reasons that so many others have come to these shores—to escape socioeconomic imbalance and poverty and to seek a better opportunity for themselves and their families. At the same time, they experience all the difficulties associated with being uprooted from familiar surroundings and extended families and entering a new cultural context.

While Catholics in the United States may no longer be considered primarily an "immigrant Church," we continue to be shaped in many important ways by the immigrant experience. Receiving the stranger, the exile, the refugee, and the economically deprived continues to be an important national and ecclesial task.

Let us now review some of the essential ingredients of effective pastoral ministry to Filipino Catholics in the United States.

PASTORAL MINISTRY TO FILIPINO CATHOLICS IN THE U.S.

Filipinos are a blend of the East and the West—oriental at heart, Western in lifestyle. They are person-oriented, warm and hospitable, easy to get along with, adaptable, flexible, and resilient in the face of crisis. Their religiosity, orientation to the present, sense of humor, and gift of music and dance, together with their love of fiestas and celebrations, reveal their capacity to enjoy life, even in difficult times. They identify closely with the region of their origin. They are creative, resourceful, industrious, and hard-working—often, willing to work at two or more jobs. But most of all—and most important—they have a deep faith which underlies their courage, daring, optimism, inner peace, and the capacity to accept tragedy and death with resignation.

The closeness of the Filipino family is legendary, and, within the family, there is a clear hierarchy of authority. Formal authority resides in the father, but decision-making is shared by the mother. Next in line is the eldest child who is given the responsibility of caring for the younger ones. In this family structure, children are expected to be seen, but not heard. The family has a wide network of kinship—the extended family—which is a main source of security for its members, especially in times of crisis. With the extended family, interdependence is encouraged, and respect for elders is held as an important value. Moreover, Filipinos often use go-betweens, particularly in situations where confrontation is necessary.

Filipino faith-life is heavily influenced by Spanish Christianity. The great majority of Filipino Catholics, whether educated or not, express their Catholic faith largely in terms of popular piety. The Christ of Filipino folk Catholicism is predominantly the Christ Child, the Santo Nino, and the suffering Christ of the Passion. Devotion to the Mother of God also plays a significant role in their religious consciousness. Traces of veneration of dead ancestors can still be found today in Filipinos' devotion to the souls in purgatory and the celebration of All Saints' Day. But perhaps the most characteristic aspect of Filipino popular religiosity is their devotion to the saints. This fits well with their natural attraction for the concrete as well as for mediators. They have a special place in their hearts for Lorenzo Ruiz, a family man from Manila, who was canonized by Pope John Paul II in 1987.

Filipino folk Catholicism puts great stress on rites and ceremonies. Fiestas, pilgrimages, novenas, and innumerable devotional practices mark the concrete, day-to-day religious life of most Filipino Catholics. Much of what they know of Christian doctrinal truth and moral values is learned through these devotional practices.

The attitude of Filipinos toward sacramental celebrations is also influenced by Spanish Catholicism. Many Filipinos tend to look upon marriage as a social event rather than a sacrament, that is, a personal encounter with the Lord. Filipino culture has the tendency to turn baptism, confirmation, and marriage into festive social events in order to create relations between families and to establish a connection with the more prominent people in the community. That is why families often tend to be more concerned with the number of sponsors and the reception afterward than with the religious aspect of the sacramental rite.

Understanding these cultural traits is a prerequisite for effective pastoral ministry to Filipino Americans.

But more than understanding is needed. The Church must also offer a warm welcome to all newcomers, a welcome which is easily perceived and felt. As I have intimated, the Church in the United States has a wonderful tradition of hospitality to immigrants, but each generation must ensure that it is kept alive and operative, and that it is passed on to the next generation. We are a Church of many nations, and we are called to develop an attitude of constant welcome, mindful of the Lord's words: "He who welcomes you welcomes me" (Matt 10:40).

As a nation and as a Church, we are greatly enriched by the diversity of cultures among our people. Immigrants bring new cultural expressions to the mosaic of our pluralistic community. They also give witness to the living communion of local churches throughout the world. Immigrants are a natural link with their countries of origin and advocates for their needs.

The commitment to welcome them is a call to dispel harmful attitudes, stereotypes, and prejudices. The Lord himself gave us the best example and motivation for identifying with the immigrant and the refugee when he said, "I was a stranger, and you welcomed me" (Matt 25:35). Hospitality is essential to the Church's mission because it educates, forms, and enlightens us. And it allows newcomers to become equal partners in the community of faith without losing their identity in the process.

Being a welcoming, understanding community significantly affects our relationship with every newcomer, especially Catholic immigrants. To minister to their needs in an effective, sensitive way, we must know them well. We must also be able and willing to understand the impact our culture has upon them, their beliefs, their values, their practices. Immigration has put a strain on Filipino family life: traditional parental authority is challenged; Filipino youth experience conflicting cultures; the extended family tends to break down. In their newly adopted land, some Filipino immigrants face an identity crisis, are forced to endure economic pressures and burdens, experience difficulties with the Church, and find their traditional faith challenged. When Filipino immigrants are separated from their extended family back home, they need new support systems.

Aware of the special needs and concerns of Filipino Catholics, the Catholic Church in the U.S. has responded to the Filipino Catholic community in many ways. Many *dioceses*, for example, have established Filipino apostolates in their local church structure. We have an Office for the Filipino Apostolate in the Archdiocese of Chicago. Its task is to reach out pastorally to the Filipinos of the Chicago area in order to nurture, develop, deepen, and enliven their faith-life, especially their unique spirituality, culture, values, and traditions. It also helps them become truly committed Catholics who see their contribution to the life of the parish, the archdiocese, and the entire Church as an integral part of their Christian vocation and an expression of their uniquely Filipino culture, and for newcomers on the process of acculturation to the structure and dynamics of the American parish.

On the *national* level, the National Conference of Catholic Bishops' Committee on Migration has proposed a National Pastoral Center for the Filipino Apostolate. Its purposes would be to provide coordination of pastoral services, evangelization, and the promotion of priestly and religious vocations at the national level. It would also assist the Filipino apostolates throughout the country by facilitating the welcome and integration of Filipinos into the local churches and acting as an advocate on their behalf.

Nevertheless, the most effective pastoral ministry to newcomers is done at the local level, in the *parish*, and this is where the greatest challenges are found. Up to this point, we have reviewed some dimensions of the immigrant experience and the Church's response as well as the essential ingredients of pastoral ministry to Filipino Catholics. Now I will address some of the challenges which lie before us, especially, but not exclusively, at the parochial level.

A GENDA FOR THE FUTURE

The challenges I will identify pertain both to the Church and to Filipino Catholics. First, challenges for the Church.

It is quite clear that, to be effective ministers to immigrants, pastors and parish teams need to have or acquire an evangelical openness, strive to learn the language and cultural backgrounds of new parishioners, and become familiar with the Church's teaching in regard to the care of immigrants and refugees.

But this is often difficult when there is so much competition for the pastor's time and energy, when the parish serves a multiracial or multiethnic congregation, and when there are fewer priests to serve an ever-increasing Catholic population. I noticed in the program notes for this convention that Father John Sandersfeld, of the Diocese of San Jose, spent a month in the Philippines to experience firsthand Filipino life and culture, and I commend him for it. That would undoubtedly be a useful experience for many pastors or members of parish staffs. But we have to face the reality that there is a growing gap in every apostolate between the availability of ministers who know the people's language and culture and the number of people needing their care. And this will undoubtedly continue for the foreseeable future.

That is why we also need to identify candidates for the priesthood, religious life, and diaconate, as well as lay ministry and leadership, within the Filipino American community and prepare them to serve their people. Past experience suggests that the second generation of immigrants is usually the first to produce vocations, not the first. (A notable exception to this is the Vietnamese community.) This implies that while we actively promote vocations in the Filipino Catholic community, we must also be patient and understanding if we do not get immediate or dramatic results.

As a partial remedy for the lack of effective ministers for immigrants, the Administrative Committee of the National Conference of Catholic Bishops approved a standard process last March for the exchange of clergy between the United States and other countries, including the Philippines. If other episcopal conferences ratify the process, it will enable us to welcome and integrate into the local presbyterate priests from other nations who will help us serve their cultural group.

At the same time, while respecting cultural differences and being sensitive to special needs, pastors—including bishops—must strive for the unity which is necessary in the local church. This means integrating people of various cultures into the Church without trying to assimilate them or strip away all that makes them different or unique. It means accepting the newcomers as equal partners in the life of the Church.

This is at the heart of National Migration Week which ends today. It is a celebration throughout this land of the rich cultural diversity *and* unity which are present today in the Church in the United States. This diversity generates a creative tension in our community of faith as cultural differences surface, and we strive to integrate them into the daily life and ministry of the Church so that we can truly be one.

In Pope John Paul's message for "World Migrants Day" 1990, the Holy Father describes some essential components of pastoral ministry to immigrants:

Today, many Catholic migrants work in countries where the seed of the Gospel was sown a long time ago. It is obvious that testimony to the faith is made within the framework of the pastoral plan of the local Church. In order to achieve this, pastoral agents should, first of all, insist on the *catechesis of adults*, which favors Christian formation and a growth in the faith of migrants; on active participation in the *celebration of the Sacraments*, starting with baptism; on *formation in prayer* of the migrant community as a whole; on a coherent commitment to giving *testimony to love*. These are the necessary means by which migrants build communion in diversity and collaborate effectively in the work of salvation.

This is not so easily implemented, however. Immigrants and their new parishes must be in personal touch with each other before these essential dimensions of pastoral ministry can occur. Parishes in the U.S. often fail to understand that many immigrant Catholics—especially those from countries where there are active missionaries—expect the Church to seek them out to welcome them. The U.S. is not a missionary country, however, and pastoral staffs often wait for people, including newcomers, to seek *them* out. This can result in an unfortunate stalemate and may give immigrants the impression that they are *not* welcome in the Church here.

Moreover, as I noted earlier, Filipinos are person-oriented, small-group oriented. Their prior experience of parish life often does not prepare them for the more regimented, impersonal style of many U.S. parishes. For example, they are not accustomed to "registering" in a parish or using weekly envelopes for their contributions. This, in turn, may give pastors the false impression that Filipino Catholics do not accept their responsibility towards the Church.

Parish staffs do not always understand that newcomers, who are struggling to adapt to the American way of life are unable, at times, to meet parish policies and requirements. At other times, the newly arrived simply do not comprehend the rigor with which certain criteria are established and implemented.

At times, Filipino Catholics do not find an understanding or respectful attitude among our parish staffs toward their popular religion, their piety and devotions. Newcomers may also be more accustomed to a more traditional liturgical expression and find it somewhat difficult to participate fully in liturgies which seem alien to them. They may hold back, giving the impression that they are lukewarm Catholics.

For these and other reasons, some Filipino Catholics are not closely associated with the Church at the local level, at least in a consistent or serious way. They may develop an attitude of passivity which, in turn, may lead to religious indifference or a search for the warmth of friendship and belonging they may encounter in other religious movements or groups. Tragically, they may remain strangers to the local Catholic church as the months and years pass, ripe for proselytization by non-Catholic groups ranging from mainline Protestants to storefront churches that reach out actively, aggressively, and persistently to them. Mrs. Nuval, the director of our archdiocesan Office for the Filipino Apostolate, tells me that a large number of Filipino Catholics are contacted five times or more by these small Christian groups. Some of these groups use standard methods of evangelization or missionary techniques while others proselytize in the worst sense of the term and make advances in the community with outright lies.

These realities prompt us to be more effective in reaching out in welcome to all immigrants, especially Filipino Catholics, in being sensitive to their special pastoral needs, and in providing effective ministry to and with them. This will continue to be a serious challenge in the future as the number of Filipino Catholics continues to increase dramatically.

Besides these challenges for their Church, there are also certain challenges for the Filipino Catholic community in the U.S.

They have many precious gifts to share with the Church in the United States—their strong faith, their wonderful bonds of family life, their rich devotions, their great intelligence and skills. Faith, in turn, requires commitment to active membership in the life of the Church, especially at the parish level, without losing one's cultural identity. This includes the challenge of responding to the call of stewardship in the Church, joining with others to share their time, talents, and possessions for the sake of the common good.

Filipino Catholics also need to work hard to preserve their culture here in the United States. There are difficulties which tend to prevent them from reaching this goal. Far from the roots which nourished their customs in the Philippines, it is more difficult for their culture to flourish here where many cultures seek to draw life from the same soil and are often in conflict. Moreover, each culture must allow the light of the gospel to help it discern and keep what is good and discard what is contrary to Jesus' teaching.

Filipino Americans also are called to keep faith in their lives, in their families, both at home and throughout this land. Last year, Jaime Cardinal Sin of Manila urged Filipinos at the First Filipino-American Catechetical Conference in Los Angeles to develop a sense of community, a sense of common good, and a common vision. "I urge you," he said, "to develop a sense of pride and solidarity as Filipinos by the way you live, by your family life, by the way you help each other, by the example of your own industry and resourcefulness."

The Catholic Church in the United States needs the gifts of its Filipino brothers and sisters. Family life has been eroded in many Western societies and has accounted for much of the disintegration of the social fabric of this nation. I call upon Filipino Catholics to show us a deep sense of, and reverence for, close family ties. Share with us your great capacity for generosity and compassion which help build community and achieve social justice. By your lives, demonstrate the importance of religious values and give witness to the transcendence of life lived in the presence of God.

My brothers and sisters in the Lord, I conclude by officially inviting you to Chicago next year for the Second National Convention on Filipino Ministry. I assure you that the Archdiocese of Chicago will make every effort to extend to you a warm welcome and traditional Midwestern hospitality.

Family Life Congress
Diocese of Phoenix, Phoenix, Arizona
—— *February 2, 1990* ——————————————————

I am delighted to have this opportunity to address you during this celebration of Christian family life sponsored by the Diocese of Phoenix.

The Church has always been deeply interested in the family. And well it
should be, because the family is *central* to the health and well-being of the
Church, as it is to all societies. The Church, therefore, works closely with
the family in fulfilling many of its basic responsibilities, such as education,
religious and value formation, socialization, religious practice, health care,
and social services. Indeed, so close is the relationship between the family
and the Church that the Christian family is known as the "domestic
church." As such, it has a unique ministry: to provide an environment in
which each person is born, grows, is strengthened, and becomes a gift to the
world. Families indeed need the services and vocational focus which the
Church offers, just as the Church needs strong families to fulfill its mission.

Living according to Christian values in a secular world is difficult. It
takes skill, not merely vision. That is why the Church's pastors, to help
families carry out their responsibilities effectively, must also suggest
strategies and help teach the skills needed for this important vocation. At
the same time, families have a responsibility to be good stewards of their
relationships and vocation. It is wise for them to remain open to, and
aware of, available resources to help them carry out their mission.

This evening I will do two things. First, I will highlight the essential role
parents play in the religious education of their children. Second, I will
share some of my personal convictions about the vocation and mission of

599

Christian parents. I will do this within the context of a parental guide to religious education which my colleagues and I developed, entitled *Growing in Wisdom, Age and Grace*. These convictions helped shape the content of that guide.

CATECHESIS IN THE HOME

Despite the influence of peers and the electronic media on the development of attitudes and values in young people, most studies indicate that children's *religious* attitudes and values are primarily shaped in the home. That should come as no surprise. It has been the Church's experience for centuries. This is why Pope John Paul II frequently refers to the family as the "Church of the home."

This, naturally, frightens many parents. They do not feel comfortable or capable of carrying out this responsibility. They feel inadequate, unprepared for the task. Some are angry that the Church seems to place the burden of their children's formal religious instruction on them. But that is not exactly what I am saying.

While I understand their feelings, I wonder if parents realize that, consciously or unconsciously, they are *continually* forming religious attitudes and values in their children. They are the models whom their children will most often imitate. Their witness to their children about how to live the faith is often expressed without words, but their actions speak much louder than words!

Parents make a unique contribution to the whole Church—and to society—when they nurture the gradual development of faith in their children. This kind of spontaneous or everyday catechesis does not require formal theological training. It enriches a child's faith naturally, almost inadvertently, because it is so closely related to the experience of daily family life.

Family celebrations, for example, often pass on the Church's traditions to children. Baptisms, first Communions, weddings, and funerals give parents the opportunity to share profound religious beliefs. This is also true of family prayer, especially if it reflects the seasons of the Church year.

Families with rich ethnic traditions frequently integrate their religious heritage into family life. In family celebrations, parents gradually weave faith into the fabric of family life, and they do so intuitively, without much studied preparation or conscious deliberation.

There are other moments in daily life which also reveal God's presence in the home. Such situations can be the occasions which put us in closer touch with God if only we can recognize them. For example, the natural, human experience of providing food and security for a child can lead a parent to realize more deeply that God nourishes and protects all of us on another level. When young people experience consistent love and concern from their parents, they are more likely to understand and respond to a loving God. If parents routinely forgive and accept their children when they do wrong, the children are more likely to understand that God forgives and accepts them too.

Moreover, if two children are fighting over a toy, a parent can use the occasion to teach the Christian values of justice, love, and peace. Sometimes these moments can be planned, but most often they occur without prior notice. If parents are alert to these opportunities, they can relate the experience of family life to our Catholic beliefs and tradition.

I hasten to add that parents also have an important role to play in the *formal* catechesis of their children. For most families, systematic catechesis takes place in parochial programs—in a Catholic school or the parish's religious education program. Both kinds of programs depend on a vital link with parents if they are to fulfill their goals. The programs' objectives, always faithful to the Church's teachings, should also reflect the traditions, values, and needs of the families of the parish. Moreover, if these programs are to be effective, the lived experience of family life must impact the catechetical content as well as the way the programs are designed, implemented, and evaluated.

Despite the fact that more formal or systematic catechesis usually takes place outside the home, informal or spontaneous catechesis in the home is simply irreplaceable. It affects all other forms of religious education and formation. Pope John Paul has said it succinctly: "Family catechesis precedes, accompanies, and enriches all other forms of catechesis." However, as we all know, it is often not easy to provide effective family catechesis in the home.

CONVICTIONS ABOUT CHRISTIAN PARENTS

That is why, when I was archbishop in Cincinnati, I published a booklet called *Let the Children Come to Me*. It was a summary of what children were expected to learn about their faith as they moved through elementary school. My staff and I, in consultation with many parents, prepared the booklet in response to requests from many Catholic parents in southwestern Ohio.

When I came to Chicago, almost immediately, an extraordinary number of parents spoke or wrote to me about how challenging it was for them to share their faith with their children. They, too, earnestly asked for help from the Church. Responding to their need became one of my first priorities. We established a task force to develop guidelines to help parents share their faith with their children. The process took a long time because over 8,000 parents participated in the consultation. I am happy to say that the final product, in my estimation, was well worth the effort!

As we developed the parental guide, I articulated several personal convictions about Christian parents. I would like to share them with you this evening because, for me, they are nine compelling reasons to celebrate Christian parenting!

Direct Help for Parents

From the beginning I resolved to provide assistance *directly* to parents. While pastors, directors of religious education, principals, teachers, and catechists all play very important roles in the religious education and formation of children, parents are closest to their children, and their influence is greatest. But while abundant resources are available for professional religious educators, very little practical and realistic help has been addressed directly to parents—until now.

The Family as an Evangelizing Community

I firmly believe that the family is a community founded and given life by love. Moreover, it is the primary community of evangelization; parents are the first evangelizers. As I noted earlier, the family is the "domestic church," the church of the home. Within it, the ordinary occurrences of daily life provide the setting where children first experience God. The human experience of living in a family becomes the foundation for encountering the divine. The natural often discloses the supernatural if only we take the time to notice it, acknowledge it, and reflect upon it.

The educational mission of the Christian family is an authentic ministry through which the first signs of faith are awakened and in which the gospel is transmitted to the next generation. Life in the Christian family can become a journey of faith and a gradual initiation into the larger community of faith. Family life is thus an important focus of the Church's mission of evangelization. The family's deliberate effort to become an evangelizing community is critical to the success of that mission.

Religious Formation and the Earliest Moments of Life

Another conviction of mine is that the religious formation of children begins at the moment of birth. They are profoundly affected by the religious experience of infancy and early childhood. Education in the faith thus begins at their earliest age.

Parents, in other words, begin to form religious values in their children long before they are enrolled in formal programs. Parents do not wait until their child is ready to go to school to begin teaching the child how to walk and talk. Neither should they wait until then to begin to form religious and moral values!

Trust in Parents

Another personal conviction about Christian parents is my abiding confidence in them as the initial and most influential evangelizers of their children. God's love is communicated to infants and young children primarily through parents. Parental love is the visible sign of God's love. Since parents instinctively share their closely held beliefs with their children, they are usually more capable of sharing their faith than they think. They influence the religious development of their children initially and powerfully, more by the example of their lives than by their words. It is important, however, that parents also speak frequently and clearly about their faith and their relationship to God, just as they speak to their children about other matters they want them to understand and treasure.

As I have intimated, parents are the fundamental models and first teachers of faith for their children. Formal programs of religious formation are important helps, but they can only supplement children's experience of living in a Christian home. To say it succinctly, programs can never replace parents in the religious formation of children.

Parental Involvement

Parental involvement in formal religious education programs is also essential. Formal catechesis—whether in Catholic schools, parish-based settings, or other contexts—can at best reinforce the more informal process of growth in faith that ordinarily happens at home within the family. Such structured programs *supplement* Christian family life. They support the efforts of parents to share their religious beliefs and practices with their children. But no amount of formal religious instruction can supplant the living witness and good example of a Christian family.

Christian family life has a character which is, in a sense, irreplaceable. Often without words, family members help one another grow in faith by the simple witness of their lives. If children do not see Christian values, attitudes, and behaviors integrated into their parents' lives, formal religious education has no solid foundation on which to build. The best education in human sexuality for children, moreover, comes from the wholesome attitude and behavior of their parents.

Parents have the right and duty to select the most suitable method of formal religious education for their children. But parents do not surrender the responsibility for their children's formation to others. In effect, they invite teachers and catechists to become their partners. Therefore, parents should not be viewed by professional religious educators as mere participants in the occasional sacramental preparation program.

A Realistic View of Family Life

If our help is to be effective, we must be committed to assist *real* parents, not idealized or romanticized ideas about families. In more stable times, it was easier for parents to transmit their values to their children. But today's society makes that task much more difficult. We all know how much family life has changed over the last few decades. The "traditional" family in which the father works outside the home and the mother keeps house and raises the children is less and less common.

Moreover, in a culture in which separation, divorce, and remarriage are common, married couples face serious challenges to living out their permanent, faithful, life-giving commitment to each other. The rising number of single parents, who raise children alone and often bear full responsibility for their families' welfare, demands that we respond to the actual experience of parents and not to some idealized concept of family life. The frequent mobility of families today places further stress on their internal relationships and reduces the amount of personal support for parents.

Many families today are hurting deeply. Chronic illness, alcoholism, and drug abuse often create painful family tensions. Poverty, hunger, unemployment, homelessness, inadequate educational opportunities, domestic violence, and many other related problems can overwhelm parents who struggle to provide adequate food, shelter, safety and security for their families. These, too, are facts that have to be taken into consideration in helping parents fulfill their responsibility regarding the religious education of their children.

Racial and Ethnic Diversity

Another factor which requires close attention is the richness of the racial, ethnic, and cultural diversity of families. Obvious differences among families are based on race, ethnicity, socioeconomic situation, or a multitude of other factors. Any attempt to remake families according to one, uniform, dominant standard, or to homogenize children's religious formation as if there were only one acceptable model, disregards the authentic religious traditions of their families. Effective religious formation is based on accurate knowledge of the various cultures, their essential components, and their significant expressions.

Family Prayer

Another conviction about Christian families is the importance of integrating prayer into family life. Prayer expresses and helps constitute our relationship with the Lord. It is the companion of everyday Christian life, and the home is a natural environment for prayer. Parents' attitudes about prayer greatly shape their children's attitudes. If parents recognize the sacredness of all creation, pray with their children regularly, and help them identify the events of their lives as experiences of God, then children are more likely to be comfortable with prayer as a daily reality.

At the baptism of their children, parents promise to teach them to pray. Parents do so by actually praying with their children and introducing them to the Church's tradition of prayer. Moreover, prayer in the home is the natural introduction for children to the Church's liturgical prayer. While setting aside time for family prayer is, admittedly, quite challenging today, parents must establish priorities in this area of life, as in all others. They have to evaluate carefully all activities that conflict with major family interests and values. Family prayer flows from family life, so family members will have to make personal sacrifices to ensure appropriate time for praying together regularly.

Interconnection of Family, Prayer, and the Church

A final fundamental conviction of mine is the necessary interrelationship of family life, prayer life, and Church life. As I said earlier, the religious formation of children basically happens within the home through the ordinary experiences of everyday family life. Moreover, a healthy Christian family incorporates the habit of daily prayer within its life. This habit of praying together, in turn, leads the family to the wider community of faith. There the family's religious traditions, values, attitudes, and practices can be reinforced completely and systematically. The integration of family life, prayer, and Church life forms an effective circle for the ongoing evangelization and catechesis of all the family members. If one part of the circle is missing, the dynamic interaction of the other parts is impaired, and the family's growth in faith is impeded.

* * *

I would like to address a few words directly to the parents here this evening. At times, being a parent may seem an overwhelming and lonely task. You may feel that society does not support your efforts, that television and other media demean your family values, or even that the Church has left you on your own to struggle with the questions you face in raising your children as Catholics.

I want to affirm and assist you in your efforts to share your faith with your children. I invite you to recognize that you are God's partner in the creation of the domestic church—your family. I also urge you to view your family as a community of persons who encounter the Lord in and with one another.

You are the first heralds of the gospel for your children. Perhaps the most fundamental contribution you can make to the religious formation of your children is to grow in faith *yourself*—both because you are a parent and because you are also a child of God. My prayer for you is that God will give you the wisdom and the strength to grow closer to him and to walk with your children on the journey of faith.

National Association of Catholic Family Life Ministers

Dallas, Texas

── *September 24, 1992* ──────────────────────────

Thank you for the warm welcome to your conference and for the very kind hospitality you have extended to me since I arrived in Dallas last evening.

I bring you greetings from the National Conference of Catholic Bishops' Committee on Marriage and Family, which I presently chair. Our committee highly values your dedication to the Church's mission, and the many efforts you make to strengthen and renew family life. As diocesan, parochial, and organizational leaders, and collectively, as members of this association, you have consistently been on the front lines of leadership in family ministry. The Plan of Pastoral Activity for Family Ministry, a Family Perspective in Church and Society, Putting Children and Families First— none of these initiatives of our episcopal conference could have taken root throughout the local churches of this country without your support, creativity, vision, and just plain persistence. And so, I express the gratitude of our committee for your important service to the Church.

Our ministry with families is *complex*—responding to changing families in a changing world. So, this ministry needs to be firmly rooted in Christ's teaching, the Church's tradition, and the realities of human life.

Our ministry is also *challenging*—sometimes even to the point of confusion and exhaustion. And so, we stand ever in need of renewal and refreshment.

The theme of your conference, "returning to the well," captures rather succinctly this desire for rootedness and renewal. The image suggests to me a "getting back to the sources" and drawing from them the energy we need to continue. A singularly important source of our life and ministry is our own family. It is a community to which we return throughout our lives, either physically or spiritually, for nurture, direction, criticism, and affirmation. Our family is, as one author put it, "the primary lens that filters the early and lasting light of every life."

Last year, I had the pleasure of visiting the ancestral home of my parents in Italy where many members of our family still live. Returning to and reconnecting with those sources of my life was a wonderful experience. On an even more regular—often daily—basis, I visit my mother who is in a nursing home in Chicago—another kind of "returning to the well." Despite her physical disabilities and loss of memory, she is both a source of, and a resource for, my ministry.

I grew up in the depression. My mother was widowed when I was only six years old and my sister only two. We had very little. But the scarcity of material goods was more than made up for by the love and care showered on us by our mother. Although a recent immigrant from Italy and handicapped, in the beginning at least, by not having a full knowledge of English, she worked hard to provide us with the basic necessities. But she worked even harder to make sure that my sister and I learned and assimilated the basic values needed to lead an integral, upright Christian life. My sister and I also had the love and moral support of several aunts and uncles and their children.

It was this experience—which unfolded in so many simple ways each day—that made me what I am and informs my approach to matters affecting family life in the Church and in society generally. I minister as a pastor, teacher, and leader in the Church and other public arenas, but I observe, discern, judge, act, and even react as a family person. My private and public roles, in other words, are simultaneous and inseparable.

I admit that it is not always easy to keep the two perspectives in balance. Despite my mother's best efforts, I can often forget that I have always been her son and, for merely ten years, the archbishop of Chicago.

And so, I am pleased to begin this dialogue session with you today, acknowledging that I speak about the lives of families in general, but from the perspective of the life of a particular family.

I mention the difference and the connection between the private and public realms in my ministry with families because it offers important guidance about how we approach the renewal and support of families.

Family life is in the spotlight today. I, for one, am pleased that there is a growing public debate in our country over how to strengthen family life. We need to devote even more attention to this matter. Unfortunately, the debate is being polarized by those on the political left and the right. Some on the right say we need better family values and more personal responsibility. Some on the left claim we need better public policies and more investment in human development. The right emphasizes the primary role of moral values and personal character, often ignoring broader social forces such as the impact of economics, discrimination, and antifamily policies which hurt families. The left focuses on the social and economic forces that undermine families, often ignoring the important role that basic moral values play in family life. The pull and tug of the recent "family values" debate in the political arena is a perfect example of this polarization and reveals the "either/or" thinking at the root of it.

An appropriate, comprehensive discussion of family values should have two parts. First, we must emphasize the beliefs or priorities which families have the unique ability to instill in their members, such as respect, commitment, trust, responsibility. Second, we must consider how and to what extent society values the family. This can be measured by the degree to which families are helped to realize their values—for example, through the provision of affordable housing and health care, decent jobs for just wages, neighborhoods free from drugs and violence. For, how can families fill their homes with love and care if they have no homes? How can they teach commitment and trust if the world outside their door offers no security or future for which to strive?

The Church believes that strengthening family life requires a "both/and" approach. Our bishops' conference proposed this in the statement, "Putting Children and Families First," when we wrote: "We believe parental responsibility *and* broader social responsibility, changed behavior *and* changed policies are complementary requirements to help families."

The "both/and" approach is a guiding principle for the work of our Marriage and Family Committee. I suggest that it function in the same way for your work as well. The family is the foundation of society and, therefore, a public entity. It is also an intimate community of life and love and, therefore, a private realm. So, inasmuch as the family spans both public and private worlds, the responsibility for its welfare should be both a public concern and a private endeavor.

I'd like to offer two examples of how the Marriage and Family Committee is addressing family issues—both as a public and a private agenda. I would like to hear your thoughts about them and about your own approach in our discussion period.

Our committee recognizes the public character of the family when, using the framework of a family perspective, it calls upon larger social systems to take the family into account and to act in its best interests. The pastoral statement, "Putting Children and Families First," which the committee helped develop, is a good example.

In this statement we urged that society reorder its priorities to focus more on the needs and potential of children by developing the necessary social supports for the families which raise those children. To focus on children is an effective way to bring into sharp relief the social and public nature of the family. For, it can be argued, children are the most obvious and critical of a family's social responsibilities.

Now we are embarked on an energetic phase of implementation of the statement nationally, called "A Catholic Campaign for Children and Families." This campaign is really the aggregate of many local efforts.

In the Archdiocese of Chicago, we have created a three-pronged approach. Education is the first component. It will consist of hearings on family and children's problems as well as my own pastoral statement on the current situation and the archdiocesan response.

Our second thrust will be to help families directly. Every parish will be invited to use resource materials which the United States Catholic Conference has produced. In a related effort, special parenting programs will be set up in as many as ten locations in the Chicago area. We are also investigating the possibility of a television series designed to help families manage or avoid problems. Finally, the archdiocese is working to transform its personnel policies toward greater "family friendliness."

The third level of archdiocesan response will engage us in efforts to change social institutions and public policies. We will begin to communicate the message of "Putting Children and Families First" to public officials who serve the people of the archdiocese. Concomitantly, we will urge greater participation by Catholics in advocacy efforts to pass legislation that will help children and families.

"Putting Children and Families First" implicitly urges that family ministry have a public awareness and advocacy dimension. Is this true of family ministry as you know it? If not, what seems to be holding back this thrust?

Last spring, I visited the Cabrini Green Housing Project, located only a few blocks from the glitter of Chicago's Magnificent Mile, North Michigan Avenue. I saw there firsthand the toll which violence, lawlessness, and hopelessness take on families. I vividly recall meeting the family of an 8-year-old boy who had just been killed by a stray bullet fired by a 13-year-old. His grandfather pleaded with me, "You must do something. This makes no sense, babies shooting babies!"

Yes, I must do something. And yes, *we* must do something together. And, perhaps, we must do things differently. Where are we to start?

I ask myself whether our family ministry needs a sharper social edge to it. Are we perceived as caring about too narrow a range of family issues? My awareness of how families struggle within the larger social system was expanded considerably when I talked with people at the Black Catholic Congress two months ago.

Despite our aspirations about diversity, do our programs still involve only certain kinds of families? Your preconference workshop on Hispanic families was a wonderful effort to enlarge the boundaries of our ministry. I hope you will continue this emphasis. For, if the Church will not stand up in the public arena for families of all types, who will? Your mission statement pledges the association to be a "voice for families." Are you being heard? What would help your voice to be amplified? How do you get the public's attention and hold it long enough to listen to your message?

The Marriage and Family Committee has also devoted attention to the inner life and dynamics of the family. Here, as before, I will offer one project as an example.

During the past year our committee has discussed a theological vision for Christian family life. This vision is more or less adequately captured by the phrase "domestic church" or "church of the home." We have asked theologians, social scientists, pastoral ministers, and ordinary family people to help us delve into the meaning and application of this concept. We have responded to Pope John Paul's eloquent plea in *Familiaris consortio:* "the family absolutely needs to hear ever anew and to understand even more deeply the authentic words that reveal its identity, its inner resources and the importance of its mission . . ." (no. 86).

What are those "authentic" and revealing words? What images will reach families, bringing them to appreciate their full Christian dignity and vocation? What symbols will reach pastoral ministers, freeing their imaginations to work with families in new, more effective ways?

The Church's teaching about the family being a "church of the home" has rich, unrealized potential. It gives us a starting point for teaching that all families have within their own unique settings many inner resources for a fully creative and redemptive life. Whether a household is composed of mother, father, and children, or a single parent and children, or an extended family with several generations, the dynamic of the Christian mysteries is still at work; sacramental moments still abound. God appears in the times of forgiveness and reconciliation, which many consider the pulse of family life no matter what its configuration. Shared meals and family rituals—graduations, birthdays, holidays, anniversaries—have their own sacred quality. The sick are cared for, the dead are mourned, the sorrowful are comforted; babies are born and guided through the stages of life. Prayers are offered, often with tears and pleading; trust is practiced. This is the Church alive in the home.

To say that every Christian family is called to be a "domestic church" is both to make a statement about the value of what ordinarily happens within family relationships and to recognize how vital families are for God's purposes in the world. For, if they are truly an embodiment of the Church, families are a sign and instrument for bringing about God's kingdom—and family values assume a transcendent meaning.

This Christian vision of family life can appear overly idealistic to some, elite and exclusionary to others, and judgmental to still others. These perceptions must be addressed honestly.

In addition, we should avoid a lopsided presentation of the "domestic church" that would cause families to turn in upon themselves and cultivate their own private holiness. If the Christian family is to be considered an authentic embodiment of the Church, it must be helped to recognize its solidarity with other families and to join with them for witness and service to the larger world.

The symbol of "domestic church" is indeed a rich one. It can shed new light on the roles and responsibilities of the family as both a private and a public community.

That is why our committee wants the ecclesial vision of family life to become better known and acted upon within families, parishes, and dioceses. We ask your help in this task. For, if communicated well, the vision can empower all families and serve as a source of renewal for the Church and society alike.

At this time the committee is working on a pastoral message to families that will be released by the U.S. bishops as part of the 1994 United Nations International Year of the Family. Our working title for the document is "Growing in Love." A foundation for our message is the theological vision I have just been discussing.

At the heart of our message—as it is now beginning to take shape—is the family as "an intimate community of life and love." We are asking what would strengthen the family's ability to be loving, life-giving, and truly an expression of the Church in the world. In the message we identify some important challenges within family life and offer guidance on them, namely, the challenge of equality and mutuality within a marriage, the challenge of change through the family life cycle, the challenge to take time for one another, the challenge to be generative through raising children and through other ways of caring for society and serving the common good. These are not the only challenges of family life, nor might they be the most critical. That is why I ask for your counsel. Will you help us find the authentic words of challenge, hope, and gratitude with which to touch families as they journey through this time of trial and grace?

As Church leaders we must also speak words of commitment to families. An important responsibility of the Church is to support families in their mission as a "church of the home." This is where our theological vision of Christian family life gives way to far-reaching, even radical, pastoral implications. Thus, our pledge to families should be one of partnership. But what does this mean concretely?

Undoubtedly, many of you have thought deeply about the meaning of such a partnership and have been working to bring it about. I would like to hear your insights. Do you think that families see themselves as partners in ministry with their parish? Do they regard themselves as partners with any social institutions? Are parochial and diocesan leaders ready to become partners with families? What attitudes and structures impede the development of a partnership—on the part of Church leaders as well as families? Are there some "success stories" to tell about partnership?

The 1994 International Year of the Family theme is: "Family: Resources and Responsibilities in a Changing World." This suggests that resources and responsibilities exist both within the family and within institutions for the sake of the family. In other words, a partnership is necessary, not only possible. I would like to see the Church and our society move in this direction. It can strengthen families, the Church, and society. It would put some flesh on the bones of our rhetoric about "family values." It will require collaboration and dialogue—to which I now invite you.

"The Church and Families: A Partnership for Life"

The United Nations, New York City, New York

— December 7, 1993 ————————————————————

On December 6, 1983, ten years ago yesterday, I came to New York City to deliver the Gannon Lecture at Fordham University. In my address I articulated the need for a consistent ethic of life. Because human life is sacred, society has a responsibility to protect and foster it in all its circumstances—from conception to natural death. In that broader context of a consistent ethic of life, I have come here this afternoon to talk about the importance—indeed, the necessity—of defending and nurturing family life in the world today.

I am very pleased to be present with Archbishop Martino as the United Nations launches the International Year of the Family. The members of the National Conference of Catholic Bishops are very grateful for his work at the United Nations, and for his frequently expressed concern for the family. I particularly appreciate his efforts on behalf of the Convention on the Rights of the Child. It is my hope that our conference will be able to issue a statement of support for the convention in the near future.

I am also grateful to Father Robert Vitello and Ms. Meg Gardinier of the International Catholic Child Bureau for arranging this afternoon's gathering. As a member of the Board of the ICCB, I enthusiastically endorse the organization's vision and goals.

The welfare of children is a deep and abiding concern of the Catholic bishops in the United States. Two years ago, we approved a statement entitled *Putting Children and Families First*, in which we said that the well-being of children is both a public policy issue and the personal responsibility of parents and families. The document blends responsibilities with rights, personal values with social policies, and individual initiatives with governmental action. Through this statement we confidently assert that we need *both* better values and better policies, more personal and more social responsibility.

Nevertheless, we devoted much of that document to the social policies needed if children are to grow up as healthy, sound members of society. But we also said that the vocation of marriage and family needed to be lifted up, that we must offer people the resources of our spiritual and sacramental heritage in effective and creative ways.

Last month, the U.S. Catholic bishops in general assembly approved a pastoral message to families entitled *Follow the Way of Love*, which is a step in that direction. *Follow the Way of Love* looks at the interior life of families and offers practical and tested ways of strengthening family life. The United Nations observance of 1994 as the International Year of the Family provided the motivation and gave a certain urgency to our task. And while we wrote the message primarily for Catholic and other Christian families, we intend it as a resource for all families in search of encouragement and hope. We wrote it in such a way that it would be easily readable and understandable. Both the bishops and the media have noted that this goal was fulfilled.

The pastoral statement is meant to stimulate reflection on the important, precious dimensions of one's life. The text is punctuated with reflection questions. What we envision is that women and men, parents and grandparents—and even children—will sit down together or alone, read a section, and reflect on and grapple with the reflection questions. In this way they will come to appreciate the strengths and gifts already present in their family; understand more fully God's abiding presence in their lives; have the courage to face their problems; and try out the message's practical suggestions for establishing stable homes of life and love.

We know that the planners of the International Year of the Family hope that this observance will provide the occasion for families to step back and consider the shape of their life together; to renew their commitment to the education and formation of children; and to enliven active concern for the world entrusted into our care. We—the Catholic bishops of the United States—hope that *Follow the Way of Love* will be one means to achieve these ends.

The theme proposed by the United Nations, "Family: Resources and Responsibilities in a Changing World," implies a sense of confidence in the future of the family, the ability of men and women to identify and use their own resources and responsibilities. The Holy See's Pontifical Council for the Family illuminated the theme with these words about the International Year of the Family:

It is necessary to have trust in families, make them aware of their dignity and of the fact that they themselves are social subjects, the protagonists in the defense and promotion of their rights. Indeed, the family "possesses and continues to release formidable energies" *(Familiaris consortio)*.

That is what we have tried to do in our pastoral message: help families tap into the energy that is the grace of family life.

Early on in our deliberations we determined to exercise a discipline of choice. We could not speak about every aspect of family. So, we chose four dimensions which our research indicated are particularly significant for families today—four of which have pastoral implications, and on which sacred Scripture and tradition could shed some light.

These four issues might also be viewed as four marks of a family trying to follow Christ's way of love in our time. They are:

1. *growing in faithful love* as spouses and as family members, one to another. Earlier this afternoon I pointed out that the witness of fidelity can be a light to the world where, too often, faithlessness is the mark. Families can demonstrate that not only is fidelity possible, it is also a source of joy; that promises kept enhance human freedom. Faithful love can be an antidote to cynicism which tends to erode free societies.

2. *giving life* as parents to children, and as families to the broader community. It is a great privilege for parents to be co-creators with God, bringing children into the world. Society has the responsibility of assisting them in this task, not hindering them. Being open to new life signals a profound trust in God as families are called to new levels of responsibility and maturity. Giving life pertains to more than procreation, however. Parents who welcome a child by adoption bless all of us by their faith and their generous spirit.

   Moreover, the vocation of giving life belongs in some measure to the whole family. This is especially urgent in our contemporary cultural situation in the United States where too often narcissism and an exaggerated individualism seem to dominate attitudes and actions.

   There are still other ways—aesthetic, philanthropic, ministerial—in which families are life-givers. *Follow the Way of Love* points out that: "Each generation of a family is challenged to leave the world a more beautiful and beneficial place than it inherited."

3. *acting in a spirit of mutuality and respect*, both in a marriage and in all family relationships. Here we affirm again the equal dignity of women and men. We do not deny differences between men and

women, but we do underscore that marriage is a partnership of equals. Drawing on our spiritual tradition, we state that mutual submission, not dominance, is the key to genuine joy. This is not a matter of measuring out tasks and keeping score. It is a matter of joint responsibility for keeping love alive and building a common life. The details of how that will be accomplished will differ according to the people involved.

4. *investing time* to develop strong family bonds and making family life a priority. Many, if not most, surveys of family life today indicate anxieties about the little time they have to fulfill their familial responsibilities. Parents—most of whom work outside the home, mothers as well as fathers—want more time with their children. And their children wish their parents had more time for them. We realize that time constraints are very real for families. Parents have to work and are grateful to have jobs. Balancing home and work responsibilities is a major challenge for our society.

Mr. Richard Riley, the U.S. Secretary of Education, recently urged parents to turn off the television sets, and read and talk to their youngsters. He reminded them that they have a powerful capacity to shape their children's lives. I agree that turning off the television is a fine suggestion. But if that seems to be unlikely, for whatever reason, we suggest in *Follow the Way of Love* that families watch programs together and discuss the values promoted in them. (We presume intelligent choice of programming.)

The point is that families must make a decision to spend time together. If a meal has to be taken in a fast-food restaurant, and it often does, then we urge families to make it a time when they share more than just food. They should talk to one another. And listen. It has been said that listening is the heart of pastoral care.

Our message to families urges men and women to work at keeping their marriages together. Aware that divorce is taking a terrible toll on children and their parents, we encourage people to move beyond a mindset that says divorce is inevitable. We urge couples to nurture their marriages, for, in so doing, they nurture both their children and themselves as well as the larger spheres of family and community life.

Caring for a marriage may mean seeking pastoral and/or professional help from time to time. Some parishes now have on staff persons trained in psychology, who are also knowledgeable about theology and spirituality. They have the skills to help people work on their problems in a spirit of faith and hope.

Caring for a marriage may mean joining with other couples dedicated to enriching and strengthening marriage and family life. We exhort parishes to consider a variety of ways to support marriage in its various stages.

Couples will certainly also need to draw on the resources of prayer, contemplation, and the sacraments, and especially to remember daily the power and grace inherent in their own sacrament of matrimony.

We have no illusions that an enduring marriage is achieved without effort. Married people tell us it is hard work. But they also tell us it is worth the effort. We want parishes and church agencies to do everything possible to assist couples to build strong, lasting, and, ultimately, joyful marriages, and to aid in the long and often arduous process of reconciliation when conflicts arise.

We are also aware of the needs and responsibilities of single-parent families. *Follow the Way of Love* says to single parents:

> To be faced with all the responsibilities of parenting by yourself is a challenge that touches the very core of your life. We bishops express our solidarity with you. We urge all parishes and Christian communities to welcome you, to help you find what you need for a good family life, and to offer the loving friendship which is a mark of our Christian tradition.

We have said to the women and men who bear the principal responsibility for families: "We rejoice with you in your happiness. We walk with you in your sorrow." And we mean it! We are pastors and church leaders, yes. But we are partners in some sense in this most important enterprise: the forming of families.

Sociologist Robert Bellah suggests that the Church is a necessary context for family life because, historically, it is a source of social support, and, doctrinally, it maintains an understanding of love that includes values of mutual service and indissoluble commitment. Furthermore, daily rituals, so necessary for an orderly family life, can find reinforcement and new meaning through religious ritual and symbols. By providing a counterpoint to the individualistic currents in society, the communal character of the Church can help families move beyond individualism. And families can help churches to be faithful to the common good.

As an interpreter of values in the culture, the Church can help families make choices that are life-giving and enhancing, and, ultimately, transformative of society. For this to be effective, however, the Church cannot be merely a gathering of passive listeners. It needs to be, at the same time, a caring community, and one prepared to act corporately on behalf of justice. It also needs to provide vehicles for its members to care for different segments of human need, to go beyond personal welfare. Many parishes do precisely that.

As a Church leader, my task is to support and help the family in all the ways I have mentioned, and in all the ways described in *Follow the Way of Love*. But my responsibility goes beyond that. It includes developing a sense of discipleship among families so that they will participate with vigor in the debates and activities of public life, bringing to these arenas fidelity, commitment, mutuality, respect, and cooperation which are public virtues as well as family virtues.

My message today, the message of *Follow the Way of Love,* is one of partnership between families and the Church, a partnership needed not only by families and the Church, but also by the world. In this we follow our Lord Jesus Christ who said, "I have come that they may have life, and have it abundantly" (John 10:10).

Pastoral Outreach

Protestant Foundation

Chicago, Illinois

── *December 15, 1982* ──────────────────────────────

I would like to open my remarks with a brief reflection on the titles we bear as we gather together this evening. I am the Roman Catholic arch-bishop of Chicago. You are members and guests of the Protestant Founda-tion. Protestant and Catholic. Those two words are pregnant with meaning.

Protestant. One thinks of Martin Luther declaring before the Diet of Worms on April 18, 1521: "Here I stand, I cannot do otherwise." Or Ralph Waldo Emerson writing about faith: "It cannot be received second hand," he said. "Truly speaking it is not instruction but provocation, that I can receive from another soul. What he announces, I must find true in me, or reject; and on his word or his second, be he who he may, I can accept nothing. On the contrary, the absence of this primary faith is the presence of degradation." The individual, committed to the Lord, striving to be true to his or her conscience in the midst of the stress and strain of life.

And Catholic. The overtones of universality, reaching out to embrace all times, all places, all cultures, all classes. Taking seriously the magnanimity of Jesus reflected in his beautiful image found in the Gospel according to John, chapter 14: "In my Father's house there are many mansions. If there were not I would have told you, for I am going to make ready a place for you." Catholicism embodies that image of a large sprawling house contain-ing an immense family, united in the essentials of faith but not always agreeing on all the implications of that faith; full of energy and vitality, somehow resolving their spats before they reach the point of fracture, striving to move together as God's people living in an ecclesial community which they see not so much as an institution as the living presence of the Lord Jesus.

These are but a few of the rich overtones of these two words. I am sure that, as you sit here listening to me, many other connotations have entered your mind, both positive and negative. Were we to share them, the room would be filled with stimulating ideas, and the conversation would go on for a good part of the evening. However, I would like to turn to another aspect of the matter.

As most of you probably know, one part of the preparation for young couples who come to be married in the Catholic Church involves some paperwork. The parish priest fills out what is called the "premarital questionnaire." It covers basic information about the bride and groom as well as their fundamental attitudes towards marriage. Lately some of our priests have noted that when they come to the question which asks "What is your religion?" some couples have responded, "Christian." The priest inquires further: "Yes, but are you Catholic or Lutheran or Methodist or Baptist or what? What specific kind of Christian are you?" In some cases, the couple's response goes like this: "Well, I was baptized Catholic (or Presbyterian or whatever) but now I'm just a Christian. I found a group in college that doesn't want to be encumbered with all that baggage from the past. It seems to distract from what's really important about God and religion. All those complicated doctrines and all those religious wars that were fought in the name of Jesus. Who needs it? What I've found is the simplicity of reading the Scriptures and sharing together and praising the Lord by leading a good, virtuous life."

What is your reaction to a statement like that?

For me, there are a number of reactions. I would like to share some of them with you now.

First of all, we can surely take some consolation from the fact that the spiritual dimension of life is still important to such young people. In a world where so many practice no faith at all, it is refreshing to encounter young men and women who see religious values and prayer as important formative elements which touch at the very heart of who they are and what they are about.

My second reaction is that the phenomenon I have just described carries a strong message of urgency to us who are leaders in the various churches, congregations and denominations. It urges us to look anew at our own respective traditions and to move forward at the same time with the work of ecumenism. It reminds us that, after the surge of interest which marked the 1960s and early '70s, it appears to the public that we have been resting on our oars. It prods us to get moving because some of our people are growing impatient. Such urgency is valuable. As Pope John Paul II himself has asked: "Have we the right to turn back? Dare we to turn back simply because the road is difficult?"

However, there are other reactions. One is a caution. It is a caution couched in the old expression: "He who does not learn from history is doomed to repeat it." Sydney Ahlstrom's excellent work, *A Religious History of the American People,* is filled with many examples of individuals and groups who rejected their traditions in order to seek a pristine experience of the purity and simplicity of a religious community unencumbered by the baggage of the past. After a period of initial enthusiasm they encountered the challenges of the human condition. Issues of responsibility, authority, disagreements, finances, structure—all of these key realities of human existence had to be dealt with, together with the attendant frictions and stresses. I say this not as an older person seeking to pour cold water on the enthusiasm of young people, but as a fellow human being saying: "Welcome to the club. We're all in this together." We are the way we are not because we are bad people, but because we are human.

Still another reaction. Our history as Catholics and Protestants is, like all history, a mixed bag. It chronicles saints and sinners, light and shadows, beauty and ugliness, generosity and selfishness—indeed the whole litany of human possibilities. The young couples are accurate, up to a point. People were killed and dealt with unjustly in religious wars and persecutions. There was corruption and manipulation. True. But it goes beyond that. We belong to a very rich tradition which embodies the hard-earned wisdom of centuries of experience—an experience that can revitalize us today.

There are two aspects of that experience I would like to underline this evening. First, our *intellectual* tradition. Second, our tradition of *service.*

I was visiting a religious bookstore recently. It was a delightful place in many ways. It had records and wall plaques. There were fragrant candles and lovely statues carved from wood. There were autobiographies of people to whom religion was vitally important. There was an abundance of inspirational literature and devotional reading of all types. And they had a pretty strong shelf of first-rate reference books on the Bible. But there was not much challenging reading in the area of theology or ethics. I do not mention this in criticism of the store because I am sure the owners stocked items in which people were interested. And the place was doing a brisk business, a good sign that people thirst for religious nourishment. My concern is for a possible softening of the vigor of our intellectual tradition. True, some of our ancestors may have wasted time quibbling over matters that were quite peripheral to the faith. But we stand in mutual admiration of the intellectual accomplishments of such people as Augustine and Aquinas, Calvin and Luther, John Courtney Murray and Reinhold Niebuhr. We need to celebrate and renew that aspect of our separate and intertwined traditions.

This is especially needed today. In particular, we need to study and evaluate the bilateral consultations which have been in progress between the Roman Catholic Church and individual Protestant churches both at the international and national level for the past ten to fifteen years. These consultations, as you know, have sought to bring into clear focus the points that unite us and those that divide us, and to indicate those areas where there could be a greater convergence of positions. Such a study must not be done superficially; neither can it resort to myths and caricatures. Rather, it must—with candor and integrity—plumb the depths of our respective traditions and in that context evaluate the possibilities which have been presented by the Catholic and Protestant theologians who have represented the churches in these consultations.

What Pope John Paul II and Archbishop Robert Runcie said last June in their joint statement about the Roman and Anglican churches applies equally to all: "(Our task) will be to continue the work already begun: to examine . . . the outstanding doctrinal differences which still separate us, with a view toward their eventual resolution; to study all that hinders the mutual recognition of the ministries of our communions; and to recommend what practical steps will be necessary when, on the basis of our unity in faith, we are able to proceed to the restoration of full communion. We are well aware that this . . . will not be easy, but we are encouraged by our reliance on the grace of God and by all that we have seen of the power of that grace in the ecumenical movement of our time."

My second concern is our tradition of service. The young couple filling out marriage papers with the parish priest are products of a world of escalating complexity. "Future Shock" has become part of our normal experience. I suppose it is a natural reaction to seek an island of simplicity in such a world. And for some, perhaps for many, that island is religion. It is a matter of God, my Father, and you, my brothers and sisters, and our shared desire to live lives of genuine goodness. And that is absolutely correct.

But what about that complex world out there? What about the needs of all those suffering people? We have to resist the temptation to withdraw from it all and disengage ourselves. I know some folks who will not watch the evening newscast because it is all so depressing and, besides, "What can one individual do about it?"

One of the keystones of our tradition of service—both Catholic and Protestant—is based upon those words of Jesus which at first seem so ordinary but, on reflection, are so rich in meaning. In the sixteenth chapter of the Gospel according to Matthew he says: "I am sending you out like sheep among wolves. So you must be wise like serpents and guileless like doves." Those who have been most effective in responding to the needs of humanity have been men and women, Protestants and Catholics, who were able to negotiate those two apparently contradictory qualities. Guilelessness or simplicity of heart and wisdom or shrewdness—or as we sometimes hear around Chicago, "street smarts." It is precisely this tradition of service that takes us into the real world and prompts us to make moral judgments about what we see and experience. Some complain about this, but Jesus' contemporaries complained about him also when he addressed the issues of his day.

I would like to conclude with one more reflection on those two words, "Protestant" and "Catholic." In his fine book, *The New Testament: An Introduction,* the now-deceased University of Chicago professor Norman Perrin makes this observation:

> Though the books in the New Testament differ from one another in their understanding of the nature of Christian faith in the world, they are in common wrestling with the problems of that faith and no other. . . . Each writer attempts to relate to and to make sense of life in the world by means of his faith in Jesus Christ. The diversity of the New Testament is matched by the diversity of Christian churches in subsequent Christian history. Over and over again a particular viewpoint in the New Testament is developed historically by a group of churches. . . . The New Testament represents the whole spectrum of possibilities of what it means to be Christian in the world, and either anticipates or inspires every subsequent development within the Christian churches. The Roman Catholic and the Lutheran, the liberal Protestant and the fundamentalist, the contemplative mystic and the apocalyptic visionary, all find themselves at home in one part or another of this collection from the literature of earliest Christianity (ch. 2, 18–19).

You and I share that dream of the young couple to whom I referred earlier. We desire simplicity and authenticity; we crave for ultimate unity among all who seek to follow in the footsteps of Jesus Christ. However, we seek that unity not by turning our backs on our traditions, but by penetrating to the deepest roots of those traditions which are found in the Gospels. As we discover our home in the Gospel of Jesus, we will, I trust, discover ourselves to be neighbors in the most authentic sense.

As I leave you, I make my own the prayer of Pope John Paul II spoken last June in the Anglican Cathedral of Canterbury: "Love grows by means of truth," he said, "and truth draws near to man by means of love. Mindful of this, I lift up to the Lord this prayer:

O Christ, may all that is part of today's encounter be born of the spirit of truth and be made fruitful through love.

Behold before us: the past and the future.
Behold before us: the desires of so many hearts!
You, who are the lord of history and the lord of human hearts,
be with us! Christ Jesus, eternal Son of God, be with us! Amen."

"This Hope Will Not Leave Us Disappointed"

Garrett-Evangelical/Seabury-Western Seminaries
Evanston, Illinois
—*January 26, 1984* ─────────────────────────────

It is an honor for me to be with you this morning. I come before you as a brother to share my reflections and my prayers for Christian unity. You and I have come together not simply because we instinctively believe it is a good thing for all Christians to witness to their common faith in the Lord Jesus, but because we sincerely believe that it is God's will that we work toward the restoration of Christian unity.

In the past two decades, dialogue groups representing the various Churches have advanced the work of ecumenism. As you know, Anglicans and Roman Catholics have been meeting in officially sponsored consultations since 1965 in the United States, and since 1970 at the international level. The Methodist-Roman Catholic dialogue has been taking place since 1966 in the United States, and for nearly as long on the international level. In these bilateral consultations, our representatives have been pursuing questions of doctrine and praxis, as well as how we might join together to proclaim the Lord Jesus and his gospel more effectively in our world.

The International Anglican-Roman Catholic Commission issued its final report at Windsor in 1981. The report consisted of consensus statements about Eucharist, ministry and ordination, and authority in the Church. The report concluded by stating: "The convergence reflected in our Final Report would appear to call for the establishing of a new relationship between our Churches as a next stage in the journey towards Christian unity" (*Origins*, vol. 11, no. 44, April 15, 1982, p. 703).

I am sure that you are aware of the impact that such ecumenical endeavors have had on your seminary programs and on our attitudes about one another. These changes, to some extent, have reached the level of the local congregation.

In a sense, then, the Week of Prayer for Christian Unity is a time for marking progress and celebrating what has happened to us because of our dialogues with one another. We praise and give thanks to God who has guided us, strengthened us, nourished us with his word.

Yet it is also clear that much remains to be done. We are not yet at the point of full unity to which the prayer of Jesus calls us. About a month ago, the Anglican-Roman Catholic Dialogue in the United States issued some reflections on Christian anthropology that highlight such concerns of the two churches as human sexuality and marriage; the role of Mary in the life, devotion, and teaching of the Church; and the admission of women to the ordained ministry. The report concludes by expressing the need and pointing the way for further studies in these areas (*Origins*, vol. 13, no. 30, January 5, 1984, pp. 505–12). These are issues of great importance about which significant differences still remain.

Two years ago, the Methodist-Roman Catholic dialogue group in the United States issued a statement on "The Eucharist and the Churches." Again, the group found "points of surprising convergence as well as remaining differences in teaching and practice about the Eucharist." While "remarkable unity and agreement on the structure of the eucharistic celebration and on the central eucharistic prayer have been discovered in the dialogue," there are still questions to be pursued regarding "church order, authority, and ministry, on which our differences are considerable" (*Origins*, vol. 11, no. 41, March 25, 1982, pp. 651–59).

It may not be misleading to suggest that, when we began this process of dialogue with the hope that it would lead to deeper Christian unity, we did not have a clear set of directions. We were not yet aware of the paths we would have to walk. We did not know the time frame to which we were committing ourselves. But the Spirit of God has been with us, leading and guiding us and it is clearer today that this is a long-range process on which we have embarked.

Sometimes it seems as though the major ecumenical efforts are being conducted at the national and international levels, while ecumenism is less of a burning issue in our seminaries and in our local congregations. Perhaps it is more accurate to say that ecumenism is taken for granted in the seminary environment today, but that it does not always receive the same emphasis that it did a decade ago. This is understandable to some extent, given our cultural preoccupation with quick results from our efforts. It is more difficult for us to sustain interest in processes that necessarily extend over decades.

However, the real test of Christian unity will take place in the hearts of individual members of our churches and in the local congregations. To continue enabling good and holy things to happen at this level, it is essential that we prepare another generation of local church leaders who are committed to the work of Christian unity.

Two years ago, Pope John Paul II met with members of the Joint Commission cosponsored by the World Methodist Council and the Roman Catholic Church. He told them: "Do not be upset by the cries of the impatient and the skeptical, but do all in your power to ensure that your search for reconciliation is echoed and reflected wherever Methodists and Catholics meet" (*Pope John Paul II: Addresses and Homilies on Ecumenism,* 1978–1980 [Washington, D.C.: United States Catholic Conference, 1980] 161–62). His words apply equally to all gatherings such as this!

As I have followed the progress of the various dialogue groups, I have become more and more aware of the pain of disunity and the need to take seriously the Lord's desire for ecclesial unity. The work of ecumenism has become a greater and more urgent reality for me in recent years. Part of this spiritual experience is the growing realization and conviction—not only intellectually, but in the very depths of my being—that the sixteenth-century separation and those that followed would not have happened if the mutual charity and openness of our dialogue today had existed then.

Regrettably, there followed more than four hundred years of mutual recrimination. During that time the record suggests that neither side heard what the other was saying. Instead of focusing on the Lord Jesus, who would have been able to help us rise above our human weakness and failure, we looked only at ourselves, at our own prejudices, whims and hurts—both real and imagined. And the result was that the chasm between us became wider.

Christian unity is God's gift to us. God bestows his gifts in sovereign freedom. In sharing his freedom with us, God gives us the power, by abusing our freedom, to frustrate his plan and block his gifts. He also gives us the capacity for relating to one another in such a way that we can be a source of ongoing strength and support for one another. In this way we may also become more effective witnesses to the teaching of Jesus and the love of God.

In this light we can join with Saint Paul in boasting about the afflictions and the suffering that derive from our disunity. These afflictions make for endurance, just as endurance makes for tested virtue, and tested virtue makes for hope (Rom 5:3-4). The work of Christian unity is a task for the long run. There is no shortcut. The way of dialogue is long and arduous at times. But the destination towards which we are learning to walk together is worth any hardships we encounter along the way.

We seek Christian unity *not primarily* because it will free us from some of the anxiety and tension that disunity and confrontation entail. We seek unity *not simply* so that we might be seen as more authentic and credible when we preach Good News to the world. In our search for Christian unity, the spotlight is not to be on ourselves but on the Lord. This work is important because it will enable us to proclaim *the Lord Jesus and his gospel more effectively*.

It will also provide us the opportunity to model in our world the processes, attitudes, and beliefs that can lead to reconciliation, justice, and peace. If, as Christians, we are going to be peacemakers, we will have to join together in a community of conscience to provide moral guidance in our world. We will have to cooperate and collaborate to ensure the establishment of a just international order that will promote peace.

This work of Christian unity demands that we be people not only of faith, but also people of hope. The hope to which we are called "will not leave us disappointed—because the love of God has been poured out in our hearts through the Holy Spirit who has been given to us" (Rom 5:5). When the Lord Jesus reconciled us with God, he called us to live in peace and harmony with one another; to love one another as he himself has done; to live with one another as brothers and sisters.

I have come among you this morning as your brother. I invite you to join with me in thanking the Lord for the good things that he has already accomplished among us—and to pray ardently that we will have the strength, courage, and wisdom to continue to walk together along the yet undisclosed paths that lead to Christian unity.

Address

Leadership Greater Chicago

Chicago, Illinois

—January 9, 1985 ——————————————————————

As I was flying here from Cincinnati two-and-a-half years ago to be installed as archbishop of Chicago, many feelings filled my mind and heart. I thought about this great city and its proud history. I thought about the many influential leaders who have left their mark on Chicago. And I thought about what kind of contribution I might make to this metropolitan area.

When I arrived, I said that I understood my role to be that of a reconciler. My task is to help create the kind of atmosphere in all parts of the archdiocese that will encourage people to come together, dialogue, and thereby create a new, united community. I can assure you that I have become more realistic about the challenge this entails, but I am even more firmly committed to its realization than when I arrived!

I very much appreciate the invitation to address the Fellows of the Leadership Greater Chicago program. I wish to share some reflections about the opportunity we find in Chicago's social diversity and the tragic obstacle we discover in its racism. I trust that each of you cares deeply, as I do, about the potential for good which exists in the Chicago metropolitan area.

One of the major impacts of Chicago on my own life and ministry has been its social and cultural diversity. There is reason to be proud of the broad range of ethnic and racial backgrounds. Each wave of immigrants has enriched our life as a community and broadened our experience of the wider world. Increasingly, many of our neighborhoods and suburbs are becoming international in population and culture. Chicago clearly is a cosmopolitan city.

633

Today's world has become a global village because of the increasing interdependence of all peoples and nations. In the Chicago area we have a golden opportunity to demonstrate to the world that people of diverse backgrounds *can* live together in harmony and peace.

Our ethnic fairs—with their exchange of foods, dance and other forms of culture—are attractive and successful events. They show how we can engage in dialogue and commerce with one another while retaining our particular cultural heritage and identity. They are one example of what we can accomplish when we work together.

Our social and ethnic diversity can, indeed, work to our advantage. But it also can lead to conflict. When such diversity becomes the focus of fear or intolerance—when it is manipulated to maintain group power, prerogatives or material gain—the ensuing hostility and conflict impact negatively on the quality of life and impede the resolution of community problems. It is to the advantage of all of us that we learn to live in harmony. Our very survival may depend upon it—because we face enormous problems in our community!

Apart from our diversity, economic change is seriously affecting the quality of life among our people. Many industries, once crucial to Chicago's economic vitality, have been declining, retooling, and choosing to move to other labor markets. Service industries are no longer growing at previous rates. Restrictions in public service affect many people, especially the poorest and most vulnerable among us. We must provide affirmative and responsible ways to develop the kind of strong economic climate in Chicago which will benefit all its citizens.

As a community, we face critical issues which affect the health and well-being of all our people—our families, our youth, our elderly. Unemployment, underemployment, crime, poor and inadequate health services, deterioration of family life, ever decreasing social service programs, violence in our streets and on our playgrounds—all these problems demand our common concern, our competence, and our collaboration.

This means that we must take down the fences which separate people from one another in this community. Robert Frost once said, admittedly somewhat with tongue in cheek, that "good fences make good neighbors." Perhaps in some other circumstances his words bespeak wisdom, but not in Chicago, not at this point in our history. The high fences around our various communities have only increased the suspicion, the fear, the distrust which threaten to isolate us from one another, thereby destroying the harmony of this community. These fences have become obsolete and destructive because they make it impossible for us to be brothers and sisters towards one another. They also make it impossible for us to confront the problems which can only be resolved through joint efforts.

Racism isn't new in Chicago. To some extent, it has lain hidden and dormant in specific periods of our history, but it has been with us for a very long time. It's not limited, of course, to the city boundaries or to the metropolitan area. It has deep roots, which will not easily be eradicated. Although efforts have been made to cope with the problem in the past, the results suggest that they have been inadequate. The number of racial incidents has escalated during the past year. While some progress has surely been made, in many ways we are still at the beginning.

Racism has many deleterious effects. It so blinds us that we do not recognize our sisters and brothers. It so deafens us that we cannot listen attentively to one another—or even to God. It diffuses our energies which are needed to build up a city and a nation where people can live in justice, peace and harmony. Racism alienates us from our better selves and allows our weaknesses to control our thoughts and behavior. In short, it causes a tremendous waste of gifts, energy and resources.

Let me be more personal for a few moments. As someone born and raised in the South, I only gradually became aware of the ugliness of racial discrimination. I remember the first time I traveled to a convention with a fine black Catholic gentleman. My head told me it was right and proper for us to be together as brothers in the Lord. But, as people stared at me (or so it seemed to me), I must admit that my emotions were very confused. Working out that inner turmoil took a long time. I say this so that you will understand that I too have had to struggle, as I assume each of you has, with this issue.

Racism is an insidious sin, but it is not confined to any single racial, social or economic group. Moreover, it is often associated with other convictions, fears or emotions. At the risk of oversimplification, let me clarify what I mean:

(1) The racism of a white homeowner whose neighborhood is experiencing racial change is sometimes expressed in ugly or violent words, feelings, thoughts. But it is coupled with profound grief at the loss of something very dear—a home, a neighborhood, a parish, close friends, a way of life.

(2) Those of us who live in the more affluent sections of the city or suburbs, far from the problem areas, must challenge ourselves on subtle forms of discrimination lest our well-intended compassion be subverted by smug self-righteousness.

(3) Racism can be found among black people as well as whites. It is coupled with a legitimate desire to have a larger house, to live in a more pleasant neighborhood, to enjoy the fruits of their hard labor. As black people at last gain greater political, economic and social power in our society, they must challenge their own attitudes and behavior lest the actors change but the drama continue with the same old story.

(4) Young people—black and white and Hispanic—are often the flash point for racist violence. But frequently they are merely acting out the attitudes and prejudices which they learn from their elders.

Last September I joined a number of religious leaders in issuing a statement about what has been happening recently in Chicago and what our response should be. We were well aware, of course, that the churches and synagogues of Chicago cannot solve all of the city's political, social, and economic problems. This is not our intention. We acknowledged that we lack not only the resources and skill to do so, but the mandate as well. However, we recognized our responsibility to model and critique the tone of social discourse and the quality of spirit which we believe is essential for this community. We also believe we have a role in motivating and encouraging civic and business leaders to develop a common, constructive approach to the city's problems.

With these other religious leaders, I feel that building up the larger community is the key to solving the social and economic problems of this metropolitan area. No greater challenge faces us today than that of overcoming the polarization and lack of a united spirit which exist in our midst. We can no longer sit back and wait for something to happen. We must begin to act, and we must do so *now!*

I have acknowledged that the problems we face are complex, difficult, and manifold. But I am a man of hope. In the relatively short time that I have been in Chicago, I have met literally thousands of citizens in all walks of life. When we appeal to what is best in all of us, the people of the Chicago area are *good*. We have the potential to make this a world-class city. We have, in our ethnic diversity, all the ingredients necessary to demonstrate to the world how people of various racial, ethnic, social, and economic backgrounds can live and work together in harmony. The tradition of this city—like the story of the phoenix—gives us hope for the future.

As archbishop of Chicago, I have a dream for Chicagoland.

I dream of a coalition of dedicated people in our metropolitan area working together to renovate the structures of our society which are at the root of poverty, crime and racism.

I dream of a society in which there are jobs for the unemployed and the underemployed, good schools for the young, and decent housing for all.

I dream of social programs which support family life rather than undermine it.

I dream of young people becoming enthusiastic about themselves and the possibilities of life rather than taking refuge in drugs, sex and violence.

I dream of Chicago presenting itself to our nation and the world not as a city of racial tension, but as a metropolis of racial collaboration and harmony.

Do you share these dreams? Do you, perhaps, feel they are unrealistic? If so, remember what Daniel Burnham wrote many years ago: "Make no little plans. They have no magic to stir men's blood, and probably themselves will not be realized. Make big plans; aim high in hope and work, remember that a noble, logical diagram once recorded will never die, but long after we are gone will be a living thing, asserting itself with ever-growing insistency. Remember that our sons and grandsons are going to do things that would stagger us."

One of our tasks is to prepare the next generation of leaders: people who have the capacity to continue developing a broad vision which can embrace the ethnic and cultural diversity of this great metropolis—people who have the courage to work collaboratively and creatively in solving the problems facing the people of this community—people who have the compassion and concern to help all their brothers and sisters, especially those who are more vulnerable.

If you are willing to become this kind of leader, know that I will stand with you, walk with you, support you and challenge you!

Humboldt Park–Logan Square–West Town Community Meeting

Chicago, Illinois

— *February 5, 1985* ─────────────────────────────

"When you wake up in the morning, you don't know if you're going to live the whole day. Parents don't know if their son or daughter will come home or not." These are the words of "Maria," a teenager who had been repeatedly harassed and threatened by "folks" and "people." A recent issue of *The Chicago Catholic* reported her story. I'm sure that her words echo in the minds and hearts of many of you here this evening!

Some of my associates advised against my coming here this evening. They reminded me of the icy walkways and my recent track record of walking on ice. They also told me that I could not wander through a large crowd and avoid having my arm bumped. I'm sorry that I won't be able to shake hands with most of you this evening. But I told my friends: the pain in my arm is nothing compared to the pain in the hearts of so many good people in Humboldt Park, Logan Square, and West Town. I'm going to their community meeting!

Why am I here this evening? I have come here—not simply to listen, although I *have* listened and I will continue to listen to you. I am here—not merely to announce an archdiocesan program to lessen the impact of gangs on this community. Basically, I am here because I want to stand with you in your present predicament. I want you to know that you are not alone. I care about you and your families. After all, you are my brothers and sisters!

I'm sure that's why so many of *you* have come to this community meeting—because you care about your families, your neighbors and your neighborhoods. Many civic and religious leaders have also joined us this evening to demonstrate that we are all in this together. They represent many of the churches and schools of this area, city and state government, the Chicago Police Department and the Park District. We want to help you, and we want to encourage you to help each other.

My particular concerns are the young people of this particular community and of our entire city. They represent our future. Their early years are so formative in preparing them for the future. They deserve every opportunity to grow into full adulthood safely—equipped with adequate education to enable them to secure employment, with moral values to guide their activities, and with a sense of their own worth and dignity.

They have a right to learn that they belong to God, *not* to a gang leader—that they belong to a family and friends, to a church which cares for them. We must prepare them to assume their full and rightful role as citizens of this great city and nation. That is the task which lies before us.

What is actually happening today, unfortunately, is quite different. Many young people, like "Maria," live in constant fear and apprehension. Their walk to school may take them across gang boundaries. A simple trip to the store may prove fatal.

Their classmates may belong to rival gangs. Their brothers and sisters may be in jeopardy unless they cooperate with ruthless gang leaders. This is no way to grow up! We must change this pattern!

This evening I would like to share my reflections with you on (1) the scope of the problem we face in regard to gang violence, (2) some things you can do as a community to solve the problem, and (3) some of our archdiocesan plans for helping communities better cope with this devastating situation.

THE SCOPE OF THE PROBLEM

Perhaps the single most important indicator of the extent of the problem is this: during 1984, this area of Humboldt Park, Logan Square, and West Town sustained the highest number of gang-related murders in the nation. Twenty-nine young people suffered a violent death in this community last year. Only last night another youth, Douglas Tomason, was shot and remains tonight in critical condition. Although the statistics are shocking enough, they do not begin to touch the deep tragedy that so many of you have felt during the past twelve months. We remember them—not as mere numbers but as fellow human beings with *names*, with *families*, with *friends*. We, too, have been diminished by their loss.

Estimates put the number of gangs in this area at about 42—compared with 110 gangs in the entire city. It is not just the number of gangs that is so alarming but the scope of their activities, especially in regard to drugs.

I'm sure you know that there are three kinds of gang members: the professional core who provide leadership, active members who want to belong to the gang, and then those who are pressured to join and stay in the gang.

New members are often recruited through intimidation and promises of false security. Sometimes mere children are set up to do some of the most dangerous deeds for the professionals who hide behind them. We all know that many young people do not really want to belong to a gang—if they are given a free choice or a better alternative.

I would not want us to give up on rehabilitating the professional core because their lives also have value. But my primary concern is for the majority of young people in this area—those who really do not want to belong to a gang but who also need alternatives to gang activities.

Something is very amiss when young people have to protect their very lives by the colors or clothing they wear. As you know, it can be fatal to wear the "wrong" color or to make the "wrong" gesture. Adolescence has always been a time to wrestle with conforming to the ideas and manners of peers. But to be forced to conform under penalty of violence or death erodes individual dignity and tends to rob the individual of a very important God-given resource—the ability to decide for oneself.

Schools often are not the places of safety that parents want for their children. This is not due to negligence on the part of dedicated administrators or teachers but to the pervasive presence of gangs. I wish to commend the efforts and sacrifices made by many of the teachers and administrators present here tonight, representing both the public and the Catholic school systems. However, because of the number of weapons brought to school, these places of potential opportunity—despite the best efforts of the school personnel—have become, instead, powder kegs storing up potential violence and destruction.

Moreover, so many young people are "dropping out" of high schools. Father Charles Kyle tells me that the "drop-out" rate in this community over the past ten years is about 70 percent! The "drop-out" problem is clearly related to the gang problem because it lessens the chances of "drop-outs" for meaningful employment and puts them on the streets where they are easy prey for gang recruitment and active gang membership.

Perhaps you have heard Father Kyle explain why he became interested in "drop-out" statistics. "I buried kids," he says. "I've buried 18 kids under age 18 who died violently. At each wake I began to ask what school the youth attended. I found out that all of them had dropped out of school. They were living on the streets." As you can see, "dropping-out" can be a matter of life or death!

Whenever we face a problem, we need to understand its causes to ensure that we do not become content with merely putting band aids on the surface or taking aspirins to chase away the pain for a limited period of time. Enough studies have confirmed what you already know in your hearts—that the environment contributes to the success of gang development, crime and violence.

In this community, more than 1 out of 4 people live below the federally established poverty level. In some sections of this neighborhood it is 1 out of every 2 people! What is the environment like when people are faced with unemployment and underemployment, when their schools are gang-infested, when they lack adequate diet or living conditions, when they have limited access to important medical and social services? There is no question that such an environment helps breed the problems we face.

These are the facts of life in this community. They are similar in many other neighborhoods across this city. They are also duplicated in many of our urban areas and rural regions throughout this nation. They are problems that city government or county government cannot solve alone. They are problems that demand state and federal assistance, as our civic leaders know so well—Mayor Washington and the City Council, State's Attorney Mr. Richard Daley, Dr. George Munoz, Mr. Edmund Kelly, Superintendent Fred Rice and other civic leaders present this evening.

In this connection, I challenge the federal administration to take these realities into account. In the admittedly necessary effort to reduce the national deficit, it is highly questionable whether this should be achieved by *reducing* the budget for social programs by 15 percent while *increasing* the military budget by 13 percent.

But, for now, I want to keep our focus on what you can do in *this* community to change the environment.

WHAT YOU CAN DO

Whenever we face a problem, we also must calculate what resources we have at our disposal to solve it. I would like to highlight two essential resources in particular: this community itself and your families.

This area of the city has a rich diversity of racial and ethnic backgrounds. Each of you brings an important cultural heritage into this community and thereby enriches it. Our prayer service this evening will clearly reflect this. But diversity can also lead to conflict when it becomes the focus of fear and intolerance. Racial and ethnic intolerance lead to deeper alienation within a community. This makes it even more difficult to solve community-wide problems such as the gang violence which cuts across racial and ethnic lines.

Violence and the fear of violence can also lead individuals and families to retreat into the safety of their homes—in a kind of isolation from others. However, in doing so, they simply become more vulnerable because, in not reaching out to help others, they can expect no help themselves.

One of the key ingredients in solving problems in Humboldt Park, Logan Square and West Town is strengthening your life *as a community*. Does that sound unrealistic to you? Does it seem, perhaps, even impossible? Well, then, just look around you and see the others—like you—who have come to this meeting because they also care. We have heard this evening what positive things have happened at Our Lady of the Angels parish because people have come together to care for one another. You don't have to stand alone against violence and the poverty which breeds it; you can stand together!!

To unite this community in the face of serious problems means that you must take down any fences which separate people from one another. These fences are destructive because they make it impossible for us to be brothers and sisters towards one another. They also make it impossible for us to confront common problems, which can only be resolved through joint efforts.

The efforts of the police, the state's attorney's office, the courts, and correctional agencies will only be successful to the extent that this *entire* community is vitally interested, cares deeply and participates fully in the elimination of crime and gang violence. Real progress can be made—and *will* be made—to the extent that each of you, each of your families, your churches, your civic organizations, your business leaders cooperates with city, state and federal agencies to improve the quality of life in this community. Again, we have heard what a good experience such cooperation has been for Our Lady of Angels parish.

We also have to learn to help one another. So often it is the most vulnerable in our midst who are taken advantage of. The poor, the aged, the young, and women are forced to bear the brunt of violence and injustice. They are the most frequent victims of crime. Families who lack adequate income, housing, education or health care too often are the same ones who have to stand by helplessly as their children are convicted and imprisoned as juvenile offenders. Repeated tragedies wear them down until they close in on themselves in shame and want. Somebody has to let these people know that we care about them! I am here to say that *I* care! I stand with you in your struggle!

The second key to our young people's future lies within our families. I know it is very difficult to raise a family today. Moreover, unemployment, financial problems, lack of adequate housing or health care, alcoholism and drug abuse—all of these further erode family ties.

Nevertheless, young people need real homes to return to after school. They need some place where they are not only safe but also where they know they are loved. They need someone to talk with—to share their dreams and their fears, their hopes and their despair. They need parents who show concern about who their friends are, what they do outside the home, where they go and why. They need parents who care enough to learn whether their children are going to school, whether they are gang members. They need parents who are willing to help them. You parents—mothers, fathers, single parents—*you* hold the key. We are here to support *you!*

Perhaps most important of all, our children need homes where they can learn values and moral principles. They need to learn personal responsibility and why it is important to defend and protect the rights of all our fellow human beings. They need to learn the dignity and worth of each human life. Where human life itself is considered "cheap" and easily "wasted," eventually nothing is held as sacred and all lives are in jeopardy.

Perhaps the two single most important things that you can do right here in this area of the city—by yourselves—is strengthen both family and neighborhood life.

The rest of us are here this evening to tell you that we will help you do this to the extent that you need help and we have the appropriate available resources. Let me now outline what the Church can do to help you.

THE ROLE OF THE CHURCH

Jesus taught us to love one another as brothers and sisters, children of the one God. The Church has consistently taught the basic rights of each human person: the right to life, the right to human dignity, the right to those things necessary for life—including personal safety and freedom from fear.

We do more than teach, however. We also work to defend and protect those rights whenever they are threatened. We stand for justice and will help those who are the victims of injustice. We are also committed to doing what we can to prevent injustice and oppression.

The most important place where the Church can help reduce and prevent crime—including gang-related violence—is in the local church. If you look around this evening, you will see many Catholic and Protestant pastors in attendance. I can assure you that this is not a command performance! Their presence underlines a point I want to make: the Church is *not* engaging in something new by its concern about gang violence. We have been here a long time, and we intend to continue serving the people of this area. The priests, religious, and laity of these local churches have labored faithfully and selflessly for many years, addressing needs as they emerged. In particular, they have committed their resources to ministering to young people—including those in trouble.

I want to be clear about a second issue: I have not come here from the Archdiocesan Pastoral Center to solve the gang problem. I simply don't have the solutions. They lie within *you*. Long-term solutions must be based in the community. They must emerge from your midst and have your full support. To be effective, they truly must be *your* solutions.

But the Church is here to help you. Your pastors and those who work with them will help you build up this community. I am here to demonstrate my heartfelt support for them and to encourage them to continue their difficult but dedicated ministry. If we were not to speak out at this time of civic crisis in our city, the very stones would cry out! I assure you I intend to speak out! I will walk every street in this city, if necessary, until this problem is resolved.

As you may know, the Catholic priests of this area have been meeting regularly to develop approaches and programs to address the problems which we are discussing this evening. Recently they developed a proposal regarding community-based gang intervention. We are currently studying it for possible archdiocesan financial assistance.

Since December 20, my staff and I have been meeting regularly with a small group of persons who serve in neighborhoods which have been particularly ravaged by gangs. Your community is represented. We have been examining the problem, listening to the voices of the neighborhoods, and considering various proposals. Of course, we are under no illusion that the Archdiocese of Chicago can solve all gang problems. The primary concern is how we use our available but limited resources to help people in various parts of the metropolitan area to cope with the problem. To me it seems urgent that some constructive steps be taken, that we move from debate and discussion to action.

This evening I would like to describe briefly a particular archdiocesan initiative which can have great impact, I believe, on your efforts in this community—Mobile Teams.

Although I mentioned that long-term solutions to the problem of gangs must come from within the individual community, it takes time to develop the needed consensus. There are also short-term, partial solutions which can bring a measure of relief to a community.

The Mobile Teams are designed to have an immediate impact. There will be two teams, each consisting of two persons, trained and ready to help specific neighborhoods assess and address gang activity in their area. In other words, these teams will be available to all areas of the archdiocese. They will be bilingual and interracial. One team is to be available primarily to Hispanic-Anglo communities, the other to black-white communities. Both will be selected, trained and based at Kolbe House, an archdiocesan center for ministry to imprisoned persons, their families, and other families in trouble.

These teams will focus on education and information. They will, for example, assist parents in identifying and responding to gang presence and pressure on their children. They will offer similar assistance to churches, schools and youth workers. They will also deal directly with young people, informing them about the implications of gang participation and about alternatives. In all of this, they will cooperate with the police, social service agencies, other churches, school authorities, and recreational programs in each area.

I want these teams operational by mid-February. My hope is that you will welcome them into your churches, schools and other neighborhood forums as you continue to address gang problems within your community. As I said, they will not solve all the problems, but they can make a significant contribution because of their expertise and mobility. I might add that all archdiocesan programs will be evaluated on a regular basis to ensure their effectiveness.

I am here to listen and to learn what other approaches we might initiate or encourage. The task is gigantic but do-able! No one solution will solve the problem with its many dimensions. But we must begin somewhere, and we must begin together.

My brothers and sisters, it has been good to be with you this evening. I appreciate your welcome and hospitality very much. I am very grateful to you and to those who minister in your midst. We have gathered here—Hispanic, black and white—Catholic and Protestant—representatives of civic and religious dimensions of our society—to address a serious problem.

We know that the killing must stop! The violence must stop! We must put an end to poverty in this city! We have many social and economic problems which tend to overwhelm us. But we must learn something very important from this evening: that, when we join together as brothers and sisters trusting in one another—and when we put our trust in God—we can solve these problems! We can do together what we could never do alone! That is the challenge before us this evening.

I dream of returning one day to Humboldt Park, Logan Square and West Town and meeting another "Maria" who will tell me that it's good to wake up in the morning—she likes going to school—she has many friends and a good family life—and this is a good place to live!

I hope that day will be soon!

Address

"Civic Unity in Chicago:
Is It Only a Dream?"

Hesburgh Forum Luncheon

Chicago, Illinois

— February 23, 1989 —————————————————————

I have been told that, at your last luncheon, a member of my staff included in his invocation a slightly veiled petition on behalf of an upcoming football game. As you can imagine, I was quite relieved when Notre Dame *did* beat Southern California that weekend! Otherwise our pastoral credibility would have been on the line.

It's no secret that I haven't devoted much time to sports since I came to Chicago. However, I live and work with people who are quite familiar with the sports scene. Moreover, a person would have to have lived in outer space *not* to know that the Notre Dame football team was quite spectacular this past season.

As you know, *leadership* was key to its success. While a number of players exhibited this quality, the quarterback, Tony Rice, displayed *special* leadership skills. And then there's Coach Lou Holtz who is quickly becoming a legend at the university. He's finding a place in our hearts similar to that enjoyed for so many years in Chicago by Coach Ray Meyer.

What strikes me most about Lou Holtz is his philosophy. He has said that "coaching is based on Bible principles—belief, faith, hope, charity"! He also has revealed that his staff encourages "athletes to pray, but mainly just to lead a good, sound life, and to grow in their beliefs and values." That sounds more like a religious educator than a football coach, doesn't

647

it? It does end runs around the standard wisdom immortalized in the words of another famous Chicago sports figure, "Nice guys finish last."

Coach Holtz has amply demonstrated that he's also *tough*. As you will recall, before *the* game of the year—the contest with USC—he sent two of his key players back to South Bend *before* the event because they had come late to practice. And when Notre Dame incurred some penalties in the last minutes of that same game, he rushed onto the field and vented some strong emotions—not by verbally abusing the referee but, rather, by letting his team know quite clearly that he was very upset by their infractions!

What makes the coach's philosophy so appealing to many people, of course, is the fact that he has developed a *winning* team. But what if Notre Dame had lost to USC? How many of us would have blamed the disaster on the forced absence of key players—or complained that the coach wasn't aggressive enough with the officials? The point is that Coach Holtz is willing to take great *risks* to uphold his values and principles.

Some may ask what inspired a major university to select a head coach like him. But that question would show that they didn't know the University of Notre Dame. Lou Holtz is simply continuing a long-standing Notre Dame tradition that includes fidelity to basic Christian principles, ethical values, discipline, and the pursuit of excellence—a tradition that took deep root during the tenure of Father Hesburgh and continues under the present leadership of Father Malloy. It extends well beyond Notre Dame's sports program and impacts all dimensions of the university.

While you may be enjoying the nice things I've just said about your *alma mater* (I really should say *our alma mater* since I received an honorary doctorate from the university five years ago), you may be wondering what all of this has to do with the theme of my address this afternoon: "Civic Harmony in Chicago: Is It Only a Dream?"

Here's the connection between the two: As Notre Dame graduates and heirs of that same outstanding tradition, *you* have a unique opportunity and a serious responsibility to help ensure that civic harmony in this great city and its metropolitan area becomes a *reality*, not a mere pipe dream. You can help shape an effective agenda for Chicago, but that will inevitably mean taking risks. You can make a difference by remaining faithful to basic Christian principles and ethical values, by directing your pursuit of excellence to civic harmony.

The responsibility, to which I have referred, is enhanced by your Notre Dame education, but it reaches all the way back to your baptism. You share in the Church's mission to the world. How this is to be understood and carried out was the theme of the 1987 World Synod of Bishops, in which I participated. Three weeks ago, Pope John Paul II issued an Apostolic Exhortation on the Laity which is based on the synod's recommendations. In this document, the Holy Father points out that Catholic lay men and women are called to participate in all aspects of public life—in his own words, "in the many different economic, social, legislative, administrative and cultural areas which are intended to promote . . . the common good" (no. 42).

That last phrase, "the common good," is the key to civic harmony. It is also a traditional concept in Catholic social teaching. As the Second Vatican Council pointed out,

> The common good embraces the sum total of all those conditions of social life by which individuals, families and organizations can achieve more thoroughly their own fulfillment (*Gaudium et spes*, 74).

The common good, in other words, is the good of *every* person in the community. No one's well-being may be excluded.

I'd like to reflect on some of the implications of this concept for present-day Chicago. I'm not suggesting that this is the only major city in the country that faces serious obstacles to civic harmony. At the same time, the current climate demands that we take an honest look at our city and metropolitan area. We have a long way to go before the pursuit of the common good, the basis for civic harmony, becomes an integral part of the fabric of social, economic, and political life of this community.

One of the realities here which has struck me very forcefully is how heavily politicized Chicago is. I am no stranger to political environments. I was born and raised in Columbia, the state capital of South Carolina. For two years I lived in Atlanta, the capital of Georgia. And I lived in Washington, D.C., our national capital, for five years before I was appointed the archbishop of Cincinnati. But I was not prepared for the Chicago scene where politics is so intensely interwoven with daily life. Even selling popcorn has political ramifications here!

Unfortunately, in some of the political discourse in this great city we continue to hear the rhetoric and to witness the politics of self-interest. I hasten to add that I am *not* referring to the mayoral candidates when I say this. They know that they cannot win the primary or the election without broad support that extends beyond their respective racial or ethnic groups.

However, that does not deter others from engaging in the kind of civic discourse that divides rather than unites. Those who champion narrow interests make claims for "their own," rejecting as part of their strategy even the possibility of compromise and sacrifice for the common good. Chicago suffers greatly from those who refuse negotiation and cooperation, who insist that their claims must be recognized and their demands met immediately without regard for those of others.

There can be no community at all if people no longer have enough faith to transcend their self-interest for the sake of a greater good. Ethnic, racial, and religious identity are proud attributes, but not when they are invoked in order to define "us against them." A city divided by prejudice or exaggerated self-interests harms every one of its citizens.

Racism is more than a regrettable reality. Whether it involves white against black, or black against white, racism is also a *sin*. On February 10, the Pontifical Justice and Peace Commission in Rome issued a document on the Church and racism. It points out that

> Racial prejudice, which denies the equal dignity of all the members of the human family and blasphemes the Creator, can only be eradicated by going to its roots, where it is formed: in the human heart. . . . To overcome discrimination, a community must interiorize the values that inspire just laws and live out, in day-to-day life, the conviction of the equal dignity of all (no. 24).

This implies that meeting the needs of all must be part of a community's agenda.

I make frequent trips to parishes and neighborhoods throughout the city and its metropolitan area, and, on these occasions, I often have an opportunity to meet people and listen to their concerns. I can tell you that all those I've talked to, regardless of the color of their skin or national origins, want their children to enjoy safety on the streets, the opportunity for an effective education, appropriate health care, the chance for honorable work and advancement, a decent home.

These are common human aspirations. And they have great potential to help create a stable and prospering human community if people in the community—like you and me—are willing to help channel those drives toward the pursuit of the common good.

Pitting group against group because of skin color or nationality constitutes a major moral problem. And, as with all great moral issues, it quickly affects the quality of life on all levels and destroys the possibilities of constructive social harmony. Guided only by the consideration of race or culture—or any other single characteristic—we harm ourselves in so many ways.

We deny opportunity to the next generation. We sentence Chicago to death by self-inflicted wounds. When factions make power at any price their prize, they seed the land for a bitter harvest. They can quickly pass the point of no return beyond which people will have only *memories* of Chicago as a city of friendly neighborhoods, of practical cooperation among all the diverse segments on behalf of the common good, of religious faith manifested in daily life rather than one day a week or on special occasions.

Religion's real test is in our relationships with one another. We must meet that test *now*, in our city, together. I speak for no one side in any current dispute. I speak for all Chicagoans who love their city and understand that we must dissipate the cloud of racial hatred and animosity that hangs over us. There are no winners in the wars incited by prejudice. For *all* of us, Chicago has to be the city that works!

Some contend that racism is on the wane here. However, I suspect that even the most naive resident of Chicago knows that this is not true. To be sure, during the mayoral campaign there have been few overt racist outcries. Even the unfortunate statements of a few in recent weeks were isolated and did not give rise to any swell of racial unrest. The candidates themselves have made efforts to avoid this kind of confrontation, and they are to be commended for this.

But in this metropolitan area there is a low-key, *chronic* racism that manifests itself every day in the usual ways: inadequate housing, jobs, health care, and education, as well as a certain distance between people of different ethnic and racial backgrounds. This form of racism has been described by the National Advisory Commission on Civil Disorders, popularly known as the Kerner Commission, as "the quiet riots" gripping our society today.

We often assume that the silent wounds of chronic racism are incurable conditions of contemporary life. So, we try to live with the "quiet riots." However, upon further reflection, even the perennially optimistic person recognizes that such silent racism is a problem waiting to turn into a deafening crisis. To put it bluntly, there will be no end to *acute* racial crises until we attend to the *chronic* problems of racism and cultural misunderstandings in Chicago.

That is why, several weeks ago, Rabbi Herman Schaalman, Reverend W. Sterling Cary, and I—members of the Religious Leaders of Metropolitan Chicago—wrote a series of articles about some of the chronic problems facing Chicago today. These articles were published in several local newspapers and reported in the electronic media. I'd like to highlight some of the challenges we raised because they will indicate more concretely what is involved in our pursuit of the common good.

In the introductory article, we noted that, while downtown Chicago is in the midst of a renaissance, this progress is not being shared equally by all sections of the community. We also shared the conviction that the current mayoral campaign offers all of us two opportunities: first, to address the critical issues facing metropolitan Chicago and, second, to move beyond the racial divisions that have too long plagued our community. We then identified five "critical issues": education, health care, employment, housing, and segregated neighborhoods.

First, *education*. Today, as you know, a high school education is the minimum needed for a decent job, even at low-entry levels. And the ability to get and hold a job, in turn, develops self-esteem, creates access to decent housing and adequate health care, and stabilizes families. But the Chicago public school system has a dropout rate of nearly 50 percent, and high-school achievement scores here are consistently and significantly below the national average.

Many of the most serious problems of Chicago's public school system have already been identified and discussed throughout this community, and initial efforts have been made during the past two years to resolve them. The second phase of this reform process must now begin. Working together, all citizens must now find ways to bring school reform into the classroom. And this, in turn, will require leadership in the schools, the neighborhoods, the teacher's union, the City Council, the Mayor's Office, and the Illinois Legislature.

Second, *health care*. Many residents do not personally face problems of access to appropriate health care. Moreover, Chicagoans are rightly proud of the marvels of contemporary medicine that are performed here every day. At the same time, as *Crain's Chicago Business* recently reported, six hundred thousand Chicagoans are *not* receiving the health care needed for their well-being.

The medical community *does* try to help these people, but many health care providers are finding it increasingly difficult to meet so great a demand for uncompensated care. As a result, hospitals either run consistent deficits, or they close their doors, as have nine Chicago-area hospitals in the past two years. Proper, accessible health care is not a *privilege* to be enjoyed only by those who can afford it. The health of every Chicagoan is a significant dimension of the common good here.

Third, *employment*. While the majority of Chicagoans have jobs, more than 155,000 are officially listed as unemployed. This statistic does not include those who are underemployed (some working only one hour a week) or those who have dropped out of the labor force in frustration. As you know, many of our other social problems relate, directly or indirectly, to employment opportunities. These include lack of access to health care and affordable housing, substance abuse, crime, racial discord, and, most importantly, an erosion of self-esteem and family life.

Some experts point out that, while Chicago has lost nearly half of its factories and about 250,000 manufacturing jobs since 1970, it has gained a comparable number of mostly higher-skilled jobs in the service sector. But what happens to those who are unprepared for these new jobs? What happens, moreover, to the nearly half of our public school students who fail to graduate from high school? Their need for job training must be a critical concern in our pursuit of the common good. As I have intimated, no one's well-being may be excluded if we are to achieve authentic civic harmony in the Chicago metropolitan area.

Fourth, *housing*. The severe shortage of decent low- and moderate-income housing borders on scandal in a nation as affluent as ours. It forces people to make, at best, some miserable choices—to accept an inadequate, run-down, overcrowded, badly located dwelling or to invest too much of their income for rent, thereby being forced to neglect other necessities. The housing shortage is one of the basic causes of homelessness. And it is clearly discriminatory; it disproportionately affects minorities, women, and children.

If we are to deal with this problem in Chicago, we need a major effort backed by ingenuity, creativity, and adequate resources. That effort will require much more attention from all segments of the community and its leaders. Adequate housing for all is also an essential ingredient in our pursuit of the common good.

Fifth, *segregated neighborhoods.* A recent study has indicated that Chicago tops the list of this nation's most segregated large cities. We pay a great price for segregation every day—in the poor quality of our public schools, in the higher rates of unemployment among minorities, in the many deteriorating neighborhoods where hope has nearly vanished.

In recent years there have been some welcome changes in several southwest and northwest neighborhoods. When black families moved across old boundaries, local community groups have mobilized to support and maintain *integrated* communities. The residents of these neighborhoods have demonstrated that people of good will, acting in their own best interest *and* for the common good, can work together for neighborhoods with high standards that are open to everyone.

Perhaps you were a bit surprised when I said that these people acted both in their own best interest and for the common good. While I have emphasized the importance of the common good, the concept does not exclude legitimate self-interest. As a matter of fact, it presumes it. Pursuit of the common good implies that individuals and groups continue to identify and work for their legitimate self-interest, but they do so in collaboration with others who may have similar or competing self-interests.

In other words, civic harmony and unity is not something static. It is not a shared state of *nirvana*. It involves a creative tension among the various groups that make up the community. It demands that all sectors engage in civility and dialogue to develop a shared vision, set communal priorities, solve common problems, and ensure that everyone's needs are met.

I invite each of you—as citizens, baptized Christians, and Notre Dame graduates—to join me and others of good will in the pursuit of the common good. As citizens, we are part of Chicago's history, but we are not prisoners of the past. We *can* make the needed changes in this community to ensure that all its members share in its benefits. As Catholic Christians, we are part of a faith tradition that binds us together as brothers and sisters and calls us to stand in solidarity with the poor, the alienated, the forgotten, the abandoned. As graduates of the University of Notre Dame, you have the responsibility of sharing its traditions of excellence with this community and passing on its vision and values to the next generation.

In honesty and humility—and in the freedom that is ours as God's children—we must repent and change our hearts—wherever and whenever necessary. We must also forgive and, at times, forget, especially now as we face a unique opportunity to build *one* united community in Chicago.

Is civic harmony a mere dream in Chicago? Not if we decide we want to do something about it! Let us join together in this worthy endeavor!

Address

National Committee for the Prevention of Child Abuse

Chicago, Illinois

— August 29, 1992 —————————————————————

For some days now we have been nearly inundated with tragic stories of the widespread devastation caused by Hurricane Andrew. As destructive as this natural disaster was, it pales in comparison with the ongoing tragedy of child abuse and neglect—a preventable force which is battering the very heart of the human family. In 1991, for example, more than 2.7 million children in this nation were the victims of child abuse and neglect. If left unchecked, the damage this problem is wreaking will irreparably harm our society.

Recently, a local media report starkly illustrated the grim reality of child abuse. A local police department had called a press conference about a child abuse case which resulted in death, but they had to postpone it because it took the coroner an hour and a half to count the bruises and bite marks on the body of the three-year-old victim! The child's parents, showing no remorse, admitted beating and biting the child on numerous occasions over several weeks.

Unfortunately, this is not an isolated incident. The increasing frequency of child abuse reports is a national scandal. According to a report issued by the U.S. House of Representatives Select Committee on Children, Youth and Families, "*homicide* as a cause of children's death in the Western world is almost uniquely a U.S. phenomenon." What possesses people to act so viciously, so inhumanely?

655

As we know, child abuse does not occur in a vacuum. Factors which put children at risk include increased economic stress due to poverty, unemployment and work concerns, mental illness, and, increasingly, the effects of drug and alcohol abuse. There are also broader cultural forces which are responsible for the increase in child maltreatment. At times, children are seen more as a liability than a precious gift from God and hope for the future. One commentator underscored the sad state of our nation's priorities by noting that, "Taxpayers in America today can receive a bigger tax break for breeding racehorses than for raising children."

In a climate of exaggerated individualism and a preoccupation with personal "rights," where many consider the option to abort an unwanted, unborn child to be a fundamental right, the climate is ripe for abuse. While I acknowledge the different views on this issue which exist, I am personally convinced that our current policy of nearly unrestricted abortion—as well as the growing interest in euthanasia—contributes to the widespread disrespect for human life in our society. Since 1983, I have often spoken about the need for a consistent ethic of life which *defends* and *enhances* human life across its full spectrum from conception to natural death, and in all its circumstances. When human life under any circumstance—including the vulnerable years of childhood—is not held as sacred in a society, *all* human life in that society is threatened. However, when it *is* held as sacred in all its circumstances, all human life is protected. What is the attitude in our society today about the value of the lives of our children?

In 1990, a report issued by the U.S. Department of Health and Human Services' Advisory Board on Child Abuse and Neglect declared child abuse and neglect in the United States a *national emergency*. The board based this conclusion on three findings:

1. Each year hundreds of thousands of children are starved and abandoned, burned and severely beaten, raped and sodomized, berated and belittled;

2. The system the nation has devised to respond to child abuse and neglect is failing; and

3. The United States spends billions of dollars on programs that deal with the results of the nation's failure to prevent and treat child abuse and neglect.

It is not only the government's responsibility to respond to this crisis. We *all* share a moral obligation to prevent and eliminate child abuse and neglect. For the sake of our nation's and the world's future, no one can afford to shirk this fundamental responsibility. All segments of society—civic, religious, educational, business, law enforcement, social and health services, as well as voluntary and professional organizations—must form a partnership to address this emergency. I commend you, the National Committee for the Prevention of Child Abuse, for your efforts and growing influence. They are sorely needed if we are to succeed in protecting and enhancing the lives of our children.

Religious communities also have an important role to play in this endeavor, working in partnership with others in the private sector and with government agencies. Children and their families are an integral part of our congregations. They attend our schools, churches, and synagogues. We have a special ready access to them, and there is a sacred trust between pastor and parishioner. Like the Catholic Church, other religious communities are becoming more aware of the national scandal of child abuse and neglect and are responding in a variety of ways. I was asked to speak on the role of the Church in addressing the tragedy of child abuse. Rather than speak in a theoretical way, I will talk this evening about the concrete efforts of my own ecclesial community because I am most familiar with its programs and future plans.

For centuries, the Catholic Church has sought to meet the human, religious, and educational needs of children, families, and individuals in many different ways. Basically, our approach includes direct services, education, and advocacy.

Direct Services. Catholic Charities of Chicago, which has its counterparts in most U.S. Catholic dioceses, is the Midwest's largest private social agency. It annually serves more than a half million people of all faiths through 200 programs at 107 locations. It addresses issues as disparate (and related) as adolescent pregnancy, gang intervention, homelessness, and suicide through services in four primary areas: children, families, seniors, and basic human needs.

Catholic Charities is strongly committed to preserving the family unit and improving the quality of life for all people. Its philosophy is service-oriented. That is why, in responding to allegations of child abuse or neglect, Catholic Charities begins to help the family rebuild itself from the initial point of intervention. Let me give you an example.

A man and his two daughters, ages 13 and 10, were brought to the attention of Catholic Charities by a report to the Child Abuse/Neglect Hotline, alleging the family was residing in an abandoned building, which was also known as a "drug house." The living conditions were deplorable: no utilities, mounds of garbage, rodents, stray animals and other hazards.

An investigator for Catholic Charities' Department of Child Protective Services immediately responded and interviewed the family, learning about the long history of problems that had besieged them over the years. The father had been granted custody of his daughters when he divorced his wife eight years earlier. He had been gainfully employed until two years ago when he lost his job, their apartment, and his feeling of self-worth. He reported that their lives took a downward spiral of transit living, abject poverty, and hopelessness. The girls had been truant from school over the past year, and they lacked proper clothing, medical and dental care, and hygiene.

Despite all this, the father refused to take his daughters to a shelter because of the horror stories he had heard about shelters. The Catholic Charities investigator observed a close bond between the father and daughters, and both girls wanted to remain in his care, even though the uncertainty and danger of their lifestyle had taken its toll on them. As a result of this intervention and follow-up, the father was able to secure temporary living quarters with a friend for a few days until the Catholic Charities investigator could initiate referrals for emergency housing. Clothing and other personal items were obtained for the family, and the three were referred to Catholic Charities' In-Home Protective Services Program for ongoing aggressive outreach services. Had Catholic Charities failed to apply a service-oriented approach in responding to the needs of this family, their lives would undoubtedly have been further disrupted.

Nevertheless, as important as intervention and follow-up care are in cases of child abuse and neglect, preventive measures are also vital. In times of widespread concern about the national deficit, it is important to note that preventive measures have proven to be much more effective and cost-efficient than programs of intervention and follow-up services after the fact of child abuse and neglect.

Education and Advocacy. Hoping to build a stronger foundation and framework for preventive measures, the U.S. Catholic bishops issued a pastoral statement last fall; it is entitled, "Putting Children and Families First: A Challenge for the Church, Nation and World." We described the document as a "call for conversion and action—a spiritual reawakening to the moral and human costs of neglecting our children and families."

In it we call for system-wide reform because of the widespread strains on our child welfare system, including lack of adequate foster homes, inadequate support services, a shortage of trained personnel, inappropriate placements, and a serious absence of preventive programs. We also stress that the "primary goal of reform should be preserving families wherever possible, through long-term, home-based services and programs designed to meet individual family needs before children's safety is jeopardized." To do this, we urge better coordination in providing family services, emphasizing prevention and replacing fragmented individual programs.

As a pastor and as the chairman of the bishops' Committee on Marriage and Family Life, I enthusiastically and wholeheartedly support this initiative. It is a way to highlight and focus attention more vigorously on many concerns we are already addressing in myriad ways. In metropolitan

Chicago, the Archdiocese of Chicago has a more sophisticated and extensive network of family services available than any other organization, including local and state government. So, in some areas, this new initiative will provide new energy for ongoing projects. But in other areas, it is the impetus for a new way of doing things, as well as a fresh context for considering new ideas for action.

This program—Putting Children and Families First—will help us bring those in need into contact with the existing network of services available from the Church and other caregivers. It will also enable us to enlarge the circle of help in order to include other resources that serve families in need and to publicize throughout Chicagoland the many services which are available. And we will continue to be advocates for social change—specifically changes in public policy—to support children and families.

This fall, the archdiocese is planning several new initiatives in this campaign:

- In September, we will open the first of eleven regional resource centers for families to help parents gain skills and confidence in handling the challenges of parenthood.

- We are inviting state and federal legislative candidates to a breakfast so we can share our concerns with them and press for legislation that will support families.

- The archdiocese will also sponsor hearings to allow children and young people to express their concerns and needs for better family life.

- We are also reviewing our own archdiocesan personnel policies in order to ensure that they are "family-friendly."

As you undoubtedly know, during this past year we have also taken significant steps regarding sexual misconduct by archdiocesan clergy and other Church personnel with minors. Last October, I appointed a commission to review and make recommendations about such cases or allegations as well as archdiocesan policies and procedures. The commission's report, issued in early June, was generally very well received. We have been translating its recommendations into archdiocesan policy, and we will complete this process by early fall. We have also planned workshops in each region of the archdiocese for priests and other pastoral ministers on professional responsibility, with specific attention to child abuse.

I assure you of my determination that the Catholic Church in metropolitan Chicago will continue to join with others in the private and public sectors to face head-on the continuing challenge of widespread child abuse and neglect—through direct services and such preventive measures as education and advocacy. Our very future as a nation depends on these efforts.

My friends, it has been said that "Every child born into the world is a new thought of God, an ever-fresh and radiant possibility." Let us work together so that these beacons of hope and love will forever brighten our world!

Keynote Address

"The Story of the Campaign for Human Development: Theological-Historical Roots"*

25ᵗʰ Anniversary of the Campaign for Human Development

Chicago, Illinois

— ***August 25, 1995*** —————————————————

I am delighted to serve as honorary chairman of this event and to welcome you to Chicago for the 25ᵗʰ anniversary celebration of the Campaign for Human Development. I thank Bishop Garland and Father Hacala for the kind invitation to speak at this gathering. This is the first address I have undertaken since my illness, so it is indeed good to be here with you!

It is fitting that we are gathered here because since the beginning, Chicago has been important to the campaign and the campaign has been important to Chicago. As you may know,

- Msgr. George Higgins of this archdiocese wrote a Labor Day message in 1969 that pointed the way to the campaign.

- Auxiliary Bishop Michael Dempsey of Chicago was CHD's first spokesperson.

*Also published in *Origins*, vol. 25, no. 12, September 7, 1995, pp. 196–99.

- Msgr. Jack Egan organized the "Friends of CHD" in the mid-1970s and for decades has been an inspiration to the campaign's work.

- The great work of community organizing began in Chicago, and Chicago has many important networks and training centers.

- CHD enjoys a rich tradition of support here, both in the form of active and enthusiastic participation by people in organizations and projects funded by CHD, and in the generous donations to the annual CHD collection. Again this past year, despite many other urgent and worthwhile requests for assistance, Catholics throughout the archdiocese donated nearly three-quarters of a million dollars.

An anniversary is a good time to reflect on the splendid accomplishments of the past and to look to the significant challenges of the future. This evening, I will highlight CHD's historical and theological roots and share some thoughts on its importance for the future.

In his Labor Day message in 1969, Msgr. George Higgins urged the Catholic Church to make "a generous portion of its limited resources available for the development and self-determination of the poor and powerless." At the bishops' meeting that fall, the late Msgr. Geno Baroni continued to lay the groundwork for this initiative by urging the bishops to take up the plight of the poor in a new, significant way.

In response, the bishops resolved (a) to raise $50 million to assist self-help programs designed and operated by the poor and aimed at eliminating the causes of poverty; (b) to educate the more affluent about the root causes of poverty; and (c) to change attitudes about the plight of the poor. The bishops were inspired by Jesus' life and mission, by almost a century of Catholic social teaching, and by Pope Paul VI, who had called for determined efforts to "break the hellish circle of poverty" and to "eradicate the conditions which impose poverty and trap generation after generation in an agonizing cycle of dependency and despair."

As general secretary of the National Conference of Catholic Bishops at the time, I was directly involved in this exciting endeavor. While enthusiasm among the bishops was high, details about how the crusade would be implemented had yet to be developed. As I have often noted, the bishops voted in this collection and left it to me and staff to work out the details! Despite the complexities involved in such an enormous undertaking, I was motivated by my strong belief that the idea behind what would become known as the Campaign for Human Development was "blessed from the beginning," and was eager to get it underway.

Even though we had to create a program, manage a national collection, and decide how to distribute millions of dollars in grants—all in only a few months—we were determined to make it a success. Thanks to a dedicated staff, and many others, some of whom are with us this evening, the campaign did get off to a good start. Indeed, the first CHD collection was the most successful national Catholic collection ever taken up in the United States, raising $8 million. And we received a thousand requests for grants!

But, as you know well, CHD is not simply a fundraising program. With the campaign's threefold mission of empowering the poor, educating people about poverty and justice issues, and building solidarity between the poor and non-poor, it is a remarkable expression of Catholic social teaching. CHD embraces the basic principles of that teaching: the God-given dignity, rights, and responsibilities of the human person; the call to community and participation in that community; the option for, and solidarity with, the poor. CHD embodies the call in the Scriptures to integrate the love of God and neighbor, and has become an integral part of the Church's response to some of the most pressing social and economic problems facing our society.

CHD funds have helped organizations effectively address the larger issues of the community by promoting changes in detrimental laws and policies and by opening lines of communication with government, banking, business, and industry. According to a recent study sponsored by The Catholic University of America, CHD seed monies have generated billions of dollars' worth of resources for underprivileged communities. That same study indicates that CHD-funded projects currently benefit in some way fully half of the poor in the United States!

CHD-funded groups have helped to shape U.S. public policy and improved life for families and communities in many ways. They helped enact legislation to ban redlining, require mortgage information disclosure, and require reinvestment in communities. They helped enact federal standards that virtually eliminated "brown lung" disease in the textile industry. They helped pass the Family and Medical Leave Act and strengthen enforcement of child support.

However, more important than *what* CHD-funded groups have done is *how* they have done it. While some political leaders have lately begun to talk about "empowerment," CHD has made empowerment its very reason for existence. CHD has successfully promoted self-determination and participation for countless people.

One of my joys as archbishop is meeting individuals who, thanks to CHD, now share more fully in decision-making processes that affect them. For example, just yesterday the following 1995 CHD grants for the Chicago area were announced at a press conference:

- Chicago ACORN received $45,000 to fund the Chicago Parents Organizing Project's efforts to unite parents and young people to improve schools in low-income communities;

- Chicago's Homeless on the Move for Equality received $30,000 to expand its operations to serve better the needs of the homeless in Chicago;

- Illinois Fiesta Educativa of Chicago received $40,000 to fund educational programs and services to Latinos with disabilities; and

- Chicago Metropolitan Sponsors, with which I have been personally involved, received $116,000 to address such social issues as crime, unemployment, and education in Chicago and surrounding suburbs.

Twenty-five years, nearly $250 million dollars, and 3,000 funded projects later, CHD remains a leader in community organizing and education about the impact of poverty, the social structures that perpetuate it, and ways to overcome it. CHD has consistently taught all of us about systemic injustice that limits people's ability to improve their lives. It has also changed attitudes among the poor by fostering self-esteem, self-confidence, and self-reliance, as well as encouraging a sense of hope about being able to address injustice effectively and create a better life for the poor. As CHD's "25th Anniversary Challenge" document notes, "CHD is an unusual combination of religious commitment, street-smart politics, commitment to structural change, and commitment to the development of the poor."

Pope John Paul II highlighted CHD's effectiveness when he was in Chicago in 1979, saying, "The projects assisted by the Campaign have helped to create a more human and just order, and they enable many people to achieve an increased measure of rightful self-reliance." In a recent letter to Cardinal Keeler, the president of our Episcopal Conference (for whose presence this evening I am very grateful), the Holy Father echoed similar sentiments of admiration and respect. And in their 1986 pastoral letter, "Economic Justice for All," the U.S. Catholic bishops underscored CHD's efforts, pointing out that: "Our experience with CHD confirms our judgment about the validity of self-help and empowerment of the poor. The Campaign . . . provides a model that we think sets a high standard for similar efforts."

Despite CHD's successes, tragically, poverty is more entrenched today than ever before in our nation's history. Indeed, reducing poverty today is even more daunting than a quarter-century ago because it is often exacerbated by other serious, societal problems that have increased significantly. Out-of-wedlock births, particularly among teens; inadequate housing, health care, education, and job opportunities; lack of community involvement; and most of all, the collapse of family structures—all are undermining our society and making it all the more difficult for people to escape from the grips of poverty. Moreover, senseless violence, rampant crime, drug abuse, and gang warfare dramatically and tragically diminish the quality of life in many communities.

As a result, our country is even more divided today between the "haves" and "have-nots." There is an increased concentration of wealth and political power alongside a growing feeling of powerlessness among many of our citizens. Rapidly developing technology, layoffs, diminishing health benefits and retirement security, and more part-time jobs offering little or no benefits have left the middle-class and working poor very insecure and growing more resentful toward both government and the nonworking poor who depend on society for aid and assistance.

Building solidarity between the "haves" and the "have-nots" is vital if we are to overcome poverty and the many other problems facing our society. So, even though the challenge of reducing poverty is greater today, the fact that one of CHD's greatest strengths is its ability to *bridge the gaps*—between the poor and the affluent, the powerful and the powerless, workers and management—will enhance its influence. However, as you and I know very well, it will require much more than "bridging the gaps."

Twenty-five years ago, Msgr. Baroni emphasized this point when he spoke to the U.S. bishops about the urgent need to address poverty, racism, and injustice in our nation. He pointed out that "something spiritual is lacking—the heart, the will, the desire on the part of affluent America to develop the goals and commitments necessary to end the hardships of poverty and racism in our midst."

Today, for example, there appears to be a great desire to address one dimension of poverty, namely, welfare reform. Unfortunately, the debate about such reform seems to spring not so much from an authentic concern for the poor as from pragmatic concerns about the federal budget deficit and taxpayers' pocketbooks. Now the federal budget and taxes are realities that must be dealt with, but they should not be resolved apart from a sincere and objective consideration of the common good of all citizens.

If we are to solve these problems, then, we must shift the discussion about welfare reform from a merely pragmatic or myopic concern to a more fully humane concern for all. To address poverty realistically and humanely involves more than appealing to people on an intellectual or a political level. It requires calling people to a real conversion of heart for the sake of the common good, which includes the well-being of the poor and needy. It means nurturing a *new spirit* in the Church and in our nation—

- a *new spirit* of compassion, generosity, and love for "the least among us";

- a *new spirit* that rejects the vicious rhetoric and the push for punitive measures that is so common today and instead encourages a new, determined approach to addressing the root causes of poverty;

- a *new spirit* that challenges those who are not poor to disavow stereotypes of the poor and shatter myths that enable people to look down upon the indigent;

- a *new spirit* that encourages an honest and informed consideration of issues in the light of human values and a moral commitment; and, ultimately,

- a *new spirit* that trusts in God's grace to transform our hearts and to empower our communities and Church—from sin and evil to love and justice!

There is no doubt that welfare reform is an urgent national priority. No one should support policies that are wasteful or counterproductive, policies that perpetuate poverty and dependence. Rather, such reform should aim to enhance the lives and dignity of poor children and families and enable them to live productive lives. Saving money in the immediate future should not be the only criterion because such short-term savings lay the groundwork for greater difficulties and costs in the future. Remember also that welfare funds amount to only 1 percent of the national budget. Reforms that effectively punish the innocent children of unwed teenage mothers, wittingly or unwittingly promote abortion, or burden states to do more with less resources are not the answer.

The success of CHD clearly shows that combining *personal* responsibility and *social* responsibility is a potent catalyst for change, renewal, success, and hope for the future. Now is the time to demand a halt to the political rhetoric and posturing, which are fueled by individual interests and those of special interest groups. Now is the time for creative solutions and bold strategies that invest in human dignity and potential rather than scapegoat and punish the poor, further exacerbating the already dire situations many poor people face today. We know that true reform will not be easy, but we also know that poor people, with the right kind of assistance and opportunities, can make a better life for themselves and can contribute to the common good. As people who have been involved with the Campaign for Human Development, you and I have seen individual lives and entire communities transformed in cities, towns, and rural areas throughout our country.

So, this evening, this weekend, and as we return home, let us renew our commitment to economic and social justice for all by continuing to engage people in their faith life and by encouraging them to put their faith into action. If we do, we can and will make a difference! I am convinced that CHD harbors a vast reservoir of untapped potential.

In a speech to students in South Africa, the late Senator Robert Kennedy said, "Each time a man stands up for an ideal or acts to improve the lot of others or strikes out against injustice, he sends forth a tiny ripple of hope, and crossing each other from a million different centers of energy and daring, those ripples build a current that can sweep down the mightiest walls of oppression and resistance." (Senator Kennedy's widow, Ethel, is featured in CHD's current radio ads, and his daughter, Kerry, now serves on the USCC/CHD Committee.)

The Campaign for Human Development began as a ripple and has become a current cascading through lives and communities—bringing new opportunity in its wake. It is a sign of hope for the poor and for all Americans who seek justice. *You,* my friends, help to make that hope possible!

My dear sisters and brothers, let us thank God for the grace of the past quarter of a century. Let us also open ourselves to the inspiration and strength of the Holy Spirit so that we will be able to

- change hearts,

- face the challenges and opportunities of the future, and

- nurture a new spirit of compassion and solidarity with the most vulnerable members of our society.

May God who has begun a good work among us bring it to fulfillment!

Appendix

Biography of Joseph Cardinal Bernardin

Archbishop of Chicago

—— *1982–1996* ——————————————————————

His Eminence Joseph Cardinal Bernardin, archbishop of Chicago, was a native of Columbia, South Carolina. He was born on April 2, 1928, the son of Mrs. Maria M. Simion Bernardin and the late Joseph Bernardin.

After attending Catholic and public schools and the University of South Carolina in Columbia, he was accepted as a candidate for the priesthood by Most Rev. John J. Russell, then bishop of Charleston.

He studied at St. Mary's College, St. Mary, Kentucky; St. Mary's Seminary, Baltimore, where he received the Bachelor of Arts degree in Philosophy; and at The Catholic University of America, Washington, D.C., where, in addition to his theological studies, he received the Master of Arts degree in Education in 1952.

He was ordained to the priesthood by Bishop John J. Russell on April 26, 1952, in St. Joseph Church, Columbia. During his fourteen years in the Diocese of Charleston he served under four bishops in many capacities, including the offices of chancellor, vicar general, diocesan consultor, and administrator of the diocese during a period when the see was vacant.

He was named a papal chamberlain in 1959 and a domestic prelate in 1962 by Pope John XXIII.

On March 9, 1966, Msgr. Bernardin was appointed auxiliary bishop of Atlanta by Pope Paul VI. Upon his episcopal ordination with Archbishop Paul J. Hallinan of Atlanta as principal consecrator, he became the youngest bishop in the country. In Atlanta he served as vicar general and rector of the Cathedral of Christ the King. After the death of Archbishop Hallinan in March, 1968, he served as administrator of the Archdiocese of Atlanta until the installation of the new archbishop.

671

On April 10, 1968, Bishop Bernardin was elected general secretary of the National Conference of Catholic Bishops (NCCB) and the United States Catholic Conference (USCC) by the administrative bodies of those conferences. During this period the bishops were reorganizing the episcopal conference according to the norms established by the Second Vatican Council. As general secretary, he served as coordinator of the reorganization until the latter part of 1972.

On November 21, 1972, he was appointed archbishop of Cincinnati by Pope Paul VI and installed by the Most Rev. Luigi Raimondi, apostolic delegate to the U.S., in ceremonies at the Cathedral of St. Peter in Chains on December 19, 1972. He served the Ohio Metropolitan See for almost ten years.

From November 1974 to November 1977 he served as president of the NCCB/USCC.

On July 10, 1982, he was appointed by Pope John Paul II as archbishop of Chicago, the See left vacant by the death of John Cardinal Cody. His installation by the Most Rev. Pio Laghi, apostolic delegate, took place at Holy Name Cathedral on August 25, 1982.

On January 5, 1983, Pope John Paul II announced Archbishop Bernardin's elevation to the College of Cardinals. During the February 2, 1983 consistory, he received the "red hat" which is the symbol of the cardinalate. His titular church in Rome was the Church of Jesus the Divine Worker.

His elevation to the College of Cardinals was the most public, but not the only recognition of his stature by the Holy See. In 1973, Pope Paul VI appointed Archbishop Bernardin to the Congregation for Bishops; in 1974, to the Pontifical Commission for Social Communications; and in 1978, as a consultor for the Congregation for Catholic Education.

Between 1982 and 1996, Pope John Paul II appointed Cardinal Bernardin to four memberships in curial groups: the Pontifical Commission for the Revision of the Code of Canon Law (1981), the Congregation for the Evangelization of Peoples (1983–1988), the Congregation for Sacraments and Divine Worship (1983–1996), and the Pontifical Council for Promoting Christian Unity (1983–1996).

He was one of four elected NCCB delegates to the synod of bishops held in Rome in 1974, 1977, 1980, 1983, 1987, 1990, and 1994. Beginning in 1974, he was elected five times to serve on the 15-member Council of the Secretariat of the Synod, serving in that capacity for 16 years. He was again elected to the council in 1994.

Cardinal Bernardin served as chairman of the NCCB ad hoc Committee on War and Peace which prepared the pastoral letter, "The Challenge of Peace: God's Promise and Our Response," adopted by the U.S. bishops at a special meeting in Chicago in May 1983. In recognition of his work with the committee, he received the 1983 Albert Einstein Peace Award. In order to follow up the pastoral letter, he chaired the NCCB ad hoc Committee to Assess the Moral Status of Deterrence between 1985 and 1988.

On September 9, 1996, President Clinton awarded Cardinal Bernardin the Presidential Medal of Freedom, the nation's highest civilian honor bestowed on individuals who have made important contributions to their communities and the nation. In presenting the medal, the President cited Cardinal Bernardin's work on behalf of racial equality and arms control and noted he "has been a persistent voice for moderation."

Cardinal Bernardin chaired the ad hoc Committee on the Structure and Function of the NCCB/USCC. He served as chairman of the NCCB Committee for Marriage and Family Life from 1990 to 1993. From 1983 to 1989, he served as the chairman of the NCCB Committee for Pro-Life Activities. He also served as chairman of the NCCB Committee for Canonical Affairs (1979–1981) and the USCC Committee for Communications.

Cardinal Bernardin was chancellor of the Catholic Church Extension Society and the University of St. Mary of the Lake. From 1985 to 1988 he served as chairman of the Board of Trustees of The Catholic University of America.

Nationally, the cardinal also served in several capacities. In 1975–1976 he served on the President's Advisory Committee for Refugees (Vietnamese), and the President's American Revolution Bicentennial Advisory Council. From 1978 to 1981, he was chairman of the Board of Trustees of The Catholic University of America.

He was a founding member and vice-chairman of the Religious Alliance Against Pornography (RAAP). He was also a member of the Catholic Charities U.S.A. National Development Task Force and the Board of Trustees of the Catholic Health Association.

Cardinal Bernardin received numerous honorary doctorates from colleges and universities in the U.S. and Europe.

Among his writings are *Prayer in Our Time*, 1973; *"Let the Children Come to Me," a Guide for the Religious Education of Children*, 1976; *Called to Serve, Called to Lead—Reflections on the Ministerial Priesthood*, 1981; and *It Is Christ We Preach*, 1982. His last work, *The Gift of Peace*, was published posthumously in 1997.

As archbishop of Chicago, Cardinal Bernardin wrote five pastoral letters: on liturgy, *Our Communion, Our Peace, Our Promise*, 1984; on Jesus and his meaning for Christian life, *Christ Lives in Me*, 1985; on ministry, *In Service of One Another*, 1985; on the Church, *The Family Gathered Here Before You*, 1989; and on health care, *A Sign of Hope*, 1995. He also wrote a weekly column for *The New World*, the newspaper of the Archdiocese of Chicago.

Cardinal Bernardin issued guidelines on *Access to the Sacraments of Initiation and Reconciliation for Developmentally Disabled Persons*, 1985. In spring 1986 he issued his *Reflections on Religious Life*. In autumn 1986 he issued *"The Challenges We Face Together,"* *Reflections on Selected Questions for Archdiocesan Religious Educators*. In October 1986 he issued *A Challenge and a Responsibility—a Pastoral Statement on the Church's Response to the AIDS Crisis*. He issued *"Come Holy Spirit," A Pastoral Statement on the Charismatic Renewal* for the feast of Pentecost, 1988. In autumn 1988 the cardinal published *Growing in Wisdom, Age and Grace—a Guide for Parents in the Religious Education of Their Children*. In 1992, he published *The Parish in the Contemporary Church*. In November 1993 he issued a pastoral statement on the occasion of the 25th anniversary of the restoration of the permanent diaconate, entitled, *"The Call to Service."* In November 1994 he issued a video pastoral statement to youth, entitled, *"Here and Now."* In May 1996 he issued *"Building Bridges Between Communities of Faith,"* a pastoral statement on parish sharing.

The *Consistent Ethic of Life*, published by Sheed & Ward in 1988, brings together in one sourcebook ten of Cardinal Bernardin's major addresses on the topic of the "Consistent Ethic," as well as response papers from eight theologians who participated with him in a symposium sponsored by Loyola University of Chicago and the Archdiocese of Chicago. *A Blessing to Each Other*, published by Liturgy Training Publications (Chicago, 1996), is a collection of addresses by Cardinal Bernardin on Catholic-Jewish relations.

In 1996, Loyola Press published *This Man Bernardin*, a collection of photographs by John H. White with text by Eugene Kennedy.

Cardinal Bernardin died on November 14, 1996.

* * *

In late 1996, Dr. Paolo Magagnotti of Trent, Italy, published *The Word of Cardinal Bernardin* (New York: Center for Migration Studies), a collection of essays on thirty topics based on Cardinal Bernardin's works. In 1997, Loyola Press published *The Final Journey of Joseph Cardinal Bernardin* with photographs by John H. White. In 1998, Georgetown University Press published *A Moral Vision for America*, edited by John P. Langan, S.J., a collection of fourteen public policy addresses by Cardinal Bernardin and his deathbed letter to the U.S. Supreme Court about assisted suicide. In 1999, the Catholic Health Association published *Celebrating the Ministry of Healing: Joseph Cardinal Bernardin's Reflections on Healthcare*, edited by Reverend Michael Place.

He has been the subject of five biographies: *The Spirit of Cardinal Bernardin* by A.E.P. Wall (Chicago: The Thomas More Press, 1983); *Cardinal Bernardin* by Eugene Kennedy (Chicago: Bonus Books, 1989); *My Brother Joseph* by Eugene Kennedy (New York: St. Martin's Press,

1997); *Bernardin, Life to the Full* by Eugene Kennedy (Chicago: Bonus Books, 1997); and *I Am Your Brother Joseph: Cardinal Bernardin of Chicago* by Tim Unsworth (New York: Crossroad, 1997).

March 2000

Index